The Cambridge Haydn Encyclopedia

For well over two hundred years, Joseph Haydn has been by turns lionized and misrepresented – held up as a celebrity, and disparaged as a mere forerunner or point of comparison. And yet, unlike many other canonic composers, his music has remained a fixture in the repertoire from his day until ours. What do we need to know now in order to understand Haydn and his music? With over eighty entries focused on ideas and seven longer thematic essays to bring these together, this distinctive and richly illustrated encyclopedia offers a new perspective on Haydn and the many cultural contexts in which he worked and left his indelible mark during the Enlightenment and beyond. Contributions from sixty-seven scholars and performers in Europe, the Americas, and Oceania capture the vitality of Haydn studies today – its variety of perspectives and methods – and ultimately inspire further exploration of one of Western music's most innovative and influential composers.

CARYL CLARK is Professor of Music History and Culture at the Faculty of Music, University of Toronto, and a Fellow of Trinity College. Editor of *The Cambridge Companion to Haydn* (Cambridge, 2005), and author of *Haydn's Jews: Representation and Reception on the Operatic Stage* (Cambridge, 2009), her research interests include Enlightenment aesthetics, interdisciplinary opera studies, Orpheus and Orphic resonances, and the politics of musical reception – all generously funded by the Social Sciences and Humanities Research Council of Canada.

SARAH DAY-O'CONNELL is Associate Professor in the Department of Music at Skidmore College. A recipient of the Pauline Alderman Award for Outstanding Scholarship on Women and Music, she has held research fellowships at Yale University, the British Library, and the Institute for Advanced Studies in the Humanities at the University of Edinburgh. She has published on Haydn, the social contexts of singing, music and gender, theories of performance, and music studies within the liberal arts.

The Cambridge Haydn Encyclopedia

Edited by

CARYL CLARK
University of Toronto

SARAH DAY-O'CONNELL
Skidmore College

CAMBRIDGE
UNIVERSITY PRESS

University Printing House, Cambridge CB2 8BS, United Kingdom

One Liberty Plaza, 20th Floor, New York, NY 10006, USA

477 Williamstown Road, Port Melbourne, VIC 3207, Australia

314–321, 3rd Floor, Plot 3, Splendor Forum, Jasola District Centre, New Delhi – 110025, India

79 Anson Road, #06–04/06, Singapore 079906

Cambridge University Press is part of the University of Cambridge.

It furthers the University's mission by disseminating knowledge in the pursuit of education, learning, and research at the highest international levels of excellence.

www.cambridge.org
Information on this title: www.cambridge.org/9781107129016
DOI: 10.1017/9781316422847

© Cambridge University Press 2019

This publication is in copyright. Subject to statutory exception and to the provisions of relevant collective licensing agreements, no reproduction of any part may take place without the written permission of Cambridge University Press.

First published 2019

Printed in the United Kingdom by TJ International Ltd, Padstow Cornwall

A catalogue record for this publication is available from the British Library.

Library of Congress Cataloging-in-Publication Data
NAMES: Clark, Caryl Leslie, 1953– editor | Day-O'Connell, Sarah, 1972– editor.
TITLE: The Cambridge Haydn Encyclopedia / edited by Caryl Clark, Sarah Day-O'Connell.
DESCRIPTION: Cambridge, United Kingdom ; New York, NY : Cambridge University Press, [2019] | Includes bibliographical references and index.
IDENTIFIERS: LCCN 2018036915 | ISBN 9781107129016
SUBJECTS: LCSH: Haydn, Joseph, 1732–1809 – Encyclopedias.
CLASSIFICATION: LCC ML410.H4 C172 2019 | DDC 780.92–dc23
LC record available at https://lccn.loc.gov/2018036915

ISBN 978-1-107-12901-6 Hardback

Cambridge University Press has no responsibility for the persistence or accuracy of URLs for external or third-party internet websites referred to in this publication and does not guarantee that any content on such websites is, or will remain, accurate or appropriate.

For my family and my students.

– C. L. C.

For Jeremy, Micah, and Gabriel.

– S. D-O'C.

Contents

List of Figures   page viii

List of Music Examples   xi

List of Contributors   xii

Preface and Guide to Readers   xv

Acknowledgments   xviii

Chronology   xx

List of Abbreviations   xxxii

List of Entries and Essays   xxxiv

A–Z Entries and Essays   1

Bibliography   407

General Index   451

Index of Compositions   483

Figures

Full publication details of works cited appear in the Bibliography.

1. Title page of program for complete performance of *The Creation* by the Handel and Haydn Society in Boston in 1835. Reproduced with permission of the Boston Public Library. — page 12
2. William Hogarth's *Analysis of Beauty* (1753), Plate 1. Courtesy of The Lewis Walpole Library, Yale University. — 20
3. The title page of the *Six Quatuors* Op. 82 printed by the Parisian publisher Jean-Jérôme Imbault in 1794. Bibliothèque nationale de France. Used with permission. — 33
4. Soproniensis map c. 1800. Map of Burgenland as a border region around Sopron/Ödenburg. Courtesy of Sepp Gmasz and the Burgenländisches Landesarchiv map collection. — 35
5. 1717 print of Hans Wurst Sauschneider image. Reproduced with permission of Wien Museum. — 39
6. Jewish wedding musicians playing on the Judengasse of Eisenstadt in the 1930s. Courtesy of the Landesmuseum Burgenland, Eisenstadt. — 42
7. Andreas Altomonte, High Mass at St. Stephen's Cathedral, on the occasion of the homage of the Lower Austrian Estates to Maria Theresia, 1740. Wien Museum HMW 19.803. Copyright Wien Museum. Reproduced with permission. — 49
8. Autograph sketch from the finale of Symphony No. 99. Österreichische Nationalbibliothek, Musiksammlung, Mus.Hs. 16835, fol. 24v. and 25. Reproduced with permission. — 68
9. Prince Anton Esterházy's 1791 installation ceremony in the forecourt of the palace at Eszterháza. Hungarian National Museum. Used with permission. — 108
10. *Las siete Palabras con su Introduccion y Terremoto, Musica del M.tro D. J. Haydn para Piano Forte*. Cover and first page of *The Seven Last Words* (first half of the nineteenth century). Piano transcription. Convent of las Claras, Sevilla (©ICCMU, CS-2-03-0957). Reproduced with permission of ICCMU. — 115
11. "Strephon and Lydia," from *A Selection of Scots Songs in Three parts, the Harmony by Haydn*. London: William Napier [1792], part 3. Reproduced by kind permission of the National Library of Scotland. — 124

LIST OF FIGURES

12   Replica of a 1788 Ignaz Kober square piano (Chris Maene – Ruiselede, Belgium, 2007). Photo by Jeremy Tusz. Reproduced with permission of Tom Beghin, Orpheus Institute.   181
13   Digitally altered map of Eisenstadt. From Prickler (ed.) 1988. Reproduced with permission of the Wiener Stadt- und Landesarchiv.   183
14   A summary of Haydn's orchestral forces c. 1761–95. Reproduced from Zaslaw 2012, 312. Used by permission of author and press.   186
15   Reconstruction of orchestral seating arrangement of Salomon's concerts in London 1791–94. Adapted from McVeigh 1993, 212, and Zaslaw 1989, 465.   188
16   A reconstruction of the seating plan of musicians at the performance of *The Creation* in the old Burgtheater, Vienna, March 19, 1798. Reproduced and translated from Feder 1999, 112. © 1999 Bärenreiter-Verlag Karl Vötterle GmbH and Co. KG, Kassel. Used with kind permission.   190
17   Title page of libretto for *Il mondo della luna*, opera buffa performed at Eszterháza in 1777. Reproduced with permission of National Széchényi Library in Budapest.   193
18   OPERA HOUSE or KINGS THEATRE in the HAYMARKET. London, published by Harrison and Co., April 1795. Image reproduced with permission of Royal College of Music/ArenaPAL.   199
19   Foldable quartet stand. English, early nineteenth century. Collection of Pierre Bouckaert (Ghent, Belgium). Photo by Jonas Tavernier. Reproduced with permission of Orpheus Institute, Ghent, Belgium.   259
20   Detail from title page of Haydn, Keyboard Trio Hob.XV:10, Artaria (Vienna) 1798, indicating ocular communication between the players. Reproduced by permission of Jean Gray Hargrove Music Library, University of California, Berkeley.   272
21   Enacting a domestic keyboard trio setting. Photo extracted from a video by marK Boone. Reproduced with permission of Orpheus Institute, Ghent, Belgium.   273
22   Comparison of the size and shape of the Schlosstheater at Schönbrunn (l) and the second opera house at Eszterháza (r). After a gallery level and partial stage plan by Carl Schütz, around 1778, Wien Museum, HMW 19.160/1, Vienna (copyright Wien Museum, used with permission); and a ground floor and stage plan by Joseph Ringer, 1789, Magyar Országos Levéltár (Hungarian National Archives), Fond T2, no. 1222, Budapest (used with permission).   282
23   *Almanach Musical* (1775–83), vol. 7 (1782), Frontispiece. Paris: Au Bureau de L'Abonnement Littéraire, 1782. https://hdl.handle.net/2027/mdp.39015027690703   312
24   *Magazin der Musik*, vol. 1 (1783), Frontispiece. Hildesheim: Georg Olms Verlag, 1971. Image courtesy of The Irving S. Gilmore Music Library of Yale University.   313
25   Title page of the London edition of Haydn's *Ariana a Naxos* with the clause "Printed for the Author & sold by him" and Haydn's signature as publisher. Copy from the former Esterházy Collection. Courtesy of the National Széchényi Library, Budapest.   320

26 An engraving of the monument to Haydn at Rohrau, published in   322
    the *Allgemeine musikalische Zeitung*, March 12, 1800. Courtesy of the
    University of Toronto Music Library.
27 The dedication page of Franz Niemetschek's 1798 biography of   323
    Mozart. Courtesy of the University of Toronto Music Library.
28 An engraving from the title page of Artaria's edition of Haydn's 352
    Piano Trio in E♭, Hob.XV:10, published in 1798. Reproduced by
    permission of Jean Gray Hargrove Music Library, University of
    California, Berkeley.
29 Plan of the stage and orchestra of the second opera house at   363
    Eszterháza. Reproduced by permission of Oxford University Press.
30 Title page and cast list from the printed program of the first   368
    production of Haydn's *Orfeo ed Euridice*. Reproduced with permission
    of the Faculty of Music Library, University of Toronto, and *Maggio
    Musicale Fiorentino*, Florence.
31 The hierarchical organization of topical categories, and the   377
    interaction of topics in String Quartet Op. 50, No. 5, first movement.
32 Map of Vienna from John Stockdale's *A Geographical, Historical, and* 393
    Political Description of the Empire of Germany, Holland, the Netherlands,
    Switzerland, Prussia, Italy, Sicily, Corsica, and Sardinia (London, 1800).
    Reproduced with the permission of Wiener Stadt- und Landesarchiv
    (WStLA, Pläne und Karten: Sammelbestand, P5: 6175).
33 Kohlmarkt with Grosses Michaelerhaus immediately beside   398
    St. Michael's church, engraving by Karl Schütz 1786. Reproduced
    with the permission of Österreichische Nationalbibliothek,
    Bildarchiv.

Music Examples

1. Comparative table of melodies for "Acht Sauschneider müssen seyn"; from Klier 1932, prepared by R. Pietsch. — page 37
2. Transcription of "Es war einmal eine Jüdin" as sung by the Deutschkreutzer Frauen; Bohlman and Holzapfel 2001, 19–20. — 43
3. String Quartet in C major, Op. 20, No. 2, second movement, Adagio: Capriccio, mm. 1–6. — 104
4. "Maggie Lauder," harmonized by Haydn for George Thomson's *Select Collection of Original Scottish Airs*, Hob.XXXIa:35bis, reduction. — 123
5. Koch's 16-measure minuet; model form. — 126
6. Cadential scheme for a sonata exposition, after Koch. — 126
7. Sonata in E minor, Hob.XVI:47bis, third movement; hypothetical *Anlage*. — 128
8. Sonata in E minor, Hob.XVI:47bis, third movement; derivation of subordinate theme. — 129
9. Sonata in E minor, Hob.XVI:47bis, third movement; derivation of the modulating transition. — 130
10. Keyboard Sonata in D major, Hob.XVI:14, first movement, mm. 1–10 and 23–37 (GA = Grundabsatz; QA = Quintabsatz). — 211
11. Symphony No. 85 in B♭ major, second movement, mm. 1–8. — 212
12. Quartet in G major, Op. 33, No. 5, first movement, opening measures, transcribed from the JHW score. — 258
13. "Quartetto I," first movement, opening measures, Artaria parts. — 265
14. "Quartetto I," first movement, mm. 182–93, transcribed from Artaria parts. — 267
15. Sonata in B♭ major, Hob.XVI:41, first movement, mm. 1–8, original edition by H. Bossler (Speyer, 1784). — 269
16. Trio in E♭ major, Hob.XV:11, first movement, mm. 1–23, Artaria print. — 271
17. Trio in C minor, Hob.XV:13, first movement, mm. 1–8, transcribed from Artaria parts. — 278
18. String Quartet Op. 20, No. 5, third movement, mm. 1–4. — 341
19. "Pleasing Pain," mm. 8–18. — 342
20. Symphony No. 40, fourth movement, mm. 46–54. — 343
21. Topics in the first 5 measures of Sonata in E♭ major, Hob.XVI:52. — 381
22. Sonata in D major, Hob.XVI:42, mm. 1–4. — 390
23. Haydn's notation of a children's chorus heard in St. Paul's Cathedral, London, recorded in his First London Notebook. — 403

Contributors

Daniel Barolsky	Beloit College
Tom Beghin	Orpheus Institute
Philip V. Bohlman	University of Chicago
Eloise Boisjoli	University of Texas, Austin
Federico Celestini	Innsbruck University
Keith Chapin	Cardiff University
Jen-yen Chen	National Taiwan University
Caryl Clark	University of Toronto
Katelyn Clark	University of Toronto
Alan Davison	University of Technology Sydney
Sarah Day-O'Connell	Skidmore College
Felix Diergarten	University of Music, Freiburg
Emily I. Dolan	Harvard University
Martin Eybl	University of Music and Performing Arts, Vienna
Mark Ferraguto	Pennsylvania State University
Michelle Fillion	University of Victoria
Andreas Friesenhagen	Joseph Haydn Institute
Wolfgang Fuhrmann	University of Leipzig
Matthew Gelbart	Fordham University
Robert Giglio	Museum of Fine Arts, Boston
James Grande	King's College London
Roger Mathew Grant	Wesleyan University
Emily H. Green	George Mason University
Andrew A. Greenwood	Southern Illinois University Edwardsville
Robert S. Hatten	University of Texas, Austin
Matthew Head	King's College London
Erin Helyard	University of Melbourne
Ludwig Holtmeier	University of Music, Freiburg
Mary Hunter	Bowdoin College
David Wyn Jones	Cardiff University
Edward Klorman	McGill University
Raymond Knapp	University of California, Los Angeles
Elisabeth Le Guin	University of California, Los Angeles
Deirdre Loughridge	Northeastern University
Melanie Lowe	Vanderbilt University
János Malina	Independent Scholar
Nathan John Martin	University of Michigan
Nicholas Mathew	University of California, Berkeley

List of Contributors

Catherine Mayes	University of Utah
Edward McCue	Independent Scholar
Nicholas McGegan	Music Director, Philharmonia Baroque Orchestra
James Van Horn Melton	Emory University
Balázs Mikusi	National Széchényi Library, Budapest
Luisa Morales	FIMTE Almeria; University of Melbourne
Mary Sue Morrow	University of Cincinnati
Martin Nedbal	University of Kansas
Markus Neuwirth	Swiss Federal Institute of Technology Lausanne
Nancy November	University of Auckland
Janet K. Page	University of Memphis
James Parsons	Missouri State University
Rudolf Pietsch	University of Music and Performing Arts, Vienna
Pierpaolo Polzonetti	University of California, Davis
Bryan Proksch	Lamar University
Armin Raab	Joseph Haydn Institute
Walter Reicher	Haydn Festival and Foundation, Eisenstadt
Annette Richards	Cornell University
Michael Ruhling	Rochester Institute of Technology
Elaine Sisman	Columbia University
W. Dean Sutcliffe	University of Auckland
Wiebke Thormählen	Royal College of Music
Thomas Tolley	University of Edinburgh
Bertil Van Boer	Western Washington University
Christopher Wiley	University of Surrey
Ulrich Wilker	Goethe University, Frankfurt
Richard Will	University of Virginia
Susan Wollenberg	Oxford University
Laurel E. Zeiss	Baylor University

Preface and Guide to Readers

Over the four years that this encyclopedia was in development, we had many conversations with contributors and colleagues about its somewhat unconventional approach. No entries on works, individuals, or genres, we'd explain. After all, we already have the excellent *Oxford Composer Companion: Haydn* (ed. David Wyn Jones) and *Das Haydn-Lexikon* (ed. Armin Raab, Christine Siegert, and Wolfram Steinbeck) – both of which continue to ably serve the reference needs of Haydn scholars, performers, and listeners. Instead, our volume would be organized around clusters of ideas. Cross-references would lead readers from one entry to another, allowing them to see the connections but also the variety of perspectives and methods that exist within Haydn studies today.

Time and again, these conversations would lead to comparisons with eighteenth-century encyclopedia-writing. We would recall that d'Alembert warned the readers (critics?) of his great *Encyclopédie* (1751–72, written and edited with Diderot) not to expect to find the lives of the saints, genealogies of the aristocracy, or the great conquerors of historical battles. Instead, he promised, they would gain "an overview of learning, as if gazing down on a vast labyrinth of all the branches of human knowledge, observing where they separate or unite, and catching sight of the secret roots between them." Likewise, Rousseau, in his *Dictionnaire de musique* (1768, a revision and expansion of his music-related entries for the *Encyclopédie*), wrote entries that at once articulated, rejected, and adapted traditional views. Theirs was the Age of Enlightenment, ours is the Age of Information; what both eras have in common is a knowledge revolution. Then as now, people ponder the nature of facts and interpretation, the role of editors, and the creation (as well as democratization) of knowledge.

Of course, to draw too many comparisons between the *Encyclopédie* or the *Dictionnaire* and the *Cambridge Haydn Encyclopedia* would be grandiose – and absurd. Rousseau produced some 900 entries, and d'Alembert and Diderot produced 28 volumes – 730 times as many entries and 1,000 times as many words, on all manner of subjects – all the while living under the threat of arrest, confiscation, and exile! Our choices as editors have not been decisions about how to avoid being thrown into the Bastille. And yet, it could be said that we two North American women (and note: there were no named female contributors to the *Encyclopédie*) are making a contribution not just to scholarship but to the evolution of scholarship, and it is indeed a contribution that bears some family resemblances to – or perhaps better, that owes debts to – the *encyclopédistes*. Like these ancestors, we toyed at first with arranging the book thematically, with lead essays introducing interrelated entries, but ultimately settled on alphabetical

xv

order, with essays interspersed. Our first editor, Vicki Cooper, had urged us to rethink this plan, and she was right to do so, for as Diderot put it in his entry on "Encyclopédie" (at over 30,000 words long, a seventh of the length of our entire book), he and his colleagues had concluded that alphabetical order is the least intrusive: it allows readers to draw connections for themselves, and to see how any detail can be related to the whole. Also like Diderot, we take particular satisfaction in providing cross-references (he called them the most important part), which expand the subject and hopefully take the readers on rewarding detours they had not anticipated. This is a book designed to be consulted, but also to stay in one's hands and be read.

In addition to organizational models, we have inherited some style cues. We encouraged our contributors – all sixty-seven of them (from thirteen different countries around the world, for a truly international perspective on Haydn studies) – to be thought-provoking and opinionated, and we allowed dissent between entries. Obviously, more than our eighteenth-century counterparts, we needed the entries to give the reader a clear sense of the state of research, but in their same spirit we encouraged contributors to leave clear traces of the real people, with real agendas, that have shaped that state. In this way, our resource is different from many present-day encyclopedias, which may have entries that read as "truth." In our case, historiography is meant to be built in. As in the case of the *Encyclopédie*, our contributors were on board with the vision and the mission to varying degrees. We likewise nudged and pushed and even championed certain directions, but also strove to allow individual authorial flavors to show through . . . and never channeled Diderot to the point of appending our own commentaries.

In the end, Diderot wrote, an encyclopedia can "throw off the yoke of authority" only when compiled by a loose association of experts. While any number of the circumstances may be different, his dictum remains true. It has been an incredible privilege to work with our association of experts (including each other!), from whom we have learned so much. But we will have to continue to aspire to Diderot's definition of an editor: "neither a genius nor an imbecile, but someone gifted with great common sense, celebrated for the breadth of [her] knowledge, the elevation of [her] sentiment and of [her] ideas and [her] love of [her] work: a [woman] loved and respected for [her] character in private and in public; never zealous, if not for truth, for virtue, and for humanity."

***

The volume consists of over seventy entries and seven longer, conceptual essays: Biography and Identity, Ideas, Institutions, Musical Materials, People and Networks, Performance, and Place. The essays often refer to and make connections between related entries. The entire volume is arranged in alphabetical order. Naturally, there are innumerable topics of interest that do not have their own entry. If you are seeking something you do not find, please head to the index, which we have tried to make as thorough as possible. There you will also find every Haydn composition that is referenced in the volume; it is listed according to genre together with Hoboken numbers. The list of entries and essays included at the outset of the volume shows the contents at a glance and should also be helpful if you are seeking something that turns out not to have an entry of its own. The Chronology, drawn from standard sources, offers an overarching summary of Haydn's life and musical productivity.

Scholars are referred to by last name in entries and by full name in essays. Each entry and each essay is followed by a Further Reading list in the short form (author, date). Full information for each of these references appears in the Bibliography. The standard reference literature and most commonly cited sources are named in abbreviated form; please consult the List of Abbreviations.

Cross-references appear in SMALL CAPITALS. They are marked in this way usually (but not always) at the first iteration within the entry or essay. Variants of entry headwords may be marked as cross-references: for example, ENLIGHTENED may be marked to draw the reader's attention to the entry ENLIGHTENMENT.

Musical examples help to exemplify points made by authors; they also acknowledge the multiple ways of engaging music in human experience. Musical notes are indicated using the Helmholtz system: CC, C, c, c′, c″, c‴, where middle C = c′. Illustrations (Figures) are meant to help readers understand Haydn's music with respect to geographical locations, spaces of performance, print culture, commodification, and acts of human communication and interaction. They are limited precisely because so many images relevant to Haydn are readily available on the Internet. So, while no images or likenesses of Haydn accompany the entry on ICONOGRAPHY, a simple search of the artist's name listed in the entry will summon forth numerous exemplars – and in color too. The 1791 Haydn portrait by John Hoppner was the inspiration for Andreas Roseneder's 2007 "retake" on the front cover (see Melanie Lowe's entry on present-day RECEPTION) – an apt visualization of our aims for this volume.

Acknowledgments

This collaboration began in a conversation during a conference at our mutual *alma mater*. We both feel grateful and proud to have studied and earned our PhD degrees at Cornell University (albeit in different decades) alongside scholars who were and who would become shapers of the discipline, especially in the areas of eighteenth-century music and culture.

From the start, a multitude of individuals have helped us to develop and ultimately bring this project to completion. Above all, we thank our many knowledgeable and generous contributors for gathering together, synthesizing, and creating knowledge while also suggesting new areas of research – the CHE (as we affectionately call it) owes its strengths to you. Caryl is grateful to her graduate-student research assistants at the University of Toronto, who helped vet and edit numerous entries, assisted with image procurement, prepared the chronology as well as several charts and musical examples, and willingly undertook all manner of tasks: Virginia Georgallas, Steven Hicks, Lindsay Jones, Kaleb Koslowski, Sarah Koval, Tegan Niziol, and Shelley Zhang – the future of music scholarship is in good hands. University of Toronto librarians Houman Behzadi, Jan Guise, James Mason, and Tim Neufeldt graciously assisted at various stages, as did many unnamed others at institutions and archives in North America and Europe. Thanks also for RA support and funding of images provided by the Social Sciences and Humanities Research Council of Canada. Sarah thanks her colleagues at the two liberal arts colleges she's called home during these years, Knox College and Skidmore College, for modeling the integrative thinking and collaborative work that inspires this volume; two groups of Skidmore seminar students (Samantha Abrams, Schuyler Borden, Matthew Borkowski, William Bresee, Alastair Canavan, Rachel Chang, Yanqi Chen, Olivia Cox, Michaela Dawe, Joseph Eisele, Taylor Fohrhaltz-Burbank, Anna Gerber, Hannah Knaul, Jules Koslow, Brennan Mitrolka, Caroline Moe, Nicole Mooers, Rachel Perez, Lea Peterson, Jordan Shedrofsky, Rebecca Sohn, Leigh Tooker, and Carder Welles) for inspiring new ways of thinking about Haydn and about encyclopedias; and participants of the 2016 "Teaching Music History" Conference (sponsored by the Pedagogy Study Group of the American Musicological Society) for constructive and empathic feedback on her presentation "Faculty–Student Research in Musicology: What, Why, How." We are grateful to Dean Crystal Moore and the Skidmore College Office of the Dean of Faculty for funding to assist with indexing.

We began at the invitation of commissioning editor Vicki Cooper, who readily supported our approach – and her successor, Kate Brett, heartily embraced it as well. Kate provided excellent advice, more-than-generous availability, exceedingly good humor, and crucial moral support throughout the long gestation process. To both of these insightful women, and to the many other extraordinarily capable folks with whom we have worked – editorial assistant Eilidh Burrett; copy-editors Gillian Cloke, Hilary Scannell, and Ken Moxham; content manager Lisa Sinclair; indexer Lisa DeBoer – we offer our heartfelt thanks.

Finally, from Sarah, loving thanks to Jeremy for countless forms of moral support. And from Caryl, as ever, love and continuing gratitude to Lou for his patient encouragement.

Chronology

	Life and Career	Musical Productivity
1732	Born March 31, Rohrau, Lower Austria, to Mathias Haydn, a wheelwright, magistrate, and amateur musician, and Anna Maria Koller; baptized Franz Joseph on April 1.	
1737	Receives his first formal training while living with a distant cousin, Mathias Franck, in Hainburg.	
	Haydn's brother and future composer, Johann Michael, is born.	
c. 1739–40	Recruited by Georg Reutter (1708–72), Kapellmeister at St. Stephen's Cathedral in Vienna, to join the choir school; receives instruction in violin, harpsichord, and vocal performance, as well as some instruction in composition and theory. In particular, becomes acquainted with Johann Joseph Fux's *Gradus ad Parnassum* (1725) and Johann Mattheson's *Der vollkommene Capellmeister* (1739).	
c. 1745	Haydn is joined by his younger brother, Johann Michael (1737–1806), at St. Stephen's Cathedral choir school.	
1747–9	Leaves the choir school at St. Stephen's Cathedral after his voice changes.	*Missa brevis* in F major, Hob. XXII:1 (1749?): rev. 1805
	Haydn moves into the garret room in the Michaelerhaus (where Metastasio and Marianna Martines also lived), and works as an independent musician.	
1750–1	Compositions in the 1750s reflect acquaintance with contemporaneous music in a wide range of genres.	
	In mid-1750s, Haydn works at several churches as an occasional singer and violinist, and augments his income performing in pick-up ensembles for	

	Life and Career	Musical Productivity
	special events at court and in the theater. His most important patron at this time is Baron Carl Joseph Fürnberg (1720–67), who commissions the earliest string quartets and recommends the composer's services to Count Karl Joseph Franz Morzin (1717–83). Haydn also comes into close contact with court poet Pietro Metastasio (1714–87) between 1751–54.	
1752	Meets comic actor and impresario Joseph Felix von Kurz.	First stage work, Der krumme Teufel, Hob.XXIXb:1a
1753	Works as valet and keyboard accompanist for the Neapolitan opera composer and singing teacher Nicola Porpora, learning the Italian language and *partimento* counterpoint, which Haydn referred to as "the true fundamentals of composition."	
	Friend of fellow violinist and composer Carl Ditters (1739–99) throughout the decade.	
1754	Approximately 1754–58 Haydn works as a singer, violinist and organist at several venues in Vienna, including the Hofkapelle, the chapel of Count Friedrich Wilhelm Haugwitz, the church of the Brothers Hospitallers (Barmherzigen Brüder), and St. Stephen's Cathedral.	
1755	Haydn's beloved student, Theresia Helena Keller, enters the convent.	
1756		Salve Regina, Hob.XXIIIb:1
		First Concerto for Organ, Hob.XVIII:1
		Earliest string quartets
c. 1757	Possibly began working for Count Morzin in Vienna during the winter, and in Lukawitz, Bohemia in the summer. Earliest symphonies were for Morzin court.	Possible first symphony: Symphony No. 1 in C major
1759		Der (neue) krumme Teufel, Hob. XXIXb:1b

	Life and Career	Musical Productivity
1760	Marries Maria Anna Theresia Keller, the elder sister of Haydn's first love Theresia Helena Keller.	
1761	Appointed to the position of Vice-Kapellmeister at the court of Prince Paul Anton Esterházy in Eisenstadt; assists Kapellmeister Gregor Joseph Werner (1693–1766) with church music, and is responsible for all secular music. Contract stipulates near equal supervision of all musicians with Werner.	Symphonic trilogy on the times of day – Symphony No. 6 in D major, "Le matin"; Symphony No. 7 in C major, "Le midi"; Symphony No. 8 in G major, "Le soir"
1762	Death of Prince Paul Anton Esterházy March 18; succeeded by Prince Nicolaus "The Magnificent." Premiere of Gluck's *Orfeo ed Euridice* in Vienna. Until 1766 the court moves between Eisenstadt and Vienna. During this period, renovations are undertaken on the palace at Süttör, which becomes the permanent seat of Nicolaus's court, Eszterháza.	
1763	Completes first Italian *opera seria*, *Acide*, for wedding of Prince Nicolaus Esterházy's oldest son, Count Anton, to Countess Maria Theresia Erdödy, on January 10.	*Acide*, Hob.XXVIII:1 *Destatevi, o miei fidi*, Hob. XXIVa:2, cantata composed for Prince Nicolaus Esterházy's name-day *La marchesa Nespola* (one aria survives, Hob.XXX:1)
1764	Prince Nicolaus Esterházy returns from Frankfurt to Eisenstadt. Theatrical performances held at Kittsee and Pressburg and over the next couple of years.	*Da qual gioia improvvisa*, Hob. XXIVa:3, to celebrate Prince Nicolaus Esterházy's return Symphony No. 22 in E♭ major, "Philosopher"
1765	Begins thematic catalogue of compositions, *Entwurf-Katalog*; contributes regularly to the catalogue into the 1770s.	Cello Concerto No. 1 in C major, Hob.VIIb:1 Capriccio in G major, Hob. XVII:1, "Acht Sauschneider müssen seyn"

	Life and Career	Musical Productivity
	Studies C.P.E. Bach's *Versuch*, affecting improvisatory nature of his keyboard works.	Symphony No. 30 in C major, "Alleluja" Symphony No. 31 in D major, "Horn Signal"
	Mid-1760s Haydn learns to play the baryton, the favorite instrument of Prince Nicolaus; encouraged to produce more works for this instrument for performance by the prince.	
1766	Promoted to Kapellmeister following the death of Werner; assumes full responsibilities for musical life of the court.	Mass in C major, Hob. XXII:5, *Missa Cellensis in honorem BVM, Cacilienmesse*
	Purchases house in Eisenstadt.	
	Prince Nicolaus issues requirements for operatic performances for the entertainment of guests.	*La canterina*, Hob.XXVIII:2
	Haydn responds to demands for more baryton works with an elegantly bound edition of trios.	First book of Baryton Divertimenti, Hob. XI:1–24
1767	As a result of his new responsibilities as Kapellmeister, Haydn increases production of both sacred and secular vocal music.	*Stabat mater*, Hob.XXbis. Second book of Baryton Divertimenti, Hob. XI:25–48
1768	Opera house at Eszterháza inaugurated with Haydn's *Lo speziale*, based on a libretto by Carlo Goldoni.	*Lo speziale* (*Der Apotheker*), Hob.XXVIII:3 *Applausus* cantata (*Jubilaeum Virtutis Palatium*), Hob. XXIVa:6
	Haydn's baryton writing in the third book for Prince Nicolaus becomes more complex, demonstrating the prince's increased technical skill by mandating use of both the bowed strings and the unusual plucked manual of the instrument.	Third book of Baryton Divertimenti, Hob. XI:49–72 Symphony No. 49 in F minor, "La passione"
	Haydn's house in Eisenstadt destroyed by fire. Rebuilt with support of prince.	
1769	Haydn's instrumental style becomes more eclectic, continuing into next decade. Resumes composition of string quartets.	*Le pescatrici*, Hob.XXVIII:4
	Prince Nicolaus establishes summer theatrical performances, possibly requiring incidental music from Haydn.	Symphony No. 59 in A major, "Fire"
		String Quartets Op. 9 underway

	Life and Career	Musical Productivity
	Haydn travels to Pressburg for five days to scout out new singers for Eszterháza.	
1770	Haydn's opera *Le pescatrici* staged at Eszterháza in celebration of the marriage of Countess Maria Theresia Lamberg to Count Alois Poggi.	Symphony No. 26 in D minor, "Lamentatione"
1771	Haydn becomes ill and is visited by his brother. Following his recovery, Haydn may have begun composing the *Salve Regina* in G minor, Hob. XXIIIb:2.	Keyboard Sonata in C minor, Hob.XVI:20 String Quartets, Op. 17
1772	Carl Wahr's theatrical troupe performs at Eszterháza for the next five years. The repertoire includes tragedies by Lessing, Goethe, and Shakespeare (*Hamlet, Macbeth, Othello,* and *King Lear*).	Symphony No. 43 in E♭ major, "Mercury" Symphony No. 44 in E minor, "Trauersinfonie" ("Mourning") Symphony No. 45 in F♯ minor, "Farewell" String Quartets, Op. 20, "Sun" Mass in G major, Hob. XXII:6, *Missa Sancti Nicolai*
1773	Haydn's *Philemon und Baucis* performed at the opening of the marionette theater at Eszterháza; attended by members of the Habsburg court including Empress Maria Theresia.	*L'infedeltà delusa*, Hob. XXVIII:5 *Philemon und Baucis*, marionette opera, Hob.XXIXa:1
1774	First authorized publication of Haydn's music by Kurzböck in Vienna—keyboard sonatas Hob.XVI:21–26 (dedicated to Prince Nicolaus)	Symphony No. 55 in E♭ major, "The Schoolmaster" Symphony No. 60 in C major, "Il distratto" Mass in E♭ major, Hob. XXII:4, *Missa in honorem BVM, Missa Sancti Josephi,* "Grosse Orgelsolomesse"
1775	*L'incontro improvviso* performed for Archduke Ferdinand and his wife Maria Ricciarda Beatrice d'Este at Eszterháza. Haydn conducts performances of *Il ritorno di Tobia* at the Kärntnertortheater in Vienna.	*Dido*, Hob.XXIXa:3, lost marionette opera, approximate composition date *L'incontro improvviso*, Hob. XXVIII:6

	Life and Career	Musical Productivity
		Il ritorno di Tobia, Hob.XXI:1, Haydn's first oratorio, commissioned by the Viennese Tonkünstler Societät
1776	Short autobiographical sketch published in an Austrian encyclopedia.	Incidental music for Der Zerstreute (Symphony No. 60 in C major)
	Theatrical offerings at Eszterháza now include a regular season of marionette and staged theater, as well as opera. The first season begins with Gluck's Orfeo ed Euridice.	
1777	Comic opera Il mondo della luna premiered at Eszterháza celebrating the marriage of Prince Nicolaus's second son.	Il mondo della luna, Hob. XXVIII:7
	Haydn's marionette opera Hexenschabbas (now lost) performed at Schönbrunn at the request of Empress Maria Theresia.	
1778	Haydn sells his house in Eisenstadt.	Symphony No. 64 in A major, "Tempora mutantur"
	Court extends stay at Eszterháza for up to ten months of the year, spending winters in Vienna.	Divertimento in F major for 4 hands, Hob.XVIIa:1, "Il maestro e lo scolare"
	Artaria & Co. enters music publishing business in Vienna.	Mass in B♭ major, Hob. XXII:7, Missa brevis Sancti Joannis de Deo, "Kleine Orgelsolomesse" ("Little Organ Mass")
1779	On January 1 Haydn signs a new contract with Prince Nicolaus Esterházy, allowing him to publish and sell his music and accept outside commissions without the consent of his patron.	Symphony No. 53 in D major, "Imperial"
		Symphony No. 69 in C major, "Laudon"
		Die bestrafte Rachbegierde, Hob.XXIXb:3, lost marionette opera
	On 18 November, fire destroys the opera house at Eszterháza; many operatic scores are lost.	La vera costanza, Hob. XXVIII:8
	Soprano Luigia Polzelli (1750–1830) is employed at court.	L'isola disabitata, Hob. XXVIII:9

	Life and Career	Musical Productivity
1780	Haydn issues first publication with Artaria, and enjoys an upsurge in commercial activity.	*La fedeltà premiata*, Hob. XXVIII:10 Artaria publishes set of six keyboard sonatas, Hob. XVI:20, 35–39, dedicated to Auenbrugger sisters
1781	Haydn's *La fedeltà premiata* opens the new opera house at Eszterháza. Librettist and theater director Nunziato Porta arrives at Eszterháza. Haydn markets his music in England with Forster.	Symphony No. 63 in C major, "La Roxelane" String Quartets, Op. 33, "Russian" Artaria publishes Haydn's first set of lieder, Hob. XXVIa:1–12, in Vienna
1782	Begins professional relationship with publisher John Bland in London. Joseph Elssler, Haydn's first copyist, dies; he is succeeded by his son of the same name and subsequently by Johann Elssler, who becomes Haydn's principal copyist by the late 1780s.	Mass in C major, Hob. XXII:8, *Missa Cellensis*, "Mariazellermesse" *Orlando paladino*, Hob. XXVIII:11 Artaria publishes Haydn's Op. 33 string quartets
1783	Growing emphasis on *seria* works over *opera buffa* at Eszterháza. Future Prince Nicolaus II marries Princess Marie Hermenegild.	Cello Concerto No. 2 in D major, Hob.VIIb:2 *Armida*, Hob.XXVIII:12
1784	*Armida*, Haydn's last opera for the court, is staged at Eszterháza to mark the completion of the estate. Carl Friedrich Cramer publishes the first issue of his *Magazin der Musik*, in which he praises the works of Haydn. First documented evidence, provided by Irish tenor Michael Kelly, of Haydn meeting Mozart at a quartet party. Haydn played first violin and Mozart played viola.	"Svanisce in un momento," additional chorus included in revival of *Il ritorno di Tobia*, Hob.XXI:1 Artaria publishes the second set of lieder, Hob. XXVIa:13–24
1785	Becomes a Freemason in January and joins the lodge "Zur wahren Eintracht" (True Concord). In September, Artaria publishes Mozart's String Quartets Nos. 14–19, K. 387, 421, 428, 458, 464, 465 (respectively), dedicated to Haydn. Increased number of commissions from abroad, including the "Paris"	First two "Paris" symphonies performed (Nos. 83 and 85)

	Life and Career	Musical Productivity
	Symphonies, and *The Seven Last Words of Our Savior on the Cross*.	
1786	Haydn composes three piano trios at the request of Artaria, Hob.XV:6–8.	"Paris" Symphonies, Nos. 82–87, Concert de la Loge Olympique
1787	Resumes composition of string quartets after hiatus of nearly six years. Haydn declines an invitation to compose an opera for Prague. Johann Elssler becomes Haydn's personal copyist.	String Quartets, Op. 50, "Prussian" *The Seven Last Words of Our Savior on the Cross*, Hob. XX/1, performed at Good Friday ceremony in Cádiz
1788	Purchases Schanz keyboard. Gluck's ballet *Don Juan* performed at Eszterháza.	String Quartets, Op. 54, and Op. 55, "Tost"
1789	John Bland visits Haydn at Eszterháza to negotiate a new set of string quartets. Haydn begins regular contact with Maria Anna von Genzinger, a Viennese aristocrat and amateur pianist married to Prince Nicolaus's physician. July 14 1789, French Revolution begins with storming of the Bastille.	Symphony No. 92 in G major, "Oxford" Solo cantata *Ariana a Naxos*, Hob.XXVIb:2
1790	Prince Nicolaus Esterházy dies in September; his successor, Prince Anton, disbands the orchestra and opera troupe, leaving Haydn free to seek employment elsewhere. In December, Haydn accepts offer from the German violinist and impresario Johann Peter Salomon (1745–1815) to go to London; enroute he meets the young Ludwig van Beethoven (1770–1827) at the electoral court in Bonn.	String Quartets, Op. 64, "Tost"
1791	Arrives in London in early January. Receives an honorary Doctor of Music degree from Oxford University in July. "Oxford" Symphony, No. 92, is performed during the ceremony. Publisher John Bland commissions Thomas Hardy to paint Haydn's portrait. Wolfgang Amadeus Mozart (b. 1756) dies in Vienna in December.	*L'anima del filosofo, ossia Orfeo ed Euridice*, Hob.XXVIII:13 (not performed) Earliest "London" Symphonies performed at Hanover Square Rooms with Salomon on violin and Haydn playing keyboard; first set of six "London" Symphonies, nos. 93–98

xxvii

	Life and Career	Musical Productivity
1792	Continuation of Salomon concert series in Hanover Square Rooms. Haydn impressed by performance of anthem, God Save the Queen. Theme woven into Symphony 98, Hob. I:98. Visits William Herschel at his observatory in Slough, West London. Leaves London in July to return to Vienna. Meets with Beethoven again on return trip.	*The Storm*, Hob.XXIVa:8 *Sinfonia concertante* in B♭ major Symphony No. 97 in C major, and Symphony No. 98 in B♭ major round out the first set of six symphonies for London
1793	Purchases house in the Viennese suburb of Gumpendorf; moves in permanently in 1796. Beethoven moves to Vienna; studies composition with Haydn. First monument erected in honor of Haydn in Rohrau by Count Karl Leonhard von Harrach.	String Quartets, Op. 71, and Op. 74, "Apponyi" F minor variations for keyboard, Hob.XVII:6
1794	Prince Anton Esterházy dies in January and is succeeded by Prince Nicolaus II. Haydn arrives in London in February for a second visit, accompanied by his copyist Johann Elssler. Publishing firm Corri & Dussek founded in London.	Symphony No. 99 in E♭ major performed during first season of second London visit. Symphony No. 100 in G major, "Military"; Symphony No. 101 in D major, "Clock"; and Symphony No. 102 in B♭ major – all performed the following year Six Original Canzonettas, Hob.XXVIa:25–30 English Psalms, Hob. XXIII, originally published in Reverend William Tattersall's *Improved Psalmody* Corri & Dussek publish String Quartets Op. 71, and Op. 74; and arrangements of the "London" Symphonies, Nos. 93–98 for piano trio
1795	Departs London in August, returns to Vienna via northern Germany to avoid	Symphony No. 103 in E♭ major, "Drumroll"

	Life and Career	Musical Productivity
	warfare in the south; reinstated as Esterházy Kapellmeister for Prince Nicolaus II; minimal court duties, responsible for the eight wind instrumentalists of the *Harmonie* and a small group of string players (primarily for performances at Eisenstadt).	Symphony No. 104 in D major, "London" Keyboard Sonata in E♭ major, Hob.XVI:52, for Therese Jansen Keyboard Trio No. 25 in G major, Hob.XV:25, "Gypsy Rondo" *Berenice, che fai?* Hob. XXIVa:10 Six Original Canzonettas, Book 2, Hob. XXVIa:31–36, published by Corri & Dussek in London
1796	Begins collaboration with Baron Gottfried van Swieten, the imperial librarian, former censor, and leader of the Gesellschaft der Associierten, an association of noble patrons. Leipzig firm Breitkopf & Härtel becomes Haydn's primary publisher.	Trumpet Concerto in E♭ major, Hob.VIIe:1 Mass in B♭ major, Hob. XXII:10, *Missa Sancti Bernardi von Offida, Heiligmesse* Mass in C major, Hob. XXII:9, *Missa in tempore belli, Paukenmesse, Kriegsmesse* *The Seven Last Words of Our Savior on the Cross*, Hob. XX:2, added choral parts
1797	In January, Haydn granted free admission to all concerts of the Gesellschaft der Associierten, and on December 11 appointed "senior assessor" in perpetuity. Made a life member of the Viennese Tonkünstler Societät.	"Gott, erhalte Franz den Kaiser!" ("Emperor's Hymn") Hob.XXVIa:43, basis for a set of variations in the second movement of String Quartet in C major, Op. 76 no. 3, "Emperor." Later the basis for the German national anthem String Quartets, Op. 76, "Erdödy"
1798	Tonkünstler-Societät performs vocal arrangement of Haydn's *The Seven Last Words of Our Savior on the Cross*, Hob. XX:2. First private performance of *The Creation* at the Schwarzenberg Palace.	Mass in D minor, Hob. XXII:11, *Missa in angustiis*, "Nelson Mass," written around the time of Horatio Nelson's victory against Napoleon's fleet

	Life and Career	Musical Productivity
		at Aboukir Bay, possibly heard by Nelson during his visit to Eisenstadt in 1800
1799	Georg August Griesinger (1769–1845) has initial visit with Haydn as a representative from Breitkopf & Härtel. Breitkopf & Härtel begins publishing its *Oeuvres complettes de Joseph Haydn*. Nine portraits and busts of Haydn produced between 1799 and 1800.	*The Creation*, Hob.XXI:2 String Quartets, Op. 77 (later "Lobkowitz") Mass in B♭ major, Hob. XXII:12, *Theresienmesse* First public performance of *The Creation* at the Burgtheater on March 19; oratorio performed again in December as a benefit for the Tonkünstler Societät George Thomson commissions British folksong arrangements, Hob. XXXIa
1800	Haydn's wife dies in Baden in March. Parisian premiere of *The Creation*.	
1801	Private premiere of *The Seasons* on April 24 at the Schwarzenberg Palace followed by the first public performance at the Redoutensaal on May 19.	*The Seasons*, Hob.XXI:3 Mass in B♭ major, Hob. XXII:13, *Schöpfungsmesse* ("Creation Mass") Publication of Op. 77 String Quartets, dedicated to Prince Lobkowitz
1802	Completes last full composition, Mass No. 14; last string quartet, for Lobkowitz, left incomplete.	Mass in B♭ major, Hob. XXII:14, *Harmoniemesse*, Haydn's last major composition
1803	Haydn is presented with a medal by the city of Vienna.	String Quartet in D minor, Op. 103, incomplete
1805	Albert Christoph Dies (1755–1822) meets Haydn. Luigi Cherubini writes "Chant sur la mort de Joseph Haydn" when rumors of Haydn's death circulate in France and Britain; it is first performed in 1810, nine months after Haydn's death.	Haydn's copyist Johann Elssler prepares comprehensive thematic catalogue of Haydn's works, known as *Haydn-Verzeichnis*.
1806	Haydn basically housebound from this point onwards.	

	Life and Career	Musical Productivity
1808	Makes his last public appearance on March 27 at a performance of *The Creation* conducted by Antonio Salieri at the Great Hall of the Old University of Vienna.	
1809	Haydn dies on May 31 at his home while Vienna is under siege by the invading French armies. He is buried the next day in the cemetery at Gumpendorf. A large memorial service is held in Vienna on June 15.	

Abbreviations

Bartha and Somfai	Dénes Bartha and László Somfai, 1960. *Haydn als Opernkapellmeister*. Budapest: Ungarische Akademie der Wissenschaften.
Beghin and Goldberg	Tom Beghin and Sander M. Goldberg, 2007. *Haydn and the Performance of Rhetoric*. University of Chicago Press.
Briefe	Dénes Bartha (ed.), 1965. *Joseph Haydn: Gesammelte Briefe und Aufzeichnungen*. Kassel: Bärenreiter.
Cambridge Companion	Caryl Clark (ed.), 2005. *The Cambridge Companion to Haydn*. Cambridge University Press.
CCLN	H. C. Robbins Landon (ed.), 1959. *The Collected Correspondence and London Notebooks of Joseph Haydn*. London: Barrie and Rockliffe.
Dies	Albert Christoph Dies, 1810. *Biographische Nachrichten von Joseph Haydn*. Vienna: Camesina.
Gotwals	Vernon Gotwals (trans. and ed.), 1963. *Joseph Haydn: Eighteenth-Century Gentleman and Genius. A Translation with Introduction and Notes by Vernon Gotwals of the Biographische Notizen über Joseph Haydn by G. A. Gresinger and the Biographischen Nachrichten Von Joseph Haydn by A.C. Dies*. Madison: University of Wisconsin Press.
Griesinger	Georg August Griesinger, 1810; rpt. 1954. *Biographische Notizen über Joseph Haydn*. Leipzig: Breitkopf & Härtel; Vienna: Paul Kaltschmid.
Grove Online	Grove Music Online, Oxford Music Online, www.oxfordmusiconline.com.
Haydn Studies	W. Dean Sutcliffe (ed.), 1998a. *Haydn Studies*. Cambridge University Press.
H-L	Armin Raab, Christine Siegert, and Wolfram Steinbeck (eds.), 2010. *Das Haydn-Lexikon*, Laaber.
Hoboken [Hob.]	Anthony van Hoboken, 1957–78. *Joseph Haydn: Thematisch-bibliographisches Werkverzeichnis*, 3 vols. Mainz: Schott.
Hunter and Will	Mary Hunter and Richard Will (eds.), 2012. *Engaging Haydn: Context, Culture and Criticism*. Cambridge University Press.

HWorld   Elaine Sisman (ed.), 1997b. *Haydn and his World*.
                      Princeton University Press.
JHW   [Haydn-Gesamtausgabe] *Joseph Haydn Werke*.
Landon I–V   H. C. Robbins Landon, 1976–80. *Haydn: Chronicle
                      and Works*, 5 vols. London: Thames and Hudson;
                      Bloomington: Indiana University Press.
MGG   *Die Musik in Geschichte und Gegenwart. Allgemeine
                      Enzyklopädie der Musik* 1994–2005, 2nd edn.
                      Kassel: Bärenreiter.
NG Haydn   James Webster and Georg Feder, 2002. *The New
                      Grove Haydn*. London: Macmillan; New York:
                      Palgrave.
Oxford Companion   David Wyn Jones (ed.), 2002b. *Oxford Composer
                      Companion to Haydn*. Oxford University Press.

Journals
H-St   *Haydn-Studien*
HYb   *Haydn-Yearbook*
ECM   *Eighteenth-Century Music*
EM   *Early Music*
JAMS   *Journal of the American Musicological Society*
JM   *Journal of Musicology*
JMR   *Journal of Musicological Research*
JRMA   *Journal of the Royal Musical Association*
M&L   *Music and Letters*
MQ   *The Musical Quarterly*
MT   *The Musical Times*

List of Entries and Essays

Note: Essays are indicated in **bold** typeface.

Acoustics – see Performance Spaces
Aesthetics
Aging
Amateurs
Americas, The
Archives – see Collections and
Audiences and Publics
Beautiful
Biography and Identity
Burgenland
Capitalism – see Commerce
Catalogues, Worklists, Nachlass
Church
Circulation
Collections and Archives
Commemorations and Festivals
Commerce and the Market
Composers and Music Professionals
Compositional Process
Correspondence and Notebooks
Cosmopolitanism – see Nationalism and
Counterpoint
Courts
Cyclic Integration
Dedicatees
Disability
Discography
Economics and Finances
Editions and Edition-Making
Education
Eisenstadt – see Eszterháza and
Empfindsamkeit
England – see London and
Enlightenment
Environments – see **Place**

Esterházy Court – see **People and Networks**; Courts
Eszterháza and Eisenstadt
European Contexts: France, Italy, Spain
Exoticism
Experiential Learning
Exploration – see Travel and
Festivals – see Commemorations and
Film – see Reception 1950s–Present
Finances – see Economics and
Folk Song Settings
Form
France – see European Contexts
Freemasonry
Friendships – see Relationships and
Gender
Genius
Harmony
Humor
Iconography
Idealism
Ideas
Identity – see **Biography**
Imagination – see Improvisation
Imitation – see Mimesis
Improvisation
Inspiration – see Improvisation
Institutions
Instruments and Organology
Italy – see European Contexts
Jewish Culture
Large Ensembles – see Leading Large Ensembles
Leading Large Ensembles
Librettos and Librettists
Literature – see Reception, 1950s–Present
London and England
Market; Marketplace – see Commerce and
Material Culture
Melancholy
Melody
Memorials; Memorializing – see Monuments and
Meter – see Rhythm and
Mimesis
Monuments and Memorializing
Musical Imaginary – see Travel
Musical Materials
Musical Societies
Nachlass – see Catalogues
National Melodies – see Folk Song Settings

Nationalism and Cosmopolitanism
Nature
Networks – see **People and**
Opera – see Theater and Theatricality
Orchestras – see Leading Large Ensembles
Orchestration
Organology – see Instruments and
Originality – see Genius
Pannonia – see Burgenland
Paris – see European Contexts
People and Networks
Performance
Performance Spaces
Philosophy – see Idealism
Place
Poets
Politics
Popular Culture – see Reception 1950s–Present
Portraits – see Iconography
Press
Printing – see Publishers and Publishing
Professionals – see Composers and Music
Programmatic Elements
Publics – see Audiences and
Publishers and Publishing
Reception – Contemporary;
Reception – Posthumous to 1959;
Reception – 1950s–Present
Recording
Rehearsal – see Vocal Coaching and
Relationships and Friendships
Religion and Spiritual Beliefs
Revivals – see Commemorations and Festivals
Revolution – see War
Rhetoric – see **Performance**
Rhythm and Meter
Science
Scotland – see Folk Song Settings
Self-Reflexivity
Sensibility – see *Empfindsamkeit*
Sociability
Societies – see Musical Societies
Spain – see European Contexts
Spiritual Beliefs – see Religion and
Sublime
Teaching and Students
Theater and Theatricality
Time

Tonality
Topics
Transatlantic Studies – see Americas, The
Travel and Exploration
Variation as Principle
Vienna
Vocal Coaching and Rehearsal
War
Women – see Relationships and Friendships; Gender
Worklists – see Catalogues

Acoustics – see Performance Spaces

Aesthetics Haydn seems to have taken a broad view of music aesthetics. Evidence of his aesthetic preconceptions is to be found, for example, in his London Notebooks, the contents of his library (Material Culture), and interviews with early biographer Griesinger, as well as the Musical Materials themselves. At root was the idea of good (melodic) invention and the ability to develop a theme in a logical and flowing manner. According to Griesinger, Haydn insisted that "fluent song" (*fliessender Gesang*) was a prerequisite for good music, and he lamented contemporary composers' lack of Vocal training: "[Haydn] also criticized the fact that now so many musicians compose who have never learned how to sing. 'Singing must almost be reckoned one of the lost arts; instead of song, people allow the instruments to dominate.'" The integrity of the "fluent song" itself was to be maintained and coherently worked out so that the resulting work would "remain in the heart" of the listener (Gotwals 61). Indeed the aesthetics of song can be considered to govern his musical output, vocal and instrumental works alike.

Central to Haydn's aesthetics, and contemporaries' reception of his music, is the concept of originality (see Genius). By his own account to Griesinger, Improvisation (*phantasieren*) at the keyboard was a fundamental first step in his Compositional Process: "I sat down, began to fantasize, according to whether my mood was sad or happy, serious or playful, [until] I had seized upon an idea" (Gotwals 61). He then sought to work out coherent musical ideas according to the "rules of art" (Bonds 136). Sisman notes that he distinguished the "rules" to which he referred from standard textbook compositional rules of the day, which he termed "artisan's fetters." These rules were to be understood, but not followed in a servile manner; rather, they were used strategically, broken when necessary, and manipulated to enhance a musical argument. Haydn's contemporaries recognized novelty as a key component of the resulting composition. His champions saw in his works the spirit of genius along the lines described by Immanuel Kant in his *Critique of Judgment*: "Genius is the talent (natural endowment) which gives the rule to art" (Sisman 9).

Aestheticians of Haydn's time such as Edmund Burke and Immanuel Kant divided the field using two key categories: the Sublime and the Beautiful. To these, a third category, the ornamental (*niedlich*) or picturesque was often added, for example by commentators such as Carl Friedrich Michaelis and William Crotch. These aesthetic ideas, which were clearly ranked in terms of status (sublime as highest, ornamental as

1

low) were applied to Haydn's music by reviewers and biographers of the day. They heard sublime elements in Haydn's *The Creation*, Hob. XXI:2, for example. The "Representation/Idea of Chaos" leading to the Creation of Light, in particular, fuses text and music to suggest something beyond comprehension – the origins of the universe – invoking, as Webster (1997) points out, the incompressibility that was central to Immanuel Kant's idea of the sublime. In applying the idea of the sublime to *The Creation*, contemporaries such as Christoph Martin Wieland went so far as to imply that the work actually effects a fusion of the persona in the work and the author of the work, thus looking back to the ancient definitions of the sublime by pseudo-Longinus.

The dyad/triad of sublime and beautiful (and picturesque) were categories of reception that stabilized towards the end of Haydn's career, and certain works of Haydn seemed to represent these categories well. However, Haydn himself was working within a much more fluid field of aesthetics. The pastoral mode is also invoked in Haydn's music, for example. A prime example is *The Seasons*, Hob.XXI:3, where it is mixed with the sublime. Webster (2005b) describes how the pastoral is invoked not only through word-painting, instrument choice, and "genre" pieces of a bucolic nature. Aspects such as run-on movements and the repetition of large-scale modulations create a sense of the cyclic passage of pastoral time.

Critics and admirers alike noted Haydn's use and mixing of the sublime, beautiful, and ornamental in his instrumental music. Brown observes that London reviewers of Haydn's later symphonies, and the scholar William Crotch, found that the sublime and ornamental featured alike in these works, although Crotch did complain that the ornamental style predominated. London reviewers found Haydn's use of the sublime, in particular, to be praiseworthy in works like Symphony in E♭ major, No. 103 ("Drumroll"). Other commentators of Haydn's day, especially north German critics, were not so enthusiastic about Haydn's "mixture." They found the serious elements in his chamber music to be problematically intermixed with wit, as did the Reverend Thomas Twining:

> [Haydn's] Quartetts spoil me for almost all other music of the kind. There are, in *them* too, some very fine, *serious* Cantabiles; – yet now & then in the midst of them, he takes a freak up to the top of the finger-board – & then, (to my ear, at least) the charm is dissolved – trick, caprice, & the difficulté vaincue, take place of expression & pathos. – It seems to me as if no Composer, or player cou'd be in earnest, in *altissimo*: – it is not the {climb-at/climate} for it (Ribeiro 400).

Earnestness and melancholy are within the scope of Haydn's aesthetics; indeed they are crucial to an understanding of his various modes of musical HUMOR. However, from the nineteenth-century onwards commentators on his works have tended to emphasize wit, jollity, and mirth, downplaying or ignoring the more serious and deeply felt aspects of his compositions. In part this was due to an ignorance of the full breadth of his vocal music in the nineteenth-century; but it was also due to a misunderstanding, or partial understanding, of the range of expression in his instrumental music. Eighteenth-century listeners recognized the serious and melancholy aspects of Haydn's aesthetics. (See also RECEPTION.)

NANCY NOVEMBER

FURTHER READING
Bonds (1997); Brown (1996); Gotwals; Griesinger; Ribeiro (1991); Sisman (1997); Webster (1997, 2005a, 2005b).

Aging Haydn was seventy-seven years and two months old when he died on May 31, 1809 – older than many, if not most of the Great Composers. He had always enjoyed reasonably good health and had a positive, largely uncomplaining outlook on life. Soon after completing *The Creation* in 1798 he started to comment about waning energy levels and, later, he repeatedly observed that composing *The Seasons* had been an unprecedentedly tiring exercise. Only one major work, the *Harmoniemesse*, was to follow, and by 1805 he had given up composing entirely. As his biographer Dies recorded in several accounts of his visits to the housebound composer, Haydn was now an old man, sometimes tired, often in pain with swollen legs, and more willing to talk about the past than the present. His condition was neatly summed up by a new visiting card that he used from about 1805. It quoted the opening of an earlier part-song "Der Greis": "Hin ist alle meine Kraft, Alt und schwach bin ich [Gone is all my strength, old and weak am I]."

Haydn lived long enough to experience many of the emerging characteristics of composer MEMORIALIZATION, nourishing a clear and proud sense of artistic legacy that sat alongside his habitual modesty. He willingly co-operated with biographers such as Griesinger and Dies, with PUBLISHERS like Pleyel and Breitkopf & Härtel who wished to produce orderly and authoritative EDITIONS of his music, and in his will he even left a sum of money to maintain a monument that had been erected in his honor in his birthplace, Rohrau (see RECEPTION).

While these actions are unambiguous in their motivation, establishing aged qualities in the music that was composed in the last phase of his life is more complex. A conference in Cologne in the anniversary year of 2009 included considerations of lateness as style and idea (Konrad, Miller, and Webster) as well as legacy writing and canon formation (Raab and Gruber; the full conference report is contained in *Haydn-Studien* volume 10). Significantly, the terms "late style" or "third-period style" are hardly ever encountered in Haydn scholarship. There are a few works, or portions of works, that deal with mortality, but they do not amount to a consistent stylistic trait. As well as "Der Greis," there is a second part-song, "Betrachtung des Todes," that deals – rather inscrutably it has to be said – with the prospect of death. A much more eloquent contemplation, followed by a picture of the life thereafter, occurs at the end of "Winter" in *The Seasons*, Simon's aria "Erblicke hier, betörter Mensch" ("Behold, deluded man") and the chorus "Dann bricht der grosse Morgen an" ("Then comes the dawn of that great morn"). But the expressive sensibility of these movements derives from the Catholic CHURCH music of a life-long believer, rather than from any newly found sense of personal quietude.

Challenging, even intellectually indulgent, complexity is often regarded as a third-period characteristic, as in Bach's *Art of Fugue* or Beethoven's late quartets and piano sonatas. The closest Haydn came to that outlook was in his last, unfinished quartet, Op. 103 in D minor. The composer was unable to find a four-movement context for the HARMONIC reach of the *Andante* and the thematic terseness of the *Menuet*, an intellectual challenge that creeping old age could not meet. The frustration of this process is well attested, as in the wording on Haydn's visiting card and, more particularly, Griesinger's reported comment that he sometimes had good ideas for composition but lacked the ability to develop them or even to remember them. Perhaps, there was, too, an underlying sense that this most engaging and inventive of composers did not want to live up to the challenge if it resulted only in cerebral abstraction.

Physical infirmity in the last five years or so of Haydn's life meant that any admirer had to make the journey to the Viennese suburb of Gumpendorf to pay their respects, and the visits of people as varied as his two biographers, Griesinger and Dies, Mozart's widow Constanze, younger COMPOSERS such as Cherubini and Weber, musical colleagues from the Esterházy COURT and a soldier from the occupying French forces all had the feeling of a pilgrimage. That sense of a settled, revered status that contrasted with, but ultimately transcended, physical and mental decline was put on public display in the celebrated performance of Haydn's *Creation* in the large hall of the university on March 27, 1808, a few days before the composer's seventy-sixth birthday. Seated in an armchair Haydn was carried into the packed hall, greeted by Beethoven, Gyrowetz, Hummel, and Salieri, presented with a three-verse adulatory poem, the sound of trumpet and timpani fanfares and shouts of "Vivat" and "Long live Haydn." Fearing that the occasion might be too much for him, the composer left at the end of Part 1, once more carried in his armchair and with the sound of unending applause ringing in his ears.

DAVID WYN JONES

FURTHER READING
Gruber (2013); Jones (2004); Konrad (2013); Miller (2013); Raab (2013); Webster (2013).

Amateurs Amateurs participated in music for recreational rather than vocational purposes, as an entertaining and self-improving pastime rather than a means of livelihood. But beyond the basic commonality of their non-professional status, amateurs were a diverse group. They were Haydn's patrons or DEDICATEES, the recipients of manuscript copies, or the anonymous consumers of his printed music. Some were highly skilled on an instrument, others less so. While amateurs were active mainly in domestic settings, the music they played ranged across public and private genres, light and serious styles. Rather than the intended audience for a specific subset of compositions, amateurs represent a lens through which one can view Haydn's entire oeuvre.

The multiplicity of Haydn's amateurs is reflected in the variety of terms for non-professional musicians current in his milieu. For gentleman, these included "Kenner," "Liebhaber," "Dilettant," and "Kunstfreunde." For women, any specification of GENDER – such as "für das schöne Geschlecht" (for the fair sex) or "à l'usage des dammes" (for the use of ladies) – signaled amateur status. Each term had different shades of meaning, and even shifts in meaning during Haydn's lifetime. The Dilettant was typically counterpoised to the Virtuoso, being characterized by his less rigorous training and lower skill level. Kunstfreunden, or "friends of art," embraced professional and non-professional musicians, on the basis of a shared devotion to ideals of BEAUTY. The terms "Kenner" and "Liebhaber" described music consumers while simultaneously distinguishing those consumers from a more general public (see Sisman). Though often translated as "connoisseurs" and "amateurs," the terms in fact described two levels of amateur engagement, and might be better rendered as "knowers" and "lovers." The Liebhaber was thought to have a "natural" appreciation for music – an intuitive sense of musical judgment based on feeling and pleasure, uncorrupted or unrefined (depending on one's point of view) by knowledge of the rules. The Kenner occupied a midpoint between the artist and the Liebhaber, having more musical training and knowledge than the Liebhaber, but applying this to the appreciation rather than to the production of works of art. As Riley has observed, the term "Liebhaber" was increasingly applied to listeners as opposed to amateur performers in the late eighteenth century, reflecting the expanding AUDIENCE (and widening skill gap) that came with the rise of public concerts (416).

From c. 1762–78, Haydn's compositional energies focused – by contractual obligation – on one particular amateur: his employer, Prince Nicolaus Esterházy (see COURTS). Prince Nicolaus purchased a baryton in 1765, and thereafter sought from Haydn a regular supply of new pieces for him to play on the INSTRUMENT, which resembled a viola da gamba with an additional set of plucked strings. The result was 123 trios – most scored for baryton, viola and cello – as well as a handful of other chamber works for the instrument. The trios are relatively short three-movement works, with baryton parts suited to the prince's limited time and skills: most are in the open-string-friendly keys of D, G, and A major, and only two call for the advanced technique of bowing and plucking simultaneously. The baryton was an uncommon instrument, and the baryton trios remained in manuscript – gathered into sets bound in leather and gold – for the exclusive use of Prince Nicolaus.

Changes to the terms of Haydn's employment in 1779 freed Haydn from the obligation to compose solely at the discretion of the Prince, and allowed him both to compose for others and to have his works published. In fact, Haydn had already seen a number of compositions find an enthusiastic amateur market domestically and abroad, including the string quartets Opp. 9, 17, and 20, published in 1771, 1772, and 1774, respectively. But 1778 nonetheless marked a decisive transition point, when Haydn turned toward the public as a main audience for his chamber music. Aiding this turn was the Viennese publishing firm of Artaria, which entered the music business in 1778 and became Haydn's primary PUBLISHER in Austria.

Unlike contemporaries such as C. P. E. Bach, Haydn titled no works "à l'usage des dammes" (or the like). Ladies were, however, the default players for his solo keyboard works, as well as for the keyboard parts in his chamber works. The title page to Artaria's 1785 edition of Haydn's keyboard trio Hob. XV:10 pictures a typical domestic music-making arrangement: a lady plays the keyboard, while gentlemen play the violin and cello (see SOCIABILITY, Figure 28).

Confirmation of these GENDER roles also comes from Haydn's dedications: all of Haydn's published keyboard sonatas were dedicated to ladies (with one exception: the first set, Hob.XVI:21–26, was dedicated to Prince Esterházy, likely because it was Haydn's first authorized publication). His string quartet publications, by contrast, all had male DEDICATEES. There are, however, exceptions to the identification of ladies with amateur status. Haydn dedicated several trios (Hob.XV:27–29, 31) and sonatas (Hob.XVI:50 in C major and XVI:52 in E♭ major) to Therese Jansen (later Bartolozzi), a piano teacher in LONDON. The professional-level bravura of these works points up the amateur features of Haydn's other keyboard compositions, such as the two-movement designs in the set dedicated to Princess Marie Esterházy (Hob.XVI:40–42), and the expressive subtleties of the set dedicated to salon-playing sisters Marianna and Katharina Auenbrugger (whom Haydn praised for their "insight into composition," a comment discussed by Beghin; Hob.XVI:35–39, 20). (See RELATIONSHIPS AND FRIENDSHIPS; COMPOSERS AND MUSIC PROFESSIONALS.)

Haydn's song publications targeted amateur performers. He described his first set of lieder (Hob.XXVIa:1–12), published by Artaria in 1781, as featuring an "ease of vocal execution" (quoted in Komlós 2005, 166). For certain critics, these lieder were a disappointment: *Cramer's Magazin der Musik* criticized them as beneath Haydn, being made only for the amusement of "male and female amateurs [Liebhabern und Liebhaberinnen] of a certain kind" (Cramer 456). The lieder indeed proved appealing to music lovers of modest skill both in Austria and abroad: the songs were published in London in 1786, with English words. Haydn also wrote English-style songs (Canzonettas) for publication in London, contributing fourteen to the English domestic music-making scene (Hob.XXVIa:25–36, 41–42).

Amateurs played Haydn's symphonies, operas, and oratorios in domestic settings in the form of arrangements (see CIRCULATION). Easy versions of such large-scale compositions were the "DESIDERATA of the Amateurs in this science," according to an English publication – Thompson's *Twelve Elegant and Familiar Canzonetts* (1788) – which supplied overtures, the slow movement from Symphony No. 47 and other selections in arrangements for keyboard with ad libitum accompaniment, made "as familiar [i.e. easy] as possible" (see Wheelock). While keyboard arrangements of large-scale works were common throughout EUROPE, arrangements for string quartet or quintet were Viennese specialties. As Thormählen has argued, these string arrangements did more than make public works available for private performance: they aimed to "inspire social interaction in and through art" and "went hand in hand with the belief in humans' innate senses of SOCIABILITY and of morality" – senses understood to be best trained through active, physical engagement with beauty (345–46). Arrangements thus highlighted what amateurs stood to gain from participating in musical performance, above and beyond the edification they might absorb through musical listening.

String quartets straddled the realms of professional and amateur. From the 1750s, "quartet parties" were popular in and around VIENNA; typically, these took place at the behest of noble amateurs, and featured at least one professional musician among the four players. The initial impetus for Haydn's compositions for string quartet has been credited to just such a party: according to Haydn's biographer Griesinger, the Baron Fürnberg invited his pastor, his manager, Haydn, and the brother of composer J. G. Albrechtsberger to make music, and asked Haydn to compose "something that could be performed by these four amateurs [Kunstfreunden]." When Haydn published his Op. 33 quartets (1781), he sought to sell advance manuscript copies to those he described as "gentlemen amateurs and great connoisseurs and patrons of music" (Heern Liebhaber und Grosse Kenner und Gönner der Tonkunst). Both the high level of compositional artifice and the technical difficulty of the string quartets were widely noted. Fending off complaints about excessive difficulty, the *Wiener Zeitung* advertised the Op. 64 quartets (1790) as appealing to professionals and non-professionals alike: "the artist [Künstler] as well as the mere amateur [blosse Liebhaber] will be completely satisfied."

While verbal evidence is sometimes available to establish for whom Haydn composed certain works, and what musical capacities he expected those people to have, there is often little testimony to such matters beyond the compositions themselves. Because amateurs possessed a wide range of musical skill levels, and often crossed ranks with professionals, what can be deduced most reliably from musical works are types of PERFORMANCE SPACES – those suited to public or intimate style, more THEATRICAL or delicate expression. Potentially distinguishing music conceived especially for amateurs, however, are features that reflect a concern with the pleasure of the performers above that of listeners. The opening to the slow movement of Haydn's Piano Trio in B♭ major, Hob.XV:20, for instance, features the instruction "the left hand alone" in the piano part. As Hunter has noted, the effect could make little difference for a listening audience, but the peculiar one-handed moment can be enjoyed by the pianist and perhaps appreciated by her nearby companions.

Throughout his career, Haydn wrote of his musical patrons and public with kindness and respect. In this he differed from Mozart, who often expressed impatience or frustration with anyone below the level of a Kenner. Haydn's faith in the capabilities of amateurs is reflected in the permeable boundary between professional and non-professional participation in his music; and it shines through the trait for which he was celebrated by contemporaries – his "artful popularity" and "popular artistry."

DEIRDRE LOUGHRIDGE

FURTHER READING

Bar-Yoshafat (2013); Beghin (2015a); Brown (1986a); Cramer (1783); Hunter (1997a); Komlós (1987, 2005); Riley (2003); Sisman (2005); Thormählen (2010); Webster (1974); Wheelock (1990).

Americas, The For generalist treatments of this topic we must hark all the way back to M. D. Herter Norton's "Haydn in America Before 1820" written in 1932 and Irving Lowen's "Haydn's Reputation and Popularity in the United States" written in 1979 – the latter itself an apparent stop-gap to what would otherwise have been a complete absence of discussion of Haydn in America at the giant Haydn festival-conference held, after all, in America (that is, Washington, DC) in 1975 (see RECEPTION and FESTIVALS). Thereafter the subject is touched upon incidentally, within research on particular American subcultures. But the year 2011 saw a burst of interest, with a conference in Eisenstadt entitled "Joseph Haydn and Die Neue Welt: Musik- und kulturgeschichtliche Perspektiven." Some of the participants operate, at least in part, from the relatively new theoretical perspective of Transatlantic Studies, a key premise of which is to understand western-Atlantic manifestations of eastern-Atlantic cultural forms not as derivative, not as peripheral, but as central – as "authentic" expressions in and of themselves.

The Herter Norton and Lowens studies are certainly ripe for historiographic critique. Both authors focus on how often Haydn was performed and how seriously he was taken. Herter Norton labels as "odd" the mixed programs that included Haydn symphony movements or songs alongside the likes of spoken recitations, glass harmonica performances, and military marches – and as "odd" (again) the settings for such performances, such as New York ice-cream purveyor Joseph Delacroix's elegant Vaux Hall Gardens in 1797–99. She wonders how, under such circumstances, Haydn's music could receive "proper" appreciation. Nevertheless, she concludes, Americans contributed their "full share of acceptance and appreciation, and may honestly say that Haydn has been taken for granted as part of our tradition ever since real musical activity came into the life of America" (337). Lowens is less sanguine: in America, he concludes, Haydn was not "appreciated at his true worth." The frequency of Haydn's name on concert programs raises what he calls a "delicate point": only a limited number of works were heard; they were just much repeated. As for publication, the American record "is nothing about which we can boast" (6): PUBLISHERS supplied songs and piano pieces for the home; the symphonies and overtures heard on concert programs, on the other hand, were sent or brought from Europe or copied by hand. Ultimately, although their assessments are somewhat different, Herter Norton and Lowens both seem to wince, apologize, and occasionally defend.

Haydn and the Americas, then, is a topic well poised for fresh research. On the one hand, there is still much more to be said in answer to key old questions. What were Haydn's perceptions of the "New World"? (See TRAVEL AND EXPLORATION.) How was Haydn perceived across the Atlantic; how were his music and his reputation understood there, and to what ends? But meanwhile, the most exigent questions are, in a sense, new. What happens when we understand the places in question not as physical locations but as NETWORKS, as "geographies of ideas"? Transatlantic historians remind us that the Atlantic Ocean was, for many, a much wider physical than ideological divide. Families had branches on both sides; companies had agents on both sides; government officers could serve in one country despite having been born in another. The factual, place-based details of Haydn's personal biography are not literally transatlantic, but the world in which his music was made meaningful – the Atlantic world in the age of revolution – was a transatlantic world, one at once diverse and closely knit.

We should start by considering the very term "New World." Obviously, it is Eurocentric; less obviously, but no less true, it perpetuates the illusion that the Americas prior to European colonization were sparsely populated, uncivilized, untouched. The notion of "newness" was, and continues to be, integral to a mythology, and one of the functions of that mythology is to obfuscate the genocide and erasure of culture that occurred. Depending on the topic and the aims of our research, the term "New World," in scare quotes, may or may not have its place.

Haydn's Perceptions Haydn's perceptions of indigenous, imperial, colonial, and revolutionary activity across the Atlantic would have been developed by reading the newspaper, *Das Wienerische Diarium/Wiener Zeitung*, and several books in his possession, such as William Robertson's three-volume *History of America*, which he owned in a 1787 Viennese edition; William Guthrie and John Gray's *Allgemeine Weltgeschichte*; and Joachim Heinrich Campe's *Erste Sammlung merkwürdiger Reisebeschreibungen für die Jugend*, which summarized real travel accounts to a variety of remote places including the Americas. He also owned an account of Captain Cook's voyages and, as Tolley posits, was familiar with the family of one of its artistic illustrators. Zacharasiewicz provides an extensive account – and notes the ambiguity – of images of the "New World" that would have been familiar among Haydn's milieu, including those found in "Letters from an American Farmer" by J. Hector St. John de Crèvecoeur, in an adaptation of "Inkle and Yarico" by C. F. Gellert (one of Haydn's favorite authors), and in the writings of Thomas Jefferson and Jean-Jacques Rousseau on native Americans in particular. Van Boer describes the tumultuous picture painted in the London press, particularly of American self-governance, during Haydn's sojourns there. Future scholarship can extend the efforts of these scholars by attending to the complexity of the representations, for they are at once sympathetic and blinkered.

Haydn had at least two personal contacts with men born in the Americas. In England, he was friendly with Pennsylvania-born John Antes, who was a Moravian clergyman (uncle of Christian LaTrobe, mentioned below), instrument builder, inventor of a pedal-operated music stand, and composer. Antes's three trios, although written during a period of missionary service in Egypt, are considered the earliest known chamber music written by an American. He is also known to have sent a set of string quartets, written around the same time (but now missing), to Benjamin Franklin. Antes was described on the title page of the trios as a "Dilettante Americano" but their "Americanness" as experienced by Haydn would have had a truly transatlantic flavor. As Crews observes, "here we have an American-born missionary in Egypt sending copies of his quartets to an American diplomat in France, quartets which he had written for an English nobleman and his associates in India! This makes his dedication of the *Three Trios* to the Swedish ambassador in Constantinople almost an anti-climax" (13).

Haydn's first personal contact was with Venezuelan revolutionary General Francisco de Miranda, who in October of 1785 arrived at Eszterháza in the middle of his European tour, on the heels of eighteen months in the United States. Miranda records in his diary (October 26–28, 1785) that he spent two days with Haydn touring the palace and gardens. "I spoke a lot about music with Haydn," he reports, but given what we know from other sources about Miranda's interactions, we can assume that non-musical topics were also raised by the admiring but garrulous guest. Miranda's aim in the United States had been to learn everything he could in order eventually to lead his own emancipation project in Spanish America. According to President John Adams, Miranda had more personal connections with Americans, and a more comprehensive grasp of key events and even minor details of the WAR, than any American officer or statesman; his "constant topic was the independence of Spanish America, her immense wealth, inexhaustible resources, innumerable population, impatiences [sic] under the Spanish yoke, and disposition to throw off the dominion of Spain" (Racine 64). Miranda was on a public-relations mission, and he liked to drop names. In conversation with Haydn he could likely have referred to his acquaintance with George Washington (whom he did not like), Thomas Paine, James Madison, and Thomas Jefferson, or his regular discussion "symposium" with Samuel Adams and Alexander Hamilton, or his love of Philadelphia and of public libraries, or his baffled aversion to the austerity of the Quakers. Very likely he took the opportunity to paint a dim picture of free enquiry in his South American home: there could be no intellectuals in New Spain, he had recently claimed to another host, "for Geniuses dare not *read* nor *think* nor *speak*, for fear of the Inquisition, wh[ich] keeps out all books lest it sh[oul]d effect sedition" (Racine 54).

The export of EUROPEAN values is the topic of one of Haydn's operas: L'isola disabitata, in which, as Sisman argues, the two heroines embody "Old World" and "New World" outlooks and, together with their rescuers, metaphorically enact a colonial encounter. Did Haydn perhaps write music that expressed revolutionary ideals? Polzonetti argues that Il mondo della luna transposed the "discovery" of the Americas to the heavenly realm; in the opera, utopia stands as a metaphor for revolution. More generally, several scholars have helped to build a sense of how Haydn and his contemporaries perceived the "New World" by describing other operas of the period. Rice reveals Haydn's heavy editorial involvement with the opera Montezuma, originally by Niccolò Zingarelli, which was performed at Eszterhàza in 1785. Mikusi considers two operas inspired by Marmontel's "Les Incas ou La destruction de l'empire du Pérou": Idalide (which Haydn produced in 1786) and Cora; he finds that both portray "EXOTIC" Peru in opposition to "civilized" European culture. Pratl identifies documents held in the Esterházy ARCHIVES pertaining to sets and costumes of the "New World" operas. (See also THEATER.)

Perceptions of Haydn Like other Austrians, Haydn may have been interested in American colonization and revolution because America's British rulers were Hanoverians – that is, loyal to the Habsburg monarchy, which ruled Austria. And perhaps his interest was further motivated by concern with his reputation and legacy abroad. In any case, it could be said that Haydn knew less about America than America knew about him, for he was known there in many ways – and to many different ends.

Haydn was a familiar name to the Moravians, descendants of Hussites (Bohemian forerunners of Protestant reformers) who established religious communities in the American states as well as Greenland, Canada, Jamaica, the West Indies, and Suriname. Theirs was an anti-rational faith that prized music for its power to move listeners directly and emotionally in every facet of life – not just worship but also labor, leisure, and school. Consequently, their musical culture was extraordinarily robust. VOCAL and instrumental ensembles were quickly established in each settlement, providing musical training and affording what was considered the "ideal" recreational pursuit. Instruments were manufactured and sold within and beyond the communities and imported from Europe. Lay women as well as men composed hymns, and members of the community generally learned to improvise hymn tunes (and texts). This was the backdrop against which Haydn's sacred music, symphonies, and string quartets were frequently obtained, copied, CIRCULATED, adapted, performed, and held up as a model. The efforts of Immanuel Nitschmann, Johann Friedrich Peter, and Johannes Herbst stand out in this regard, but were far from unique. Because the Moravians were diligent record-keepers, documentary evidence abounds; many items are yet to be mined in the archives of Moravian communities, particularly the Moravian Music Foundation in Bethlehem and Winston-Salem. (See foundational work by Knouse, Lamkin, and Strauss.) For example, Cassaro recently uncovered virtually forgotten copyist manuscripts of works by Joseph and Michael Haydn (and especially Johann Matthais Kracher, student of Michael) at the Saint Vincent Archabbey in Latrobe, Pennsylvania, and has begun determining a stemma of dissemination. (The city is named after the nephew of Christian Ignatius LaTrobe, the friend and influential publishing advocate of Haydn in England.) Now, as Eyerly has indicated, research should more often incorporate theories of cultural encounter. The Moravians retained close ties to the European continent while also participating in the syncretic amalgamation of European, African-American, and indigenous musical traditions. They promoted Haydn as their own but also repurposed his music for their internal use (such as for hymnody) and external use (for example in missions to the Mohican and Delaware communities of Pennsylvania and New York). What might have been the transformative effects of native musical customs on the "Moravian Haydn," and how was he heard by native listeners?

In Boston, Haydn's music was promoted by one of its foremost musicians, Gottlieb Graupner, who could boast of having played oboe in Haydn's London orchestra in the 1790s. Graupner established Boston's Philoharmonic Society in 1810 for gentlemen of various backgrounds to play Haydn symphonies, and the collective, meeting in Graupner's Music Hall, soon gave rise to a choral counterpart in 1815, the Handel and Haydn Society (see MUSICAL SOCIETIES). Haydn's name continues to be familiar today thanks to this still-prominent ensemble. Its first formal concert included portions of *The Creation*, and the complete oratorio was presented (spread over three nights) the following April along with Handel's *Messiah*; this was advertised as an opportunity to determine which work was superior. Various solos, anthems, and miscellaneous religious and patriotic pieces separated the two halves of the performances. Ruhling suggests that *The Creation* in fact came to be seen as symbolic of the mission, ambitions, and values of the Society itself (see Figure 1). How was this connection made, and how was it adapted over time? More broadly speaking, what explains the immense significance of Haydn to a society that trained most of its attention on just one of his works? It could be argued that the fortunes of the Society have tracked or indeed determined the image of Haydn in America – from

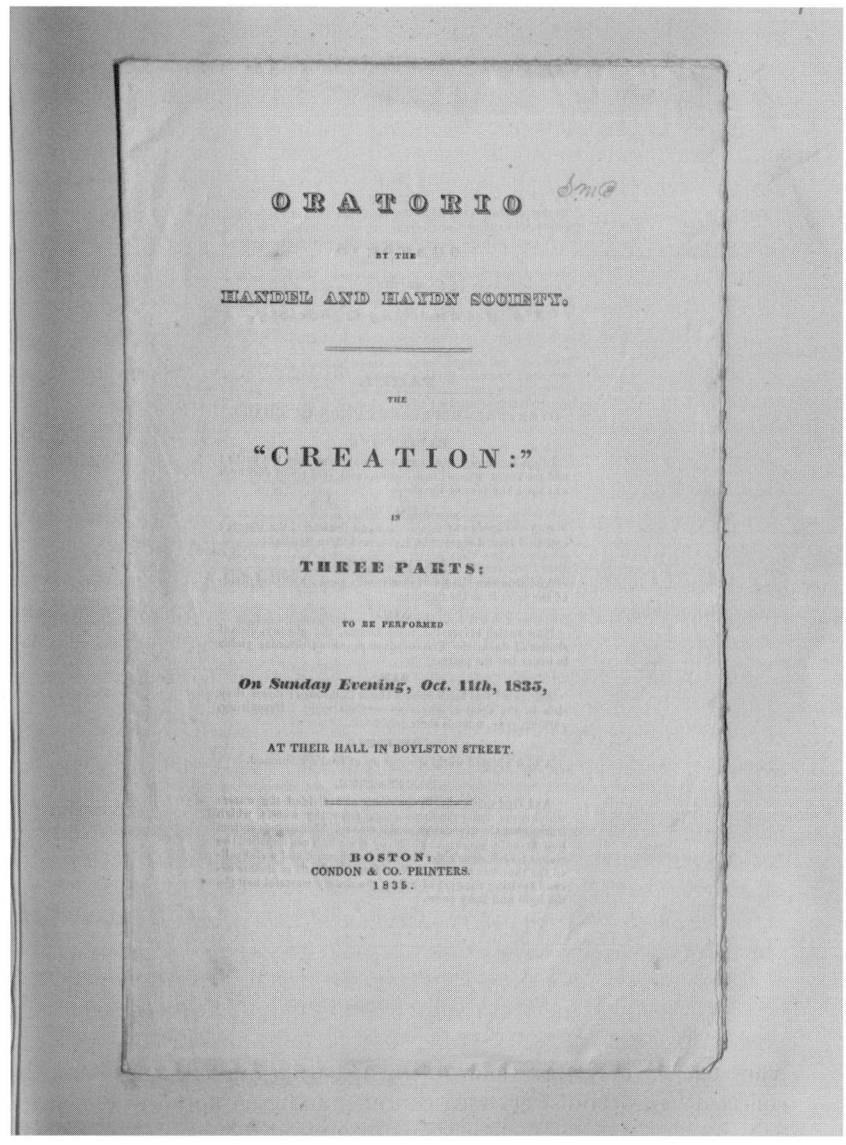

Figure 1 Title page of program for complete performance of *The Creation* by the Handel and Haydn Society in Boston in 1835. Reproduced with permission of the Boston Public Library.

"quintessential" in the nineteenth century to "heroic" during World War II, from old-fashioned in the 1950s to slimmed down, professional, and anti-Romantic in the 1960s and beyond. Research on these questions would reward attention to the intersections of GENDER (women participated but were barred from membership until 1967), POLITICS, and religion (the culture of oratorio singing). There are extensive histories by Johnson and Broyles, but a vast quantity of primary sources continue to want scholarly attention: programs, correspondence, annual reports, meeting minutes, presidential addresses, scrapbooks, posters, photographs, and newspaper clippings held by the Music Department Special Collections of the Boston Public Library since 1978 were only recently (just in time for the 200th anniversary of the Society in 2015) catalogued.

Since the 1980s the Handel and Haydn Society has sponsored education programs in the public schools. This mission can be said to date back to Lowell Mason, president of the society from 1827 to 1832. Mason's *Boston Handel and Haydn Society Collection of Church Music* (1822), which consisted of hymn arrangements of tunes from Haydn and some of his European contemporaries, propelled Mason's career of composing, conducting, anthologizing, and, above all, powerfully influencing American musical instruction and musical taste. Mason continued to revere and to promote Haydn as he went on to spearhead the establishment of a music curriculum in public schools, lead teacher conventions, and found the Boston Academy of Music and the New York Normal Music Institute. Meanwhile, collections of hymn arrangements continued to be a common means by which Americans were introduced to Haydn. In 1850 B. F. Baker and L. H. Southard named their contribution to the genre *The Haydn Collection* and put the composer's portrait on the title page, despite including, as was conventional, tunes from a variety of composers. In other words, the composer's name was synonymous with good, desirable, appealing: Haydn was a brand. And yet, critics have generally been dismissive of hymn tune collections, charging them with trivializing or failing to convey the essential harmonic, formal, motivic, and textural qualities of their sources. This amounts to perpetuating the metric of the European ideal that Mason and his nineteenth-century contemporaries subscribed to – and charging those same agents with falling short. Mercer-Taylor finds instead that *The Haydn Collection* presents some ingenious arrangements that are sensitive to higher-order compositional concerns. His assessment is different but his metric is the same. What might it look like to use a different metric?

A clear example of contrasting approaches to the question of how Haydn was understood in the Western Atlantic world is found in scholarship on Thomas Jefferson. Music was Jefferson's "favorite passion" and one of his many talents; he played violin (often practicing multiple hours in a day), collected harpsichords, attended concerts, and even hoped to establish an orchestra at Monticello. His years as ambassador in Paris coincided with the rage for Haydn's music there; he heard Haydn symphonies at nearly every performance of the Concert Spirituel that he attended, just as he did at Alexander Reinagle's concerts, to which he subscribed after his return to Philadelphia in the 1790s. Taking a more conventional approach, Lowens includes a catalogue of Haydn's works in the Monticello Collection – all songs and symphony adaptations for keyboard – and what he believed to be a 1783 list of the Haydn works Jefferson wished, but never managed, to acquire. Larsen, reviewing Lowens, is befuddled: "Haydn," he concedes, "apparently did not take the place in Jefferson's musical world that we would like to reserve for him" (84). Kidd corrects Lowens, demonstrating that

Jefferson did in fact own eight collections (making Haydn his "second favorite composer"); the Monticello collection reflects not the taste of Jefferson's daughter (and her teacher) in Paris, but of Jefferson himself and the music available in Philadelphia in the 1790s, making it valuable as "an indication of music-making in the young capital and for a study of 'Haydn in America'" (332). But taking a categorically different approach, Gordon attends to the full soundscape of the noisy plantation at Monticello. Though some music-making (especially certain kinds of drumming) by slaves was restricted, some slaves played violin and most sang (indeed, were encouraged to sing at work). Jefferson's daughters sang with them. And yet Jefferson said little about the musical sounds of his enslaved population in his correspondence and documents. The effect is "a repressive and discursive silence or erasure," which is in turn perpetuated by the source- and text-basis of modern and present-day histories of Jefferson; they take Jefferson at his word, and thereby achieve a kind of "diachronic silencing" (110). Haydn's music was a vehicle for that erasure – and arguably, so too is our continued interest in Haydn at Monticello.

Haydn was the most renowned foreign composer in Latin America during the late eighteenth and early nineteenth centuries. Foundational scholarship on the region's Haydn imprints and hand copies was conducted by Stevenson. Pointing out that Haydn's most famous work for Spain, *The Seven Last Words*, was in fact commissioned for a service established there by a Mexican-born priest who was drawing on Peruvian traditions, he identifies a link that should inspire further work on transatlantic exchange and dissemination of ideas. (After all, Haydn was said to have been heavily influenced by a vivid description of the tradition, particularly the preparation of the space with black fabric; see EUROPEAN CONTEXTS – SPAIN.) Magalhães-Castro begins to take up this charge, exploring the lavish collection of the Mexican music merchant José Fernandez Tauregui (fl. 1780s), which contains a predominance of works by Haydn. She proposes an approach "done locally from local points of view," analyzing "*in loco* cultural miscegenation that took place in specific contexts and structures of colonial and post-colonial societies" (360–61). Kühl similarly advocates for a move away from the center-and-periphery model, with its attendant ideas of a singular, uni-directional influence. Indeed, there is massive scope for scholarship in this vein. Buenos Aires, for example, was itself both a periphery and a center, with its own multiple and co-terminus peripheries in Uruguay, Chile, and Bolivia. To the extent that Brazilians adopted Haydn as a model for good Brazilian music, they often did so on multiple terms, including by attesting to Haydn's universality and catholicism. Particularly after 1817, with the arrival of the Austrian Princess Maria Leopoldina in Rio de Janeiro, and Haydn's pupil Sigismund Neukomm the year before, Haydn's music was treated as an antidote to Italian – read Portuguese – influence. And yet the instinct to ask how much Haydn was played and to what extent he and his Viennese classicism were "appropriately" appreciated "in the periphery" is hardly anachronistic. Neukomm, who stayed in Rio until 1821, himself contributed reports in this vein to the *Allgemeine musikalische Zeitung*. His assessment was critical: "people listen, at most, to the beginning or end of a mass, to a cheerful rondo from one of Haydn's symphonies," he wrote in an oft-quoted letter. "Since I have been here I could not gather a string quartet. Music here is in its childhood" (Kühl 82).

In the nineteenth century, interest in Haydn waned in the Americas as it did in Europe (though *The Creation* never left the repertoire). But if the twentieth-century revival of Haydn was politically motivated in Europe (see RECEPTION), in America it appeared in tandem with support for modernism. Proksch describes how critics such as Lawrence Gilman, Paul Rosenfeld, and Oscar Sonneck depicted Haydn's music as demanding and rewarding attentive listening – unlike that of the Romantics, which, they claimed, fostered passivity. In a "sudden jolt" for Haydn's re-emergence, the 1925–26 New York season saw six different conductors direct six symphonies and two concertos (Pablo Casals performing the Cello Concerto in D major and Wanda Landowska performing the Harpsichord Concerto in D major); Gilman's program notes for the New York Philharmonic described Haydn as "daringly futuristic." Arturo Toscanini and Leonard Bernstein championed Haydn with their respective American orchestras into the 1960s. The revival also paved the way for numerous American composers to write music inspired by Haydn. Siegert considers works by Kirke Mechem, George Crumb, Lalo Schifrin, and William Bolcom; others include John J. Becker and Norman Dello Joio. Perhaps German composer Werner Thomas-Mifune's string quartet *Haydns Südamerikanische Saitensprünge* of 1984 (whimsically yet perspicaciously translated not as *String-leaps* but as *Lapses*), with its amalgamation of Haydn quotations and Latin rhythms, brings Haydn's transatlantic journey full circle. Certainly circles – and loops, spokes, and bi-directional lines – provide the visual schematic for future studies of Transatlantic Haydn.

SARAH DAY-O'CONNELL AND BERTIL VAN BOER

FURTHER READING
Broyles (1992); Cassaro (2016); Crews (1997); Eyerly (2008); Gordon (2014); Herter Norton (1932); Johnson (1981); Kidd (1987); Knouse (2008); Kühl (2018); Lamkin (2018); Larsen (1984); Lowens (1979); Magalhães-Castro (2009); Mercer-Taylor (2015); Mikusi (2018); Polzonetti (2018); Pratl (2018); Proksch (2015); Racine (2002); Reicher, Siegert, and Fuhrmann (2018); Rice (2018); Ruhling (2018); Siegert (2011); Sisman (2011); Stevenson (1982); Strauss (1976); Tolley (2018); van Boer (2018); Zacharasiewicz (2018).

Archives – see Collections and

Audiences and Publics Because Haydn wrote many types of works for a variety of MARKETS, it is impossible to circumscribe his audience in a single word or phrase. From part-songs to masses, keyboard VARIATIONS to THEATER pieces, nearly each genre had a different vector for meeting the eyes and ears of its public – and thus attracted a different audience. Haydn's contemporaries had three ways of encountering his music: listening at COURT (including in theatrical and sacred contexts), listening at concerts, and reading or playing scores. This entry describes the audiences associated with one example of each point of contact: ESZTERHÁZA, subscription concerts in LONDON, and the PUBLISHING market in VIENNA.

Haydn himself seems to have conceived of the taste of listeners and performers as tied to PLACE, as evident in the letter explaining the performance practices of the *Applausus* cantata (Hob.XXIVa:6, 1768): "Finally, I ask everyone, and especially the musicians, to apply the greatest possible diligence in order to advance my reputation as well as their own; if I have perhaps not guessed their taste, I am not to be blamed for it, for I know neither the persons nor the place, and in truth the fact that these were concealed from me made my work very difficult. For the rest, I hope that this *Applausus* will please the poet, the most worthy musicians, and the honorable reverent *Auditorio* [i.e., the commissioning audience at the abbey of Zwettl]." The taste associated with the venue and its attendees, Haydn implies, is crucial information to the composer. Further, Haydn acknowledges performers as a crucial part of his audience, alongside patrons and others – a classification that defies the modern-day notion that listeners were merely divided into connoisseurs and AMATEURS. As Sisman and others have recognized, these categories do not adequately capture the variety of people and groups who encountered Haydn's music.

The audience at the Eszterháza court is the most challenging to describe, aside from the obvious fact that it included the Esterhazy family, and that many works from the Eszterháza years had limited exposure outside of the court. Some works, like early string quartets (Opp. 1 and 2) and the baryton trios (Hob.XI) were certainly performed for a limited group, whereas masses and larger-scale pieces written for celebrations – like the *Festa teatrale Acide*, premiered for the marriage of Nicolaus's son Anton, and the operas *L'isola disabitata* (1776) and *Orlando paladino* (1782), premiered on Nicolaus's nameday – would have been attended by the Esterhazy court and, from time to time, the Imperial family. We know, for instance, that Empress Maria Theresia visited Eszterháza in 1773. On the other end of the spectrum, there is also evidence (noted by Green) that local peasants attended some of the events for celebrations in the 1770s, though which music they would have heard is unclear.

Subscription lists to the London concerts provide a partial catalogue of a subset of Haydn's London audience. Haydn's music appeared on the Professional Concert series as well as Salomon's Concert series in Hanover Square. According to McVeigh, these events were probably attended by around five hundred people, though the capacity was close to eight hundred. London dailies printed references to "fashionable" subscribers and "foreign Noblesse," though a healthy degree of skepticism is appropriate regarding these descriptors; as McVeigh notes, we can assume that they were not comprehensive, and that aristocratic, titled names were listed more readily in print than others, in order to emphasize the status of the event. Though it is likely that, based on their price, these concerts were technically affordable to all but the working class, it is unlikely, for a number of reasons, that an extensive population of bourgeois attendees could be found at any given event. McVeigh also points to evidence that suggests that Salomon's concerts drew a broader audience than the Professional Concert. Works written expressly for subscription audiences in London include most famously the Symphonies Nos. 93 to 104 and *Berenice, che fai?*, a cantata written for prima donna, Brigida Giorgi Banti, premiered at a benefit concert on May 4, 1795. Performers at these concerts were decidedly foreign in their make-up, including a number of German and French musicians.

Haydn's foray into publishing in Vienna, beginning in the 1770s, made his music available to a wider audience. The Keyboard Sonatas Nos. 21 to 26 (the *Esterházy* sonatas) were the first set of works to appear in "an edition authorized by Haydn," according to Larsen, and were published in Vienna by Kurzböck in 1774. Haydn's relationship with Artaria began early in the publisher's career and was occasionally fraught with difficulty (see PUBLISHERS AND PUBLISHING). Some of his music was sold on subscription from the 1780s on, including the full score of *The Creation* (1799), a work that reached a yet broader audience in the first decade of the nineteenth century in cheaper and easier-to-navigate arrangements, as in Anton Wranitzky's version for string quartet and Sigismund Neukomm's piano/vocal score (see CIRCULATION). While their appearance in print implies a process of tailoring to a broad taste and market, many of these published works were in fact simultaneously written for particular audiences, either commissioned by patrons or written for specific performers. The string quartets, Op. 76, for instance, were dedicated to Count Erdődy and published in 1799 by Artaria and Clementi, while the set of three of trios, Hob.XV:6–8, was dedicated to Countess Marianne Witzay and published by Artaria in 1787. Similarly, the trios Hob.XV:27–29 were dedicated to the pianist Therese Jansen and published in 1797 by Longman & Broderip. (In general, DEDICATEES should be seen as of one of many types of intended audiences, a type that is signaled directly on the title page.) These specific instances are yet another reminder of the ways in which Haydn and other contemporaneous composers designated their works to be suitable for multiple audiences simultaneously. Beghin suggests that all of these audiences, in addition the persona of the composer himself, can (indeed, must) be embodied in today's performer.

Also published in Vienna, perhaps Haydn's most well-known and continuously performed piece, "Gott erhalte Franz den Kaiser," should be acknowledged here, as it has had a long and broad distribution in the Habsburg realm and beyond. It was written for and reached a national audience when it was performed in many theaters in 1797, and lives on today as the German national anthem. It has had a further life encountering several types of audiences, particularly as a subject both of the theme-and-variations second movement of the string quartet, Op. 76, No. 3, and of the set of keyboard variations.

Haydn's own conception of his audience is evident in a number of sources. He assumed the Op. 33 string quartets would appeal to "gentlemen amateurs and great connoisseurs," according to the subscription announcement (1781). Haydn's advertisement for the subscription to *The Creation* publications in 1799 shows that he believed that publication was meant for "the connoisseur" (or at least demonstrates that that he wanted to attract that kind of audience). The Capriccio in G major "Acht Sauschneider müssen seyn" (Hob.XVII:1; composed in 1765, published in 1788) would "meet with approval from connoisseurs and non-connoisseurs alike," according to the composer in a letter to Artaria. Haydn understood there to be a difference in taste between these various audiences. For instance, *Orlando paladino* was first premiered at Eszterháza, but Haydn shortened the orchestral sections when preparing the score for publication by Breitkopf twenty years later, a change that we can only presume was inspired, at least in part, by the differences in audiences. There are of course counter-examples, as in the fact that Haydn used the Symphony No. 92, "Oxford," for four distinct settings without revising it, including for the Comte d'Ogny in Paris and Prince Oettingen von Wallerstein (along with Symphonies Nos. 90 and 91), as well as for the Salomon's Hanover Square concerts and the event at which he received his honorary doctorate in Oxford in 1791.

In the composer's lifetime, we can thus count patrons, performers, publishers, purchasers of print EDITIONS, as well as listeners at court, concerts, and in the home, as the broad spectrum of audiences to encounter his music. As Proksch describes, the nineteenth- and twentieth-century publics of Haydn's music have also varied by time, place, and even work – sometimes including mainstream, popular audiences – but have primarily been more limited and high-brow than before 1809. Today, Haydn's works are less often presented beyond the concert hall than those of Mozart and Beethoven. They are seldom used in film or anthologized in children's pedagogical volumes (except the occasional appearance of not-much-reduced versions of the opening measures of the *Andante* of the "Surprise" Symphony), unfortunately restricting their wider exposure. (See also RECEPTION.)   EMILY H. GREEN

FURTHER READING
Beghin (2005); Brown (1986a); Fuhrmann (2010b); Green (2005); Hunter (1997a); Larsen (1939); McVeigh (1989, 1993); NG *Haydn*; Proksch (2015); Sisman (2005); Somfai (1995).

B

Beautiful The beautiful was a key AESTHETIC category in Haydn's day, theorized by leading philosophers of the late eighteenth century such as Edmund Burke and Immanuel Kant. In *A Philosophical Enquiry into the Origin of Our Ideas of the Sublime and Beautiful* (1757) Burke located the beautiful in objects that are well formed and aesthetically pleasing, enumerating smallness, smoothness, and delicacy as qualities that give rise to beauty. He emphasized the feminine in his examples, as did William Hogarth, who located the exemplary "line of beauty" in the form of a female torso (see *The Analysis of Beauty*, 1753 [Figure 2]).

In his *Observations on the Feeling of the Beautiful and Sublime* (1764), and the *Critique of Aesthetic Judgment* (*Critique of Judgment* Part I, 1790), Kant loosened the conception of the beautiful from a particular object, relocating it within the subject or self. Whereas the SUBLIME gives rise to a sense of awe and a temporary blockage of cognition, an object is beautiful when its form fits our cognitive powers and enables "free play" between the cognitive powers of imagination and understanding, which is pleasurable (Kant 1790, §22). The judgment that something is beautiful means that it has the "form of finality" (Kant 1790, §9): the beautiful object seems to have been designed with a purpose, but does not have any apparent practical function or use. Neither Burke nor Kant related the sublime explicitly to music, but Burke identified smoothly undulating melody as the key source of "the beautiful in sounds," citing Milton's *L'Allegro*: "With wanton heed, and giddy cunning/The melting voice through mazes running" (111–12).

Christian Friedrich Michaelis, writing in 1805, related the beautiful more concretely to music. As was typical, he defined it in contrast to the SUBLIME: "the beautiful relates to form, *outline, limitation*, the easily apprehended *image* of the object in space, or the easily apprehended melody, the gentle harmonic and rhythmic play of emotions in time" (1805, 179). The sublime, on the other hand, gives rise to feelings of awe and astonishment, which is achieved "by the use of unconventional, surprising, powerfully startling, or striking harmonic progressions or rhythmic patterns" (1805, 180). Taking up Kant's notion that beautiful objects are not tied to a particular purpose, and Burke's idea of the enchanting beauty of voice, he noted:

> [M]usic's aesthetic quality, as in everything where beauty captivates us, does not ... have anything to do with what is stated or expressed, but with the order and manner in which ideas are presented. Just as a lover rejoices to hear his beloved speak, bewitched by the sound of her voice and oblivious to what she is saying, so music often enchants us simply by its very existence,

Figure 2 William Hogarth, *Analysis of Beauty* (1753), Plate 1. Item 26 shows the "line of beauty." Courtesy of The Lewis Walpole Library, Yale University.

by the union of melody and harmony in a manifold interplay of the most intimate kind which reverberates in our innermost being, whatever the content may be (1807, 676).

The sublime has been much discussed in relation to Haydn. Yet the AESTHETICS of the beautiful, especially as they were related to melody and song, were arguably more fundamental to him. To his biographer Griesinger, Haydn insisted that "fluent song" (*fliessender Gesang*) was a prerequisite for good music (Gotwals 61), and vocal music and VOCALLY based aesthetics were a matter of personal and professional identity and pride to Haydn throughout his career. Haydn's champion Johann Karl Friedrich Triest went so far as to observe: "everything in his works, even the most complex passages, sings so beautifully," thus suggesting that beautiful song is to be found throughout Haydn's oeuvre, in instrumental and vocal music alike (Triest 1801, trans. Gillespie 1997, 372).

Day-O'Connell and November argue that some of the most explicit examples of the beautiful in Haydn's music can be found in his English songs. In 1818, for example, William Gardiner noted "a perfect example of the line of Beauty" in Haydn's "A Pastoral Song," from the first set of English Canzonettas, thus drawing on Hogarth's ideal. He went on to detail qualities of the beautiful in this work: "The intervals through which the melody passes," he wrote, "are so minute, so soft, and delicate, that all the ideas of grace and loveliness are awakened in the mind" (Day-O'Connell 83). In Haydn's "O Tuneful Voice," on the other hand, the listener *seeks* (though various modes of experience – feeling, hearing, watching) to become entranced by the sound of a voice with which he or she can strongly identify, as in the case of the bewitched lover in Michaelis's definition of beauty (November 56–58).

NANCY NOVEMBER

FURTHER READING
Brown (1996); Burke (1757); Day-O'Connell (2009a); Griesinger; Kant (1764, 1790); Michaelis (1805, 1807); November (2008a); Triest (1997 [1801]).

Biography and Identity The aim of this essay is not so much to recapitulate the factual events in Haydn's life but rather to discuss the larger social, political, and intellectual forces that shaped the way the composer and his contemporaries made sense of his life, as they (re-)constructed it in biographical narratives. An outline of some of these shaping influences will be followed by a more in-depth discussion.

When Haydn was born in 1732, the Early Modern world-order still seemed very much intact. He had a rural upbringing in a Catholic region which was (and would remain) a backwater to ENLIGHTENMENT EUROPE. The values he experienced there were the RELIGIOUS, POLITICAL, and AESTHETIC values of the *ancien régime* – epitomized in the seemingly eternal rule of the House of Habsburg over the Holy Roman Empire; this had a deep and lasting influence on Haydn throughout his life.

Yet when Haydn died in 1809, the world around him had changed dramatically: the Holy Roman Empire was no more, and the head of the Habsburg dynasty had, in reaction to Napoleon's new world-order, chosen the imposing but more humble title "Emperor of Austria." Haydn himself, though formally still an employee of the Esterházy COURT, had become a European celebrity. His fame as a composer outshone that of his noble patrons by far, and after enjoying the massive success of *The Creation* – and self-PUBLISHING the score in both English and German – he could aptly consider himself more a bourgeois entrepreneur or a quite well-to-do gentleman than a servant of the aristocracy.

The musical changes that reflected the social and historical transformations in European society during Haydn's lifetime – in conventional textbook terms, the transition from Late Baroque to Classical style – had been brought about, to a considerable degree, by the composer himself. Yet Haydn remained, even in his latest years, still profoundly under the influence of his traditional upbringing and the aesthetic assumptions of his youth. This is not to say that the common view of Haydn as a pivotal representative of the musical Enlightenment is totally misleading; rather, it is to suggest that one should not underestimate the more conservative or traditional aspects of his convictions.

A second factor to hold firmly in mind is Haydn's social background. Unlike the Bachs, Mozart, or Beethoven, Haydn did not come from a family of musicians. But neither was he a peasant's boy, as has sometimes been claimed in popularizing accounts. His father, Matthias, was a master wheelwright and

Marktrichter (a sort of mayor) in Rohrau; Joseph's social background was, therefore, an Early Modern bourgeois one, rooted in a handicraft trade. During the Enlightenment, a new concept of the bourgeois emerged, one based on intellectual rather than manual labor, and Haydn, in accordance with this eighteenth-century social revolution, earned his money by doing the largely intellectual work of overseeing a courtly musical establishment and composing for it (although there were still some elements of handicraft involved in being a Kapellmeister; an orchestra, even today, is the last remnant of the great manufacturing tradition of the Early Modern Period – a manufacturer of musical sounds, as it were, if we take the word "manufacture" at its literal sense: produced by hand).

Finally, Haydn's international fame rested almost exclusively on this intellectual work and not on his activities as a performer. To be sure, according to many reports from visitors to the Esterházy court, he was an accomplished orchestral leader, but in contrast to most COMPOSERS of the eighteenth and nineteenth centuries, Haydn was by no means a virtuoso on any instrument (let alone a travelling one) and was thus, in a way, publicly "invisible." Nor was he an opera composer/impresario, the single path that led to not only artistic, but economic success for a non-virtuoso composer before the eighteenth century. Haydn's fame – and this makes him a quintessential representative of Enlightenment – was almost entirely due to the emerging musical public sphere: his works were PUBLISHED by a thriving and seemingly insatiable music MARKET, and the rising trade of music criticism gradually recognized him as the most important innovator in the field of instrumental music. Haydn's success as a composer was intimately bound to both publications and publicity, and in this respect his success is rather more comparable to that of Telemann than to that of Handel. But like Handel, by the end of his life Haydn would become a musical "classic," one whose works would continue to be performed to the present day (see also RECEPTION).

Man of the *Ancien Régime* Haydn's indebtedness to the value system of the *Ancien Régime* was threefold: political, aesthetic, and religious – though in a sense, all the aspects addressed below are of a "political" nature, as the term has been understood in recent decades. Certainly, Haydn's political stance (in the narrower and more conventional use of the term) spills over into the two other aspects, for they are all concerned with the representation of a hierarchical world-order.

Political Haydn may be considered a conservative supporter of the standard aristocratic regime throughout his life, as a glance at his CORRESPONDENCE makes clear. The humble and self-deprecatory salutation formulas of his letters are entirely conventional, probably deriving from contemporary letter-writer's guides, but they give a clear indication of the composer's devotion to the social order. Though he, like many of his contemporaries, expressed a spontaneous but passing enthusiasm for the first stage of the French revolutionary WAR, he very soon afterwards sided firmly with the Habsburg cause. His passing remark to Griesinger that he preferred to keep to "people of my own status" instead of emperors and kings (Gotwals 55) is a testimony of this devotion, just as is his fondness of showing his visitors the many honorific gifts he had received from the high-born. The most evident visual sign of his attachment to the old regime – and the one that contributed most to his denigration after his death – was his insistence on wearing the wig, definitely out of fashion by the first decade of the nineteenth century. This old-fashioned habit was remarked upon with amazement by many visitors during his last years.

Aesthetic The genres that Haydn would come to know in his youth, and which he would start to enrich as a budding composer, were the traditional ones of the "representational" public sphere: church music, court opera, and chamber music for the educated (aristocratic or bourgeois) AMATEUR. Haydn's musical career also ran along the lines established by the *ancien régime*: from church musician (first as a choir boy, then as freelance singer and instrumentalist) and occasional keyboard teacher for the higher social orders to, finally, Kapellmeister, first to Count Morzin, then to four Esterházy princes in direct succession – aristocrats who used the arts to cultivate a "representational public sphere" or "representative publicity," as described by Jürgen Habermas in *The Structural Transformation of the Public Sphere* (1989), with varying strategies.

The traditional stylistic division (and, by implication, genres) – opera, church, instrumental music – as Haydn knew it, served as a frame for his 1776 autobiographical account of his most remarkable works (CCLN 19–20). Two aspects of this account are significant: first, Haydn measures "success" on the degree of approval (beyfall) his works have found with the audience (he starts his work-list with the remark "inter alia the following compositions of mine have received the most approbation"); second, the ordering of the genres also implies a hierarchic system of values. The most prestigious genre is opera, then comes church style, and lastly and rather generally, instrumental music ("in the chamber style"). Equally in descending order is the social status of listeners that Haydn mentions, starting with "of Her Imperial and Royal Majesty Maria Theresia", for the opera *L'incontro improvviso*, singling out the favorable reaction to the *Stabat mater* by Johann Adolf Hasse, a composer closely associated with the Imperial court and revered by Haydn as his "musical and spiritual father" (Scott 136), and ending with anonymous, and by implication bourgeois, listeners to instrumental music in all parts of Europe. Thus, the "father of instrumental music," as he would come to be called, put vocal music at the top of his list in 1776, conforming to standards of taste in the later eighteenth century. And nothing leads us to suspect that Haydn revised this value system later on.

Religious Even in his later years, Haydn's religious practices were firmly rooted in Catholicism, though his ideas on religion were obviously mitigated by a certain amount of ecumenical tolerance and philanthropy, as Jen-yen Chen notes in his entry on RELIGION AND SPIRITUAL BELIEFS. Haydn conversed freely with Anglicans and Protestants, and *The Creation* can even be regarded as a conscious attempt at a trans-confessional (though Christian) oratorio (Fuhrmann 2011). At the same time, Griesinger reported that Haydn "was never so devout" than when composing this work, and he would pray every day (Gotwals 54–55). Griesinger provides the most cogent summary of

Haydn's religiosity at the very beginning of his section on Haydn's character, which might be taken to mean that he ascribed fundamental significance to it. Among other things, he notes that the AGING composer, suffering from swollen limbs, would take refuge in the very traditional Catholic belief in saintly miracles: "in 1807 and 1808 at the Feast of St. Peregrinus, the patron of diseased limbs, he had himself taken to the Servite Monastery and had a Mass said" (Gotwals 54). Haydn's will and testament amply reveal his belief in pious donations (including several masses to be read for his soul) and foundations (see Müller; Landon V). His piety mirrored the Habsburgian "*Pietas Austriaca*" (see Jones). Even more than his old-fashioned outward appearance, his religiosity reminded contemporaries of "the era of Albrecht Dürer and other artists of the German past" – a past revived and sentimentalized by Early Romanticism (Gotwals 55; see also Reichardt, column 176).

Arguably Haydn's most popular composition, the Emperor hymn "Gott! erhalte Franz den Kaiser," epitomizes his indebtedness to the values of his upbringing, synthesizing all three strands: political, aesthetic, and religious. Originally the setting of a prayer, which served as a politically loaded acclamation in honor of the Emperor's twenty-ninth birthday in 1797 during the War of the first Coalition, the melody was reworked in the string quartet "Emperor" Op. 76, No. 3 in the way of a sacred cantus firmus. Conceived amidst the crisis that would bring the world-order of the *ancien régime* to an end, the hymn was played by the elderly Haydn (who referred to it as "my prayer") daily on his piano until the frailty of AGE no longer permitted. A sounding echo of the past, the hymn also served the modern form of a "national hymn" for a supra-NATIONAL empire from 1826 through 1918; indeed, in 1831, it was reprinted with the text in German, Russian, Polish, Hungarian, Czech, Italian, and Latin, but without the composer's name. In one of history's ironic moves, since 1922 the melody has served as the German national anthem, with a text by Hoffmann von Fallersleben, severely curtailed after 1945.

"Something May Come from the Nothing" – Haydn's Enlightened View of his Life and Music History While the foregoing has stressed the "backward-looking" traits of Haydn's character, it is also apparent that he was a representative of the Enlightenment. Indeed, his biography served in his own eyes to mark the quintessential Enlightened idea: progress. According to Albert Christoph Dies, Haydn once stated: "Young people . . . can see from my example that something still may come from the Nothing. What I am today, moreover, is the product of utmost misery" (Gotwals 80–81, translation modified; Haydn, in a pre-Heideggerian vein, spoke of "das Nichts").

Time and again, Haydn would stress this point in his autobiographical statements, including the 1776 letter, and his accounts to Griesinger, Dies, and Carpani. It is tempting to see the composer succumbing to the "legend of the artist," as debunked by Ernst Kris and Otto Kurz: rising from low social breeding, the artist shows his artistic superiority at an early age and emerges, almost self-taught, as a natural genius. But though we may regard such an obvious indebtedness to a literary trope with all due scepticism, the little we know about Haydn's upbringings largely confirms his statements.

Child prodigies are always also the product of their environment. The most eminent examples – Mozart, Mendelssohn, and Korngold – came from musical backgrounds (or were encouraged to study music from a young age, like Saint-Saëns) and were exposed to music of the highest quality in their childhoods. Haydn's father Matthias was musically illiterate, though obviously talented, as he played the harp and sang. The Count of Rohrau seems not to have maintained a chapel, meaning that the local manor was not a place of musical enrichment for the young Haydn. Musical incitements must have been negligible, and any sort of musical entertainment non-existent. That Haydn managed under these circumstances to attract attention to his musical talent is no small feat. In Hainburg, and certainly at St. Stephen's Cathedral in VIENNA, he was exposed to large amounts of high-class, up-to-date music. But even in Vienna, Haydn's musical training seems to have been limited exclusively to singing and instrumental practice (violin, harpsichord). There is no evidence to contradict his claim that his compositional education was largely self-taught "until at last I had the good fortune to learn the true fundamentals of composition from the celebrated Herr Porpora" (CCLN 19). (See also EDUCATION; VOCAL COACHING AND REHEARSAL.)

For all we know, then, Haydn's biography did, at least up to this point, realise the "legend of the artist." As always, there is room for scepticism, given that we only have his own word for most of the story. But Haydn's version of the legend has important further ramifications. Though he was certainly aware of the current fashion of the aesthetics of "original" GENIUS – he uses it himself in a famous phrase (Gotwals 17) – he also voiced his distance to the modish idolatry of the artist (see anecdotes in Gotwals 55 and 152–53, and comment to Neukomm in Seeger 1959, 30). Personally, he attributed his talent to God (Gotwals 54–55, and CCLN 19–20). Furthermore, he always emphasized his personal "study," and the necessity of training and learning based on "the rules of the art" (Gotwals 61), even if he was opposed to pure theory and pedantic rules (see his comments on Albrechtsberger in Gotwals ibid., and also the liberalness of his TEACHING practices, as described in the entry by Federico Celestini).

Insufficient training may lead to mistrust in one's own competence. If Anton Reicha's report is to be trusted, Haydn "began again, at the age of forty, a complete course in composition, to strengthen himself in his art and to learn its secrets better." Bonds has plausibly suggested that the string quartets Op. 20 and the symphonies Hob.I:45–47 are fruits of this "'recommencement' of [Haydn's] compositional career" (163). But it is also possible that Reicha's remark concerned an earlier stage, possibly around March 1766, when Haydn was raised to the rank of chapel master after Gregor Werner's death, now assuming responsibility for church music. Though this was hardly one of Prince Nikolaus's main interests, Haydn was to compose three major sacred works through the next year – the *Missa Cellensis* (1766–?), the *Stabat mater* (1767), and the stile antico *Missa "sunt bona mixta malis"* (1768) – works that employed "learned" techniques he had rarely used before but which were deemed necessary for the "church style." It was here that he broke free from the cliché of a being a fashionmonger [*Modehansl*] and a cheap tunester [*G'sanglmacher*], epithets that Werner allegedly had coined for him (Pohl 1875

221–22, referring to the recollections of Esterházy musicians; cf. Landon II 347).

Whatever the case may be, the belief in personal development by way of education – the idea encapsulated in the German word Bildung – may be seen as the underlying trope of Haydn's retellings of his biography. This was not restricted to music. Indeed, his ideas on Bildung were informed by the Viennese enlightened circles he moved in from the late 1770s onwards, such as the salon of Franz Sales von Greiner and later with the circle of Marianne von Genzinger (see RELATIONSHIPS AND FRIENDSHIPS; SOCIABILITY). As Thomas Tolley describes in his entry on MATERIAL CULTURE, Haydn's personal library also provides a broader outlook on intellectual interests – its main part being a direct outgrowth of his contact with the enlightened Viennese circles. In addition to books on music and aesthetics, and a collection of poetry and literature, Haydn's library contained works on geography and history, and a broad range of the sciences, among them astronomy, botany, medicine, and chemistry (see Hörwarthner). Learning, a constant expansion of his own knowledge (and self-knowledge), was as important to Haydn as it was for his educated contemporaries, and the idea to become "something out of nothing" was a way of understanding his own biography from an enlightened point of view.

This has important ramifications, however, not only for our conception of Haydn's position in the history of music, but for Haydn's own understanding of music history. That he considered himself a "self-made man" who had literally started from scratch – whatever the factual basis of this claim – was also relevant for his conception of music and the history of music. Until old age, Haydn considered "the art of music" as a highly dynamic, expanding field, with new discoveries waiting around the next corner. On his seventy-fourth birthday he said (according to Griesinger), "that his field was limitless; what could still happen in music was far greater than that which had already happened. Ideas oftentimes came to him whereby his art might still be carried much further, but his physical powers no longer permitted him to put them into execution" (Gotwals 8). Such a dynamic understanding of the art of composition was probably typical for an autodidact who never felt he knew or had mastered enough. Reicha also reported on two separate occasions that the very old Haydn committed himself to harmonizing Scotch FOLK TUNES in order to stay in practice (Bonds 1998, 161–63).

It is possible that the idea of "something coming from the Nothing" also inspired some of Haydn's most original musical movements. Time and again, he would start with hardly more than the merest trifle of a musical idea, for instance a cadential cliché (e.g. String Quartet in G major, Op. 33, No. 5 (first movement) (see also PERFORMANCE); Symphony No. 57 in D major (second movement); String Quartet in D major Op. 76, No. 5 (fourth movement)). In other cases, a seemingly banal accompaniment figure opens a movement without anything to accompany (Symphony in D major No. 62/II), a signal that it will play almost as important a role as the "MELODY"; in Symphony in B♭ major No. 68/III, such an accompaniment figure suddenly comes impertinently to the fore, an effect taken up much more subtly in Symphony in A major No. 101/II. The locus classicus of such "something from nothing" movements is, of course, the first movement of Keyboard Sonata in C major, Hob.XVI:50. (See also Musical Materials.)

The presentation of apparently insignificant material is just the reversion of Haydn's usual strategy of breaking themes up into simple motives. But here the effect is spirited or downright funny – another of Haydn's character traits, which early biographers readily brought into connection with his music (see Humor). Humor and wit are, above all, social qualities: they always depend on the appreciative listener. Just as much of Haydn's music was intended for amateur music-making, and many compositions, especially from the 1750s and 1780s, were demonstrably intended for Viennese social circles, the idea of a social conversation or dialogue is also inherent in Haydn's compositional approach. Indeed, Haydn's music, especially his string quartets, has often been likened to the kind of conversation prevalent in urban (and urbane) social circles. But Haydn's music, in its playful exchange of motives, elastic treatment of time and fondness of surprise effects, also embodies a "dialogue" with the listener sometimes found also, to a lesser extent, in C. P. E. Bach, Mozart and Beethoven.

Social Contexts: Kapellmeister and Businessman It is a well-worn cliché that the three Viennese classical composers represent the "break-through" of bourgeois culture at the turn of the nineteenth century. Haydn is routinely portrayed as still being content with serving in the frame of Esterházy patronage; Mozart as breaking free from the "shackles" of the Archbishopric of Salzburg, but finding a miserable end as a freelance artist in Vienna; Beethoven, finally, as representing the revolutionary citizen and the autonomous subject both musically and socially. Though there is a grain of truth in this dialectic model, it oversimplifies massively; none of the three composers would have been able to survive without aristocratic patronage – especially not Beethoven. But at the same time, each of them was active (in widely varying degrees of intensity and success) both in the concert business and in the music market – both spheres dominated by aristocratic as well as bourgeois consumers.

Haydn was simultaneously the Kapellmeister of an aristocratic prince *and* a bourgeois artist working in the public sphere. Although it is true that Haydn remained in Esterházy service throughout his life, and with good reason, it is also true that his *habitus*, in a Bourdieusian sense, changed ever so subtly over these nearly five decades to embrace a self-understanding as an autonomous artist.

After having been dismissed from St. Stephen's chapel in 1749 or shortly afterwards, with insufficient training as a composer, the dire experience of eking out "a wretched existence for eight whole years" in Vienna changed Haydn's outlook on life forever (*CCLN* 19). Making ends meet as a free musician in Vienna during the 1750s must have been extremely stressful; it was at times not easy even for Mozart, working thirty years later under considerably more encouraging preconditions. Much of what has been censured by nineteenth-century music historians as "old-fashioned" or "backward-looking" in Haydn's career, especially his humble submission under the demands of the Esterházy princes and aristocratic society in general, must be accounted for in the light of the existential insecurities experienced at a young age.

The hardships of the 1750s (and earlier) probably help explain his concerns about money in business dealings (see ECONOMICS), most memorably phrased in a letter to the publisher Boyer: "for my case is now and at all times: he who pays me best shall get my works" (Raab 238; my translation). Monetary concerns also most probably played a role in why Haydn, though he was quite well-to-do after his London trips, never formally resigned from Esterházy service. He was right to maintain a connection with the court since, at the end of his life, the Esterházys would have paid for his physician and medications – major expenditures in an era without public health care. (Mozart's financial troubles during the late 1780s were in all likelihood at least partly caused by his wife's medical treatments.)

The nearly three decades that Haydn spent in the service of his second prince, Nicolaus I, Haydn's most creative and innovative years, are somewhat shrouded in mystery. We are well-supplied with documents but their mostly bureaucratic nature offers few insights into Haydn's private or musical development. What little we know of Haydn's personal outlook during this time comes from a very few letters, mostly the autobiography of 1776 and the letters to Marianne von Genzinger from the late 1780s; and sometimes his letters contain tantalizing references to friendships and acquaintances about which we know little. For all we know, Haydn's outward life was that of a Kapellmeister (Vice-Kapellmeister under Werner until 1766), perfectly in tune with the traditional duties of this post. As an orchestral leader, he was performing with his musicians on a regular basis; as an administrator, he was responsible for everything: good behaviour of his musicians, well-organised tidiness of the musical archive, good repair of musical instruments, and so forth. He provided cantatas and operas for festive occasions, symphonies and other instrumental music for entertainment, music for the baryton to satisfy the prince's demand. From the early 1770s onwards, his main occupation was music for the stage (see THEATER) – first for the theatrical troupe of Carl Wahr, and from 1776 for the opera house in ESZTERHÁZA, where opera was now performed on a regular basis, alternating with marionette operas and stage plays, for which Haydn also composed; there was theatrical entertainment almost every evening. This enormous workload added practically nothing to the ever-growing community of Haydn admirers outside Eszterháza, or his historical picture – though it was central, as we have seen, to his own self-esteem. Disagreements between Emperor Joseph II and Prince Nicolaus I (who nevertheless stayed loyal to the Habsburgs) meant that the Esterházy court spent less and less time in Vienna in the 1780s, and we know that Haydn was both frustrated by this isolation and yet also content to write his own music devoid of outward criticism.

During the 1770s and 1780s Haydn rose to European fame. This story is so familiar that it is hardly surprising today. And yet, there are good reasons to find this narrative puzzling. While Haydn was seemingly buried alive within Eszterháza, his music was distributed, sold, and eagerly listened to in Spain, England, Russia, and even Philadelphia and Calcutta (Tolley 20–21). While Haydn would fulfil the traditional duties of an ancient regime court Kapellmeister – composing the occasional opera on celebratory occasions – his music was transferred along the supply lines of the emerging Western bourgeois music MARKET. Haydn would never have achieved this status without the development of a musical public sphere, consisting mainly in thriving publisher-houses, a bustling scene of public concerts and the emergence of musical criticism.

And this, in turn, had its own aesthetic and compositional consequences. If the music-market is ever keen for novelties, the Enlightenment aesthetics of original genius can be understood as a marketing principle, and Haydn's often-praised inexhaustible inventiveness as well as his conscious bridging between "popular" and "learned" styles may be interpreted as a consequence of his musical entrepreneurship (Fuhrmann 2010b). In striking contrast to many of his contemporaries (especially Mozart), however, Haydn was loath to act as an entrepreneur, if we define that term (as William Weber does) as someone who "takes up an opportunity at his or her expense" (6). But he took full advantage of the commercialization of music by copyists and printers. Though a business at least since 1501, the music market really took off in the 1770s. Haydn was a global player in it – and a sly businessman too.

In his later years, Haydn downplayed his awareness of his own fame. According to Griesinger, Haydn "did not know himself how celebrated he was abroad, and he heard of it only occasionally from traveling foreigners who visited him." This is flatly contradicted, at least regarding Haydn's mature years, by the composer's demonstrable awareness of his public renown, documented as early as 1776 in the autobiographical sketch. Griesinger goes on to tell how Gluck and others advised Haydn to go to Italy and France, and how the Prince (and Haydn's timidity) prevented that. "Haydn himself believed that ... he would have become an excellent opera composer if he had had the fortune to go to Italy" (Gotwals 17). Haydn's operas had limited CIRCULATION in the German-speaking lands; for instance, *Orlando paladino* was especially popular in German translation (Fuhrmann 2010a 283–84). But it is certainly correct to assume that an opera produced in Italy would have more easily circulated internationally. It is tempting to speculate how differently Haydn's life may have turned out if he had gone to Italy and France, or, perhaps more likely, stayed in England. Historically Haydn became far more important as an instrumental composer than he could ever have aspired to as an opera composer – even though he held vocal music in such high esteem.

Two paradoxes characterize Haydn's insulated position at Eszterháza. First, Haydn's compositions were regarded by the Esterházys as their rightful possession, not as a public commodity, which they became – witness the famous and often-quoted fourth clause of his first contract of 1761: the order to compose at the command of his prince, and the explicit prohibition to communicate such new compositions to anyone (Jones 37). This has caused considerable moral indignation among music historians. But in the end the claim to own Haydn's music was no more (or less) disputable than the claim to own any painting, statue, or other piece of work produced while in Esterházy employ. Moreover, that the contract explicitly speaks of "new compositions" arguably means that Haydn should not communicate his works to anyone as long as they were new to the prince.

Whatever the exact scope of the clause, Haydn's music routinely circulated outside Eszterháza. Even the baryton trios, expressly composed for the prince, were eagerly rearranged as string trios and sold by Viennese copyist-publishers. It is hardly plausible that all this could have happened without Haydn tolerating this constant leaking of music, if not his actively promoting it. Moreover, around the late 1760s, Haydn begins to group his compositions into an "opus," a set of six (sometimes three) works – for instance, his first three "real" string quartet sets, Opp. 9, 17 and 20, thus arguably intending them for a patron, and for publication in copy or print. As Elaine Sisman (2008) argues, the multi-work opus enabled composers to imagine the collected work as an achievement as well as a multiplex site for rhetorical exploration within the opus. But as an opus is also conceived as a publication, the rhetorical variety within the opus also serves to satisfy both a patron and a broader audience. The two viewpoints – the commercial and the artistic-rhetorical one – complement rather than contradict each other. The Op. 20 set, for instance, contains three quartets with fugues and three without, so it was arguably destined for a patron (or market) with interest in such kinds of contrapuntal feats.

The second paradox is that Haydn's compositions were intended to be understood and appreciated in the context of the Esterházy court, not of a general audience. Especially, they were conceived to be listened to by the Esterházy princes in the first place. There are more than a few pieces that contain references to courtly life; for instance, the first movement of Symphony No. 31 in D major (1765) is dominated by a traditional post-horn signal, which is taken up at the very end of the final movement – obviously an inside joke, perhaps connected with a specific situation. Other prominent symphonic uses of the horn signals have been taken to pay tribute to Prince Nicolaus's passion for hunting. The most notable instance is Symphony No.73 in D major, "La chasse," where the finale is shared with the overture to the opera *La fedeltà premiata*, depicting the goddess Diana's hunting, but its dual use as a symphonic movement arguably shows that it pleased the prince. Symphony No. 60 in C major, "Il distratto," is a theater composition to a play by Jean-François Regnard, *Le Distrait* (1697), performed in 1774 by the theater troupe of Carl Wahr at Eszterháza. And several other symphonies from this time contain strange turns that suggest they could also have served as theatrical music (see Sisman 1990). An extreme example is the musical non-sequitur in the slow movement of Symphony No. 65 in A major (c. 1769–72?). Another famous example is the Symphony No. 45 in F♯ minor, "Farewell" (1772), whose "theatrical" performance (conveying a message from employees to employer) was already linked to anecdotes during Haydn's lifetime. (The one Haydn himself used to tell is particularly benign towards his princely employer and probably more diplomatic than truthful, though there is no way of knowing for sure – but see Seeger 29).

These symphonies with their insider references and many comparable ones were often distributed and printed decades after their composition – as if they had been intended for the public all along, as was the case for practically all symphonies from No. 76 onward. In general, Haydn's music seems to have always met with audience approval, if not always from the critics, as he himself noted in some acid remarks (see CCLN 20; Seeger 31).

A Public Figure: Canonizing Haydn To say that Haydn's two journeys to England had a profound effect on him is an understatement, as Wiebke Thormählen summarizes in her entry on LONDON AND ENGLAND. Similarly, as Laurel E. Zeiss demonstrates, the four London NOTEBOOKS show (as does his library) Haydn's equally manifold interests and observations – ranging from political events, diary entries, and lists of musicians to seemingly random anecdotes (often of a scandalous nature), notes on customs, prices, expenses and all sorts of statistical data, as well as excerpts from poetry in various languages, and the letters of his lover, Rebecca Schroeter (see RELATIONSHIPS AND FRIENDSHIPS; DEDICATEES). These notes bear witness to the many new impressions and intellectual opportunities Haydn was encountering and engaging with far beyond the only other major capital city he had known (Vienna). But the main upshot of his sojourns that is of primary interest here is his physical encounter with his fame as a composer, including tokens of personal reverence bordering on idolatry.

To be sure, when Haydn arrived in England he was already aware of his contemporary reception and international reputation. Another way to think about it is this: Haydn was already receiving his own reception by the mid-1770s. His biographical letter of 1776 shows a clear awareness of his international standing, and his extended network of correspondents is insufficiently mirrored in his extant letters. Many visitors to Eszterháza included a personal encounter with or at least a general appreciation of Haydn in their accounts, and composers like Joseph Martin Kraus (1783), Giuseppe Sarti (1784), and Johann Abraham Peter Schulz (already in 1768) made a point of coming to know Haydn in person in Vienna or travelling to the remote Hungarian residence of his prince. But in London, evidence of his renown was even more intense, continuous, and (one might say) extreme at the same time – contributing immeasurably to his monetary rewards, as Haydn noted with satisfaction. Moreover, London provided Haydn with the idea of posthumous fame to a degree he may not have previously imagined. This idea manifested itself in the English veneration of Handel, arguably the first "classical", i.e., canonized, composer in modern times; Haydn was deeply impressed by Handel's statue in Vauxhall and even more by the Handel Commemoration in Westminster in 1791.

This inspired Haydn to attempt not only to ensure his fame for eternity, but also to correct his public perception. In the eyes of his contemporaries, Haydn's success rested mainly on his achievements as a composer of symphonic and chamber music; he was slightly displeased with this reputation, and sometimes at odds with the veneration of younger listeners, as he saw himself underestimated as a vocal composer. Haydn's own view of himself and of his wondrous path of life did also not translate satisfactorily into the accounts of Griesinger (intended as a sort of accompanying volume to the Breitkopf edition), Dies, Carpani, and others. His complaint to Griesinger (noted above) that he might have become one of the foremost opera composers is just one example (Griesinger 118, cf. 24; Gotwals 63, cf. 17). Ironically, just when the early Romantics started to advocate the contemplation of "pure" instrumental music around the turn of the century, Haydn stuck to the old-fashioned aesthetic outlook in his advocacy of vocal music, which in turn had detrimental consequences for his music legacy. He virtually stopped composing instrumental music after his return from London in 1795, specializing, with few – albeit significant – exceptions, in oratorios, masses, part-songs, canons, and "Folk Song" arrangements.

The late Haydn's humble, petty bourgeois existence at Gumpendorf near Vienna should not lead us into thinking that he was unambitious. At least from the 1770s, he had been, and would remain, an industrious self-promoter: for instance, he was always fond of portraits of his own person, though very critical if he did not find them flattering (see Iconography). In 1799, he enthusiastically embraced the publisher Breitkopf & Härtel's suggestion to publish his "Oeuvres complettes" (which were, in fact, mainly restricted to chamber music), an endeavor that, once again, showed him on a par with Handel, whose "Collected Works" had been published by Samuel Arnold. "Honor and fame were the two powerful motives that ruled him," wrote Dies, who knew Haydn in his old age – though he added: "but I know of no instance where they degenerated into ambition. His natural modesty prevented that" (Gotwals 203). The Creation, publicly pronounced as Haydn's chef-d'oeuvre, was an attempt at self-canonization – the very choice of genre unmistakably evoked Handel. This was not Haydn's first attempt at self-promotion through the act of composing a large work for orchestral and vocal forces; his Stabat mater, composed three decades earlier and taking Hasse rather than Handel for a model, was very consciously conceived as a show piece, and Haydn deliberately performed it at least twice in Vienna (1771 and 1783, and possibly already 1768) for an educated, mostly aristocratic audience. The international success of his first oratorio, Il ritorno di Tobia (charted in Heine 2005), ten years later, already owed something to Handel's model, as a contemporary review pointed out (Schmid 297–98). The Creation, however, was his first work (and probably, alongside C. P. E. Bach's Heilig, the first work ever) composed with posterity in mind; Haydn explicitly stated that his first German oratorio had been composed in order to "set myself a monument" (Feder 123; see also Richard Will's entry on Monuments and Memorializing; see also Figure 3).

Haydn's attempt at self-canonization was not unanimously embraced by his contemporaries. As is well known, the frequent word-paintings in The Creation were met with severe criticism, and some of his contemporaries regarded the work more as a monument to Haydn the instrumental composer (see Mimesis; Programmatic Elements). One author (identified today as J. K. F. Triest) aptly summarized the common opinion when he noted that the work "will neither detract from nor augment Haydn's genuine fame as an artist" (373–41). And though it is true that The Creation and, to a lesser extent, The Seasons popularized Haydn's name, helping to promote a genre that would have important consequences for German patriotism in the nineteenth century, these monumental oratorios did not prevent the emerging music historiography around 1800 from immortalizing Haydn already during his lifetime as the "father of instrumental music."

WOLFGANG FUHRMANN

Figure 3 The title page of the Six Quatuors Op. 82 printed by the Parisian publisher Jean-Jérôme Imbault in 1794. The print contains what is today known as Opp. 71 and 74, the two string quartet sets composed for public performance in London (Hob.III:69–74). Haydn's ever-growing prominence as a public figure during his London sojourns is reflected in this allegorical drawing on several levels. It shows the Greek god Apollo holding an image replicating Thomas Hardy's portrait of the composer. The portrait construes Haydn as an authority, holding a score in his hand like a lawgiver, but it also establishes Haydn as a sales-promotional figure; Hardy specialized in affordable portraits, and this was one of a series of musicians made for the London publisher John Bland. The engraving that was distributed served to popularize the public figure of Haydn. When it was reused by the nameless engraver in the service of Imbault, the publisher was able to endow Haydn with the cultural capital of Greek mythology: in the inscription, Apollo, leader of the muses, says (referring to the composer), "I open for him all my treasures." Bibliothèque nationale de France. Used with permission.

FURTHER READING
Bonds (1998); Feder (1999); Fuhrmann (2010a, 2010b, 2011); Gotwals; Griesinger; Habermas (1989 [1962]); Head (2000a); Heine (2005); Hörwarthner (1997); Jones (2009); Kris and Kurz (1979); Landon I–V; Müller (1932); Pohl (1875, 1882, 1927); Raab (2003); Reichardt (1800); Schmid (1959); Scott (1932); Seeger (1959); Sisman (1990, 2008); Triest (1997 [1801]); Tolley (2001); Weber (2004).

Burgenland The Burgenland in which Haydn lived and composed during his years of service to the Esterházy family was complex and COSMOPOLITAN, locally and regionally diverse, and globally expansive. The culture of eighteenth-century Burgenland – which first became a province in modern Austria after 1921 – contributed to the musical materials upon which Haydn drew; indeed, it helped to shape an aesthetic and musical style that would become increasingly modern and global already during Haydn's lifetime (see Figure 4). It is the influence of Burgenland on both the local and the global, but above all as a cultural contact zone in which aesthetic and musical differences converge, that provides the focus for the present entry. Difference and distinction coalesce around the two areas of exchange and influence in the eighteenth-century Burgenland region examined here: (1) the musics broadly referred to as FOLK MUSIC, itself a new and modern concept of the late ENLIGHTENMENT; and (2) the musical texts and contexts determined by the processes of difference and diversity generally described as multicultural. Historically, this area has been a contact zone cohabited by folk music and the musics of cultural diversity, extensively influencing myth and modernity in Haydn's world and beyond to the present.

Folk Music as Everyday Enlightenment Haydn engaged with the sounds, sources, and sentiments of folk music – together embodying the aesthetic of the *Volksmusikalisches* (lit., "the folk-music-like") – at every level of his musical creativity, from the songs to the chamber music to the masses. In his use of folk music, he was not primarily interested in quotation or composition in a folk style, but rather in creating a complex sound world in which folk-music practices represented the capacity to unify aesthetic and stylistic differences and parallels in ways recognizable to a wide spectrum of listeners. In Haydn's music, the relation between folk music and art music proliferated, depending on genre, audience, and style (see below). Burgenland and its music culture served these goals remarkably well (cf. Winkler 2005):

1. Folk music as citation
2. Folk music arranged in an art-music setting
3. Folk music as the basic theme of an artistic composition (e.g., stylization)
4. Composed music as an approximation of folk music (e.g., genre portraits)
5. Folk music as the basis for caricature or ironic material (e.g., cabaret)
6. Composed melodies appearing in folk music

Among the Haydn compositions that moved across the soundscapes of difference and parallels, none is better known than the "Kaiserlied" or Emperor's Hymn. The broad strokes of its history from string quartet to imperial anthem for the Austro-Hungarian Empire and then beyond to the setting of Heinrich Hoffmann von Fallersleben's 1841 "Deutschlandlied" and eventually to the contested text of the German national anthem from the 1920s

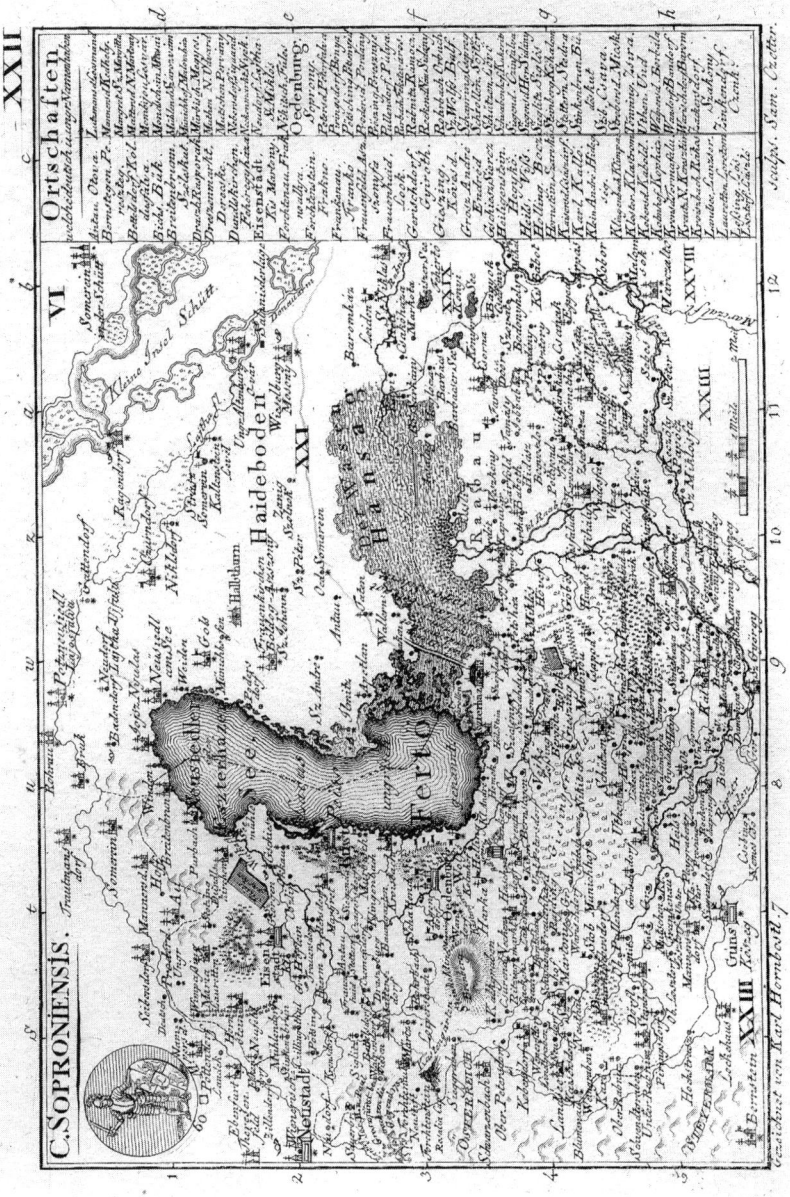

Figure 4 Soproniensis map c. 1800. Map of Burgenland as a border region around Sopron/Ödenburg. Courtesy of Sepp Gmasz and the Burgenländisches Landesarchiv map collection.

to the present are generally familiar to most readers (see NATIONALISM, COSMOPOLITANISM). More pertinent for understanding Haydn's Burgenland, however, are the ways in which the "Kaiserlied" first appears in 1797 as a song designated "Volck's Lied," and as a setting of Lorenz Leopold Haschka's "Gott erhalte Franz den Kaiser" (Fink-Mennel and Rainer). At the end of the eighteenth century, the term "folk song," first introduced only in the 1770s by Johann Gottfried Herder (Herder 1778/79) would not have a designated single object from oral tradition, but rather a constellation of sounds and structures that formed a common musical subject. Haydn's "Volck's Lied," indeed, emerges from multiple origins, the work of poet and composer, of course, but also the probability that something akin to it circulated as a country-style gavotte in a graceful tempo – only after Hoffmann von Fallersleben's setting does it become a military march – or perhaps one of the Burgenland–Croatian courting songs that have circulated in oral tradition in the Burgenland villages around Eisenstadt from the eighteenth to the twenty-first centuries (e.g., "Jutro rano sam se ja stal [I Wake before the Dawn]"; audio tracks 33, 34 and 35 on the CD accompanying Bohlman 2011). The "Volck's Lied," moreover, moved remarkably quickly into oral tradition in the many languages of the Habsburg Monarchy, where it was also widely known as the "Volkshymne." Its widespread circulation in oral tradition occurred within a generation, as evident in the variants called "Volkslied" and appearing in the first canonic collection of Austrian folk songs, the 1819 *Sonnleithner-Sammlung* of the Gesellschaft der Musikfreunde (Deutsch 1969). In its extensive biography, therefore, Haydn's "Volck's Lied" came into being out of myth in late eighteenth-century Burgenland only to move across the vast musical, cultural, and POLITICAL landscapes of European modernity.

Mobility, movement, motion – these are the processes made available in such abundance by Haydn's Burgenland. The borders between styles, repertoires, and cultural distinctions were opened to enhance the possibilities of synthesizing the new. Just as the mobility of the "Kaiserlied" illustrates the transformation of folk and art traditions, so too did Haydn turn to folk music to reposition the borders between folk and popular traditions. Again, we can turn to a case of extensive exchange with folk music, the Capriccio for harpsichord on the tune "Acht Sauschneider müssen seyn" (Hob.XVII:1; composed 1765, published 1788). The melody of the Capriccio has existed in many different forms in oral tradition across Austria (see Example 1), but Haydn turned to the popular *Volkstheater* (folk theater) piece, *Hans-Wurst*, itself a distant variant of eighteenth-century *commedia dell'arte* theater (e.g., the title role, Hans Wurst, is a Harlequin character; see Figure 5). (See also THEATER AND THEATRICALITY.)

Musically speaking, the Capriccio is not a set of variations, but rather a "musical joke" (see HUMOR) in which the theme returns, rondo-style, in a variety of characterizations with a strong IMPROVISATORY character, to be enriched by surprises and lively, almost certainly intentionally crude moments. It is clear that the "Sauschneider Capriccio" afforded Haydn the opportunity to write a popular piece tailored to the public's taste for the refined humor found at folk and popular THEATER in Vienna. To a considerable degree, Haydn even outdid this popular form of entertainment. Through his artful musical setting

Example 1 Comparative table of melodies for "Acht Sauschneider müssen seyn", from Klier 1932, prepared by R. Pietsch.

Example 1 (cont.)

Figure 5 1717 print of Hans Wurst Sauschneider image. Reproduced with permission of Wien Museum.

of the complex traits of the Hans Wurst character, Haydn was able to transform that figure's popularity into his own. As the different versions of the melody from across the Habsburg lands in Example 2 illustrate, the "Sauschneider Capriccio," published in comparative form by the Austrian folk-music scholar

Karl Magnus Klier (1932), moved widely through oral tradition, with the transformations between folk and popular music moving in various directions across the contact zones of the Burgenland that Haydn musically navigated. Some versions from oral tradition may have become known in the eighteenth century as a standardized street song, available in printed form and associated with the character of Hans Wurst, leading Beghin to suggest the transformation from oral to written, folk to popular, tradition as Haydn's source (Beghin, 77–125, and the companion website; cf. Deutsch 2000 and Winkler 2005, 2011). Ironically, Haydn's own version was introduced to Burgenland folk singers in the 1970s by the Austrian folk music scholar Walter Deutsch, who later found that the song had thereafter assumed a place with other songs in the Burgenland folk-song canon.

Burgenland's Heritage of Multiculturalism Burgenland is inseparable from one of the most complex histories of multiculturalism in Europe. Long before Haydn came to serve the Esterházy Court, at least from the earliest written records in the Middle Ages both urban and rural settlement patterns formed around ethnic and religious groups long resident in Burgenland, as well as the arrival of newcomers to the region. Political and economic structures, which encourage rather than discourage the flow and exchange of cultural practices, music significantly among them, have continued to make the region's multiculturalism distinctive, from the era of Haydn's Burgenland until the early twenty-first century. It is multiculturalism, in its many forms, that distinguishes the historical *longue durée* of Burgenland from the other provinces of Austria, in the past and in the present.

Of the historical factors contributing to Burgenland's multiculturalism, three are dominant: linguistic/national, ethnic, and religious. The linguistic/national identities that spread across Burgenland have resulted from the region's position along the borders between nations and empires, and have often formed because of the need to defend those borders or, in contrast, facilitate exchange across them. The most prominent linguistic/national groups are the "Heanzen," or indigenous German-dialect-speaking Austrians, and the Hungarians, together with the Slovaks along the northern border. Croats and Germans largely from Saxony have also made considerable contributions to the region's culture, especially since the sixteenth and seventeenth centuries, during which large numbers from these groups were brought to Burgenland when it formed one of the bulwarks of defense against the Ottoman Empire. Jews and Roma are the largest ethnic groups in the area, in both cases constituting some of the largest settlements in Central Europe. The stable communities already recorded by the fourteenth and fifteenth centuries provide striking evidence to counter the common descriptions of Jews and Roma as itinerant peoples. Diversity is also extensive among Burgenland's religious groups. As elsewhere in Austria and Hungary, Catholicism has a long history and provided religious underpinnings for the Habsburg and Esterházy courts. Judaism and Protestantism, however, have also influenced the cultural and musical history of the region. The repertoires of Jewish music, from liturgical to para-liturgical, from folk to semi-classical and classical, are some of the most extensive in all of Europe, displaying a religious diversity also within Judaism. The Protestantism of Augsburg Confession Lutherans from Germany, though referred to as "Saxons," but largely from the southern German regions of Swabia, Bavaria, and Franconia, who began settling in Burgenland in the immediate aftermath of the Reformation, provides one explanation for the extensive presence of narrative genres of folk song (e.g., ballads), which are much less common elsewhere in Austria.

Burgenland settlement patterns bear witness to the region's multiculturalism and to the extensive exchange and transnational flows that distinguish its musical culture. Burgenland has historically been a region of borders, indeed, of borders that functioned culturally, politically, and musically in very distinctive ways. Politically, the province both separates and connects Austria and Hungary, and it has done so throughout the history of Habsburg and Esterházy alliances. During the course of that history, Burgenland served also as a crucial military border, no less against the Ottoman Empire in the sixteenth and seventeenth centuries than against the nations aligned with the Soviet Union during the mid- and late twentieth century. In its position at the center of Europe, Burgenland not only connected north and south, but also east and west.

The political economy of Burgenland, similarly, forms around the flow and exchange characteristic of border regions. Whereas the local and regional economy of Burgenland has depended on agriculture and other forms of rural economy – large- (e.g., wine) and small-scale – many Burgenlanders have found it necessary to work outside the region, especially in Vienna, to earn a viable living. Such movement across political–economic borders has always been critical for musicians, surely for the court musicians in Haydn's Burgenland just as well as for folk and popular musicians recently and today. The iconic Jewish string ensemble performing for a wedding in Eisenstadt's Judengasse in the 1930s, for example, was based in the Jewish town of Kittsee – childhood home of Joseph Joachim – but its main livelihood resulted from performing light-classical and popular music in Vienna and its surrounding suburbs (see Figure 6).

Burgenland villages, accordingly, were dependent also on the flow of labor, capital, and music that connected them to the many small cities in the region, among the most important of them the "Burgen" that give the region its name and form its borders (e.g., Ödenburg/Sopron, Pressburg/Bratislava). Rural–urban borders also formed according to centers and peripheries. The "Sieben Gemeinde," Seven Holy Cities, or *Shevah kehillot*, of the Burgenland Jews – Eisenstadt (Hebrew, "Ash") being among them – form a geographical orbit around the administrative city of West Hungary in the northern part of the region, Sopron. Accounts of the movement of music and musicians between center and periphery, for example, those in the autobiography of Karl Goldmark, who grew up in the Jewish town of Deutschkreutz (Hebrew, "Zelem") and walked to Sopron for violin studies, are common across Burgenland's literary history (see Goldmark; for a fictional account of a twentieth-century Jewish pianist from Eisenstadt, see Werfel).

Burgenland's multiculturalism provided Haydn not only with a source of inspiration, but also with methods that expanded the ways in which he treated

Figure 6 Jewish wedding musicians playing on the Judengasse of Eisenstadt in the 1930s. Courtesy of the Landesmuseum Burgenland, Eisenstadt.

musical materials from the everyday world in which he lived. We find the music of Burgenland, thus, both in the representational practices and in the COMPOSITIONAL PROCESSES employed by Haydn. His use of *csárdás* in chamber music (e.g., in the third movement of the Piano Trio No. 39 in G major [Hob. XV:25]) builds upon the structures of the Hungarian folk dance, following the contrasting shifts in mode, tempo, and style that distinguish *csárdás* in the rural settings of Hungarian communities in Burgenland. References to it as a "Gypsy rondo" come from afterthought and stereotyping, failing to recognize the more organic sound with which Haydn began (see EXOTICISM). The Croatian soundscape of the villages surrounding Eisenstadt, similarly, provided a point of melodic departure for Haydn when he transformed the FORM and structure of folk song and dance into new compositions, as in the case of the "Volck's Lied" and the "Kaiserhymne" (employing German Bar-Form). The search for Burgenland in Haydn's compositions, therefore, is not simply a matter of locating and identifying individual traces, but rather it leads us to chart again the many parts of a complex eighteenth-century soundscape.

The Music of Jewish Burgenland Burgenland's multicultural soundscape cannot itself be reduced to a collection of discrete ethnic identities and repertoires. At any given historical moment, it would be misleading to reduce a Burgenland musical identity to Hungarian, Croatian, Austrian, Roma, or JEWISH. Such categories were capacious and inclusive, and always changing. The long history of Jewish music in Burgenland offers one among several cases in point. The sacred and the secular, the rural and the urban, Ashkenazic (from several Yiddish-speaking areas of Central and Eastern Europe) and Sephardic

Example 2 Transcription of "Es war einmal eine Jüdin" as sung by the Deutschkreutzer Frauen; Bohlman and Holzapfel 2001, 19–20.

(from Southeastern Europe), and the traditional and the hybrid were constantly in contact.

Jews, moreover, did not make music only in their own communities and for themselves. As Bohlman (2006) describes, the exchange of Jews and Roma musicians for weddings and other rites of passage was widespread, so much so that in central Burgenland it was common for Roma to perform the music for many Jewish weddings. Sacred music specialists, such as cantors, came from Vienna, Budapest, and the area of modern Slovakia, which supplied several communities, including Eisenstadt, with some of its most elegant liturgical and ritual objects (e.g., *haggadah* texts used for Passover Seder).

Burgenland's Jewish folk music attracted scholars from throughout Europe, several of whom were to publish influential studies of Yiddish folk song from the centuries prior to their destruction in the Shoah (Grunwald 1924/25; Cahan 1957). Many questions about where and how to distinguish a Jewish presence in Haydn's music may remain open (see Clark's important study of Jews and Jewish music on Haydn's operatic stage), but they lead to critical new ways to listen to and for Haydn's Burgenland. (For in-depth studies of Jewish music and folk culture in Burgenland, see Hörz; Winkler 2006.)

We turn briefly to a single song, "Die Jüdin" (The Jewish Woman), to illustrate the ways it can lead to a more complex understanding of Jewish music in Burgenland (see Example 2). "Die Jüdin" is an exemplary case of the struggle between self and other, object and subject, folk song as sound and folk song as history. The German and Yiddish ballad first appeared in the twelfth and thirteenth centuries in the Rhine valley, thereafter entering written tradition at the advent of publishing through fifteenth-century song collections. Folk-song and art-song variants alike appeared in the earliest anthologies of song, in Johann Gottfried Herder's unpublished *Alte Volkslieder* of 1774 (Herder 2017) and then in the first edition of *Des Knaben Wunderhorn* (Arnim and Brentano 1806/1808). The ballad's narrative moves across linguistic, cultural, literary, and musical forms. Among the art-song settings of "Die Jüdin," the best known is that by Johannes Brahms from 1893 (for other variants see Bohlman 1992; Bohlman and Holzapfel 2001, 15–23).

"Die Jüdin" circulated in oral tradition in Burgenland until the turn of the present century (see Dreo and Gmasz), and it is that variant that so fully realizes the complex soundscape of the region's multiculturalism. This variant bears witness to many different histories of Burgenland. It was recorded from the oral tradition of women living in one of the Jewish cities of the Shevah kehillot, Deutschkreutz/Zelem; it is a ballad (DVldr 158) in the German-language ballad canon, which in Austria is common only in Burgenland (Dreo and Gmasz); the ballad's narrative is ultimately about crossing borders between the Jewish community and the world outside that community. This variant also represents the ways in which Jewish music in Burgenland cannot represent a single identity, but rather must reveal an extensive and intensive multiculturalism. Though they sing from the oral tradition of a Jewish city in Burgenland, these women, recorded a half-century after the Shoah, are not themselves Jewish; they sing the ballad in the High German characteristic of literary ballads, not in the Burgenland dialect of oral tradition; they sustain a tradition from the past that reached Burgenland from the outside, only to become integrated into the local culture. "Die Jüdin," historically and in contemporary practice, serves as a text that transforms the context of a Burgenland distinguished by its incorporation of difference.

The Musical Contact Zones of Haydn's Burgenland The conditions for enhanced mobility and movement in Haydn's Burgenland were such that it became increasingly difficult to answer the questions: "What came first? The composer's work that was subsequently absorbed into the music-making of the folk, or folk music as a source of material and inspiration for the composer?" Comparing Haydn's creative work to the folk music and multicultural music from Burgenland leads us to hear the musical practices of difference and diversity in new ways and to understand Haydn's music differently. For example, it becomes possible to understand Haydn's "London" Symphonies as his most folk-like compositions, rather than his least. The theoretical issue central to considering Haydn's Burgenland is not one of rewriting musicians' biographies or music history so that they include rather than ignore folk music. Instead, Burgenland's complex soundscapes highlight the ways in which the borders between folk and art music – and popular and sacred music – are often indistinct, drawing the listener and the musician into the musical contact zone that joins the two. It was the motion and mobility that filled the contact zone so richly with musics of difference that Haydn knew so very well. (See also RELIGION AND SPIRITUAL BELIEFS.)

PHILIP V. BOHLMAN AND RUDOLF PIETSCH

FURTHER READING
Arnim and Brentano (1806/1808); Beghin (2015a); Bohlman (1992, 2006, 2008, 2011); Bohlman and Holzapfel (2001); Cahan (1957); Clark (2009a); Deutsch (1969, 2000); Dreo and Gmasz (1997); Fink-Mennel and Rainer (2009); Goldmark (1922); Grunwald (1924/25); Herder (1778/79, 2017); Hörz (2005); Klier (1932); Werfel (1982 [1955]); Winkler (2005, 2006, 2011).

C

Capitalism – see Commerce

Catalogues, Worklists, Nachlass As Jones notes of Haydn: "No other major composer has left so many lists or catalogues of his music" (Jones 33). Scholars have used them primarily to establish authenticity and chronology of Haydn's compositions. Yet these documents also shed light on Haydn's career, the increasing impact of the PUBLISHING trade on eighteenth-century musical life, and the pre-occupations of nineteenth- and twentieth-century scholars (see RECEPTION). They also reveal, perhaps, Haydn's tangential status among canonic composers. The Hoboken numbering system, unlike Köchel and BWV numbers, for example, has not been universally adopted. Undoubtedly, the catalogues reflect his industry as a composer ("one should never let a single day pass without occupying oneself with one's art") and the "fruitfulness of his mind" (Bonds 162; Landon 294).

The Entwurf-Katalog (EK): Catalogue of a Court Composer The earliest surviving catalogue, later shortened to the *Entwurf-Katalog* ("Draft Catalogue"), apparently was prompted by an order from Haydn's employer Prince Nicolaus to compose more frequently and prove "his diligence" by submitting "the first copy ... of each and every composition" (CCLN 5). The catalogue's nickname is a misnomer, as Haydn recorded finished compositions into it, probably before sending them to his employer. Initially organized by genre, the EK was designed to be regularly updated. Early entries include neatly written titles accompanied by musical incipits. This systematic organization later became muddled as the composer added more and more entries to pages, sometimes squeezing them messily onto margins. Thus, the catalogue also reflects how Haydn's output expanded in unexpected ways. Baryton trios, a genre favored by the prince, appear on pages initially set aside for minuets, and keyboard compositions crowd out sacred works. Haydn's steady output of symphonies necessitated more pages, as the composer made regular entries into the EK between 1765 and approximately 1777. Scholars agree that the surviving manuscript is incomplete and that the current order of pages is not the original one. Larsen (1974) and Gerlach posit different theories about what the missing pages may have contained. Nevertheless, the surviving pages have proven invaluable to scholars for authenticating earlier works by the composer, particularly those composed prior to 1780 when Haydn began dealing directly with publishers.

Fourth London Notebook: Self-Assessment At the end of his second trip to LONDON, Haydn entered a list of works written specifically for that city into his personal notebook. His tally of "768 sheets" suggests that the composer was proud of his productivity at the conclusion of what had been a grand adventure (CCLN 309–10). The list also reflects how MARKET forces, performers, and British patrons influenced what he composed between 1791–95. Many entries stress for whom the pieces were written (e.g., "3 Sonates for Broderip ... 3 Sonates for Miss Janson ... March – Prince of Wales"). Some works on this list have been lost. (See also CORRESPONDENCE.)

Haydn-Verzeichnis (HV): Impact of Publishers While a reprimand from the Prince prompted the creation of the EK, interactions with publishers and collectors instigated other inventories of Haydn's music. For instance, when the firm Breitkopf & Härtel planned to publish a complete EDITION of Haydn's symphonies, the publisher compiled a list and sent it to the composer asking him to check it for accuracy; Haydn's corrections eliminated some duplicated and misattributed works. Concern for his legacy, decreased creative energy, and efforts by Pleyel and Breitkopf & Härtel to publish complete editions of Haydn's music, sparked the composer's next catalogue. During 1804–5, Haydn and his copyist Johann Elssler assembled a comprehensive list entitled *Verzeichnis aller derjenigen Compositionen welche ich mich beyläufig erinnere von meinen 18ten bis in das 73ste Jahr verfertiget zu haben* (Inventory of those compositions that I roughly remember having written from my 18th to my 73rd years), cobbled together from various sources, including the EK, Pleyel's edition of the string quartets, and a catalogue of symphonies owned by patron Franz Bernhard von Kees. The list eventually became known as the *Haydn-Verzeichnis* or HV. Three copies were made: one for Haydn, one for Breitkopf & Härtel, and one for Pleyel. Haydn's personal copy eventually went into the Esterházy family archives. This copy and that of Breitkopf & Härtel were lost during World War II, but fortunately their contents were partially replicated elsewhere. Haydn's copy resurfaced in 2008 and re-entered the Hungarian National Library. The copy given to Pleyel, unknown to scholars until its discovery in 2007, now resides in the Gesellschaft der Musikfreunde in VIENNA. The accuracy of HV went largely unquestioned until the 1930s. Modern scholarship has revealed that Haydn mistakenly took credit for compositions by others (i.e., the Op. 3 string quartets by Roman Hoffstetter) and omitted a number of pieces.

Estate Inventories (Nachlass) Perhaps as part of creating the HV and/or in preparation for the eventual transfer of Haydn's music collection to the Esterházy family upon the composer's death, Haydn and Elssler created an inventory of the manuscripts and printed editions in his possession. They also catalogued his music theory books and his collection of opera and oratorio LIBRETTI. These lists show that the composer retained only a few autographs of his own works, and that he possibly had disposed of many books and scores prior to moving to Vienna in 1795. Haydn's entire estate was inventoried again after his death. This list, also known as the *Nachlass*, encompasses 614 items, including a large collection of engravings, two fortepianos, and a talking parrot.

Mandyczewski and Hoboken: Establishing Authenticity and Chronology

Because many works were attributed to Haydn – sometimes incorrectly – during his lifetime through to the 1900s, establishing the authenticity and chronology of Haydn's vast output occupied a number of nineteenth- and twentieth-century scholars. As a result, Haydn's catalogues and work lists, particularly the EK, became and remain important sources for authenticating and dating Haydn's compositions.

The work of two scholars has endured. Eusebius Mandyczewski's thematic catalogue of Haydn's symphonies (1907) established a chronological numbering system for the symphonies (nos. 1–104) still in use today. Anthony van Hoboken's thematic catalogue remains the most comprehensive listing of the composer's musical output. The Hoboken catalogue, which is currently being updated, also offers the most systematic taxonomy of Haydn's music, and the numbering system instituted therein remains the standard method for identifying individual pieces by Haydn. Drawing on the HV and delineating authentic and spurious works, Hoboken divided the corpus into thirty-two categories, with each piece within a category assigned an Arabic numeral based on chronology (e.g., Op. 33 quartets are III:37–42). Unlike Köchel and BWV numbers, Hoboken numbers have not been universally adopted; the string quartets, for example, typically are referred to by Pleyel's system of opus numbering.

Haydn's catalogues remain intriguing mainly because their contents do not match the surviving musical sources. None of them is complete, and none of them is wholly accurate. The catalogues also hint at what has been mislaid or lost – including three early operas, arias written in London, six keyboard sonatas, multiple concerti, and more – works that may yet be rediscovered.

LAUREL E. ZEISS

FURTHER READING
Bonds (1998); *Briefe*; CCLN; Gerlach (1998); Gotwals (1961); H-L; Hoboken; HWorld; Jones (2002a); Larsen (1974, 1988a); Olleson (1965); *Oxford Companion*; Sothebys (2007).

Church Haydn had connections with many churches and RELIGIOUS institutions. As a young child he went to Hainburg an der Donau, where he sang in the choir led by his relative the *Schulrektor* and *Chorregent* Johann Mathias Franck. According to Haydn, "Almighty God ... endowed me with such proficiency, especially in music, that in my sixth year I was already able to confidently sing some masses in the choir loft" (*Briefe* 76; see also EDUCATION). The Philippus-und-Jakobus-Kirche, Hainburg's pretty Baroque parish church, is compact and the choir loft is small, but the church had the usual variety of music, the festive music presumably on a small scale. Instructions for Franck, dating from 1734, stipulate that on feast days the mass was to be accompanied by full orchestra, including horns, trumpets, and timpani; on ordinary Sundays, it was to be performed with strings.

St. Stephen's Cathedral in VIENNA, where Haydn arrived around 1740, is among the most magnificent churches in Austria, a Gothic edifice founded in 1137 and receiving many alterations and accretions over the years. The cathedral's Kapellmeister was Georg Reutter Jr., who served provisionally from c. 1736 and officially 1738–72. According to Ebenbauer, the main musical ensemble (the *Essentialisten*) included five boys and twelve singing men, twelve string players, and an organist. Wind players included a cornettist and a bassoonist; trombones, trumpets, and timpani were hired from among the court or city musicians. A second musical ensemble, the *Gnadenkapelle*, consisted of three boys and three men; two violins, cello, and violone; an organist; and two cornetti and three trombones. Trumpets and timpani were hired from the court. The *Gnadenkapelle* was led by a second Kapellmeister: Johann Georg Reinhardt served 1720–42 and Ferdinand Schmidt in 1743–56. This group performed a sung mass and litany daily and a festive mass with trumpets and timpani on Sundays and feast days before the Maria Pötsch *Gnadenbild* (icon with miraculous powers – thus the ensemble's name) at the high altar. They also participated in processions and performed at other Viennese churches on special occasions (see Hochradner and Vörösmarty). Musicians from St. Stephen's regularly performed festive music at the female convents of St. Joseph, St. Nikolai, and St. Agnes zur Himmelpforte in Vienna. The Cathedral's choirboys also sang in the chapels at the Hofburg and Schönbrunn and at Klosterneuburg Abbey on imperial occasions.

    The choirboys lived in the *Kapellhaus* next to the church, attended the choir school, and were instructed in singing and playing by members of the musical ensemble and by the older choirboys. Haydn had little formal instruction in composition, but as Griesinger reports he was encouraged by Reutter to make "whatever variations he liked on the motets and Salves that he had to sing through in church … this practice early led him to ideas of his own, which Reutter corrected" (Gotwals 10).

    The *Essentialisten* usually performed in the music gallery, a wooden structure built in 1701 on the left side of the church near the high altar opposite the imperial oratory (Figure 7). The gallery contained a single-manual organ of ten ranks by Ferdinand Römer, built at the same time. This INSTRUMENT was "used daily for worship services and well known for its pure and loud sound" (Ogesser 84). Römer built another organ in the west gallery in 1720 (rebuilt several times subsequently); this large organ of thirty-two ranks was played on Sundays and feast days to accompany processions through the long church, especially when the imperial family appeared. The latter organ was little used after its early years.

    For the most elaborate ceremonies, those attended by the COURT, the music was provided by the Hofburgkapelle. As the years 1740–48 were a time of WAR, St. Stephen's was the site of many imperial victory celebrations featuring festive masses and performances of the Te Deum. The cathedral's musicians performed daily masses and other services, provided music with choir and orchestra on Sundays and feast days, and performed for weddings and funerals. Their repertoire ranged from music "alla romana" (vocal music in antique style) for Holy Week, through masses, motets and other works for SATB, strings, organ, trombones and bassoon, to magnificent music with trumpets and timpani for church celebrations, feast days, and the festivals of the university faculties, brotherhoods, and "nations" of the realm. The feast of St. Ivonis (St. Ivo of Chartres), patron saint of the law faculty of the university, was, for example, celebrated "most magnificently with a triple choir of trumpets and timpani as well as extraordinarily beautiful vocal and

Figure 7 Andreas Altomonte, High Mass at St. Stephen's Cathedral, on the occasion of the homage of the Lower Austrian Estates to Maria Theresia, 1740. Wien Museum HMW 19.803. Copyright Wien Museum. Reproduced with permission.

instrumental music" (*Wienerisches Diarium*, May 19, 1742). Charles Burney heard the responses during mass performed in four-part harmony, the soprano part sung by boys (214) – a practice that might be related to the Viennese love of processions, in which the participants sang in harmony.

A small portion of the cathedral's eighteenth-century music collection survives in the ARCHIVE of the Gesellschaft der Musikfreunde in Vienna and in the Cathedral's own collection; a nineteenth-century catalogue of the collection also survives. The repertoire in Haydn's time included music by COMPOSERS Italian, Austrian, and Central European, in old styles and new. Composers included Caldara and Fux; Marc'Antonio Ziani, who wrote in both the *stile antico* imitating Palestrina and the Italian concerted style of the early eighteenth century; Matteo Palotta and František Ignác Antonín Tůma, both of whom wrote in the then-antique style of Fux and Caldara; and Georg Christoph Wagenseil and Reutter Jr. (see COUNTERPOINT). A mass with music included instrumental pieces to accompany liturgical action, and Haydn thus would have frequently heard symphonies and concertos.

Following dismissal from the choir in 1749, Haydn visited the pilgrimage church of Mariazell, where he sang. He retained a fondness for this church, as two later masses allude to it in their titles *Missa Cellensis in honorem BVM* ("Cäcilienmesse"), Hob.XXII:5 (1766) and *Missa Cellensis* ("Mariazellermesse"), Hob.XXII:8 (1782); the works seem more likely to have been premiered in Vienna. As a young, freelance musician in the 1750s Haydn performed in Viennese churches as violinist, singer, and organist. According to his own account, he served as first violinist and leader of the orchestra (*Vorspieler*) to the Barmherzige Brüder (Brothers of Mercy, The Brothers Hospitalers of St. John of God) in the Leopoldstadt. He played in their church at eight o'clock in the morning on Sundays and feast days, went from there to Count Haugwitz's chapel (probably in his palace on Wipplingerstrasse; see Steblin), where he played the organ at 10 am, and then to St. Stephen's, where he sang at 11 am. Among his compositions from this period are a *Missa brevis* in F (Hob.XXII:1, his earliest preserved work) and a concerto for organ and violin (possibly Hob. XVIII:6) performed at the ceremony for his sister-in-law's profession at the Clarissan convent of St. Nikolai in 1756.

As Vice-Kapellmeister to the Esterházy court, Haydn was not at first involved with church music. Responsibility for the *Chor-musique* (church music) was officially added to his duties after the death of Kapellmeister Gregor Werner in March 1766. Haydn himself played organ in the chapel of the Esterházy Palace at EISENSTADT in the winters from 1773. There were also chapels at ESZTERHÁZA Castle and in the Esterházy family's Vienna palace in Wallnerstrasse.

Music by Haydn was performed in Eisenstadt at St. Martin's church, at the Bergkirche, and at the chapel of the Brothers of Mercy (see PERFORMANCE SPACES). The *Missa brevis Sancti Joannis de Deo*, "Kleine Orgelsolomesse," Hob.XXII:7, dedicated to the patron saint of the Brothers of Mercy, is thought to have been first performed in that chapel, on account of its title and small-scale scoring. The organ solo in the Benedictus may represent the capabilities of the chapel's fine small organ by Johann Franz Frey (1732, moved to the chapel 1759/60). The music COLLECTION of St. Martin's includes eighteenth-century parts for motets and other smaller pieces of church music by Haydn. Apparently, a favorite was the choral motet *Ens aeternum*, for SATB, strings and organ, for which there is a score in the Esterházy archive, and parts at St. Martin's, Göttweig Abbey, and the Musikwissenschaftliches Institut, Graz (from the Brothers of Mercy, Graz).

Under the reign of Nicolaus II Esterházy (from 1794) Haydn composed six festive masses, five of them (excluding the *Missa in tempore belli*) intended for the name-day of Princess Marie Hermenegild; these were premiered at St. Martin's or in the Bergkirche (see also COURTS). Both of these Eisenstadt churches contain organs by the eminent Viennese builder Johann Gottfried Malleck, built during Haydn's lifetime, in 1778 and 1797 respectively; the St. Martin's organ was restored in 1992 by Karl Schuke Orgelbauwerkstatt. The names of Haydn and his wife appear frequently in the records of the parish church (now cathedral) of St. Martin, as they stood as godparents to many children of the Esterházy musicians.

Austrian monasteries were among the earliest and most enthusiastic purchasers of music by Haydn, both sacred and secular, and the abbeys of Göttweig, Kremsmünster, Melk, Lambach, St. Florian, and Zwettl, among others, retain important collections of the composer's music in their libraries (see PUBLISHERS AND PUBLISHING; CIRCULATION). The Brothers of Mercy in Graz received music by Haydn during his lifetime. For Zwettl, Haydn wrote his *Applausus* cantata (Hob. XXIVa:6, 1768), commissioned for the fiftieth anniversary of profession of the Abbott. In 1786 Haydn received a commission to compose *The Seven Last Words of Our Savior on the Cross* for the grotto San Cueva in Cádiz (see EUROPEAN CONTEXTS).

Viennese churches such as those of the Brothers of Mercy and the Piarists, St. Stephen's, the Hofburgkapelle, and the Michaelerkirche also saw performances of music by Haydn during his lifetime. The *Stabat mater* (1767) was performed at the church of the Brothers of Mercy in 1768 and in the Piaristenkirche on Good Friday (March 29) 1771, the latter with Haydn directing. The *Missa in tempore belli* was premiered in the latter church on December 26, 1796.

During his first visit to LONDON, in 1791–92, Haydn heard musical events at St. Paul's (the annual Charity Children's service) and Westminster Abbey (Handel Commemoration). In his last years he visited the Peregrinikapelle of the Servite church in Rossau (in Alsergrund, about two-and-a-half miles (four km) northeast of Haydn's Vienna house). His funeral took place in the Gumpendorf parish church of St. Ägyd. He was buried in the Hundsturmer Friedhof, but his remains were moved to a mausoleum in the Bergkirche, Eisenstadt in 1820. Haydn's skull, detached from the body shortly after his death, was reunited with the body on June 5, 1954.   JANET K. PAGE

FURTHER READING
Black (2007); Burney (1773); *Cambridge Companion*; CCLN; Ebenbauer (2007); Fastl (2003); Gotwals; Gotwals (1982); Haselböck (1982); Hochradner and Vörösmarty (2000); Jahn (2005); Kassal-Mikula and Pohanka (1997); Klampfer (1959); Kretschmer (2009); Landon I–V; Merten (1986); Ogesser (1779); Organ Database; Page (2014); Rice (2012); Salinger (2009); Spink (2005); Steblin (2000); Tschischka (1843).

Circulation In his *Biographical Accounts of Haydn* (1810) Dies told of a French officer who visited the dying composer to pay his respects and express his admiration, delighting Haydn by singing the tenor aria from *The Seasons*, Part II. Griesinger told the same tale in a slightly different guise. There may be much mythology attached to both accounts, yet this very mythology indicates how Haydn was received during his lifetime and immediately after his death (see Reception). It also attests to the wide circulation of his music, both geographically and sociopolitically. And yet, scholarship on the dissemination of Haydn's music has traditionally focused on ascertaining authenticity and singular authorship, taking an interest less in the patterns of Publication and dissemination and more in the small section of his disseminated music that can be linked to him authoritatively so as to establish original texts (see Editions). Viewing his works through this lens, however, has constricted our view of the meaning of Haydn's music, as the composer himself partook in a wider playing of – and play with – his compositions.

The publication Market and strategies for publishing by and large determined Haydn's dissemination. While in the employment of Prince of Nicolaus Esterházy, Haydn's music belonged, strictly speaking and according to the normal custom of the time, to the prince. Nevertheless, his music did, in fact, circulate outside of the court: itinerant musicians could scarcely avoid taking parts on their travels and introducing them to new audiences, whether as physical objects or through performance. In the absence of copyright laws, copying music in parts was an unregulated and frequent practice, so Haydn's music was disseminated widely, but in copies that were often riddled with mistakes. More importantly, this kind of circulation offered the composer no Financial gain. Even though Haydn would proofread copies of his music made at court, he had no right to offer this music to anyone else.

The agreement of Prince Nicolaus to waive the sole ownership clause when Haydn re-signed his contract in 1779 is perhaps a more significant amendment than is customarily acknowledged, despite the suspicion that the prince had long since turned a blind eye to the composer's supplying other courts with part copies of some of his music. Only after the clause was officially removed could Haydn enter into contracts with publishers and music dealers, enabling him to establish Europe-wide dissemination of his music and, crucially, refocus his output onto the types of music that this European market demanded: chamber music to be played primarily by the upper classes (gentry and aristocracy) rather than exclusively listened to in smaller settings at Court.

Especially in Vienna, music was commonly disseminated in manuscript copies as well as in print. The lack of an official court copyist in Vienna after 1755 resulted in a de facto open market made visible through shop fronts in the city and advertisements in the Press. The court became one customer among others for copyists such as Therese Ziss, Boniface Charles Champée, and Simon Haschke (see Eybl). In 1777, shortly before Haydn's contract allowed him to exploit this market freely, the music engraver Antoine Huberty moved from Paris to Vienna, where his collaborations with publishers such as Christoph Torricella and the Artaria family, Franz Anton Hoffmeister and Anton Thomas Kozeluch strengthened the music printing business considerably, enabling the Viennese printing market to compete with publishers in other European cities. With the growing number of publishers and sellers operating in Vienna came increased trade between publishing houses in other cultural centers, including Paris and London, allowing Haydn's music to be disseminated widely across Europe.

Whereas before the 1780s, repertoire would appear in publishers' CATALOGUES in Germany, France, Holland and England, copied most likely from parts that had been brought by musicians themselves, now publishing houses struck agreements with each other across the continent. Moreover, as composers themselves became increasingly aware of the need to control publication of their music, they began developing direct relationships with publishers starting in the 1780s.

The publication market, especially from the 1780s onwards, was influential in determining what types of music would be disseminated. For instance, while Haydn was busy writing and producing mainly opera for Eszterháza, the loosening of the contractual agreement with the prince meant he could write music demanded by the Viennese market, such as string quartets, sonatas, songs, and a large body of piano music – all marketed by Artaria. Rather than music for the CHURCH and THEATER, the bulk of the music available for purchase was a large and varied repertoire aimed at the AMATEUR performing consumer. As such, the changing publication market and the cultivation of amateur music-making among a growing Bildungs-conscious class went hand in hand. In London alone, Haydn had publishing agreements at different times or concurrently with Bland, Corri, Hyde, Longman & Broderip, and Clementi. He used these agreements to ensure the circulation of his music in different European centers, but he was less concerned with accuracy in the music's dissemination than the modern scholarly focus on the idea of a "Fassung letzer hand" might suggest. Publishers similarly were less concerned with authenticity and more with the label "Haydn" because the name assured commercial success. As Ridgewell has shown, the same works were frequently reissued under different opus numbers by publishers in different countries to give the impression that these were new pieces. Furthermore, Mace has documented a legal battle that ensued between Forster and Longman in London over the rights to Haydn's music. These cases demonstrate a deep interest in Haydn's music as well as the status it had gained by the late 1780s. They also reveal the swiftness with which the composer's music was disseminated across France, Holland, England, and German-speaking lands.

During his time in London, Haydn understood his music not as an authoritative representation of himself and his GENIUS, but as the means to becoming part of a culture and a market. Jones has shown that in London, the composer was frequently led by POLITICS, prominently publishing nationalist pieces that promoted Austrian–British relationships during the time of the Napoleonic wars, including "The Battle of the Nile" and the ode The Invocation of Neptune. Similarly, Haydn readily adapted his music to fit into new local contexts. For example, a couple of his Notturni for King Ferdinand IV of Naples written for lira organizzata, an instrument unknown in London, were adapted for performance in Salomon's concert series in London in 1792. PERFORMANCE circumstances and surviving parts suggest that these pieces may have circulated in London as chamber music as well as larger ensemble pieces (see Searle), indicating that Haydn happily – even opportunistically – viewed his pieces in different guises. His Six Original Canzonettas are perhaps the best example of buying his way into a particular local culture, as poet and salon host Anne

Hunter contributed the texts to at least the first set; Grigson discusses how his publisher Domenico Corri and playwright Thomas Holcroft were equally part of this collaboration.

Haydn's music, then, appeared in myriad guises, adapted at times to local fashions. Wheelock has shown that, in London, Haydn's instrumental music was reset or rearranged to fit the local predilection for vocal and piano music while also satisfying the English audience's steadily increasing taste for Haydn. Several melodies from his keyboard sonatas and chamber works were even set to poems – mostly taken from collections by fashionable English poets such as John Cunningham, William Shenstone, Charlotte Smith, and Mary Whateley – to create songs and ballads. The English AUDIENCE appears not to have valued these any less than his original songs, even though Haydn's publisher for the latter, Corri, Dussek and Co., marketed them as "Original Canzonettas" (see Komlós). Haydn also engaged in collaborative authorship when furnishing William Napier with his *Selection of Original Scots Songs in Three Parts, the Harmony by Haydn*; the subscription list, which includes Salomon and Arnold, suggests that this type of music, rather than belittling Haydn's reputation, was understood as an integral part of the composer's ingenuity and appeal (see FOLK SONG SETTINGS).

A substantial way of spreading Haydn's fame was the dissemination of his music in arrangements, a practice that he endorsed, at times giving the job of making piano, string quartet or quintet arrangements to one of his students and overseeing the process himself (see Thormählen). Again, local tastes determined the manner of arrangement, with Vienna showing a particular predilection for string quartets and quintets for the amateur market, while in London the preference was for arrangements involving the flute. To illustrate these local differences: on March 8, 1800, Artaria announced in the *Wiener Zeitung* an arrangement of Haydn's *Creation* for string quintet by Anton Wranitzky and another for piano alone by Sigismund Neukomm. Further arrangements of this work were made for *Harmoniemusik* and piano trio. Accounts of performances of this oratorio in private papers also suggest that these smaller versions were received to great acclaim. Similarly, in London Johann Peter Salomon offered Haydn's symphonies "arranged for five Instruments viz two violins, a German flute, a tenor and a violoncello with an accompaniment for the piano forte ad libitum" (*The Times*, June 19, 1798). Here, Salomon chose to offer reductions of the symphonies rather than face competition from European publishers, who would likely issue them in parts for symphonic performance (see Hogwood). Arrangements would also capture a larger amateur market. In his chamber arrangements, Salomon ably responded to the orchestral texture of the originals by electing to have the three top parts represent the orchestral string and woodwind sections, relegating the keyboard to a truly accompanying function. The arrangements also took into account the English predilection for the flute, thus distinguishing them from the typically Viennese quintet of two violins, two violas and cello. The fact that this was Salomon's second arrangement of the symphonies indicates their considerable commercial appeal.

The reception of *The Creation* in England provides a sense of the significance of these arrangements in disseminating Haydn's music. The string quintet arrangement of the complete work was offered nearly a month before the first public performance by a full chorus and band. In addition to these arrangements of complete works, numerous arrangements of individual arias appeared most prominently for piano alone, for piano and voice or – following the amateur fashion in France and England – as accompanied sonatas for piano and violin or flute, with or without a cello. Publishers' catalogues across Europe abounded with these offerings, and it must be assumed that Haydn's large-scale music gained the fame and popularity that would carry his reputation well into the nineteenth century through these arrangements. Also, when it came to making arrangements, other composers were acutely aware of the reputation of particular works: Joseph Wölfl, for instance, composed a set of sonatas for accompanied piano based on both the melodies from Haydn's *Creation* and, significantly, on the orchestral effects for which each of the chosen *Creation* movements was famous. As such, the arrangement paid tribute to Haydn, the great ORCHESTRATOR.

These arrangements, often belittled today, were a cornerstone in cementing Haydn's fame through a particular social class of musicians who practiced their "Haydn knowledge" through the possession and performance of his music in many different formats. The composer himself had paved the way for this seemingly commercial reception of his music – both through his publication practices and by following closely the markets in London as much as Vienna. His publication of *The Creation* in English and German simultaneously certainly assured the work's reception in both cities while facilitating the dissemination of its most popular arias. Indeed, Haydn's extraordinary popularity is visible in the trickling down of his music from these arrangements into even popular dance collections, stripped bare of everything but the tune. It was the memorability of these MELODIES, and the memory of his grand orchestral effects which accompanied them, that helped to solidify the idea of Haydn's genius.

WIEBKE THORMÄHLEN

FURTHER READING
Eybl (2008); Grigson (2013); Hogwood (1996); Jones (2013); Komlós (2012); Mace (1996); Ridgewell (2013); Searle (2013); Thormählen (2010); Wheelock (1990).

Collections and Archives Haydn's music survives in over fifteen thousand manuscript sources, most of them written by professional or non-professional copyists; roughly a third are preserved in the composer's own hand. Together with contemporary EDITIONS (there are some five thousand prints of compositions by Haydn from the eighteenth and early nineteenth century) these manuscript sources are kept in hundreds of libraries and archives around the world. Some collections are of particular importance because of their provenance and/or the large number of sources in their possession. These include: the National Széchényi Library in Budapest; the Staatsbibliothek zu Berlin; the Archiv der Gesellschaft der Musikfreunde in VIENNA; and the Národni Museum in Prague.

These collections are modeled on Haydn's own music collection, the stock of which can be inferred from the *Haydn Bibliothek-Verzeichnis* (MS London, The British Library, Add. 32070) and the *Haydn Nachlass-Verzeichnis* (MS Vienna, Archiv der Stadt und des Landes Wien, Persönlichkeiten, 4/2; 2436/1809). In 1807, Haydn and Prince Nicolaus II agreed that, after the composer's death, Haydn's musical property would be merged into the Esterházy estate. In 1949, however, the estate was nationalized, and the collection incorporated into the National Széchényi Library, Budapest. The autographs, copies, and contemporary editions from Haydn's collection thus became part of the library's music collection, where today they are housed side by side with Haydniana of other provenances. The Budapest collection consists of some seventy autograph scores, all of which originate from Haydn's collection, among them the autographs of twenty symphonies and eight operas. The manuscript copies are about two hundred in number, and here again the symphonies predominate. Since the copies are of varied origins, their quality differs. There are also several manuscripts written by copyists, many of whom worked with Haydn, as well as manuscripts of a more remote origin, which are very often of little value.

In addition to the fifty-two Haydn autographs of the Staatsbibliothek zu Berlin there are also some partial autographs, fragments, and sketches. Of particular importance are the complete autograph scores of Symphony No. 102 in B♭ major, the *Sinfonia concertante* (Hob.I:105,) the Masses (Hob. XXII:8 and 10), and the *Salve Regina* (Hob.XXIIIb:2). Well over half of the Berlin autographs originate from the former collection of the Viennese PUBLISHING house Artaria, which in 1901 was incorporated into the holdings of the Staatsbibliothek, at that time still the Königliche Bibliothek. Artaria had acquired these items during the 1830s from Johann Elssler, Haydn's amanuensis, who himself had over the years created a collection of Haydn manuscripts (autographs as well as copies). It is not altogether clear in what manner they came to be in his possession, but it can be assumed that the autographs originally belonged to Haydn's own collection. However, not all the autographs in Artaria's possession found their way into the Königliche Bibliothek, since some of them were sold beforehand to other libraries. Interestingly, the autographs of compositions by Haydn that Artaria had published are not preserved; he apparently destroyed them systematically after publication. Of the 370 or so manuscript copies of Haydn's works housed in Berlin today, a good many had already been acquired during the nineteenth century, beginning in 1841 with the acquisition of the bequest of the Berlin collector Georg Poelchau. In 1870, Haydn materials in the collection of the Mozart biographer Otto Jahn were added to the Berlin library.

Even though the Archiv der Gesellschaft der Musikfreunde in Vienna does not hold as many autographs as the Berlin Staatsbibliothek, this collection is nevertheless of vital importance for Haydn scholarship. Autographs of eighteen complete compositions – including the twelve string quartets Op. 17 and Op. 20 – are among them. Numerous contemporary manuscript copies and early prints of Haydn's works – altogether more than seven hundred items – came into the possession of the Gesellschaft by way of inheritance or acquisition, a process that started shortly after the founding of the Society in 1812. Through the bequest of Erzherzog Rudolph of Austria, one of the patrons of the Gesellschaft der Musikfreunde, sets of manuscript parts of seventy-three symphonies from the former collection of Franz Bernhard Ritter von Kees passed into the Musikfreunde collection after 1831. Rudolph also bequeathed the autographs of the horn concerto and the *Missa brevis Sancti Joannis de Deo* to the Musikfreunde. Haydniana from the estate of Johannes Brahms became part of the Musikfreunde collection after the composer's death. The Haydn scholars Carl Ferdinand Pohl and Eusebius Mandyczewski (both of them archivists of the Gesellschaft) also left their Haydn treasures to the Archiv.

In the early 1950s the stock of the music collection of the National Museum in Prague was significantly enlarged by incorporating ancient collections from the confiscated properties of the CHURCH and the nobility. Sizable Haydn collections from all over Bohemia, such as those of the monasteries Osek and Kuks, and of many aristocratic families, including the Counts Waldstein (Doksy), Counts Clam-Gallas (Frýdlant), and the Counts Kolowrat (Radenín), all came to Prague. The last-mentioned collection contained the only surviving source of the Cello Concerto in C major (Hob. VIIb:1), a work long considered lost until the discovery of a copyist's manuscript in this collection in 1962. In general, these collections consist of manuscript copies, mainly of instrumental compositions, though the former monastery collections, as one would expect, also contain many sources of church compositions. In the course of reprivatization, some collections have already been restored to their original owners, for example the collection of the Princes Lobkowitz, which is now located at Nelahozeves castle north of Prague.

Numerous monasteries in Austria possess a great number of Haydn manuscripts in their archives, including the Benedictine abbeys of Kremsmünster, Melk, and Göttweig (over two hundred items each). Of comparable size in Germany are the Haydn collections of the Princes Thurn und Taxis in Regensburg, and the Princes of Oettingen-Wallerstein, which is now part of the Augsburg University library. The latter boasts an extraordinary rich collection of symphony sources. Today, more than three hundred manuscripts of works by Haydn are in the possession of the Sächsische Landesbibliothek – Staats- und Universitätsbibliothek Dresden, deriving from collections of aristocratic families and other private collectors as well as from church archives. Some of these sources even come from Haydn's immediate surroundings, while others were originally manufactured for sale by retailers of manuscript copies, such as the Breitkopf firm in Leipzig (besides its publishing activities Breitkopf was also selling musical manuscripts).

Outside of Europe important collections include the Library of Congress in Washington, with more than one hundred manuscript sources of Haydn's music, as well as the Moravian Music Foundation in Winston-Salem, North Carolina. The New York Public Library for the Performing Arts, Music Division (Lincoln Center), owns important sketches for *The Creation* as well as the autograph of the F minor Variations for keyboard (Hob.XVII:6), whereas the Morgan Library and Museum in New York holds some original letters by

Haydn and autograph scores of Symphony No. 91 in E♭ major and the composer's last String Quartet, Op. 103 in D minor.   ANDREAS FRIESENHAGEN

FURTHER READING
Biba (1982); Fojtíkova (1997); Jaenecke (1990); Landmann (1986); Larsen (1939); Vécsey (1960).

Commemorations and Festivals Haydn's compositions are frequently, but far from exclusively, heard in the context of a commemoration or a festival – that is, as part of either a unique isolated or non-recurring commemorative celebration, or a recurring annual celebratory event.

Extensive commemorations were held in the anniversary years of Haydn's birth and death (see RECEPTION). The first major special celebration was the Viennese Haydn centennial commemoration of 1909, which featured a large musicological congress and a number of concerts focusing on Haydn's significance and historical position, but with minimal repositioning of the simplified legacy perpetuated throughout the nineteenth-century (as described by Botstein and Garratt). In 1932, 1959, 1982, and 2009, commemorative performances and symposia took place in diverse locations – most notably in EISENSTADT – leading to a much broader understanding of Haydn's achievements. Other significant individual and non-continuing Haydn celebrations have included:

Festival Date	Name	Location
1975, Sept 22–Oct 11	Haydnfest	John F. Kennedy Centre for the Performing Arts, Washington D. C., USA
1982, Sept 5–12	International Joseph Haydn Congress	Vienna, Austria
1983, May 29– Jun 18	Haydn-Fest	Basel, Switzerland
1997, March 14–25	Haydn Festival	Royal Festival Hall, London, UK
1999, Jan 8–10	RNCM Manchester Haydnfest (performance of all sixty-nine quartets)	Royal Northern College of Music, Manchester, UK
2002, May 1–5	Haydn Streichquartett Weekend (performance of all sixty-nine quartets)	Eisenstadt, Austria Haydn Festival Burgenland
2009, March 19–22	Haydn 2009 (performance of sixty-eight quartets)	Montreal, Canada Arte Musica Foundation, in collaboration with the

(cont.)

Festival Date	Name	Location
		Montreal Museum of Fine Arts and the Schulich School of Music, McGill University

The first recurring Haydn festival was organized by H. C. Robbins Landon in conjunction with the Gesellschaft der Musikfreunde. Held annually in March from 1984 to 1994, the "Haydn Days" (*Haydn-Tage*) featured concerts in the historic Musikverein in VIENNA as well as sacred music concerts at various churches throughout the city – historically appropriate venues for Haydn's CHURCH music (see Fritz-Hilscher and Kretschmer). Beginning in the late 1980s, early music specialist Nikolaus Harnoncourt also offered nuanced readings of Haydn's music with Concentus Musicus Wien, a period-instrument ensemble, in the newly renovated Musikverein Grosser Saal. Although the focus was on music by Joseph Haydn, compositions by his brother Michael also featured prominently in the festival.

Meanwhile, attempts to establish an on-going festival in Eisenstadt continued. After World War II, the BURGENLAND government renovated the so called "Haydn-Saal" in the Esterházy palace at Eisenstadt with the purpose of using it as a central venue for a Haydn Festival. Although in Haydn's time the hall was mainly used for balls and THEATER, it has undergone various changes since then, and today the 600-seat hall – much prized for its excellent acoustics – serves as a venue for concerts. Finally, in 1986, earlier endeavors to institutionalize a Haydn festival were realized with the founding of the Haydn Festival Society in Burgenland (the *Verein Burgenländische Haydnfestspiele*) by the Burgenland government and the town of Eisenstadt. At this time, the entirety of the *Haydnpflege* project was also handed over to the Society. In 1993 its spin-off – the International Joseph Haydn Foundation Eisenstadt – has taken over most of the scientific research of the festival, and has built up an important collection and ARCHIVE. Since its founding, the Society has organized regular performance festivals dedicated specifically to Haydn's music, along with other multifaceted events. Since 1989 the performance festivals have also been held every September alongside the annual *Internationalen Haydntagen Eisenstadt* festival, with cyclical performances of the complete works of Haydn taking center stage. Full stagings of Haydn's twelve extant operas were presented as a cycle from 1994 to 2005, as well as multiple performances of the composer's complete symphonies, string quartets, keyboard trios and sonatas. The Austro-Hungarian Haydn Orchestra, under the direction of Adam Fischer, has been a frequent participant over the years, and works by other composers also feature regularly on the program with this and other chamber and choral ensembles. In 2017 the Society extended the *Internationalen Haydntage* to *Haydn-Land-Tage* with performances taking place in venues historically connected to Haydn throughout the region (e.g., Schloss Rohrau, Schloss Kittsee, the Basilica in Frauenkirchen, etc.)

Other ongoing festivals include:

Date(s)	Name	Location	Festival Organizers
1984–94	Haydn-Tage	Musikverein, Vienna, Austria	Gesellschaft der Musikfreunde und Kulturamt der Stadt Wien
since 1989	Internationale Haydntage (since 2017) Haydn Land Tage	Eisenstadt and surroundings, Austria	Verein Burgenländische Haydnfestspiele
since 1993	English Haydn Festival	Bridgnorth, UK	The English Haydn Festival in partnership with Bridgnorth Councils
1993–2017	Haydn-Festival	Dolní Lukavice, Czech Republic	Czech Haydn Society
since 1996	Haydn Biënnale (since 2012, Amazing Haydn)	Mechelen, Belgium	Haydn-Gnootschap Vlaanderen
1998–2009	Haydn at Eszterháza	Fertőd, Hungary	Hungarian Haydn Society
2002–7	Performances of Haydn's first 80 symphonies	Fertőd, Hungary	Orfeo Orchestra and György Vashegyi
since 2002	Haydn-Woche (since 2012?, Haydn-Festival)	Brühl, Germany	Brühler Schlosskonzerte
2004–12	Haydn-Van Hoboken Festival	Rhoon, Netherlands	Stichting Kasteel van Rhoon
since 2004	Haydn-Tage Schloss Rohrau	Rohrau, Austria	Vienna Haydn Society
since 2005	Les vacances de Monsieur Haydn	La Roche Posay, France	L'association "les vacances de Monsieur Haydn"
since 2017	Herbstgold Festival	Eisenstadt, Austria	Esterházy Betriebe GmbH

Recently Haydn's music has appeared with increasing frequency at festivals and concert events not specifically dedicated to him or his musical oeuvre, but where his works were programed as main attractions or foci – for example, the *Kuhmo Kammermusik Festival* (2004) in Finland, and the *Musiktage Mondsee* (2015). The music festival *Klang und Raum* – held annually

at Kloster Irsee from 1993 until 2011 – continued a nineteenth-century tradition by prominently featuring regular performances of *The Creation* on its program.
WALTER REICHER (TRANS. KALEB KOSLOWSKI)

FURTHER READING
Adler (1909); Badura-Skoda (1986); Botstein (1998); Fritz-Hilscher and Kretschmer (2011); Garratt (2005); Larsen et al. (1981); Reicher (2017); Weibel (2006).

Commerce and the Market The musical marketplace changed significantly for both composers and their employers in Haydn's lifetime. Some commercial behaviors persisted from the composer's first decade to his last, such as self-PUBLISHING by subscription, evident in the careers of Georg Philip Telemann in the 1730s, C. P. E. Bach in the 1770s, and Domenico Corri in the early nineteenth century. Composers also continued to seek and maintain relationships with patrons throughout this period, a fact obvious to any who study the careers of German composers in particular. But Haydn's seventy-odd years witnessed a gradual transformation in the livelihoods available to composers with the establishment and expansion of publishing houses across the continent. His catalogue of works – and their publishing histories – reflects the opportunities for success in both the capitalist marketplace and patronage system of his time.

A number of factors enabled Haydn's successes in print. First, publishers engaged in a brisk and international business of collaborative distribution. Publishers distributed their CATALOGUES far afield and generally bought from each other at a discount, as Adams and Beer have both explained, citing publishers' CORRESPONDENCE and printed advertisements. Without these mechanisms, Salomon might never have known Haydn's published music or invited the composer to London. (The distribution of manuscript copies is discussed in CIRCULATION.)

Haydn's reputation may also have benefited from the lawlessness of the publishing marketplace. ENGLAND was the only area with firm copyright law – law that was strained by the furious pace, volume, and opportunism of the publishing business. After the establishment of the Statute of Anne in 1709, authors in England were granted rights over their own works but often had to resort to court cases to enforce those rights. The systems of privileges on the continent protected publishers from piracy – and granted authority over print culture to a central body – and was gradually phased out of the German-speaking lands in the second half of the eighteenth century and altogether removed in France in the 1790s (see Gieseke and Reiber). As a result of these legal inconsistencies, Haydn's music appeared in many pirated editions by the 1780s, while several works now known to be spurious circulated under his name, such as the "Op. 3" string quartets and many cello concertos (see Brook). While this confusing and problematic activity may have furthered Haydn's international reputation in a general sense, the composer certainly suffered both injury and lost profits.

Perhaps in hopes of recouping these losses, Haydn conceived of a number of works for the broader marketplace. He revised the Keyboard Trio in C minor (Hob. XV:13), to include VARIATIONS in order to please the publisher Artaria, who presumably demanded this change because he thought it would suit consumers. In another appeal to the public, the Op. 30 Keyboard Sonatas (Hob.XVI:35–39 and 20), published by Artaria in 1780, were accompanied by a warning about thematic similarities in the set: "Among these 6 Sonatas there are two single movements in which the same subject occurs through several measures: the author has done this intentionally, to show different methods of treatment." Haydn's remarks – referring to the nearly identical musical ideas in the opening measures of the first movement of the Sonata in G major (Hob.XVI:39), and the second movement of the Sonata in C♯ minor (Hob.XVI:36) – seem designed to ensure the commercial success of his sonatas in an increasingly competitive and learned marketplace. Arrangements of Haydn's music, such as those of *The Creation* for string quartet or piano and violin, also served to increase the commercial appeal of his works.

The appearance of Haydn's music in print, like that of many of his contemporaries, was influenced by publishers who could wield authority not only over the timing of publications, but over their opus numbers, DEDICATEES, and even sometimes content, as mentioned above. Opus numbers are particularly confusing in Haydn's output, and they signal the complex workings of the marketplace at this time. The string quartets known today as Opp. 71 and 74, for instance, first published by Corri & Dussek in 1795 as Opp. 72 and 74, and soon after by Artaria as Opp. 73 and 74 in 1795–96, were in fact most likely written as one single set in Vienna. The opus numbering of these early editions was not only inconsistent but failed to reflect the compositional integrity of the set as a whole. Further, the DEDICATION of the Op. 30 sonatas to sisters Caterina and Marianna von Auenbrugger was, to Haydn's dismay, made by the publisher. Haydn gently complained to Artaria in 1780: "I only regret one thing [about the publication], that I cannot have the honor of dedicating these Sonatas to the *Demoiselles* von Auenbrugger myself." He evidently worried about the dedication's authenticity of sentiment when directed from the publisher, and his dissatisfaction concerned not the choice of dedicatee but the privilege to write it.

That Haydn balanced financial support from publishers alongside that of patrons, beginning in the 1770s, reflects the mixed marketplace in German-speaking lands during his lifetime. Haydn's experiences with patrons range from on-demand creation of particular works to general authorship of periodic entertainment to the maintenance of ensembles and musical personnel. (See COURTS; RELIGION; ESZTERHÁZA AND EISENSTADT; AUDIENCES AND PUBLICS.) Certainly, his works circulated beyond their points of origin, as discussed above.

Partly because of the material endurance of printed matter, the genres that were published in some form in Haydn's lifetime, including keyboard sonatas, string quartets, and symphonies, have as a whole (with some exceptions, in the keyboard trios, for instance) proved more commercially successful posthumously, as defined by the subsequent frequency of performance and publication, than the works that existed only in manuscript (like the operas, many of the concertos, and – to give a cliché example – the baryton trios). As with the works of many composers, the longevity and positive RECEPTION of Haydn's music has depended chiefly on the inertia established by early commercial success. (See also ECONOMICS.)

EMILY H. GREEN

FURTHER READING
Adams (1994); Aversano (2008); Beer (2000); Brook (1975–76); Gieseke (1957); Green (2017); Hortschansky (1993); Landon II; NG *Haydn*; Rabin and Zohn (1995); Reiber (1994); Sachs (1973); Tolley (2001).

Composers and Music Professionals Despite spending much of his career in relative isolation at ESZTERHÁZA AND EISENSTADT, Haydn fostered RELATIONSHIPS with many prominent musical contemporaries. Through his studies, his TRAVELS, and his work as an opera impresario, he encountered composers, singers, and instrumentalists from across EUROPE. He also inspired a new generation of composers and performers through his teaching (see STUDENTS).

As a young man, Haydn gained a foundation in liturgical music from Georg Reutter, Kapellmeister at St. Stephen's in VIENNA and perhaps the most influential musician in the city. While such training might have prepared him for a career as a church musician, a course of lessons in singing, composition, and Italian with opera composer Nicola Porpora expanded his musical horizons. Through a combination of instruction, self-instruction (via the treatises of Fux and Mattheson), and interaction with Vienna-based musicians, Haydn developed the COSMOPOLITAN musical outlook that he would refine throughout his career. (See EDUCATION.)

In 1759, Haydn became director of music for Count Morzin, whose orchestra was probably comprised largely of domestic servants. This year also marked the premiere of the two-act opéra comique *Der neue krumme Teufel*, a successful collaboration between Haydn and actor-director Joseph Kurz (known by the stage name Bernardon). Kurz, whom Haydn had impressed by improvising a six–eight keyboard accompaniment while the actor feigned swimming, directed a traveling company of German actor-singers who performed regularly in Vienna's Kärntnertortheater. In setting both *Der neue krumme Teufel* and possibly also its predecessor *Der krumme Teufel* (c.1752) to music, Haydn interacted with a different, perhaps tawdrier, side of Vienna's professional music scene. Haydn's music for both works is lost; he doubtless designed the vocal numbers to showcase singers in Kurz's company, especially the talented Teresina Morelli, Kurz's second wife (see Heartz).

As detailed in his contract of May 1, 1761, Haydn's duties as Vice-Kapellmeister (and later Kapellmeister) at the Esterházy COURT included assembling and directing the court's instrumental ensemble, the Cammer Musique (see LEADING LARGE ENSEMBLES). He recruited twelve core musicians, led by violinist Luigi Tomasini, hiring additional personnel when finances allowed. His duties were not merely musical: he was also responsible for the conduct of his musicians, ensuring that they showed up in uniform and on time and managing conflicts as they arose.

With the formal opening of the new THEATER at Eisenstadt (1762) and later the completion of the opera house (1768) and marionette theater (1773) at Eszterháza, Haydn's professional network expanded greatly. Beginning in July 1781, he collaborated with theater director Nunziato Porta, a librettist with the extensive experience in Italian opera that Haydn lacked (see VOCAL COACHING AND REHEARSAL). Porta's arrival coincided with an increase in operatic productions, and between 1781 and 1790, Haydn directed the music for roughly a hundred opera performances per season, working with an ever-changing roster of domestic and imported singers (see Jones 2009). Gradually, the court phased out the local German singers who constituted the original company, replacing them with Italian virtuosos. While some singers stayed on for a season or less, others (such as Porta's wife Metilde Bologna and Haydn's mistress Luigia Polzelli) served the court for many years.

In his role as opera impresario, Haydn took great care to tailor his music (or the music of others) to his available forces. When producing operas by other composers, he often made substantial revisions or cuts, reassigning (or eliminating) vocal parts as needed and simplifying "empty" coloratura. He composed about twenty insertion arias, of which the majority were intended for Polzelli, a mezzo-soprano for whom Haydn altered musical passages. He likewise took his performers into account when writing instrumental works: the extended high-register passages in the Cello Concerto in C major (Hob. VIIb:1, c. 1761–65), for instance, required the thumb-position technique possessed by cellist Joseph Weigl, as Badley has argued. (A later example of this tendency is the highly chromatic Trumpet Concerto in E♭ major (Hob.VIIe:1, 1796), designed for virtuoso Anton Weidinger's keyed trumpet.)

Because he so often worked outside the city, Haydn stood in a somewhat oblique relationship to his Vienna-based peers. To be sure, he was acquainted with and/or knew the music of his close contemporaries Albrechtsberger, Dittersdorf, Gassmann, Hofmann, Ordonez, Starzer, and Vanhal. Much of their music was produced in Eszterháza under his direction. He developed a close friendship with Dittersdorf, whom he first encountered through Porpora and who later encouraged him to defend himself against the Berlin critics who censured his chamber music. Haydn also knew the talented composer Marianna Martines, whom he instructed in keyboard and singing in exchange for free board at the Altes Michaelerhaus from about 1751 to 1754. The lessons had been arranged by Metastasio, who oversaw the young girl's education and who, along with Porpora, lived on the third floor beneath Haydn's drafty attic room (see Godt). Whether Haydn and Martines remained in contact after their lessons remains unknown.

Older Vienna-based composers such as Monn and Wagenseil exerted compositional influence on Haydn, but of this generation it was Gluck who made the greatest impression. Haydn knew Gluck through Porpora and Metastasio, though their interactions are not well documented. He produced Gluck's *Orfeo ed Euridice* during the first full opera season at Eszterháza in 1776, and would go on to compose his own version of the Orpheus legend – *L'anima del filosofo*, which exhibits some Gluckian tendencies – for the London stage (it was never performed). Haydn twice quoted the popular aria "Che farò senza Euridice" from Gluck's *Orfeo* – in the first movement of Baryton Trio No. 5 in A major (Hob.XI:5) and in Act IV of *L'anima del filosofo*. Another Gluck melody – "Je n'aimais pas le tabac beaucoup" from *Le diable à quatre* – provides the main theme for the first movement of Symphony No. 8 in G major, "Le Soir." (See also Programmatic Elements.)

Gluck's exact contemporary C. P. E. Bach was also an important influence, albeit from afar. Haydn studied Bach's celebrated treatise on keyboard playing, and as Harrison has shown, after c. 1765 his manuscripts incorporate several of Bach's distinctive notational features. Though he never met Bach, he called on him in Hamburg in 1795 (unaware that the elder composer had passed away years earlier) and claimed his music as his primary model. He harbored a similar reverence for Hasse, who unlike Bach was active in Vienna and overlapped with Haydn. In 1767, Haydn sent Hasse a copy of his *Stabat mater*, which Hasse praised in a letter to the composer; Haydn stated he would "treasure this testimonial all my life, as if it were gold; not for its contents, but for the sake of so admirable a man" (CCLN 20).

Younger Vienna-based composers with whom Haydn interacted included Salieri, Paul and Anton Wranitzky, and Mozart. Both Wranitzky brothers studied with Haydn; Paul would go on to be Haydn's preferred conductor of his own works. Salieri played fortepiano in the first performance of The Creation in April 1798 and conducted the same work a decade later (in Carpani's Italian translation) in celebration of Haydn's 76th birthday. His operas were frequently performed under Haydn's direction at Eszterháza. Mozart occupies a special place among Haydn's peers. The two may have met as early as the 1770s; however, their first documented encounter was in 1784. According to tenor Michael Kelly, it was in this year that they played quartets together at the residence of Stephen Storace, with Haydn on first violin, Dittersdorf on second violin, Mozart on viola, and Vanhal on cello. Two years earlier, Haydn had published his path-breaking set of six string quartets, Op. 33. Inspired by this example, Mozart composed six highly innovative quartets of his own and DEDICATED them in flattering language to "my dear friend Haydn" (they were published in 1785). Three of these (K. 458, 464, and 465) were performed at a quartet party on February 12, 1785 that Mozart organized in honor of Haydn's initiation as a FREEMASON the day before; Haydn had heard all six in the presence of Mozart on January 15. While the relationship between the two composers has often been romanticized, there is ample evidence of their mutual respect and admiration. According to Mozart's sister Nannerl, Haydn considered Mozart the greatest composer he had ever encountered, a sentiment that is corroborated in Haydn's CORRESPONDENCE. He especially revered Mozart's operas, so much so that he declined an invitation to compose an opera for Prague in part due to an unwillingness to compete with Mozart on that front.

Shortly after the death of Prince Nicolaus II in September 1790, Haydn was "informed" by impresario Johann Peter Salomon that he would be going to London, where his professional network expanded still further. Keeping track of local talent proved a task in and of itself, and Haydn regularly jotted down the names of musicians in his London NOTEBOOKS. In the first notebook of 1791–92, he made a catalogue of professional and AMATEUR musicians under the headings "Singers, male and female," "Composers," "Pianists," "Violinists," "Violoncellists," "Oboists," and "Doctors" (CCLN 262–66). There are more than ninety entries in all, with some duplications across categories; among the professionals are sopranos Mara, Storace, and Billington; tenor Kelly; composer Gyrowetz; pianists Clementi, Dussek, and Cramer; violinists Salomon, Clement, and Giornovichi; and music historian Burney, whose address Haydn also noted and who would later help solicit subscriptions for The Creation. The list, however, is far from encompassing all those musicians Haydn encountered during his two London residencies. Among Haydn's acquaintances in 1794–95 were the violin virtuoso Viotti, the soprano Banti – for whom he composed the cantata Berenice, che fai?, and of whom he wrote, in broken English, "Mad. Banti (She song very scanty)" – and the twelve-year-old John Field, "a young boy, which plays the pianoforte Extremely well" (CCLN 306, 301).

While headlining Salomon's concert series in 1791–92, Haydn was surprised to encounter a former pupil, Ignaz Pleyel, as a rival. Pleyel had been appointed to lead the Professional Concert series in direct competition with Haydn and

Salomon. Upon hearing the news, Haydn joked, "so now a bloody harmonious war will commence between master and pupil" (CCLN 128). But the two remained friendly, in spite of attempts to stoke tensions between them in the London PRESS. "Pleyel's presumption is sharply criticized," wrote Haydn, "but I love him just the same. I always go to his concerts, and am the first to applaud him" (CCLN 132).

Of Haydn's many talented pupils, Pleyel undoubtedly developed the greatest reputation as a composer in his day (despite the fact that his music was sometimes criticized for being too derivative of Haydn's). But it was another pupil, Beethoven, who would go on to achieve the kind of lasting fame that Haydn himself had attained. Haydn met Beethoven, presumably for the first time, in December 1790 while passing through Bonn on the way to London; they met again there in July 1792. Beethoven showed him some compositions, including one of his two cantatas (both dating from 1790), and Haydn agreed, with the consent of Elector Maximilian Franz, to take Beethoven on as a pupil in Vienna. Their lessons lasted for about thirteen months from November 1792 to December 1793 (or January 1794, when Haydn departed for his second London tour). The extent to which Haydn's tutelage benefitted Beethoven has historically been a source of debate. Uncorrected errors in some of Beethoven's counterpoint exercises (see Ronge), combined with the fact that Beethoven produced no new major works during the period of his studies (as Maximilian Franz bitterly pointed out in a draft letter to Haydn), led some scholars to suggest that Haydn did not take their lessons seriously. But neither the uncorrected errors nor the absence of new compositions necessarily implies that the lessons were unproductive; on the contrary, Beethoven's stylistic development in the late 1790s and early 1800s owes much to Haydn's example. Johnson has observed that a newfound compositional control is already evident in Beethoven's three Op. 2 piano sonatas dedicated to Haydn. Beethoven's assimilation of Haydn's approach is even more apparent in the symphonies and string quartets, particularly regarding motivic manipulation, rhythmic variability, and cyclic integration.

Most significant, perhaps, is that at the time of their lessons, Haydn was at the height of his powers. At sixty-one years old, he was already the most celebrated composer in Europe: he understood the intricacies of patronage and PUBLICATION, appreciated the importance of adapting one's works to specific AUDIENCES, and had experienced musical life as a freelancer, a servant, an entrepreneur, and a culture-hero. How much of this experience he shared with the twenty-two-year-old Beethoven is undocumented, but it seems clear (particularly from the ways in which Beethoven later modeled his publication practices on Haydn's) that written counterpoint exercises were just one facet of a multifaceted curriculum. That Haydn's celebrity also created anxiety for the young Beethoven should be no surprise; nonetheless, as Webster 1984 has shown, the idea of a falling-out between them is largely based on apocryphal remarks.

MARK FERRAGUTO

FURTHER READING

Badley (2012); Bonds (1993); CCLN; Geiringer (2002b); Godt (2010); Harrison (1997); Heartz (1995); Johnson (1982); Jones (2005, 2009); *Oxford Companion*; Ronge and Wilson (2013); Webster (1984).

Compositional Process Three types of documents shed light on Haydn's compositional process: early biographies, surviving sketches, and evidence from Haydn's early training as a composer. Taken together, they present a coherent picture of Haydn as composer.

The accounts of Haydn's early biographers Griesinger and Dies are based on conversations with Haydn near the end of his life. Griesinger reports: "Haydn always composed his works at the Clavier ... He laid out the entire plan of the principal voice in each part, marking the main passages by few notes and figures; afterwards he breathed spirit and life into the dry skeleton through the accompanying voices and dexterous transitions" (78 and 116; Gotwals 61 and 62). Dies is less precise about the sketches but includes a description of the composer's daily routine: "At eight Haydn had his breakfast. Immediately afterwards Haydn sat down at the clavier and IMPROVISED until he found some ideas to suit his purpose, which he immediately set down on paper. Thus originated the first sketches of his compositions ... About four o'clock he returned to musical tasks. He then took the morning's sketches and scored them [*setzte sie in Partitur*], spending three to four hours thus" (211f.; Gotwals 204).

Dies's term *setzen* also appears in a famous letter by Haydn to his PUBLISHER: "for lack of time I have not yet been able to score [*setzen*] the fifth [quartet], but it is already composed [*componiert*]" (*Briefe* 172). These documents indicate that Haydn's compositional process unfolded in three phases: in Haydn's own terms, *Phantasieren*, *Componieren*, and *Setzen* (see Schafer). These correspond to the triad of *inventio*, *dispositio*, and *elaboratio* known from classical rhetoric and frequently adapted in eighteenth-century treatises on composition (see Arlt). Heinrich Christoph Koch, for example, in his *Versuch einer Anleitung zur Composition* refers to *Erfindung* (invention), *Anlage* (layout/disposition) and *Ausarbeitung* (elaboration).

These accounts are corroborated by Haydn's sketches, which survive for more than 170 single works. Most of these date from 1785 and beyond, shedding particular light on his later years. The sketches capture the ideas Haydn discovered during the *Phantasieren* phase; simultaneously, they are also the working documents of *Componieren*. Haydn first noted the main ideas of a movement as monophonic lines. When the MELODY moves to the bass or a middle part, Haydn sketches that part. This is "the plan of the main voice" mentioned by Griesinger. If an idea includes polyphonic elements, Haydn writes what Griesinger calls a "Skelett," which usually designates the outer-voices framework of the melody and bass, sometimes specified with thorough-bass figures. Having invented "the main passages" of a movement, Haydn worked on transitions between them. A most instructive example of this process is found in the sketch of the finale of Symphony No. 99 in E♭ major (Figure 8; discussed by Nowak, Schafer, and Konrad). Haydn opened a double-sheet of music paper, so that he had two facing pages before him like an open book, probably on his keyboard, as Ludwig Guttenbrunn's portrait shows (see ICONOGRAPHY). On the left Haydn started with the twenty-measure opening subject of the movement, notating the principal thematic voice continuously (sometimes shifting to the bass when it takes over the melodic lead, m. 13ff.), and the other parts only when they held special importance: for instance, when

Figure 8 Autograph sketch from the finale of Symphony No. 99. Österreichische Nationalbibliothek, Musiksammlung, Mus.Hs. 16835, fol. 24v. and 25. Reproduced with permission.

the melodic thread moves to the bass and back, Haydn writes more parts to notate his idea for a smooth transition. Having arrived at the end of the main theme where the orchestra tutti enters, Haydn sketched the secondary subjects in the dominant key on the right-hand page. This time he tested and crossed-out several versions. Having settled on one, he went back to the left-hand page and wrote it directly below the first subject. Next he had to compose what Griesinger called a "dexterous transition," that is, a link from the first to the second subject. Since Haydn fashioned the finale as a sonata-rondo, he also had to invent a retransition from the second subject to the first, the re-entrance of which he abbreviated "da capo." Running out of space on his double-sheet, Haydn was forced to use the remaining free staves, leaping back and forth across the page. Finally, he numbered the scattered components consecutively from one to eleven to fix their order. At this point, the first part of the movement was essentially "componiert" until the onset of the development.

Haydn's sketches for the development are of special interest. Haydn turned the double-sheet over and used the back side. Again, he noted several single ideas first and linked them. Obviously dissatisfied with this version, he took the single items and reordered them with a new numbering. This accords with Griesinger's report that Haydn sketched single ideas first to link them later. He did not compose "organically" from beginning to end; rather, he rearranged a collection of passages. A comparison of Haydn's sketches with the final score shows that only slight changes took place between *Componieren* and *Setzen*.

Composition of vocal music took place in a similar fashion, as sketches of Recitative No. 30 from *The Creation* show. Again, a double-sheet served as a working space for one movement, the single parts spread over both pages (see Oppermann). And again, Haydn sketched the main ideas first, in this case the beginning of the orchestral introduction in the upper left corner, and the beginning of the vocal part in the lower left. Haydn entered single problematic passages on the right-hand page until, at the end, the complete movement was drafted.

The least documented phase of Haydn's compositional process is *Phantasieren*, since the sketches always start with the results of that phase. We have little information about Haydn's keyboard phantasies. He probably received basic instruction in keyboard composition during his time at St. Stephen's Choir School in Vienna (see EDUCATION; COUNTERPOINT). In this case, a special role in the development of these abilities was played by Nicola Porpora (see Diergarten). In his autobiographical sketch of 1776, Porpora is the only person mentioned by Haydn as a composition teacher: "I wrote diligently but not in a well-founded way until, finally, I had the good fortune to learn the true fundamentals of composition from the celebrated Herr Porpora (who was at that time in Vienna)" (*Briefe* 77). In the vocal studio of Nicola Porpora, Haydn acted in the capacity of an accompanist/coach, and had to realize difficult thoroughbasses. Porpora was brought up in the Neapolitan *partimento* tradition, in which the ability to improvise and realize a bass line based on a repertoire of voice-leading patterns – including various types of cadences, the rule of the octave (a common-practice way of harmonizing each note of a scale in the bass), and numerous sequential progressions – that students learn to apply above given bass lines (see also HARMONY).

Even before working with Porpora, however, Haydn had received one of his first commissions as a composer through his ability to improvise. Around 1752 Haydn met the comedian Joseph Felix von Kurz, called Bernadon:

> Haydn must go home with Kurz. "You sit down at the piano and accompany the pantomime I will act out for you with some suitable music. Imagine now that Bernadon has fallen in the water and is trying to save himself by swimming." Then he calls his servant, throws himself flat on the stomach across a chair, makes the servant pull the chair to and fro around the room, and kicks his arms and legs like a swimmer, while Haydn expresses in 6/8 time the play of the waves and swimming. Suddenly Bernadon springs up embraces Haydn, and practically smothers him with kisses. "Haydn, you're the man for me! You must write me an opera!" (Dies 41; Gotwals 97).

This anecdote also illustrates how Haydn's keyboard phantasies were inspired by extra-musical impulses. They could be Haydn's own mood – "I sat down, began to improvise, sad or happy according to my mood, serious or trifling" (Griesinger 114; Gotwals 61) – but also certain established characters: "he said that he oftentimes had portrayed moral characters in his symphonies" (Griesinger 117; Gotwals 62; see also PROGRAMMATIC ELEMENTS).

Whether and how his compositional process changed throughout his lifetime – whether, for example, the process of *Componieren* became more difficult or more assiduous during the decades, or if the transition from *Phantasieren* to *Setzen* was more direct when Haydn composed keyboard music – remain open questions.

FELIX DIERGARTEN

FURTHER READING
Arlt (1983); Buelow and Marx (1983); Diergarten (2011); Dies; Feder (1979); Gotwals; Griesinger; Konrad (2014); Nowak (1970); Oppermann (2003); Schafer (1987).

Correspondence and Notebooks Secret missives to rival parties, epistles from a confidant going astray, methodically copied love letters, couriers rushing dispatches between distant royal palaces – these may sound like scenes from an eighteenth-century novel, yet Haydn's personal correspondence encompasses all of these and more. The composer's letters and notebooks reflect how inseparable life-writing and literature were during the 1700s, as epistles dominated both fiction and non-fiction publications.

During certain periods of his life Haydn wrote copious letters: "this is the tenth letter I have to mail," he states in one missive (CCLN 82). The two-hundred and eighty letters that survive, then, constitute only a fraction of what he produced.

Just as Haydn tailored his music to specific performers and AUDIENCES, he adjusted his rhetoric and persona in accordance with the letter's addressee. In a letter of December 5, 1766 addressed to Prince Nicolaus I, for example, Haydn first secures his patron's goodwill before making a series of requests. The letter opens:

MOST SERENE HIGHNESS AND NOBLE PRINCE OF THE HOLY ROMAN EMPIRE ... The most joyous occasion of your name-day ... obliges me not only to deliver to you in profound submission 6 new Divertimenti, but also to say that we were delighted to receive, a few days ago, our new Winter clothes ... despite YOUR HIGHNESS's much regretted absence, we shall nevertheless venture to wear these new clothes for the first time during the celebration of High Mass on YOUR HIGHNESS's name-day.

The composer then asks the Prince to return some scores, so that he can ensure they are "neatly and correctly copied and bound" as the Prince has commanded. "Incidentally," he continues, the "oboes are so old they are collapsing." Haydn justifies the cost of purchasing new ones before he seeks the Prince's consent to do so in the letter's final section (CCLN 6–7). Haydn advocated for and protected the court musicians in letters written throughout his career (e.g., CCLN 11–12; 17; 88–89; 221; 226–27).

Haydn's letters to publishers and friends likewise provide glimpses into the exigencies of his position. One to Artaria dated November 20, 1784, for example, laments "Half the theater is sick or away ... [thus] I constantly have to amuse His Highness" (CCLN 87). In others he apologizes for not saying good-bye due to the "abrupt decision of my Prince to leave Vienna" and not being given permission to travel (CCLN 80, 102). The bulk of the surviving correspondence consists of business letters. Haydn conducted much of his business via the post because the Prince's palaces were remote. Neither EISENSTADT nor ESZTERHÁZA were on the imperial postal route, so the family maintained its own network of couriers to transport missives and goods between estates, and the composer relied on a combination of these private and public systems to send and receive letters. Correspondence with Artaria shows that in the 1780s it customarily took two to three days for a letter from Eszterháza to reach Vienna. Letters and packages sent from the rural palace to William Forster in LONDON took two and a half to three weeks to arrive.

In letters written after 1779, the year he gained permission to deal directly with PUBLISHERS, Haydn emerges as a somewhat calculating, sometimes duplicitous, businessperson. He notes that pieces that are not "overly lengthy" or difficult to perform will appeal to consumers, "brevity will make the engraving very cheap," and a famous dedicatee will help sales (CCLN 42, 38, 41). In some cases, he markets his works directly to potential subscribers (e.g., Op. 33 and *The Creation*) or the same work to more than one publisher simultaneously (e.g., Op. 50 and the "Paris" Symphonies). Occasionally, Haydn adopts an irascible tone, as in his disputes with the Tonkünstler Societät and Artaria. He also repeatedly requests that his music "be neatly and legibly engraved" (CCLN 85) and complains vehemently when it is not.

Haydn's business letters also disclose his AESTHETICS. His claim that a collection of lieder exhibits "variety, naturalness, and ease of vocal execution" is not only a sales pitch, but also an assertion of musical values (CCLN 28). Other brief comments shed light on Haydn's musical principles and perhaps some of his teaching practices as well, such as the need for "light and shade" and "ideas" that can undergo "different methods of treatment" (CCLN 31–32 and 25) (see COMPOSITIONAL PROCESS; STUDENTS). He also claims that accompaniments should not overwhelm the voice and that a composer can learn much from writing accompaniments to pre-existing tunes (CCLN 195 and 198). The letter concerning the *Applausus* Cantata (1768), written because Haydn would not be present for REHEARSALS, provides related insight into PERFORMANCE practice issues. For instance, the composer recommends using two violas "because the inner parts sometimes need to be heard more than the upper parts" and suggests three timbrally distinctive instruments (cello, bassoon, and double bass) render the bass line (CCLN 9–11).

Letters written to his close friend Maria Anna von Genzinger reveal that Haydn was a man of feeling, one familiar with the language of EMPFINDSAMKEIT, sensibility. In one of his most famous letters (February 9, 1790) Haydn exaggerates the sentimental mode for jocular effect in order to thank Genzinger for her gracious hospitality. The letter opens with the dashes and exclamation points characteristic of sentimental novels: "Well, here I sit in my wilderness – forsaken – like a poor waif – almost without any human society – melancholy – full of memories of past glorious days – yes! past alas! – and who knows when these days shall return again?" (CCLN 96–7). In other letters, his use of sentimental language seems genuine and heartfelt. Haydn's correspondence with Genzinger reveals that epistles did sometimes go astray (CCLN 100–2) and that occasionally other means were used for delivery. Genzinger, for instance, sent one letter through a jeweler, noting, "he is a trustworthy man" (CCLN 91).

The composer's London Notebooks can be construed as letters to himself, *aide-mémoires*, about professional and political events, the costs of objects great and small, and the oddities (to him) of life in LONDON AND ENGLAND. With the exception of Schroeter's letters, the contents of Haydn's notebooks resemble other travel diaries from the time; it is possible the composer intended to publish an account of his TRAVELS. The second notebook preserves romantic letters from widow Rebecca Schroeter, presumably copied because she requested that they be returned. The pair may have been afraid of a scandal similar to one that had engulfed soprano Elizabeth Billington. The singer's correspondence had been stolen, held for ransom, and then published without her permission. Haydn comments on the affair in the first notebook (CCLN 255 and Fuchs); Billington had studied with Schroeter's late husband (see RELATIONSHIPS AND FRIENDSHIPS).

Haydn's final letters carry the tone of an elder statesman. He graciously thanks various societies for honors bestowed. He recommends pupils for jobs and fellow COMPOSERS AND MUSIC PROFESSIONALS for pensions. He despairs about the state of his health and his lack of creative energy ("I only wish I could brush away 10 years of my old age, so that I could still send you some new compositions" CCLN 213), but also expresses gratitude that he devoted his life to art. Touchingly, several of his last letters return to the realm of the COURT. But instead of interceding for his fellow musicians, Haydn's words suggest that the musicians and members of the Esterházy family were advocating for him. One of his final letters thanks Prince Nicolaus II for covering his medical bills.

The composer died a wealthy man (see ECONOMICS). His last will and testament could be considered his final epistle to his family, friends, and employer. In it, he left funds to help the poor in VIENNA, Eisenstadt, and his birthplace Rohrau and he made bequests to relatives, long-time colleagues, and his servants. Haydn also remembered those who had helped or honored him. For instance, he bequeathed 100 gulden to the granddaughter of a lacemaker who had lent him "150 gulden without interest in my youth and great need" (Landon V 53, 381). The composer left a gold medal from Parisian musicians, along with its accompanying letter, to the Prince of Esterházy. In return Haydn asked to be remembered via masses said in his name.

Most of Haydn's letters are in German, but a few are in other languages. The composer's original letters are scattered in various ARCHIVES, COLLECTIONS, and libraries. Haydn's complete correspondence is available in two editions, one edited by Dénes Bartha, the other by H. C. Robbins Landon; the latter presents the letters in English translation. Although modern scholars often tweak Landon's translations they have proved remarkably serviceable. Landon and Bartha worked together on their compilations, as a subheading on Bartha's title page makes clear. It reads "using the source collection of H. C. Robbins Landon." Landon's and Bartha's editions (1959 and 1965, respectively) reflect the multi-national nature of Haydn's career and the impact of the shifting tides of history on Haydn scholarship. A number of important collections resided (and reside still) in Hungary, which suffered an extended siege during the closing days of World War II. After an unsuccessful uprising against Soviet control in 1956 the government restricted travel and business with the west. As a result, Landon's edition predates Bartha's. Thus, the editions are monuments to musicological cooperation during the Cold War as well as to Landon's indefatigable energy, wide network of contacts, and dedication to Haydn's music.

As more letters and documents have been discovered since these collections were published, updated editions are needed. Moreover, it is time to re-examine the surviving originals with fresh eyes and minds. The eighteenth century is often referred to the as the "Century of Letters." Haydn's correspondence shows how public and private, fact and fiction, actual letters and literature intertwine in the era's writings. Beghin (2015a), Fuchs, and Sisman have examined Haydn's correspondence and notebooks through the lens of *Briefkultur* and life-writing, but much more could be done in this regard. Hörwarthner and Schroeder (1990) both point out that Haydn owned several letter-writing manuals, including two influential ones by Gellert, an author he admired. The ideal letter in the 1700s, like Haydn's music, balanced artifice and naturalness, prescribed formulae with original content. A charming or cleverly written missive was admired and valued, even though recipients rather than authors frequently paid the postage. Letters to and from Genzinger and from Schroeter can be interpreted as gifts of gratitude, exchanged alongside presents of food, music, copying services, and companionship. The composer's letters to Genzinger probably were shared and read aloud within the family circle, thus adding aural and communal components to the words on the page.

Letters were also physical objects of MATERIAL CULTURE. Missives had to be sealed and/or a wrapper or envelope created, which added to the weight and cost. (Some surviving autographs have a wax seal with the initials JH.) Haydn's letters, obviously, were written by hand. He employed Old German and Latin scripts, depending on the language of the letter and/or etymology of the word. Typeset versions cannot fully convey the arrangement of the text on the paper or the size, the formalness, and boldness of the handwriting. Both Landon and Bartha note that the composer often wrote important points in larger letters; they attempt to transmit that in their transcriptions via capital letters. At times, however, Landon's edition does not always accurately transcribe the originals' punctuation and paragraph breaks or their absence (as Beghin [2015a] points out). Nor can they convey the time and care it took to create an envelope or wrapper and the placement of the seal.

It perhaps goes without saying that a prolonged exchange of letters involves reciprocity: writers alternate as authors and receivers. For the most part, what survives is only one side of the correspondence: Haydn's. Nevertheless, much can be learned from these documents that Haydn often marked "mppria" (signed with my own hand). LAUREL E. ZEISS

FURTHER READING
Beghin (2005, 2015a); Beghin and Goldberg; *Briefe*; *Cambridge Companion*; CCLN; Fuchs (2013a); Gates-Coon (1994); Gotwals (1961); Green (2005); Hörwarthner (1997); H-L; Landon; *Oxford Companion*; Schroeder (1990); Scull (1997); Sisman (2007); Webster (2005a).

Cosmopolitanism – see Nationalism and

Counterpoint The denotations and associations of the term "counterpoint" in Haydn's time partly differ from connotations of that term in modern scholarship. A thorough and multifaceted understanding of "counterpoint" in Haydn's environment requires consideration of three general observations. First, in the eighteenth century, the term "counterpoint" was not equivalent to the "strict" or "learned" style; the latter is "imitative counterpoint" in the narrow sense, while "counterpoint" in a broader sense referred to the fundamentals of voice leading, independent of style. Second, eighteenth-century contrapuntal training is not equivalent to written exercises in the tradition of treatises like Fux's *Gradus ad Parnassum*; the function of Fuxian exercises within eighteenth-century music EDUCATION can only be understood in their interaction with a practical keyboard-based instruction. Third, elements of the learned style in Haydn's works cannot be regarded as esoteric artifice for connoisseurs in opposition to more "popularizing" strategies (see AMATEURS); rather these elements should be seen in specific generic and rhetorical traditions and as strategies of communication.

"The terms counterpoint and harmony are synonymous," writes Anton Reicha, a friend of Haydn and a connoisseur of his works in the early nineteenth century (711). Reicha's use of the term "counterpoint" in this case must be interpreted broadly as a synonym for voice-leading and polyphonic composition. In Heinichen's *General-Bass in der Composition*, a book Haydn had in his library, "counterpoint in the broad sense" is defined as "composition in general," while counterpoint "in the strict sense" is a kind of composition, where "subjects" are treated "artificially" (6). In the broad sense, "counterpoint" occurs even in the outer voices of a tune with simple accompaniment. That Haydn was familiar with this conception of "counterpoint" can be seen in his *Elementarbuch*, an excerpt he copied from Fux (see Mann). To demonstrate the different contrapuntal movements, Haydn provides new musical examples in the style of galant instrumental music, far removed from Fux's original examples.

The boundary between counterpoint in its broad and strict senses is fluid. The difference between the so-called "contrapuntal" style and the purported "free" style, therefore, is less fundamental than it might seem. Throughout the century, a spectrum of countless compromises between the two can be found, which are well-reflected in contemporary writings. The integration of "contrapuntal" artifice into "free" instrumental music, often described as a specific achievement of Haydn, was actually a well-known technique that Haydn mastered with exceptional inventiveness. In 1773, for example, Johann Friedrich Daube in his Viennese treatise *Der musikalische Dilettant*, a manual for amateurs, reports that even a galant minuet can "stand" some "imitations," if only the "artificial" is integrated in a way "that one hardly takes notice of it" (71 and 73). Haydn had written such minuets with imitations in two orchestral works, Symphony No. 32 in C major and Symphony No. 21 in A major, both of which show short imitations between melody and bass at the opening. Daube also shows how canons can be used in THEATER and chamber music, or how invertible counterpoint can be blended into "brilliant passages" of a quartet (279). Contemporaneously to the writing of Daube's treatise, Haydn blended such artifice into the slow movement of Symphony No. 47 in G major. The theme of this VARIATION movement is designed as a rounded binary FORM, where the first section returns in invertible counterpoint upon its recapitulation. Daube even brings up the idea that thematic-motivic processes, as found in the development sections of classical sonata-form in particular and in classical instrumental music in general, can be seen as an integration of the "contrapuntal" devices of imitation and fugue into the free style: "What are the good things composed today – symphonies, arias, concertos – if not free fugues?" (216).

In 1717 Friedrich Erhardt Niedt wrote that "to play thoroughbass means to produce proper counterpoint on a keyboard" (68). In the eighteenth century, counterpoint was widely taught on keyboard instruments. Training based on the extempore realization of given bass lines enabled the student to produce polyphonic music from simple bass-melody frameworks up to imitative counterpoint and complete fugues. In his autobiographical sketch, Haydn mentions that he had "clavier" lessons "by good masters" during his time at St. Stephen's Choir School. Since instruction on keyboard instruments was always linked to at least a rudimentary training in thoroughbass, his training there probably enabled him to perform organ services at a young age, as noted by early biographers, and to improvise on the keyboard when engaged by Joseph "Bernadon" Kurz (see COMPOSITIONAL PROCESS). Contrapuntal procedures in Haydn's works are conspicuously connected to sequential progressions, a possible indication that they originated in keyboard counterpoint that relies widely on sequences. Still, Fux's treatise played an important role, since

Gradus ad parnassum offered multiple levels of instruction. On the one hand, Fux could be used as an introduction into counterpoint in the broad sense: when studied before or alongside practical training on a keyboard instrument, *Gradus ad parnassum* provided a theoretical basis for the voice-leading principles that also define thoroughbass. In that sense, Fux's species also helped to elucidate the polyphonic structures implicit in thoroughbass-progressions and their ornamentation. On the other hand, it has been thoroughly documented that Fux was also studied by advanced students, already familiar with thoroughbass and free composition, as the final steps to Parnassus. In contexts and at institutions where polyphonic CHURCH music was an essential part of musical life, the ability of writing vocal counterpoint in *stile antico* (old style) – and its countless variations blended with more modern styles – was an important and prestigious skill.

In a 1787 polemic that probably refers to Haydn specifically, Heinrich Christoph Koch complains about composers who blend "exceptional difficulties" into their otherwise "fashionable" compositions out of "thirst for the applause of the crowd" (Diergarten 2010, 87). Against this backdrop, it becomes clear that Haydn's more "contrapuntal" compositions should not be considered as works for "Kenner" as opposed to purportedly more "popularizing" works. In certain contexts, nothing proved to be more popular than artificial counterpoint. TOPICS like the learned style and other "ancient languages" (see Konrad) clearly served expressive and dramaturgical purposes through their stylistic markedness, if not motivated directly by certain traditions of place or genre.

Few works by Haydn are actually in the pure old style. For instance, the *Missa "sunt bona mixta malis"* and the (probably connected) Offertory, *Non nobis domine*, explicitly entitled "in stile a cappella," were both probably intended for performances during Advent or Lent. Haydn's more than fifty vocal canons can also be considered a purely contrapuntal genre; the custom of singing canons in society and the meaning of the word itself ("rule") correspond with the epigrammatic character of most of the texts. His masses and oratorios usually integrate culminating symphonic fugal sections, evoking the atmosphere of the sublime in strict contrapuntal writing, but not in actual *stile antico*.

In his instrumental music, Haydn preferred to combine techniques and forms typically recognized as contrapuntal into otherwise free compositions, some of them annotated with explicit specification ("fuga a 2 soggetti," "in contrapunto doppio") as if to ensure the appropriate appreciation of these "difficulties." In several works, Haydn made use of what Reicha termed the "fugue phrasée" (1089): as opposed to the traditional fugal style that avoided caesuras, the "phrased fugue" adopts the incision and caesuras of galant style and combines aspects of fugue and sonata (see the finale of Haydn's Symphony No. 3 in G major as an example). Actual full-movement fugues are found predominantly in compositions of the late 1760s and the early 1770s, all of them final movements of cyclic works. Beyond one Notturno and one piece for mechanical organ, the only genres that feature fugues are the baryton trios and the quartets (Scheideler provides a list). Haydn's instrumental fugues have been subject to much speculation. Specifically, the fugues of the String

Quartets Op. 20 have been seen as symptoms of a "crisis" in Haydn's compositional biography, or as a reaction to accusations of being unable to write proper counterpoint. Rather, Haydn's fugues for string quartet follow a tradition of fugal writing for small ensemble, a tradition Haydn was able to continue with much ingenuity (Landon and Jones 163f.).

A good example to demonstrate the interaction of these multiple aspects of Haydn's counterpoint is Haydn's Symphony No. 70 in D major. The first movement, a sparkling sonata allegro in three–four time, involves effortless contrapuntal techniques in developing sections, such as simple invertible counterpoint of oblique motion (mm. 26ff) or imitative strettos of the main subjects (mm. 92ff.) – an easy device in this case given the arpeggio shape of the main subject. The second movement is announced (somewhat boastfully) as a "specie d'un canone in contapunto doppio." It consists of a fragmentary cycle of double variations on a *minore* and a *maggiore* theme, each of them only varied once, plus a final return of the *minore*. The *minore* is not a canon, but a rounded binary form with the repetition of the A-section written out with inverted outer parts. The emphatic use of suspension (m. 1 and m. 5), the continuous bass, the dotted rhythms, and the muted violins in octaves further contribute to the eerie atmosphere of the *minore*, which sets the scene for the contrastingly serene *maggiore*. In the last movement, a capricious introduction and its witty recapitulation(s) frame a fugue announced as "a 3 soggetti in contrapunto doppio." The concept of this fugue is closely related to the finale of the String Quartet in A major, Op. 20, No. 6 (see Diergarten 2011). The three "subjects" are the constituents of an invertible three-part sequential progression that is presented in all possible inversions (see Diergarten forthcoming). In both fugues, sequences of dissonant suspensions evoke the old style within the free. Both fugues rely on scales as their first subject. In Symphony No. 70 in D major, a stretto of the first subject (m.105ff.) leads to a climax and to the punchline of a symphony that brilliantly justifies Gerber's famous 1790 praise of Haydn's counterpoint: Haydn has at his command "every harmonic *Künsteley*, even if from the Gothic age of grey contrapuntists," but "instead of their former stiff character they take on a pleasing character, as soon as he prepares them for our ear" (610f.).

FELIX DIERGARTEN

FURTHER READING
Daube (1773); Diergarten (2008, 2010, 2011, forthcoming); Gerber (1790); Heinichen (1728); Konrad (2008); Landon and Jones (1988); Mann (1973); Niedt (1717); Reicha (1832); Sanguinetti (2012); Scheideler (2012); van Tour (2015).

Courts The world of European nobility was an ever-present dimension of Haydn's artistic and professional life. For nearly all of his career – from the 1750s until his death in 1809 – Haydn was employed by imperial and aristocratic courts, with the only significant hiatus occurring between 1790 and 1794 during the reign of Prince Anton Esterházy. Beyond these salaried appointments, however, the multifarious interactions that marked Haydn's relations with elite members of Austrian, English, French, Russian, and other contemporary societies of his day (which included commissions, DEDICATIONS, and sponsorship of "bourgeois" endeavors), but also notable limitations upon his musical choices, represent in their totality a basic mode of cultural practice. They underscore the significance of "courts" not as mere institutional sites but also as a general ethos of human interaction whose productivity and impact did not remain limited to the aristocracy *per se*. Haydn's overwhelming fame at the turn of the nineteenth century actually owed much to the composer's extensive associations with society's highest echelons. The extraordinary adulation he enjoyed during the late stages of his career illustrates a reformulation of the traditional structure of artistic patronage by the nobility, to which the emergent middle class stood in both a collaborative and a competitive relationship. Traditional hierarchies of privilege did not enter irreversibly into an antiquated past as the result of a supposed decline of this nobility, but rather preserved their force within a reconfigured culture of prestige of which Haydn arguably represents the first major example within the domain of music, followed later by the even more striking example of Beethoven. Elias has rightly noted this complex indebtedness to central values of the *ancien régime*:

> aristocratic court society developed a civilizing and cultural physiognomy which was taken over by professional-bourgeois society partly as a heritage and partly as an antithesis and, preserved in this way, was further developed. By studying the structure of court society and seeking to understand one of the last great non-bourgeois figurations of the West, therefore, we indirectly gain increased understanding of our own professional-bourgeois, urban industrial society (67).

The early phases of Haydn's participation in Austrian court society leaned towards the conventional relationship of servitude. His very first musical engagement, as choirboy at St. Stephen's Cathedral in VIENNA during the 1740s, already manifested an important court aspect, if an indirect one. Recruited by Georg Reutter, Jr., Kapellmeister of the cathedral (and after 1751, also Kapellmeister at the imperial court, holding the two appointments simultaneously), the young Haydn became familiar with a liturgical repertoire that greatly overlapped with that performed at the nearby palace of the Habsburg monarchs, who regularly attended worship services at both sites. After his voice changed and he was dismissed from the cathedral choir, Haydn experienced for the first time the inescapable condition of musicians' lives in this period, namely, a complete absence of security against circumstances beyond their control. In his own words, for "eight whole years" he was "forced to eke out a wretched existence by teaching young people" (CCLN 19) The arbitrary exercise of authority on the part of Haydn's employers is perhaps most famously illustrated by Nicolaus I Esterházy's reprimand in 1765 of his vice-Kapellmeister for an alleged neglect of duties, accompanied by an order to produce more works, especially for the baryton, an instrument cultivated by the prince himself. Jones has characterized this directive, which resulted in 126 baryton trios from Haydn's pen, as "one of the most indulgently self-interested in the history of musical patronage" (56). Further examples of the social distance between artist and patron include the abrupt disbanding of the Morzin and Esterházy Hauskapellen following the deaths of their ruling heads in 1761 and 1790 respectively, though in the latter case Haydn and the concertmaster Luigi Tomasini nominally retained their positions and also received generous pensions in addition to their salaries. Leopold Dichtler, a tenor who had performed at court since 1763 (Landon II; E. R. Landon), and later served as a double bassist and music copyist, was also awarded a pension. The generosity accorded them may well indicate a new social capital accessible at least to some musicians. (See COMPOSERS AND MUSIC PROFESSIONALS.)

With his appointment (probably in 1757) as Kapellmeister to the Bohemian nobleman Count Morzin (Franz Ferdinand Maximilian or perhaps his son, Carl Joseph Franz), Haydn entered the world of the aristocratic Hauskapellen, a form of private resident ensemble that proliferated in the Austrian imperial lands during the second half of the eighteenth century. Institutions like this helped shape the composer's activities to the very end of his career, as epitomized in the sponsorship of his two late oratorios by Gottfried van Swieten's Gesellschaft der Associierten Cavaliere. In 1761 Haydn transferred to the service of Prince Paul Anton Esterházy, who died only one year later and was succeeded by his younger brother, Nicolaus I. With unquestionably the most impressive musical resources in the Austrian lands apart from those of the Viennese imperial court, the Esterházy orchestra provided a rich framework for the development of Haydn's GENIUS, and remains the most outstanding instance of fostering creativity within the context of eighteenth-century aristocratic Kapellen. This facet of musical life is easily overlooked from a modern, post-ENLIGHTENMENT standpoint, which has emphasized the limitations imposed upon the musical activity of Haydn and his contemporaries by their conditions of service. An alternative perspective foregrounds court structures as a positive shaping force in eighteenth-century musical life, as witnessed in the extraordinary nature of Haydn's achievements during the Esterházy years – most notably his developments in the genre of symphony and the many operas written for ESZTERHÁZA from the mid-1770s which, as argued by Rosen, played a fundamental role in the composer's formation of a revolutionary new language of the string quartet (119). As Haydn observed to Griesinger: "I could as head of an orchestra make experiments and observe what made an impression, what weakened it and, in that way, improve, add, delete and experiment. I was cut off from the rest of the world, there was no one in the vicinity to annoy or disturb me, and so I had to become original" (Gotwals 17).

The geographical remoteness of Haydn's employment circumstances did not hinder his association and beneficial interactions with other members of the noble classes. For example, Prince Anton Grassalkovics, son-in-law of Nicolaus I, engaged Haydn in 1772 for the direction of dance music at his palace in Pressburg (now Bratislava). And during the 1780s, the composer's fame spread across much of the EUROPEAN continent in large part due to commissioned and published instrumental works connected with eminent personages such as Grand Duke Paul Petrovich of Russia, later Tsar Paul I, for whom the Op. 33 quartets were performed in 1781; King Friedrich Wilhelm II of Prussia, dedicatee of the Op. 50 quartets; and Count Claude-François-Marie Rigoley d'Ogny, who commissioned the Symphonies Nos. 82–87 ("Paris") and Nos. 90–92.

During the last two major phases of his active life as a composer – the LONDON sojourns (1791–95) and the years of the late oratorios (1796–1803) – Haydn enjoyed the status of what Webster terms a "cultural hero" (150). Esterházy servitude having receded far into the background, numerous European aristocrats fêted the most celebrated musical artist of the day. Yet it would be erroneous to view this as a diminution, rather than redirection and dissemination, of the social power of the noble classes. Rather, Haydn cultivated new forms of aristocratic patronage, illustrated especially by the subscription list for the first published score of *The Creation*, a bilingual edition in German and English. Mutuality of social capital, more than authority, formed the basis of late eighteenth-century interactions (see COMMERCE AND THE MARKET).

Haydn's notable contacts with the English nobility during his London visits began with his attendance at a ball held at the Court of St. James, home of British royalty, on January 18, 1791, in honor of Queen Charlotte's birthday. The following day he performed in a concert organized by the Prince of Wales (the future King George IV). Later that year he also became acquainted with the Duke of York, brother of the heir and newly married to Princess Friederike Charlotte Ulrike of Prussia, joining the young couple for a visit to the Duke's Oatlands estate on November 24–25. These connections deepened and flourished during his second English sojourn in 1794–95. On February 1, 1795, Haydn was invited by the Prince of Wales to a soirée held at the Duke of York's, at which compositions by him formed the whole of the musical program. As reported in the *St. James's Chronicle*, the official journal of the court, Haydn personally met the king on this occasion. Thereafter followed numerous subsequent exchanges with the royal family, including a concert for the Prince Regent two days after his marriage to Princess Caroline of Brunswick, on April 10, at which Johann Peter Salomon's opera *Windsor Castle* received its premiere, with its overture composed by Haydn.

Upon the death of Prince Anton Esterházy in 1794, his successor Nicolaus II reinstated Haydn as an active Kapellmeister. Haydn's duties were now limited to the composition of one concerted Mass per year, long held to be a name-day Mass for the prince's wife, Marie Hermenegild, though re-evaluations of the available evidence suggest a broader set of associations which also include the Feasts of the Nativity of Mary and the Most Holy Name of Mary – with the latter established as a general Catholic observance following the liberation of Vienna from the Turkish siege of September 1783 (see McGrann and Clark). Without the necessity to spend more than a brief period each year at the Esterházys' principal ancestral city in order to prepare and direct the performance of the work, Haydn lived mostly in VIENNA following his return from London. Here he experienced an even greater celebrity among the Austrian nobles who helped to bring *The Creation* and *The Seasons* before the public. Led by Baron Gottfried von Swieten, the Gesellschaft der Associierten Cavaliere, whose membership, according to Griesinger's biography of 1810, consisted of "the Princes Lichtenstein, Esterhazy, Schwarzenberg, Lobkowitz, Auersberg, Kinsky, Lichnowsky, Trautmannsdorf, Sinzendorf, the Counts Czernin, Harrach, Erdődy, Apponyi, Fries," provided the material and logistical resources for the early performances of these two works. In particular,

Prince Joseph Johann von Schwarzenberg, whose palace on the Neuer Markt served as the venue for both premieres, offered especially impressive financial support, as Croll has detailed in his study of documentary records contained in the Schwarzenberg family archives in Český Krumlov. In all, this aristocrat supplied a total of 2,468 florins towards the patronage of the oratorios between early 1798 and the end of 1801. The expenditures included one-tenth of the fee of 2,250 florins paid by the Associierten to Haydn for The Creation, a further 450 florins following the first performance of the work on April 30, 1798 (equivalent to the annual salary of the best-paid musician in the prince's Kapelle, the oboist Philipp Teimer, during this period), and a contribution again of 450 florins towards the fee for The Seasons in 1801. Although this extraordinarily copious support indicates a renown unmatched by any other composer of the time, the relationship between patrons and artist was a mutually profitable one, for, as Webster has observed, "both oratorios reflected and revalorized the enlightened-conservative sensibility of the Viennese elite at the turn of the century" (153). A comparable notion applies also to the publication of The Creation, advertised by Haydn in the Allgemeine musikalische Zeitung and other journals and intended as a presentation edition rather than one for practical use, as it consisted only of a score. The aspect of doubly reinforced social distinction emerges in the list of subscribers, which eventually numbered over four hundred. The print included their names in a long roster following the title page, carefully arranged with the most impressive personages at the head, among them the Austrian empress and crown prince, the Grand Duke and Duchess of Tuscany, the Elector of Cologne, the British king and queen, the Prince and Princess of Wales, and the Duchess of York. Haydn's lifelong association with the aristocracy reached its culmination in this exceptional symbolic display of the social and cultural interdependence which deeply marked the passionate investment by Europe's courts in the arts.

JEN-YEN CHEN

FURTHER READING
Cambridge Companion; CCLN; Clark (2009a); Croll (1973–74); Elias (1969); Griesinger; Jones (2009); Landon II; E. R. Landon (2002); McGrann (1998); Pohl (1875, 1882, 1927); Rosen (1971/72); Webster (2005b).

Cyclic Integration Eighteenth-century writers took for granted that individual movements within a work would be connected in a coherent and cohesive way from moment to moment, but few writers addressed relationships across movements, the fundamental premise of cyclic integration, during Haydn's lifetime. Galeazzi (1796), typically for the era, recognized different possible levels of integration, from the phrase up to the movement, but his language is too general to indicate a concern with the cycle as a whole. H. C. Koch (1787 and 1802) described generic expectations at the work-level while noting "unity in variety" or "many-sidedness" (mannigfaltigkeit) as a compositional goal, indicating his belief that a multi-movement work should have certain affinities from movement to movement. Thinking along similar lines, A. F. C. Kollmann (1799) urged that "a calculation must be made of the variety as well as the relation of character between those movements [of a work]; so that one general character may be found in the whole … set off by a judicious variety" (6–7). Kollmann cites

Haydn's *Seven Last Words* as a specific example of this practice, perhaps an indication of the PROGRAMMATIC, TOPICAL nature of his conception of integration given that there are few if any motivic connections among its movements.

Like his contemporaries, Haydn never commented explicitly on the topic of cyclic integration, though scholars have tried to coax out clues to his views from the early biographies. His well-known remark to Griesinger about developing an idea – "Once I had seized upon an idea, my whole endeavor was to develop and sustain it in keeping with the rules of art" – while bearing striking similarities to the writings of Koch and Kollmann, seems only to apply to a single movement when read in context (Griesinger 114; Gotwals 61; see also COMPOSITIONAL PROCESS). Yet only a few paragraphs later Greisinger records that "Haydn always worked out his compositions as a whole." In his section on *The Seven Last Words*, he further noted the difficulty with which Haydn strove to write seven successive adagios without "wearying the listener," a clear indication that Haydn was conscious that the movements of a work did not exist nor act in isolation from one another. The specific strategies used by Haydn to overcome these problems remains unstated, however, and because this work is one of Haydn's most unusual, his statement provides little guidance in assessing cyclic integration in his more conventional works. Griesinger also inquired about the images or programmatic content underlying Haydn's instrumental works. To this the composer coyly mentioned his depiction of moral characters (*moralische Charaktere*) in his symphonies and remembered a slow movement (which he claimed not to be able to recall in specific) in which God and a sinner were in dialogue. While Symphonies Nos. 26 and 49 have noteworthy connections to Holy Week and additionally have overt thematic connections among movements, Haydn's remarks to Griesinger on moral characters again avoids directly addressing cyclic integration.

Cyclic integration in Haydn's music, or the lack thereof, became a subject of debate in the early years of the nineteenth century as Beethoven's inter-movement connections, both programmatic and motivic, became increasingly apparent. E. T. A. Hoffmann's 1810 review of Beethoven's Fifth Symphony changed the discourse on cyclic integration in a way that remains heavily influential to the present. Hoffmann did not question the existence of cyclic connections in Haydn's works so much as he argued that Beethoven's approach in the Fifth Symphony was a breakthrough. He argued that the Fifth Symphony's connections are stronger in quality, more readily apparent to the ear, more pervasively present, and, most critically, necessary to the listener's comprehension of the work's meaning and importance. Thereafter most nineteenth-century commentators avoided discussions of cyclic integration in late eighteenth-century music, an indication of increasing doubts. While Hoffmann seems to have taken connections for granted in Haydn and Mozart's works, a broad consensus was reached by the early twentieth century which presumed that their works included only such connections as required by convention (shared keys for outer movements, for instance). That is, their connections were judged to be too weak to be intentional or too limited in scope to presume an active interest in unifying a cycle meaningfully. For instance, a section heading in Vincent d'Indy's 1909 *Cours de Composition Musicale* (Proksch 2015, 102–11), entitled "The Cyclic Sonata as Influenced by

Beethoven" agrees in principle with his overarching view of Beethoven's pivotal role in integrating movements in a tangible way on a regular basis.

Under the auspices of organicism, scholars began to reassess cyclic integration in the music of both Haydn and Mozart in the mid-twentieth century. Rudolph Réti and Hans Keller – themselves heavily indebted to twelve-tone analytic techniques – focused on motivic cells in an effort to show underlying connections even in instances where themes appeared to be quite different on the surface (see Proksch 2006). Jan LaRue assumed the position of skeptic, arguing that there was a distinct difference between "significant" and "coincidental" thematic relationships. LaRue contended that analysts needed to take nonmotivic factors (RHYTHM and HARMONY specifically, and the element's broader contexts generally) into consideration when evaluating potential connections. This, in turn, opened up the possibility that cyclic integration could be fostered through a variety of musical gestures previously overlooked because of the overarching focus on thematic materials.

Webster's *Haydn's "Farewell" Symphony and the Idea of Classical Style* (1991) brought about a fundamental reappraisal of Haydn's approach to cyclic integration that continues to be the central line of inquiry to the present. His "through-composition" implies the evolution of ideas in a work over time and across movements, while his analytic approach broadly accounts for thematic, harmonic, and other connective possibilities (drama, rhetoric, etc.). Webster's study relies on one of Haydn's most unconventional symphonies (Symphony No. 45 in F♯ minor, "Farewell") but has broad implications for all of the composer's output. The "Farewell" Symphony closes with a run-on movement pair, an overt indication that Haydn was thinking beyond the conventional double barline. To this Webster adds a variety of similarities across movements, while for the most part avoiding the pitfalls of motivic cell analyses by dismissing those that are seemingly due to convention or coincidence. Refinements to Webster's arguments have been posited by others in the years since. Haimo added the idea of "disruption" as a factor, for example. Others have made the point that all works are inherently integrated as a cycle simply by virtue of being grouped by the composer with the presumption of being non-interchangable, thus cyclic integration exists in a continuum from very weak to very strong.

While most analyses of Haydn's cyclic integration focus on the instrumental works, both his *Salve Regina* in G minor and his oratorio *The Creation* have been cited as cyclic in their approaches to dramatic unfolding and large-scale design. His purely instrumental works include demonstrable connections writ large through a variety of techniques. In the area of thematic recall, Symphony No. 46 in B major is among the strongest, given that eighteen measures from the *Minuet*'s primary theme return verbatim in the finale. Symphony No. 31 in D major, "Horn Signal," likewise includes a prominent return to the opening movement's "horn signal" in the finale. A convincing non-verbatim reuse of thematic material can be found in Symphony No. 49 in F minor, where all four movements (as well as the second key area of the opening movement and the trio section of the third movement) begin with the same basic structural pitches (C–D♭–B♭, followed by either a C or an A♭). The thematic connections observed in this symphony may have stemmed from Haydn designing the work for use during Holy Week, a tantalizing extra-musical factor in evaluating his compositional choices. A more intervallically based approach can be seen in Symphony No. 104 in D major, "London," where the initial perfect fifth and perfect fourth leaps reappear conspicuously in the outlines of many of the themes used in the remaining movements. The closest parallel to the "motto" opening of Beethoven's Fifth Symphony in Haydn's oeuvre may be Symphony No. 93 in D major, where unison tutti Ds appear at key points within three of the four movements. Prominent run-on movement pairs – breechings of the double barline – occur in the aforementioned Symphony No. 45 and the Keyboard Trio in A♭ major (Hob.XV:14). In both of these cases Haydn accommodates a remote-key modulation between two movements. Similarly, a number of his keyboard sonatas include *attacca* indications or somehow enable a distant modulation between movements in a way that provides an opening to examine further connections. Rhythmically, the closing measures of the second movement of Symphony No. 95 in C minor, in the same key as the next movement, are connected by a shared eighth-note motivic gesture in the absence of an *attacca* indication.

Beyond his use of specific musical elements as a means towards fostering a sense of cyclic integration, there are a handful of instrumental works in which Haydn includes what might be called larger conceptual connections across movements. The liturgical contexts of some of the works discussed above provided him with just such an opportunity; Symphony No. 26 in D minor references Gregorian chant in two movements. In a more secular context, Symphony No. 103 in E♭ major uses themes with FOLK SONG-like qualities in all four movements, though whether these melodies are actual folk song quotations or merely partake of the style remains unclear. The numerous bird-like themes across the movements of his String Quartet in C major, Op. 33, No. 3, "Bird," is another instance, and also an indication of the way in which the inauthentic nicknames applied to his works often betray an underlying unifying feature. Here the themes heard at the openings of the first and fourth movements, the trio of the second movement, and potentially m. 14 of the third movement are all bird-like, broadly speaking (see NATURE).

Given the quantity and variety of these, Haydn's most overt gestures towards cyclic integration, a scholarly consensus has emerged in the decades since Webster's study was published that a large percentage of Haydn's works have at least a few unconventional (and hence "significant") connections across movements. When viewed as a whole, the composer's enduring interest in integrating his multi-movement cycles to varying degrees is apparent. (See also TONALITY; RECEPTION 1950S–PRESENT.)   BRYAN PROKSCH

FURTHER READING
Galeazzi (1796); Gotwals; Griesinger; Haimo (1990); Hoffmann (1989); Koch (1787, 1802); Kollmann (1799); LaRue (1961); Proksch (2006, 2015); Webster (1991).

Dedicatees Looking at Haydn's dedications and dedicatees provides the opportunity to consider the many professional connections, personal RELATIONSHIPS, and patronage situations that were fostered throughout the composer's career. In the process, a variety of questions may come into play, such as: what were the relative interests of the composer and the PUBLISHER? Which party chose the dedication? Was it offered, sought out, or purchased? A single Haydn work could be "composed for" and "dedicated to" different individuals, or dedicated to different individuals in different editions, further complicating the meaning of his dedications. Beghin considers these issues at length; Green, meanwhile, points out that Haydn was himself the dedicatee of over forty composers during the height of his fame (1784–1809), thereby becoming a pseudo-patron whose reputation was capitalized on by both publishers and dedicators.

During Haydn's long service to the Esterházy family his dedicatees were members of the princely family (see Fuchs). Following the 1779 renegotiation of his contract, his commissioned and published works clearly demonstrate a strong association with figures outside of COURT. These dedications imply a general association between GENDER and FORM, with string quartets typically dedicated to male figures and keyboard works (trios and solos) generally created for female recipients. Haydn's dedications also reflect the differences between amateur and artist musicians, with specific classes of players echoed in dedication choice.

An especially noteworthy dedicatee for several of Haydn's published keyboard pieces is Princess Marie, wife of Nicolaus II and lifelong friend to Haydn. Works for Princess Marie may reflect a private bond between composer and dedicatee, as demonstrated by the almost conversational nature and form of Keyboard Sonatas, Hob.XVI:40–42 (published by Hummel in 1784). Similarly personal in nature is Keyboard Sonata in E♭ major, Hob.XVI:49 (1790), composed for Haydn's close friend and gifted amateur pianist Marianne von Genzinger, but dedicated to Eszterháza housekeeper Maria Anna Gerlischek on the manuscript.

Haydn's LONDON sojourns (1791–92 and 1794–95) also produced several works dedicated to pianists with personal connections to the composer, albeit more formal in compositional style. Rebecca Schroeter (*née* Scott) was the dedicatee for Trios, Hob.XV:24–26, which include the "Gypsy Trio" in G major (see EXOTICISM). The set was composed in 1795, shortly before Haydn left England. Schroeter's place as a named dedicatee is an open reflection of her personal relationship to Haydn. Virtuosa pianist-composer Therese Jansen (*mariée* Bartolozzi) was the recipient or dedicatee for all of Haydn's larger-scale London keyboard works. Works written for Jansen include three Trios, Hob.XV:27–29 (1797), Sonata in C major, Hob.XVI:50 (1794), and Sonata in E♭ major, Hob.XVI:52 (1794); the manuscript states "Sonata composed for the celebrated Miss Teresa de Janson [sic]." Interestingly, Hob. XVI:52 was later dedicated to Magdalena von Kurzböck on the title page of the Viennese Artaria publication (1798), possibly as a marketing strategy, since dedication to a local, familiar figure helped promote sales (see COMMERCE).

Haydn's string quartets reveal his use of dedication as a social device and commodity, in contrast to the more personal nature of his keyboard compositions. His string works are exclusively dedicated to men, reflecting a tendency for string players to be male. As Sutcliffe has shown, the "Prussian" Quartets, Op. 50 (1787) follow a telling order of composition and dedication, demonstrating both Haydn's judicious understanding of publication and Artaria's power to assign dedicatees. Haydn made arrangements with Artaria to publish the set of six quartets in 1786, with the stipulation of receiving "either 12 copies or my choice of the dedication." Haydn requested that Friedrich Wilhelm II, King of Prussia be the named dedicatee in May, 1787. Although the quartets were performed in Vienna before publication, a delay of one year was necessary for Prince Esterházy to have initial exclusivity.

Haydn's astute choice of dedicatees developed through the 1790s, as exemplified by the "Apponyi" Quartets, Op. 71/74 (1792–93). Count Anton Georg Apponyi commissioned the set of quartets, a privilege that included exclusive performance rights until the quartets' publication in 1795. Notably, Artaria kept the Count as named dedicatee on its EDITION. The quartets are beyond the skill of most amateurs. Haydn's final complete set of string quartets, the "Erdődy" Quartets, Op. 76, was commissioned by Count Joseph Erdődy and composed in 1796–97. Like the "Apponyi" Quartets, the set was reserved for the Count's private use during a short period of exclusivity, and its publication by Artaria (1799) maintained the connection to Erdődy as named dedicatee.

KATELYN CLARK

FURTHER READING
Beghin (2015a, 2015b); CCLN; Fuchs (2013b); Green (2011); Landon III–IV; NG Haydn; Sutcliffe (1992); Temperley (1984–87).

Disability As the discursive binary of "abled" versus "disabled" gives way to "diversely abled," as we come to understand all of our human research subjects – composers, performers, listeners, and ultimately even ourselves – as possessing myriad dis/abilities, and as we come to see those dis/abilities as multiple and varied conditions (visible and invisible) that are socially constructed, performed, and (accordingly) always in flux and evolving, the field of Haydn studies is poised both to gain and to contribute fresh insight.

In a June 1799 letter to his PUBLISHER Breitkopf, Haydn wrote "there are some days in which my enfeebled memory and the unstrung state of my nerves crush me to the earth to such an extent that I fall prey to the worst sort of depression, and thus am quite incapable of finding even a single idea for many days thereafter; until at last Providence revives me, and I can again sit down at the fortepiano and begin to scratch away again." For Grave (2016), this comment neatly captures a trajectory from affliction to recovery – "something from the composer's own life experience" (577) – that can be heard as reflected in his choices of MUSICAL MATERIALS. For example, in the Part Two trio of *The Creation*, terror (the result of being abandoned by God) is conveyed by a unison E♭ minor scale, agitated string triplets, and a vocal line descending to the point of almost literally disappearing (at "vanish into dust"); then, through an augmented-sixth chord, "life with fresh vigor returns" in E♭ major. "In reading the excerpt from Haydn's letter," Grave suggests, "we can perhaps hear – and imagine the composer himself hearing – a musically embodied contrast between minor-colored darkness, dissonance, and despair ("crush me to the earth"), and the unmistakably major-illuminated, restorative moment that follows ("Providence revives me"), perhaps with a pivotal augmented-sixth chord to articulate the transitional "until at last": that anticipated moment when the cloud of incapacity lifts to allow for a time of health and well-being regained" (578).

Here (and in Grave 2008, on Haydn's Quartet Op. 76, No. 1) Grave grounds his understanding of the musical signifiers of affliction, transformation, recuperation, and recovery in period sources, showing us that today's familiar binaries of ability and disability are not entirely anachronistic. Rameau, for example, promoted a conception of ability and its opposite, impairment of ability, when he described the minor mode in terms of an imperfect, weakened, compromised, and subordinate form of the major. But when Grave describes his intention to "search for words, phrases, and images by which to sharpen our focus on palpable musical relationships," with a focus "specifically on ways in which the music being examined may be seen to embody the experience of disabling conditions and their remediation" (564) he suggests that his interest lies in describing music in terms that resonate with our own experiences as much as those of Haydn's contemporaries. As such, his foregrounding of disability feels of-the-present-moment, while his conception of disability as negative may not.

Meanwhile, Sisman, focusing specifically on MELANCHOLY, posits that the eighteenth-century mind was "capacious enough to hold many contradictory ideas [about this dis/ability] simultaneously" (590; see also November). There were those who defined melancholy with an emphasis on moral failing, a reflection of the sorry state of the soul; but there were others who stressed positive attributes such as inspiration (see IMPROVISATION), creativity, profundity, heightened perception, and GENIUS. Add to this the contemporary valorization of sensibility (EMPFINDSAMKEIT) and solitude, the wallowing in the seemingly paradoxical "joy of grief" in purpose-built spaces (gardens, shrines), and the supposition (recognition) that mania could be melancholy run amok – and it becomes clear that within Haydn's personal NETWORKS and the networks created by his music, there existed an expansive understanding of this particular dis/ability, one that was willing to embrace rather than erase inherent paradoxes. Perhaps we could even say they "got it" (melancholy at least) in a way that we are learning now, thanks to the disability rights movement and Disability Studies, to "get it."

Sisman goes on to describe three compositions (by C. P. E. Bach and Beethoven) that represent the experience of melancholy by way of the metaphor of a labyrinth – tacking between order and disorder, circles and lines, senses of infinitude and limitation, stasis and seeking. She suggests that it might be productive to view Haydn's many movements marked *mesto* (melancholy or mournful) through this lens. To do so is to acknowledge a multiplicity of interpretive possibilities: even if one of the expressive potentials of music is to convey the human experience of dis/ability, there is no univalent sense of that experience. Just as important, we should keep in mind that, as with GENDER or ethnicity, to discuss music in terms of its representation of dis/ability is also to participate in the construction of disability.

Following on this last point, it is worth considering the language we use to describe the FORMAL aspects of Haydn's compositions, especially given the significant (admittedly even outsized!) role Haydn's symphonies, sonatas, and quartets play in the teaching of music theory fundamentals on both sides of the Atlantic. Darcy and Hepokoski's sonata theory has made common the term "deformation" to indicate a "strain or distortion of the norm," as in a recapitulation subjected to a deformation. "We do not use this term in its looser, more colloquial sense, one that can connote a negative assessment of aesthetic defectiveness," they write, and while also acknowledging that "however carefully one might insist upon one's intentions ... words have connotational, lateral slippages and past histories that can escape our control" they go on to insist that deformations are "encouraged," "positive features," "charged [with] edginess and [the] flavor of aesthetic risk" – signs of "health and aesthetic integrity" (614–18). Whether or not they were persuasive on this point at the time of their writing (2006), the connotations of "deformation," and another of their key terms, "norm," have continued to change and their many layers of meaning have only grown thicker. Meanwhile, classrooms where their sonata theory is taught (with countless examples from the Haydn repertoire) are increasingly guided by principles of accessibility, equal access, and universal (i.e. barrier free) design. Darcy and Hepokoski are clear about their intention, but as with many words and phrases throughout the vocabulary of identity – nationality, ethnicity, gender, sexual orientation, and dis/ability – the impact or effect of their use may differ from the intention.

In fact, tuning in to the ways in which words mean different things in different contexts is a skill that can be exercised through engagement with dis/ability studies. Music Studies and Dis/ability Studies are strong allies in this regard. This is the point Kielian-Gilbert makes when she offers us the opening of Haydn's Quartet Op. 76, No. 2, "Fifths" as a sort of exercise in "rethink[ing] the fixity of material perceptions by hearing and listening for the metamorphic potentials" – potentials that both music and dis/ability have in common. Her lens of dis/ability does not lead her to hear the music as a narrative of dis/ability (affliction, suffering, overcoming, recovery or whatever else); rather, she describes the motivic material (descending fifths) as "interacting and in motion with surrounding material" in the same way that dis/abilities change according to contexts of time, place, and social relationships. We are urged to consider "musical subjectivity as *dis/able* and thus materially and immaterially incomplete, partial, contingent, and expressive." Is this not very different from saying that musical subjectivity is like gender, or any number of other expressions of identity that can also be understood as "contingent"? Perhaps, but for almost anyone engaged in the field of Music Studies, rethinking ability – thinking critically about the ontology of ability – could be especially challenging, even uncomfortable, and, as a result, enlightening. After all, musicians are by and large highly concerned with ability: its cultivation from a young age, its development over countless hours of practice under the guidance of master teachers, and its manifestation as talent and in renown. To construe ability, as Kielian-Gilbert does, instead as "emergent" would be a paradigm shift, probably a more significant shift than it might be for practitioners of many other fields.

In the end, Disability Studies joins an auspicious list of humanistic endeavors that equip us to understand ourselves and others better, to appreciate our differences and our commonalities, and to hone our ability (!) to empathize. With respect to Haydn and his music, where specifically might we apply these broad insights? To just about any topic covered in this book: to all aspects of Haydn's biography, his compositions (opera plots and characters spring quickly to mind, for example), PERFORMERS and AMATEUR players, AUDIENCES, and analysts. And beyond: to our colleagues and our students, and to ourselves.
SARAH DAY-O'CONNELL

FURTHER READING
Grave (2008, 2016); Hepokoski and Darcy (2006); Kielian-Gilbert (2006); November (2007); Sisman (2016).

Discography The Haydn repertoire has been relatively well represented throughout the eras of audio and video recording. Kemp provides a broad discography (to 2002) and Lowe lists selected recordings of the symphony cycles (Paris and London cycles up to the 1990s and complete cycles up to Adam Fischer's), and Symphonies Nos. 45 in F♯ minor and 94 in G major (to the 1980s). *The World's Encyclopædia of Recorded Music* (WERM, Clough and Cuming) from 1952 includes a wealth of untapped historical recordings for Haydn scholars, and record ARCHIVES such as those at the British Library and the International Piano Archives (University of Maryland) contain a range of unpublished or rare recordings, including many privately made recordings and radio broadcasts. An entry on Discography also appears in H-L, but an updated and comprehensive Haydn discography is needed.

It can nevertheless be noted that two particular trends have characterized, and continue to characterize, the field of Haydn discography. The first is a close and reciprocal relationship between recording and scholarship. From the Haydn Society's tandem production of EDITIONS and recordings in the 1950s, to the historically informed efforts of Christopher Hogwood's Academy of Ancient Music advised by James Webster in the 1980s and 1990s, audio recordings have often both contributed to and been influenced by scholarship on Haydn and his music. Recent productive intersections between recording and scholarship appear in *Haydn and the Performance of Rhetoric* (2007) co-edited by Beghin and Goldberg, in which several contributors make arguments based on unique audio and video examples included in the book's accompanying DVD. In 2008 Beghin joined forces with engineers at McGill University's Multimodal Shared Reality Laboratory at the Centre for Interdisciplinary Research in Music Media and Technology (CIRMMT), taking acoustical readings of nine rooms in which Haydn's keyboard music was likely played; these were then recreated using an array of speakers in the studio, where Beghin recorded each of the keyboard sonatas on contextually suitable period instruments. The aim was to think at the same time about rooms and instruments, in order to render PERFORMANCES that conveyed specifically tailored rhetorical intentions. In contrast to scholarship where recorded examples are provided as a kind of supplemental bonus above and beyond the (sufficient) printed musical example, this kind of work exemplifies the term "born digital": recording is not merely assisted by scholarship, it *is* scholarship.

At the same time, the close relationship of research and recording has at times perpetuated a perception that Haydn's music is primarily for the learned, unlikely to be enjoyed by the larger public AUDIENCE (see also RECEPTION). Today the sheer availability of recordings (and in particular, videos) effectively counters that notion. Anyone with access to the internet can hear and view, just for example, all three oratorios, many symphonies and quartets (even performed at Eszterháza), and several operas. Of particular interest in terms of the way it harnesses recording technology for the sake of not only educating and challenging but also appealing to the audience is the 2010 Unitel Classica/ORF video of *Il mondo della luna*, recorded at the Theater an der Wien in 2009. The music is provided by the period orchestra Concentus Musicus Wien conducted by Nikolaus Harnoncourt, while the sets and costumes convey the technological and scientific revolutions of the 1960s: color television, space exploration, computers (which are used, rather than the traditional microscope, to dupe the character Buonafede). Recordings will no doubt continue to propel the study, appreciation, and accessibility of Haydn's music, a topic that is critically explored under RECORDING. MICHAEL RUHLING

FURTHER READING
Beghin (2007, 2008, 2015a); Clough and Cuming (1952); H-L; Kemp (2002); Lowe (2005).

E

Economics and Finances As many contemporaries remarked, Haydn was a less-than-scrupulous businessman and was sometimes even considered a miser (see Beer and Burmeister 1997). It may be that Haydn's "wretched existence" as a freelance musician in Vienna during the 1750s (CCLN 19) caused him to become overly cautious regarding money. But just as Bourdieu expanded the concept of capital beyond the pecuniary sphere, so Haydn's economics should not be reduced to monetary transactions. Every kind of social transaction, even the gift (as Mauss has demonstrated), establishes its own kind of economy. Haydn's economies can also be understood in terms of two further spheres: an economy of artistic reputation, and an economy of charity.

Finances (Monetary Economy) When Haydn was dismissed from St. Stephen's Cathedral, probably in 1749, he started to carve out an existence as a practical musician. His income as a keyboard teacher and church and dance musician was meagre (Gotwals 12–14; Svoboda). During his early freelance years this may have amounted to something between 100 and 200 gulden per year, and later perhaps closer to 300. To help put this into perspective: a contemporary Austrian day labourer earned 85 gulden per year, a primary school teacher 120–250, and an artisan 260. In contrast, COURT secretaries received an annual income of 1,500–2,000, and state ministers approximately 14,000–20,000 Gulden (see Sandgruber).

Probably in 1757, Haydn became chapel master to Count Morzin with a salary of 200 gulden, free room and board at the staff table (according to Griesinger; Dies speaks of 600 gulden, perhaps including the monetary value of lodging and meals; Gotwals 15, 99). When Haydn signed his contract as vice-Kapellmeister of the Esterházys in 1761, his yearly income rose to 782 Gulden 30 Kreuzer (his salary was officially 400 gulden, plus 200 from the prince's private funds (*Kammerbeutel*) to which the financial equivalent of his meals must be added). He also received the monetary equivalent of a princely uniform, if a new one was not actually necessary, and (from 1771 on) he got a yearly amount of wood and wine. From then on, his salary would not rise until the death of Nicolaus I – although the prince sometimes rewarded him with financial "bonuses" for opera premieres and the like. In 1773, he managed to secure a raise in the quantity of wood and wine he received (amounting to 200 gulden) by taking up the post of organist in EISENSTADT during winter. When in 1790 the new Prince Anton dismissed the chapel, Haydn received a pension of 1,400 gulden (of which 1,000 came from the late Prince Nicolaus's estate). Due to inflation resulting from WAR, Haydn's salary increased under

Nicolaus II to 1,700 gulden in 1797, and to 2,300 gulden in 1806. The Esterházys also paid for the elderly composer's expensive medical treatments (see Siegert; see also AGING).

Haydn died a wealthy man. His last will contains bequests totalling 24,000 gulden, and the auction of his estate yielded nearly the same sum. Furthermore, he owned bonds worth 14,800, and his house in Gumpendorf was sold for 17,100 gulden (Landon V 383). These sums are clearly beyond what the most economical of householders could save (even if Haydn's characterization of his wife as a spendthrift was untruthful), and they must be due to his other sources of income – including the selling of his compositions to PUBLISHERS and patrons, and money earned during his very profitable trips to LONDON. A rough estimate of his fees amounts to between 450 and 1,000 gulden for six symphonies, and 300–450 gulden for six quartets (Fuhrmann 257–60). It is unclear, however, exactly how many compositions Haydn sold, and how often. In an age where copyright was virtually non-existent outside of England, Haydn would often sell his music simultaneously to publishers in different countries, a practice that seemed fraudulent to some of his contemporaries, including Beethoven (see Biba), but one that was routinely adhered to by later composers in the first half of the nineteenth century – again including Beethoven (see Fuhrmann). Haydn's single most spectacular COMMERCIAL success was certainly his self-publishing of the score of *The Creation* with German and English text; a rough calculation suggests that, all in all, he earned about 16,000 gulden after expenses, a sum equivalent to ten yearly salaries from the Esterházy court (see Fuhrmann).

Economy of Artistic Reputation "Honor and fame were the two powerful motives that ruled him," Haydn's biographer Dies flatly stated (Gotwals 203). But it must be kept in mind that for Haydn, commercial and artistic success were complementary rather than contradictory (as they would come to be seen by the Romantics). In 1780, he wrote to Artaria on behalf of the Auenbrugger sonatas: "I hope to gain some honor by this work, at least with the judicious public . . . should they have a good sale, this will encourage me to further efforts in the future" (CCLN 24–25). Artistic success for him rested in the "effect" of his works, an effect he always saw as intimately linked to the "right" performance (CCLN 73, 89, 162, 187, 205), and sometimes even to the right keyboard INSTRUMENT (CCLN 105). In the letter on the *Applausus* cantata, for instance, he pleaded to the musicians "for the sake of my reputation as well as their own, to be as diligent as possible" (CCLN 11). And in a late letter to Nicolaus II he still worries that two masses will be performed in Pressburg in his absence and thus "lose much of their effect and this will be greatly to the detriment of my industry," while at the same time claiming: "meanwhile I am labouring *wearily* on the new Mass, though I am *anxious* whether I shall receive any applause because of it" (CCLN 205). Haydn's economics of reputation are also perceptible in an increased susceptibility to receiving presents and honors during his advanced years.

Economy of Charity His biographer Griesinger, who also served as agent for the Leipzig publisher Breitkopf & Härtel, had himself witnessed Haydn's more dubious dealings on several occasions (see Biba). But in his biography,

Griesinger took pains to point out that Haydn was a generous man, paying debts and donating freely to poor relatives and acquaintances, and consciously leading a very modest life-style to save money for such occasions (Gotwals 59–60). Such charity may be seen as an outgrowth of Haydn's devout Catholicism (see Religion and Spiritual Beliefs) – particularly as it is documented in his last will and testament (Gotwals 1961), but it was also very much in accordance with Enlightened philanthropism. Griesinger reports that Haydn "had noted down the very considerable sums brought in for the benefit of the poor by performances of his oratorios, partly in Vienna, partly in other places." This, according to Haydn's own words, was to let the world know "that I had not been a useless member of the Society, and that one can also contribute to charity by music" (Gotwals 47).

WOLFGANG FUHRMANN

FURTHER READING
Beer and Burmeister (1997); Biba (1987); Bourdieu (1984 [1979]); CCLN; Dies; Fuhrmann (2010); Gotwals; Gotwals (1961); Griesinger; Landon V; Mauss (1966 [1923–24]); Sandgruber (1985); Siegert (2010); Svoboda (2001).

Editions and Edition-Making Editions have important responsibilities. Not only do they provide dependable musical texts for musicians and scholars, but they also separate Haydn's genuine compositions from the many works falsely attributed to him.

The quest for determining authentic and non-authentic works started already in Haydn's lifetime, when various attempts to Publish "complete editions" were made. Each encompassed only a single genre. The *Oeuvres complettes de Joseph Haydn* published by Breitkopf & Härtel in Leipzig (twelve volumes, 1801–6) consisted of works for keyboard (trios, sonatas, and other pieces, including some arrangements, as well as songs and part-songs with keyboard accompaniment). Haydn himself was involved in the undertaking, as he checked lists with incipits to make sure that "nothing would be included in this collection to which hitherto my name has been attached illegitimately," though he was not involved with the preparation of the musical text itself. In addition, Breitkopf & Härtel published seven of Haydn's masses (1802–8 and 1823) in a format resembling the *Oeuvres complettes*, and several other late choral works.

In close competition with Breitkopf & Härtel, the Leipzig publisher Christian Friedrich Lehmann released a collection of piano music also entitled *Oeuvres de J. Haydn*. Less competitive, though similar in content, is the *Collection complette des Sonates de Piano d'Haydn* (six volumes, 1801–2), including keyboard trios and other pieces, published by Haydn's former pupil Ignaz Pleyel, a successful composer as well as a publishing entrepreneur in Paris. His *Collection complette des quatuors d'Haydn* (1801–6), in parts, became canonical and served as a model for several other collections of Haydn's string quartets during the nineteenth century (especially those by the publishing house of Hoffmeister, which later became C. F. Peters). Unfortunately, Pleyel's collection included some non-authentic works, such as the notorious "Op. 3," thereby establishing the wrong number of eighty-three quartets instead of the actual sixty-eight. Of great momentousness was Pleyel's invention of the pocket score for two of his collections, the *Oeuvres d'Haydn en partitions / Symphonies* four symphonies) and the *Oeuvres d'Haydn en partitions / Quatuors* (thirty quartets in ten volumes). There were also several early collections of symphonies in parts (Artaria, Birchall, Bland, Forster, Sieber, Simrock) as well as in score (Bote & Bock, Breitkopf, Le Duc, Rieter-Biedermann), though none can make any claim to even approaching completeness.

During the nineteenth century, several complete editions were created as MONUMENTA to great composers, commencing with Johann Sebastian Bach's works in 1851, followed by Beethoven, Schubert, Schumann and many others. But only in 1907 was a first attempt made to establish a "Haydn monument" of this kind. The initiator (and one of the main editors) was Eusebius Mandyczewski, curator at the archive of the Gesellschaft der Musikfreunde in VIENNA. Only eleven volumes of this edition were completed, with the last being printed in 1933. One of the enduring merits of this edition is Mandyczewski's list of 104 authentic symphonies, distinguished from doubtful and spurious works (listed in two further indices), a first attempt at authenticity research.

The determination of authenticity has been a crucial endeavor of Haydn edition scholarship up to this day. Already during his lifetime many works had been attributed falsely to the composer – some of them well known, like the Divertimenti Hob.II:41–46 (called "Feldparthien"), from which Brahms selected the theme of his "Haydn Variations," as well as the above-mentioned quartets "Op. 3" and the infamous "Toy Symphony" Hob.II:47. In some genres the number of misattributions is higher than those of the authentic works; for instance, there are nearly two hundred "false" Haydn symphonies and more than two hundred masses (although here it is sometimes unclear whether the attribution targets Joseph or his brother Michael Haydn).

In 1949 H. C. Robbins Landon helped found the Haydn Society Boston–Vienna. The aim of the society was to propagate Haydn's oeuvre with recordings, concerts, and not least by completing Mandyczewski's edition (see RECEPTION; RECORDING). Jens Peter Larsen, who established modern Haydn scholarship with his pioneering dissertation *Die Haydn-Überlieferung* (1939), was entrusted with overseeing the scholarly foundation of the *Joseph Haydn Kritische Gesamtausgabe*, the critical edition of the composer's complete works, but only four volumes were published in 1950–51. Several more were being prepared at the time by scholars like Friedrich Blume, Karl Geiringer, Ernst Fritz Schmid, Otto Erich Deutsch, among others.

The failure of the first two attempts at producing a scholarly Haydn edition were partly caused by the lack of financial security. Crucial, however, was the complexity of Haydn transmission. Only one in three of Haydn's works has come down to us in autograph form; and for the remaining two thirds, one must rely on a (sometimes) great number of manuscript parts and (more rarely) scores and early prints (usually in parts as well). To collect and to assess the Haydn sources as a whole, the *Joseph Haydn-Institut* in Köln was founded in 1955 by Larsen together with several other Haydn scholars, including Landon, Anthony van Hoboken, and the publisher Günter Henle. Soon Georg Feder became head of the institute, defining the guiding principles and editing practice for more than thirty years.

These principles converge with those of other new, complete editions initiated in the 1950s, again commencing with J. S. Bach. In the *Neue Bach Ausgabe*, *Neue Mozart Ausgabe* and *Neue Schubert Ausgabe*, the adjective "new" is an integral part of the names of these editions, which replace the "monuments" from the nineteenth century. All are scholarly editions, with extensive critical reports, that claim to serve both scholars and performers. These editions closely follow the sources, and indicate editors' additions by diacritical markings. This also applies to *Joseph Haydn Werke* (JHW), the first volumes of which were published in 1958. Up to now (2017) 108 (of 113) volumes have appeared. As in the two previous projects (and complete editions generally), the JHW is organised in "Reihen" or series: for instance, series I symphonies (eighteen volumes), IX trios with baryton (five volumes), XII string quartets (six volumes), XXIII masses (six volumes), XXV Italian operas (fourteen volumes), and XXXII Scottish songs (five volumes). Many of these volumes present works in modern editions for the first time. For each work, all the available sources are examined. If no autograph survives, many sources have to be collated in detail to put together a genealogical tree ("stemma"), which enables the reconstruction of Haydn's original. Once the volumes with Haydn's works are completed, two further parts will be added: a new edition of Haydn's Correspondence, as several documents have resurfaced since the publication of Landon's (1959) and Bartha's (1965) editions; and a new thematic Catalogue – not to replace Hoboken's catalogue completely, but to correct the many mistakes contained therein, especially with regard to authenticity and transmission.

Besides the JHW there are additional critical editions, some of which were widespread before their respective complete works editions appeared, namely Landon's editions of the symphonies (Philharmonia), the trios and (together with Reginald Barrett-Ayres) the string quartets (Doblinger). The keyboard sonatas were edited by Christa Landon (Wiener Urtext) and later by Miklós Dolinszky (Könemann). A publication of Haydn's masses and some church music (Carus-Verlag) has recently been completed; a new edition of the string quartets by Simon Rowland-Jones und David Ledbetter (Peters) will replace the canonical old edition of the same publishing house, which is still in use with many quartet players.
ARMIN RAAB

FURTHER READING
Larsen (1939); Raab (2010, 2017).

Education Haydn attended two schools during his youth. The first was a small parish school (*Pfarrschule*) in the Lower Austrian town of Hainburg (not far from the village of Rohrau, Haydn's birthplace), where he was a pupil from the age of six until eight. The second was the Choir School (*Chorschule*) in Vienna, which he attended from 1740 to 1748. As with education in general in the Habsburg lands at this time, both schools were closely connected with the Catholic Church. The *Pfarrschule* in Hainburg was a parochial school attached to the Philippus-und-Jakobus-Kirche, while Vienna's Choir School adjoined St. Stephen's Cathedral. The formal academic training he received in both was uneven; in neither did it go much beyond the acquisition of basic skills in what would today be called the three Rs, with some religious instruction and a smattering of Latin added to the mix.

In another respect, however, Haydn's schooling proved indispensable to his musical evolution. That his formal education was so rudimentary had precisely to do with the fact that both schools, because of their connection with the Church, placed heavy emphasis on music instruction. Melton (1988) has noted that parish schoolmasters commonly had at least some musical ability, since in addition to their teaching duties they were usually expected to serve as church organist. Their responsibilities could also include training pupils to sing in the church choir, or to play an instrument during masses. His pupils might also perform musically as participants in processions on Holy Days or during local religious celebrations. Occasions for such performances were abundant in the late baroque, Catholic milieu of Habsburg Austria. Melton (1988) found that when Haydn was a pupil in Hainburg, Catholics in the Habsburg monarchy universally observed around eighty-six religious holidays, including Sundays; added to these were the locally celebrated full or partial feast days that could number as many as thirty, depending on the region. On most of these occasions it was common for the schoolmaster to assemble his pupils and provide some sort of choral or instrumental performance. The influence of Austrian baroque piety, rooted in what Evans described as a symbiotic partnership between the Habsburg COURT and the Catholic Church, had reached its zenith by the time of Haydn's birth. Sacred music was integral to that culture, of which schools – often in relatively remote towns and villages – were an important incubator.

So it is no accident that Haydn's first music teacher was his Hainburg schoolmaster, Mathias Franck, under whose tutelage young Joseph studied not only voice but organ, keyboard, violin, and timpani. The parish church where Franck was schoolmaster was relatively well equipped musically. A 1762 inventory of the instruments stored in its choir loft listed eight trumpets, two hunting horns, six violins, one cello, one double bass, and a pair of kettledrums. Haydn later recounted arriving in Hainburg as a boy of six and being immediately pressed into musical service by schoolmaster Franck, who had lost his drummer and hastily trained Haydn as a replacement so that the boy could perform in the various religious processions scheduled for that week.

Haydn left Hainburg in 1740 to continue his schooling as a pupil at the Choir School of St. Stephen's Cathedral in Vienna. The Kapellmeister at the cathedral, Georg Reutter, was a friend of Hainburg's parish priest and sometimes visited the town to recruit choirboys. On one occasion the priest recommended Haydn, whom Reutter later enrolled in the school. Haydn remained a pupil there for eight years and continued his musical education. The main function of the school was to train students to perform in the cathedral's annual cycle of ordinary masses, requiems, Te Deums, and solemn processions. So while Haydn received instruction in reading, writing, and rudimentary Latin, the focus of his education was musical. Reutter, his teacher at the Choir School, was a major (if now largely forgotten) composer in his own right. Sacred vocal music dominated his oeuvre, as befit his position as cathedral Kapellmeister. It is therefore unsurprising that one of Haydn's earliest compositions was a *Salve Regina* (no longer extant but mentioned by his early biographer Dies), a Marian antiphon sung at different phases of the Catholic liturgical calendar. According to Jones, the *Salve Regina* was the most frequently performed Marian text of the period. Reutter himself composed nineteen musical settings of the hymn, and as a choir boy Haydn would have sung it frequently. Around 1756 Haydn composed his earliest extant version, the elegant and graceful *Salve Regina* in E major (Hob.XXIIIb:1), which Dack and Landon see as exemplifying his early mastery of sacred composition. Though he received little formal training in composition during his school years, the experience he had acquired in school choirs left its mark. It explains, among other things, why vocal music, much of it sacred, would make up half of his musical corpus.

Melton (2007) views Haydn as only one example of how schools in the Habsburg monarchy helped nurture musical talent (see COMPOSERS AND MUSIC PROFESSIONALS). The Bohemian composer Johann (Wenzel Anton) Stamitz (1717–1757), an important symphonist in Mannheim, acquired his earliest musical training from his schoolmaster father. Josef Mysliveček (1737–1781), for a brief time the most prolific composer of *opera serie* in Europe, took his first musical lessons with his Prague schoolmaster. Ignaz Pleyel (1757–1831), one of Haydn's STUDENTS, grew up the twenty-fourth child of a parish schoolmaster in a village outside of Vienna. The tradition continued into the nineteenth century. Franz Schubert's father taught in a parish school in the Viennese suburb of Lichtental, where Franz was a pupil and had his first violin lessons; he later worked as an assistant schoolmaster at his former school. Anton Bruckner's father was a village schoolmaster in Upper Austria, as was Johann Baptist Weiss, Anton's first music teacher. Bruckner later taught several years in Upper Austrian parish schools. All of these examples illustrate the ways in which the parish schools of the Habsburg lands, long after Haydn had attended one, continued to play a key role in fostering the monarchy's musical culture. JAMES VAN HORN MELTON

FURTHER READING
Dack (2005); Dies; Evans (1979); Jones (2009); Landon I; Melton (1988, 2007).

Eisenstadt – see Eszterháza and

Empfindsamkeit. Notwithstanding the currency of a putative "empfindsamer style" in surveys of musical history, with reference to the sighing, chromatic, nervous keyboard music of C. P. E. Bach, "Empfindsamkeit" in eighteenth-century usage was not principally a category of musical style or TOPIC but an aspect of human character (see Cowart; Berg 1990). Like its English cognate "sensibility," "Empfindsamkeit" lent emerging nerve-based physiology metaphysical significance, connecting organic sensitivity with virtuous action via a notion of sympathetic responsiveness to others and the world (see Sauder). In literary contexts, which (following Frye) dominate current understanding, sensibility concerned infinite shades, objects, and consequences of love – and love was the antonym of indifference and selfishness. Narratives of sensibility typically contained tableaux-like scenes of feeling, authenticated with the real tears of the reader, in which characters' full-hearted attachment to a lover, parent, child, or friend, to a society or nation, to nature or faith, to a moral principle and even to death, were accorded exulted ethical import. The boundary between sensibility and its "Other" – mawkish sentimentality – was necessarily tense, because unclear, but the moment of feeling to which narratives of sensibility progressed was ethically high-minded, an apotheosis of sympathy, not (officially at least) of feeling for its own sake.

Only recently have scholars begun to explore the relationship between Haydn's life, music, and what is now often deemed the culture of sensibility. (Sensibility is styled a "culture" because it exceeded purely artistic concerns, drawing in and linking the disparate disciplines of physiology, psychology, ethics, POLITICAL economy and anthropology [see Barker-Benfield]). That Haydn was aware of and compositionally responsive to this culture is demonstrated by Waldoff in a study of the representation of sensibility in the dramma giocoso, La vera costanza (1778). Belonging to a group of operas drawing on Pamela by Samuel Richardson, La vera costanza is a study of sensibility – ordered and disordered – embodied by its main characters Rosina (a fisherwoman whose constancy is rewarded) and the Count, whose seemingly unmotivated mood swings and erratic behaviour show the dangerous flip side of disordered passions. Working towards a cure – a peculiarly common goal in dramas of sensibility – the opera takes on a quasi-medical, didactic role in relation to the Count's "madness" and Rosina's suffering. As Waldoff traces, Haydn's music seeks realism, fostering the audience's absorption in the fiction, with musical forms that (breaking with the prim distinction of recitative and aria) are hybrid, broken, and open-ended. In Rosina's aria "Con un tenero sospiro," Haydn provides a "sentimental singing style," a sort of noble simplicity that falls between the poles of buffa and seria styles and which included musical imitation of breathlessness, faintness, and palpitation. But more than this, Haydn models the heroine's changing state of mind in something like real time – her movement from happy memory to current anguish seeming to determine the musical FORM.

In appraising sensibility as the "subject" of operatic representation, Waldoff stands on solid ground. Related studies of the English Canzonettas, and of select German lieder have begun to trace how Haydn responded to the literature of sensibility in a range of generic and social contexts (see Day-O'Connell; Webster). However, scholars have yet to clarify questions of chronological priority – was music always and already a medium of sensibility because it was widely understood from the beginning of the century as a language of feeling that fosters virtue? Or is something musically specific at stake under this rubric that arose from the composer's commerce with new types of opera libretto and poetry? Presumably the answer to both questions is yes. Webster's desire to broaden the scope of discussion, and make sensibility more central to Haydn studies, is understandable, but it can seem that he elides the broad issue of music's expressiveness with the literary sensibility of the mid- and later eighteenth century. His contention that even in orchestral and chamber works we hear "Haydn's persona" – thus a single lyric voice – squares such music with the first-person and confessional narratives of literary sensibility but assumes too much about how people listened – and listen – to Haydn.

By definition, the topic of Haydn and sensibility belongs to the cultural history of music; to begin to understand it we need to return to documents of reception. Both Griesinger and Dies present the composer and his music through the lens of sensibility, even as Dies, in particular, is explicit that this culture was all but swept aside by the Napoleonic wars. For both writers, Haydn's music is not a craft but a fine art, a realm of cultivated instinct free from rigid rules; a product of natural genius and learning, it is imagined as an orderly "outpouring of [Haydn's] soul" (Gotwals 95), even if this is offered more as a critical fiction than a literal fact. Incorporating natural, universal signs of the passions in melodic RHYTHM and pitch inflection, Haydn's music acts directly on the listener's body, setting the internal clavier – the nervous fibres – in motion. This *empfindsam* fantasy of immediacy rested on a conviction that music and feeling shared a material basis in movement and vibration. The theory was dramatized by both biographers in their accounts of an exhausted, AGED Haydn persecuted by musical ideas too energetic and forceful for his frail body to withstand. In this context, it was logical that the composer's fortepiano was put out of harm's way on doctor's orders, and that the composer was carried out of a Viennese performance of *The Creation* on March 27, 1808, "for fear that a storm of emotions too long continued might endanger the health of an old man" (49). Haydn's calling card from 1806 tapped into this corporeal thinking; a simulacrum of his failing body, it featured a listless musical phrase from his setting of Gleim's "Der Greis" (The Old Man), the words "alt und schwach bin ich" (old and weak am I) broken up with faltering rests. The flip side of this poetics of infirmity is Dies's sense, apparently confirmed by the composer, that the teasing humor of Haydn's music arose from a youthful "abundance of good health" (145; see also DISABILITY).

Griesinger and Dies measured Haydn's success in no small part by the ability of his music "to touch the heart" (Gotwals 125). That Haydn shared this view is suggested by his words of praise for Mozart's keyboard playing (56). Even technical features of Haydn's, that might appear to modern eyes to concern unity and coherence, serve that goal – an idea must be sustained and developed, Haydn advised, so that it "remains in the heart" of the listener – a phrase that links MELODY, feeling, and memory. Somewhat ritualistically, *empfindsam* criticism renounced artifice in favour of (various concepts of) NATURE. Simple melody, theorised as preserving original, passionate accents of humanity, was often lent greater affective power than elaborate composition. Both biographers report that "no music moved [Haydn] so greatly" as the hymn singing of "four thousand charity children" in St. Paul's Cathedral (154, 25), a scene of innocence, devotion, and benevolence that also highlights the importance to music's reception of context and mental association (see Example 23). The *empfindsam* aesthetic of music, though eschewing dogged service to words or social function, was too concerned with emotional effect on the listener to privilege musical autonomy. Words, in the form of titles, incipits, or poetry, were considered necessary not to give music meaning, or provide formal scaffolding, but to "guide" the feelings music roused (106). At the same time, as Griesinger observed of *The Seasons*, "sentiments merely hinted at in flat, often ordinary prose are here by the magic of musical poetry really ennobled and idealised" (40; see also IDEALISM). As primarily a matter of RECEPTION, sensibility turned on a moving performance, which Dies glossed as "enchanting" and "graceful" and measured against "the lifeless playing of clockwork" (123). An affectionate, loyal RELATIONSHIP between the composer and musicians assisted this: "out of love" for Haydn, Dies reported, the LONDON musicians "rose to the level of inspiration required" for the performance of Haydn's symphonies.

The culture of sensibility linked Haydn's life, his compositional activities, and the telling of both. Old age and illness, like farewells, poverty, charity, male friendships, family, STUDENTS, INSTRUMENTS, memories, children, pets, storms, WAR, the crucifixion, and heavenly bliss, punctuate the earliest Haydn biographies, inviting the reader to "know" the composer in a "feeling" way and to connect the subjects of his music with his life. Notably, this is as true of Griesinger – whom scholarship has deemed the more reliable witness – as Dies, who is routinely dismissed as "sentimental" (a term that serves rhetorically to validate sensibility as something more than self-indulgent and false). Haydn's romantic friendships and love affairs with women leave evidence of his knowledge of the epistolary language of sensibility, which, like Sterne, he enlivened with humor. (See CORRESPONDENCE.) To Marianne von Genzinger he employed the intimate apparatus of dashes, dots and exclamations, to signal the limits of writing and the intensity of his feelings, even if, in the famous letter "from the wilderness" (dated February 9, 1790) he enlivened heartfelt pathos with HUMOR – "that horrible North wind woke me and almost blew my nightcap off my head" (CCLN 97). The slow movement of the Sonata in E♭ (Hob.XVI:49), written expressly for her and which he described as "full of feeling," projects a musical corollary for this type of prose (CCLN 105). Within the delicate framework of a minuet, Haydn's yearning, melodic gestures push against the meter with a refined, but passionate second-beat emphasis, resolving at phrase endings in the quintessential musical marker of sensibility – the sighing appoggiatura. It is as though the music might break its boundaries – which, in a fictional sense, it does in the central section (starting at m. 57), a purple patch in B♭ minor that calls for sustaining pedal, hand crossing, and fragmented "crying" figures across the bass and soprano registers that comprise distinct voices. In leaving enough traces for performers and listeners to savor the possibility of a musical love letter, Haydn continues to coax his audience into the subtle riddles of sensibility.   MATTHEW HEAD

FURTHER READING
Barker-Benfield (1992); Berg (1990, 2009); Blasius (1996); Castelvecchi (1996); CCLN; Cowart (1984); Day-O'Connell (2009a); Frye (1956); Gotwals; Head (2014); Heartz and Brown (2001); Hirschmann (1995); Hunter (1985); Sauder (1974, 1980, 1990); Waldoff (1998); Webster (2009).

England – see London and

Enlightenment The Enlightenment is typically understood as the "age of reason" where European societies gradually rejected outmoded authoritarian and absolutist political and religious structures of the *ancien régime*. It is also commonly characterized in terms of new forms of political and social organization that responded to an emerging desire for human freedom and democratic representation, where science, reason, and rational thought were identified as the means of attainment of those ideals. Yet the focus on science and reason has often obscured other modes of human expression that in fact served important roles in shaping the Enlightenment period as a whole. The arts, understood broadly to include eighteenth-century literature, painting, and music, have often been marginalized in classic studies of the Enlightenment – music perhaps most of all.

Rather than think in terms of Haydn's relationship to "the" Enlightenment (as a singular phenomenon), we should consider Haydn's engagement with a multiplicity of Enlightenment movements (national, regional, thematic, etc.) Drawing on Wittgenstein's theory of family resemblance in his *Philosophical Investigations*, we can describe a "core" family of socially situated, dialectically related IDEAS and authors. Each particular Enlightenment shares multiple ideas in common with others, but not all ideas are essential to each. Core Enlightenment ideas include SOCIABILITY, SENSIBILITY, COSMOPOLITANISM, the SUBLIME, FOLK SONG, technology, SCIENCE, social development, knowledge, and reason. The last of these, reason, forms the focus of a classic study by Geiringer of Haydn's instrumental music. In contrast, the "multiple Enlightenment" approach includes Haydn within an important family of *philosophes*, *literati*, and other key individuals, and it should spark a broader conversation between Haydn scholars and those working in related fields of eighteenth-century studies more generally. This dialectical approach is consistent with developments in scholarship in other disciplines that recognize the significant challenges of defining such a complex social and intellectual formation known as "Enlightenment." Often stereotyped in terms of abstract and universal notions, Enlightenment must be understood as constituted through diffuse NETWORKS that include transmissions of texts, ideas, and media; geographical and national contexts (PLACE); INSTITUTIONS; and social actors.

We might consider, for example, Haydn's engagement with Enlightenment sensibility and EMPFINDSAMKEIT, the Catholic Enlightenment, and theories of Scottish Enlightenment sociability and social development. In the wake of the 1707 *Treaty of Union*, Scots had lost their national parliament yet retained key social institutions such as the Kirk, the legal profession, the universities, the club, and society city culture – which, partly in lieu of a sovereign political life, became the center of much Scottish social life. MUSICAL SOCIETIES played a central role, and the Edinburgh Musical Society (formed 1728) was the largest of all clubs and societies. By the late eighteenth century, Scotland had become one of the most literate and economically prosperous countries in Western Europe. A thirst for knowledge, curiosity about the world, travel, education, and intellectual ferment lay at the center of what is now termed the "Scottish Enlightenment." In this context, many *literati* considered Scotland itself as a sort of cultural laboratory for the testing of ideas concerning human social development.

This is the context in which George Thomson commissioned Haydn to arrange dozens of Scots songs as part of his extensive national song project *A Select Collection of Original Scottish Airs for the Voice* (see FOLK SONG SETTINGS). The project was presented to the public by Thomson as a musical-cultural manifestation of a four-stage anthropological theory of human development. Stadial theory, as defined by Scottish Enlightenment philosopher and political economist Adam Smith in his 1762–63 *Lectures on Jurisprudence*, consisted of the following process: "four distinct states which mankind pass thro [sic]: first, the Age of Hunters; secondly, the Age of Shepherds; thirdly, the Age of Agriculture; and fourthly, the Age of Commerce" (14). In Thomson's "Dissertation Concerning the National Melodies of Scotland," appended to various editions of his song project, he alludes directly to these four "states" of stadial theory:

> There is hardly any people, however rude, that has not its music. The warrior, the hunter, and the shepherd, sing their triumphs, their exploits, and their loves, in strains dictated by nature, and inspired by feeling. Even among the most barbarous tribes, if there are any traces of the softer and better emotions, it is in their Songs that these traces are to be found; and music is thus, not merely the most innocent and refined pleasure which a rude people can enjoy, but a powerful instrument in quickening the progress of improvement, by cherishing the best feelings of our nature (3).

In this example, Thomson explicitly identifies music (and by implication, the musical settings for Scots songs by Haydn and other composers in his collection) as an agent that could be used to "quicken" the development of culture through the four stages or "states." By setting Scots songs using techniques of art music, for Thomson, Haydn's settings manifested the notion that Scots musical culture could be "progressed" out of the earlier stages and "modernized" in accordance with stadial theory outlined by Smith and others (for Chandler, this progression is nonlinear and an "uneven" development, while Sher recognizes the diverse range of philosophies and authors associated with stadial "conjectural history"). In Thomson's prefatory commentaries, Haydn's settings of Scots songs are compared with those of earlier composers (William Thomson's *Orpheus Caledonius* of 1725/33 is a popular but not exclusive target) and are consistently evaluated as "superior" musically to those of earlier settings of the same songs, thus demonstrating the capacity of Scottish culture to be "modernized."

Theories of stadial development linking Haydn to the Scottish Enlightenment were part of larger Enlightenment discourses of sociability, sensibility, and sentiment. Dwyer aptly suggests that the phrase "age of sentiment" better characterizes some Enlightenment thought than does "age of reason." Haydn owned copies of Adam Smith's seminal *Theory of the Moral Sentiments* (1759) – a work Smith considered his magnum opus and the intellectual architecture for his theory of COMMERCE in his *The Wealth of Nations* of 1776. As Schroeder has discussed, Haydn also owned the Earl of Shaftesbury's 1711 treatise on sentimental sociability, *Characteristics of Men, Manners, Opinions, Times* that was vital to early Scottish Enlightenment thinkers such as Francis

Hutcheson and David Hume. While the direct extent of Haydn's intellectual engagement with these two works is unknown, Hörwarthner has suggested the fact that he owned English-language editions rather than readily available German translations is at least evidence of his contact with the wider circulation of Scottish sentimental moral philosophy. Smith's treatise was translated into German very quickly after its initial appearance and was vital to the musical thought of Johann Gottfried Herder including his coining of folk song, a notion attempting to fuse the moral sentiments of particular peoples and cultures musically with song. At the same time, as Will has described, Haydn's folk song settings participated in the kind of international cosmopolitanism that could appeal to various AUDIENCES depending on circumstances.

Haydn's interest in the newly coined folk song together with the rise of *Empfindsamkeit* ("sensibility" or "sentimental") and the related literary movement *Sturm und Drang* ("Storm and Stress") all serve to situate Haydn within a broader context of Enlightenment sensibility and AESTHETICS that crossed musical thought in the Scottish and German Enlightenments (Baker and Christensen). For instance, Waldoff has connected Haydn's vocal music, particularly his opera *La vera costanza*, with the cult of sensibility that emerged from the English sentimental novel *Pamela* by Samuel Richardson. Haydn's instrumental music, too, has long been linked to a *Sturm und Drang* musical equivalent, with much symphonic music of the 1760s/70s originally intended for use on stage (Sisman 1990). To take one of the best-known examples, the incessant and insistent descending arpeggios found in the opening measures of the Haydn's "Farewell" Symphony No. 45 in F♯ minor (1772) clearly evoke a restless mood that matches the literary equivalent. Haydn is not unique here (Mozart's affinities with *Sturm und Drang* are well documented, as in the opening of his "Little" Symphony No. 25 in G minor and the "Introduzione" to *Don Giovanni*, to name just two examples) but Haydn's music more often exhibits qualities manifesting *Empfindsamkeit* (popularized by C. P. E. Bach's use of a "sensitive style" in his "Prussian" and "Essay" sonatas) than his most famous contemporaries. Connections between Haydn's music and a "sensitive style" illustrate the composer's broader contact with multiple Enlightenment movements – sometimes through a "core" idea such as sensibility, sociability, or one of those listed earlier in the family of ideas.

An example of Haydn's deployment of a sensitive style can be seen in the Adagio Capriccio of his String Quartet in C major, Op. 20, No. 2 (1772) from the "Sun" quartets, identified by Schroeder as important precursors to his later 1781 Op. 33 quartets written, as put by the composer in an effort to appeal to his subscribers, in a "new and special way" (see Example 3). As Brown and Heartz put it, one of the most common strategies for a composer to evoke *Empfindsamkeit* or a sensitive style was to invoke the style of operatic obbligato recitative. This can be observed in the dramatic, weighty, and emotionally intense style of writing present from the beginning of the Adagio Capriccio, written in the parallel key of C minor. In mm. 1–4, this effect is achieved through the use of monophonic texture, dramatic descending and ascending leaps (e.g. down from the third scale degree E♭ to the leading tone of B♮ in m. 1, followed immediately by an upward leap to the fifth scale degree of G rather than the tonic scale degree, both played staccato), through the use of

Example 3 String Quartet in C major, Op. 20, No. 2, second movement, Adagio: Capriccio, mm. 1–6.

repeated trills that leave the listener dwelling on the poignant emotive content of the music, and through the use of weighty dotted rhythms in m. 4.

These same techniques are used repeatedly throughout the movement for similar effect, sometimes coupled with the use of insistent and ominous sixteenth notes as seen in mm. 5–6. Unlike some of Haydn's symphonies that allude directly to a more aggressive *Sturm und Drang* through the use of faster tempi, this slow movement evokes a sentimental and sensitive musical style that situates Haydn in relation to an *Empfindsamkeit* musical aesthetic. Both were central to German Enlightenment musical thought. But how might we explore Enlightenment in Germanic and Austrian contexts beyond the philosophical and musical-aesthetic?

Eighteenth-century developments in science, technology, optical and musical INSTRUMENTS, astronomy and "solar poetics," and audiovisual culture have been increasingly recognized as key to a better understanding of Haydn's relationship to particular AUDIENCES and emergent cultures of listening. Recent musical studies in these areas have reconceptualized understandings of Enlightenment that have tended to privilege philosophical treatises over other forms and circulations of media, MATERIAL CULTURE, and technological artifacts (Siskin and Warner). At the same time, it is important to recognize the potential danger in collapsing all distinctions of genre, MUSICAL MATERIALS, EDITIONS, PUBLISHING, and PERFORMANCES to simply Enlightenment "mediations." What is refreshing about new approaches focusing on Haydn and scientific technology is that they have not privileged abstract notions of science and reason as pinnacles of Enlightenment achievement in the way identified at the beginning of this essay. Rather, music and science are approached inclusively in a spirit of a holistic Enlightenment "arts and sciences" – a better reflection, perhaps, of how the arts and sciences were far more intertwined during Haydn's lifetime than they are today. As Klancher describes, the Enlightenment discourse of arts and sciences resulted in the production and organization of new forms of knowledge and the emergence of new cultural institutions.

One particular institution that underwent transformation in the Enlightenment was the Catholic CHURCH. Haydn can be situated within the "Catholic Enlightenment" or the tradition of reform Catholicism within Sorkin's larger category "Religious Enlightenment." At first glance, the notion of a "Religious" Enlightenment seems antithetical to a movement often typified as inherently secular, grounded in reason above all else, and opposed to unthinking religious dogma as Kant famously addressed in his 1784 essay "What is Enlightenment?" Yet an exclusively secular view overlooks the fact that religious reform in Catholic, Protestant, JEWISH (e.g. Moses Mendelssohn), and other traditions was a central part of Enlightenment movements across Europe – especially outside of France where social and political conditions had largely prevented a Catholic reform movement. As Rosa defines it: "Catholic Enlightenment was, therefore, a reform movement within the Church that was linked, though in discordant harmony, with the Enlightenment reform movement and with interventions by reforming sovereigns who were inclined to welcome the collaboration of religious forces with the state in a more general process of cultural and social transformation" (472). When coupled with EDUCATION and FREEMASONRY, the Catholic Enlightenment served as a vehicle for larger Enlightenment ideals discussed earlier. Haydn's visits to Vienna in the 1780s included the company of numerous intellectuals of an "enlightened-conservative" orientation – most whom were Freemasons open to Enlightenment ideals yet grounded in a devout (but not dogmatic) Catholicism, much as Haydn was. Haydn was inducted as a Freemason on February 11, 1785 after applying the previous year, although little evidence exists that the organization specifically shaped his outlook. Evidence of his devout Catholic RELIGION AND SPIRITUAL BELIEFS is actually much stronger – for instance writing "In nomine Domini" (In the name of the Lord) and "Laus Deo" (Praise be to God) at the beginning and end of his autograph manuscripts (see NG Haydn).

The above cases clarify the connection between Haydn and the Enlightenment(s), not merely because it is possible to identify characteristics in his music that conform to particular stylistic traits, but rather because Haydn participates dialectically in a family of core ideas that manifest differently across multiple Enlightenment movements. Haydn can thus serve as a touchstone not only for musicologists interested in Enlightenment thought, but for multiple disciplines working across the field of Enlightenment studies, thus bringing our discipline into closer contact with others.

ANDREW A. GREENWOOD

FURTHER READING

Agnew (2008); Baker and Christensen (1996); Beales (2005); Bonds (1991a); Chandler (1998); Dwyer (1998); Edelstein (2010); Freeman (2002); Gay (1966–69); Geiringer (2002a); Gelbart (2007); Grave and Grave (2006); *Grove Online*; Head (2005); Heartz and Brown (2001); Hörwarthner (1997); *HWorld*; Kant (1991); Klancher (2013); Kors (2002); Lehner (2016); Lehner and Printy (2010); Loughridge (2016); Lowe (2015); McCue (1993); Mullan (1998); *NG Haydn*; Porter and Teich (1981); Robertson and Timms (1991); Rosa (2002); Schroeder (1990); Sher (1985, 1995); Siskin and Warner (2010); Sisman (1990); Smith (1978); Sorkin (2008); Sutcliffe (1998a, 2013); Thomson (1822); Waldoff (1998b); Webster (1998b); Will (2012); Wittgenstein (2009).

Environments – see Place

Esterházy Court – see People and Networks; Courts

Eszterháza and Eisenstadt Haydn's nearly five-decade connection with the Esterházy family and their places of residence inevitably determined many aspects of his professional and private life. Whereas the Esterházy Court palace in the Viennese Wallnerstrasse played a relatively minor role in the composer's career, the family's traditional residence in Eisenstadt, located approximately twenty-five miles (forty kilometers) southeast of Vienna, and to a greater extent the splendid palace Nicolaus I erected in Eszterháza another twenty-five miles to the east, were important in Haydn's life. Regular movement between these locations created a cyclical rhythm in the composer's creative life.

After signing a contract as vice-Kapellmeister to Prince Paul Anton Esterházy on May 1, 1761 in Vienna, Haydn gradually relocated to Eisenstadt (Kismarton in Hungarian). Following Paul Anton's death in March 1762, Haydn is documented as being a subtenant in the house of Adalbert Kussenics, a member of the local council, in October 1762 (Pratl 2009c). He eventually bought a house in the Klostergasse (no. 82, today Joseph-Haydn-Gasse 21, now the Haydn-Haus museum) on May 2, 1766, several weeks after the death of first Kapellmeister Gregor Joseph Werner. While the acquisition of a house (together with a tiny kitchen garden nearby) undoubtedly reflected a change in Haydn's position and prestige, his ownership proved a burden in the longer run (see Economics and Finances). He struggled to pay the remaining installments after the ground-floor tenant died in 1767, and two fires devastated the town in August 1768 and July 1776. Thanks to the generosity of Prince Nicolaus, who helped with the costs of reconstruction, Haydn avoided financial ruin. Indeed, after the 1768 fire, Haydn took the opportunity to add another room to his house for an extra fee of 50 gulden. He eventually sold the house on August 27, 1778, since by this time his services were needed at Eszterháza virtually all year round.

Although Prince Nicolaus's decision to leave the traditional princely residence in Eisenstadt has (rightly) been interpreted as an extravagant gesture, his palace in Süttör – which was by no means a simple hunting lodge – had served as his primary residence since 1737, when he received his inheritance. Following his installation in 1762, the prince initiated plans to turn this residence into a major palace. The move of the princely center proved but partial, however, since Nicolaus himself spent more and more time in Süttör, and his wife Maria Elisabeth, together with the entire princely administration, remained in Eisenstadt. In forsaking the traditional family seat, Prince Nicolaus took the unprecedented step of reimagining his primary residence as a *"maison de plaisance"* (*Lustschloss*). However, the vastly augmented and expanded palace complex known as Eszterháza was much more than a place of retreat and summer refuge; paradoxically, it combined the roles of long-term residency with that of leisure. The striking combination of the original terracotta and light green colors (not restored during the recent reconstruction) signaled the informal and pleasurable character of the residence (Lászay).

Even though construction at Eszterháza commenced immediately, Prince Nicolaus's ambitious project, based on plans by architect Nicolas Jacoby (1733–1784), was not completed until the mid-1780s. During the first phase (1762–64) the separate buildings erected by the Viennese mason Anton Erhard Martinelli from 1720 onward were connected by L-shaped extensions and horseshoe-shaped wings to embrace the *cour d'honneur* (see Figure 9). The second phase (1765–68) included topping the central ceremonial hall with a belvedere, constructing fountains with statues, building a quadruple-armed exterior staircase leading from the south end of the courtyard up to the antechamber of the ceremonial hall, and modernizing the interior rooms and their furnishings after French models. Finally (in 1775 and 1778), a third storey was added to the central section of the building together with the construction of two single-level wings on either side: a picture gallery to the west and a winter garden to the east.

A crucial feature of the Eszterháza palace – reinforcing its pleasure palace function – was the organic connection between the inner spaces and their outer environment, most notably the ornamental park, the Lés woods (an exquisite hunting area), and the surrounding Lake Fertő (Neusiedlersee) region with its swamps and marshy plains. The palace's original ornamental garden (probably designed by Anton Zinner) was considerably reshaped in the mid-1770s and visually enclosed by two cascading waterfalls in 1784. As early as 1762 the line between the elegant garden and the Lés woods was blurred by the removal of the bordering hedges, and much of the woods was converted into a park with new avenues and allées. Similarly, the ornamental floral designs on the walls and ceiling of the Sala Terrena, the central ground-floor room of the palace which provided a cool respite in the hot summer months, evoked the surrounding natural world: statues of autochthon animals and plants appeared side by side with fountains reminding one of the life-giving element of the Fertő region. This intricate dialogue between the "artificial inside" and the "natural outside" also permeated the many attractions of the vast parklands, which offered visitors the opportunity to rest, contemplate, and delight at the same time. These included four temples dedicated to Diana, Fortuna, the Sun, and Venus (complete by 1773), an "Eremitage" (a secluded retreat), and – most famously – a ballroom in Chinese style, which incidentally caused, through the explosion of a stove,

Figure 9 Prince Anton Esterházy's 1791 installation ceremony in the forecourt of the palace at Eszterháza. Hungarian National Museum. Used with permission.

the fire that destroyed the (first) opera house in 1779. (The Chinese ballroom was not identical to the so-called Bagatelle, a pavilion also in Chinese style erected in 1783.)

This ambitious project inevitably raised the interest of many contemporaries. Indeed, the Prince seemed intent upon spreading the news about Eszterháza after officially decreeing the new name on January 3, 1766. (Contemporary documents in German frequently refer to "Eszterház," while Haydn typically dated his letters from "Estoras"; during the Communist era following World War II the place was renamed Fertőd, obscuring the formative role of the Esterházy family.) The brief 1772 sojourn of the French ambassador to Vienna, Prince Louis de Rohan, was carefully documented in György Bessenyei's Hungarian poem *Az eszter-házi vígasságok*, and Maria Theresia's famous visit the following year, coinciding with the opening of the grotto-designed marionette theater with Haydn's *Philemon und Baucis*, was recorded in a detailed anonymous report entitled *Relation des fêtes données à sa Majesté L'Imperatrice par S. A. Mgr le Prince d'Esterhazy Dans son Château d'Esterhaz Le 1r & 2e 7bre 1773*. The completion of the seventy-year-old Prince Nicolaus's *chef d'oeuvre* was marked by the publication of the famous *Beschreibung des hochfürstlichen Schlosses Esterhász* (1784), which includes artful engravings and maps of both the buildings and the park. The ever-more famous Kapellmeister's presence at Eszterháza formed an integral part of the Prince's grand project, contributing to its success in no small measure. While travelers of the 1780s found much to object to in Eszterháza's old-fashioned gardens and the moral dissonance of its luxurious existence within swampy surroundings where inhabitants suffered from poverty and disease, Haydn's reputation remained intact. At the same time, those undertaking the troublesome five- or six-hour (and oftentimes twice as long) journey from Vienna to Eszterháza to visit Haydn were rewarded not only by the famous composer's company but also his equally venerable surroundings.

After Nicolaus's death in 1790 the "Hungarian Versailles" waned. Although his son Anton was installed as governor of the County of Sopron (Oedenburg) at Eszterháza, the new prince had little interest in maintaining the glory of his father's palace. He reduced court music to a minimum, offering pensions to the two longest-standing members, Haydn and Luigi Tomasini, and moved the court back to Eisenstadt. There he put his mark on the palace by filling in the moat, redesigning the square before the palace, and adding a balcony supported by twin columns above the portico. Anton's efforts were furthered by his successor Nicolaus II who called upon the renowned French architect Charles Moreau to give the old palace a new classical guise. Financial difficulties prevented the full realization of Moreau's plans, which were launched in 1803 when Haydn was already retired and living in Gumpendorf, a suburb west of Vienna. Two conspicuous changes to the palace in Eisenstadt included replacing the four onion-shaped domes dating from the time of Prince Paul Anton (1635–1713) with tent-shaped roofs, and the erection of an elegant new hall with pillared portico on the garden side.

Haydn's musical activities changed according to the location of the princely court (see Performance Spaces). The three "Times of Day" symphonies (nos. 6–8) were probably written and first performed in Vienna, where the composer spent most of his initial year of Esterházy employment. Eisenstadt was the primary location for much of Haydn's output up to about 1768, including *Acide* (a *festa teatrale* first performed at the wedding ceremony of Prince Nicolaus's eldest son) and a few Italian cantatas written for festive occasions (*Destatevi o miei fidi*, Hob.XXIVa:2 and *Qual dubbio ormai*, Hob. XXIVa:4 for Prince Nicolaus's name-day, *Da qual gioia improvvisa*, Hob. XXIVa:3 for the return of the prince from the 1764 Frankfurt coronation of Joseph II). Around 1766 Eszterháza gradually usurped Eisenstadt as the prime location for courtly representation. The first opera house opened in September 1768 with *Lo speziale*, followed by the erection of a residence for musicians in 1769. During the 1768–75 period it is difficult to connect concrete works with this or that location, apart from two characteristic genres: Haydn's operas were typically staged at Eszterháza (see THEATER), while several of his CHURCH compositions were connected with different churches in Eisenstadt. In the last two decades of his active service at court (c. 1770–90) Haydn spent the overwhelming majority of his time at Eszterháza, and it is tempting to view his path-breaking symphonies and string quartets as musical reflections of Prince Nicolaus's powerful achievements with his Eszterháza project (even though performances of Haydn's quartets are as good as undocumented at the Esterházy court). While geographical and psychological isolation increasingly frustrated Haydn in the 1780s, during the late 1760s and early 1770s when Eszterháza was comfortably habitable and attracting visitors from all walks of life, it proved an inspiring environment – despite the conservative and oftentimes technically facile baryton trios Haydn was required to write for his patron (see INSTRUMENTS). The start of regular operatic seasons in 1776 burdened the Kapellmeister with many other duties, including arranging operas to suit local conditions, rehearsing the orchestra and the singers, and conducting the regular performances. Gradually, the winter break between the "summer" seasons was reduced to a mere 2 to 3 months – and fewer for those musicians who returned earlier to prepare the first productions of the new season. Haydn's oft-quoted letter (to Genzinger on February 9, 1790) about being more a "*Capell*-servant" than a "*Capell*-master" reflects on this state of affairs. Soon after the Prince's death, Haydn moved not to Eisenstadt, but directly to Vienna, and a few months later on to London, making up for lost opportunities resulting from his daily service at the Esterházy court. Following Haydn's London sojourns, his connection with Eisenstadt was revived under Nicolaus II, who called upon Haydn to help reorganize musical life at the court. From 1796 to 1803 the composer spent part of each summer and early fall in Eisenstadt, in order to complete and perform an annual mass for the name-day of Princess Marie Hermenegild. Most of these performances were held in the Bergkirche, where the composer's tomb was also erected later on.

The exact locations of "musical academies" held in the palaces of Eszterháza and Eisenstadt are difficult to determine. Local oral tradition suggests that, at Eszterháza, the first-floor antechamber (the room at the top of the open stairs ascending from the courtyard) is where Haydn's symphonies were performed, while others have assumed that these performances took place in the ceremonial hall overlooking the gardens to the south. Recent research by Malina, however, suggests that in Haydn's time the antechamber was primarily used for dining, and the regular *Accademien* – including performances of Haydn's symphonies – took place in the opera house from 1768 onwards. Little evidence supports the hypothesis that the famous "Haydn-Saal" on the east side of the Eisenstadt palace, constructed at the time of Paul I and later transformed by Moreau, was a venue for symphony performance in the composer's lifetime. A decree issued by Prince Nicolaus on November 4, 1765 in response to Werner's complaints against Haydn ordered that academies be held twice a week in the "officiers zimmer" of the Eisenstadt palace, a term suggesting a room of much more modest dimensions. Today the Haydn Hall in Eisenstadt and the ceremonial hall at Eszterháza are both venues for Festival performances.   BALÁZS MIKUSI

FURTHER READING
Bartha and Somfai; Dávid (2006); Feder (1970); Gabriel and Winkler (2009); Gürtler and Kropf (2009); Horányi (1962); Kopp and Wolf (2014); Lászay (2009); Malina (2006, 2016a, 2016b); Mőcsényi (1999); *Oxford Companion*; Pratl (2009a, 2009c); Somfai (1982, 1989); Szentesi (2013); Szentesi, Mentényi and Simon (2013); Winkler (2009b); Zaslaw (1989a).

European Contexts: France, Italy, Spain Haydn reached a turning point in his career when, in 1779, he signed a new contract with Prince Esterházy, effectively freeing himself from exclusive obligations. With this newfound independence, Haydn was free to accept commissions from individuals and organizations across Europe. In the following years, as concert Societies cultivated by the rising bourgeoisie provided patronage equal to that of the aristocracy and the church, Haydn received numerous commissions from patrons in France, Italy, and Spain, resulting in some of his most creative and unique works. Extant scores in Archives as well as contemporary accounts of performances also testify to the overwhelming success of Haydn's instrumental music within Europe, including chamber music and symphonies in their original dispositions, and arrangements mainly for string quartet or keyboard. His vocal music Circulated less widely, and was generally limited to the *Stabat mater* together with the late oratorios and selected operas.

During the 1780s, Haydn's symphonic reputation became firmly established throughout Europe, with the most important cities performing his symphonies in their original instrumentation or in a wide array of arrangements, depending on local performing forces and practices. Haydn initially gained popular success across Catholic Europe with his *Stabat mater* (1767). Performed at the Concert Spirituel in 1781, the work was a grand success, and praised by the Parisian reviewers for being noble and touching, most worthy of the excellent master (see Harrison). Subsequently, the "Paris" Symphonies (nos. 82–87) were commissioned by the Concert de la Loge Olympique, a private masonic lodge with a very fine orchestra. Composed around 1784–85, they date from the period of Haydn's own initiation into the lodge "Zur wahren Eintracht" in Vienna (see Freemasonry). Haydn's popularity in France had never been greater than at the end of the 1780s: of the 110 symphonies performed by the Concert Spirituel in the years 1788–90, no fewer than 94 were by Haydn, with 20 performances during the month of March 1788 alone. Haydn's symphonies were also performed as part of other kinds of entertainments, particularly as entrac'te music at the Comédie Française, as part of the balles de la Cour impériale and as preludes to tragédies lyriques – proof of the great popularity of Haydn's symphonies in the French capital. Detached movements were also used as part of the ballets-pantomimes at the Paris Opéra, most notably in Pierre Gardel's 1793 Jugement de Pâris (see Dratwicki).

Circulation of Haydn's music on the Italian peninsula was more broadly based. As early as 1767, Giuseppe Cambini, a member of the Florentine Quartetto Toscano (quite possibly the first established string quartet), is known to have studied some of Haydn's string quartets. Thanks to the high number of academias by philharmonic societies, Haydn's symphonies were widely played in Italian theaters across the entire peninsula. Bologna was a major center for the performance of Haydn's music, while Venice is notable for the publication of editions of the composer's instrumental music. As outlined by Gon, the Venetian-based editor Antonio Zatta published four instrumental collections in the mid-1780s: the first in 1783, containing six Trios per violino, viola e violoncello (Hob.XI:57–62), was followed in 1787 by several more works, including the Quartet in D minor, Op. 42, a series of Divertimenti per cembalo o pianoforte facili e piacevoli (Hob.XVII:9), and three Sonate per cembalo con accompagnamento di violino e violoncello (Hob.XV:6–8). Zatta's last catalogue from 1798 listed twenty symphonies by Haydn.

The kingdom of Naples developed a privileged relationship with the composer following the marriage of King Ferdinand IV to Maria Carolina of Austria in 1767. Haydn's symphonies were performed during the intermezzi of the French comedies held at the Teatro Reale on March 3, 1786 at the personal request of the king. Moreover, Ferdinand IV was the recipient of the Five Concertos for Organized-Lyre (Hob.VIIh: 1–5) dated 1786–87, and Eight Nocturnes for 2 Organized-Lyres (Hob.II:25–32, dated 1790). The lira organizzata, an instrument popular with the French aristocracy in the eighteenth century (Ferdinand was a Bourbon), combines a hurdy-gurdy mechanism with an organ mechanism. Haydn adapted two of these Notturni for Salomon's concert series during his first visit to LONDON (see ORCHESTRATION).

The first Italian performance of The Creation occurred on March 20, 1804 in the Neapolitan Real Teatro del Fondo, with the libretto translated into Italian by Haydn's admirer and biographer Carpani. Antonio Salieri used Carpani's translation when conducting the performance of The Creation at the Old University in Vienna on March 27, 1808 – Haydn's last public appearance.

A concert dedicated exclusively to Haydn's vocal works took place on April 12, 1786 in the Accademia Filarmonica Ducale of Modena, which had nominated Haydn as its honorary member in 1784. The performance, probably as part of the Lenten season concerts, included the oratorio Il ritorno di Tobia, the Salve Regina and the Stabat mater. The opera Armida was performed on December 27, 1804 at the Teatro Regio in Turin. Based on Torquato Tasso's late sixteenth-century epic poem, Gerusalemme liberata, the subject matter of this opera would have appealed to local audiences (see THEATER).

The impact of Haydn's music in Spain can be measured by the great number of manuscripts and print-copies of his works that are contained in private and public collections, together with eighteenth- and nineteenth-century reports of the regular sale of his instrumental music in shops (see Commerce) and the significant number of performances of his music. Further evidence of Haydn's importance can be seen in other artistic manifestations, including literature and painting: Tomas de Iriarte's poem *La música* (1779) is an appraisal of Haydn's art; and Francisco de Goya's portrait of José Alvarez de Toledo, Duke of Alba and Marques of Villafranca (c. 1795), depicts the subject holding a book entitled "*Cuatro canciones con acompañamiento de fortepiano del Sr. Haydn*" (see Reception).

During the eighteenth century and up until the Ecclesiastical Confiscations of Mendizábal (1835–37) the production, transmission, and consumption of music in Spain took place in religious institutions, including cathedrals, monasteries and convents, and at public concerts held in theaters, as well as in private concerts given at the royal court in Madrid and at the academies hosted by members of the aristocracy. The libraries of religious institutions account for the highest percentage of Haydn's music preserved in Spain. Copies of Haydn's symphonies, usually containing the instrumental parts, are preserved at several cathedrals, among them twenty-five symphonies in Jaén, fourteen in Granada and thirteen in León. Vocal music is also preserved in many of the Spanish religious institutions, including copies of the *Stabat mater*, *The Creation*, and *The Seasons*.

Of particular interest is a notebook entitled "*Overturas Para Piano, o Organo. Hayden*," which contains transcriptions of the first two movements of Symphony No. 69 in C major, known as the "Laudon" Symphony, and the first movement of Symphony No. 75 in D major. A keyboard transcription of the whole of Symphony No. 75, held in the archives of the Royal Monastery of las Descalzas in Madrid, contains a note on the title-page of the collection indicating that these symphonic movements were performed as part of the Introit of the mass, a practice documented not only in monasteries but also in Spanish cathedrals. Movements from Haydn's symphonies were also performed during the mass in the early 1790s at the Benedictine monastery of Montserrat, as described by Fernando Sor (1778–1839): "The morning Mass was accompanied by a small orchestra composed of violins, violoncellos, contrabasses, and oboes ... During the Offertory they performed the Introduction and Allegro of one of the symphonies of Haydn in the key of D; during the Communion the Andante was played, and at the last Gospel, the Allegro" (Heartz 286; see also Church).

According to notices in the *Diario de Madrid*, Haydn's music was also performed in Madrid's three main theaters: Teatro de la Cruz, Teatro del Príncipe and Teatro de los Caños del Peral, where *tonadillas* (comic intermezzi), operas and ballet were the chief musical entertainments. To give just one example, the 1792–93 opera season at the Teatro de los Caños del Peral lasted from April to February, with 197 staged performances consisting of 13 operas and 12 ballets. At Madrid theaters, purely instrumental concerts were performed only during Lent when, because of religion restrictions, opera performances ceased. It is precisely in these Lenten series that Haydn's music was heard. The *Diario de Madrid* from March 6, 1788 contains a description of the performance of individual movements of Haydn symphonies interspersed with works by Cimarosa, Pleyel, and others, performed by a variety of different ensembles. At a concert given on March 13, 1790 in the Teatro del Príncipe, a symphony by "Haydem [sic]... one of the most moderns" was performed. The second half of this concert began with an "alegro de sinfonia de Haydem [sic]" and concluded with another *Allegro* by Haydn, the whole interspersed with works by other composers. The number of performances of Haydn symphonies peaked in the 1790 Lenten concert series, with a total of nine. Haydn symphonies spread out over the Spanish peninsula, and were widely performed in different spheres and concert venues, including the Royal Palace, aristocratic salons and enlightened societies, churches, cathedrals, and public theaters. Today, symphonies by Haydn represent the highest percentage of the total number of symphonies by all composers in musical manuscripts and editions from the late eighteenth century preserved in Spanish ARCHIVES.

About two hundred works by Haydn formed part of the Royal Palace collection during the reigns of Carlos III, Carlos IV and Fernando VII – a collection that today is scattered among the Royal Palace archives, the library of the Conservatorio de Madrid, and the US Library of Congress. Symphonies in both their original scoring and in different arrangements constitute the core of this collection. This collection also includes some chamber music, two operas – *L'isola disabitata* and *Laurette*, a French adaptation of *La vera costanza* – and the three oratorios: *Il ritorno di Tobia*, *The Creation*, and *The Seasons*. Haydn's chamber music was highly praised, famously so by the House of Benavente-Osuna and the House of Alba. From 1783 to 1789 Countess of Benavente regularly acquired works by Haydn, and her library contained more than a hundred works by the composer, including most of his quartets, trios, sonatas, symphonies as well as some masses and the opera *Orlando paladino*.

In 1783 Haydn was commissioned to write a piece for the Good Friday observances by the Brotherhood of the Santa Cueva chapel in the Andalusian port city of Cádiz, which resulted in one of his most unusual compositions. As Will observes, *The Seven Last Words of Our Savior on the Cross* (1786) formed part of the *Tres horas* (Three Hours) passion service traditionally observed from twelve noon to three in the afternoon on Good Friday. A series of seven slow instrumental movements or musical mediations on the last words of the crucified Christ as recorded in the Gospels of Matthew, Luke, and John, the structure of the work corresponds to the ritual theatricality demanded by the service. Prefaced by an introductory adagio in D minor, the seven "sonatas" (sounding pieces) alternate with scripture readings and reflective sermons, culminating in a presto movement in C minor, *Il terremoto*, that depicts the tumultuous earthquake unleashed by Christ's death. It is uncertain if the original orchestral version was ever performed in the Santa Cueva chapel. About 200 square meters in size, the small performance space would barely have accommodated an orchestra of some twenty to twenty-five players alongside a congregation of Brothers and worshippers (see LEADING LARGE ENSEMBLES; PERFORMANCE SPACES). Díez reasons that Haydn's own arrangement of the work for string quartet was used at this first performance, a tradition that continues to this day in Cádiz. In 1787 the Viennese PUBLISHER Artaria issued three different versions of *The Seven Last Words* – the original orchestral score, the string quartet reduction prepared by Haydn, and a reduction for solo keyboard sanctioned by him – suggesting how both performance contexts and MARKET forces helped shape the form, presentation, mediation, and CIRCULATION of Haydn's later works. After hearing a choral arrangement of the work by Joseph Frieberth in Passau in 1795, Haydn created his own choral–orchestral version with librettist Gottfried van Swieten, which was performed in Vienna the following Lent.

Keyboard arrangements of *The Seven Last Words* proliferated in Spain up to the end of the nineteenth century, in part because of the great number of keyboard performers in the cathedrals, monasteries, and convents of Spain. The Ecclesiastical Census of 1768 for Castile records a total of 1,026 female monasteries and convents, most of which had at least one nun who was an organist (while many had up to four), as well as students or *educandas* to whom the nuns taught music on a range of keyboard INSTRUMENTS, including organ, harpsichord, clavichord and, later in the century, the fortepiano and the square piano. (See also GENDER.) Sonatas by Domenico Scarlatti, Antonio Soler, Haydn, and others comprise the largest body of eighteenth-century keyboard

Figure 10 *Las siete Palabras con su Introduccion y Terremoto, Musica del M.tro D. J. Haydn para Piano Forte*. Cover and first page of *The Seven Last Words* (first half of the nineteenth century). Piano transcription. Convent of las Claras, Sevilla (©ICCMU, CS-2-03-0957). Reproduced with permission of ICCMU.

Figure 10 (cont.)

music in the archives of the female monasteries of San Pedro de las Dueñas (León) and Santa Ana de Ávila. The manuscripts in these monastic institutions show that keyboard sonatas were performed by nuns as part of their private recreation in the cloisters or during the liturgy. For instance, the archive of the convent of Las Claras in Seville, today housed at the Library of the Universidad Complutense in Madrid, contains six keyboard notebooks dating from the early nineteenth century with works by Haydn. Among these are two versions for fortepiano of *The Seven Last Words*. Figure 10 shows one of these.

LUISA MORALES

FURTHER READING
Acker (2007); Bordas et al. (2011); Brown (1986b); Díez (2011); Dratwicki (2005); Gon (2013); Harrison (1998); Heartz (1995); Montero (2011); Morales (2011a); Stevenson (1982); Will (2002).

Exoticism As a composer living within the multicultural Habsburg Empire, Haydn was surrounded by diversity, and its representation colors many of his works. Although Haydn's own family was primarily of German descent, Croats, Slovakians, and Hungarians were also numerous in the area of Lower Austria where he was born and spent his early childhood, and ethnic diversity abounded in and around Vienna, ESZTERHÁZA, and EISENSTADT, where Haydn was later active (see also BURGENLAND). Given this context, it remains unclear to what extent the music of various peoples might have been considered exotic or "Other" by Haydn himself rather than integral to the complex cultural fabric of the Habsburg Empire, of which he was also a part. Exoticism – the evocation or representation of difference – however, is largely a matter of reception, and to Haydn's international audiences, the Central and Eastern European music that he evoked in his own compositions would have sounded quite foreign.

Titles of movements and performance indications in Haydn's music often clearly identify specific exotic referents; examples include the "Rondo all'ungarese" from the Keyboard Concerto in D major, Hob.XVIII:11 and the "Menuetto alla zingarese" from the String Quartet in D major, Op. 20, No. 4. Yet the intermingling of influences within the Habsburg Empire complicates even apparently straightforward examples. Szabolcsi has traced the rebounding thirds characteristic of much music *alla turca*, for instance – as in Volpino's aria "Salamelica, Semprugna cara" in Haydn's opera *Lo speziale*, discussed by Head (2000, 2005) – to the Hungarian *törökös*, a parodic dance dating from the Ottoman occupation, and Clark (2014, 2016) has suggested that the "dadl, dadl" refrain in this same aria may reference the Jewish *niggun*.

More often Haydn did not identify his musical stimuli, and scholars have variously claimed the rustic themes of many of his symphonic trios and finales as Hungarian, Gypsy, Croatian, or more generally Balkan or Slavonic in origin. Evidence for the exotic inspiration of these passages is scant, however; Ferraguto suggests they are perhaps better understood as instances of Haydn's "minimal" aesthetic, reflected through a limitation of scoring, dynamics, texture, and motives.

Less often discussed is the unlabeled second movement of Haydn's String Quartet in C major, Op. 54, No. 2, which strongly evokes the *hallgató* style (for listening, rather than for dancing) of Hungarian–Gypsy musicians through the improvisatory and impassioned quality of the first violin's line, replete with ornamental filigree, varied rhythms, and augmented seconds. This movement is in fact one of the few from the substantial late eighteenth-century repertoire of Hungarian–Gypsy representations that is indebted to this particular style of music, perhaps bearing witness to Haydn's familiarity with the whole range of music performed by Hungarian–Gypsy musicians. From Haydn's perspective, many of his works are perhaps best understood as reflecting submerged exoticism (incorporating musical gestures often associated with exoticism into his general compositional style) or even transcultural composition (writing music for Western contexts that employs musical conventions typical of foreign works arising from quite different performance contexts), categories that Locke has explored, though not in connection to Haydn. Yet for his bourgeois and aristocratic publics throughout Europe, these works most likely sounded distinctly Other, evoking cultures and socio-economic classes far removed from their own.

Scholars have interpreted the meaning and context of exoticism in Haydn's works in a wide variety of ways. Clark (2009a) has traced representations of Jews in Haydn's operas from stereotypical comic portrayals in his early works *Der krumme Teufel* (c. 1752) and *Lo speziale* (1768) to his later *Il mondo della luna* (1777), in which the absence of the comic stereotype may signal increasing acceptance and integration of Jews in European society. More generally, Head (2005) has read Haydn's exotic works, many of which mix national referents and interweave them seamlessly into the fabric of Haydn's own musical language, as reflections of the ENLIGHTENMENT values of universal brotherhood and tolerance, which he suggests the composer himself espoused. Lowe nuances this idealistic interpretation of Haydn's engagement with difference by suggesting that his exotic works might best be understood as reflections of the multiple publics – aristocratic patrons, public concert audiences, musicians of varying abilities, publishers, and critics – to whom he consciously and astutely addressed his music. The finale of Haydn's Piano Trio in G major, Hob.XV:25 ("Rondo in the Gipsies' style"), for instance, written initially for cosmopolitan London audiences, invokes Westernized Hungarian–Gypsy and *alla turca* styles as well as a contredanse topic, which at once contains the difference of the two exotic styles while simultaneously challenging autocratic rule through its democratic spirit.

Explicit in or underlying scholarship on exoticism in Haydn's and other late eighteenth-century music is the recognition that engagement with the Other was always at least in part an attempt better to understand or to critique the Self. One of the most interesting examples of Self-reflection in Haydn's oeuvre is his opera *L'incontro improvviso*, which, although it includes no European characters, highlights the civility of the Sultan of Egypt, an enlightened ruler much like the Habsburg monarch, for whose visiting representatives it was premiered at Eszterháza in 1775, along with a multitude of other entertainments. This mirroring flattered the court, and moreover, the lavish spectacle of the opera itself (including the vocal sensuality of the female captives in the harem), together with displays of *turquerie* through multiple media – including Haydn and his musicians in Oriental dress performing in the Chinese Pavilion – all heightened the splendor and exoticism of the festivities surrounding the courtly visit, abundantly displaying the power of the nobility and royalty (Clark 2005a; Head 2005, 2012). CATHERINE MAYES

FURTHER READING
Christiansen (2008); Clark (2005a, 2009a, 2014a, 2016); Ferraguto (2010); Head (2005, 2012); Locke (2009, 2015); Szabolcsi (1956).

Experiential Learning Haydn's musical EDUCATION was a combination of formal training, self-study, and formative musical experiences in VIENNA. He received his first musical training at his childhood home in Rohrau. Haydn's father Matthias, a wainwright by profession, played the harp, and sang with his wife Anne Marie. In 1737 or 1738, the schoolteacher and choral conductor Johann Mathias Franck, a cousin who lived in Hainburg, witnessed their music-making; so impressed was he with the child's performance that he offered to give him regular tuition. In the late sixteenth century, a network of Catholic parish schools was established across Austria and Bohemia with the aim of counteracting the propagation of Protestantism (see CHURCH). In accordance with the cultural program of the Counter-Reformation, Catholic education aimed to enhance the visual, aural and theatrical aspects of a basically non-literate culture – with musical education assuming an important role. Not only Haydn profited from this: the composers Johann Wenzel Anton Stamitz, Josef Mysliveček, Haydn's student Ignaz Pleyel as well as later Franz Schubert and Anton Bruckner were all sons of schoolmasters. According to Griesinger, for approximately three years Haydn received lessons in reading and writing, catechism, singing, and almost all wind and string instruments as well as timpani. His own autobiographical sketch from 1776 relates that he could sing the vocal lines of masses and play some violin and piano at the age of six (*Briefe* 76). In Hainburg, Haydn also had the opportunity to experience the musical activities in the main Philippus-und-Jakobus-Kirche, where he learned by observing and listening to performances of works by Johann Joseph Fux, Antonio Caldara, Georg Reutter Sr. and Jr., and local masters.

The year 1740 marked a decisive turning point in Haydn's musical education, when Georg Reutter Jr., the Kapellmeister of St. Stephen's Cathedral in Vienna, chose him as a chorister. In the choir school, music tuition was of highest importance. While the focus was primarily on singing, Haydn also received keyboard and violin lessons (*Briefe* 76). General studies included reading, writing, mathematics, and basic Latin. Several of the cathedral ensemble members tutored Haydn, including the singing teachers Adam Gegenbauer and the tenor Ignaz Finsterbusch (Griesinger 9) – perhaps instructing him with Fux's handwritten treatise, *Singfundamente*. Possible keyboard and violin teachers included Georg Ignaz Keller, who later became a member of the *Hofkapelle* (chapel choir), as well as the aforementioned Gegenbauer, who was also a violinist, and the organist Anton Reckh. In later years, Haydn criticised the lack of formal compositional training at the choir school, noting insufficient lessons in COUNTERPOINT (*Briefe* 76). Griesinger reports that Reutter gave Haydn only a few counterpoint lessons, but encouraged him to make his own variations of pieces he was required to sing in church. These exercises, which Reutter then corrected, enabled the young Haydn to develop his own ideas (10). Indeed, several sets of VARIATIONS dating from the 1760s are listed in Haydn's catalogue, including Hob.XVII:1, 2, and 7. Single variation movements also appear in the string trios Hob.V:7/2, 8/1, 11/2, and 18/3, the Divertimenti for winds and strings Hob.II:1/4, 11/4, and the String Quartet Op. 2, No. 6. These reports and later recollections allow us to see the particularity of Haydn's path to composition, namely the creative acquaintance with contemporary works. After leaving the choir school, Haydn acquired Fux's treatise on counterpoint, *Gradus ad Parnassum* (1725), and undertook intensive self-study. He later used this treatise in his own compositional TEACHING, suggesting that he did not necessarily view his own path to composition as being a correct one, but believed that a well-founded basis in counterpoint was important for the training of COMPOSERS.

Haydn had plenty of opportunities to hear contemporary works at St. Stephen's Cathedral, one of the most important church music centers in Europe. Here Haydn witnessed and participated in many grand performances, including a performance of Fux's so-called *Emperor Mass* (1720) for Emperor Charles VI's requiem mass. A distinguished composer, music theorist, imperial court conductor and former St. Stephen's Kapellmeister, Fux died a few months later and was buried in the cathedral following a festive requiem mass, in which Haydn performed. As the cathedral and court ensembles were closely connected, Haydn also frequently heard musicians and singers from the imperial court. He composed his *Missa brevis in F a due soprani* (Hob.XXII:1) around the time his connection with the school ended. The instrumentation, two violins and continuo bass, conformed to the "Viennese church trio" praxis of the time. If Landon's supposition is correct about the soprano solos being composed for Haydn and his younger brother Michael (who joined the choir school in 1745), then this piece shows that both boys were virtuosic singers.

After leaving the cathedral choir when his voice broke (c.1749), Haydn soon came into contact with the court poet Pietro Metastasio, his neighbor in the Michaelerhaus in Vienna. Through Metastasio, Haydn met the celebrated opera composer Nicola Porpora, for whom he worked as a servant in exchange for composition and singing lessons. Haydn reported that he learned "the true fundaments of the art of harmony" from Porpora (Briefe 77). He also played for Porpora's vocal lessons, acquainting himself with the Italian style of singing and accompanying. Metastasio may also have introduced Haydn to the keyboard sonatas of Domenico Scarlatti, since handwritten copies were circulating in Vienna (see Badura-Skoda 1985). According to Griesinger, Haydn also studied the keyboard works of C. P. E. Bach, though his preoccupation with the latter's *Versuch über die wahre Art das Clavier zu spielen* (*Essay on the True Art of Playing Keyboard Instruments*, Part I, 1753; Part 2, 1762) probably only began in the 1760s. Griesinger also testifies to Haydn's interest in music theory, reporting that Haydn studied Johann Mattheson's *Der vollkommene Capellmeister* (1739) and Fux's *Gradus ad Parnassum* (1725), which he annotated in Latin. Both works are listed in Haydn's book inventory from 1804 (see MATERIAL CULTURE).

A more complete picture of Haydn's musical education emerges when one considers the extraordinarily rich musical life of mid-eighteenth-century Vienna. In 1748, the rebuilt Burgtheater featured operas by Christoph Willibald Gluck, Georg Christoph Wagenseil, Giovanni Battista Pergolesi, Johann Adolph Hasse, and Baldassare Galuppi, but the contemporary bourgeoise public preferred the Kärntnertortheater, where lowbrow German-language comedies with sung arias were performed (see THEATER). A selection of such arias from productions in the 1750s featuring comic and ethnic stereotypes includes several pieces that were either composed by or closely connected to Haydn (see Clark). Neapolitan opera symphonies by Porpora, Leonardo Vinci, and Leonardo Leo were soon introduced in Vienna, influencing composers such as Wagenseil, Georg Matthias Monn, and František Ignác Tůma to develop a distinctive style of symphonic writing that formed a direct link to Haydn. Contemporary trends in keyboard and chamber music important to Haydn's musical development include the Vienna Divertimento, as represented by Wagenseil.

Haydn was sensitive to his AUDIENCE and the effect of his works on the general public. The idea that the quality of a work should not be judged by its conformity to a pre-established system of rules, but by its power to move an audience, is one of the most important consequences of Haydn's experience with the Baroque sensualism that pervaded Catholic education in Austria.

FEDERICO CELESTINI

FURTHER READING
Badura-Skoda (1972, 1985); Briefe; Clark (2009a); Dies; Griesinger; H-L; Landon I; Mann (1970a); Melton (2007).

Exploration – see Travel and

F

Festivals – see Commemorations and

Film – see Reception 1950s–Present

Finances – see Economics and

Folk Song Settings Claims about Haydn's supposedly effortless engagement with "folk" idioms, including his apparent use of existing tunes for thematic material, constitute running tropes in the RECEPTION of his music – sometimes enhancing his reputation, while at other times working against it. His huge corpus of approximately four hundred settings of British "national song" MELODIES is thus a rich source of evidence about the composer and the milieu in which he was working.

His earliest Scottish song settings, written at the request of the publisher William Napier, date from 1791. Having already released a volume of Scottish songs with harmonizations by Pleyel, Barthélémon, Shield, and others, Napier sought Haydn's assistance in reversing his troubled finances. During Haydn's two London visits, the composer set a hundred and fifty songs for Napier – an act of apparent charity that he undertook with care. The songs are printed using a format common in British collections: a violin descant on the top stave, a vocal melody shared with the keyboard right hand in the middle, and a figured bass on the bottom. Then, in 1799, the Edinburgh-based George Thomson asked Haydn to participate in a more ambitious PUBLICATION project, for which he solicited the most famous EUROPEAN composers to write introductions ("symphonies") and accompaniments to a huge body of melodies collected as a NATIONALIST project. (He had already worked with Pleyel and Kozeluch, and after Haydn would engage Beethoven and Weber.) To promote these melodies to a patriotic middle-class AUDIENCE, Thomson also employed Robert Burns and other POETS in a bowdlerized retexting project – sometimes providing side-by-side (English and Scots) texts to the same melodies – and asking composers to write full obbligato keyboard parts as well as optional violin and cello accompaniments. Working with Thomson via correspondence until 1805, Haydn also set some Welsh songs. In 1802 a third publisher, William Whyte, also engaged Haydn, and for twice the rate, prompting Thomson to raise his own payments; there was money to be made in the commodification of the folk.

Given the Romantic values associated with art-music reception in the nineteenth and twentieth centuries, Haydn's Scottish song settings have frequently been considered insignificant (e.g., Landon III). The songs suffer in several ways when measured by later criteria. First, the melodies were not "original" to Haydn. Second, the composer often worked without seeing the words, reducing his ability to craft music around them. (When Thomson sent the tunes to be set, he withheld the texts because he feared print piracy, and he also wanted to be able to switch texts from one setting to another). Third, Thomson demanded settings that were easy to play by the young AMATEUR women pianists he was targeting. And to top it off, Haydn delegated around thirty harmonizations to his student Sigismund von Neukomm, apparently overseeing the process but ultimately passing them off as his own.

Entrenched dismissals of these settings, however, miss what is most rewarding and interesting about them. Besides the fact that many are little gems, the settings help to illuminate a moment when "folk music" as a concept was in formation but not yet solidified. In the mid-eighteenth century, certain old or orally transmitted melodies had been claimed as national property, but soon they would also be conceived as relics of a pure and lost organic stage of humanity, a salve for modern civilization's follies, and a repository of Ur-national and Ur-human nature. These latter qualities, which would come to define idealized folk music, were increasingly associated with Scottish music around 1760, when James Macpherson claimed to discover the ancient Celtic "Ossian" epics in the Highlands. Macpherson's publications in turn inspired J. G. Herder to urge the collection of *Volkslied* across Europe (see Gelbart). Yet even as the idea spread that setting "folk" or "national" melodies in art music was reaching across an imagined gulf in time to compensate for a loss of natural ways, older modes of treating pre-existing melodies persisted, unburdened by Schillerian sentimentality. Whether due to personal temperament or to the richly multicultural interaction of old and new melodies in the BURGENLAND where he spent much of his time, Haydn's attitude to pre-existing and national melodies fully embraces this older approach, treating such melodies as shared, fluid material in a synchronic and kaleidoscopic mix of peoples and social classes (see COSMOPOLITANISM). This was Haydn's approach to rustic *topoi* in general (see TOPICS), and it remained so when he set British tunes; indeed, he is perhaps the last composer to engage with the modal features of these Scottish melodies in an easy manner rather than treating them as a barbaric throwback (as Kozeluch already had), or as primitive inspiration (as Beethoven would a few short years after Haydn's song settings). Unlike the letters of Kozeluch and Beethoven, for whom such melodies had become folk music in the modern sense, Haydn's CORRESPONDENCE with Thomson is devoid of observations – positive or negative – about the striking "Otherness" of the melodies. Thus, "foregrounding ... an authorial voice" (Will 45), Haydn employed his usual idioms and techniques to frame the tunes rather than using the presumed purity and EXOTICISM of the tunes to inspire him toward a new, Romantic style. In other words, any exoticisms served "as topics and melodies that can participate fully in the musical discourse" (Head 79).

True, the national song settings exhibit some features that set them apart from anything else Haydn wrote, and which he did not try to erase. The strophic melodies (containing many verses) are short, rigid in phrase length, and use

Example 4 "Maggie Lauder," harmonized by Haydn for George Thomson's *Select Collection of Original Scottish Airs*, Hob.XXXIa:35bis, reduction.

jagged RHYTHMS such as the "Scotch snap." Nevertheless, despite some unique modal features – such as abrupt shifts in TONAL center by a whole step, ubiquitous in Scottish music – the style Haydn applied to the song settings is rarely at odds with his manner in general. He draws on a variety of *topoi* from his usual palette. "Maggie Lauder" (Example 4, for Thomson) juxtaposes, in comic style, overwrought *coup d'archet* and march figures, both in its introduction and under the vocal line. "Strephon and Lydia" (Figure 11, for Napier) gave Haydn the chance to provide one of the most beautifully contrived countermelodies he ever wrote, in the violin part.

Even some aspects of the melodies that make them relatively unique squared with stylistic features that Haydn relished. The frequent alternation of minor and relative major in the melodies was a feature he had already employed as a melodic game, as in the second theme of the first movement of the Quartet Op. 20, No. 6 (where the expected E major arrives only after alternating

Figure 11 "Strephon and Lydia," from *A Selection of Scots Songs in Three Parts, the Harmony by Haydn*. London: William Napier, [1792], part 3. Reproduced by kind permission of the National Library of Scotland.

playfully between G major and E minor). Likewise, the alternation of relative keys sees an extended use in the English Canzonetta "Fidelity" (Hob.XXVIa:30) dating from the same period as the Napier song settings (in this case it is combined with modal mixture on the same tonic).

The settings remind us of an eighteenth-century ability to see music as collaborative, motley, and outward-reaching. In performance, the songs offer much potential for improvisation, with the Napier collections in particular inviting combination, variation, and experimentation. They demonstrate Haydn's cultivation of versatility both in performance and in appeal. At this transitional moment in the ideas of folk and art music as we know them, Haydn used the material he was given to contribute unself-consciously to a musical language that – as he proudly noted on the eve of his first London trip – all the world could understand. (See also ENLIGHTENMENT.)

MATTHEW GELBART

FURTHER READING
Bohlman (2017a, 2017b); Edwards (2004); Gelbart (2007); Head (2005); Landon III; Rycroft (2004); Weber-Bockholdt (2005); Will (2012).

Form Haydn's music poses considerable challenges to received ideas about musical form. Monothematic expositions (Brown), continuous expositions (Hepokoski and Darcy 1997), three-part expositions (Larsen; Martin 2014), "false" recapitulations (Bonds; Hoyt), and recomposed recapitulations (Neuwirth) abound. It is therefore no surprise that Haydn's music has figured prominently in twentieth- and now twenty-first-century attempts to reconfigure traditional *Formenlehre*, whether those of Caplin (1998), of Hepokoski and Darcy (2006), or of latter-day exponents of Heinrich Christoph Koch's "punctuation form" (*interpunctische Form*) such as Diergarten (2012) and Burstein (2010, 2015). The study of Haydn's formal processes has likewise attracted attention from scholars concerned less with theorizing form in general than with analyzing Haydn's forms in particular (e.g., Haimo; Larsen, Webster 1991, see also COMPOSITIONAL PROCESS). Throughout the literature, commentators have concentrated on Haydn's instrumental music, to the relative neglect of his music for the CHURCH or the operatic (THEATER) stage. And within the corpus of Haydn's instrumental music, first-movement forms have received the lion's share of attention from critics.

An alternative is to take seriously the late eighteenth-century injunction – expressed in particular by Joseph Riepel and Koch – that composition pedagogy should begin from the minuet (compare Budday; see also EDUCATION). "Since the minuet is no different than a concerto, an aria, or a symphony," Riepel wrote in 1752, "we therefore want always to start with something small and base in order to arrive from there at something bigger and more praiseworthy" (1). Koch likewise sets the student composer to composing short minuets at first, and then shows how to elaborate these small forms into ever larger musical constructs.

For Koch, a minuet consists at minimum of four four-measure phrases (see MELODY and HARMONY). The ending of each of these phrases is marked by a "closing formula" – in modern terms, by a half-cadence (HC) or a perfect authentic cadence (PAC). And the form is defined by the succession of these punctuation formulas. Various schemes are possible, but the most salient is that diagrammed in Example 5: the first phrase ends with a tonic HC (*Quintabsatz*), the second with a subordinate-key PAC (in the dominant if the tonic is major, in the mediant if minor), after which this entire first half (*Periode*) is repeated; the

Example 5 Koch's 16-measure minuet; model form.

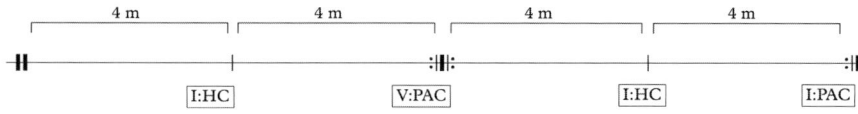

Example 6 Cadential scheme for a sonata exposition, after Koch.

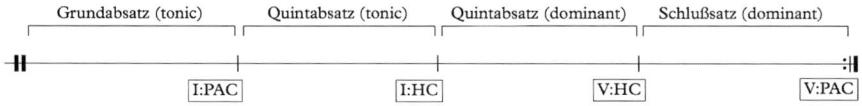

third phrase concludes with a I:HC (tonic half-cadence, or *Quintabsatz*), and then some part of the first half is reprised as the fourth phrase, with its ending formula revised so as to close with a I:PAC (perfect authentic cadence in the tonic, or *Grundabsatz*), after which the entire second half is repeated as well.

Once the student can reliably produce minuets of this type, the next task is to learn how to expand this formal template's modest dimensions. Koch gives an elaborate typology of phrase-expansion techniques and also allows for numerous repetitions and interpolations. By means of these techniques, the sixteen-measure template of Example 5 can be expanded into the much larger "first-movement form," the first part of which (corresponding to the minuet's first half) is shown in Example 6. At its maximum dimensions, the first period now consists of four successive cadential spans (*Sätze*): a first span ending I:PAC placed before the I:HC of the minuet template, and a third span ending V:HC (half cadence in the dominant) interpolated between the I:HC and V:PAC (authentic cadence in the dominant) of Example 5's first half. Either of the HCs can be omitted, and the initial phrase ending I:PAC is similarly optional (if it is omitted, the piece begins directly with a tonic *Quintabsatz*). Expanded in this way, the first period is equivalent to a sonata exposition in any of its various possible dispositions (see Caplin 2001). If all four cadence points are present, then the first phrase is the main theme, the second a non-modulating transition, the third either a modulating transition (making a two-part transition with the second phrase) or, if it begins already in the subordinate key, a first subordinate theme leading to an internal half-cadence, and the fourth is a subordinate theme. The medial caesura, if present, is typically placed after the second or the third of these spans (Hepokoski and Darcy's first- and second-level defaults). In the still more expansive forms of Haydn's later symphonic practice, multiple subordinate themes all ending V:PAC may appear. At the opposite extreme, the scheme may be condensed by fusing successive functions (typically the transition and first subordinate theme) into a single cadential span (Caplin and Martin 2015).

The minuet's second half becomes the development plus recapitulation. The third phrase's I:HC is the development's closing half-cadence, after which a "double return" of the tonic key and main-theme material normally ensues. Koch provides detailed accounts of how the composer might arrange the development, including recommending repetition of the main theme in the dominant at the section's opening (Pre-core), medial tonic returns (the apparent tonics of Schenkerian theory), and a prominent PAC in the submediant region. Still, development procedures remain the least thoroughly scrutinized of Haydn's formal processes, despite the important insights of Caplin and Ratz (the Pre-core–Core scheme), Hepokoski and Darcy (rotation), and Schenker (the notion that the development, at its most background level, prolongs the dominant). Haydn's recapitulations are also notoriously free, and would reward further study along the lines sketched out by Neuwirth. (See also COUNTERPOINT.)

Koch's advice to budding composers is thus to work out an initial "plan" (*Anlage*) consisting of a maximally concise version of the eventual piece and then to expand this template into the desired fully worked form. Though Koch's concern is always with composition pedagogy, his approach can be reversed, and so made analytically productive, by inverting his procedure and reverse-engineering a pre-compositional plan from a finished movement. The *tempo di minuetto* finale of Haydn's Sonata in E minor (Hob.XVI:47bis) can serve as an example (on the work's contested attribution, see Somfai). Example 7 presents a synopsis of the movement distilled down to its smallest dimensions in accordance with Koch's techniques. A moment's observation confirms that its cadential scheme corresponds to that diagrammed abstractly in Example 5. To work back from this *Anlage* to the movement's finished text, do the following:

1. Copy mm. 1–4 of Example 7, changing the cadence from a I:HC to a I:PAC. These become mm. 1–4 of Haydn's Hob.XVI:47bis, third movement.
2. Repeat measures 3–4 (i.e. the new cadential idea ending I:PAC) immediately as an "appendix" (*Anhang*) to form mm. 5–6.
3. Copy mm. 1–4 of Example 7 again, now verbatim, as mm. 7–10 (varying the right-hand rhythm in m. 2 and changing the register of the cadential idea in mm. 3–4).
4. Skip over mm. 11–14 for the moment, and move to the subordinate-theme material in m. 15ff.
5. To build this subordinate-theme material out of mm. 5–8 of Example 7, expand those four measures as shown in Example 8.
6. Copy the final version of the theme in Example 8 into mm. 15–21, leaving off the final tonic to the V:PAC, so as to create an evaded cadence (Schmalfeldt).
7. Copy this same passage, now with its final tonic added, once more as mm. 22–29, lightly ornamenting and embellishing the right-hand part.
8. Finally, engineer a modulating transition ending in a V:HC and incorporating both an echo of the main theme's opening and a pre-echo of the subordinate theme's as shown in Example 9. Copy this material as mm. 11–14.

The result of applying these steps is to transform mm. 1–8 of Example 7 into the concise, but nonetheless fully worked, sonata exposition that Haydn in fact wrote. In terms of modern accounts of sonata form, mm. 1–6 are that exposition's main theme; mm. 7–10 are a non-modulating transition ending with a bifocal close (see Winter); mm. 11–14, which begin already in the dominant, are a first

Example 7 Haydn, Sonata in E minor, Hob.XVI:47bis, third movement; hypothetical *Anlage*.

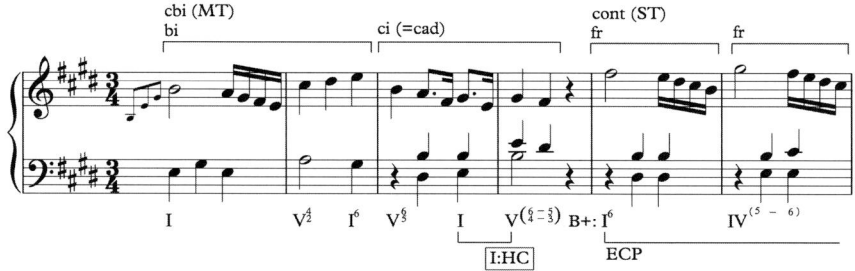

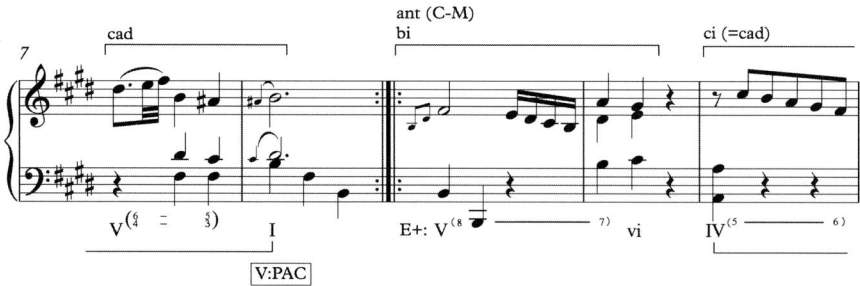

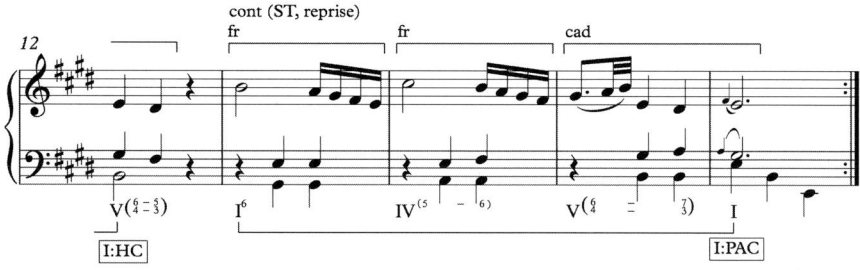

subordinate theme leading to an internal half-cadence; mm. 15ff resume continuational activity following that internal HC and lead to an evaded cadence at m. 22, whereupon that entire span is repeated to bring about the exposition's final cadence at m. 29. The movement's medial caesura separates m. 14 from m. 15, and its EEC (essential expositional closure) is the final V:PAC. A similar set of instructions would serve to turn mm. 9–12 into the movement's brief development section, and mm. 13–16 into its recapitulation. The minuet of Example 7 thus stands to Haydn's finished composition as a hypothetically reconstructed *Anlage*.

A movement such as Hob.XVI:47bis, iii could be easily made into a sonata–rondo (Type 4 in the nomenclature of Hepokoski and Darcy) by

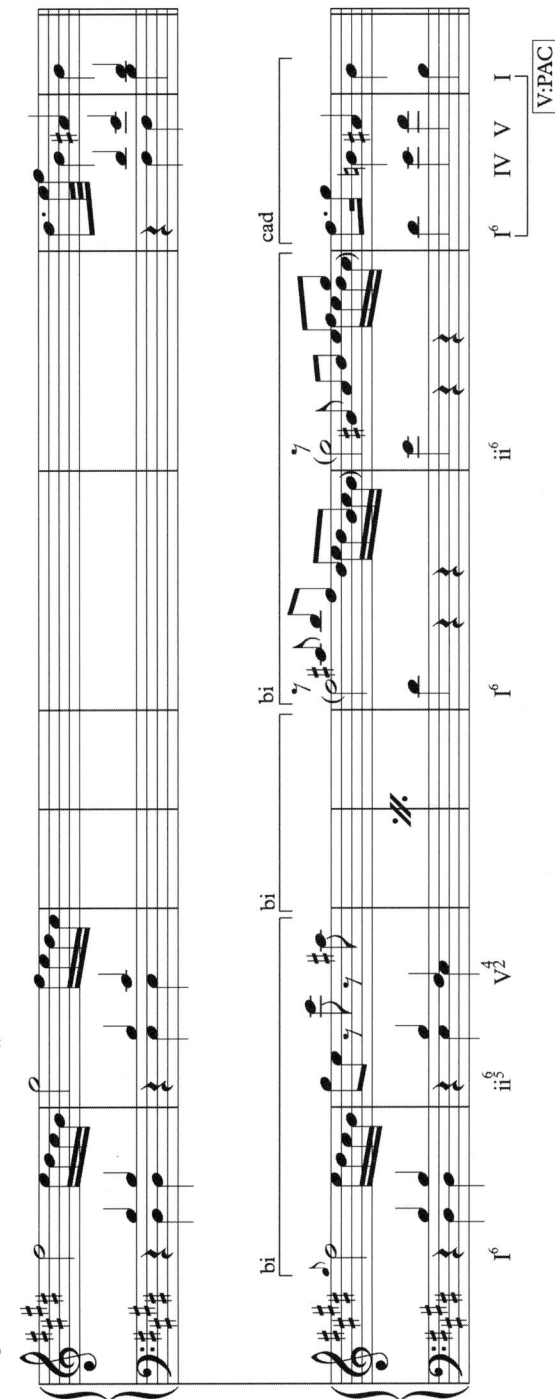

Example 8 Sonata in E minor, Hob.XVI:47bis, third movement; derivation of subordinate theme.

Example 9 Sonata in E minor, Hob.XVI:47bis, third movement; derivation of the modulating transition.

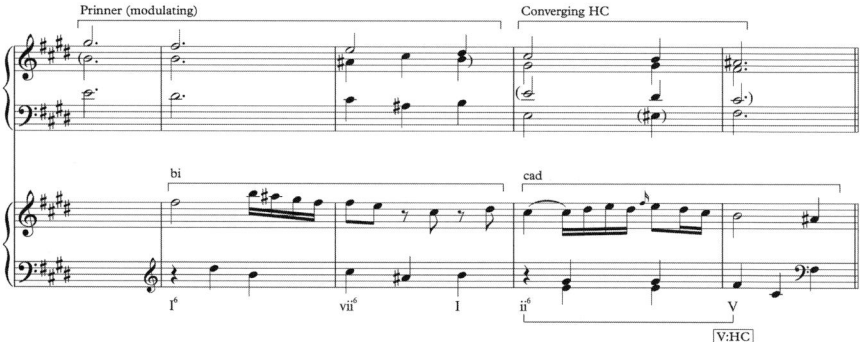

interpolating a return of the main theme between the end of the exposition and the beginning of the development (i.e., between mm. 29 and 30), or into a rondo proper by also substituting an appropriate second couplet in place of the development section. Suppressing the return of the main theme in the recapitulation would produce a Type 2 sonata; deleting the development a Type 1. Transforming the finished Type 3 sonata into the first movement of a concerto (Type 5) is a matter of interpolating appropriate orchestral ritornelli: the first ritornello belongs before the (solo) exposition, the second between the exposition and the development, and the third after the end of the recapitulation (Diergarten and Neuwirth 2018).

In Haydn's instrumental music, first movements typically follow the Type 3 scheme (or Type 5 in the case of concerti). Finales are frequently rondos or sonata–rondos (Type 4). Minuets, when present, follow lightly expanded versions of Koch's scheme (Example 5). Slow movements, finally, are variously Type 1 sonatas, large ternaries (in which a main theme bookends a middle section cast as the second couplet of a rondo), or VARIATION sets. In these last, the theme and each variation is typically formed on the model of Example 5. (For discussion of Haydn's variation procedures, see Sisman 1993a.)

Arias are formed much like instrumental slow movements (see Hunter; Martin 2010), though a variant form that is rare in instrumental music – in which the second couplet of a large ternary is replaced by a subordinate theme or transition plus subordinate theme (i.e., the first couplet of a sonata-rondo) – is common in that context. The formal organization of Haydn's masses, finally, would reward further study (see Gibbs; Webster 1998).

As an analytical and music-theoretical category, "form" is of course a modern construct more or less coeval with the appearance of A. B. Marx's *Lehre von der musikalischen Komposition* (1837–47). Koch, Riepel, and Haydn's other contemporaries generally make no concerted reference to the category. Their concern, moreover, is with teaching composition, not with analyzing "masterworks." And much of their discussion turns on matters that might strike a modern reader as pertaining more to style or to genre. The polysemous mutability of the word "rondo/rondeau" in eighteenth-century usage offers a case in point: some late eighteenth-century pieces bearing the title "rondo" are rondos in the modern, post-Marxian formal sense, while others are not (see Fillion). To talk, therefore, about form in the abstract is a uniquely modern predilection, and there is thus an unintended irony to attempts at reconstituting a "historically informed" *Formenlehre* from contemporaneous writings (see Budday). Still, scholars working within the disciplinary context of a robust and institutionally ensconced music theory need make no apology for approaching Haydn's music on their own terms. Whether these terms also imply a commitment to some kind of "formalism" as a matter of philosophical AESTHETICS, as has sometimes been asserted, is unclear. (Certainly, the charge is nonsense if directed at Hepokoski and Darcy's Sonata Theory, which functions in effect as a vast machinery for producing hermeneusis.) More probably, the choice to bracket out ancillary matters in accounting for formal processes is a methodological decision – one motivated primarily by the fact that, as Gertrude Stein is alleged to have said, "not everything can be about everything all the time."

Beyond the confines of academic music theory, however, observations regarding form have sometimes been used to shore up critical or historical judgments, or some mixture of the two. As Webster (1991) complains, Haydn's early music has not infrequently been denigrated as evincing an immature, "pre-Classical" style, with the reproach sometimes (as in Rosen 1971/72) cast in terms of formal categories such as periodicity. Webster, in contrast, uses an extensive battery of analytical techniques to argue for the aesthetic value of Haydn's early music, with the "Farewell" Symphony (no. 45) as the lead example (see RECEPTION 1950S–PRESENT; CYCLIC INTEGRATION). Such attempts to found critical appraisal upon analytic observation seem unlikely to persuade skeptics, and raise the natural suspicion that what is being presented as an argument is less what Dahlhaus called "a discovery of what always underlay subjective judgment" (1982, 4) than a post hoc rationalization of a prior aesthetic judgment. More formally, such attempts would seem to violate both Hume's injunction against using an "is" to establish an "ought" and Kant's reiteration of the classical dictum *de gustibus non est disputandum*.

Especially in the wake of Kerman and the New Musicology, aesthetic judgments are not always segregated off from historical ones. Arguably, the conclusion of Webster's analysis is meant to be both that the "Farewell" Symphony is good and that it is (historically) important. If the mustering of analysis towards criticism seems suspect (*pace* Kerman), its historiographical use appears problematic in more subtle ways.

Traditionally, the exploitation of formal categories for historical purposes has been especially characteristic of historians of style. Wilhelm Fischer (1915), for instance, coined his celebrated opposition between the *Lied-* and *Fortspinnungstypus* with the aim of charting the (alleged) evolution of the Classical style from the Baroque. Fischer's argument, which bears a family resemblance to the analysis of Hob.XIV:47bis, iii offered above, treats Baroque binary dance forms as the historical progenitors of Classical sonata form: the *Fortspinnungstypus*, which is typical of the first half of a Baroque dance, becomes, in Fischer's view, the sonata exposition by means of internal expansions and interpolated *Liedtypen* (this is the point of his extended analysis of Hob.XVI:14). This view is now obsolete, thanks to Gjerdingen on the one hand and to Heartz and his students on the other. The fact that, however, one can be persuaded by the music-theoretical argument while rejecting the spurious history serves to signal the distance between the two disciplinary registers: that a sonata-form movement can be compellingly analyzed as an expanded minuet does not mean that the one emerged historically from the other, and the gap between the analytic and the genetic claim should be acknowledged. Riepel's and Koch's views are *post facto* rationalizations recommended, in their own time, by their pedagogical usefulness and, in ours, by their music-theoretical suggestiveness. Just where – aside from foundering as Fischer's also does on historical facts – historical arguments invoking formal categories go wrong, however, is a more delicate diagnosis. Probably, categories like *Fortspinnungstypus* are ideal types in something like Max Weber's (1968) sense (Dahlhaus 1978). If so, then Fischer commits the methodological error, against which Weber warned, of hypostatizing his ideal types and mistaking them for historical entities (cf. Braunschweig). Such categories are in fact irreducibly etic: form is our problem, not theirs, and one should therefore be deeply suspicious of any argument attributing historical agency or efficacy to the etic constructs of recent *Formenlehre*. At the same time, Fischer's article stands as a cautionary tale for the precariousness of claims regarding style change and influence based solely on intrinsic evidence. The virtuosity with which the exemplary analyst may deploy the conceptual apparatus of modern theories of form – whether those theories claim to be grounded in contemporaneous writings or not – in itself says little that can be marshalled towards the music historian's purposes without considerable circumspection. Like a social scientist performing inferential statistical tests, the historical musicologist borrowing music-theoretical tools needs to understand the presuppositions and limitations of those tools in order to avoid putting them to spurious uses.

NATHAN JOHN MARTIN

FURTHER READING

Bonds (1988); Braunschweig (2015); Brown (1975); Budday (1983); Burstein (2010, 2015); Caplin (1998, 2001); Caplin and Martin (2015); Dahlhaus (1978, 1982); Diergarten (2012); Diergarten and Neuwirth (2018); Fillion (2012); Fischer (1915); Gibbs (1972); Haimo (1995); Hepokoski and Darcy (2006); Hoyt (1999); Hunter (1982); Kerman (1980); Koch (1782–93); Larsen (1962); Martin (2010, 2014); Neuwirth (2013); Ratz (1951); Riepel (1752); Rosen (1971/72); Schmalfeldt (1992); Sisman (1982, 1993a); Somfai (1995); Weber (1968); Webster (1991, 1998); Winter (1989).

France – see European Contexts

Freemasonry Haydn's official connection with the Freemasons is fairly well documented. His application for membership to the Viennese lodge "Zur wahren Eintracht" (True Concord), submitted on December 29, 1784, was approved on January 24, 1785, but the initiation ceremony was delayed until February 11. On this occasion, Joseph von Holzmeister gave a speech, later published in the *Journal für Freymaurer*, emphasizing that the harmony between different layers of society can guarantee the happiness of the state just as the cooperation of diverse instruments can bring about enjoyable music. Following this ceremony, however, Haydn's name appears in the archives of the lodge only among the absent members, and – following the merger of his lodge with another in late December 1785 to create "Zur Wahrheit" (Truth) – his name was eventually omitted from the attendance lists in early 1787.

Scholars have suggested diverse explanations for the composer's conspicuously short-lived Masonic career. At the one extreme, Brand insisted that Haydn should not even be labeled as a Mason, since his first and only personal encounter with Freemasonry apparently proved so frustrating that he turned his back on the fraternal organization forever. Others, however, have pointed out that the reason why the composer's initiation had to be postponed – his countless duties at Eszterháza – could have also prevented him from attending the weekly meetings of his lodge in Vienna. Even so, Haydn's consistent absence suggests a modest interest at best in the craft, and there is no evidence that he would have taken the opportunity to attend the meetings of other lodges closer to ESZTERHÁZA. Nor did he attend meetings in LONDON, where his host Johann Peter Salomon was a member of the German-speaking Pilgrims Lodge, which included a number of German musicians, and convened in Freemasons Hall, a popular concert venue of the time.

With these circumstances in mind, the motivations for Haydn's joining the craft invite speculation. It is possible that, by joining a lodge whose ranks included court and government officials, diplomats, lawyers and doctors, clerics, natural scientists, university professors, artists and musicians, he may have been declaring his leanings towards progressive societal ideas. It is equally possible, however, that Haydn was primarily following the high vogue of Freemasonry in contemporary VIENNA. At the time of Maria Theresia's death in 1780, there were about two hundred Masons in the Imperial City, while under the favorable intellectual climate fostered during the early years of Joseph II's reign, "Zur wahren Eintracht" alone numbered that many members.

By late 1785, the Emperor reversed his opinion and came to view the Masonic movement as a potential nest of anti-government criticism. His *Freimaurerpatent* of November 9 restricted the number of lodges, prompting yet another merger of Haydn's lodge with two others at the end of the year, and eventually bringing about its quiet dissolution in 1789. Remarkably, Haydn never moved beyond the initial grade of *Lehrling* (Apprentice), when doing so would have been a natural step not only for the few aristocratic members of the lodge, but also for the professionals, scientists, artists, and musicians who swelled its ranks. (Mozart became a member of "Zur Wohltätigkeit" two weeks prior to Haydn's similar request.) Thus, the flattering words in Haydn's letter of application about "the highly advantageous impression" he had about the craft, and his "sincerest wish" to appropriate its "humanitarian and wise principles" should not necessarily be read as a heartfelt confession, especially since the letter itself is in a foreign hand, and was only signed by the composer. Haydn may primarily have intended to mix with the leading circles of Vienna, just as he did around the same time in Gottfried van Swieten's or Franz von

Greiner's salons – and precisely at a time when his interest in writing works for commissions arriving outside of the Esterházy court was on the rise (see PUBLISHERS AND PUBLISHING). Haydn's only documented later connection with Masonic circles are related to such commissions. The "Paris" Symphonies (nos. 82–87) were written for a Mason-sponsored series (the Concert de la Loge Olympique) in 1785–86, a period when Viennese Masons could easily have acted as go-betweens, though we have no direct evidence. In the case of Symphonies Nos. 90–92, written in 1788–89 probably also for Count d'Ogny, the representative of the Loge Olympique, such mediations were hardly necessary.

Whether Haydn's Masonic experiences and connections had an impact on his music is difficult to judge. Advocates of Freemasonry have pinpointed outward features, including triple meter, key signature of three flats, etc. (analogous to Mozart's *Die Zauberflöte*), but few musicologists have found such efforts convincing. Haydn certainly had some knowledge of the actual music used in the lodges – his estate, for example, included the songbook of "Zur wahren Eintracht" with printed music for eleven lieder by B***j (perhaps Joseph Anton von Bianchi, who is known to have written music for Masonic purposes) and one by Giuseppe Sarti (see MATERIAL CULTURE). Nevertheless, the characteristic choral refrain structure, so typical of the Masonic song repertory, does not appear in Haydn's works; nor are other kinds of Masonic elements evident in the symphonies specifically commissioned by Paris Masons. By contrast, potential Masonic resonances in *The Creation* have often been discussed, especially as regards certain aspects of the plot: the dissolution of Darkness through Light, the portrayal of God as the "great architect" of the universe, and the harmony between the different parts of the world created by him (a topic also raised in Holzmeister's speech for Haydn's induction). These ideas, nonetheless, are hardly specific to Freemasons; they should better be viewed as elements of a larger set of ideas promoted in the ENLIGHTENMENT period, which the Masonic movement also relied on. Overall Haydn's relationship with Freemasonry appears to have had little significance for his intellectual or creative life, even though he was inevitably in touch with a number of people who were active Masons during parts of their lives. (See also RELATIONSHIPS AND FRIENDSHIPS.)

BALÁZS MIKUSI

FURTHER READING
Brand (1941); *CCLN*; Hurwitz (1996).

Friendships – see Relationships and

G

Gender "We cannot expect to understand any new repertory other than the traditional ones if we are not prepared to invent new methods appropriate for its study." So wrote Don Randel in his whimsical yet potent "Canons in the Musicological Toolbox" in 1992. Haydn's music, particularly his symphonies and quartets, were "traditional repertory," kept canonic (to paraphrase Randel) by the musicologist-mechanic who genuinely believed his toolbox was comprehensive – but whose tools, it turned out, were not all-purpose tools. Indeed, the very tools that he used to determine whether a work was "great" were in fact tools designed to *demonstrate* that the music was great, so, mission accomplished. How then would Haydn scholars respond to Randel (and others making similar appeals)? They heard the call: they addressed new repertories, they borrowed and developed new methods, and, perhaps most importantly, they began to circle back and apply the new methods to the "traditional repertory." Very often, this work hinged on the idea or the lens of gender. For as was the case throughout the humanities, Gender Studies was on the vanguard of musicology's turn to cultural analysis, and it helped forge a path for a variety of modes of analysis, including music and race/ethnicity and (more recently) music and DISABILITY.

Some of the "new repertories" that came under purview were written by women; see Godt on COMPOSER Marianna Martines, a STUDENT of Haydn (and Metastasio), and duet partner of Mozart; see also Fortino on composers Anna Bon, Marianna von Auenbrugger, and Maria Theresia von Paradis, all women in Haydn's NETWORK (see also RELATIONSHIPS AND FRIENDSHIPS). Likewise, attention was paid to music played by women: keyboard music (see Wheelock), songs (see Brown), and the salon settings in which they were heard (see Fuchs). This work opened the door for serious treatment of domestic, AMATEUR, or private sphere music, such as Mikusi's 2010 study of Haydn's part-songs.

The work of developing new tools warmed up by calling attention to the gendered language within contemporary musical discourse; see Morrow's study of reviews in the PRESS of instrumental music, and Head's demonstration (1995) that even genres were understood in gendered terms (for example, rondos as feminine or effeminate) – and furthermore, that these metonymic connections figured into composers' COMPOSITIONAL PROCESSES. The work reached a steady simmer with Leppert's elucidation of the ICONOGRAPHY of female music-making as modes of "containment" and Head's subsequent exploration (1999) of how that same conflation of music and discipline was presented – but also potentially resisted – in music designated "for the fair sex."

Did the images discussed by Leppert reflect actual practice, or did they, as Head put it, "seek to produce and control that practice through an ideal, fantasized image" (1999, 205)? Here then lies a methodological crux: music exists in time, through performance, and as such its articulation of rhetoric can change and range from affinity to dissent and everywhere on the continuum in between. And it is largely the study of music-as-performance that has fueled gender studies in, of, and through Haydn's music. For example, it is exactly because she envisions and describes not so much music but musicking that Le Guin is able convey the ways in which Haydn's Trio in A♭ major, Hob.XV:14 (first movement) can be understood as a manifestation of a salon, and as such, a manifestation of the female role in civil society. A salon participant suggests that the gatherings "require a certain power to temper them," a power which is "no better held than in the hands of a woman." "What in fact does this woman do," another counters, "beyond providing us her house, serving us dinner, and policing the free play of our minds?" A third responds: "With their attention and their attentiveness, women fill intervals of conversation and of life, like the padding that one inserts in cases of china; they are valued at nothing, and yet everything breaks without them." Le Guin herself concludes: "it is toward the cultivation of this nameless and yet essential capacity that a composer such as Haydn directed his accompanied sonatas" (33). Each elucidates the other: we learn something about both music/music-making and the construction of gender.

In fact, during Haydn's life, gender was in fact very much "under construction" – significantly more so than in the early decades of the nineteenth century, by which time the norms around, and agency of, musical women had in many ways narrowed. Eighteenth-century ENLIGHTENMENT egalitarianism promoted the twin ideas that the ability to reason was a universal human attribute independent of class, and at the same time, the only criterion for participation in the public sphere. The motivation to circumscribe gender was a by-product of this logic, for if both claims were true, then the public sphere could be open to women. As a result, science and medicine were gradually marshalled to describe "essential" gender differences locatable in the female body. These efforts were widely discussed and therefore available as the terms through which depictions of women and femininity in music (for example in songs about bodies, death, or TIME) would have likely been understood by performers and listeners – and commented on through choices in performance (Day-O'Connell 2009a). It is above all thanks to Head's landmark collection of essays *Sovereign Feminine* (2013) that we can appreciate the breadth of what femininity signified during Haydn's lifetime. Through a deep dive into an array of primary sources, he shows how the feminine could operate as a positive AESTHETIC signifier: natural and uncorrupted, cultivating sympathy, civilizing, and inspiring (see GENIUS; EMPFINDSAMKEIT; BEAUTY), for example in the preface to the published NACHLASS of Charlotte (Minna) Brandes, which Haydn owned. This is not to deny or lose track of the fact that idealization has to do, after all, with what is ideal, not real. Feminine idealization has often functioned as a replacement or substitution for real-world, everyday rights and opportunities. But Head shows that ideal and real overlapped – the symbolic was reflected in actual practice: "in this period the very means of containing female authorship also facilitated it and made it meaningful" (2013, 122).

Beghin uses a "performance-anchored paradigm" to explore Haydn's keyboard music for female DEDICATEES. "I found myself more interested in playing Haydn *her* way than in playing him *his* way," he writes, which leads to a "quest ... to learn as much as possible about the personalities of my female counterparts" (xxviii) as well as a case-by-case consideration of who the performing and/or listening personae of the pieces might be. For example, playing the sonatas dedicated to the talented Marie Esterházy, one can become the student of Haydn-the-teacher who is striving to strike a balance: "to teach, but not to lecture; to demonstrate, rather than to explain; to befriend, not to paternalize" (159). Haydn, then, is "a composer who actively communicates with his dedicatee, who is a wonderful and patient mentor, and who through his music remains in touch with etiquette and life." Exhilaratingly engaged at every juncture, Haydn is "in touch" with the very lives of his DEDICATEES and his interaction with them. Beghin is up-front about the paradox this presents: his performance-anchored paradigm reveals the performer–dedicatee interaction as the "essence" of Haydn's musicking, but this in turn makes (or reduces?) present-day performance into an act of making "adjustments" – to suit the needs of the recording studio, say, or the concert stage, or the performer's other considerations, "including self-promotion" (128). Or, perhaps it is the engagement itself, the deep and multifaceted engagement with biography, with instruments, with acoustics, etc., that is the present-day performance? Performativity, after all, is a key concept of gender studies, and it is similarly paradoxical: the idea that gender is at once a choice and an assignment, fluid yet culturally entrenched and reinforced. It is no wonder that music and gender work – perform – hand in hand.

And if that is true, then of course any repertory, including "traditional repertory," is ripe for consideration through the lens of gender. On that count, Haydn scholarship (especially compared to Mozart and Beethoven scholarship) has much work to do. Dietrich and Mikusi (2009) both consider gender construction in (or through) *The Creation*; Head (2012) does the same for Haydn's "seraglio opera" *L'incontro improvviso*, as does Will (indirectly) for the *Stabat mater* and Lowe for Symphony No. 88 in G major. Future study will draw on a rapidly evolving, intersectional and inclusive toolbox, responding to and applying more (for example, non-binary) understandings of gender and sexuality. Hopefully, we will also remember that the result of applying the toolbox of gender studies is social change and activism. As we continue to strive to dismantle or reconfigure the toolbox of implicit masculinity in our Haydn scholarship and performance, we also interrogate and challenge the present, everyday norms about men, women, power, and privacy that characterize the institutions in which we do our work.

SARAH DAY-O'CONNELL

FURTHER READING

Beghin (2015a); Brown (2002); Day-O'Connell (2009a, 2009b, 2012); Dietrich (2008); Fortino (1997); Fuchs (2009); Godt (2010); Head (1995, 1999, 2012, 2013); Le Guin (2007); Leppert (1993); Lowe (2007); Mikusi (2009, 2010); Morrow (1997); Randel (1992); Wheelock (1999); Will (2004).

Genius Every age has recognized exceptional creative ability among artists, but each age recognizes this talent in its own way. These culturally specific notions of talent go hand in hand with practices, aims, and ideals, such that the notion of exceptional ability can be seen as a key – a key not only to our contemporary understanding of the past, but also a key that locked into place configurations of approaches to musical production and reception. Thus, by understanding how contemporaries singled out Haydn and other musicians of his time, we understand better what guided Haydn in his compositions and what guided his listeners and critics in their RECEPTION. At the height of his career, Haydn was celebrated as a genius, a term of ancient if unstable pedigree that resonated strongly in eighteenth-century English and German circles. After his death, Haydn's ability ensured his canonization as a classic, but shifts in the ideal and culture of genius also led to his partial marginalization. Central in distinguishing genius from other contemporaneous notions of ability were ideals of novelty and originality, as well as moods and behavioral types such as MELANCHOLY and the characteristic effects of the SUBLIME. Prejudices about class, masculinity (GENDER), and race were seldom far from the surface. Thereby the genius distinguished himself from other eighteenth-century types of musicians of aptitude, such as the learned musician (with consummate mastery over a range of styles and genres) or the virtuoso (endowed either with great moral character or with great technical ability).

It is possible to illustrate these different conceptions of ability by comparing Haydn with some of his contemporaries. Both family members and professional musicians recognized Haydn's talents early in his life. His father's cousin-by-marriage, Johann Mathias Franck, took him into his house and instructed him in the rudiments of music. The Kapellmeister at St. Stephen in VIENNA, Georg Reutter, was attracted to his "thin but pleasant voice" and admitted the young boy to the choir school at the Cathedral of St. Stephen in Vienna. Ability as a performer as well as facility and speed in various simple musical tasks recommended Haydn to those around him, but these capacities were hardly enough to qualify a person as a genius according to the terms of the time. One sees comparable early success amongst a range of musicians that neither contemporaries nor later generations thought fit to crown as genius. As did many other young boys of the day, Johann Georg Albrechtsberger (1736–1809) had both early success as a boy soprano and early training from a leading light of his day, Georg Matthias Monn. Yet Albrechtsberger became known as a learned musician, excelling in instruction and COUNTERPOINT. A generation earlier, Carlo Broschi (1705–82), who achieved fame as a virtuoso performer under the stage name of Farinelli, trained as a child in composition as well as performance. Women such as Charlotte "Minna" Brandes (1765–88) and Corona Schröter were exalted for the beauty, grace, and dignity of their music, as well as their roles as muses to male artists, but (as Head explains) such celebration closed to them the strong authorship associated with genius. Such were some of the alternative paths to the variety of practices that moulded talent along the road to success and renown. Genius was linked to composition more than pedagogy or performance, to masculinity rather than femininity, and, increasingly, to a bourgeois public sphere rather than aristocratic or domestic spaces.

To examine Haydn's self-image is to take a first step towards understanding his version of creativity, though it is difficult to know exactly how Haydn perceived his own creativity at different points of his career. Both CATALOGUES of his library and many of his attested statements date from the early nineteenth century, after trips to LONDON and international fame had perhaps shaped his self-image along lines amenable to the cultural climate of the time. Nonetheless, the late conversations with Griesinger and other friends are essential indications of Haydn's values. Often cited is Haydn's comment to Griesinger on his development in the relative isolation of ESZTERHÁZA: "My Prince was satisfied with all of my works; I received applause. As head of an orchestra, I could make experiments, observe what created an impression and what weakened it, and thus improve, add, make cuts, take risks. I was isolated from the world; no one in my vicinity could make me lose my way or harass me, and so I had to become original" (24–25).

Originality and novelty distinguished the creative type of the genius from that of the learned musician, who was esteemed for his mastery of time-honored tradition. But the same qualities also joined together the genius and the virtuoso. Where the originality of the former was linked to strong notions of authorship, self, and eventually subjectivity, the latter was associated with consummate control over the process of communication. Eventually, the two would be associated with composition and performance respectively, but at a time in which musicians cultivated both skills and in which composition was conceived as a communicative act, the two types easily cohabited. Haydn's statement points in both directions: his awareness of "impression" shows his social orientation, even as his grouchy wariness of outside influence betrays melancholy inwardness.

Even within composition, primary markers of genius such as originality and novelty could be displayed in different ways. In his conversations with Griesinger, Haydn expressed aversion to textbook rules alongside respect for the musical laws of HARMONY, belief in the primacy of inspiration but also awareness of the need that initial inspirations needed to be corrected and worked out (see COMPOSITIONAL PROCESS; IMPROVISATION). Griesinger pulled in Immanuel Kant as an authority on genius; the philosopher had attained unparalleled prestige by the beginning of the nineteenth century (113). As Harrison points out, Kant's analysis of genius in the *Critique of Judgment* (1791) did nicely synthesize beliefs shared by many eighteenth-century artists, in particular the need for a balance between spontaneous inspiration and critical acumen, review, and selection.

Yet originality and novelty were not just a matter of critical control of spontaneous inspiration for Haydn's contemporaries. In celebrating Haydn, less philosophically inclined commentators often highlighted important issues of musical production and dissemination through their comparisons of Haydn to men celebrated as geniuses in the eighteenth century, especially William Shakespeare, Laurence Sterne, and Isaac Newton. Sisman (in *HWorld*) and Chapin describe how the comparison with Shakespeare emphasized the opposition to overly normative versions of neo-classical poetics, that is to the application of rules without consideration of effect. Bonds, Wheelock, and Finscher suggest that the comparison with Sterne stressed ironic play with convention rather than its direct suppression, as well as wit (Humor) and combinatorial play with Musical Materials, rather than subjective immediacy and the birth of original melodies. Newton served to emphasize Haydn's immense prestige, his role in solidifying new norms of style and genre, and his status as a model for other musicians. Comparisons with other artists abounded; Tolley indicates how they could be used to articulate and encourage close attention to these and other aspects of Haydn's creative art.

The notion of genius locked into place practices of the Market no less than those of composition and reception. The concept could spur concert attendance, ticket sales, and orders of sheet music, as well as ward off competitors. This was entirely characteristic of a time in which the absence of copyright laws and other author protections made it necessary for artists to develop strong arguments to protect their rights, a history explored by Woodmansee.

Genius did not need to imply novelty and originality, however. In antiquity, the "genius" simply indicated the respective daemon or protective spirit that accompanied individuals on their life journeys. Later, the term could refer to the particular character of an artist's creative gift. Writing for the *Oracle* about Salomon's concert February 10, 1794, a reviewer wrote that silence was the only appropriate praise of Haydn's greatness, only then to comment briefly, "VIOTTI gave a Concerto, *simple* and *affecting*, like his genius" (Landon III 234). Understood thus, the ascription of genius specified an approach to music as much as it did abstract ability.

While these usages still echoed in the eighteenth century, as the century progressed force, unruliness, and subjective autonomy increasingly dominated the semantic field of genius. Haydn was celebrated in these terms, especially in London, but the terms do unequal justice to Haydn's creative output. They favored symphonies, in particular first movements, as the expansive Orchestrations, complex textures, sharp dynamic contrasts, and surprising twists and turns linked nicely with contemporaneous understandings of the sublime. In addition, the absence of texts encouraged commentators to luxuriate in imaginations of free creativity. Haydn himself valued his late mass compositions as his finest works, a judgment that shows his sensitivity to contemporaneous hierarchies of genre but also that throws a strong light on his own understanding of his creative powers. While the late masses exhibit the same formal unruliness and wealth of contrasts as the symphonies, they suggest a composer in dialogue with tradition rather than standing above it. The creative individual stands as part of divine creation, rather than as a god controlling an autonomous world of tones.

This same tendency to associate genius with power, unruliness, and subjective autonomy eventually led to Haydn's marginalization within the classical canon. E. T. A. Hoffmann's influential review (1810) of Beethoven's Fifth Symphony, subsequently integrated into the literary *Kreisleriana* essays of the *Fantasiestücke in Callots Manier* (1814), staged a gradual entry into the world of tones. Hoffmann celebrates Haydn for his "childlike optimism" and portrays the symphonies as leading "through endless, green forest-glades, through a motley throng of happy people." Mozart "leads us deep into the realm of spirits," while "Beethoven's instrumental music unveils before us the realm of the mighty and the immeasurable" (237–38). Haydn is one of Hoffmann's chosen few, no doubt, but Haydn's marriage of individual talent with social collectivity would wait for a later century to regain full appreciation.

KEITH CHAPIN

FURTHER READING
Bonds (1991a); Chapin (2008); Finscher (2000); Griesinger (1810); Harrison (2009); Head (2013); Hoffmann (1989); HWorld; Landon III; Tolley (2001); Wheelock (1992); Woodmansee (1994).

Harmony The eighteenth-century use of the term "harmony" can easily be misunderstood today because it inevitably carries the connotations and denotations of modern music theory, with its distinct sub-disciplines. But in an eighteenth-century context, it should in fact be understood as largely synonymous with the term thoroughbass. Diergarten has shown how Haydn learned his compositional craft as practical *accompagnateur* and *répétiteur* in the Italian *partimento* tradition (see COMPOSITIONAL PROCESS). Building on the following quotation from Carpani's early biography, Diergarten demonstrates that even modulation, the centerpiece of modern harmony instruction, was an integral part of practical thoroughbass instruction in Haydn's time: the composer learned from Porpora the "true Italian style of singing, and the art of accompanying on the harpsichord, an exercise much more delicate than is commonly supposed ... He frequently had to accompany Porpora's difficult compositions, full of learned modulations and basses difficult to work out ... He laid the foundations for the theory of modulation and chords there" (57; see also EDUCATION).

Beethoven famously stated that "religion and thoroughbass are self-contained objectives and should not be further discussed" (Schindler, 430). The "self-containment" of thoroughbass to which Beethoven refers is its function as a foundation within the (scientific) system of musical composition (*Compositionswissenschaft*). Gustav Nottebohm later stressed that, in Haydn's time, thoroughbass had a twofold meaning: "1) the epitome of the rules for the (practical) accompaniment of a figured bass; 2) as systematic teaching of the inner structure and the combination of intervals and chords (harmonies) with or without regard to practical accompaniment" (5). Haydn owned a copy of Heinichen's *Der General-Bass in der Composition*, which assumes a distinction between "accompanist" and "composer": both musical professions are understood to be based on a foundation in thoroughbass instruction, although with different objectives and orientations. Heinichen's distinction became commonplace in the eighteenth century. Johann Friedrich Daube's *Der Generalbass in drei Accorden*, also in Haydn's possession, makes a clear distinction between the "practice" and the "theory" of thoroughbass (VII). Johann Georg Sulzer even speaks of the "science (Wissenschaft) of thoroughbass" (456): the boundaries between practice and theory might be fluent, but nevertheless their reciprocal relation is subjugated to a strict hierarchy – "without a complete knowledge of harmony it is impossible to perform a thoroughbass in the correct way" (456). Daube defines the relation between the theory and the practice of thoroughbass as follows:

Besides the practical execution [thoroughbass playing] includes a theoretical knowledge about the facts 1) where most of the chords stem from, 2) where they can be directed to, 3) how to conclude from the first chord to the following ones ... An accompanist should understand the practice but also the theory of thoroughbass because only then will he be able to understand how the rules of composition are directly derived from it ... A good composer might lack the practice of thoroughbass, but he must always be in complete command of its theory. Mastering both is always the best. The complete knowledge of the thoroughbass will always remain the fundament on which the melodic edifice can be erected (VIII).

Although thoroughbass was not a "basic harmonic shortcut" (*rudimentäre Akkordschrift*) at this time (see Dahlhaus 125), its teaching included a theory of harmonic progression. This theory was dominated by two competing concepts: the "natural progression of the scales (*Tonarten*)" (Daube XIII), the so-called "rule of the octave," and the (German–northern Italian) principle of the *Grundbass* or fundamental bass (see Holtmeier 2017). It is one of the characteristics of thoroughbass instruction (not only) in German-speaking countries of the eighteenth and early nineteenth centuries that both concepts exist side by side and mutually enrich each other. The thoroughbass treatises of this period differ from each other in the way they weigh the relation between *Grundbass* (or inversional thinking) and the rule of the octave. Both concepts find their definitive form around the same time, at the beginning of the eighteenth century. They originate from different musical repertoires and genres and they imply different theoretical contexts. For the rule of the octave the scale is the primordial principle of tonality, whereas for the fundamental bass tradition it is the concept of inversion and of chord generation based on the stacking up of thirds. The scale step is the archetypal harmonic progression for the rule of the octave, while for the fundamental bass it is the leap of fifths and thirds. One could go as far as to speak of "scale-tonality" and "chord-tonality."

Haydn's concept of harmony was fundamentally shaped by this symbiotic juxtaposition of the Italian *partimento* tradition and fundamental-bass thinking, stemming from the German–northern Italian *Trias-harmonica* tradition (see Holtmeier 2017). Although Haydn owned some of the central treatises of the Grundbass tradition in his library (such as Friedrich Wilhelm Marpurg's *Handbuch bey dem Generalbass und der Composition*, popularized by Georg Andreas Sorge's groundbreaking formulation of the Grundbass teaching), inversional thinking – associated with the concept of "extensive" harmonic prolongation – plays a lesser role in his works than in those of Mozart and Beethoven.

The "schema" (see Heinichen) of the rule of the octave dominated the understanding of harmonic progression in the eighteenth and early nineteenth centuries (see Holtmeier 2007). Heinichen shows in the second part of his monumental treatise that the rule of the octave is the basic principle of modern harmony by which any harmonic progression could be explained. David Kellner's successful popularization of Heinichen's concept (1743) emphasizes and reinforces the significance of the rule of the octave.

The fundamental principle of the rule of the octave is stepwise motion, where distinct chords are assigned to each scale degree. The distinction between ascending and descending harmonic functions is crucial to the understanding of the rule of the octave. Its basic form is driven by the old principle of harmonic progression with an interchange between perfect and imperfect consonances. Perfect triads are assigned to the first, fifth and – under certain circumstances – also to the fourth scale degree, and imperfect sixth chords or their harmonic enhancements (6–5 chords etc.) to the remaining, mediating scale degrees. Thus, with the help of the rule of the octave, any arbitrary bass voice could be harmonized after determining the specific scalar context in which the bass voice was located. As Budday argues, the basic form of the rule of the octave can be progressively extended like a modular system (176–77). Haydn's harmonic language mainly moves within the limits of a traditional thoroughbass harmony and its common schemata. A small practical treatise like Kellner's *Treulicher Unterricht im General-Bass*, which was also in Haydn's library, may inform Haydn's "linear" concept of harmony.

It is difficult to speak of an inner dynamic or development of Haydn's harmonic language. The baroque-galant thoroughbass idiom, with its dominance of cadential and sequential schemata, is most prevalent. The stylistic development in the second half of the century resulted in an integration of a more extensive "classical" harmonic architecture, with its dominance of cadential schemata. Later works employ an enlarged modulatory radius as exhibited in the Sonata in E♭ major, Hob.XVI:52 or the Keyboard Trio in F♯ minor, Hob.XV:26. But these expanded gestures never completely cover the underlying thoroughbass structure. A special kind of harmonic style shapes Haydn's late oratorios, testifying to the same "tendency towards pomposity and harmonic monumentality" that Theodor W. Adorno found in Beethoven's *Missa solemnis* (149). With their slower harmonic rhythm, extensive prolongation, and straightforward cadences, these works represent a distinct harmonic idiom within Haydn's oeuvre.

LUDWIG HOLTMEIER

FURTHER READING
Adorno (1982 [1959]); Budday (2002); Christensen (1992); Dahlhaus (1967); Daube (1756); Diergarten (2011); Heinichen (1728); Holtmeier (2007, 2017); Kellner (1743); Marpurg (1755a); Nottebohm (1873); Schindler (1988 [1860]); Sulzer (1771/74).

Humor Commentators on Haydn's personality and his musical style have frequently focused on humor and wit. Works cited that support the image of jolly "Papa Haydn" include, classically, the String Quartet Op. 33, No. 2 ("Joke"), and his Symphony No. 103 ("Drumroll"), both of which excite mirth with their unexpectedly abrupt pauses and shocking shifts in music material. Wheelock and Mastic acknowledge bold, but carefully calculated, departures from audiences' expectations as a central aspect of Haydn's musical wit. Historically, this aspect of Haydn's musical persona has been underscored and at times overemphasized. An early writer, Frederik Samuel Silverstolpe, set the tone for later accounts of Haydn's own personality by finding him to be alternately earnest or jovial. In the nineteenth century, the jovial aspect of his personality, and by extension his music, was underscored at the expense of other, more serious or deeply felt humors. In 1814, for example, Stendhal (Marie-Henri Beyle) found

Haydn to be incapable of MELANCHOLY in his music, on account of his supposedly uniformly jolly personality and supposed lack of experience with the deeper, more troubled emotions in his own life. Botstein argues that the traditional image of Haydn's personality, that of pious, good-humored "Papa Haydn," proved particularly tenacious, whereas as the RECEPTION of Mozart, Beethoven, and their music underwent radical changes during the nineteenth century.

In Haydn's day, writers clearly pointed to and praised a serious side to his music. The north German critic Carl Ludwig Junker thought that this was to be found especially in his Adagios: "Does someone wish to refer to Hayden's adagio? Good, because it is serious, interest-engaging humor [Laune]; like the tragic sentiments of a Schakespear" (Sisman 22). Michaelis commented in a similar vein:

> Humorous music is either witty and of a jovial, pleasing character, or else it is on the whole more serious, bearing the traces of a wayward humor in which the impressions conflict strangely with each other and in which the imagination cannot quite enjoy free play. One rarely encounters these categories in their pure form ... [In the capriccio], the composer seems to be too dependent on his immediate mood and upon ideas that are generated by it to have in mind an audience or to attempt to entertain it and engage its sympathy by means of comprehensible ideas. He seems rather to be impelled by an inner urge to lay bare his immediate soul and to express the strange succession and transformation of emotions and ideas to which he is subject ... the capriccio tends towards the sublime (725).

Michaelis championed Haydn as the leading modern composer in the field of musical humor: "There is ... a considerable element of "humour" in modern music, especially since Joseph Haydn, the greatest master in this genre, set a pattern, particularly in his highly original symphonies and quartets" (Le Huray and Day, 205). He made it clear, too, that the humor he found characteristic of modern music (in which he obviously includes Haydn's works) is equally of the serious, high comic sort, as of the jesting, low comic variety, and that these two states of humor are rarely found unmixed. The former variety of works do not straightforwardly engage these listener's affections through a "free play" of their imaginations, as is the case in Michaelis's definition of musical BEAUTY. He associates this serious brand of musical humor with the SUBLIME, and finds it to be epitomized in the capriccio or free fantasia. One thinks of works like the C minor Capriccio in Haydn's String Quartet Op. 20, No. 2 (second movement), in which arioso, recitative, dramatic unisons, and beautiful song follow one from the other. Works such as this engage the audience's sympathy obliquely, through a surprising and striking sequence of "vocal" transformations. The listener might indeed seem to gain from this an insight into the succession and transformation of emotions of the compositional persona.

Regarding the low comic, Bonds argues that "wit" signifies intelligence as well as humor in Haydn's music, and contemporaries found that his musical wit was often admixed with irony. Writing in 1802, Johann Karl Friedrich Triest observed: "Haydn might perhaps be compared, in respect to the fruitfulness of his imagination, with our Jean Paul [Richter] (omitting, obviously, the latter's chaotic design; transparent representation is not the least of Haydn's virtues); or, in respect to his humor and original wit (*Laune*), with Lor. Sterne" (Triest 1801, trans. Gillespie 1997, 373). Bonds further notes that contemporaries recognized the writings of Laurence Sterne, in particular, as touchstones of irony. In likening Haydn to Jean Paul, Triest recognized a new kind of irony in Haydn's instrumental music, which had little to do with the affectionate sociability that Sterne had established with knowing readers of his novels. Rather, this irony could operate at the level of the musical work itself, turning an entire musical argument on its head. Whether one heard this kind of irony in Haydn's music depended on one's aesthetic stance and mode of listening. The extravagant "performance" of closure, involving registral extremes and repeated cadential gestures in Haydn's String Quartet in C major, Op. 54, No. 2, might on the one hand be heard to call to question the whole idea of resolving a musical argument. Chua makes such claims in connection with Haydn's Romanticism and SELF-REFLEXIVITY. On the other hand, this kind of artifice can be understood as manipulation of a language of conventions – both sonic and visual. Where this language is shared by audience members, it can contribute to the wit and SOCIABILITY of the quartet, creating an aura of intimacy, of experience shared by knowing listeners and performers.

NANCY NOVEMBER

FURTHER READING
Bonds (1991a); Botstein (1998); Burnham (2005); Chua (1998); Le Huray and Day (1981); Mastic (2015); Michaelis (1807); November (2007); Russell (1985); Sisman (1997a); Stendhal (1814); Triest (1997 [1801]); Wheelock (1992).

I

Iconography Not unexpectedly, portraits of Haydn reflect the contexts of his employment, professional activity, and social standing during the various stages of his career. Interest in portraits of Haydn during his lifetime was considerable, a measure not only of his success as a composer but also of the late eighteenth-century craze for portrait-print collecting. The creation and subsequent consumption of portraits was motivated by a range of factors, including their role in presenting one's self to the public, their value for self-improvement through the study of notable physiognomies, and an urge to collect portraits as part of emerging celebrity culture. Haydn himself was a keen collector of portrait prints especially, with his own collection numbering over sixty, including several Music Professionals (see also Material Culture).

The representation by artists of Haydn's physical appearance, and his actual appearance in person, is important because of the weight given to Lavatarian physiognomy. As inner qualities were reflected in outward appearance, facial features provided a "window to the soul." While Haydn's physiognomy was widely considered less than attractive, it was not – as intimated by Dies – in its fundamental form but rather in its surface qualities. Given that the role of portraitists was to underscore their sitter's true physiognomy, portraits of Haydn that see past any blemishes should not necessarily be dismissed as merely flattering.

The provenance and even authenticity of several Haydn portraits is surprisingly problematic, even given Somfai's attempt to list a complete iconography of twenty-six "verified" portraits. Detailed knowledge of the context of production is crucial for understanding Haydn's connections to artists, engravers, Publishers, and patrons, so uncertainty here presents an ongoing challenge to research. Difficulties arise immediately with the widely accepted earliest portrait: an oil attributed to the Eszterházy Court painter J. B. Grundmann, dated from early 1760s by Robbins Landon or late 1760s by Somfai. The painting appears to have been destroyed in 1945 with only a black and white photograph extant, showing a young man resplendent in court uniform. There is no direct evidence of the portrait being of Haydn, with the circumstantial evidence at best weak.

We are on firmer ground with the portrait (in two versions) by Ludwig Guttenbrunn, another painter at Eszterháza, from 1770–72. It shows Haydn composing at the keyboard, quill hand raised, eyes looking into the distance as if in mid-thought. The engraving by Luigi Schiavonetti, published in 1792 in London, is based on a later and more visually complex version of the painting.

The most influential likeness through the 1780s was the print by Johann Ernst Mansfeld for Artaria, published in 1781. Even before his triumphant visits to LONDON in the 1790s, Haydn's likeness was well-known via the engraving after Mansfeld by J. Newton, published by J. Sewell in 1784. (The engraving accompanied the biography published in *The European Magazine and London Review* for October 1784.) Replete in its symbolism, the print shows Haydn's likeness within a roundel, surrounded by multiple references to antiquity, and including musical instruments and scores. This rich iconography was in fact typical of Artaria's portraits from the time, as seen in similarly styled prints of the musicians Anna Morichelli and Adalbert Gyrowetz. Haydn's CORRESPONDENCE with Artaria suggests he was happy with the portrait, and also indicates that he provided an oil painting on which it was based (the details of which are unknown). The print itself identifies Mansfeld as designer and engraver, with no reference to an original painter or oil portrait.

Haydn's trips to London brought much attention and some important portraits resulted. A print by the famous engraver Francesco Bartolozzi was published by Hannah Humphrey in April 1791, after a miniature by A. M. Ott. Humphrey published many satirical caricatures during the 1780s and 1790s. The significance of Bartolozzi as the engraver is that it would have added much to the desirability of obtaining the print. The painting by Thomas Hardy, commissioned by the music seller John Bland, was hung at the Royal Academy Exhibition in 1792, notably along with that of the impresario Johann Peter Salomon. The portrait was part of a series of oils and subsequent prints of leading musical figures in London including Salomon, W. Cramer, I. Pleyel, and M. Clementi. The stipple engraving of the portrait (also by Hardy and published by Bland) was widely distributed and formed the basis of further prints. (See also BIOGRAPHY.) John Hoppner's unfinished oil portrait (on the back of the dustjacket for this book) was the result of a commission from the Prince of Wales, and as a consequence is on a larger scale than other oils. Holding a quill, the portrait is otherwise quite unlike the Guttenbrunn in that Haydn engages with the viewer directly. The fact that the Prince had sought a portrait of Haydn by one of his favorite painters was news in itself, and caught the attention of the press at the time. A profile drawing (plus a study) by the Royal Academician George Dance stands out for its veracity in showing Haydn with a protruding lower lip and open mouth, and yet according to Schlesinger Haydn approved of it. Again, seen in context, the portrait was one of hundreds by Dance of notable sitters in the intellectual and social world of his time, later widely available as a print engraved by William Daniel.

In summarizing this rather disparate iconography, we could say that portraits of Haydn presented him as a professional, creative, successful ENLIGHTENMENT man of social standing. Given the status of music as a profession, this is no mean achievement. Apart from gaining better understanding of the portraits created in his own lifetime, there remains the intriguing question of how the iconography of Haydn after his death aligns with shifts in his posthumous fate, with reiterations of his images contributing to or contradicting the trajectory of his overall RECEPTION from GENIUS of originality to scene-setter for Mozart and Beethoven.　　　　　　　　　　ALAN DAVISON

FURTHER READING
Davison (2009); Muller (1932); Somfai (1969); Tolley (2001, 2003).

Idealism German Idealism is a philosophical movement grounded in the writings of Immanuel Kant and first extensively promulgated by a group of intellectuals at Weimar and the nearby University in Jena toward the end of the eighteenth century and the beginning of the nineteenth, overlapping the period of Haydn's greatest fame and international success. Among early adherents at Weimar/Jena were the philosophers Johann Gottlieb Herder, who had studied with Kant; Karl Leonhard Reinhold, whose elucidations of Kant brought the philosophy into the mainstream; Johann Gottlieb Fichte, whose work further intensified German Idealism's already intense subjectivity; Friedrich Wilhelm Joseph Schelling, who elaborated an "Aesthetic Idealism"; and Georg Wilhelm Friedrich Hegel, credited with achieving a dialectical synthesis between subject and object. But notwithstanding Schelling's alliance of German Idealism with AESTHETICS, that wing of German Idealism was dominated by a group of Romantic POET/writers working at Weimar/Jena, including Johann Wolfgang von Goethe, Friedrich Schiller, Jean Paul Richter, the brothers August Wilhelm and Friedrich von Schlegel, Friedrich Hölderlin, Wilhelm Heinrich Wackenroder, and the latter's close friend Johann Ludwig Tieck. While the full complexities of German Idealism and its development are not specifically relevant here, key aspects of the philosophy had a profound influence on the development of music, especially through the doctrine of "Absolute music" (see Bonds) and evolving concert and critical traditions (see Pederson), most immediately in the German lands but eventually affecting virtually all European-derived concert and opera music. In particular, it is German Idealism's enduring sway over what we now call "classical music" that has relegated Haydn to a respected but secondary status among history's most esteemed composers (see Botstein; Garratt; Proksch; see also RECEPTION).

In general terms, German Idealism places its primary emphasis on the subjective self, aligning the philosophy with some aspects of Protestantism and making it enormously appealing to the Romantic poets who took it up. Like Protestantism, Idealism identified something all-encompassing that was both present in the self and exterior to it, something toward which the self strove to merge, bypassing the real (phenomenal) world and making it of secondary importance. Whereas for Protestants this larger something was understood as God, German Idealists at different stages identified a variety of other noumenal realms, whether a kind of collective identity (nation, Kultur, or Fichte's "collective consciousness"), or something understood to be beyond the human as such (the absolute, infinity, or, slightly later, Schopenhauer's universal Will). Music's indefiniteness and its appeal to the emotions made it suspect from an German Idealist perspective until quite late in the eighteenth century, when the growing belief that music's removal from phenomenal reality could make it serve as a conduit to the noumenal allowed music to flip from being considered the lowest of the arts to being considered the most

Romantic and therefore the highest art, potentially more capable than any other art of assisting the self in its quest for the absolute. Herder, who had (with others) earlier ranked music below the literary arts, in *Kalligone* (1800) became the first important figure to express this sentiment in direct terms, although he was influenced by recent writings by Schiller, Christian Gottfried Körner (a jurist, amateur musician, and friend of Schiller's), Wackenroder, Schlegel, and Tieck.

The belief that music was the highest of the arts was of course highly seductive to composers, performers, music critics, and all others who cared deeply about music, but its elevation came with conditions. If music were to make good on its heady but still speculative promotion, new paradigms had to be enforced across the board: composers had to compose in a new way, performances had to reflect serious, even reverent attitudes, and repertory and histories had to be reconsidered according to the new (and still evolving) paradigms. In a word, serious music had to be *cultivated* (see Gramit). The latter project was particularly pressing, at first, in the German lands, where music's elevation interacted with nascent NATIONALIST sentiments that understood Germans to have a special affinity for serious music. If Beethoven was the first composer to work under the sway of the new paradigms – who, indeed, helped establish those paradigms for his and subsequent generations – the specific Germanness of those paradigms required that they also be grounded in German musical history. (The Bach Revival was one of the cornerstones of that project.) But Beethoven's music, though considered revolutionary, was also obviously much indebted to his immediate predecessors, in particular to Mozart and Haydn, the latter (ostensibly) his teacher. Yet neither Mozart nor Haydn fit the new paradigms particularly well. Early advocates for a German music more congenial to Idealism considered Mozart's music too ornate, too eager to gratify (thus, Joseph's II's probably apocryphal pronouncement that Mozart's *Die Entführung aus dem Serail* had "too many notes"). And Haydn's music, though readily entertaining and written with consumate skill, lacked "GENIUS," newly understood in German Idealist terms.

Thus, already in 1792, Count Waldstein wrote in his famous inscription to Beethoven that "the Genius of Mozart . . . has found a refuge but no occupation with the inexhaustible Haydn. Through him she wishes to form a union with another. With the help of assiduous labor you shall receive: *Mozart's spirit from Haydn's hands.*" Two decades later, in 1813, E. T. A. Hoffmann would articulate the heirarchies among these composers in similar terms, if more explicitly based in German Idealist aesthetic paradigms:

> [Instrumental music] is the most romantic of all the arts, one might almost say the only really romantic art, for its sole object is the expression of the infinite. . . . Music discloses to man an unknown kingdom, a world having nothing in common with the external sensual world which surrounds him . . .
>
> Beethoven's instrumental music discloses to us the realm of the tragic and illimitable. . . .
>
> Haydn conceives romantically that which is distinctly human in the life of man; he is, in so far, more comprehensible to the majority.

Mozart grasps more the superhuman, the miraculous, which dwells in the imagination.

Beethoven's music stirs the mists of fear, of horror, of terror, of grief, and awakens that endless longing which is the very essence of romanticism (quoted from Locke and Hoffmann 127–28).

Both Waldstein and Hoffmann were prescient in so closely anticipating how history would judge these three composers, guided by the German Idealist paradigms that have shaped serious music over the past two centuries (within a tradition Weber aptly calls "musical idealism"). Over time, Mozart and many other older composers were reclaimed for the new paradigms (see Knapp). But despite attempts to reclaim Haydn, his music, with its gratifying penchant for entertaining its audiences, was much more resistent, while also resiliently securing secondary status based on his having developed ways to align elements of musical logic with narrative and a sense of musical ontology, which proved extremely useful to Beethoven and later composers. That Haydn's effective demotion was overwhelmingly due to German Idealism may be ascertained by considering two aspects of his career and music: his reception in LONDON during the same historical moment when music was being elevated by Idealist aesthetics (early to mid-1790s), and the ways his music treats topics that may be considered, potentially, within the purview of Musical Idealism.

As Schroeder has demonstrated, the English PRESS understood Haydn in moral terms, in ways compatible with how Shakespeare was then being understood: his symphonies instilled Aristotelian virtues, such as tolerance, first of all by entertaining, and then by using the platform of an engaged audience to elevate his listeners' thoughts and sensibilities. In this way, the English celebrated Haydn's music precisely for attributes that German Idealism would find intractable to their project of reclaiming him for their new paradigms, which project would, time after time, bump up against the fact that Haydn's aims were not only incompatible with Idealist aesthetics, but also often openly antithethical to them.

Thus, for example, Haydn's *Sturm und Drang* period (in the early 1770s) was by that borrowed designation allied with Goethe's youthful Romanticism as parallel expressions of the Zeitgeist (even though Haydn preceded the latter by some years) (see TOPICS). Yet, in his 1785 Symphony No. 85 ("La Reine"), Haydn evokes his *Sturm und Drang* style, not as an expression of subjective *angst*, but as an abstract *object*, an extremity reached through an elaborately worked out thematic process managed and contained by sonata FORM, in which an opening theme of exquisite geniality is transformed, step by step, into a near-quotation of the torment-driven theme that opens his 1772 Symphony No. 45 ("Farewell") (see Webster 1998b).

Thus, for example, Haydn in his oratorio, *The Creation*, sets the initial Act of Creation – one of the most SUBLIME moments available to music – in such a way that we "hear" the stage machinery of creation itself, as the single separate stroke of the pizzicato strings suggests the divine equivalent of striking a match or (for later audiences) throwing a switch (see Kramer 1992; Kramer 2008; Webster 1997). From an Idealist perspective, there are two main ways of understanding the piece's odd profile: either Haydn is not fully up to the challenge of the occasion, or he is deliberately drawing attention to the artifice of his own creation (see SELF-REFLEXIVITY), opting to entertain rather than to allow a more effective evocation of the void to engulf us with its scary sublimity.

Thus, for example, Haydn in the slow movement of his 1791 Symphony No. 93, sets up an elaborate formal and thematic procedure (described in Lowe), within a movement of surpassing loveliness, to highlight, as a moment of release that is both surprising and aesthetically satisfying, a loud, isolated blat by the bassoon, obviously meant to be heard as a fart. While the event itself may be regarded as simply crude, the skill and effectiveness of Haydn's elaboration belie any notion that the joke is incidental to the proto-idealist procedures that set it up (see HUMOR).

Thus, for example, Haydn in the slow movement of his 1794 Symphony No. 100 ("Military"), limns a narrative that closely parallels events of the previous century in which his countrymen – including many blood relatives – were brutalized and butchered by the Turks; Haydn then caps the movement with a dramatic "rescue" strongly redolent of the last-minute Polish intervention that saved VIENNA from the Turks in their seige of 1683 (see Al-Taee; EXOTIC). Despite the seriousness of the evoked historical events and the coarse "Janissary" style that Haydn uses to set the conquering Turks, the movement's overall tone is comic, and the rest of the symphony may be heard as the Turks' rehabilitation, so that all parties celebrate together at symphony's end, when the "Janissary" instruments return (see Knapp).

In these examples, and in the ways that Haydn routinely entertains, establishes modes of SOCIABILITY (for example, in the "conversational" quality of his quartets and other chamber works), engages playfully and intelligibly with the mechanics of music-making, or otherwise may be understood to support human flourishing in the here and now, his music stands well apart from the musical paradigms of German Idealism even as it uses – indeed, in many cases pioneers – the very means by which Beethoven and others pursued a German Idealist musical aesthetic. This combination of exemplary means and disparate ends has, perhaps, predetermined Haydn's historical fate, of remaining always just outside the main tent, too exemplary of musical processes esteemed within the tradition to give up entirely, but too embarrassing in his lapses of religious decorum to allow into the inner sanctum.

RAYMOND KNAPP

FURTHER READING
Al-Taee (2010); Bonds (2014); Botstein (1998); Dahlhaus (1989); Garratt (2005); Gramit (2002); Knapp (2018); Kramer (1992, 2008); Locke and Hoffmann (1917); Lowe (2007); MacIntyre (1984 [1981]); Pederson (1994); Proksch (2015); Schroeder (1990); Weber (2008); Webster (1997, 1998b); Wheelock (1992).

Ideas Haydn and Ideas; Or, The Idea of Haydn This essay addresses an elusive group of entries in the encyclopedia: those that fall under the heading "ideas." This apparently unwieldy category is understood here in a particular way: "ideas" stands for things relevant to Haydn's compositional style – concepts that inform our analytic approaches to and hermeneutic understandings of his music – that are not explicitly musical techniques. These range from the BEAUTIFUL and SUBLIME, to TIME, EXOTICISM, POLITICS, and WAR.

An underlying assumption is that Haydn's music does not simply speak for itself in purely musical terms: our experience of it is mediated by our assumptions – by ideas. It is no surprise then that more than any other section of the encyclopedia, this collection of entries gives us a vivid snapshot of the issues and concerns that are most relevant to Haydn studies in the early twenty-first century. Haydn has long been an ideal composer on which to project the musicological concerns of particular eras. Classical Haydn has given way to (or been joined by) Modern Haydn and occasionally Romantic Haydn. Haydn has entered (and exited) the laboratory of musical experimentation; it seems genial Papa Haydn was also a revolutionary.

Before delving into the entries in this section, it is useful to reflect on the nature of these ideas and on the idea of Haydn. The changeability we note reflects the status of Haydn's biography and our access – or lack thereof – to Haydn the man. We have no robust, agreed-upon understanding of Haydn's interior life. While Mozart scholarship has worked to distance the composer from his colorful biography and the sundry myths that cling to him, Haydn scholarship – precisely because his nineteenth-century RECEPTION did not produce the same kinds of Romantic narratives – has constantly striven to reconstitute the man through the music. We have had, in other words, a hard time resisting reading Mozart's music through his biography while we have struggled to read Haydn's biography through his music. If we approach this from the angle of Foucault's (1994) idea of the "author function," we might say that Haydn has been a proper noun, circulating at a distance in the medium of print, and subject to a range of investments and fantasies, many authorizing themselves as true to Haydn himself. For these reasons, our introduction does not seek to capture and endorse a current consensus about Haydn. Rather, we reflect on the scholarly desires that shape the entries, highlight their particular relationship with the complex idea of "Haydn," and invite readers to challenge orthodoxies and generalizations past and present.

While imposing no unity on the entries, we nonetheless note some common motifs and provide the reader with a context for these in recent scholarly trends. Anglophone scholars today, though not only that subset, tend to resist the modernist idea of Haydn's music as disembodied, playfully self-referential, and devoid of representational elements that was prominent in the early and mid-twentieth century. In a peculiar conjunction, this idea was often elided with another construct – that of "Viennese Classical Style." Indeed, Haydn was credited as the first composer to achieve that uniquely coherent and self-referential idiom, through the reconciliation of seemingly antithetical Baroque and galant styles. In technical terms, this meant the fusion of counterpoint and melody-dominated textures, of periodic phrasing and the spinning out of an opening motif. Towards the end of the twentieth century, however, Anglophone scholarship – reappraising its institutionalized musical values and ways of writing history – sought to free Haydn from so prestigious a yoke. Webster (1991) subjected the idea of Viennese Classical Style to a withering deconstruction, stressing the ways in which the very idea of the Classical served narratives of Romantic progress (or progress towards Romanticism). In place of classicism, Webster instead emphasized Haydn's contemporary reception as a bold pioneer. One might note, however, that the musical values Webster discovered in the "Farewell" Symphony – including CYCLIC INTEGRATION and motivic unity – were to a large extent familiar from the construct he so passionately demolished. His study belongs to a group of seminal works of the 1990s – including Burnham (1995) and Goehr (1992) – that interrogated the foundational ideologies that underpin Western art music. These works share the desire to unmask and reveal the origins of these ideologies, and have largely succeeded in doing so, fundamentally altering the field of musical studies. But, even as they historicized these concepts, these works also reinforced certain musical and philosophical values – be they motivic unity, heroic overcoming, or the work concept.

Change came gradually and is on-going. With specific regard to Viennese Classical Style, Will (2002), drawing on Sisman (1990), has raised the issue of representation in a study of "characteristic symphonies," works whose affiliation with scenes of battle, nature, national or regional dances, and human passions, was signaled by titles and programs. The broader issue of whether the characteristic is a specific category or bleeds out into the symphonic repertory as a whole remains unexplored. The theory of musical TOPICS, inspired by semiotics, could provide a way into that issue. Introduced by Ratner (1980), and recently rationalized by Mirka (2014a), this theory emphasizes the playful cross-referencing of musical styles and genres – a technique that concerned more conservative critics of the period – and is sensitive to the discursive associations of different types of material. Specific constellations of topics may suggest characters, plots, ideas, scenes, and symbols existing beyond the piece itself, or may simply rub shoulders as a sort of meta-musical argument. In either case the pervasive presence of topics and other communicative devices demonstrate that Haydn did not compose "pure" or absolute music.

In her posthumously published monograph, Allanbrook uses the opening of Haydn's Symphony No. 59 in A major to illustrate her anti-Classical theory of comic mimesis in later eighteenth-century music. Highlighting a "theatre of surface [gestures] and stylistic heterogeneity," she observes that "the opening is successively annunciatory, misterioso, purposeful, agitated, urbane, rollicking, valedictory, and all in just over a minute of music ... There is nothing 'Classic' about it" (Allanbrook 2014; 26). Inspired by the fragmentary and mercurial rhetoric of *opera buffa*, such music, she implies, was received as if endowed with a vital energy, a life force. It risked spinning out of control, but was pulled back by the exigencies of the comic muse – the generic requirement for a happy ending, for difficulties to be overcome and comic confusions resolved. A similar, if more highbrow vitalism informs Polzonetti's revelatory study of metamorphic principles in Haydn's music. Through analogy with Ovid's metamorphoses, he translates notions of stylistic mixture, topical play, and motivic development into matters of wonder – a sort of "kinetic" and "metaphoric" beauty (232):

> Ovid reduces all kinds of bodies – men, bats, ants, nymphs, wolves, bears, etc. – to archetypal shapes or qualities, such as long, curved, rough, whole or divided, empty or filled. These shapes or qualities are then susceptible to transformation through the action of simplified

types of motion, such as going away, coming back, melting and reshaping, shrinking, and growing larger or narrower ... Like Ovid, Haydn often builds his thematic material from simple, geometrically composed cells that can be broken apart into smaller segments, keeping their identity intact by preserving either melodic or rhythmic content, or both. The segments can be recombined in different ways, or transformed quite radically, by changes in the direction and pace of the movement, which may become faster or slower, more ascending or descending, stretched or compressed (227–29).

In resisting appropriation of Haydn for a later conception of absolute music, Will, Sisman, Allanbrook, and Polzonetti revitalize our sense of MIMESIS (or representation) – an aesthetic principle of the eighteenth century that musical scholarship has often struggled to take seriously. Mimesis also proves essential to understanding how "expression" operates in Haydn's music. As period aesthetics predict, "feeling" in Haydn's music is not free floating or autonomous, but relational, conjuring experiences *of*, *for* or *about* something either specified in the piece or supplied, imaginatively, by the audience. The name for a feeling of this kind was a passion. As for the "something" to which a passion was directed, this encompassed the entire order of a divinely created universe, thus God, nature, institutions, other people, even oneself. Passions retained something of their earlier danger – that is, they were still clouded with associations of irrationality and immorality – but the idea of eradicating them gave way to projects of recuperation. The passions were accorded moral and epistemological dignity as ways of knowing, understanding and acting virtuously in the world.

Today, Haydn's vocal music sits comfortably in this broad project of what Hirschman has called "the rehabilitation of the passions" (47). As the entries imply, Haydn's passions form affective constellations around the anchors of faith, the rhythms of rural life, princely magnificence, and literary–visual topoi. The latter include such venerable scenes as the ages of "man," the characteristics of the sexes, farewell, absence and return, and the joys and sufferings of love. Deploying characteristic musical styles, or topics in Ratner's sense, affiliated with the sacred, the pastoral, the ceremonial, and the intimately subjective, Haydn's music directs attention, filters perception, and fosters sympathy, conveying a sense of what things feel like and, thus, what they mean. In select instrumental music, this art of sensual knowledge turns mirror-like on the performers and listeners. The ticking of a clock morphs into heartbeats, and an affinity is discovered that links the domains of time and body.

Few argue that the range of things Haydn represents, or the feelings he attaches to them, project a radical subject position. This may help to explain why his muse flourished for whomever was paying, be that a Spanish cathedral, a Hungarian Prince, or a LONDON concert audience. Haydn's music engaged with the political revolutions of the 1780s and 1790s only through commission and appropriation. Didactic and regulative, his masses, oratorios, occasional pieces and secular songs point listeners to approved passions for God, the natural world, institutions, others, and themselves. Judging by the entries in this category, Haydn is celebrated for the vividness, nuance, and persuasive force of his representations of things and of feelings for them, but not for any essential novelty in his approach to expression.

As already mentioned, this emphasis on representation nudges Haydn back into the eighteenth century and the framework of IMITATION AND MIMESIS from which many have sought to liberate him. Conventionally, Haydn is still understood as the father of autonomous instrumental music, a view that is given more vitality, but not fundamentally challenged, when he is described as a "pioneer" and "radical" in the genres of symphony, string quartet, keyboard trio, and solo sonatas. The idea of Haydn as revolutionary provides an attractive corrective to the neutralizing effect of canonic discourses, but can obscure Haydn's relationship with traditions of genre, institutional ritual, and the aesthetic principles of his day. Ultimately, the twin notions of the conservative and the pioneering need to be questioned: what precisely do they mean, and are they in fact oppositional in Haydn's case?

Questions like these invite us to reflect on our values and compare them with those of the past. Sometimes we risk writing-off entire genres of Haydn's music because we lack the ideas – the critical frameworks – through which to appreciate them. His large corpus of baryton works are generally subject to polite but lukewarm reception as works too intimately tied to aristocratic patronage for the comfort of bourgeois historical writing. But looked at in a different way, they belong to a larger trend within his output: throughout his career, Haydn composed for a wide range of unusual or less common INSTRUMENTS, from musical clocks to the baryton to the lira organizzata, to Anton Weidinger's experimental keyed trumpet. While this engagement seemingly belongs more squarely to the issue of compositional technique – that is, questions of instrumentation and ORCHESTRATION – the idea of technological specificity also ties into larger questions of ENLIGHTENMENT aesthetics and mediation. While we have traditionally understood some of the aesthetic shifts in the eighteenth century in terms of imitation and expression, more recent scholarship on the Enlightenment has emphasized the shifting understandings of media and mediation. Indeed, in This is Enlightenment, Siskin and Warner suggest that we might understand the Enlightenment as "an event in the history of mediation" (1). The concept of mediation allows us to connect a wide range of concepts relevant to Haydn's career: it can frame, for example, the importance of print and its CIRCULATION to his international fame. AESTHETICS itself – as the study of sensitive cognition – is also a study of mediation: in its original Baumgartenian sense, it is a study of the mediation between the outside world and our higher orders of cognition. Haydn's works, sensitively written for the particularities of specific instruments can be seen to engage creatively with the question of technological mediation.

Aesthetics also proves fundamental to the entries BEAUTIFUL (by Nancy November), SUBLIME (Keith Chapin), EMPFINDSAMKEIT (Matthew Head) and MIMESIS (Annette Richards) that explore modes of perception for, the expressive character of, and representation in Haydn's music. These summaries invite understanding of Haydn's art as like a convex mirror that captured and framed but also shaped the composer's world – and reflected it back to the audience. According to the then-ruling principle of mimesis, "all art ... [is] an imitation of nature."

The seemingly straightforward maxim proved contentious, however, in arguments about the standpoint from which musical imitations are made, their proper subjects, the appropriate degree of realism, and the morally didactic purpose of music's "reflections." Must musical imitations be human-centered, providing accounts of how things feel, or, taking cue from Baroque practice, can they seek to paint things more objectively, as if unmediated by human subjectivity? Was it hubris to represent the divine act of the creation of the world, or was the realm of musical imitation infinite? When representing objects variously terrifying or irrational, such as the supernatural or states of excessive passion, how could truth to the alterity of the object be reconciled with the decorum required by artistic representation? Did art gain legitimacy, or suffer under an inappropriate burden when it was tasked, didactically, with making human vice feel ugly, and virtue beautiful? Though not specific to Haydn, and so not featuring in the entries themselves, these were the broader debates surrounding the art of music in the German-speaking eighteenth century which readers can begin to explore through, for example, Hosler (1981), Baker and Christensen (1996), and Nedbal (2016).

In the entry AESTHETICS, November begins with the exemplary status of (a notion of) song in Haydn's thinking about music. In line with the music-theoretical writings of his contemporaries (particularly Jean-Jacques Rousseau, Johann Georg Sulzer, Heinrich Christoph Koch and Francesco Galeazzi), Haydn affirmed that a fluent, songful MELODY should provide the thread, and the focus, of both vocal and instrumental compositions. A rather specific, bourgeois sense of the voice underwrites this period maxim, one already present in Johann Mattheson's *Der volkommene Kapellmeister* (1739), a treatise Haydn is known to have studied (Jones 2010). Both Mattheson and Haydn imagined singing as natural, coherent, intelligible, and rich in human presence. Acting as a critical shorthand, Haydn's reference to song alluded not simply to restraint in exploring the artificial resources of instruments, nor to melody-dominated texture alone, but a sense of music as human utterance. In turn, this mimetic standard informed principles of melodic–rhetorical construction, or, in Galeazzi's memorable word from his *Theoretical-Practical Elements of Music* (1796), the "conduct" of the melody (cited from Allanbrook 1998, 86).

November also sets melody center stage in her entry on the aesthetic category of the BEAUTIFUL. For Burke at mid-century, the beautiful turned on qualities of smallness, regularity, delicacy, and "feminine" curves, and was musically embodied in "smoothly undulating melody" (111–12). Half a century later, Michaelis, a disciple of Kant, retained this emphasis on regularity and smoothness affirming in proto-formalist terms that "music's aesthetic quality, as in everything where beauty captivates us, does not . . . have anything to do with what is stated or expressed, but with the order and manner in which ideas are presented" (676). But Michaelis quickly backtracks from this fledgling formalism, invoking gentleness and love as expressive zones of beautiful music, and suggesting a tender, loving mode of apprehension:

> Just as a lover rejoices to hear his beloved speak, bewitched by the sound of her voice and oblivious to what she is saying, so music often enchants us

simply by its very existence, by the union of melody and harmony in a manifold interplay of the most intimate kind which reverberates in our innermost being, whatever the content may be (676).

Though November understandably avoids speculation, it might be concluded that beautiful music is music we fall in love with and it models a condition of intimacy in the way that its elements – such as HARMONY and melody – move together, and move listeners. A human-centered imitation indeed!

The culture of sensibility mapped in Head's entry EMPFINDSAMKEIT sets these somewhat abstract ideas of human presence, beauty, pleasure, and intimacy in ethical and social contexts. Not a musical style but a human disposition, "sensibility" (a cognate of *Empfindsamkeit*), valorized sympathetic feelings for others as morally elevated and as the wellsprings of virtuous action. Informing Haydn's choice and setting of POETRY and LIBRETTI, his RELIGIOUS faith, his personal RELATIONSHIPS, his musical values and technique, and the way he conceived of and told the story of his life (BIOGRAPHY), sensibility is among the most neglected and misunderstood issues in Haydn scholarship. Part of the problem lies in the redundancy that arises when sensibility is mistakenly equated with "expression": isn't all Haydn's music "expressive," we might ask, and therefore doesn't sensibility explain everything and nothing? Nonetheless, music *was* privileged in the culture of sensibility, in part for the perceived immediacy of its affective impact on the nervous (and quasi-musical) fibers of the body, and in part because of the conception of musical passions as feelings "for" something or someone, not just feelings in the abstract (see above).

The sublime stretched the culture of sensibility to its limits. Though sometimes applying to art works themselves, it more often described "emphatic experiences characterized by sudden transport rather than persuasion." Ironically, given the subsequent elision of Beethoven and the sublime – in which context, as Chapin notes, Haydn was relegated to the less heroic realm of the beautiful – Haydn's late oratorios *The Creation* and *The Seasons* were touchstones of sublimity around 1800. The divine mystery of chaos, the creation of light, sunrise, storm, and the extremes of human passion were burnished with a music of superhuman grandeur, baffling complexity or monumental simplicity. Though Chapin rightly emphasizes the divine reference of Haydn's sublime effects, it appears that in such moments as the orchestral blast of C major in *The Creation* for the oft-cited line from Genesis ("Let there be light"), a more worldly and human-centered development was also at stake: the emergence, in Schleuning's memorable phrase, of "a typically bourgeois God–artist ideology" (Schleuning 1984).

This ideology of creative GENIUS had bubbled away from mid-century in composer-centered theories of original genius, imagination and inspiration, HUMOR and MELANCHOLY. Though often operating within the framework of mimesis, these ideas about original creativity challenged and ultimately overturned that framework. They did so by focusing less on acts of musical representation than on exceptional creativity. Linking inner and outer spheres, these theories figured Haydn's music as both self-expressive and as "illuminating" – shining light into the world. Of course, they were not applied to

Haydn exclusively. Nor was the direction of travel one way: Haydn's music was not simply subject to theories of originality but inspired critics to develop them. Though well established in recent literature on Haydn and his period they may still strike readers as surprisingly Romantic.

Genius was a buzzword of the period and did not always allude to truly exceptional talent, sometimes indicating a more modest but innate facility to learn. In the sense explored by Chapin, however, genius was the source of original creativity and was distinguished from other kinds of exceptional musical ability, "such as the learned musician ... or the virtuoso." Though in part recognition of talent, it was also a patriarchal and national ideology, thus rarely applied to women or to "foreigners." Connected to the ideal of personal autonomy, and to the notion of the fine arts as self-governing and free, notions of genius also helped to elevate the status of music, securing its inclusion in a republic of arts and letters. As Chapin puts it, comparison with Shakespeare emphasized Haydn's freedom from rules; comparison with Sterne highlighted Haydn's irony, and comparison with Newton posited Haydn's discovery of "new norms of style and genre."

The theory of inspiration, hypothesizing a state when ideas flow unbidden, put genius into action. As Richards emphasizes for C. P. E. Bach, inspiration was associated with IMPROVISATION and is evoked in the seemingly spontaneous, digressive, and abrupt unfolding of written keyboard fantasias and the neighboring solo genres of sonata and rondo. For Haydn keyboard improvisation was also a way of arriving at ideas. This first step in the COMPOSITIONAL PROCESS involved some notion of self-expression at odds with the modernist construct of Viennese Classical Style. In his famous anecdote about beginning his composing with improvisation at the keyboard (cited in various entries), Haydn indicates that he played "according to whether my mood was sad or happy, serious or playful." This element of self-expression or (so to speak) self-mimesis is subject, however, to complex mediation and is difficult to grasp in all its historical difference. Haydn *seems* to suspend it, in commenting that "once I had seized upon an idea, my entire effort went toward elaborating and sustaining it, according to the rules of art" (Gotwals 61). Yet Haydn's devotees, and many readers of the anecdote, know those rules were also subject to Haydn's agency: he variously upheld, suspended, and invented rules anew. Thus, the initial impression that affective self-expression yields to purely musical technique is complicated by the recognition that this technique is also, in another sense, personal – subjectively colored.

That said, writers from the late eighteenth century to today do not agree on "who is speaking" in Haydn's music. Answers are diverse, seeming to rest less on argument and evidence than writers' intellectual contexts, critical frameworks, and musical values. For Rosen (1971/72), Haydn, the man, is absent in his music; for Webster, "Haydn" is a construct of the music itself, an implied author (2007). Haydn's contemporaries possessed less polarized but also even less consistent views. The idea that Haydn's character was manifest in his music was conveyed through the notion of his humor, a slippery term meaning not simply his wit but his temperament (the balance of his humors). In a play of universality and individualism, Haydn's humor was both something distinctive to him, and *of a type* that could be recognized, categorized, and imitated. Haydn's humor – which he was sometimes felt to share with Shakespeare and with Sterne – coupled the jovial and the serious, wit and melancholy. Michaelis notes this tendency for different emotional states to blend together under the banner of humor. His observation concerns not Haydn specifically but rather the genre of the capriccio:

> [In the capriccio], the composer seems to be too dependent on his immediate mood and upon ideas that are generated by it to have in mind an audience or to attempt to entertain it and engage its sympathy by means of comprehensible ideas. He seems rather to be impelled by an inner urge to lay bare his immediate soul and to express the strange succession and transformation of emotions and ideas to which he is subject ... the capriccio tends towards the sublime (725).

Panning out to Haydn's broader contexts, Andrew Greenwood, Elaine Sisman, and Jen-yen Chen address several large, overarching concepts that functioned as fundamental categories that structured late eighteenth-century life: ENLIGHTENMENT, TIME, NATURE, SCIENCE, AND RELIGION AND SPIRITUAL BELIEFS. Importantly, these are not static ideas that merely framed Haydn's life or his compositional output; rather, the very ideas of time and nature and the basic understandings of science and religion were themselves in flux in this period. Furthermore, as Sisman and Chen show, Haydn's music reflects this flux, whether in the choice of subject or the music's broader function. We might say, in other words, to understand Haydn's life, one ought to wrangle with these basic concepts; but one can also understand these concepts and what they meant in the late Enlightenment through Haydn's music.

To this end, in his entry on ENLIGHTENMENT Greenwood urges us to understand this period not just in terms of "science and reason," but to think more broadly about "how other modes of human expression" – that is, the arts – shaped the Enlightenment. To do so is to move away from thinking of the Enlightenment as a singular concept and instead to embrace "a multiplicity of Enlightenment movements." In place of overarching ideas, Greenwood emphasizes the importance of media and modes of transmission, technology, and institutions, as well as to the many different and distinct strands of the Enlightenment: the Scottish Enlightenment, the Catholic Enlightenment, and the centrality of *Empfindsamkeit*.

To do so alters how we view Haydn's oeuvre, shifting which works we might invoke as exemplary of Enlightenment thought. In place of purely instrumental works and talk of formal procedures – as paragons of reason – one might turn, and Greenwood does, to Haydn's settings of Scottish FOLK SONGS. George Thomson, who commissioned these settings, believed in the power of music to aid the development of culture, pushing it to a more advanced stage; this belief directly reflected Adam Smith's stadial theory. Greenwood likewise places emphasis on those works, especially those from the 1770s, that manifest Haydn's "sensitive style." These include his opera *La vera costanza*, Symphony No. 45 in F♯ minor ("Farewell"), and the second movement of his String Quartet, Op. 20, No. 2. Greenwood argues for Haydn's importance to understanding the Enlightenment, not just for musicologists, but also for all scholars engaged with Enlightenment thought. Greenwood's main argument – the multiple Enlightenment in which the arts and feeling are central – is supported by scholarship that has argued for the importance of sensibility in the history of empiricism (Riskin) and in the history of technology (Voskuhl). The divisions between the sciences and the arts and between reason and feeling have been becoming increasingly porous.

Time and nature were especially slippery concepts in this period, encompassing a range of meanings and values. Even confining one's focus to Haydn's music, as Sisman shows, time is a concept that worked in many ways: it was "a musico-poetic theme, a source of humor, and a characteristic topic." Understood as RHYTHM, time was an element for Haydn to be manipulated and distorted to a variety of rhetorical and dramatic ends. As a subject, Haydn addressed time and its passing in works across his career, from the "Times of Day" symphonies to *The Seasons*. Sisman connects Haydn's own engagement with the broader preoccupation with time and how it was tracked and measured in this period, whether in the context of longitude and the invention of the Harrison H4 clock or in the calendrical reforms associated with the French Revolution. Sisman cites Berger's provocative argument that it was precisely this period that witnessed a shift from "a cyclic to a linear sense of time," a transformation that could be seen to mark the emergence of modernity.

Nature likewise was a capacious concept that was subject to much theorizing during the Enlightenment: for thinkers like Rousseau and Herder, nature was a place of origin, the departure point for the development of humanity and therefore something that functioned in counterpoint to human culture. Nature was something to be controlled (by industry), admired (through nature tourism) and understood (via taxonomical research). At the same time, as Sisman emphasizes, nature was a "source for artistic imitation and aesthetic values," which spans ideas of the Beautiful and Sublime to questions of representation and tone-painting.

While we do not have robust statements from Haydn detailing his views on nature – apart from brief references to his admiration of gardens and mentions of his outdoor pastimes – we do have Haydn's numerous musical representations of nature, from storms, to animals, to hunting. In compositional style, Haydn was, in Sisman's words "strikingly attuned to the natural world." Furthermore, Sisman notes how these kinds of representations connect directly with invocations of human emotions (a storm topic can simultaneously represent a tempest but also pained emotions). This connection between the natural world and human feeling echoes the three stages of "musical painting" described by Johann Jakob Engel, who laid out a spectrum of possibility starting with the direct painting of a sonic object with sound and ending with the imitation of the impression that a particular object makes upon the human soul.

In his entry on RELIGION AND SPIRITUAL BELIEFS Chen emphasizes the complexity of both Haydn's own personal Catholic faith – which was sincere – and the diversity of Haydn's liturgical and sacred compositions, which took pride of place in Haydn's valuation of his own output. Chen divides Haydn's sacred vocal output into two distinct phases: the first, which spans from 1749 until 1782, encompasses a "stylistically heterogeneous" collection of works that reflect Haydn's "accomplished familiarity with the prevailing styles and techniques of Catholic religious music in Haydn's milieu." The second period, from 1796 until 1802, comprises Haydn's late masses and his oratorios. Chen, following Webster, connects Haydn's late sacred vocal to the aesthetics of the sublime: "the gestural forcefulness of this style ... manifests the exploratory, searching bent of the composer's religious temperament." Though Chen stresses the originality of Haydn's late style, we should also emphasize the influence of Handel, whose music – especially in the commemorative performances that Haydn himself experienced in 1791 in London – were moving models that equated divine power with musical might.

Sisman paints a vivid picture of eighteenth-century natural philosophy in her entry on SCIENCE (a titular anachronism, as she points out). Haydn lived in an exciting period of discoveries across a wide range of scientific and technological subjects, many of which are reflected in Haydn's personal library (see MATERIAL CULTURE). Sisman stresses the importance of astronomical events, of which there are many in Haydn's lifetime, including the appearance (and reappearance) of comets, the Transit of Venus, and Herschel's discovery of Uranus. Sisman's emphasis on the astronomical (over, for example, the botanical or geological) reflects the connections that can be drawn between contemporary celestial discoveries and Haydn's compositional output. The Transit of Venus, for example, led to widespread obsession with the diurnal solar positions, which in turn are embodied in Haydn's Symphonies Nos. 6–8 (see Sisman 2013); Haydn's *Il mondo della luna* features an astronomer, telescopes, and musical effects of distance (see Loughridge 2013); Tovey has tempted us to connect Haydn's depiction of chaos in *The Creation* to the nebular hypothesis of Kant and Laplace. Yet we might note the overlap between the works invoked here with those in nature, which reflects the inevitably blurred boundaries between the two concepts. It raises the question of how we consider these words: can Haydn be said to represent concepts from natural philosophy in the same way that he represents nature? Or is it more productive to imagine work in natural philosophy shaping Haydn's view of nature, which is then in turn embodied in his compositional output?

In the next group of entries, James Grande, Nicholas Mathew, Catherine Mayes, and Richard Will address the complex issues surrounding national identities in this period as well as Haydn's own politics and the roles played by his music in the broader culture of his time. In his entry on POLITICS, Grande notes that Haydn's conservative image has more recently been replaced by a much more revolutionary one. He traces this dual reading back to Haydn's own time period, in which, in Grande's words, Haydn's music could be "appropriated both by the politics of nationalism and utopian project of the radical Enlightenment." This duality also applies to Haydn's audiences: Grande stresses the ways in which Haydn's music – most strikingly, his instrumental music – could appeal both to European elites as well as "the burgeoning commercial culture." Mathew compellingly shows the many ways in which WAR had a defining influence on Haydn's life: from birth until death, he was surrounded by wars; he worked for princes who had military careers; and, as Mathew emphasizes, in his late career he was part of a culture in both Britain and Austria that "increasingly required musicians and other artists to shape and mediate wartime public sentiment in newly prominent ways." The list of works with a "broadly martial character" from the 1790s is long and generically diverse, including symphonies, masses, songs, incidental music, and an unfinished cantata.

To this one can also add the commission of "Gott erhalte Franz den Kaiser" for Franz II's birthday in 1797; Mathew describes it as "a song of state loyalty" while Mayes, in NATIONALISM AND COSMOPOLITANISM, invokes it for the hymn's accessible and easily singable *Volkston* style. And though Haydn's music clearly participated in a burgeoning idea of national style, the broad circulation of Haydn's music easily crossed national boundaries. Haydn's language, Mayes emphasizes, was the "universal musical language of the ruling classes of Europe." What emerges from Mayes's entry is a productive categorical ambiguity: the ideas of nationalism and cosmopolitanism are not easily opposed.

Indeed, this blurriness extends further to EXOTICISM, which, as Mayes shows, was also a slippery category in Haydn's music. As Mayes points out, the diversity of Haydn's contexts makes it difficult to understand what musics would have been heard as exotic. One can identify styles that might be evocative of Hungarian, Turkish, "Gypsy," and Jewish musics, but it remains unclear how one might interpret such invocations: an enlightenment statement of tolerance and brotherhood or as a way of reaching and entertaining multiple audiences and publics. The challenges posed by these categories reflects their still-nascent state in the late Enlightenment; their status as truly separate – even opposing – categories does not arrive until the nineteenth century.

The works invoked by Mathew and Mayes point to the broader question of the larger cultural and political ends to which Haydn's music was used, both in his time period and beyond. Will tackles these questions in his entry on MONUMENTS AND MEMORIALIZING. He identifies three ways in which we might engage with the idea of the monument in Haydn's music. First, there are the works that themselves might qualify as such – as much as we can apply the term to a temporal art. These, Will suggests, are "Gott erhalte Franz den Kaiser" and perhaps *The Creation*. But if two seems a small number, Will argues that "most of Haydn's works do not praise famous men, nor memorialize recent events as monuments tend to do." Instead, Will suggests that "perhaps Haydn did not create monuments so much as write music appropriate for memorializing." But if we turn our attention away from political monuments – a focus surely influenced by early nineteenth-century music and Beethoven – one can alight on a whole different form of monument making: Haydn's secular cantatas honoring his princes, and his five volumes of music for the baryton, Prince Nicolaus's beloved instrument. Finally, we might consider the ways in which Haydn himself is commemorated, in monuments, poems, medals, and even in his status as Europe's greatest living composer (see RECEPTION). This is to avoid singling out individual works as monumental and instead to see Haydn's music more generally as a "monument to creative genius and cultural achievement."

***

At this point, it is illuminating to step back and reflect upon how the authors engage with Haydn's oeuvre across the entries. A partial canon begins to emerge: the one work mentioned more than any other is by far

The Creation, which is invoked by nearly half of the entries. Also prominently featured is The Seasons, which appears in a quarter of the entries. Symphonies Nos. 6–8 and No. 100, and the Kaiserhymne "Gott erhalte Franz den Kaiser" each appear in roughly three entries. With the exception of the early symphonies, these works all date from the 1790s and 1800s. This emphasis on Haydn's later works helps explain Haydn's more recent transformation into a revolutionary composer, both in terms of the political ends to which his music was used and in terms of his influence on later composers.

And yet we might also consider all the ends to which these works are invoked. Take, for example, The Creation. The brilliant moment of divine fiat – the blinding C-major light – has long invoked the language of the sublime and served as an invitation to connect Haydn to a range of philosophers (Longinus, Burke, Kant); indeed, it serves that purpose within this encyclopedia. But then again, The Creation has been an extremely obliging work in Haydn scholarship of the past two decades, accommodating a wide range of scholarship. It heralded a new era of hermeneutic approaches to Haydn's music with Lawrence Kramer's essay on representation in the oratorio; its length and musical diversity makes it a useful work for thinking about Haydn's approaches to his orchestral forces (see ORCHESTRATION); the work's text painting and moments of representation not only invite reflection on the status of mimesis in this period, but also connect the work to contemporary entertainments, such as the magic lantern show and shadow puppetry, as Loughridge (2010) has shown; more recently, The Creation shows up in Waltham-Smith's study of musical belonging carried out through the lens of Alain Badiou.

One could argue that this capaciousness is a straightforward symptom of the work's canonic status (after all, Beethoven's Ninth Symphony has functioned in similar ways in musical scholarship). But it is critical to note that much of this scholarship – even as it seeks to provide a deeper understanding of richness of The Creation – instrumentalizes the work in order to get at other aspects of late eighteenth and early nineteenth-century culture, whether we want to access religion, philosophy (of both the eighteenth and twenty-first centuries), the enlightenment, intertextuality, globalization, media, technology, or analysis. Just as Haydn has been reinvented to meet the needs of different musicological generations, so too The Creation functions as a gateway to initiate conversations about Haydn's broader contexts and as a vessel that conveniently holds together a tangle of sometimes contradictory ideas. And though we can situate the work in a dizzyingly complex network of Enlightenment thought, we might question whether the work transcends its status as an "*example of.*" What agential power, we could ask, does The Creation have? Has it served as a proving ground for robust hermeneutic and analytic interpretations? Have musicologists argued about what the work means on a fundamental level? To ask this is not to deny The Creation's status as a powerful precursor, one whose influence can be felt in works ranging from Carl Maria von Weber's Der erste Ton (1808, rev. 1810), to Rossini's

Mosè in Egitto (1818, revised 1819), to Beethoven's Ninth Symphony. But this status as precursor is yet another instance of the work's status as a gateway to other things.

That we can cite *The Creation*, *The Seasons*, or Symphonies Nos. 6–8 as examples of so many things reinforces the notion with which we opened this essay, namely, that Haydn's works have always required a set of ideas through which to speak, and that set of ideas has been in constant flux. The enthusiasm in Haydn scholarship for particular concepts, such as the sublime, is linked less to the sublime itself – which for all its glamour tended to uphold the authority of church and state, faith and aristocracy – than the potential it offers for innovation within the academic discipline of musicology. The ease with which we can identify the sublime in Haydn's works reassures us that the perpetually enigmatic and slightly distant authorial figure of Haydn had robust ideas.

At the moment, it seems we are poised at the trailheads of two possible futures for Haydn studies. Along one path, one could imagine that ideas that matter in the early twenty-first century – and the works they help animate – might change radically in the coming years. Will future musicologists find the ideas contained in this category quaint? Will they question why certain ideas were included or marvel over those that were left out? This is to imagine Haydn studies as an ever-changing kaleidoscope: beautiful crystal-line constellations of ideas that come and go, telling us as much about Haydn as their contemporary moment in scholarship. Alternatively, Haydn studies could continue, like the universe, to expand. Just as the notion of a "multiple Enlightenment" could take hold, we might also come to embrace a "multiple Haydn." Future musicologists might add countless new ideas to this category without draining the importance or interpretive power of the ones already established. As this encyclopedia captures, this multiplicity is already present in Haydn scholarship. And perhaps Haydn's ability to continue to stockpile countless ideas can itself be understood as a form of the sublime.

EMILY I. DOLAN AND MATTHEW HEAD

FURTHER READING

Allanbrook (1998, 2014); Baker and Christensen (1996); Burke (1757); Burnham (1995); Engel (1780); Foucault (1994); Galeazzi (1796); Goehr (1992); Hirschman (2013 [1977]); Hosler (1981); Jones (2010); Kramer (1992); Loughridge (2010, 2013); Mattheson (1739); Michaelis (1807); Mirka (2014a); Nedbal (2016); Polzonetti (2012); Ratner (1980); Riskin (2002); Rosen (1971/72); Schleuning (1984); Siskin and Warner (2010); Sisman (1990, 2013); Tovey (1935–39); Voskuhl (2013); Waldoff (1998); Waltham-Smith (2017); Webster (1991, 2007); Wheelock (1992); Will (2002).

Identity – see Biography and

Imagination – see Improvisation

Imitation – see Mimesis

Improvisation The practice of improvisation (*fantasieren* in German) was closely associated in later eighteenth-century Europe with theories of inspiration, originality, and the imagination. A long tradition of musical training gave the experienced musician tools for composing at the instrument, and in the moment, in strict styles and genres, but musicians, writers, and theorists alike became increasingly interested from the mid-eighteenth century on in "free" improvisation. Improvisation might occur as a mode of PERFORMANCE (in the public spur-of-the moment creation of cadenzas by a solo instrumentalist in a concerto, or by a solo keyboard player improvising alone or for a small group of friends), or as an aid to the imagination of a composer beginning to work on a composition in another genre, or as a composition based on, or imitating, actual improvisation (such as the Freie Fantasie in C minor, published as the final piece in C. P. E. Bach's 18 *Probestücke* that accompanied his widely circulated *Versuch über die wahre Art das Clavier zu spielen* [1753]). In music-aesthetic terms in the period, improvisation at its finest not only made manifest the effects of inspiration, it could also provide a window into the soul of the artist.

In improvisation, the artist's imagination was stimulated, or fired, by inspiration in a process often described as the communication of a higher power, or the ecstatic experience of being swept up in the transports of the SUBLIME. The musician and writer C. F. D. Schubart described an experience shared by many of his contemporaries when he wrote in the 1780s that: "I improvised with passionate creativity. I could play to myself in this fire – the principal trait of musical genius – in such a way that everything around me faded, and I lived only in the music, which my imagination created" (1: 50). Perhaps the most famous improviser of the late eighteenth century, whose music Haydn knew and admired, was C. P. E. Bach. Bach's improvisations for small groups of friends were demonstrations of inspiration in action, as the musician gave himself up, trancelike, to the musical imagination: according to the composer J. F. Reichardt, during these performances "his soul appeared to be wholly absent, his eyes swam as if in a sweet dream, the under-lip hung down over the chin, face and body suspended lifeless over the clavichord" (31–32).

Haydn's well-known account of his own COMPOSITIONAL PROCESS, as reported by his first biographer Griesinger, begins with improvisation. Inspiration is courted and the imagination nourished through fantasizing at the keyboard: "I sat down at the keyboard and began to fantasize [*fantasieren*], according to whether my mood was sad or happy, serious or playful. Once I had seized upon an idea, my entire effort went toward elaborating and sustaining it, according to the rules of art" (78). Improvisation at the keyboard was held by many to be a vital mode for unleashing inspiration in as nearly an unmediated manner as possible, not least for the composer. H. C. Koch explained in his *Musikalisches Lexikon* (1802) that: "this improvisation .... can very often be a means by which the composer arouses the activity of his genius or puts himself into that state known as inspiration" (col. 778). Compositional improvisation, as Webster has written, was as central to Haydn's musical imagination as it was to C. P. E. Bach.

Recently scholars including Webster, Richards, Fillion, and Beghin, have begun to point out improvisatory elements in Haydn's work, discussing the ways in which "the rhetoric of improvisation" runs through Haydn's music in many genres. Compositional devices such as digression, dynamic surprise, sudden silence, and formal and generic ambiguity may be seen to partake of the aesthetic of fantasy, as the composer appears to play freely, spontaneously, and audaciously with his ideas and with the rules of the game. Such music, in its turn, challenges attentive listeners to engage in a free imaginative play as they attempt to follow the composer through what eighteenth-century writer on original genius Edward Young described as "excursion and deviation" on the errant tracks that are the necessary path of the original GENIUS (14).

One might look to Haydn's Fantasia in C major, Hob.XVII:4 (1789) for an example of music that is overtly imaginative and risk-taking: after the initial statement of its folksy presto theme in three–eight, structural articulation is blurred as cadences are avoided, and sudden caesuras interrupt the progress, to be followed by surprising harmonic swerves or textural changes, with ambiguity, silence, and sudden stillness calling into question not only genre but also the temporal fabric of the piece itself. In that moment of stillness, the mind is challenged to open itself to inspiration, to vault into the void and produce meaning: the classical rules of structure and syntax momentarily checked in favor of the rewards of risk. Demanding and rewarding attentive listening, notated works such as this stage the interaction between composer, performer, and listener. Shying away from the stormy unpredictability of the free fantasia, the Fantasia Op. 58 nevertheless demonstrates how an idea can be worked on, and worked out, without losing what Koch called the "prominent and striking traits" (col. 554) that the composed fantasia shares with the spontaneous improvisation. (See also SELF-REFLEXIVITY.) ANNETTE RICHARDS

FURTHER READING
Beghin (2015a); Bonds (1991b); Fillion (2005); Griesinger; Koch (1802); Reichardt (1814); Richards (2001, 2007); Schubart (1839); Webster (2007); Young (1759).

Inspiration – see Improvisation

Institutions Two decades into the twenty-first century the persistence of the view that major creative figures from the past achieved greatness predominantly through relentless self-will rather than through constant engagement with their environment is remarkable. It is a seductive conceit, tapping into the very human need to understand the impulses of exceptionally gifted individuals. The continuing popularity of biographies of kings, presidents, authors, film stars, as well as musicians, feeds that fascination. When an author explains the wider environment, it is usually to shed light on the steadfast ambition of the individual. Of course, a biography that is all context and no personality would be a contradiction, yet understanding a composer's world is clearly a pre-requisite for understanding the composer.

In Haydn's case, it is a particular challenge, not only for the simple fact that he lived for a long time, from the first half of the eighteenth century to the first decade of the nineteenth, but because the world of the composer saw so many new developments during that time, many enthusiastically embraced by him, and that determined fundamental changes in his creativity. But it was never an entirely linear process of one set of circumstances replacing another, rather the interaction of the continuing with the new, the permanent with the intermittent. For Haydn, it was also one of expanding horizons as he engaged, indeed became a key figure, in the internationalization of music in the eighteenth century, a particular product of Capitalism and the MARKET. Other individuals and groups of individuals played their part: princes, PUBLISHERS, impresarios, patrons, performers, and music SOCIETIES, but each of these agencies of tradition and change had its own identity that was also changing. "Institutions" is a convenient portmanteau word for these diverse forces – religious, political, social, cultural, and commercial – that shaped Haydn's character and career.

Church and Court One institution that governed Haydn's behavior and wider outlook for his entire life was the Catholic CHURCH. As Janet Page indicates in her entry, Haydn's piety is frequently commented upon by biographers but, reflecting social attitudes that are more of the nineteenth century than the eighteenth, it is often presented as something incidental, an allowable comparative weakness that fed into the idea of the innocent Haydn. But for Haydn himself, as for wider society in Austria in the middle of the eighteenth century, it was all-embracing and a source of security and strength. The Catholic church was not so much an institution within society as society itself. In earlier centuries, the Habsburg dynasty had spearheaded the Counter-Reformation, creating an indivisible link between religion and politics. In the process, it created a visual identity for much of the Austrian territories that persists to this day: churches, monasteries, chapels, and shrines. In the Austria of Haydn's youth, it represented a way of life that went far beyond religious observance and had acquired a label, *Pietas Austriaca*, that signaled this all-encompassing outlook (see Coreth). While it emphasized piety it also promoted broader moral virtues of duty, modesty, and moderation – core attributes in Haydn's mature personality. It was the only institution that mattered in Haydn's childhood and youth, reflected in the fact that early biographies mention the church more frequently that they do Haydn's mother, father, or indeed any other individual. It seems also necessary to point out that though it may have been conservative in European terms, for Haydn and others *Pietas Austriaca* was thoroughly contemporary, not least because many of the churches and abbeys that celebrated Catholicism were comparatively new, part of a Baroque building boom in the early decades of the eighteenth century. As was common practice, Haydn was given two Christian names reflecting saint days that were close to his birthday, Franz (Francis of Paola, April 2) and Joseph (March 19). Along with Leopold, Karl, and Maria, Joseph was a particularly popular name, the husband of the Virgin Mary and, since the end of the seventeenth century, identified as the protector of the Austrian hereditary lands. In 1741, eight years after Haydn's birth, Maria Theresia's first son was born and was given the name Joseph because she had repeatedly prayed to Saint Joseph during her pregnancy for a male heir. As Joseph II he was to reform several aspects of society (including, very notably, the role of religion) with many indirect effects on Joseph Haydn's career, but never on his faith.

As James Van Horn Melton points out, Haydn's EDUCATION in Rohrau, Hainburg, and VIENNA was entirely in the hands of the Catholic church, and his parents thought he might become a clergyman. Indeed, until he joined the service of Count Morzin, Haydn probably felt that a career as a church musician (violinist, organist, singer, and composer) represented his likely future, an important component of *Pietas Austriaca* and not something that would have been regarded as second-rate or lacking in ambition.

The second institution that was to be a constant presence in Haydn's life was the COURT, the focus of Jen-yen Chen's entry. The centrality of the Esterházy court in Haydn's life and music from 1761 onwards is key to his image, amply attested in surviving documents and the source of many familiar anecdotes. But this was only one court amongst many that featured in his life, directly and indirectly, representing a form of patronage that was ubiquitous though not uniform in its application. Whereas the church can be described as one overriding institution, courts consisted of any number of defined individual institutions, largely autonomous in their day-to-day authority, but with shared characteristics and shared allegiances. The most important was the Habsburg court itself, located in the Hofburg in Vienna and very much a physical presence in the city altogether, especially in Haydn's youth. It had a long-standing musical tradition that stretched back to the sixteenth century, providing music for Catholic services and private performances of opera on the birthdays and name-days of the most important members of the families, as well as special occasions such as weddings. When Maria Theresia became empress in 1741, a few years after Haydn had arrived in Vienna, she instigated a period of reform, fueled by financial concerns and, in the case of opera, the wish to make it available to the public in general. Although Haydn was a member of the choir in the cathedral of St. Stephen's rather than the chapel in the Habsburg court (the Hofkapelle), there had always been a close connection between the two establishments, with many politically significant church services taking place in St. Stephen's using the combined forces of the court and the cathedral. In turn, these two musical bodies were part of a wider network of church musicians, numbering around 2,000, that afforded full-time and occasional work. In his early twenties Haydn was fully integrated into this network: singing in church services at court and in St. Stephen's, playing the violin in court balls, leading the orchestra in the church of the Barmherzige Brüder in the Leopoldstadt, and playing the organ in the private chapel of the Bohemian Chancellery.

The musical courts of the aristocracy were largely independent of this civic network, even though the historical impulse for the setting up of such musical courts had been to mirror the imperial example. Successive Habsburg emperors had astutely nurtured the loyalty of the aristocracy, partly by encouraging them to establish their winter palaces in the city. The principal Esterházy palace was in the Wallnerstrasse, two streets away from the Hofburg; nearby palaces included the Lobkowitz palace and the Schwarzenberg palace, both of which were to feature in Haydn's life. The aristocracy, together with their musical retinues, followed the imperial practice of moving to one or more summer palaces, either in the outskirts of Vienna or, more commonly, in the distant countryside, especially Bohemia and Hungary. Some members of the aristocracy chose to spend most of their time outside Vienna; Prince Nicolaus I's preference for the summer palace of ESZTERHÁZA over the summer palace of EISENSTADT, and for both palaces over the one in the Wallnerstrasse, resulted in the Esterházy court spending very little time in Vienna in the 1770s and

1780s. For Kapellmeister Haydn, it led to a feeling that he did not belong to Vienna's musical life in the same way as when he lived there in the 1750s.

Hereditary members of aristocracy were not the only social grouping to operate with a court system in the Austrian territories. When the church was the local landowner, then the local ruler was an archbishop or bishop whose musical retinue served secular as well as sacred needs. Haydn's brother, Michael Haydn, worked for two such courts, in Grosswardein and, together with Leopold and Wolfgang Amadeus Mozart, in Salzburg (then part of the Holy Roman Empire rather than the Austrian hereditary lands).

The vast quantity of documents that survives from the Esterházy court relating to the musical provision reveals a continuing administrative and financial accountability within a system that was hierarchical, controlling, and broadly efficient: the players and singers reported to the Kapellmeister, the Kapellmeister along with other individuals to the Estates Director, Peter Ludwig Rahier, and, ultimately, to the prince. Typically, INSTRUMENTS belonged to the court rather than to the individual, summer and winter uniforms together with board and lodge were provided together with annual allowances of anything from flour to wine, cabbages to firewood; for some senior employees, like Haydn, there was access to medical care too. Any music composed for the court also belonged to the court rather than to the employee but, as Haydn's career in the 1760s and the 1770s reveals, this does not seem to have been rigorously enforced. Haydn was a skilled operator within the court system, as in the familiar (and well-founded) story of the "Farewell" Symphony, and biographers have often drawn attention to the fact that he was able to circumvent some of the court processes and speak directly to the prince, on his own behalf as well as of others. There is wider evidence that court life could be socially informal, with the habitual use of the familiar "Du" rather than "Sie" in conversation; certainly, as one of Haydn's pupils Sigismund Neukomm recorded, the composer was most offended when Prince Nicolaus II pompously addressed him in the third person, "Er," the standard address for anonymous male servants (Seeger 29; Landon IV 43).

All courts – imperial, aristocratic, sacred – were constituted in the name of the titular head – emperor, dowager empress, prince, count, archbishop, bishop etc. – and were formally re-established, partially re-established, or completely disbanded at the accession of the new ruler. The most enthusiastic of the four Esterházy princes that Haydn served, Prince Nicolaus I (r. 1762–1790), willingly took on the retinue of his brother Paul Anton; but Nicolaus's successor, Prince Anton (r. 1790–1794), disbanded almost the entire retinue, keeping only Haydn, first violinist Luigi Tomasini (see MUSIC PROFESSIONALS), and a small ensemble for church music, a telling instance of continuing religious values; when he, in turn, died, his son, Prince Nicolaus II (r. 1794–1832), began a rather fitful process of rebuilding.

The social fabric of church and court was a binding one throughout the Austrian territories, as important in rural Bohemia and Hungary as in Vienna itself; it also encompassed major towns and cities, such as the Bohemian capital of Prague and the Hungarian capital of Pressburg. For much of Haydn's career these two institutions also managed to resist or marginalize the influence of other, newer developments. Haydn was clearly comfortable in this environment; it was what he knew, it enabled success and promoted his self-worth.

Newer Impulses Haydn was not, however, a socially conservative individual. His career shows a willingness to explore, accommodate, and, indeed, exploit newer institutional practices. The process began in the late 1770s, gained momentum in the 1780s and culminated in his engagement with a whole new set of interlocking institutional practices during his two visits to LONDON in the 1790s. Two complementary forces were at work. Within the Austrian monarchy Joseph II accelerated the process of reform begun by his mother, Maria Theresia, affecting all aspects of society, including the church, education, trade, censorship, and the legal system. And from outside, there was the ever-increasing internationalization of musical life.

Haydn's relationship with developments in Viennese musical life in the 1780s was by no means an all-embracing one, mainly because he was not often in residence. The traditionally inward-looking nature of music at the imperial court meant that his music featured very little there and since, for much of the decade, Joseph II took a direct role in the management of the opera at the two court theaters (Burgtheater and Kärntnertortheater) Haydn's operas were almost unknown. Susan Wollenberg's entry draws our attention to another collection of institutions, MUSICAL SOCIETIES, that evolved along with Haydn's role in Vienna. The composer's dealings with the Tonkünstler Societät, for example, began awkwardly. Set up in 1771, it organized two charity concerts a year, at Easter and Christmas, each given twice, where Viennese instrumentalists and singers gave their services voluntarily to raise money for widows and orphans of musicians. Haydn joined the society in 1778, but when it subsequently indicated that they expected him to compose music voluntarily for the society, the composer resisted and eventually resigned. Although Haydn's music was subsequently performed at some of its concerts, the institution did not formally acknowledge its clumsy behavior until 1797 when it made the composer a life-long member. This in turn paved the way for a key element in Haydn's Viennese persona in the last period of his life, namely his willingness to be associated with charity concerts in general, especially performances of *The Creation* and *The Seasons*. That emblematic image – Haydn the benign supporter of musical life in Vienna – remained in the collective memory long after his death, signaled by the incorporation of Haydn's name – not that of Mozart or Beethoven – into that of the society from 1862 onwards; as "Haydn: Musicians' Society for the Care of Widows and Orphans in Vienna" it existed until 1939, when the society was dissolved by the Nazi government.

By far the most influential institutional development of Viennese musical life on Haydn in the 1780s was the rapid rise of music printing, as captured in the entry on COMMERCE AND THE MARKET by Emily H. Green (see also CIRCULATION; PUBLISHERS AND PUBLISHING). For much of the eighteenth century, music was disseminated in the Austrian territories in the form of manuscript copies, very efficiently serving the needs of courts, churches, and salons. While the skills of music engraving and printing were known in Vienna, there did not seem to be a need for an established music publisher in the imperial capital – unlike the more cosmopolitan musical cities of Amsterdam, Berlin, London and Paris. Members of the family firm of Artaria, originally from Lake Como, had established a business presence in Vienna from 1770 onwards, selling engravings, maps, and the occasional item of imported printed music. In 1778 it began engraving music, initially no more than a handful of items a year, gradually rising to two dozen or so. By 1790 it had issued over three hundred works. As this gradual approach suggests Artaria was not attempting to replace the still-flourishing trade of manuscript copying; it was instead very skillfully carving out a presence in the musical life of Vienna, primarily serving domestic music-making (see AMATEURS), especially keyboard music, songs, and quartets. In that way, it became an active catalyst in the formation of musical taste, also in the increasing sense of authority and permanence that accrued to musical works that were printed rather than just distributed in manuscript (see CIRCULATION). Haydn both benefited from and promoted this development. By 1790, approximately a fifth of Artaria's catalogue was by Haydn, by far the best-represented composer in the catalogue of the firm. Many of the works themselves would not have been composed without this significant change in musical COMMERCE in the 1780s. This is especially true of quartets: Op. 33, Op. 50, Op. 54/55, *The Seven Last Words* and arrangements of three of the "Paris" symphonies were all published by Artaria. The firm represented a new form of incidental and negotiated patronage that sat alongside the traditional one of a musical court, and Haydn was able to combine the two.

Artaria's patronage had another dimension, which was to influence the composer's status. Like many publishers elsewhere in Europe Artaria established business connections with firms in other cities, notably Longman & Broderip in London and Le Duc in Paris; in that way Haydn's existing reputation in those cities was significantly boosted. Since both cities had a much longer tradition than Vienna of publishing music, the vibrancy of the resultant market economy was unrivalled in EUROPE. While much of the music published by Artaria was by local composers, firms in London and Paris were more internationally minded. Long-standing arguments about national styles, French, German, and Italian, became increasingly irrelevant in instrumental music even if they were still evident in operatic music; the emergent sense of a universality of taste chimed with wider ENLIGHTENMENT values and were integral to Haydn's wider RECEPTION.

As a result of the internationalization of music publishing, Haydn became a popular composer in Paris and London long before he was asked to write the "Paris" Symphonies and long before he travelled to London. The role of London in Haydn's musical development in the 1790s is richly documented and well understood. But Paris continued to influence Haydn's reputation too, despite the upheaval of the Revolutionary and Napoleonic period. Haydn received and declined occasional invitations to write new music for the city, but the continuing vitality of Paris's music publishing industry encouraged a former STUDENT of Haydn, Ignaz Pleyel, to set up his own publishing company, the Maison Pleyel, that issued the first complete edition of Haydn's quartets (1801) – a pioneering act of canon formation that resonates to this day.

Artaria's increasing presence in the musical market of Vienna in the 1780s encouraged the setting up of other firms, Torricella, Kozeluch and, most enduring, Hoffmeister, all of whom played a part in Haydn's career. As well as the composer, the publisher, and buying public there was a fourth element in this network of transmission that was begin to emerge: the DEDICATEE. Although only a minority of music publications by Haydn carried a dedication in this period – for instance, Symphonies Nos. 76–78 to Prince Nicolaus, the German lieder (Hob.XXVIa:1–24) to Franziska Liebe Edle von Kreutzer, the Op. 50 quartets to King Friedrich Wilhelm II, and the Op. 64 quartets to Johann Tost – there was already a sense of shared connoisseurship in the process rather than dutiful or opportunistic obligation, a quality that was to become more pronounced in later years. Uniquely amongst composers Haydn himself began to be the recipient of dedications, especially as the master of the medium of the string quartet. Pleyel led the way with his Op. 2 of 1784, followed the next year by Mozart's celebrated set of six, Op. 10; both included warm-hearted letters of dedication as part of the publication.

If music publication in Vienna in the 1780s was gradually catching up with practice elsewhere in Europe, there was another institution, addressed in the entry by Mary Sue Morrow, that remained wholly undeveloped: the musical PRESS. Vienna had only one newspaper, the *Wiener Zeitung*, which appeared twice a week, an official court newspaper rather than an independent critical voice. It did contain announcements of performances in theaters and advertisements for manuscript and printed music, and, in that sense, it reflected and promoted something of a busy musical environment, but there are very few accounts of public performances and, to the enduring disappointment of music historians, virtually no accounts of private performances in aristocratic palaces or elsewhere. The combined presence of an absolutist imperial court and an exclusive aristocratic network ensured that flourishing public debate of the performing arts, especially music, was not so much actively suppressed as made to appear unnecessary and irrelevant. Sources like the entertaining autobiography of Dittersdorf, the occasional letter by Haydn and the rather more numerous ones by Mozart hint at musically informed opinion and debate but it was largely an oral discourse rather than a written one. As Morrow points out, this was a very different environment from that which existed in Berlin, Leipzig, London, and Paris, where the musical press was an active and influential one, including accounts of Haydn, his life, and his music. Haydn's autobiographical sketch from 1776 – prepared for a rare venture in Austria, a small and rather haphazard dictionary of national biography *Das gelehrte Oesterreich* ("Learned Austria") – reveals the composer's considerable irritation with "the Berlin gentlemen" – namely, writers who had commented on his music, sometimes favorably, sometimes critically. Haydn's irritation has often been construed as over-sensitivity; more fundamentally, it represented a discomforting clash of two musical cultures, the intellectually informed and the intellectually circumscribed.

If Haydn had written a second autobiographical sketch just ten years later, in the middle of the 1780s, he might well have been more understanding, certainly more grateful, recognizing that his emerging status in London and Paris, in particular, was closely linked to a liberal, inquisitive, and critical musical press in those two cities. Newspapers in London in the 1780s commented regularly on performances of his symphonies and the almost-annual attempts to get the composer to travel to the city. The *European Magazine* satisfied wider curiosity about the composer by publishing a four-column biography in 1784 together with "an excellent engraved likeness." At the same time in Paris the *Mercure de France*, a journal that had originated in the seventeenth century and had a long history of featuring contested debates on all manner of subjects, including art, music, and philosophy, was including regular reports, mainly enthusiastic, on performances of Haydn symphonies, also the *Stabat mater*, in the city.

At this mid-way stage in Haydn's career, public concerts were another institution that signaled fundamental differences between Vienna and practice elsewhere. In Vienna, Haydn's symphonies were routinely performed in the non-public arenas of aristocratic and ecclesiastical courts, though the practice of including symphonies (often single movements rather than whole works) within liturgical services in churches and monasteries provided a particular public experience that bound them to the long-standing religious and social values enshrined in the composer's church music and, more generally, the all-enveloping *Pietas Austriaca*. Public performance in a secular venue, however, was the exception rather than the rule. In 1780s London and Paris, on the other hand, Haydn's popularity was sustained by public performances of symphonies. The fact that these took place without the presence of the composer encouraged critical commentary on the music itself as much as on its creator, the beginning of a process that was to elevate the symphony to the pinnacle of musical ambition in the nineteenth century and inform the concept of absolute music.

Continuity, Change, and Creating a Legacy In Haydn's long career 1790 is seen as a major turning point. The composer had served at the Esterházy court for twenty-nine years when Prince Nicolaus died in September; although his successor, Prince Paul Anton, retained Haydn as Kapellmeister there was very little to do, certainly in comparison with the previous decades. The standard biographical narrative continues with Johann Peter Salomon's hurried journey to Vienna and the successful signing of a contract that enabled Haydn to travel to London, the first time the composer had left the Austrian territories. This was to be a tale of personal and musical triumph. The fact that Haydn continued to compose symphonies, quartets, piano trios and even an opera (the aborted *L'anima del filosofo*) have tended to obscure how fundamental the change in the musical environment was. From an existence that was enabled by traditional courtly practice and developments in music publishing in Vienna, Haydn moved to a diverse environment with a range of institutions that nourished a reputation that was noticeably public. As well as the range of bodies – concert organizations, publishers, newspapers, societies devoted to old music, the King's Theatre, the pleasure gardens, the Anglican church, and universities – there were a number of interlocking and interacting NETWORKS of individuals whose interest and energy enabled the institutions to flourish and to create an environment that was greater than the sum of its parts. Haydn's letters and, especially, his four London NOTEBOOKS are full of names of organizations and individuals, an informal attempt to map out the social and musical landscape.

Although Salomon the violinist-impresario was to gain sole credit for inviting Haydn to London, the initial visit was the result of a three-way collaboration between him, John Gallini, the manager of the newly rebuilt King's Theatre (the home of Italian opera; see THEATER) and John Bland, a music publisher. Within a matter of months Haydn's direct experience of these institutions was supplemented by that of several others: a rival concert organization, the Professional Concert, the numerous end-of-season benefit concerts, the Handel FESTIVAL in Westminster Abbey, the least regulated press in the whole of Europe, courtesy visits to the Austrian and Italian embassies, the acquaintanceship of another music publisher, Napier, dinner parties with the music historian Charles Burney and his friends, the musical company of the Prince of Wales, and the award of an honorary DMus. At the University of Oxford (music as a discipline did not exist in the University of Vienna).

As well as the profusion of institutions in England and the vicissitudes of their changing relationships, Haydn would have experienced their combined capacity to promote his status as a creative individual, most obviously reflected in the repeated use of the appellation "the Shakespeare of music." Haydn was placed on a pedestal for public admiration, a course of action that signaled ownership and mutual prestige. It was this pluralist, energetic, and sometimes exhausting environment that led Haydn to comment that he first became "celebrated" ("berühmt") in England.

The final phase of Haydn's life, from 1796 through to his death thirteen years later, saw the return of the composer to the environment that he had known in the 1780s, including court life as Kapellmeister and engagement with musical institutions in Vienna and major European cities. But the details and emphases of Haydn's working environment, local and international, were now rather different, inevitably influenced by the legacy of the two London visits and the unsettled political climate of the time, the French Revolutionary and Napoleonic WARS. The fourth of Haydn's Esterházy patrons, Prince Nicolaus II, revitalized musical life at the court, but rather than the constant, daily presence that it had enjoyed in earlier times, it tended to coalesce around particular occasions, such as the celebrations of Princess Marie Hermenegild's name-day in September and one-off visits by individuals as varied as Archduke Johann (the Hungarian palatine) or Admiral Nelson. For performances of church music, court musicians were often supplemented by the casual employment of others, for performances of opera by the engagement of an entire theatrical company. Such pragmatism was not peculiar to the Esterházy court but is evident in the musical patronage of other aristocrats at the time, notably Prince Lobkowitz. Other aspects of Haydn's tenure at the Esterházy court reflect much longer institutional practice, even though they are sometimes portrayed as uniquely sympathetic responses to the composer's particular circumstances: employment for life, the appointment of a deputy to gradually take over his duties, and the successful request in 1806 for an increase in pay.

One much newer aspect of the institution of aristocratic patronage of music played a decisive role in Haydn's career at this time, namely the increasing willingness of aristocrats to act together to promote music, and to do so in public (or semi-public) rather than in private. The composition and first performances of The Creation and The Seasons were the direct result of the patronage, financial and in-kind, of Gottfried van Swieten and an informal group of aristocrats, including Prince Nicolaus Esterházy, known as the "Associierte Cavaliers," an artistic oligarchy that sought to lead public taste in Vienna. When the two oratorios by Haydn were subsequently taken up by particular charities such as the Tonkünstler Societät, the sense of a broader, civic ownership was further enhanced.

Haydn lived long enough to see the beginnings of a wider public awareness of his symphonies in Vienna too. During the 1807–8 season a group of aristocrats came together to promote a semi-public series of twenty concerts, variously known as the Liebhaber Concerte, Musikalisches Institut, Freunde der Tonkunst, and Gesellschaft von Musikfreunden. Six performances of some of the "London" Symphonies were given, over a decade after they had established themselves in the affection of London audiences.

In music publishing, while Artaria in Vienna and Longman & Broderip in London were the main publishers of new music by Haydn in those two cities, there was a new firm in Leipzig that was to have a major influence on establishing Haydn's reputation, not only in the remaining years of his life but posthumously too. Breitkopf & Härtel was founded in Leipzig in 1797, uniting the long experience of the former as a music dealer and printer with the shorter experience and financial resources of the latter. Although their base was in Leipzig, their market was German-speaking Europe, and, later, Europe as a whole. As well as issuing several individual works by Joseph Haydn, such as orchestral scores of The Seasons and excerpts from L'anima del filosofo, Breitfkopf & Härtel began to publish multi-volume EDITIONS of parts of Haydn's output: twelve volumes of a variety of keyboard music and songs (1799–1806), six volumes devoted to six of the "London" Symphonies (1806–8), and seven volumes of masses containing five of the late masses plus two earlier works (1802–23). Published in hefty tomes with a similar format and appearance, they were visually imposing, intended for libraries as much as performance, and they created a firm sense of authorized legacy. Several volumes of the keyboard music series have title pages attractively adorned with standard images of the power of music (e.g. an entirely docile lion in the presence of a mother and her children, vol. 11) and memorialization (a hovering angel carrying a laurel wreath, vol. 4; three women before a memorial stone, vol. 3).

Breitkopf & Härtel also established in 1798 a new music journal, the Allgemeine musikalische Zeitung, that included not only regular reports on musical life in Vienna and other major cities but also detailed reviews of printed music (including its own publications). Many issues of the Allgemeine musikalische Zeitung contain extended biographies of composers as the opening article and, later in the issue, short and engaging, if not always well-founded, anecdotes. It was against this wider interest in the lives of composers that the firm's representative in Vienna, Griesinger, set himself up as an official biographer of the composer, regularly meeting him to gather information. His account first appeared in installments in the Allgemeine musikalische Zeitung and then as a single volume. In short, within a matter of a dozen years or so Breitkopf & Härtel had created an authorized view of Haydn's life as well as much of his music, one that posterity was to expand – greatly – and amend – punctiliously – but never alter in its fundamentals.

DAVID WYN JONES

FURTHER READING
Coreth (2004); Gates-Coon (1994); Jones (2009, 2016); Lamkin (2007); Landon IV; McVeigh (1993); Morrow (1989); Seeger (1959).

Instruments and Organology The extant compositions by Haydn represent a period of over fifty years – c. 1749 to c. 1803 – and in considering such a large window of time, instruments of regional and chronological distinctiveness present myriad choices for the historically informed performer. Haydn's compositional activity is divided here into three periods: c. 1749–61, the freelance years in VIENNA and the Morzin court appointment; 1761–91, the years at the Esterházy COURT; and 1791–c. 1803, the LONDON excursions and the later years in Vienna. Superimposed onto this chronology will be four examples of broad-scale conceptual shifts in EUROPEAN wind, string, and keyboard design, each section drawing information from the most relevant organological and musicological research.

In wind instruments, flutes with one or two keys (for which Johann Joachim Quantz wrote his lessons) met with competition from multi-key instruments. A six-key flute was introduced in mid-eighteenth-century England, with the first extant example built around 1753–58, most likely by John Just Schuchart. English flutes were most certainly exported to the Continent in the coming decades; however, Continental builders only began building keyed flutes in the 1780s. In 1785 J. G. Tromlitz of Leipzig built a seven-key flute, which was the first to provide a tone-hole for every semitone. The Grenser workshop of Dresden began making multi-key flutes in the 1780s while continuing to build single-key flutes. In France, a flute resurgence coincided with the 1795 establishment of the Conservatoire, where François Devienne tolerated the use of, at most, four-key flutes by his students. The full lower register achieved by added key-work was not universally admired, and it may well have catalyzed a divide between performative ideals: Englishman John Gunn writes in 1793 of the distinction between "an equal fullness of tone" on one hand, and "tender expression" on the other.

In 1766 at ESZTERHÁZA, Haydn expressed a preference for the oboes of Viennese builder Mathias Rockobaur, who was also known to have made single-key flutes. It is possible, then, that works of the 1760s – such as the Divertimento in D major (Hob.II:8, for two flutes, two horns, two violins, basso) and the Symphony No. 7 in C major, "Le midi" – were played with single-key flutes from Vienna or elsewhere on the Continent. In the years preceding Haydn's first journey to London, it is likely that he encountered multi-key flutes of German or English design. The Keyboard Trios (Hob.XV: 15–17), composed in 1790 for keyboard, flute, and cello, may have been performed at court by flautist Zacharias Hirsch. By this time, the possibilities for Hirsch's instrument are numerous: he could have played a Tromlitz seven-key flute, a flute by a Viennese maker working under the influence of either English or German models, or indeed, the fact that Hirsch began his employ in 1776 could mean that he was trained on, and continued to use, a Continental flute with only one or two keys. These trios were sold to the PUBLISHER John Bland in London, where multi-key flutes by the prominent English maker Richard Potter were mass-produced.

Eighteenth-century brass instruments saw the coexistence of two types of crooked orchestral horns: those with crooks inserted into the mouth-pipe, and those with crooks fitted into the coiled tubing of the horn's body. Evidence of horn crooks appears as early as 1703, when an itemized bill from Viennese trumpet and horn-maker Michael Leichnamschneider included "1 pair great new Hunting-Horns [Jägerhorn]" and "4 new double Crooks [Krumbögen]" (Fitzpatrick 32–33). These early crooks were likely of the terminal type. The development of internal crooks occurred in the 1750s and was attributed to hornist Anton Joseph Hampl and instrument maker Johann Werner of Dresden. Crooks placed internally provided an advantage in that the mouthpipe – and therefore the distance between player and instrument – remained fixed. Despite this ergonomic advantage, both types of crooking retained popularity throughout the century.

In 1782, Forkel wrote of the appearance of internal crooks in Vienna. "For six years or so one has been able to buy the so-called Inventions-horns as well, which have their crooks in the middle of the horn on extending sockets instead of on the mouthpipe" (Fitzpatrick 132). Fitzpatrick suggests that, despite such references in lexicons by Forkel and Gerber, there is insufficient evidence in the Viennese trade literature to suggest that the *Inventionshorn* was taken up wholeheartedly in the city. Four bills are extant from horn-maker Anton Kerner for services rendered to the Esterházy court; two dated 1773 and 1780 specify the delivery of horns with full sets of crooks (see Bryan). There is further documentary evidence that, at some point in Kerner's career, he made horns following the pattern of Werner's internal crooking scheme, but extant examples – including those examined by Fitzpatrick (132–34) and another dated 1760 in the Mährischen Nationalmuseum, Schloss Jevisovice, Brno Czech Republic – seem to suggest a terminal crooking scheme.

As for violin bows, the midpoint of the eighteenth century likely saw the coexistence of short bows and long bows, with the latter gaining favor. Short bows – with lengths in the immediate area of 61 cm (24 inches), weights from 36 to 44 grams (1.3 to 1.5 ounces), very little or no concave cambre, and hair mounted within a "pike's head" on one end and through a "clip-in frog" on the other – were championed by Arcangelo Corelli and his later followers. Long bows measured from 66 to 72 cm (26 to 28 inches) and weighed from 44 to 55 grams (1.5 ounces to 2.4 ounces). Generally, they were without concave cambre and had either a pike's head or commonly a higher "swan bill" shape at the tip. The option of a frog with adjustable hair tension was available in long bows around mid-century but was not immediately popular. In a 1731 account of the differences between short and long bows, the Prince of Monaco bemoans that his violinist returned from Paris with a long bow and a loss of articulation. The violinist was then sent to Turin in order to replace the long bow technique he acquired in Paris with a short bow technique from Corelli student Giovanni Battista Somis (this story is relayed by Seletsky). Likewise, around 1741, Italian virtuoso Pietro Locatelli is reported to have said: "No fiddler can play anything with a long bow that he can't play with a short one" (Seletsky 292).

Transitional bows entered the musical scene in the 1760s, overlapping with long bows. The new bows, made with differing lengths and weights, shared both the characteristic of even higher "battle-axe," "hatchet," or swan bill shapes at the tip as well as varying degrees of inward cambre. The Tourte bow of the 1780s – longer and heavier than what came before at 74.5 cm (29 inches) and 57–60 grams (2–2.1 ounces), and often with more severe cambre – gained popularity in the closing years of the century, but did not completely outmode the long bow or the transitional bow during Haydn's lifetime.

During his freelancing years in Vienna, Griesinger tells us that "in the evenings, Haydn often went 'gassatim' [street performing] with his musical comrades ... and he recalled having composed a quintet for that purpose in the year 1753" (Landon I 62). Though their dates are uncertain, a number of *cassatios* (perhaps derivative of the term "Gasse" or "little street") exist, which may have been composed for this purpose. If the young Haydn performed one of these pieces at an evening serenade on the streets of Vienna during a temporal crossroads in bow construction, it is conceivable that he played with the declining short bow. Later, during his first decade at Eszterháza, Haydn composed the Violin Concerto in C major (Hob.VIIa:1) for first violinist Luigi Tomasini. Although the long bow was gaining favor by this time, Tomasini may have adhered to the Italian (Corellian) tradition of short bow performance. Of Italian birth, Tomasini had also studied for a short time in Venice in 1759.

The baryton, a favorite instrument of Prince Nicolaus I, resembles the bass viol in size and shape, is held upright, and has a flat back, a fretted fingerboard, six bowed (gut) strings tuned in varying combinations of thirds and fourths, and a set of resonating strings positioned behind the fingerboard (see Gartrell). In contrast to the norm, the prince's instrument, constructed by Johann Joseph Stadlmann in Vienna in 1750, featured seven bowed strings, tuned A, D, G, c, e, a, d', and ten sympathetic strings, tuned A, d, e, f♯, g, a, b, c♯ d', e', which could vibrate independently or be plucked by the left thumb. The bowed strings afford the player more direct control over sound production while the plucked strings produce a short, quieter, lower-pitched sound. The scalar tuning of the plucked manual also enables the performer to provide a bass line of contrasting timbre in counterpoint with the bowed melody – typically in alternation, although on occasion Haydn requires the bowed and plucked strings to be played simultaneously. The bowing and plucking action increases the sense of virtuosic display since the performer's left hand produces two separate sound-actions, one visible, the other having no visible sound source – creating a ghosting effect that adds a sense of mystery to the performance. In general, Haydn's music for the baryton rarely exploits the instrument's full virtuosic potential. In addition to Haydn, Esterházy musicians who played the baryton included Andreas Lidl, horn player Carl Franz, cellist Joseph Weigl, and Tomasini, suggesting a broader SOCIABLE dimension to the performance of baryton duets and trios at court. (For an overview of Haydn's nearly two hundred baryton duets and trios, see *Oxford Companion* 14–17.)

In keyboards, the harpsichord with "multiple-broken" short octave in the bass (Beghin 2015a) was commonplace in Austria in the mid-eighteenth century. At least six harpsichords, one spinet, and one clavichord with this layout are extant, and in 1793, a Viennese advertisement still referred to a chromatic keyboard as "French." During the second half of the eighteenth century, the emerging fortepiano existed with incredibly diverse mechanism types, all of which fell into one of two general categories: a mechanism that pushed the hammer up toward the strings (Stossmechanik), or a mechanism that pulled the hammer up toward the strings (Prellmechanik). These fundamental principles were both employed in the non-escapement actions of square pianos – for instance the *stoss*-action of English instruments by Zumpe and the *prell*-action of various Rhineland area instruments. Throughout the last three decades of the eighteenth century, *stoss* and *prell* were also employed in a diverse European selection of escapement actions, for instruments of both square and grand design: the *stoss*-action of Cristofori, with intermediate lever between key and hammer, persisted in various permutations throughout the eighteenth century; forms of hopper propelled *stoss*-action (without intermediate lever) appeared in England, Germany, and Austria; and the Prellmechanik, with a hammer directly connected to the key, became widely influential in Germany and Austria.

Four pieces by Haydn require left-hand stretches that can only be played on a short octave keyboard: the Sonata in E minor (Hob.XVI:47), the Variations in A major (Hob.XVII:2), the Divertimento "Il maestro e lo scolare" (Hob.XVIIa:1), and the "Sauschneider" Capriccio (Hob.XVII:1). The Capriccio alone can be dated to 1765 through an autograph manuscript in Haydn's hand. Using a replica of a short-octave harpsichord, made after a 1755 instrument by Johann Leydecker, Beghin reimagined the Capriccio as a kind of THEATER piece for the keyboardist, one in which the short octave constellation of keys is a part of the performance (Beghin 2009/2011, Chapter 3 of the book and Program 1 of the recording). No harpsichords from the Esterházy court are extant, and written records of the harpsichords do not describe the key configuration. However, the short octave was certainly a mainstay of the musical scene in Haydn's Vienna, from his freelancing years in the 1750s to his earlier years at Eszterháza. In October 1788, a letter from Haydn to the publisher Artaria explains that he had obtained, by necessity, a fortepiano from Wenzel Schanz. The Viennese builder was *schutzverwandt* (protected) by a government license to build keyboard instruments even though he was not an indoctrinated *Meister* of the guild. Although no instruments by Wenzel Schanz survive, some by his younger brother Johann have come down to us; but because Johann did become a *Meister*, he could not have officially trained with Wenzel, which only complicates the case for the similarity between the brothers' instruments. Using Haydn's letters, the historical price of instruments, and the currents of fortepiano construction in the 1780s as guiding factors, Maunder and Beghin have argued that the Wenzel Schanz fortepiano was a square, and furthermore, that it could very well have contained a Viennese *Stossmechanik*, much like that in a contemporary square piano by Ignaz Kober (1788; see Figure 12). The pieces that necessitated his purchase of the Wenzel Schanz were the Keyboard Trios, Hob.XV:11–13 for fortepiano, violin, and cello. In 1795, after playing fortepianos of square and grand design in London, Haydn brought home an English grand fortepiano by Longman & Broderip. Instruments such as this one, with English *Stossmechanik*, were active influences in Haydn's composition of works during the London period, including the Sonata in E♭ major, Hob.XVII:52. (Regarding organs, see CHURCH.) ROBERT GIGLIO

Figure 12 Replica of a 1788 Ignaz Kober square piano (Chris Maene – Ruiselede, Belgium, 2007). Photo by Jeremy Tusz. Reproduced with permission of Tom Beghin, Orpheus Institute.

FURTHER READING

Beghin (2009/11, 2015a); Bryan (1973); Cole (1998); Fitzpatrick (1970); Gartrell (2009); Hiebert (1992); Landon I and II; Maunder (1998b), *Oxford Companion*; Powell (2002); Seletsky (2004); Walter (1970).

Italy – see European Contexts

J

Jewish Culture In the mid-eighteenth century, Jewish stereotypes were engrained in European culture (see HaCohen) and frequently caricatured in a comedic manner in the THEATER. Early in his career, Haydn incorporated coded Jewish caricatures in two comedic works for the stage: *Der (neue) krumme Teufel* (The [new] limping devil, 1752; rev. 1759) for the German Theater in Vienna; and *Lo speziale* (The apothecary, 1768) for Eszterháza. During this period Haydn had many occasions to observe and possibly interact with Jews near his places of employment in both VIENNA and EISENSTADT. In the Habsburg capital, he worked with the well-known comic actor Johann Joseph Felix von Kurz (Bernardon), who specialized in portraying Jewish caricatures in lowbrow German comedies. Also, Leopoldstadt, home to the Jewish ghetto in Vienna, was located directly across from the church of the Barmherzige Brüder (Brothers Hospitallers) where Haydn worked in the later 1750s. Similarly, in the small town of Eisenstadt, Jews lived in a protected community – one of the "Sieben Gemeinde" or seven Jewish communities on Esterházy lands – located immediately west of the Esterházy palace. The windows of the communal synagogue as well as the western gate of the ghetto opened onto the main thoroughfare connecting the palace and the Bergkirche in Oberberg – a road Haydn would have travelled frequently when moving from his home or workplace within the town walls to the church on the hill (see Figure 13; see also BURGENLAND; TRAVEL AND EXPLORATION).

Traveling theatrical troupes visiting the rural outpost of Eszterháza also included actors skilled at playing the Jew (see Horányi; Och). These include Carl Wahr's travelling troupe (1773–76) and Franz Diwald's company (1784). Unlike other stereotypical characters, such as young lovers, old fathers, noblemen, servants, soldiers, and country bumpkins, the Jew was the only category of stage character identified by ethnicity or religion. *Lo speziale*, composed for the opening of the new court opera house in 1768, is Haydn's only Italian opera alluding to Jewish stereotypes – especially notable in the depiction of the apothecary (see Clark 2009a). Despite issuing Edicts of Toleration in 1782, Joseph II and subsequent Habsburg rulers also seem to have shared Prince Nicolaus's predilection for Jewish characterizations on stage, since repertory presented at the National Theater between from 1788 onwards also included musical works featuring Jewish stereotypes (see Buch).

In Act 3 of *Lo speziale*, the cross-dressed female playing the role of the young male suitor, Volpino, masquerades as a Turkish ambassador when attempting to lure the apothecary to Constantinople to work for the sultan. In the aria "Salamelica, Semprugna cara," Haydn invokes the *faux* Turk through the use of

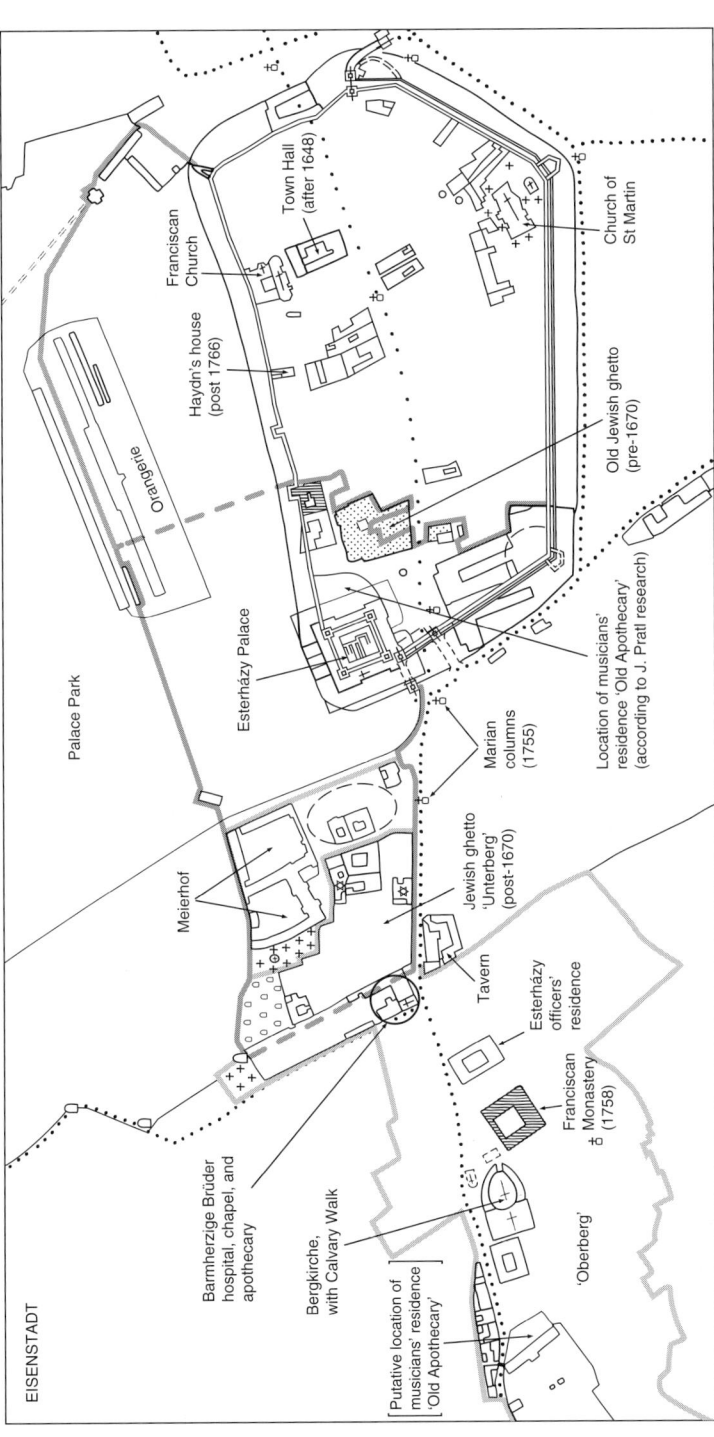

Figure 13 Digitally altered map of Eisenstadt showing the Unterberg ghetto in relation to the Eszterházy palace, the Freistadt to the west of the Barmherzige Brüder complex, and the Oberberg where the Bergkirche and Kalvarienberg are located. From Harold Prickler (ed.), Österreichischer Städteatlas, 3: Eisenstadt (Vienna: Wiener Stadt- und Landesarchiv, 1988). Reproduced with permission of the Wiener Stadt- und Landesarchiv.

a garbled Muslim greeting accompanied by a rebounding rhythmic figure in duple meter featuring the oscillation of the first and third scale degrees to signal the Törökös – a dance "in Turkish style" developed in central Hungary under Ottoman rule and performed at weddings by dancers dressed in pseudo-Turkish costumes (see Head; EXOTICISM). Later, mock synagogue music effecting the lamentation style of the Jewish *niggun* (Yiddish *nigun*) underscores the "dadl dadl" phrase, a wordless babble repeated within the Allegretto section and expanded at the close of the Presto section. Dittersdorf, Haydn's formative busking partner in mid-century Vienna, similarly uses a disguised character to impersonate a Jew as a ruse to fool a jealous and gullible character in Act 3 of *Das rote Käppchen* (1788). Strong stylistic consistency characterizes musical depictions of Jews on the stage.

Selected settings of the mass by Haydn suggest accommodation to non-Catholic listeners. His setting of the *Missa brevis Sancti Joannis de Deo* (c. 1775), honoring St. John of God, the patron saint of the Brothers Hospitallers, may have been designed to accommodate congregants in the process of transitioning to the Catholic faith. In the *Credo* of this mass, the second article of faith, which describes Jesus Christ as the only Son of God, is omitted, its absence disguised by the mellifluous texture created by the *missa brevis* style, with different lines of text delivered simultaneously by the soprano, alto, tenor, and bass vocal parts (see Clark 2009b; see also RELIGION AND SPIRITUAL BELIEFS; CHURCH). Although textual omissions in this and other mass settings (e.g., *Missa in angustiis* and the *Theresienmesse*) have traditionally been attributed to Haydn's absentmindedness, the consistency of the omissions suggests they were intentional, and may have symbolized the composer's discontent with the authoritarian nature of the Church, revealing his sociopolitical ideals, empathetic ENLIGHTENMENT views, or efforts toward easing the process of conversion.

The Judeo-Christian text of *The Creation* (1798), whose bilingual English–German text acknowledges difference, also benefits from a multi-faith investigation through the lens of the Jewish *Haskalah* (Enlightenment), a socially transformative period in European Jewry. Interconnections between the secular Enlightenment and the religious Enlightenment (see Sorkin) offer avenues for exploring the creation narrative in relation to both Handelian oratorios on Old Testament texts as well Haydn's transnational experiences, transcultural exchanges and growing COSMOPOLITANISM in the 1790s – including Haydn's close interpersonal RELATIONSHIP with the violinist, impresario, and converted Jew, Johann Peter Salomon, as well as his engagement with the writings of Moses Mendelssohn, whose final book was in Haydn's library. John Milton's *Paradise Lost* also conveys a close understanding of Hebrew scholarship and exegesis (see MATERIAL CULTURE). Haydn's and Swieten's representation of prelapsarian life in *The Creation*, which is indebted to Book 7 of Milton's epic, conveys the poet's understanding of Mosaic law as the principal source of Eden's polity before the Fall (see Rosenblatt).

CARYL CLARK

FURTHER READING

Buch (2012); Clark (2009a, 2009b, 2010, 2016, 2017); HaCohen (2011); Head (2005); Horányi (1962); Och (1995); Rosenblatt (1994); Sorkin (2008).

L

Large Ensembles – see Leading Large Ensembles

Leading Large Ensembles During his long working life, Haydn witnessed tremendous changes in large ensemble performance practice. Early in his career he probably led performances of his symphonies from the violin, while late in life he conducted the premiere of *The Creation* with a baton in his hand. The job of leading large ensembles was a role in transition.

It has long been assumed that the frequent concerts (*Accademien*) at Eszterháza took place in the splendid main hall or ceremonial room (see Performance Spaces). Recently, however, Malina has persuasively argued that this room was in fact used mainly for entertaining aristocratic visitors. There may have been music played here, but most likely as background entertainment or for dancing. Some concerts were given in the picture gallery, but the main venue was the opera house, which sadly no longer exists. The rooms in the central block of the palace were for nobles and the family only. Concerts, operas, and any events that might be open to the public took place in special buildings situated away from the palace itself.

Haydn's initial orchestra was small. The basic ensemble started with only eleven strings, which may have been increased by some wind players who doubled on string instruments, and soon growing to fourteen strings; the total, including winds, was never more than twenty-four. Modern experience shows that a bassoon doubling the bass line helps to augment the sound in the small ensemble, while three (later four) violins in each section helps improve blend and intonation. (See Figure 14; see also Instruments and Orchestration.) Haydn certainly led the orchestra, but it's unlikely he did so from the keyboard – given recent research by Malina that updates that of Webster. (See also Lowe.) The opera house certainly had a keyboard, and the surviving programs show a mixed repertoire of instrumental and vocal music, so it's plausible that Haydn led the symphonies from the violin and then directed the vocal numbers from the keyboard.

Haydn's first known encounter with a large musical ensemble occurred in 1775 when he was commissioned to compose an oratorio, *Il ritorno di Tobia*, for the Tonkünstler-Societät. By far the largest group of performers in Vienna, their ranks were increased by solo singers from Eszterháza. Haydn's oratorio was not the only work on the program; there were also two concertos played by members of the Esterházy orchestra – a violin concerto performed by Tomasini on April 2 and a cello concerto performed on April 4, 1775. Haydn directed the performance, presumably from the keyboard, given the large number of musicians on stage in the Burgtheater. Performing forces (chorus and

ESZTERHÁZA – EISENSTADT

c. 1760 – c. 1767:
  Strings: 3 vi, 3 v2, 1 va, 1 vc, 1 db
  Winds, etc: 0–1 fl, 2 ob, 1–2 bn / 2 hn, [2 tr, timp] = 13–16.
  Haydn: violin (instrumental music), or, harpsichord (vocal music)

c. 1768 – c. 1775:
  Strings: 4 vi, 4 v2, 2 va, 1 vc, 1 db
  Winds: 0–1 fl, 2 ob, 1–2 bn / 2 hn [2 tr, timp] = 16–18.
  Haydn: violin (instrumental music), or, harpsichord (vocal music)

—

1780s:
  Strings: 6 vi, 5 v2, 2 va, 2 vc, 2 db
  Winds: 1 fl, 2 ob, 2 bn / 2 hn, 2 tr, timp = 22–24

L'ORCHESTRE DE LA LOGE OLYMPIQUE, PARIS (1786)
  Strings: 14 vi, 14 v2, 7 va, 10 vc, 4 db
  Winds: 2–3 fl, 2 ob, 2 clar, 2 bn / 4 hn, 2 tr, timp = 65

1790s:

SALOMON CONCERTS, LONDON (1792–94)
  Strings: 8 vi, 8 v2, 4 va, 5 vc, 4 db
  Winds: 1–2 fl, 2 ob, 2 bn / 2 hn, 2 tr, timp = 37–38

PROFESSIONAL CONCERTS, LONDON (1795)
  Strings: 10 vi, 10 v2, 5 va, 6 vc, 5 db
  Winds: 2 fl, 2 ob, 2 clar, 2 bn / 2 hn, 2 tr, timp = c. 60
  Haydn: on keyboard

Figure 14 A summary of Haydn's orchestral forces c. 1761–95. Reproduced from Neal Zaslaw, "Haydn's Orchestras and His Orchestration to 1779, with an Excursus on the Times-of-Day Symphonies," in *Engaging Haydn: Culture, Context, Criticism*, Mary Hunter and Richard Will (eds.). Cambridge University Press, 2012: 312. Used by permission of author and press.

orchestra) numbered as many as two hundred at the semi-annual performances of Italian oratorio in the 1770s. In 1781 when Mozart first appeared with the ensemble, the orchestra numbered ninety-two and the chorus fifty-four. The string section consisted of forty violins, eight violas, nine cellos, and eleven basses, while the winds and brass included two flutes, seven oboes, six bassoons and four horns (see Edge). The main reason for the enormous numbers was that AMATEURS, some noble, joined the ranks of the professional performers. It was considered a badge of honor to perform: as Mozart observed in a letter to his father, "everyone who has any inkling of music plays gratis" (March 24, 1781). But Paul Wranitzky complained about the poor acoustics when the musicians were behind the proscenium arch. He raised money to have a temporary shell built to improve the sound but when it was used in a performance of Haydn's *Creation* in 1807, it was found ineffective and was eventually abandoned (see Spitzer and Zaslaw). It is doubtful if all the orchestra members played in every piece, especially in the concertos and arias; some of the less talented amateurs likely omitted the trickier passages. Haydn's music was performed often by the Society, with a revised version of *Tobia* given in 1784. His symphonies were played with some regularity, enabling the composer to hear what his music sounded like when performed by large forces in a 1,350-seat theater (see Cole). In 1783, the program included music by both Haydn and Mozart, and as Heartz (2009) observes, this may be the first time that the two composers met, beginning a friendship that would last until Mozart's death.

Haydn never visited Paris in person, but his music was often performed there. At the Concert Spirituel in the 1770s and 80s, it became the norm to begin each concert with a Haydn symphony. Harrison provides two tables of how popular Haydn's symphonies were in the years 1777 to 1790. The concerts were given in the Salle des Cent-Suisses at the Tuilleries, a cube-shaped hall. There was much criticism of the placement of the musicians. As noted in the *Journal de musique* in 1771: "The first and second violins neither see nor hear each other; consequently, they often lack good ensemble. The flutes and oboes are buried among the bass instruments and lose their effect; the horns are no better placed, and the miserable organ, which is in the midst of the violas, divides and destroys all the harmony" (Heartz 2003, 208–9). By 1773, the stage had been elevated and the orchestra rearranged. The band was now led by the concertmaster and the principal second violin rather than in the old style by a *batteur de musique*. In 1775, the orchestra numbered sixty: twenty-six violins, four violas, ten cellos, four basses, two flutes, three oboes, two clarinets, four bassoons, pairs of horns and trumpets, plus timpani (Zaslaw 1989b).

After 1786 the concerts moved to the Salle des Gardes, which was, as Lister shows, of a similar size to the Hanover Square Rooms in LONDON. The final concert in the Salle des Cent-Suisses on April 13, 1784 most appropriately ended with Haydn's "Farewell" Symphony (see Heartz 1993).

In 1784 the Comte d'Ogny, one of the directors of MASONIC Le Concert de la Loge Olympique, approached Haydn with a prestigious international commission to write six symphonies. Delivered in 1786, the "Paris" Symphonies (nos. 82 through 87) soon appeared in print in Paris, London and VIENNA (see PUBLISHERS AND PUBLISHING). In 1786, L'Orchestre de la Loge Olympique totalled sixty-five players, of whom twelve were gentleman amateurs who each shared a stand with a professional (see Figure 14). Lister provides a projected seating plan of the orchestra along with some poignant old photographs of the venue before it was destroyed in May 1871. He also shows how the total roster of musicians changed slightly from year to year. The orchestra had often been directed by Le Chevalier de Saint-Georges, but during the performances of the "Paris" Symphonies he was in London taking part in a fencing exhibition.

After the death of Prince Nicholas Esterházy in 1790 and the subsequent reduction in the size of the musical establishment, Haydn accepted an invitation to travel to London. Contracted to write a dozen symphonies and an opera, he still found time to attend other musical events. He was said to have been deeply moved by the Handel Commemoration performance featuring over 1,000 musicians in Westminster Abbey in May 1791 (see Rice). At the concerts held in the Hanover Square Rooms, Haydn and concert master Johann Peter

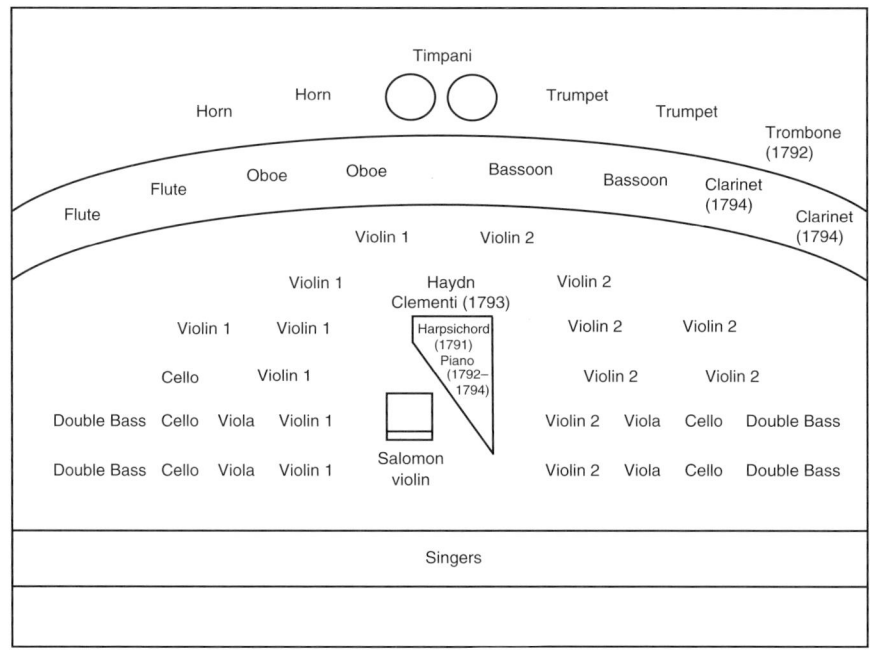

Figure 15 Reconstruction of orchestral seating arrangement of Salomon's concerts in London 1791–94. Adapted from Simon McVeigh, *Concert Life in London from Mozart to Haydn* (1993), 212, and Neal Zaslaw, *Mozart's Symphonies: Context, Performance Practice, Reception* (1989), 465.

Salomon co-directed – the composer from the fortepiano and Salomon from the violin. In 1792 the band consisted of up to thirty-eight musicians: sixteen violins, four violas, five cellos, four basses with pairs of wind and brass, plus a trombone, and timpani; and the following year this number increased to forty-one, with the addition of more string players. The Hanover Square Rooms where the concerts took place was seventy-nine feet by thirty-three with a ceiling about twenty-eight feet high (see Zaslaw 1976–77). One thing immediately noticed by the approximately six hundred audience members was Haydn's novel arrangement of the musicians: the violins were divided, as was customary, but so were all the rest of the strings, while the winds sat in a semi-circular amphitheater arrangement above them. (See Figure 15; I have used this set up with the all the string instruments sitting in stereo on several occasions and find that it works very well.) However, given that the Bach-Abel concerts featured symphonies for double orchestra, was this string seating arrangement totally novel in London? Whether the upper strings and winds stood to perform, which was the norm at the time, is not known. At center stage, Haydn sat at a fortepiano facing the audience, while Salomon stood approximately where a conductor might stand today. (Reconstructions showing Haydn with his back to the audience may reflect REHEARSAL positioning.)

Salomon would have directed the performance, but Haydn seems to have been in charge of the rehearsals. According to his biographer, Dies:

> [Haydn] had laid out a symphony which began with a short Adagio. Three notes of identical pitch opened the music. But since the orchestra played these three notes too forcefully, Haydn stopped the music by waving and "Sh! Sh!" During the following silence, a German violoncello player quite near to Haydn said his mind to his partner in German: "Hey, he doesn't even like the first three notes, how's he going to like the others?" (Gotwals 84f.; Landon III).

Landon posits that the symphony was probably No. 92 in G major, "Oxford." A review in *The Times* (February 20, 1792) of the concert featuring the premiere of Symphony No. 93 in D major credits Salomon as director: "The Orchestra under the direction of SALOMON, produced an effect, that may with propriety be said, was A SOUL AND BODY OF HARMONY" (Landon III 134).

Haydn's final season of concerts in 1795 was held in the Music Room in the recently renovated King's Theatre. Slightly larger than the Hanover Square Rooms, the Music Room was ninety-five feet long, forty-six feet wide and thirty-five feet high and accommodated an orchestra of about sixty players (see Zaslaw 1977; see also PERFORMANCE SPACES). For his benefit concert on May 4, 1795, an annotated program survives in which the Symphony No. 100 in G major, "Military" is described as being "grand but very noisy" (Landon III 307).

On his return to Vienna, Haydn was able to put into practice what he had heard in London, especially in his performances of *The Creation* and *The Seasons*. Of the forty-plus performances of *The Creation* that were given in Vienna during Haydn's lifetime, nearly half were directed by the composer. Since a keyboard player is often listed, it becomes clear that Haydn is actually leading – most likely with a baton. For the private performances in the Schwarzenburg Palace, it is not known exactly how many musicians took part, but for the public performances at the Burgtheater the following month, several commentators, including Constanze Mozart, put the figure at about 180, but whether that is the total or just the orchestra is difficult to say. Brown estimates that 120 would be in the orchestra and 60 in the chorus. This may seem to be a strangely small choir for such a large group of players, but it was not uncommon then for the chorus to be placed in front of the orchestra on either side of the soloists. One can see this type of seating plan in the reconstruction of the 1799 Burgtheater performance by Feder (described below) and in the Balthazar Wigand painting of the last performance of *The Creation* that Haydn attended in the Old Hall of Vienna University on March 27, 1808, as well as in the reconstruction of the first public performance prepared by Georg Feder. (See Figure 16; see also the reconstruction in Brown 30.)

I conducted a performance of *The Creation* with this set up – with choir out in front – in 1992 at the Herbst Theater in San Francisco. Haydn had an extra choir director nearer the chorus, but even without this assistant, I found it surprisingly easy to lead the entire ensemble once everyone got the hang of it. Fewer choristers were needed, the balance was very easy to control, and the

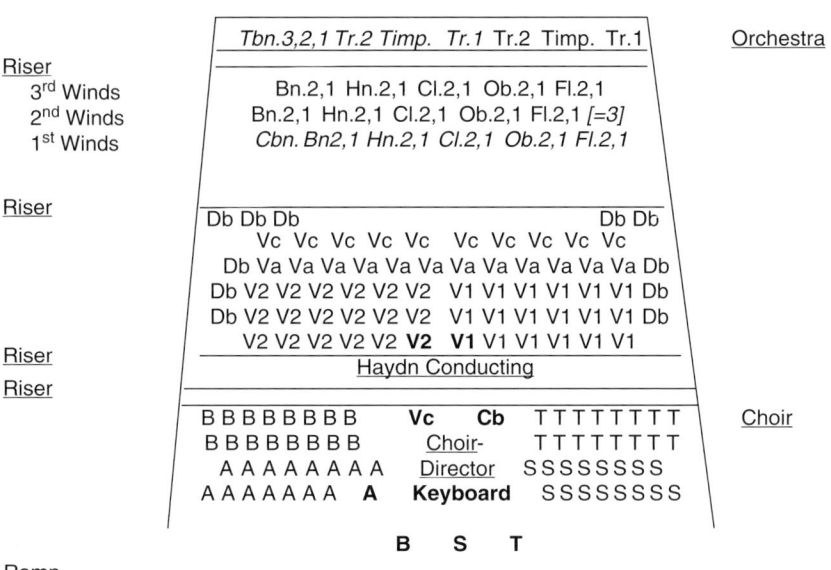

Explanatory Notes

V – Violin
Cursive Print – obbligato/solo
Bold Print:
    V1 & V2 – First and second principal violins
    Vc & Cb – Recitative accompaniment
    A – Solo Alto in the closing chorus
    B, S, T – Bass, Soprano, and Tenor solo

Figure 16 A reconstruction of the seating plan of musicians at the performance of *The Creation* in the old Burgtheater, Vienna, March 19, 1798. Reproduced and translated from Georg Feder, *Joseph Haydn: Die Schöpfung* (Kassel: Bärenreiter, 1999), 112. © 1999 Bärenreiter-Verlag Karl Vötterle GmbH and Co. KG, Kassel. Used with kind permission.

blend between soloists and chorus was perfect. The orchestra and choir begin a movement together in only two choruses, so coordinating entries was easily accomplished. PERFORMANCES where the soloists are placed behind the orchestra just in front of the chorus are, in my estimation, poorly balanced.

Johan Berwald gives an excellent description of the seating plan for the performance in the Burgtheater on March 19, 1799:

> When we entered, we saw that the stage proper was set up in the form of an amphitheatre. Down below at the fortepiano sat Kapellmeister Weigl, surrounded by the vocal soloists, the chorus, a violoncello and a double bass. At one level higher stood Haydn himself with his conductor's baton. Still a level higher on one side were the first violins, led by Paul Wranistzky

and on the other the second violins, led by his brother Anton Wranitzky. In the centre: the violas and double basses [sic cellos?]. In the wings, more double basses; on higher levels the wind instruments, and at the very top: trumpets, kettle drums, and trombones (Brown 29).

The wind parts were usually doubled or even tripled in these large-scale performances. The third flute, which plays only at the opening of Part 3 of *The Creation*, is not an extra who has to sit there unemployed during Parts 1 and 2. Haydn is always careful to write SOLO if he only wants one player on a line.

Performances on this grand scale generally took place during the day. For instance, the Handel Commemoration Concerts in Westminster Abbey started at noon (see Burney). Light is visible through the windows in Edward Edwards's painting of the 1791 Handel Commemoration in Westminster Abbey, now in the Centre for British Art at Yale, and also in Wigand's forementioned painting of the celebratory performance of *The Creation* in 1808 (although this could be attributable to artistic license). Candles were expensive as well as dangerous, and well into the nineteenth century only theaters and opera houses were equipped to provide enough illumination for both audience and performers. Concert halls remained small for this reason, and also typically had windows – as in the opera house at Eszterháza. Low level of light is one of the reasons that conductors began to use batons, and some even wore white gloves so that the musicians could better follow them. Rehearsals generally took place in the morning for the same reason.

NICHOLAS MCGEGAN

FURTHER READING
Brown (1986b); Burney (1785); CCLN; Cole (1998); Edge (1992a); Gotwals; Harrison (1998); Heartz (1982, 1993, 2003, 2009); Landon III; Lister (2004); Lowe (2005); Malina (2016b); McVeigh (1993); Rice (2012); Smidak (1996); Spitzer and Zaslaw (2004); Webster (1990); Zaslaw (1976–77, 1989b, 2012).

Librettos and Librettists The majority of Haydn's music-dramatic output is Italian *opera buffa* (eighteen out of twenty-six operas listed in *New Grove*). Haydn favored authors and texts already set decades earlier by other COMPOSERS, but the extent to which he altered these libretti reveal an intention to enhance possibilities for musical dramatization as well as to renew and modernize the tradition.

During his tenure at ESZTERHÁZA, Haydn's responsibilities were not only to compose new operas, but also to edit and produce operas by other composers. He served as artistic director, impresario, stage director, and conductor; he also edited librettos that he did not set to music and that were never produced at Eszterháza (see Bartha and Somfai; Biba). For instance, a copy of the printed libretto of Marco Coltellini's *Piramo e Tisbe* (Vienna 1777), with music by Venanzio Rauzzini, contains handwritten comments and alterations by Haydn himself prepared for possible production at Eszterháza. From recent research conducted by Malina we know that many printed libretti from the Esterházy archives – including operas performed there and elsewhere over a period of 150 years – were selected and for a long time jealously preserved by archivist János Hárich, resurfacing only after his death in 1990. Malina's survey of seventy-six libretti belonging to seventy-three operas performed under

Haydn's direction confirms that this repertory, which many believed to have been dispersed or destroyed during World War II, survived nearly intact.

Comic libretti by the Venetian playwright Carlo Goldoni were frequently adapted for Eszterháza. La buona figliuola, one of the century's most popular operas, based on Richardson's Pamela, was performed during the earliest theatrical season in 1776, followed by other Goldoni comedies set to music by Haydn, Gassmann, Dittersdorf, Gazzaniga, and Righini. Two other important comic librettists whose works were represented at Eszterháza (both set by composers other than Haydn) were Gennaro Antonio Federico, who gained long-lasting fame through his intermezzi La serva padrona, and the best-selling fiction writer, journalist, and playwright Pietro Chiari. While Chiari, Federico, and Goldoni were mostly active in the first half of the century, many other authors of the Esterházy repertory were contemporaries of Haydn, such as Nunziato Porta, Giuseppe Petrosellini, and Antonio Palomba. Two operas by Palomba deal with North AMERICAN themes. For Palomba's and Guglielmi's La quakera spiritosa, one of the most radical operas representing America during the Revolutionary era, Haydn wrote a new aria for the 1787 Eszterháza production: "Vada adagio signorina" (Hob.XXIVb/12) (discussed by Polzonetti 2011). Among Giovanni Bertati's many libretti in the Esterházy collection is Il convitato di pietra (Don Giovanni), set as a dramma tragicomico by Righini. Interestingly, as Biba shows, neither Mozart and Da Ponte's Don Giovanni nor Le nozze di Figaro were presented at Eszterháza. The court, however, did not oppose Paisiello and Petrosellini's Il barbiere di Siviglia, the prequel of Le nozze di Figaro, which was performed there in 1790 (see THEATER).

Goldoni remains to this day the only Italian librettist who has secured a strong presence in the literary canon. In his libretti, Goldoni challenged the old commedia dell'arte conventions, using them to establish new comic operatic conventions based on a tripartite system of dramatic roles – buffa, mezzo carattere and seria – each characterized by a different rhetorical level. For this reason, the Goldoni–Haydn operas may appear today more conservative than the Da Ponte–Mozart operas, as they show a stricter adherence to the conventions of buffa roles. Nevertheless, the degree to which Haydn alters and ideologically recontextualizes Goldoni's libretti is remarkable, offering a reading of these old texts that is perfectly in line with the philosophical and political ideas of the late ENLIGHTENMENT and even with proto-Romanticism. Lo speziale (1768), for instance, appears on the surface as a simplification of Goldoni's text, as it eliminates the seria roles or parti serie; however, in Haydn's setting the protagonist is represented as a stereotypical Jew, obsessed with news and gazettes (i.e., with the world around him), but unable to integrate into society (see Clark 2009a; see also JEWISH CULTURE). Le pescatrici (1770) is a libretto in line with the topos of interclass marriage and recognition of noble birth that Goldoni successfully exploited in La buona figliuola. The libretto then allowed for an exploration of a broader variety of stylistic levels and sentimental overtones, but with a dangerously problematic representation of class interaction and social fluidity reflecting reformist POLITICS adopted by the Esterházy COURT (see Green). A similar cross-genre contamination of buffa and semiseria is clear in Francesco Puttini's libretto of La vera costanza, which solidly belongs to the sentimental subgenre as described by

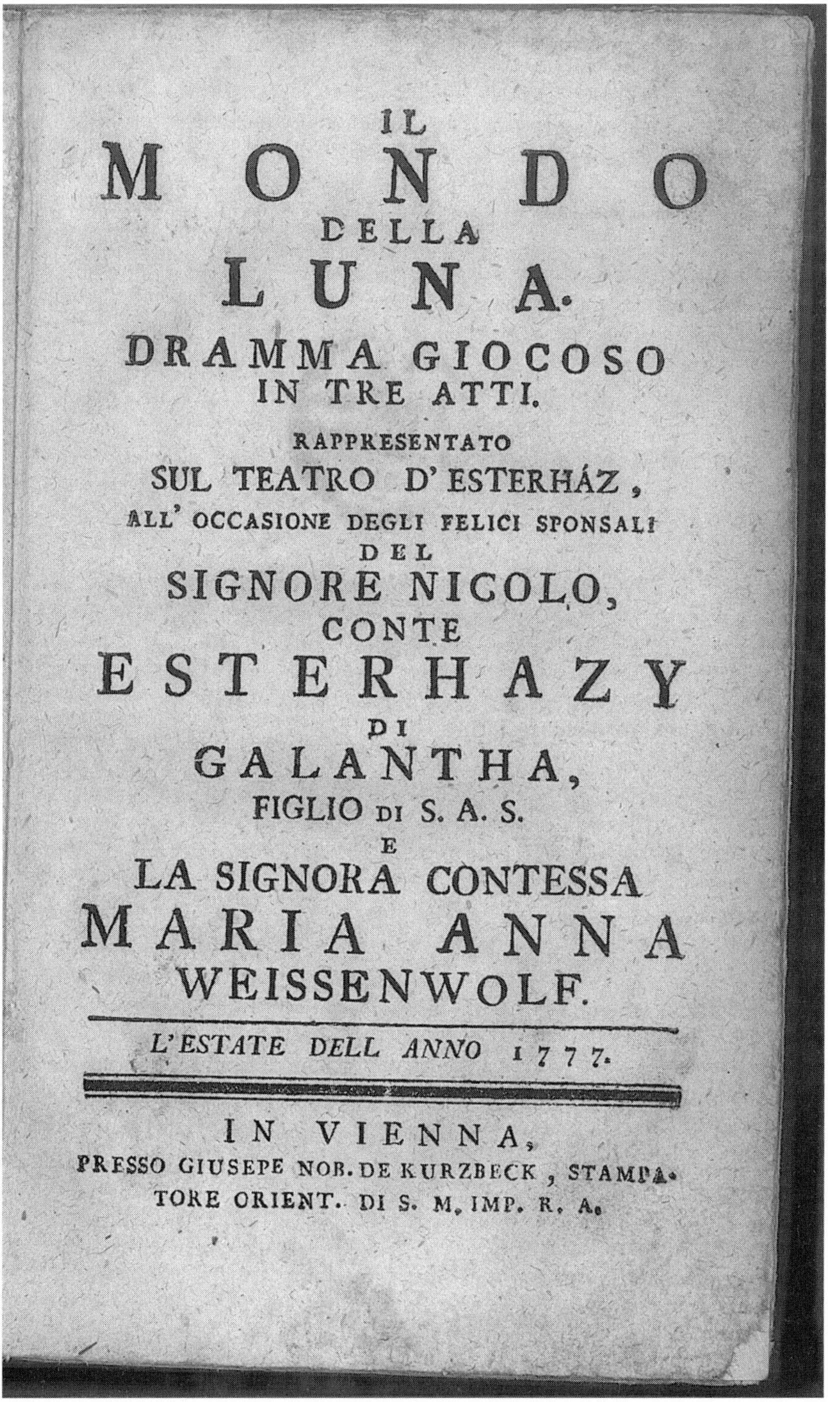

> IL
> # MONDO
> DELLA
> # LUNA.
> DRAMMA GIOCOSO
> IN TRE ATTI.
>
> RAPPRESENTATO
> SUL TEATRO D'ESTERHÁZ,
> ALL' OCCASIONE DEGLI FELICI SPONSALI
> DEL
> SIGNORE NICOLO,
> CONTE
> # ESTERHAZY
> DI
> GALANTHA,
> FIGLIO DI S. A. S.
> E
> LA SIGNORA CONTESSA
> # MARIA ANNA
> WEISSENWOLF.
>
> L'ESTATE DELL ANNO 1777.
>
> IN VIENNA,
> PRESSO GIUSEPE NOB. DE KURZBECK, STAMPA-
> TORE ORIENT. DI S. M. IMP. R. A.

Figure 17 Title page of libretto for *Il mondo della luna*, *opera buffa* performed at Eszterháza in 1777. Reproduced with permission of National Széchényi Library in Budapest.

Waldoff (see EMPFINDSAMKEIT). Polzonetti (2011) shows how, for Goldoni's *Il mondo della luna* (1777; Figure 17), meaningful revisions to the libretto made at Eszterháza celebrate the lunar utopia represented in the comedy with key concepts and terms related to the reception of the American Revolution in Europe at the time of the Declaration of Independence. Haydn's interest in America is further demonstrated by the choice of his lost first Singspiel, *Der neue krumme Teufel*, also titled *Arlequin, der neue Abgott Ram in Amerika*.

Haydn's setting of Metastasio's *L'isola disabitata*, first presented for Prince Nicolaus Esterházy's name-day in 1779, is also emblematic of his commitment to revamping canonic librettists and promoting innovation and reforms within an existing tradition. In this opera Haydn recontextualizes an old libretto to celebrate Eszterháza as an idealized social and cultural island and, more significantly, compounds "the sublimity of the text, its perfect amalgam of elemental emotion, elevated sentiment, and wit," to create a Metastasian reform opera (Sisman 40; see also SUBLIME; HUMOR). Haydn recognized in this libretto the potential for a cross-genre form of musical theater, already latent in Metastasio's text, which he labeled *azione teatrale* (renamed *operetta eroicomica* by Sisman). The text evokes parallels with Calzabigi's reform opera *Orfeo* set by Gluck, which Haydn emphasizes by providing detailed indications on dramatic action and stage sets. Like *Orfeo*, *L'isola disabitata* insistently invites reflection on the classical iconography of the labyrinth charged with philosophical and spiritual meanings. At the same time, it opens a window on typical Enlightenment themes of the exotic, distant natural ecosystem, and a societal isolated microcosm (see SCIENCE).

Haydn's use of libretti based on Classical and Renaissance authors reveals a similar forward-looking attitude towards the literary canon and experimentation in cross-genre opera types. Examples include the *festa teatrale* entitled *Acide* (a revision of Metastasio's adaptation of Ovid's myth), Nunziato Porta's *Orlando paladino* (after Ariosto), labeled *dramma eroicomico*, *Armida* (after Tasso), also a *dramma eroico*, and two marionette Singspiel libretti: *Dido* (after Virgil) and *Philemon und Baucis* (after Ovid). Haydn's last opera is based on Carlo Francesco Badini's libretto *L'anima del filosofo*, which revisits the Orpheus myth after Ovid and Virgil from a contemporary perspective. Composed in 1791 in ENGLAND, the opera was never performed in public during Haydn's lifetime, and was likely banned from the stage because of its metaphorical representation of current societal upheaval during the initial stages of the French Revolution. As Clark explains, in Badini's unusual alteration of the myth's ending, a mob of Bacchants poison Orpheus. In doing so, he presents the hero's death as a parallel of Socrates's execution, widely understood as a symbol of the death of reason and of tyrannical degeneration of democracy. Badini's libretto, although unmistakably tragic, presents (like many other works set by Haydn) cross-genre elements.

Libretti for Haydn's oratorios *Il ritorno di Tobia* and *The Creation* are both based on the Old Testament (see Polzonetti 2015). *Il ritorno di Tobia* was first performed during Lent 1775 in one of Vienna's opera theaters, the Kärntnertortheater, and revised in 1784, with Nancy Storace (the first Susanna in Mozart's *Le nozze di Figaro*) interpreting the role of Anna. Original sources for the libretto by

Giovanni Gastone Boccherini, brother of the composer Luigi Boccherini, provide indications for stage settings and action that may suggest that the oratorio was staged and enacted like an opera rather than performed statically as a concert piece. Extant copies of the libretto and scores indicate that the oratorio circulated widely. Remarkably it was also produced in Protestant centers such as Berlin (1777) and Leipzig (1787 and 1790), even though after the Reformation the *Book of Tobias* (or *Tobit*) remained in the canonic Bible only in the Orthodox and Catholic Churches. The interdenominational success of this oratorio is a sign of the ecumenical appeal of Haydn's sacred works. Set in the city of Nineveh, the fundamental contrast of light and darkness in the oratorio is dramatized through old Tobit's personal journey as a blind man who eventually regains his sight. Both text and music encourage a metaphorical interpretation of this central dichotomy, which was recurrent in the culture of the Enlightenment, especially in FREEMASONRY circles. Moreover, Tobia and his bride Sara celebrate a new marital ideal, abandoning old patriarchal values (a pervading theme in Haydn's comic operas) in favor of equality and mutual respect (see GENDER).

The libretto of *The Creation/Die Schöpfung*, like Haydn's 1798 musical dramatization, embodies a perfect synthesis of both RELIGIOUS and secular Enlightenment ideas with the emerging Romantic sensibility of the SUBLIME and the picturesque. Designed to appeal to Catholic, Protestant, and enlightened sensibilities of English-speaking countries, the bilingual (English and German) text by Gottfried van Swieten was initially disseminated in England and other European countries, and soon found favor abroad. Internal and contextual clues suggest that *The Creation* was conceived as an interfaith cultural endeavor during the composer's prolonged sojourns in England where he was exposed to local philosophical trends (see IDEALISM; SCIENCE). One such trend was the theory of Transformationism, which had started to gain credibility against traditional pure creationist cosmogony without immediately challenging – and yet beginning to erode – the idea of a divine, intelligent cosmogonic design. In *The Creation*, NATURE is celebrated for its creative force as well as for its ability to reveal and regenerate the beauty impressed on it by its maker. Haydn further pursued this naturalist aesthetic in his last oratorio, *Die Jahreszeiten*, based on a libretto also by Swieten after James Thomson's poem *The Seasons*. The libretto of *The Creation*, based on Genesis 1–2:3, recounts the six days of God's creation but omits almost everything from the second Biblical account (Genesis 2:4–3:24). The quotations from the English Bible in the German text are close translations from the King James Bible (as noted by Olleson). All early biographical sources, including a letter by the librettist, report that the libretto was based on a previous English source of uncertain authorship. This source, possibly edited by Thomas Linley the elder, quoted or paraphrased several lines from Milton's *Paradise Lost*. For this reason, critics have assumed that Milton's *Paradise Lost* was the oratorio's main literary model (see Landon IV; MacIntyre). However, differences with Milton's poem are as many and as striking as the similarities, which, as Bertoli suggests, explains why scholars have recently begun to approach the issue more cautiously. At a macroscopic level, whereas Milton's narrative focuses on the aftermath of the creation, specifically on the original sin and loss of Paradise, Haydn's oratorio is a joyful celebration of creation and prelapsarian life, skipping entirely the narrative of sin and fall. The orchestral "Representation of Chaos" at the beginning of the oratorio suggests that Haydn had directly consulted Milton's literary source, Ovid's *Metamorphoses*, which gained immense popularity in England during the 1790s (see Polzonetti 2012). The climactic hymn, the duet of Adam and Eve with chorus (no. 30), reviews the entire creation, adjusting the order of created things to make it more compatible with current scientific theories. More than any other libretto set by Haydn, that of *The Creation* reflects his willingness to engage in a dialectical relationship that could reconcile different religions and religious denominations, literary and philosophical traditions, and world views.

PIERPAOLO POLZONETTI

FURTHER READING
Bartha and Somfai; Bertoli (2006); Biba (2013); Clark (2005a, 2009a, 2012b); Green (1997); Hárich (1962); Landon IV; MacIntyre (1998); Malina (2017); Olleson (1966); Polzonetti (2011, 2012, 2015); Sisman (2012); Waldoff (1998).

Literature – see Reception, 1950s–Present

London and England Haydn's status as the father of the symphony and the string quartet suggests an old and wizened image, a man hovering above the mundanities of musical life with its social interactions, political interventions, and commercial endeavors. But the relationship of Haydn with London, and in particular of London with Haydn, reveals a distinctly worldly bustle; commercial and sociopolitical machinations both precipitated and determined the RECEPTION of his music, and recent studies of the composer in this metropolitan context have in turn precipitated an idealization of the composer as indicator of sociopolitical developments.

"Haydn" and "London" have become the hubs for topics that form a complex web of interrelations. The traditional view of Haydn emancipated from the fetters of COURT employment has long since been replaced with a more complicated picture of Haydn engaging with and, crucially, influencing developments in the English capital. Recent literature on Haydn in England suggests a period of work and life saturated with opportunities and developments that would prove crucial to posterity (see in particular the collection *Land of Opportunity* edited by Chesser and Jones). But it also suggests a time fraught with rivalry and intrigue, rife with struggles between warring factions – defenders of modern versus ancient music, opera impresarios and subscription concert organizers – whose members co-opted him for their purposes and who shoe-horned his music into their differing ideologies. The picture is complicated further by current historiographical interests, broadened far beyond Haydn's music to embrace the wider study of social and political history in which the composer was embroiled, and the various interests he served.

Haydn visited England twice, between January 1, 1791 and the end of June 1792, and returning on February 5, 1794, this time staying until the middle of August 1795. Yet, the conflation of the topical circles around Haydn and London predated his first visit by nearly a decade, and its resonances were felt far beyond the mid-1790s – not least in the establishment, four years after the composer's death, of the Philharmonic Society in 1813, described in its Foundation Book as devoted to "the best and most approved instrumental music" and prominently featuring Haydn's music. As Taylor has shown, Haydn's influence on London's musical life was perpetual until this formalization in the Society's statutes.

The earliest English BIOGRAPHY of Haydn appeared in *The European Magazine and London Revue* in October of 1784. Though inaccurate in many respects, this biographical account was a cornerstone in the edifice erected strategically in the British press to promote Haydn as the ingenious composer of instrumental music – possibly to boost the Bach-Abel Concerts, for and through which the Earl of Abingdon was promoting Haydn's instrumental works as the pinnacle of a modern music. As early as 1782 Haydn was described in the *Morning Herald* as the "Shakespeare of Musical composition," a conscious effort (as Sisman has explored) to entice audiences but also a nomenclature designed to herald Haydn's compositions as elevated art. This was, however, a very particular type of elevated art, one that belonged to the modern style of music advocated by the equally modern subscription concert series: music that played with the traditional rules of COUNTERPOINT and that broke the conventions of tragedy and comedy to fuse them into one and the same work. The debate of ancient versus modern music mirrored critical socio-POLITICAL divides, not because – as is often assumed – ancient and modern repertoires divided aristocratic and middle-class audiences (in fact, both repertoires relied heavily on aristocratic patronage), but because the ancient concerts promoted the establishment of an English and principally sacred repertoire, whereas the concerts of modern music thrived on the reputations and exoticism of foreigners.

Both opera and concert life in London were thriving in the later eighteenth century, and both were dominated by foreign COMPOSERS AND MUSIC PROFESSIONALS. In the mid-1780s the Italian Giovanni (John) Gallini (who was related to the Earl of Abingdon) attempted to seize control of the King's Theatre on the Haymarket, London's prime location for Italian opera since Handel's day, but his endeavors were frustrated initially by competition from Drury Lane and Covent Garden, staging popular English opera and, after the loss of the Haymarket theater to fire in 1789, the rival opera house, the Pantheon (see THEATER). Haydn's newly composed opera *L'anima del filosofo* may have fallen victim to the disputes surrounding licenses for the Italian opera waged between opposing groups of nobles supporting Gallini and the impresario O'Reilly, for the opera was never performed during Haydn's lifetime. Its performance may have been suppressed on deeper political grounds related to its radical retelling of the Orpheus myth – an allegory of events unfolding in revolutionary France (see Clark). In the field of concert music, Haydn found far greater success.

Concert life was equally dominated by an influx of foreign visitors. Two of these, J. C. Bach and C. F. Abel, established the first regular subscription series in the metropolis in 1765, soon inhabiting their purpose-built, glamorous yet exclusive concert venue at Hanover Square, built in partnership with Gallini. Other subscription series followed, yet each one was subject to the ebb and flow of London fashion and had to be reinvented time and again. Haydn's music was co-opted into perhaps London's largest phase of reinvention when, under the management of yet another German, Wilhelm Cramer, the Professional

Concerts (1785–93), as successor to the failing Bach-Abel Concerts, rode the wave of the Haydn craze. The latter phenomenon was perpetuated in the Press from the mid-1780s onwards, and relied on Haydn regularly sending new music to London. Yet another foreign-naturalized musician, Johann Peter Salomon, went to great lengths to bring Haydn to London in 1790; seeking to capitalize on the growing interest in instrumental music, Salomon recruited the greatest instrumentalists from Germany for his own concert series (1786 and 1791–94). Indeed, his success was a milestone in the cabals of London concert life, since the Professional Concerts eventually folded and Salomon's series continued to thrive on Haydn's presence and on the impresario's ability to procure exclusive rights to the composer's symphonies in London.

The illustrious London audience relished these cabals, with press reports comparing the music scene to a political scenario that required competition to achieve the greatest goals. As a result, vocal music was pitted against instrumental, ancient against modern, Italian against German and Foreign against English. An alliance was reached in the joint venture of the Opera Concert in 1795, which brought together rivalling factions; nevertheless, foreign musicians remained dominant in this series as well. The predominance of exotically named foreigners – mostly German and Italian – in London's concert scene was indeed striking. Some like Bach and Abel, later Salomon, Cramer, and Clementi, settled in London permanently, whereas others such as Pleyel and Haydn himself came for a few seasons to cement their musical fame across Europe with the help of London's press.

Haydn concluded his stay in the city by partaking in a series of benefit concerts at the King's Theatre Haymarket in May 1795 (see Figure 18). At the concert held on May 4, 1795, Haydn himself was the beneficiary. "The whole company was thoroughly pleased and so was I," Haydn wrote of the experience. "I made four thousand Gulden on this evening. Such a thing is possible only in England" (CCLN 306). Such benefits were used as both an enticement to bring foreign stars to the city and as a reward for their continued involvement in subscription concerts, as the presence of these luminaries alone made the concerts attractive and lucrative. The pattern was already established in the Bach-Abel concerts and continued through the 1780s and beyond with the Pantheon Concerts (1774–85), the Professional Concerts and eventually the Salomon Concerts. Haydn's final season in London was unusual insofar as no other subscription series followed afterwards. The composer's involvement in the benefits, however, continued the usual pattern: Haydn performed in all concerts, each one featuring a symphony by him, which he directed from the keyboard (see Leading Large Ensembles). Moreover, each benefit concert was typically given over to a musician with strong foreign associations yet adopted into the London concert scene, such as the Italian–Scottish Miss Corri, the German-born Wilhelm Cramer, the Italian Domenico Dragonetti, and even the Irishman Andrew Ashe (who was adopted by a British naval captain). It was almost as if Londoners lived out the empire's expansion by heralding the exotic as local heroes.

The aristocracy had upheld a predilection for all things German for some time, not least because they were loyal to their Hanoverian ruler. In the highest houses, then, music-making was a means of remembering one's roots and

Figure 18 OPERA HOUSE or KINGS THEATRE in the HAYMARKET. London, published by Harrison and Co., April 1795. Haydn's opera arias and duets were performed here, inserted into other composers' operas; Haydn's Benefit Concert was held at the King's Theatre's "New Room" on May 4, 1795. Image reproduced with permission of the Royal College of Music/ArenaPAL.

home, and Haydn seemed altogether happy to play to this nostalgia – especially as he described himself (in a letter to Marianne von Genzinger, dated December 20, 1791) directing his own music for four hours with the recently married daughter of the King of Prussia by his side "humming all the pieces from memory, for she had heard them so often in Berlin" (CCLN 123). As Jones has pointed out, the popularity of the generic German was also replaced in the 1790s by a more specific predilection for what Charles Burney called "the music of the Austrian school" (*General History of Music*, II, 963). In tandem with this, we can detect a shift in interest from the individual performer and his stage persona – largely perpetuated by the Italian opera heritage – onto the music, and instrumental music at that (see IDEALISM). This change mirrors a shift in perspective – a transition from perceiving the modern concert as an ephemeral amusement (albeit highbrow) to a place for perpetuating a repertoire that would outlast its composers and performers. In the first instance this appeared in a linguistic guise, with instrumental music sublimating the Italian/English musical divide in favor of a music that was formulated to communicate a new freedom to the COSMOPOLITAN and self-confessedly ENLIGHTENED, leisured, debating, and COMMERCIAL London AUDIENCE; it also heralded a new universality of brotherhood, even if the pan-European roots of its cosmopolitan self-understanding were dangerously rattled by the aftermath of the French Revolution and the early Napoleonic WARS.

When Haydn arrived in London for a second time, Austria and Britain were firmly united in the first of three coalitions against France, a unity that endured in the face of peace treaties signed between France and various other European countries. Throughout 1794, when the city's prosperity was threatened by the war efforts, Haydn's renewed presence served to assure the British of Austria's continued alliance while also affirming their belief in the glamour, glory, and universality of art. Quite apart from Haydn's own agenda, the British press depicted the composer as a symbol of brotherhood between the nations so as to ease the minds of audience members. That Haydn himself was resolved to play the role of cultural ambassador became clear in the summer of 1794 when he used the end of the concert season to travel to Portsmouth, viewing a captured and heavily damaged French vessel that had become an icon for British victory over the French, before travelling on to more luxurious and lucrative summer towns such as Bristol and Bath.

The inevitable difficulty of travelling across a Europe embroiled in hostile action made itself manifest in London in 1795 when Salomon declared that it was too difficult to hire first-rate singers from southern Europe. By this point, London was suffering the effects of the war, which worked to Haydn's advantage; the cutting-edge culture of London's musical life, fueled by political exiles from France who brought with them an astute sense of business and accomplishments in the instrument manufacturing trades, and the city's deep-seated engagement with politics had, as Mathew describes, been co-opted in a reverse move to establish Haydn's heroic aesthetic and with that the heroism of an artistic GENIUS. This heroism now had to be sustained in the absence of paid musical specialists from the continent.

The press had already sown the seeds for this transfiguration in the dispute over the virtues of ancient and modern music. And philosophical debates raged over the responsibility of the listener. That Haydn's music was praised for its inventiveness by some meant that others deemed it "desultory and unaccountable," claiming that his inventiveness was too demanding of listeners. John Marsh, writing after Haydn had already left London, stipulated that several hearings were necessary to understand and perform Haydn's music. Although he presented this in a disparaging tone, his views prepared the way for Haydn's lasting influence; indeed, as Davison describes, the composer's music was understood as demanding serious REHEARSAL and performance while containing enough riches to gain with every hearing. Historian John Hawkins had, in his *General History of the Science and Practice of Music* (1776), inadvertently aided this reception with his derogatory comments about "modern music" that "urges men to assume the character of judges of what they do not understand" (II, 919), when it was exactly this requirement of judgment that made Haydn attractive to audiences. What Hawkins read as the reflection of a far-reaching social malaise, those actively promoting the commercial world a decade later would read as the primary quality for a music fit for the London metropolis; discourse about genius and commercial discourse on audience "participation" were both flourishing in London.

Haydn, on the other hand, was focused on commercial success and immediate glorification rather than on his lasting impressions on the city. Besides playing and composing for Salomon, the project of bringing Haydn to London had been connected to the scheme of reopening the King's Theatre Haymarket and to publishing music through John Bland. Salomon, Bland and Gallini were planning a market-driven tripartite coup – a complete package that involved Haydn directing the opera, Salomon leading the orchestra and running a concert series, and the composer teaming up with Bland to publish music from the concert. (See CIRCULATION; PUBLISHERS AND PUBLISHING.)

This type of commercial concert culture relied heavily on London's flourishing press whereby concerts were advertised, a foreign visitor could be discussed and promoted, and his music offered for sale. An astute businessman, Haydn willingly participated in these market-culture endeavors and on occasion was a harsh critic of the work of his competitors. Well aware of the financial implications of these schemes, he celebrated his glorious reception when he first arrived (CCLN 115) but clearly felt the effort and exertion of doing "the round of all the newspapers for 3 successive days" and having to "dine out six times up to now" (CCLN 112). Equally, he expressed his delight at the audience's continued obsession with his music, boasting in a letter to Luigia Polzelli in Vienna in March 1791 that "at the first concert of Mr Salomon I created a furor with a new Symphony, and they had to repeat the Adagio: this had never before occurred in London" (CCLN 116).

Haydn took great interest in the eclectic London intellectual life inextricably linked to the city's commercialism. He composed for Salomon (in 1791, 1792, and 1794) and for the Opera Concerts (in 1795), and he also attended and possibly composed for various social gatherings such as POET Anne Hunter's weekly evening parties (see Grigson). His compositions of the mid-1790s bear testimony to his active engagement with English musical fashions and with manners of musical consumption in the city: they ranged from the *Twelve Sentimental Catches and Glees* honoring Lord Abingdon to the *Six Original Canzonettas* setting Anne Hunter's poems to music (see Day-O'Connell), from the trios for two flutes and cello that reflect the particularly English predilection for a gentleman's flute to the *Sonatas with an accompaniment for a violin and violoncello* that immortalized his RELATIONSHIP and infatuation with Rebecca Schroeter. He also acquired a large collection of sheet music, and delved into the fads and fashions of high society by purchasing a number of miniatures and popular engravings as well as numerous books (see Mikusi). Some of these acquisitions may have been gifted to him, but even if this was the case, he kept them as small mementos in honor of the great jigsaw puzzle that was London. As Tolley describes, his interest in British print culture appears to bear witness to his fascination with the London audience and its politics per se. In return, he furnished his noble patrons with (mock) FOLK SONGS that were the latest craze in English drawing rooms and pleasure gardens (see Will). Haydn's pattern of composition, then, was a fundamentally different one in London to what he had known in the VIENNESE sphere, and his various letters suggest that he enjoyed the metropolis for its lucrativeness and for the sheer pleasure of its market culture. Yet his connections with the burgeoning leisure industry and its uneasy relationship with artistry is one that still needs to be teased out.

If Haydn was titillated by the city's commercial opportunities and by the cult of stardom that London afforded him, there are hints that he may nevertheless have struggled with it. While his publishing contract with Longman &

Broderip assured the lasting dissemination of his music within England, it may also have hampered the wider circulation that a broader engagement with the publishing industry might have guaranteed (see Rowland). Similarly, his parting gesture of signing his so-called "London" Symphonies over to Johann Peter Salomon on leaving the English capital for the last time assured his legacy, but could also reflect him relinquishing his participation in the city's heady commercial MARKET. (Salomon reaped further financial benefit from these symphonies by publishing arrangements for piano trio and quintet.) Nevertheless, the twelve symphonies would eventually make their way into the possession of the Philharmonic Society, securing Haydn's permanent place in London's concert life, albeit long after the Society had begun to promote a serious concert culture by playing his music. In return, London's legacy inspired Haydn to bring forth *The Creation*, which he published and marketed with the help of his old London friends, especially Charles Burney, as a bilingual oratorio (English and German) that sealed his fame across Europe in the early nineteenth century (see RECEPTION).

"London" and "Haydn" entered into a dialogue that reached far beyond the composer or the city. Embracing politics and war, the burgeoning market culture and commercial rivalries, social interaction and a developing leisure industry, immigration and integration, aesthetics and the rise of the Romantic artist, this nexus of topics is as current today as during Haydn's own lifetime and continues to co-opt the composer and an understanding of his music.

WIEBKE THORMÄHLEN

FURTHER READING

Chesser and Jones (2013); Clark (2012b); Davison (2013); Day-O'Connell (2009a); Grigson (2009); Jones (2013); Mathew (2007); McVeigh (1993); Mikusi (2013); Milhous et al. (2001); Rowland (2013); Sisman (1997); Taylor (2010); Tolley (2013); Will (2012).

M

Market; Marketplace – see Commerce and

Material Culture When means and time were available, Haydn accumulated material possessions appropriate to his position. Sometimes his tastes proved expensive. Items of personal dress he owned at the time of his death, for example, were recorded as extensive and opulent. His wardrobe featured no fewer than twenty-nine waistcoats; one was described as "richly embroidered" with gold and silver trimmings. Other collections were less lavish, though no less passionate. By the time he himself drew up a catalogue of his personal collection of printed libretti (written before 1805), it numbered over 250 items, including not only libretti of his own operas and those by contemporaries performed at Eszterháza, but examples by numerous other composers acquired during the course of his career. Most of the items represented in this collection, such as Antonio Bertali's *La Zenobia di Radamisto* (composed for Vienna in 1662), are works he could never had heard performed. Outdated texts, such as this one, are unlikely to have been acquired for any relevance to composing or performing opera in his own time. Haydn may have had a genuine interest in the history of opera Libretti; but like other aspects of his worldly goods, it seems likely that part of his motivation in collecting was situating his own considerable achievements within contexts conceived to project his personal standing in broader spheres, for his own satisfaction and notionally for others.

Material Possessions Amassed by 1768 Documentation provides useful insights into the furnishings and works of art Haydn owned at the time his house in Eisenstadt was destroyed by fire in 1768. Losses sustained by the composer, then recently promoted to the position of full Kapellmeister to Prince Esterházy, reveal a taste for glazed display cabinets and expensive furniture with inlaid decoration. The most surprising item in his possession was an extensive collection of "drawings," on which he himself set a very high value in the official record of his losses. There were no fewer than fifty, all framed and glazed, presumably decorating the walls of the home he had recently purchased as a residence for himself and his wife, and many of these can be identified. Since Haydn's income had only very lately provided him with the means to purchase significant works of visual art, his decision to acquire this collection implies a strong impulse to collect at the earliest opportunity. It signals the relevance of visual culture in sustaining his position as a leading figure in Esterházy employment. It also arguably acted as a creative stimulus.

Haydn's Library An inventory of his possessions made shortly after his death shows that Haydn collected a significant number of books covering a large range of subjects other than music. These ranged from works of fiction in most Western European languages, to guidebooks on health and gardening (see also MUSICAL IMAGINARY). Accounts of Haydn written by his early biographers and by other visitors show that he reserved time in his daily routine for reading, which included newspapers as well as books. Favorite volumes were kept in one or more glazed cabinets. Although many items were probably gifts, the dates of publication suggest that the books were acquired over a long period of time. Many of the volumes appear to have been selected not only on account of their texts, but also because of their illustrations.

The most opulent book he owned was the first volume of Jean Benjamin de La Borde's *Choix de chansons mises en musique*, published in Paris in 1773 with a dedication to the Dauphine Marie-Antoinette, one of the most esteemed illustrated books of the eighteenth century. Although this publication featured the music for La Borde's songs, its distinction lies in its twenty-six magnificent plates. All but one of these were designed by the leading French artist Jean-Michel Moreau le Jeune, who also engraved and signed them, something noted by the compiler of Haydn's inventory in 1809. Haydn's acquisition of this fabulous volume is likely to have stemmed from his early connections with Baron Gottfried van Swieten.

Haydn as Print Collector CORRESPONDENCE from the 1780s shows that Haydn collected prints. He claimed to be especially interested in those published in England, which in German-speaking countries at the time were supplanting the taste for French prints on the part of amateur collectors. Haydn's two visits to England in the early 1790s provided him with ample opportunity to indulge this enthusiasm through visiting print shops and galleries that offered prints of pictures on show, enabling him to purchase those he particularly fancied. The inventory of Haydn's possessions formed after his death lists over three hundred prints, almost all English, mostly kept in a portfolio – the most widely used receptacle for preserving prints kept loose in the eighteenth century. The details preserved by the compiler of the inventory allow all these prints to be identified, offering a valuable insight into Haydn's taste and interests. There were also separate collections of printed portraits and of "theater scenes," probably reproductions of well-known episodes from Shakespeare plays.

Haydn's "Cabinet" Several visitors to the last house in which Haydn lived, in the Viennese suburb of Gumpendorf, record the impression made on them of seeing framed pictures hanging on the walls of his home, especially in his "cabinet," the room in which he worked, often entertained, and sometimes slept. These pictures included portraits (see ICONOGRAPHY) – including paintings representing the composer himself and his wife, drawings showing Cherubini and Gyrowetz, and images in varied media of Mozart, Michael Haydn, and C. P. E. Bach among others – and some favorite prints, especially examples of caricatures by the English artist Henry Bunbury (see Tolley 2013). But the most extraordinary "pictures" the composer displayed were sheets of his own compositions, a series of about fifty individual canons, all separately framed and glazed. These compositions were the only examples of his mature work that he withheld from publication during his lifetime. Various accounts indicate that these "pictures" were autographs, that many were written using more than one color of ink, and that some or perhaps all of them included floral embellishments, probably additions to the autographs commissioned from a professional artist. It is clear that Haydn conceived these particular compositions pictorially – the visual form of some had clear iconographic associations – a circumstance that shows how seriously Haydn took the visual artists in relation to his work as a composer.

"My Treasures" After Haydn achieved international fame by the 1780s, he regularly received gifts from highly placed admirers or as acknowledgments for dedications. Many of these gifts were conventional for the period. For example, he received several gold snuffboxes and rings; however, there were also more individual, tailored gifts, such as the six pairs of cotton stockings inscribed with musical quotations from several vocal compositions by Haydn, sent to him by the Leicester industrialist William Gardiner in 1804. As a youth Gardiner saw Haydn at one of the Handel commemoration concerts in 1791, and thereafter became an active promoter of Haydn's music, and later of Beethoven's.

Another kind of gift Haydn especially appreciated were medals commemorating his compositional achievements received from various music institutions throughout Europe. Haydn took pleasure in amassing such gifts and showing them to guests, particularly as he grew older. He told one visitor that they were "an old man's toys." By contrast with other COMPOSERS, Haydn was never tempted to profit from any objects of value he received by selling them. For him the items he received functioned as a unique record of his personal successes. Their display later in life enabled him to present himself as guardian of his own reputation, a testament to his distinction as a composer complementing his actual compositions (see RECEPTION). Visitors shown this collection of objects, however, were not always positive in their assessment of Haydn's motivation. One saw in them "signs of avarice in the midst of his riches which he could not even use any more" (Landon V 374). Haydn, however, claimed they enabled him to count his life "backwards": "for a few moments I am young again" (see AGING).

The Music Library Aspects of Haydn's music collection pertain to his concerns with material culture. For example, from the time of his visits to England Haydn acquired printed music by younger composers, notably of compositions DEDICATED to him. Like other items Haydn received, these were kept together not so much for their intrinsic (in this case musical) worth, for which there is little to suggest he had special appreciation for any particular example, but as testaments to his own standing – all the composers in question paying him tribute, a distinctive honor for a composer in the late eighteenth century. This emerges from the catalogue of Haydn's music library drawn up c. 1805 by his faithful copiest Johann Elssler (see Hörwarthner; Landon V).

Haydn appears to have valued publications that featured elaborate decorative title pages, which he encouraged for his own compositions where influence on PUBLISHERS might be exerted. He was perhaps initially influenced in this by knowledge of conventions in France for publishing *opéras comiques*. His collection of eleven such works, issued in Paris between 1761 and 1775 and probably all acquired during this period, presents several instances of sophisticated music publications, many with elaborate pictorial decoration. Publications of complete operas in score or in arrangements were rare in German-speaking regions throughout his lifetime. But Haydn seems always to have taken the trouble to investigate those that became available. At some point early in 1761, for example, he recommended to a STUDENT study of *Il mondo alla roversa*, an opera by Galuppi (1750). The evidence for this is an inscription in a copy of the vocal score of this opera published by Breitkopf in 1758, probably the actual publication the pupil studied alongside his teacher. Later published music in Haydn's music library suggests his interest in advances in the technology of music printing, such as lithography (see SCIENCE).

Late in life Haydn retained relatively few autographs of his own compositions. Many Haydn autographs were probably deemed at an early stage the property of Prince Esterházy. About 1807 Haydn entered into an arrangement that all personal musical effects still in the composer's possession at the time of his death, including autographs he had retained, would be purchased by the prince directly from his chief beneficiary, the composer's nephew Mathias Frölich. As a result of this "bequest" the greater part of the musical items from Haydn's COLLECTIONS are now in the National Széchényi Library (Budapest), which acquired this part of the Esterházy collection in 1948. Although Haydn probably anticipated that his archive would be best preserved as an entity by its passing into the hands of the family he served for the greater part of his career – a kind of guarantee of his musical legacy – he also appears to have taken care to ensure that autographs of major compositions were given to distinguished younger composers, perhaps partly as a means of honoring them and ensuring their lasting respect for the older composer, but conceivably also as a means of enhancing his reputation through association. For example, both Beethoven and Cherubini (among others) received gifts of autograph symphonies from Haydn, and Neukomm was presented with the autograph of the *Harmoniemesse*. This marks the moment when autographs by leading composers became collectors' items, and for those who could not afford such purchases, facsimiles of autograph pages started to be reproduced.

Musical Instruments While Haydn's attitude to his own autographs, at least late in life, shows that he conceived them as items of significant material value, the musical INSTRUMENTS he possessed were not assigned the same significance despite being substantial and expensive. They did not form part of the "bequest" that passed to Prince Esterházy. His Schanz fortepiano, which he himself described as "beautiful," was sold less than two months before his death for 200 gulden, at a time when he was hardly in need of the money. No record was kept of its purchaser. An Érard mahogany fortepiano, valued at 200 gulden following his death, was retained by Frölich. His Longman & Broderip fortepiano, also with a mahogany case, fetched 700 gulden at the auction of his household effects, and was later acquired by the Abbé Stadler, who clearly valued its association with Haydn. The only instrument from Haydn's personal collection now extant is a Bohak clavichord made in

Vienna in 1794, on which he performed at home for visitors, sometimes accompanying performers in his own compositions. At an unknown date late in life, he gave this to a friend with the intention that the friend's young son might learn to play on it. Haydn's biographer Dies sheds light on his attitude: "It amused him in particular that I said a few words about his *Klavier*. He thought it comical that I called it a 'priceless treasure'." When Dies suggested that the *Klavier* must be worth at least as much as the 100 guineas offered for the bullet that killed Nelson, Haydn retorted "In LONDON they care for such nonsense! I saw Handel's *Klavier* at the Queen's House, where she keeps it as a relic having purchased it from the family" (Gotwals 143–44). Haydn's purpose on this visit to the Queen's house was to see the royal collection of Handel autographs, the most important testimony to the earlier composer. For Haydn, the harpsichord was merely an additional curiosity.

THOMAS TOLLEY

FURTHER READING
Gotwals; Hörwarthner (1997); Landon V; Tolley (2001, 2013).

Melancholy Since the nineteenth century, Haydn has been a composer known more for mirth than melancholy. (See HUMOR and RECEPTION.) But this one-sided view disregards comments from his own letters, in which he refers to himself as melancholy, and ignores contemporary reviews of certain works, which acknowledge a melancholy voice in the music. In his CORRESPONDENCE, the composer presented himself as one to whom nostalgic sentiments and *Weltschmerz* (world-weariness) were well known, as were the relevant typical "cures": retreat into letters, friendly society, and especially music. In an open declaration of his love to the singer Polzelli in a letter from London of January 14, 1792, for example, he suggested that his melancholy was a product of his removal from her midst: "I am quite well, but am almost always in an 'English humour,' that is, melancholy, and perhaps I shall never again regain the good humour that I used to have when I was with you. oh! my dear Polzelli: you are always in my heart, and I shall never, never forget you" (November 2007, 83). Haydn associated himself with the melancholic (here the depressed artist/lover), and thereby also built up his Austro-British identity: melancholy had long been considered a particularly 'English' malady.

Melancholy was an important idea in aesthetic and medical thought alike. Key thinkers of the time, notably Edmund Burke, Henry Home (Lord Kames) and Immanuel Kant, discussed the main attributes of the melancholy state. Late eighteenth-century English writers, like their late Renaissance forebears, considered music as both a cause and a cure for melancholy, a complex temperament that yielded both pleasure and pain. Burke made the connection between "beautiful" music and melancholy at the corporeal level. The involuntary responses induced by the soft, sweet, *legato* strains – "that sinking, that melting, that languor" – were strikingly similar to the lethargic bodily responses that Burke and the medical practitioners of his day associated with melancholy. Indeed, he found that this "beautiful" music could produce something akin to "a species of melancholy" (November 2008a, 41).

Kames, and later Kant, identified melancholy with the ability to step back from one's troubles in self reflection – to maintain a detached stance that encompassed both pleasure and pain. In his *Anthropologie in pragmatischer Hinsicht* (1798), Kant located the conception of melancholy within the subject or self. Here melancholy was characterized not so much by sadness as by a tendency to brood deeply on a single idea: "[In the melancholy temperament] sense impressions are less striking [than those associated with the sanguine temperament], but they get themselves rooted deeply. It is in this, and not the tendency to gaiety or sadness, that we must locate the distinction between these temperaments of feeling." In his *Observations on the Feeling of the Beautiful and Sublime* (1764), Kant described melancholy further, linking it to the SUBLIME and heroism (GENIUS): it is "a gentle and noble feeling so far as it is grounded upon the awe that a hard-pressed soul feels when, full of some great purpose, he sees the danger he will have to overcome, and has before his eyes the difficult but great victory of self-conquest" (November 2007, 78).

The melancholy of Haydn's music is arguably as varied as definitions of the temperament itself. In English criticism of the early nineteenth century, Haydn's popular "A Pastoral Song" (from the first set of English Canzonettas), is described as "a perfect exhibition of the line of beauty in music"; one listener noted a drooping into "pleasing languor" (compare Burkean discourse), which he connected to the representation of melancholy. Musical melancholy can be understood, further, to arise in Haydn's music when the protagonist of a work – be it the vocal character in a song or the "composer's voice" in an instrumental work – takes a position of distance, possibly ironic distance, with respect to his or her own pain (see SELF-REFLEXIVITY). Paradoxical contrasts in his works prompt listeners, for their part, to take a step back from the work itself in order to contemplate the borders and limits of emotional experience and communication. In Haydn's "She Never Told Her Love" (from the second set of English Canzonettas), the protagonist maintains a self-reflective stance throughout, signified by the extreme restraint of the vocal line, while the feelings that lie beneath this calm exterior are signaled in the keyboard part (which engages in vivid word-painting), and in the inability of the protagonist to effect a conclusive cadence until the very end.

Haydn's invocations of melancholy are not confined to this vocal music, although they are arguably easiest to trace there. A reviewer for the *Allgemeine musikalische Zeitung* (1799) drew attention to melancholy as the dominant affect in Haydn's Variations in F minor, Hob.XVII:6, commenting in particular on its quasi-improvisational quality and its technical challenges: "A melancholy Andante in F minor, varied as only a Master can, which sounds almost like a free fantasia. Even the first section is not easy; thus one can surmise that the further development of the same will have its own difficulties." An anonymous reviewer for the *Allgemeine musikalische Zeitung* (1800) described a dialectical experience of an arrangement of the Adagio movement in Haydn's String Quartet Op. 76, No. 6, invoking an experience of "floating" through the climbing keys, and encountering unexpected, deceptive turns in the musical argument. The experience seems akin to being in a maze or labyrinth, which, as Sisman notes, figures in discourse about melancholy of this time.

NANCY NOVEMBER

FURTHER READING
Chua (1998); November (2007, 2008a); Sisman (2016); Wald-Fuhrmann (2010).

Melody All three of Haydn's earliest biographers stress the crucial role that melody plays for the composer's creative process as well as for his personal style and AESTHETICS. According to Griesinger, Haydn placed a strong emphasis on the ideal of a "fluent melody" as an important prerequisite for a good (i.e. natural) composition (113). In a similar vein, and entirely in keeping with an ENLIGHTENED music aesthetics, Dies referred to Haydn as a composer who sought to elicit emotions in his listeners by making use of an "easy, fluent, pleasing, and appealing" melody (83). Finally, Carpani defines melody as the "soul of music" and the "essence of a composition," required to reach the hearts of an audience (33). None of these biographers misses the opportunity to point out the importance of melodic invention for Haydn's COMPOSITIONAL PROCESS.

It is a truism in Haydn research that Haydn, unlike Mozart, who has always been praised for his extraordinary melodic inventiveness, seems to have been more economic in the use of his melodic material, showing across genres a tendency toward deriving a multiplicity of melodic units from a common source ("monothematicism"). Although Haydn was by no means alone in using this device – for instance, Muzio Clementi and Leopold Koželuch had a similar penchant for it – he is undoubtedly the composer who adopted a monothematic approach to a hitherto unprecedented extent. In Haydn's sonata expositions, main theme restatements in the secondary key area range from loose motivic references to a complete thematic repetition (one of the rare instances of the latter case can be found in the final movement of the Symphony No. 47 in G major).

For the enlightened aesthetics of the eighteenth century, evident in the writings of Griesinger, Dies, and Carpani, and largely absorbed by Haydn, the concept of melody features two intertwined and virtually inseparable components, one technical, the other aesthetic. Viewed from a technical perspective, larger melodic utterances called Perioden are subdivided into constituent parts (Sätze) by means of hierarchically ordered points of caesuras, which Heinrich Christoph Koch famously referred to as "resting points of the mind." These punctuation formulae – incises (Einschnitte), Absätze, and cadences – are ordered in time such that they give rise to a form-functionally meaningful trajectory. Koch's main form of melodic punctuation for what we now call a sonata exposition consists of two Absätze in the main key (a Grundabsatz followed by a Quintabsatz) as well as a Quintabsatz and a strong cadence in the key of V, thus gradually weakening the home key and increasingly confirming the secondary key (see HARMONY and FORM).

If Haydn the orator wanted to ensure the comprehensibility of his music, he needed to take into consideration the cognitive constraints of his listeners as implied in Koch's theory. It is, therefore, by no means coincidental that Koch in his *Versuch einer Anleitung zur Composition* cites an example from Haydn's oeuvre to discuss his model of melodic punctuation, the *Andante* from his Symphony No. 42 in D major (1771), which shows the unusual heading *Andantino e cantabile*. In this movement, Haydn employs various techniques of melodic elaboration, including phrase repetition combined with subtle VARIATIONS of the melodic substance. In addition, it is a commonplace in

Haydn research that the composer's creative play with normative phrase lengths constitutes one of the hallmarks of his style.

Haydn's music evinces a considerable inventiveness in dealing with the Kochian models of melodic punctuation, to the extent that he even decided to entirely dispense with any unequivocal points of closure, as is the case in the slow movement of his Symphony No. 64 in A major ("Tempora mutantur"). A less extreme example of creative engagement with Koch's main form can be found in the first movement of the Keyboard Sonata in D major, Hob.XVI:14 (see Example 10). The first two stages of the main form appear already within the opening eight measures: each four-measure half contains a La-Sol-Fa-Mi voice-leading model (Gjerdingen calls this pattern the Prinner) that first leads to an imperfect authentic cadence (mm. 3–4), then to a half-cadence (mm. 7–8). By contrast, the third caesura alone requires considerably more space to be attained, stretching from mm. 9 to 24. However, particularly intriguing is the way in which the Schlußsatz is treated: although the first Schlußsatz reaches a förmliche Cadenz, it is not followed by an appendix but by a minor-mode interpolation featuring motivic imitation and ending with a Phrygian half-cadence. This necessitates the repetition of the Schlußsatz, in which Haydn enhances the sense of closure by merely melodic means: the second Cadenz is much more emphatic, owing to the more expansive melodic gesture (starting on a higher pitch, g♯ instead of e) and the replacement of the earlier soprano clausula by a more conclusive tenor clausula.

The concept of melody also features strong aesthetic implications, as the then-prevalent aesthetics required the composer to write melodies in a vocal idiom, i.e., melodies that were "singable" (*cantabile*) as well as clearly perceivable in a preferably homophonic, lucid texture. Harmony, by contrast, was considered an auxiliary domain that was primarily needed to enhance the desired effect of the melody on the listener's soul. As Day-O'Connell demonstrates with respect to Haydn's Canzonetta "A Pastoral Song" (Hob.XXVIa:27), the melody in this song can very well be described in terms of Edmund Burke's aesthetic category of the BEAUTIFUL.

However, as Griesinger pointed out, Haydn tended to think in vocal terms even when composing purely instrumental music, thus doing justice to the ideal of *cantabile* across virtually all genres. According to Griesinger, Haydn complained about those composers who "had never learned to sing" (114). As Seedorf suggests, Haydn's first teacher, the renowned Neapolitan opera composer Nicola Porpora, who taught Haydn the "true fundamentals of composition," may have had some impact on the young master's earliest attempts to design instrumental lines in a vocal manner (see EDUCATION). For instance, the *cantabile* markings in the Adagio movement of his String Quartet in B♭ major, Op. 1, No. 1, nicely exemplifies Haydn's notion of instrumental *cantabile*. In Haydn's later career, it was the "new proximity of symphony and opera" that, in Webster's view, became "characteristic of Haydn's music ... after 1774" and is responsible for the appearance of "beautiful melodies" in his symphonies (388). This suggests that the emphasis on melody was not merely an aesthetic ideal without any stylistic correlate, but manifested itself in the late eighteenth-century compositional style in general and Haydn's music in particular.

MELODY

Example 10 Keyboard Sonata in D major, Hob.XVI:14, first movement, mm. 1–10 and 23–37 (GA = Grundabsatz; QA = Quintabsatz).

The relation of melody to song has another implication as well. It is important to note that Haydn showed an increasing predilection for using "popular" or Folk tunes, in the "London" Symphonies even more than in the symphonies composed for Paris. These tunes may even be subject to excessive contrapuntal treatment, as in the final movements of the Symphonies Nos. 103 in E♭ major and 104 in D major, the latter of which opens with the Topics of peasant

211

Example 11 Symphony No. 85 in B♭ major, second movement, mm. 1–8

dance and musette. "Popular" tunes are typically symmetrical in formal design (conforming to the periodic theme type), feature triadic and stepwise motion within a limited pitch range rather than excessive leaps, and tend to avoid chromaticism. The humor invoked by the famous opening theme of the Symphony No. 94 in G major ("Surprise"), second movement, derives from this very sort of simplicity (and predictability) of the theme – precisely because it is juxtaposed with an unexpected forte stroke at its end.

Some of these tunes are only vocal in nature (e.g., the popular tune in the *Andante* from his Symphony No. 53 in D major); others seem to be derived from pre-existent vocal songs stemming from a variety of sources: operas, liturgical contexts (Symphonies Nos. 26 in D minor and 30 in C major), and folk song as well as street music. For an operatic source, one may think of the opening movement of Haydn's Symphony No. 8 in G major ("Le soir"), in which Haydn uses the then-popular tobacco aria from Gluck's opéra comique *Le diable à quatre* as the material for both the primary and (slightly varied) secondary themes in a monothematic exposition. Furthermore, it is hypothesized that the sources of Haydn's folk-tune-based melodies are not only Austrian (e.g. "Acht Sauschneider müssen seyn"), but also Hungarian or Gypsy ("Alla zingarese") and Croatian, pointing to Haydn's Exoticism. Also French sources can be identified: following Carl Ferdinand Pohl, Harrison suggests that in the second movement of the Symphony No. 85 in B♭ major ("La Reine"), the French folk song *La gentille et jeune Lisette* is cited as the opening theme, which is subsequently subject to a series of variations (see Example 11). Undoubtedly, the Parisian audience would have readily recognized the origin of this theme.

Haydn's frequent use of popular tunes in his symphonies may be seen as a deliberate strategy to reconcile the increasing complexities and learnedness of the symphonic genre of the 1780s and 1790s with the still-existent aesthetic concerns for (melodic) simplicity, naturalness, and popularity espoused by Rousseau and many other philosophers of the time. In this light, the choice of familiar melodies can be explained by reference to Haydn's desire to please his (anticipated) AUDIENCES in Paris, London, VIENNA, and elsewhere; and by subjecting simple melodic material to highly artistic contrapuntal procedures, he likely succeeded in also satisfying the demands of the Kenner among his listeners.

MARKUS NEUWIRTH

FURTHER READING
Carpani (1812); Day-O'Connell (2009a); Dies; Gjerdingen (2007); Griesinger; Harrison (1998); Koch (1782–1793); Schroeder (2002); Seedorf (2002); Webster (1981).

Memorials; Memorializing – see Monuments and

Meter – see Rhythm and

Mimesis The concept of mimesis was fundamental to eighteenth-century AESTHETICS of music. To French neo-classic theorists in the first part of the century, all art was first and foremost an imitation of NATURE. Jean Baptiste du Bos, in his widely read *Réflexions critiques sur la poësie et sur la peinture* (1719), claimed that "Just as the painter imitates the forms and colors of nature, so the musician imitates the tones of the voice – its accents, sighs and inflections. He imitates in short all the sounds that nature herself uses to express the feelings and passions" (quoted in Hosler 45; Le Huray and Day 18). Du Bos' formulation that music "imitates" nature's tools for "expressing" the passions points to the intertwining of the concepts "imitation" and "expression" across the eighteenth century. M. H. Abrams' influential model notwithstanding (in which an early eighteenth-century concept of art as the imitation of an action is seen to give way in the second half of the century to an expressive one, in which art is, as Wordsworth put it, the "spontaneous overflow of powerful feelings"), "imitation" in eighteenth-century music aesthetics should be discussed, as it was in the period, alongside terms such as "painting," "depiction," and "expression."

For Batteux, whose *Beaux-arts réduits à un meme principe* (1746) had as its express purpose to demonstrate that imitation of beautiful nature is the basis of all the fine arts, music's imitations included both what we might call "pictorialisms," and what we might think of as "expression": "There are two kinds of music. The one merely imitates unimpassioned sounds and noises and is equivalent to landscape painting. The other expresses animated sounds and relates to the feelings. This corresponds to portrait painting" (quoted in Lippman, 49). Music can imitate the sounds we hear in nature, but the value of art lies in its ability to move: and it can only move if it expresses – not merely imitates – the passions: "Musical compositions that fail to move us can unequivocally be equated with pictures that have no merit other than their coloring, or with poems that are no more than well-constructed verses" (Lippman 21). As Hosler has summarized, the most important questions, assuming that music could or must represent the emotions, were what those emotions were, what aspects of the emotions and which emotions could be musically represented, with what musical means, how the listener understood the emotional content, whether words were necessary for this, and whether music had moral or spiritual value.

The necessity, and power, of music to imitate passionate utterances underlies French writing on aesthetics into the 1770s, also deeply influencing

German thinking on the subject. With the emphasis on musical mimesis as the high art of expressing the passions and moving the listener, the "pictorial" imitation of natural phenomena (birdsong, storms, etc.) risked accusations of tastelessness. A concomitant debate concerned the problem of instrumental music and the necessity for titles and other verbal texts to make explicit the subjects of musical imitation – the particular passion or set of passions being expressed; a definite subject, especially an emotion, could rescue instrumental music from accusations of moral vacuity (see Will). (Critics of the mimetic/expressive theory could see music's indistinctness as an advantage: Adam Smith, for example, described listening to orchestral music as the work of the intellect: like "the contemplation of a great system in any other science.") Obvious examples are to be found in character pieces by François Couperin and his contemporaries, with such titles as "Les Moulins à Vent" (The Windmills), "La Distraite" (The Distracted One), or "Le Rossignol en amour" (The Nightingale in Love). Yet as Allanbrook has suggested, instrumental music of the period, with its quick-changing characters and emotions as exemplified in the first movement of Haydn's Symphony No. 59 in A major, may be understood as quintessentially imitative, rooted in the dramatic exchanges of comic theater: "what are these postures if not the energetic – mimetic – units [of] *opera buffa*" (26).

In Germany, Johann Georg Sulzer, stressing the moral role of art in his widely read *Allgemeine Theorie der schönen Künste* (1771–74), claimed that "the chief intent of the arts is the steering of the soul by means of pleasant and unpleasant feelings" (quoted in Hosler, 147). Music's role was to express the passions, and to inculcate feeling. Tolley describes how these notions stemmed from Sulzer, Johann Jakob Engel, and others. Sulzer, in his articles on "Tone-Painting" and "Painting in Music," explained that music could be made to imitate wind, thunder, or the gurgle of a brook, but even in the hands of the most skilled composers "such painting *violates* the true spirit of music, which is to express the sentiments of feeling, not to convey *images of inanimate objects*" (Tolley 272). Engel, meanwhile, was more open to pictorial imitations in his *Über die musikalische Malerey* (1780), and to the idea that painting may be a kind of expression, but he still explained that music should always "paint *feelings* rather than *objects* of feelings" (273). Heinrich Christoph Koch summarized the issue in the article on "Malerey" in his *Musikalisches Lexikon*: because music's function is to stir the feelings, he claimed, it is inappropriate to merely describe inanimate nature, although occasionally musical painting can be justified when it relates directly to the "expression of the inner soul" (272–73).

Perhaps the most famous moments of musical imitation in Haydn's oeuvre are to be found in the late oratorios, from the foggy harmonic ambiguities and tonal wanderings of the Chaos, to the sudden blazing C major trumpet-and-drum fortissimo representing the creation of Light in *The Creation* (1798), or from the whistling plowman in Spring to the croaking frogs at the end of Summer in *The Seasons* (1801). Such "imitations" range from literal evocations of the sounds of nature (birdsong, wind, running streams, thunder) to more oblique, even rhetorical, effects that conjure in the listener the SUBLIME impact of divine intervention.

After the enormous initial success of both *The Creation* and *The Seasons* – which were praised, especially in ENGLAND, for their vivid pictorialism – critics steeped in earlier aesthetic debates over musical mimesis took issue especially with Haydn's imitations of nature. (On the initial reception of both of these works, see Webster 2005a and Tolley.) An early critic of *The Seasons* complained that, while the work as a whole was moving and sublime, "the imitation of the crowing cock at dawn [and] the exploding gun in the hunt represent for me a false notion of tone-painting in music, possibly even disgracing this heavenly art" (Tolley 272). Haydn, for his part, was aware of the terms of the debate. He famously blamed the notorious frogs in *The Seasons* on his librettist, Swieten ("This Frenchified trash was forced on me," quoted in Webster 2005a, 152), and, as Fredrik Samuel Silverstolpe reported, spoke humorously of word-painting:

> He showed me the aria [No. 6, "Rolling in foaming billows"] from *The Creation* that is intended to portray the motion of the sea and the rocks rising out of it. "Look," he said in a joking tone, "see how the notes run up and down like waves? See too there the mountains, which rise out of the depths of the sea?" (Webster 2005b, 32)

However, such imitations did not preclude the all-important moving of the listener: "But as we came to the clear stream [in the contrasting section 'Softly purling glides the limpid brook'], oh! I was entirely carried away ... [He] sang at the piano with a simplicity that went straight to the heart." As Webster has suggested, many instances of pictorialism in these two oratorios may be understood as not merely naive representations but rather revelations of profound compositional shaping and even psychological insight.

Haydn's oratorios, with their vivid pictorialisms, brought many of the eighteenth-century debates over musical mimesis into high relief and offered the opportunity for a new consideration of music's power to signify. Webster's remark that such musical painting, long an important aspect of the genre of Pastoral (in which *The Seasons*, in particular, is deeply rooted), may be seen as combining naive entertainment with high moral purpose and sophisticated artistic technique, echoes early nineteenth-century criticism. Reflecting a need to justify Haydn's musical pictorialism, Carl Friedrich Zelter heard the birdcalls in "Auf starkem Fittiche schwinget sich" (*The Creation*, No. 15, "On mighty wings uplifted soars") as contributing to the expression of purity and innocence, and overtly pictorial moments in *The Seasons* as not superficial but "serious." As Will has shown, Zelter goes on to suggest that such musical mimesis provides material for the play of the imagination, so that the oratorios might be understood like the instrumental works, as a medium for a kind of transcendent listening: musical evocations of hunting, harvesting, or divine interventions "lose substance when translated from language into the indefinite and ephemeral medium of sound" (147). (See also PROGRAMMATIC ELEMENTS; TOPICS.)

ANNETTE RICHARDS

FURTHER READING
Abrams (1953); Allanbrook (2014); Batteux (1746); du Bos (1719); Engel (1780); Hosler (1981); Koch (1802); Le Huray and Day (1988); Lippman (1992); Mathew (2012); Rehding (2009); Sulzer (1771–4); Tolley (2001); Webster (2005a, 2005b); Will (2002).

Monuments and Memorializing We tend to think of monuments as public, permanent, and grand. By those standards, the most obvious candidates among Haydn's works come late in his career. His patriotic song "Gott erhalte Franz der Kaiser" (Hob.XXVIa:43) is an example; or his wildly successful oratorio, The Creation. Both were very public, and both became permanent in two senses, appearing quickly in printed editions and receiving sufficient performances to be fixed in memory. Indeed, they count among the first musical "works" in the modern sense, conceptual objects rather than fleeting experiences, casting long shadows in their own time and since (esp. Rehding, Riethmüller, and Temperley). As for "grand," The Creation redefined the term with its opening blast of light and endless cascade of choral-orchestral climaxes. The grandeur of "Gott erhalte" differs, its tuneful melody designed for the powerful experience of collective singing. Yet though Haydn called it a "FOLK SONG," he departed from most of the British melodies he arranged during the same years by incorporating a systematic ascent to a glorious high note – which is then repeated for good measure. The moment is as stupendous in its own way as anything in The Creation, and reinforced in Haydn's orchestral arrangement by a Creation-esque tutti. Expressing broad public sentiments in an expansive language, these and other works of his final productive years seem like exemplary musical monuments.

Monuments to what, though? Or to whom? The answer is clear enough in "Gott erhalte" or the solo song "Lines from the Battle of the Nile," two of a handful of pieces that explicitly engage the POLITICS of the Napoleonic era (see Mathew). But most of Haydn's works do not praise famous men, nor memorialize recent events as physical monuments tend to do. His objects are creation, the seasons, God, the Holy Trinity – timeless and divine (see RELIGION AND SPIRITUAL BELIEFS). When his music engaged earthly matters, it did so by way of dedicated performances. This was of course customary during his lifetime, especially in Catholic EUROPE where one wrote a Requiem to commemorate a death, a Te Deum for a military victory, a mass for almost anything else. Musical monuments differ in this regard from their architectural counterparts, expressing generalized sentiments that are easily redirected by new circumstances or PLACES.

So perhaps Haydn did not create monuments so much as write music appropriate for monumentalizing. Seen from this perspective, much more of his oeuvre appears relevant. He composed sacred music throughout his life, much of it for celebratory occasions such as name-days, and all of it open for repurposing in the manner of The Creation. The same was possible, if less common, for instrumental music: in 1783 Haydn accepted his PUBLISHER's suggestion that he append the name of Ernst Gideon von Laudon, a war hero of the Habsburg Empire, to a keyboard arrangement of an appropriately militaresque Symphony in C, No. 69 (see Will). As Mathew notes, a whole range of works beyond "Gott erhalte" acquired patriotic associations during Austria's wars with France, from the famous

"Military" Symphony (No. 100, 1794) to the now-obscure incidental music to *Alfred, King of the Anglo-Saxons*. Haydn did not have to write a battle symphony, like Beethoven's *Wellington's Victory* with its explanatory text and opposing orchestral armies, for his music to get caught up in the memorialization of WAR and battlefield exploits.

His long service to the Esterházy family (see COURTS) suggests yet another dimension of monument-making. Early in his tenure he wrote a number of secular cantatas specifically honoring the Princes; one for a wedding, two for name-days, two for Prince Nicolaus's safe return from journeys (Hob.XXIVa:1–5). The tradition did not last, but the works may be symptoms of a broader truth, namely, that everything he composed for the family amounted to a cumulative monument to its wealth and artistic taste, a kind of musical equivalent to ESZTERHÁZA, the elaborate palace that Nicolaus built for himself during Haydn's tenure. Until 1779, the composer had to obtain permission to sell his music or accept commissions from elsewhere, meaning that his works were literally a possession of the Prince, another material enhancement of his grandeur (see PUBLISHERS AND PUBLISHING; CIRCULATION). Any music could contribute, not just the large-scale or celebratory. When Nicolaus ordered Haydn to compose more music for baryton, the Prince's favorite oddball viol, the resulting trios were preserved in bound collections of twenty-four each. In addition to their practical purpose, these volumes served as a testimonial to the Prince's musical skill and participation in chamber music PERFORMANCE – a proprietary monument.

Haydn lived long enough to see his music become a monument to someone else as well. During the last two decades of his life he experienced a good deal of personal commemoration; an architectural monument went up in his home town of Rohrau, while poems and medals celebrated his trips to LONDON, his composition of *The Creation*, and his general status as Europe's greatest living composer (Landon IV–V; see also RECEPTION). The same period witnessed the first attempts to produce retrospective EDITIONS of his music, as well as his own efforts to compile a complete CATALOGUE of works. Again, these projects encompassed much more than the grand expressions of his late years: the first "complete" editions were of quartets and keyboard music, and the catalogue listed even his settings of Scottish folk song melodies – accompaniments for keyboard and strings, often brilliant but decidedly small-scale. They nonetheless inspired him to hope that he would "go on living in Scotland many years after my death" (*CCLN* 195). Haydn and his contemporaries had begun to see his music – all his music – in a way that was new at the time but familiar now, as a monument to creative genius and cultural achievement. Their vision was confirmed by a famous concert of 1808, the composer's last public appearance, at which *The Creation* was performed in honor of Haydn himself. The musical monument came full circle to commemorate its maker. (See also SUBLIME.)

RICHARD WILL

FURTHER READING
CCLN; *Grove Online*; Landon IV–V; Mathew (2007); Riethmüller (1987); Temperley (1991); Will (2002).

Musical Imaginary – see Travel

Musical Materials Our judgments about Haydn's choice and use of musical materials are, quite naturally, filtered through our own current scholarly preoccupations, whether these be historical or music-theoretical. Yet, just as naturally, they are also determined by previous patterns of thought. Taking issue with existing views – which can range from completely contradicting to more gently inflecting them – is an intrinsic part of the process, as this helps to determine just what our current preoccupations are. (It will also follow that as these new views seem to coalesce into "received opinion," they will in turn be subject to revision.) More than most, though, Haydn scholarship has in recent generations felt obliged to combat what seems like a dead weight of earlier views, including those concerning his creative attributes and significance. It has thus for a long time had an especially pronounced reactive strain. In the revised image that has emerged Haydn could be said to have changed from a classical to a radical figure, from a law-giver to a law-breaker; in sum, a Reception premised on various kinds of simplicity, whether personal or creative, has been replaced by one that favors a more complex grain. In Tonality, for example, Roger Mathew Grant traces how a nineteenth-century emphasis on the "simplicity" and restraint" of the composer's tonal language has more recently given way to an emphasis on its exploratory aspects.

However, it is easy to overlook that some supposedly defining attributes have been less subject to changing evaluation over time; they have remained relatively constant. Economy is one such attribute. It has been invoked repeatedly over many generations, and so seems to constitute a fundamental term of reference when we consider Haydn's treatment of his musical materials. For example, it often arises when a writer draws attention to Haydn's habit of reusing all or part of a primary theme at the start of the secondary-theme area of a sonata-form structure. The arguably unfortunate term "monothematicism" is often used to describe this feature: unfortunate since it tells us nothing of what contrast may lie around the corner later in the section, or indeed elsewhere in the movement. The term might more appropriately be applied to those movements in which the composer, regardless of formal layout, seems to concentrate on a small amount of material. In Form Nathan John Martin notes how this and other formal features of Haydn's music have continued to challenge theoretical orthodoxy.

The existence of compositional economy seems to have been affirmed by the composer himself. In one of his meetings with the elderly composer, biographer Griesinger reports Haydn's words to the effect that "once I had seized upon an idea, my whole endeavor was to develop and sustain it in keeping with the rules of art" (also cited in Bryan Proksch, Cyclic Integration), whereas too many younger composers "string out one little piece after another, they break off when they have hardly begun" (Gotwals 61). Ludwig Finscher rightly reminds us that this source, together with the biographical accounts of Dies and Carpani, represents "'oral history,' with all its advantages and problems," and so all three "demand caution in their use," a stricture that has by no means always been heeded in the literature (87). In other words, we cannot use this material, as often happens by implication or quite explicitly, as a straightforward account of Haydn's attitude to composing and his art in general. It may not apply even to the later works, let alone the entire sweep of his creative production, or across all genres.

This is not to cast serious doubt on this particular creative attribute. Compared with others in his orbit, Haydn is certainly inclined to make much of seemingly little, and even through the typically varied gestures and topical allusions of later eighteenth-century musical language we may readily hear a particular kind of intense concentration on small amounts of material. Yet one might ask whether we are interpreting this feature in the appropriate spirit, indeed whether we are really attempting to interpret it at all. As Levy points out, economy is one of those "covert and casual" values that automatically confers legitimacy on the music in which it is found. She specifically notes the reception of Haydn's music in such terms, which brings approving references to "unity" and "maturity" as part of a larger "organicist orientation" (7). Within such an orientation, economy needs no further justification. She writes, "critics have perhaps been too quickly satisfied with 'economy' as an explanation of what is special and valuable in Haydn's music. The 'discovery' of economy – in Haydn or others – may well short-circuit analysts'/critics' searches for other, and possibly more important or telling attributes of value" (8). But even if we adhere to this particular value, there are questions we might raise about it, such as what economical music is like to listen to. Does musical economy mean, for example, that there is less for an audience to process, that listening is in some way lightened? That must seem doubtful when the most "economical" Western musical idiom we know, minimalism, is not universally perceived to constitute easy listening. And the "success narrative" (Sisman 6) that has been applied to Haydn's career means that we have been inclined to overlook contemporary evidence of the difficulty that was experienced with Haydn's often "economical" procedures.

However, contemporary evidence also suggests that Haydn's economy was often understood to exist in a dialectical relation to variety – that what was admired was less the economy as such than the composer's ability to see so many possibilities in a single musical idea, to draw so many consequences from it. And the idea itself was often an apparently simple, artless one. Haydn was thus revealing the versatility of a model ENLIGHTENMENT thinker, able to see all sides of a story, able to probe all the nuances of a (musical) argument. Take the description by Johann Baptist Schaul, for whom Haydn's GENIUS "knows, like a chameleon, how to assume every possible form." In his quartets,

> once he has determined the motive of an Allegro, he delivers it in a hundred different ways, now giving it to the bass, now the viola, then to the second or the first violin, now transforming the whole in a trice, with a single brushstroke, and yet he always lets the theme shine through, so that one cannot help but be astounded (Schaul 10).

In VARIATION AS PRINCIPLE Michelle Fillion notes how Haydn used developing variation to offset his characteristic economy ("concentration on relatively few musical ideas"), but from the current perspective the two properties are not so much to be conceived as being in a causal relationship, variety offsetting economy, as being interdependent.

Schaul's image of a chameleon represents a nice way of capturing this relationship: the chameleon is always one and the same thing, but what captivates us is the number of apparently different forms it can take – a supreme adaptability to circumstances. This duality can be found in many different Haydnesque musical environments. We find it, for example, on those many occasions when the same material is made to fulfill different formal functions – a clear instance of where "economy" does not make for a smooth listening experience, since the initial aural impression may be one of confusion. Thus, the finale of the String Quartet in D major, Op. 76, No. 5, opens with forceful alternations of dominant and tonic chords, widely spaced not only texturally but also temporally, with distinct gaps left between each pair of chords. This is plainly material that belongs at the end of a movement; the music therefore immediately sends signals that it is about to close, which is bound to bring a listener up short. More than that, this ending formula is particularly incongruous. The alternating chords represent quite grand gestures, and could only be musically convincing if they were to be worked up to by a good deal of preceding material, material that operates at a high-energy level. And so, to start a movement in this vein is doubly confusing. Needless to say, the same material does eventually return in its proper position, at the end of the movement, approached by much brilliant propulsive writing that makes the chords sound like a natural climax to proceedings, an idiomatic post-cadential affirmation of the tonic key.

However, not all such games with formal function are as extreme as this. The first movement of the Keyboard Trio in G major (Hob.XV:15), for example, opens with a short two-measure motto figure that seems like a brief call to attention before the theme proper begins in the flute. Yet that theme consists of a compressed sentence structure that lasts for six measures, meaning that motto plus theme seem to belong together in creating a broader symmetrical eight-measure unit. The two elements then appear in conjunction at a number of points later in the movement, so that the two-measure motto appears to be inseparable from the material that follows. Yet at the very end of the movement the motto returns to close the movement all by itself, thus changing at this last minute from having an opening to a closing function. The difference here from the Op. 76 quartet movement is that the material seems plausible in both positions, both as announcement and as peroration, though once again a certain kind of economy is used to give the listener a jolt, to renew perception and so to encourage an active type of listening.

In neither of these cases does the compositional economy concern the most prominent thematic material of the movement, and it is such cases that have occasioned the greatest critical attention. Contemplating the first movement of the String Quartet in F major, Op. 74, No. 2, Polzonetti invokes a different kind of animalistic transformation, those found in the *Metamorphoses* of Ovid, as a way of accounting for the transformations undertaken by the theme, which "contains as its essential characteristic a readiness to change" (231). The author also proposes a new term, "metathematicism," to cover this kind of protean changeability (229), which, if more widely adopted, would be a great improvement on the seemingly entrenched "monothematicism." On many occasions, it is not in fact a theme as such, but some of its internal elements that form the focus – the more concentrated phenomena we call motives. But the same sort of flexibility within economy is evident, as in the finale of the Keyboard Trio in C major (Hob.XV:27), in which the dominating three-note motive, a simple neighbor-note figure, is quite content to adopt all sorts of roles within the discourse, whether thematic or transitional, melodic or accompanying. Such treatments can readily entail an epigrammatic style of writing in which economy, once more, turns out to be highly demanding of its listeners, as with the *Minuet* of the String Quartet in D major, Op. 50, No. 6, which features the detailed interaction of several short rhythmic units. Floyd Grave and Margaret Grave describe the resulting movement as "plainly eccentric," with "quizzical Lombard rhythms and jarring accents" (243).

These last two movements sound highly comic, which reminds us that the flexible creative attitude exemplified by Haydn's economical procedures can also be accounted for under the rubric of wit – which is of course the art of making unexpected connections (see HUMOR). While we can comfortably contextualize this as another desideratum of Enlightenment thinking, it is important to note that wit and comedy need not overlap. "Witty" transformations of a musical element so that it seems to mean something quite different can occur under any affective regime. Wit, in other words, is better thought of as an operating procedure, an intrinsic expression of a particular creative mentality, rather than necessarily determining the musical mood. For example, the choir's unison chanting on a single note of the text within the "Et resurrexit" section of the Credo of the *Missa in angustiis* ("Nelson Mass") is certainly economical, and may even be said to display wit, since it refers to the congregational intonation of prayer, but it is unlikely to be heard as humorous. On the other hand, an ultimate in economy is represented by the *Minuet* from Symphony No. 51 in B♭ major, which is built on the same four-note bass figure played eight times at various transpositions. This means that in the original part the figure is written out just once, with various clefs attached, in the manner of a musical cryptogram. But not only is the bass absolutely repetitive, so is the rest of the material, which recycles the same two-measure module. Here the economical has become mechanical, a *reductio ad absurdum*. The concentration on a limited amount of material produces a sort of caricatured rigidity – a negative image of our prized versatility of utterance. On the other hand, by being repeated in all possible positions within the larger eight-measure phrase, the material does in fact manage to appear in beginning, middle, and end positions, which is certainly versatile in theory, if not in sound or gesture.

These two cases confirm that Haydn's economy can take many forms and lead to very different musical outcomes. We might even understand it as a key ingredient in those many SUBLIME moments that critics have found especially in the late choral works: a certain economy of thought is required to create the maximum musical effect from simple elements, to create a sense of awe or elemental power out of basic forms of contrast or juxtaposition. It can also explain a compositional habit of Haydn's that is especially striking in this repertoire – endings that seem to arrive almost before the listener can possibly expect them to. Contemplating one such instance, at the conclusion of *The Seasons*, Webster notes how its final cadence arrives "with breathtaking swiftness," which he terms an instance of "Haydn's dynamic sublime" (Webster 1998a, 67). At such points, less can definitely be more.

This also highlights a creative taste for reduction that is related to our theme of economy. It involves stripping materials back to their simplest possible form, bespeaking a thoroughly galant conviction that the greatest eloquence can be achieved with the simplest means, as opposed to the *horror vacui* of Baroque music, which translates into consistently fuller textures and a much more even rate of musical progress. This taste for reduction can most readily be recognized when Haydn employs chains of repeated notes, the most reductive form of musical action possible. The second-movement Trio from the Baryton Trio in D major (Hob.XI:95), for example, consists of very little but repeated-note shapes, changing with the downbeats in outer voices but sticking to a repeated d′ almost throughout in the viola part, at the expense of some not very functional harmonies towards the end of the second section. Or, to take one of many such instances, the finale of Symphony No. 88 in G major features a delicious retransition from mm. 140 to 158 based on the common device of anticipating the return of the theme via teasing repetitions of its anacrusis. This anacrusis consists of repeated notes, dispersed between the various instruments of the orchestra in a dialogue between higher and lower voices: the music seems to hold its breath, and surely the listener does too. Even the smallest possible elements of a musical discourse can be made special, objects of attention and wonder.

At the same time, what results from this reductive aesthetic can of course be rich and complex in effect. A nice instance of this is the Trio from the String Quartet in E♭ major, Op. 76, No. 6, which is built on alternating rising and falling scales of E♭ major passed canonically between the four players, a plan of seemingly nursery-rhyme simplicity; as Georg Feder notes, "it is as if one is consciously hearing a scale for the first time" (106). Yet this in itself, by drawing our attention to a feature that we would normally take for granted, creates a certain richness of perception – a "thin" element becomes "thickly" described by the composer. Furthering that sense of enrichment, on the basis of an initial unaccompanied tonic scale played by a single instrument, the texture is again and again built up from scratch into ever-new forms. Out of a simple scale played in iambic rhythm, we end up hearing a virtual compendium of harmonic and contrapuntal techniques, like an exercise in the rule of the octave run riot (see Ludwig Holtmeier's entry on HARMONY for an explanation of this fundamental part of Haydn's compositional equipment). It is a display of compositional virtuosity built on the merest of means.

The characteristic feeling that arises out of such procedures – "thinning out" so as to "thicken" our actual listening experience – is one of imaginative liberation, of inhabiting a (musical) world of seemingly endless possibility.

Holloway captures this when writing that Haydn's music suggests "a still small voice telling of the strange within the normal, the vast within the modest" (334). At the same time our social virtue of versatility comes once more to the fore. This is also evident in one of Haydn's most distinctive compositional traits, his tendency to avoid large-scale formal rhymes in favor of new developments, or of new combinations of previously heard material. While most commonly observed of the composer's recapitulation sections in his sonata-form structures, this in fact applies much more widely to his output. Why, after all, say the same thing twice; why not show the material in a new light?

All these characteristics stand at odds with some of the implications of "economy" as often found in the literature: economy becomes cognate with a "careful husbanding of resources" or "good housekeeping," linked seamlessly with a common biographical image of the composer. Much of the evidence points to Haydn's having been methodical and well organized in his creative routine, cemented by the late accounts to his biographers of how he went about composing, as reported in COMPOSITIONAL PROCESS. The fact that he left so many lists or catalogues of his output (as described by Laurel E. Zeiss in CATALOGUES, WORKLISTS, NACHLASS) would seem to confirm this, and among biographers Finscher has made much of what he sees as Haydn's systematic approach to composition, both in how the composer "works systematically through the possibilities of a given compositional situation" (116) and, on a larger scale, in how he planned at the level of a whole set of instrumental works.

The problem lies not in whether Haydn was indeed like this in his real-life routine – though if he was, it may not be so remarkable, since one imagines that few composers of the time (or indeed, any other time) managed to survive professionally without a good deal of self-discipline. Rather, the difficulty lies in the way in which such attributes are absorbed into the construction of Haydn's artistic persona. It is hard to hear Haydn as systematic or tidy given some of the characteristics we have already outlined – such as drawing attention to, and magnifying, features that we should normally be able to take for granted, whether these be beginnings and endings or simple repeated notes. Such operations distort the "natural flow" of a musical discourse. The aversion to literal large-scale repetition of material is another feature that proclaims not the artistically "small" virtue of tidiness, but rather an open mind, a more dynamic approach to musical art. Similarly, in his account of compositional process, Felix Diergarten, assuming that the written traces faithfully reflect the actual compositional process, suggests that Haydn "did not compose 'organically' from beginning to end," but effectively in neat blocks, with thematic material being fixed before transitions were considered. This may indeed have been generally the case, but it would not account for the dynamic succession of musical materials that we may experience as a particular piece unfolds. LaRue illuminates an important element of this with his concept of "multi-stage variance": "Haydn ... develops his material in a tight linkage of variants on variants ... creating thematic richness without lessening the tensional drive of his structural logic or the unity of his overall design" (265). LaRue also notes the inadequacy of the term "monothematicism" for this technique, "since it suggests limitation, the very opposite of the sense of boundless variety one experiences in the continual unfolding of Haydn's ideas."

Indeed, as already noted, this synergy between "tightness" and "boundless variety" was appreciated by many of Haydn's own contemporaries. And some of the most striking reception of it can be traced in other music of the time, with composers like Brunetti in Madrid and Clementi in London palpably being inspired by the challenge that such economy posed, to say nothing of those closer to Haydn's own orbit. Others were inclined to hear the variety but not the control, and this could include other composers who tried to replicate the composer's apparent eccentricity without managing to bring it off. This at least was the opinion of a Paris reviewer in 1787, who praised a new symphony by Marie-Alexandre Guénin for avoiding this trap: "One was particularly grateful to this composer for having retained his own manner, and for refraining from the all-too-common mania for imitating the style of M. Haydn ... It is believed all too often today that in accumulating extraordinary modulations, in cutting up phrases, in favouring strange and even baroque melodies, one has found this style" (quoted in Harrison 16–17). Such a reception stands at odds with any implication that Haydn was a neat and tidy artist, and of course one controlling factor in that image is the very label still widely used to characterize his era, "Classical." This word inevitably implies a degree of sobriety, of care taken to be lucid at every turn, and the need for self-contained utterance. We should not forget that this was largely a retrospective understanding of what Haydn and his contemporaries were about. As Taruskin puts it: "what we now call 'classical' virtues, especially the virtues of artistic purity and self-sufficiency, are really romantic values in disguise. Calling them 'classical' expresses the nostalgia ... that the artists and thinkers of post-Napoleonic Europe felt for the imagined stability and simplicity of the *ancien régime*" (647).

One particular difficulty with the concept "Classical" is that it mutes the desideratum of variety that was so clearly felt in the later eighteenth-century musical world. And this pivotal term of reference could be applied not just at the level of an individual movement, but also on a larger scale, when one considers the possible cyclic integration of multi-movement works. We might note Haydn's nervousness when "cyclic integration" occurs in the most literal possible way between separate keyboard sonatas of an individual set published in 1780. The first movement of the Sonata in G major (Hob.XVI:39) and second movement of the Sonata in C♯ minor (Hob.XVI:36), begin with the same theme, albeit in different keys and with differences of rhythmic detail. The fact that Haydn asked the publishers to append an "Avertissement" to note that this was "done intentionally" suggests that such cross-reference would by no means necessarily have been viewed in a positive light. It might have been seen as indicating poverty of invention, the composer repeating himself instead of offering the expected variety of material.

As Proksch points out in Cyclic Integration, the reception of Beethoven's Symphony No. 5 from E. T. A. Hoffmann onward set the terms for the debate, which in fact includes an assumption that themes carry the burden of proof when it comes to multi-movement connections. It also seems to set up a binary opposition whereby the overtly cyclic or integrated is automatically attributed positive value, whereas "not integrated/cyclic" is the problematic side, the term that needs special justification. But for the later eighteenth century it seems that variety, or multiplicity, was the normal state, one that could go unquestioned. It was instead lack of variety – which might be felt to suggest overinsistence as well as simply failing to provide the pleasure of contrast – that was aesthetically problematic. This is something we can grasp from most individual movements alone, which are much less consistent in their application of musical materials than was the rule in Baroque times – pronounced contrasts of texture, rhythmic values, dynamics, musical TOPICS and the like are the norm. Movements are no longer likely to be monothematic – and, as we have seen, that rubric is only weakly applicable to those movements of Haydn's that have often been described in that way. Thus, when it comes to assessing the relationships between numbers or movements, we should not feel obliged to "explain" their differences from each another, contrast being a self-evident property of the style.

These differences can be extreme, to the extent that movements may seem incompatible. Kramer considers one instance in the case of the String Quartet in D major, Op. 76, No. 5: after the famous *Largo cantabile e mesto* in the remote key of F♯ major, with its exalted expressive atmosphere, the ensuing *Minuet* "is so sturdy and earthy that it seems . . . false," suggesting that Haydn's work is refusing to allow its individual parts to add up into a "self-evident whole" (62–63). Compared to say the slow movements of Beethoven's Rasumovsky Quartets, which "all seem to respond to something in the movement preceding them rather than to step unforeseeably into an alternate expressive universe," as Haydn's seem to do (63), "Haydn shows more confidence in simple difference," since he inhabits a "culture of feeling where emotions more often coexist than interact" (65). Difference, in other words, can be left to stand, and in fact contrasts can often be equally abrupt and unmediated within individual movements. As Emily I. Dolan points out in ORCHESTRATION, Haydn's symphonic slow movements "often pit sweet, lyrical themes against loud, aggressive intrusions." One example would be the slow movement of Symphony No. 88 in G major, where the conflict between two basic gestures – long-breathed melody and obsessively accented chords – is never rationalized, never "overcome," as our nineteenth-century-centric instincts might lead us to expect, but is instead left for us to contemplate.

On the other hand, to return to the more specific matter of overt inter-movement integration, where materials are recognizably shared between movements, this is in fact much more common in later eighteenth-century music than is generally acknowledged. It can be readily encountered in the works of such composers as Boccherini, C. P. E. Bach, and Kozeluch, for example. From this vantage point, Haydn's relatively sparing use of such overt connections suggests a different mentality, perhaps a stronger drive always to be offering something different. This can clearly be related to the sort of firm forward projection that LaRue's "multi-stage variance" aims to capture. However, there is no question about the less thematically focused form of cyclicity found in Haydn along the lines mentioned by Proksch (and indeed by Webster 1991, with his notion of "through-composition") and we need to be careful not to let perceptions of nineteenth-century practice determine the argument, whereby connections are made primarily through themes and their transformation.

Variety, if not indeed unpredictability, seems to be a byword if we consider the composer's orchestration, with Dolan stressing Haydn's "creation of variation through instrumentation" as well as his attention to individual instrumental sonority. These attributes can be evident on a large scale, for instance in the *Andante* of Symphony No. 16 in B♭ major, in which the upper line is carried, as one might expect, by muted violins, but these are doubled one octave below by a solo cello, to create a subtle and mellow flavor. In the extra movement for wind ensemble ("Introductione: *Largo cantabile*") in A minor that Haydn inserted into his choral version of *The Seven Last Words*, the plurality of individual timbres creates a collective sonority that Landon describes as "austere, gaunt and cold" (182). But the penchant for unexpected colors can also be felt on a much smaller scale. On the darker side of the timbral spectrum, for instance, there is the development section of the first movement of Symphony No. 67 in F major, where a sudden sustained line low in the violas helps point up a harmonic pivot (from m. 147), or the passage when the same instruments double the vocal line two octaves below from m. 96 of the *Scena di Berenice* of 1795 (Hob.XXIVa:10). And in this domain too we find a critic cautioning other composers against slavishly imitating Haydn; Dolan quotes Carl Zelter's admonition to this effect, referring in particular to Haydn's use of trumpets and drums in some later slow movements.

Another constantly enlivening aspect of Haydn's compositional style, one that we can also understand as taking shape under an imperative of variety, is often overlooked: his manipulation of phrase rhythm, often marked by ambiguities or outright irregularities (noted by Markus Neuwirth in MELODY). But even when no such irregularities seem to exist, there is often something very distinctive about Haydn's rhythmic style – it seems to be inhabited by a particular kind of nervous energy. For Johann Triest, writing in 1801, this was a key to the composer's greatness: "his exceptionally light treatment of rhythm, in which no one can compete with him" (373). In RHYTHM AND METER Grant notes how this rhythmic virtuosity expresses itself in a penchant for metrical transformations within an individual movement, and a recent study of metrical manipulation in several sets of Haydn string quartets by Mirka suggests just how much we still have to grasp about this side of the composer's art. This study also helps to make concrete the active type of listening implied by Haydn's style: understanding the composer's metrical strategies, and indeed those of fellow composers of the time, helps us to approach the mindsets of "historical listeners" of the time. An added benefit is how this can change current approaches, "turn[ing] today's listener from a passive consumer into an active partner of the eighteenth-century composer in a game played with the compositional rules of the time" (xii).

If we seem to be collectively under-appreciative of Haydn's rhythmic invention, the same might apply to his orchestration, as Dolan points out: "The power of Haydn's legacy is attested to by its later invisibility: during the nineteenth century, rich, colorful orchestration became the norm." And in fact, this invisibility might apply more widely, to Haydn's handling of musical materials in every sense; much of what was most innovative has lost the sharp edge that it originally carried. This can be understood very broadly. Taruskin suggests that Haydn changed the terms of reference for what composition meant altogether, at the level of technique in general. The "London" Symphonies, in particular No. 104 in D major, "set a benchmark for structural efficiency toward which composers have ever afterward aspired," an efficiency that "came to command … authority" (578). But surely composers were judged according to their perceived technical prowess before this time, so what has changed? What might have changed is that technique is now "staged," a clear example being the equivocation with beginnings and endings that was discussed earlier, when one cannot but be aware of the figure of the composer making choices about what material to present when. More globally, "technique" becomes foregrounded when – for the first era in musical history – variety becomes such a strong desideratum within an individual musical utterance. The introduction of difference – from simple contrast all the way to outright incongruity – naturally raises awareness of how we get from one thing to another, of how the composer manages the process. And this encourages the development of a strong authorial voice, bringing in its train a high degree of technical self-consciousness. As Mary Hunter points out in Self-Reflexivity, this was not peculiar to Haydn, but he "was the composer who most consistently, pervasively, and brilliantly deployed these processes."

Yet this self-consciousness by no means accords with the prevailing image of Haydn today, which retains strong traces of the nineteenth-century reception of the composer as unself-conscious and "natural," both personally and technically. This certainly reflects the enduring power of the label "Classical" and its aesthetic implications, but it also in fact reflects something intrinsic to later eighteenth-century musical thought, and certainly Haydn's. This is what we could describe as a "pastoral" orientation, which amounts to saying complex things with a straight face, "in all innocence." Charles Rosen has addressed this quality in Haydn, which involves a "combination of sophisticated irony and surface innocence" (162), "a naïveté or simplicity that demands … to be taken at face value, even though it is belied by everything else in the work" (163). Counterbalancing the tough, self-conscious, "radical" side of the composer is a pronounced orientation towards accessibility and transparency of musical materials, without which of course any meaningful interplay with a listener would become impossible. This orientation was shared by most of the composer's contemporaries, and was encapsulated by the designation "galant," which produced the "unmarked, dominant style" of the time (see Topics).

Yet "pastoral" might do just as well as galant for the purpose. As Eloise Boisjoli and Robert Hatten point out in Topics, the pastoral can be understood not so much as a clearly delimited topical signal as something broader, a basic level of discourse described as a "mode." Yet the sense intended above is considerably broader even that that, since it describes a fundamental approach to all musical materials. At the same time, more obviously than galant, "pastoral" also allows for the presence of popular elements that is so striking in Haydn's output. In Melody, Neuwirth proposes that the composer's use of popular tunes in the 1780s and 1790s was a way of trying to retain galant simplicity in the face of the symphonies' increasing technical ambition, though in fact popular elements are already frequent in Haydn, and in many genres, before this time. As Matthew Gelbart notes in FOLK SONG SETTINGS, Haydn does not condescend to such materials. Late in his career, when setting Scottish (and Welsh) songs for his British publishers, the composer did not treat as the tunes as EXOTIC or primitive, as "a musical inner child that could inspire new individual art." This latter possibility was left for a later generation, once the concept of "folk music" had solidified into something like its modern form. In the context of newly composed art music, the treatment of popular-sounding or folk-like materials often accords with our concept of the pastoral: here too they are "taken at face value" and at the same time often subjected to artful complexity of treatment. Even in music that presents apparent extremes of exotic color, such as the "Menuet alla Zingarese" from the String Quartet in D major, Op. 20, No. 4, or Volpino's Act III aria "Salamelica" from *Lo speziale*, Haydn does not, as Head notes, "present them simply as exotic curiosities" (79).

Nor does this mean, of course, that such materials are treated sentimentally, as some sort of "deeper human truth" – that is a later form of folk or pastoral mythology. What it does suggest is rather that they are treated, like any and all other musical materials, with a certain reserve, showing "an attitude of skepticism or relativism about the nature of musical utterance" (Sutcliffe 119). In a pluralistic musical world, there is no absolute ordained mode of expression, only many varied possibilities. And while sometimes the stylistic identity of the material that forms part of the bigger mix is clear, as it often is when PROGRAMMATIC ELEMENTS may be discerned, this is not always so. In TOPICS we discover that there are many gradations of signifier, and in COUNTERPOINT Diergarten throws into doubt one of the most seemingly fixed areas of the "topical universe," whereby contrapuntal textures are associated with learned style.

The sense that topics can approximate to a musical garment that one puts on and then takes off must have been promoted by Haydn's experiences in opera. It is literally embodied in a series of arias sung by Vespina in *L'infedeltà delusa* in her attempt to win back her lover Nencio. She adopts a series of disguises that are musical as well as sartorial. In "Ho un tumore in un ginocchio," dressed up as an old woman, she presents a catalogue of devices signaling (mock) pathos: two-note sigh figures to denote weeping (mm. 25–28), further two-note figures to denote being out of breath (mm. 34–38), to the accompaniment of diminished-seventh harmonies, and loud upward sweeping figures for a touch of self-dramatization, such gestures most commonly being found in *accompagnato* recitative. In addition, a syncopated *alla zoppa* rhythm is literally used to illustrate lameness. That this is all a show is proved by some very healthy vocal lines sung in between the pantomime, which would be unlikely to issue from the mouth of an old woman. Vespina's next aria involves her adopting the guise of a German servant, and takes the form of a drinking song, "Trinche vaine," written in a rapid six–eight with generous use of pedals, both signs of rusticity. Here it is the operatic character who is the chameleon, able to bend musical materials to her particular needs.

Many of the traits commonly regarded as intrinsic to Haydn – such as playing with expectation and convention, or the creation of a dialogue between listener and composer – were in fact more widely shared by his contemporaries. However, Haydn was undoubtedly a MARKET leader in such respects; he created frames of reference which many other composers of the time felt obliged to square up to. While there are of course fingerprints and distinctive characteristics, what stands out most is not so much the "what" as the "how": the composer's sheer handling of his musical materials and the artistic, ethical, and social implications of such handling. Haydn's intense intellectual and musical curiosity helped to ensure that his particular brand of discursive and technical richness was highly influential, making his music a significant "event" in the history of later Enlightenment EUROPE.

W. DEAN SUTCLIFFE

FURTHER READING
Feder (1998); Finscher (2002); Gotwals; Grave and Grave (2006); Harrison (1998); Head (2005); Holloway (1998); Kramer (2009); Landon IV; LaRue (1982); Levy (1987); Mirka (2009); Polzonetti (2012); Rosen (1971/72); Schaul (1809); Sisman (2005); Sutcliffe (2014); Taruskin (2005b); Triest (1997 [1801]); Webster (1991, 1998a).

Musical Societies The eighteenth century was notably an age of clubs and societies reflecting the diverse tastes and pursuits of the time. The musical societies with which Haydn's name is linked represent a significant and rich strand in his life and compositional career. These associations range over a wide geographical area encompassing the EUROPEAN capitals, LONDON, Paris and VIENNA, and stretching to the provinces, including the university city of Oxford which Haydn visited in person during his first London sojourn.

Embedded in the concert life of these cities were societies formed by enthusiasts for music, whether connoisseurs or AMATEURS, constituting a pool of likely patrons and entrepreneurs. Typically, such societies might be able to offer larger orchestras for the performance of Haydn's works than were available to him in his regular employment, and to attract larger AUDIENCES. The repertoire they cultivated generally ranged from "ancient" music (famously defined by the London concerts of that name as music that was more than twenty years old) to new commissions from contemporary composers. Within the broader genre are numerous sub-types including concert organizations emanating from larger societies such as the FREEMASONS, and musical societies set up specifically for charitable purposes, such as the New Musical Fund, "established for the relief of Decayed Musicians, their Widows and Orphans, residing in England" (McVeigh 74; its conductors for the annual performances included Philip Hayes, Heather Professor of Music at Oxford, who hosted Haydn on his visit to the University in 1791). Professional organizations in England that inspired Haydn to provide music included the Royal Society of Musicians, for whom he made a version of his *Prince of Wales March* in 1792.

Further inflecting the topic are societies that came into existence beyond Haydn's lifetime, pertaining to the composer and his works, and constituting a vital conduit for his music in a variety of ways that reflect changing trends in the production and consumption of musical performance, as well as in musical scholarship, and in the RECEPTION of classical repertoire. Among significant contributory factors, the role of the German immigrant community in nineteenth-century AMERICAN musical life was linked with the cultivation of this repertoire, as Newman observes. A selection of all the different types of society is considered in what follows, highlighting in each case their particular impact on Haydn in his lifetime, or their implications for the cultivation of his music and his reputation posthumously. The topic of musical societies has long been embedded in the Haydn literature. A sharper focus on the structures such organizations represent has emerged alongside the increasing attention to concert history, as is reflected in the pioneering work of Fauquet, Holoman, McGuinness, McVeigh, Morrow, Newman and others.

The culture the musical societies represented in the eighteenth and nineteenth centuries was overwhelmingly male, yet it also enabled female access to its musical offerings as both performers and listeners, by differing routes in various times and places. Thus, while the Musical Society at Oxford was run by a committee of stewards from the all-male colleges of the University, "ladies" were numerous among the subscribers purchasing tickets to the concerts at the Holywell Music Room, where they too could experience Haydn's chamber, orchestral, and vocal music in what was regarded as a safe place for them to mingle socially (see Wollenberg). Among the chamber music societies proliferating in nineteenth-century Paris, and offering concert series, a 'quatuor féminin' that formed (and re-formed with changing personnel) in the middle decades, was applauded for their performance of Haydn, among other repertoires (see Fauquet).

The structures underpinning concert life in Vienna offered Haydn a plethora of stimulating opportunities to mingle with high society, to produce new works to commissions, and to attend – and on many occasions to direct – performances. As a general rule, where there was membership of a society or at least a link with it, there would be networking opportunities for musicians. But the benefits of these associations went further, offering a chance to encounter precious sources of stimulus to artistic creativity as well as significant sources of patronage. Such was the role (for Mozart as well as Haydn) of Baron Gottfried van Swieten's prestigious Gesellschaft der Associierten Cavaliere, whose sponsors included such influential musical patrons as Prince Kinsky, Prince Lichnowsky, and Prince Lobkowitz (names associated also with Beethoven). Constituted more as an informal group of aristocrats than a formal society, the Associierten promoted repertoire dating from the 1780s onwards as well as Handel's oratorios and other vocal works. Swieten also cultivated music of the Bach family, with whom he had direct links via C. P. E. Bach.

Among Haydn's own works, his oratorios were particularly prominent in the programs of the various musical societies in Vienna. *Il ritorno di Tobia*, commissioned by the Tonkünstler-Societät, a musicians' association founded to benefit members, their widows and orphans, featured periodically in their Lenten concerts after its successful premiere, as did the later oratorios, *The Creation* and *The Seasons*, and also *The Seven Last Words* (*Die sieben letzte Worte*), all three being based on texts by Swieten. The Associierten sponsored these works, offering generous support to Haydn for the original production of *The Creation* in April 1798 (see Webster) and financing the premiere of *The Seasons* in April 1801 at the Schwarzenberg Palace in Vienna, "with the same soloists as in the later performances of *The Creation*" (Landon V 37). They also paid the costs of the first public performance of *The Seasons* in the Redoutensaal put on for Haydn's benefit in May 1801, although on this occasion the event, as Rosenbaum recorded, was disappointingly "not too well attended" (Landon V 59).

Haydn later in life received gratifying attention from the musical societies. Thus, the Tonkünstler-Societät, with which he had a longstanding relationship, made him an honorary member in 1798 (thereby repairing an earlier injustice towards him and securing his loyalty to the society). In 1802 the Musikverein of Bergen, having performed *The Creation* with notable success, wrote in gratitude to Haydn, whose appreciative reply expressing wonderment and satisfaction at this evidence of the spread of his works to distant regions "has subsequently become one of the composer's most famous documents" (Landon V 232). The *Liebhaber Concerte*, set up on a similar model to Swieten's Cavaliers, put on a gala performance of *The Creation* in March 1808 to mark Haydn's seventy-sixth birthday, with the composer and many other luminaries in attendance (detailed in Brown).

Although Haydn never visited Paris in person, his music travelled there and a number of organizations put out tentacles towards the composer, enabling him to attract a considerable following and gain a lasting popularity there for his music. Among them was the Concert de la Loge Olympique, supported by a group of Freemasons under the leadership of Comte d'Ogny, an ambitious enterprise which with its large orchestra rivaled the Concert Spirituel in programing Haydn's works, notably commissioning from him the six "Paris" Symphonies (1785–86). (See also European Contexts; Leading Large Ensembles.) The Freemasons formed a prominent element in Parisian concert culture, with lodges having their own music master and orchestra; masonic ceremonies are documented as finishing with a "concert vocal et instrumental" (Brévan 54). The Concert des Amateurs, founded 1769, not a masonic organization but with connections to the Freemasons, had built a tradition of performing Haydn's works in Paris before the mid-1780s (see Brévan; Harrison). Like the Viennese concert societies, the Parisian equivalents reflected back to Haydn the esteem in which he was held, presenting him with medals specially struck in his honor. In December 1801 Haydn was elected a non-resident member of the Paris Institut National des Sciences et des Arts, Literature and Fine Arts section.

Haydn's music was in the repertoire in England long before his visits in the 1790s brought him into contact with the lively culture of musical clubs and societies in London and beyond. His appetite for social contact and musical happenings was fed by a wide range of institutions, including the entertainments offered by London's pleasure gardens. Early in 1791 he attended the concerts of the Academy of Ancient Music, finding their performances of early musical repertoire impressive. The Anacreontic Society, meeting at the Crown and Anchor Tavern, "which had been so hospitable to Haydn when he arrived in London" continued to give "flattering attention to his music" (Landon III 115). Particularly important to highlight here as a national speciality are the popular genres of English catch and glee. These figured in the meetings of the Anacreontic Society (involving the members in performances) alongside musical entertainment of a more elevated kind, and with dinner in between. Haydn contributed to the genre most notably with his piano or harp accompaniments supplied for the Earl of Abingdon's *Twelve Sentimental Catches and Glees* (published in London in 1795; see Robins).

Haydn declared that his honorary doctorate from the University of Oxford, bestowed in July 1791 when his "Oxford" Symphony was performed in the University's Assembly Room, the Sheldonian Theatre, had brought him "the acquaintanceship of the most prominent men and the entree into the greatest houses." It also brought him election to the Musical Graduates' Society formed in the wake of the success of the original Glee Club. As its name implies, its members were musical graduates of Oxford and Cambridge. As Dr. J. W. Callcott, fellow member of the society and graduate of Oxford, recorded in his handwritten "Account of the graduates meeting, a society of musical professors established in London, November 24, 1790, at Dr. Arnold's":

> A new and illustrious member was then added to the list by the University of Oxford, who conferred the degree of Dr. in music upon the celebrated Haydn, and it was with much concern to Mr. Callcott, who held the sixth meeting ... on the third of August [1791] that Dr. Haydn's summer engagements prevented his attendance. At the eighth meeting, however ... the presence of the new member was highly gratifying to all. (Recorded in the *Musical Times and Singing Class Circular* in article entitled "A Musical Graduates Society" in 1892.)

Haydn gave the graduates a farewell dinner in June 1792 at Parsloe's coffee house, "to which, at his particular request, Mr. Salomon was admitted, partly as the intimate friend of Dr. Haydn, partly as an interpreter, Dr. Haydn having not made sufficient progress in the English tongue."

Beyond the occasion of the degree ceremony in 1791 Haydn demonstrably had connections with the Oxford Musical Society and its weekly subscription concerts given at the Holywell Music Room (opened in 1748 as the earliest purpose-built concert room in Europe). Philippe Jung, violinist in the Holywell Band, came originally from Vienna, as did Andreas Lidl, a baryton player. Haydn's music was regularly programed by the Society at Holywell for several decades both before and after his visit, and indeed continuing after his death, with the Symphony No. 100 in G major ("Military") among the "London" Symphonies, and the earlier Symphonies No. 53 in D major ("L'Impériale/Festino") and No. 63 in C major ("La Roxelane"), recurring as particularly popular items. Hayes's successor, William Crotch, conducted a performance of *The Creation* at the Holywell Music Room in 1801 with Madame Mara among the soloists. The students attending these performances were destined mainly to enter such professions as the clergy or some form of public service, whereby the musical tastes acquired during their time in Oxford could impact on the wider communities they served.

In the Victorian period the Sacred Harmonic Society (founded in 1832) performed *The Creation* every year at London's Exeter Hall. It was enthusiastically adopted on the provincial scene, becoming a staple of choral societies in the north of England, and across the Atlantic where the Boston Handel and Haydn Society included it in its repertoire from the year of their foundation in

1815, and indeed may have been inspired by the work to couple Haydn's name with Handel's in their title (see Temperley). The Boston society was founded specifically "for cultivating and improving a correct taste in sacred music and also to introduce into more general practice the works of Handel, Haydn and other eminent composers" (Herter Norton 328). By early September 1815 the secretary of the newly formed society had been deputed "to purchase a suitable number of copies of Haydn's Creation of the World of Mr. Graupner, at 5 cents a page", and at their meeting on September 7 they performed "The Heavens are Telling" as well as the Hallelujah chorus. By Christmas that year they were able to put on an apparently "entirely successful" public performance of Part I of *The Creation*. Between 1818 and 1880 *The Creation* was performed by the society more than sixty times (and *Messiah* over seventy times; see Dwight), while the New York Oratorio Society performed *The Creation* and *The Seasons* in full, among other vocal works by Haydn, during its first seven years starting in 1873 (see Proksch; see also THE AMERICAS).

The work of the Handel and Haydn Society in Boston has continued through to the present day. Gottlieb Graupner, a founding member of the society, was a versatile German-born instrumentalist who had played oboe in Haydn's orchestra for Salomon's London concerts (1791–92): he emigrated to America by 1795, and by 1797 had settled in Boston where among other activities – including music publishing – he set up a Philharmonic Society around 1810–11. As music critic John Sullivan Dwight put it in 1881, "in their small way they practised Haydn's Symphonies, etc., for their own enjoyment" (416).

Threaded through the history of the Handel and Haydn Society in the mid-nineteenth century is the record of participation in their performances by the Germania Society, as noted by Newman. This orchestral body of German musicians who fled their native land to seek a society free of the ills of patronage (as they saw it) remained dedicated to the Viennese classics among more modern, and lighter, repertoire. The programs drawn up for their six-year tour of America from 1848 to 1854 featured Haydn's symphonies as well as those of Mozart and Beethoven. The motivation for preserving this canonic repertoire went beyond the purpose of mere entertainment, it being regarded, as Broyles observes, as reflecting moral values. The founders of the Harvard Musical Association (1837) urged that music be "looked upon, not as an amusement, but as a serious pursuit" (Ritter, writing in 1884, 241). According to Dwight, the programs for the ten seasons of symphonic concerts the Association put on in Boston between 1865 and 1875 included twelve Haydn symphonies, as well as six of Mozart's, alongside more recent repertoire in a variety of genres (445).

As Lesure writes, the trinity of Haydn, Mozart, and Beethoven was revered in nineteenth-century Paris as representing "the acknowledged models of classicism" (9). Haydn's chamber works were cultivated both by amateur societies and by professional groups, in public concerts and in private performance sessions: indeed, Arthur Pougin referred in 1869 to the "sanctuaries" remote from the noise of the world, where the devotees of chamber music could give themselves up to the cult of the "venerable goddess, divine inspiration of Haydn, Mozart, Beethoven and Boccherini" (Fauquet 32). At the opposite end of the spectrum were the "*Séances populaires de musique de chambre*" put on by the Société Lamoureux from 1860 onwards, which offered a wider public the opportunity to form a taste for the chamber music of Haydn, Mozart, and Beethoven.

Haydn's string quartets – from the earliest to the last – and also his keyboard trios, were assured of their place in the programs presented by performers of the calibre of violinist Pierre Baillot (1771–1842), who wrote to his friend François de Montbeillard: "What Haydn has said is full of justice, of elevation, of reason." He also considered Haydn "the mentor to whom all the young composers should listen" (Fauquet 55). Baillot was among subscribers to Pleyel's edition of the Haydn quartets (1802), alongside Cherubini, Kreutzer, Méhul, and Montbeillard and others.

The opportunities for orchestral performance also helped to secure the continuing cultivation of Haydn's music in Paris. After the Treaty of Paris in May 1814, while the city was "no longer, as it had been under Napoleon I, the political centre of the continent ... Paris was soon to recover through the arts the hegemony which it had lost through arms" (Mansel 38). Among the strands making up the network of musical organizations that developed, the renowned Société des Concerts of the Paris Conservatoire, founded in 1828, sustained a continuous presence in the concert life of the city through to the next century. Its seeds were sown in the statutory student performances at the Conservatoire under the rubric of *exercices publics des élèves*; at these Sunday afternoon orchestral concerts, "Haydn was to be heard on every concert" (Holoman, 10–11). Haydn's symphonic compositions in the programs of the Société des Concerts du Conservatoire (inheriting the Sunday afternoon slot) ranged from the Symphony No. 45 in F♯ minor ("Farewell,") to the "Paris", "Oxford," and "London" Symphonies (Nos. 82–87, 92, 93–104). Deldevez, who served as chef d'orchestre of the society, documented for their seasons of 1860–67 a total of sixty-six performances of Haydn's Symphonies, including No. 82 "L'Ours/the Bear," No. 85 "La Reine" (seven performances), No. 94 the "Surprise," and No. 100 the "Militaire" (five performances), as well as selections from "*La Création du monde*" and "*Les Saisons de Haydn*" with French text (225–26). In these concerts, as in those of the various chamber music societies, it was customary for Parisian audiences to request movements to be repeated, especially slow movements; the Austrian "*Hymne de Haydn*" (Op. 76, No. 3, ii) was a particular favorite, performed at the Conservatoire by the whole string band (see also WAR).

Widening the net to encompass non-musical societies that commissioned musical works, among those devoted to philanthropic purposes was the Vienna Pensionsgesellschaft bildender Künstler, to which Haydn (and also Beethoven) contributed music for their charity balls held at the Redoutensaal. Other groups provided venues for musical performances, as with the Freemasons Hall in London, used by the Academy of Ancient Music among others. Finally, societies established after Haydn's time were important in preserving sources of his works, notably the Gesellschaft der Musikfreunde in Vienna (founded 1814) with its extensive holdings of source material relating to Haydn and his contemporaries (see COLLECTIONS), besides its cultivation of Haydn's music in performance. The Society also helped promote musicological scholarship on the composer and making his music newly available in critical EDITIONS and RECORDINGS, as with the Haydn Society (originating in Boston) founded by H. C. Robbins Landon and others in 1949. The Haydn Society of Great Britain (director: Denis McCaldin) declares as its mission the promotion of knowledge and understanding of the composer and his music, while the Haydn Society of North America aims to disseminate information about Haydn's music to researchers, performers, and devotees; and the Society for Eighteenth-Century Music (founded 2001 in Atlanta, GA, at the annual meeting of the American Musicological Society) has also generated important scholarship on Haydn: these latter two societies have held joint meetings resulting in publications (e.g. Murray). An anthropological study of the phenomenon of musical societies considered more broadly has yet to be produced.

SUSAN WOLLENBERG

FURTHER READING

Brévan (1980); Brown (1986); Broyles (1992); Burchell (1996); *Cambridge Companion*; Clark (2000); Deldevez (1887); Dwight (1881); Fauquet (1986); Harrison (1998); Herter Norton (1932); Hogwood (1980); Holomon (2004); Landon I– V; Lesure (1986); Mansel (2001); McGuinness (2004); McVeigh (1993); Morrow (1989); Murray (2001, 2011); Newman (2010); Proksch (2015); Ritter (1884); Robins (2006); Smither (1987); Taylor (2010); Temperley (1991); Webster (2005b); Wollenberg (2001).

N

Nachlass – see Catalogues

National Melodies – see Folk Song Settings

Nationalism and Cosmopolitanism The modern concept of nationalism – the feeling that one's primary allegiance is to the nation and that one's identity is chiefly determined by an overriding sense of belonging to the nation – was only beginning to emerge during the ENLIGHTENMENT, bolstered by the French and American revolutions. For Haydn as for his contemporaries, society was structured in horizontal layers – by classes – rather than by vertical slices cutting across class lines, which would ultimately be necessary to the full development of nationalism in the nineteenth century and beyond. Haydn's career was dominated by his service to an aristocratic patron, and much of his music was thus a product of and for the uppermost classes of society, both within the Habsburg Empire and abroad. Haydn's (perhaps apocryphal) response when Mozart admonished him for speaking so few languages – "But my language is understood all over the world" – might be interpreted in this context: the cosmopolitanism to which he was pointing was the universal musical language of the ruling classes of EUROPE, a language dominated in the late eighteenth century by the Austro-German compositional style, which Haydn himself played a key role in shaping.

Nations and national styles in music existed before the advent of nationalism, but it was not until the nineteenth century that rustic or folk-inspired styles carried national connotations rather than simply lower-class – and therefore, to the aristocracy and bourgeoisie, exotic – ones. Haydn's autograph superscript "Volck's Lied" on his *Kaiserhymne* ("Gott! erhalte Franz den Kaiser") denoted not a song *of* the people but *for* the people, accessible and familiar enough for the purpose of raising their voices in celebration of their emperor's birthday while the revolution raged in France. In 1796, the Deputy Minister of Police, Count Joseph Franz Saurau commissioned Haydn to set Lorenz Leopold Haschka's text to music in time for it to be sung simultaneously in cities throughout the Empire on Franz II's birthday on February 12, 1797. Hiles explores how Haydn composed his hymn in the *Volkston*, which, as J. A. P. Schulz explained in the preface to his *Lieder im Volkston*, is defined by its appearance, or illusion, of familiarity. In the case of the *Kaiserhymne*, the *Volkston* is manifest through an easily singable, largely stepwise and diatonic strophic melody contained within a comfortable range. Crucially, the *Volkston* was a cosmopolitan European style associated with no particular national, linguistic, or ethnic group, therefore it was perfectly suited to a hymn destined to be sung by subjects throughout Franz's multicultural realm. As Hiles notes, both the text and the context of the hymn at its inception were clearly royal, but they were not narrowly national (in the sense of specifically Austro-German), and the various performances on the emperor's birthday preserved some of the cultural differences among the numerous regions of the Empire; at war with revolutionary France, the emperor had to be a supra-nationalist, emphasizing unity among his very diverse subjects. Yet by 1825, the "German hymn" in Rossini's opera Il viaggio a Reims ossia Il giglio d'ora was none other than Haydn's Kaiserhymne, sung by the German Ambassador to the King of France to a text that Winkler has read as a legitimization of the French Restoration and of monarchy more generally, celebrating "tranquil harmony govern[ing] all men and nations" (39).

Similarly, Haydn's unfulfilled agreement or proposal, in a letter of August 1789 to the Parisian publisher Jean-Georges Sieber, to write a National Symphony points to the political potential of the composer's cosmopolitan musical style. As Bonds has suggested, although we know little about Haydn's political leanings, he would certainly have been aware of the details of the situation in France in the summer of 1789, which were reported without downplaying their violence in Vienna's and Pressburg's press. Bonds also suggests that Haydn understood the particular valence of the term "national" in France at this time: "public" or "anything having to do with the Third Estate and the forces of change" (15). It was thus likely no coincidence that the "national" work Haydn was considering was a symphony, the most public of all genres of the late eighteenth century. Since he never wrote the symphony, we can only speculate as to how it might have sounded, but as Bonds points out, a National Symphony for France may not necessarily have been a symphony in French style or quoting French melodies. The single work Haydn did write that includes the word "national" in its title, the Hungarischer National Marsch, Hob.VIII:4 (1802), essentially corroborates Bonds's conjecture: with the possible exception of a few melodic ornaments, this short piece of Harmoniemusik does not contain strikingly "Hungarian," or even particularly exotic, colorings. (See also FOLK SONG SETTINGS; BURGENLAND.)

CATHERINE MAYES

FURTHER READING
Bonds (2011); Fuhrmann (2013); Grasberger (1968); Hiles (2009); Winkler (2009a).

Nature Described as "the key Enlightenment concept" but "deeply enigmatic" (Porter 295), Nature in Haydn's era functioned as ideal, as place, as source of artistic imitation and aesthetic response, as subject for minute description and taxonomy, and as object of mediation, improvement, and control. Its reassuring reminder of the divine plan paradoxically focused attention on its opposites: artifice, disorder, industrial production. Some of its profoundest musical evocations were analogical or metaphorical, or stemmed from what might be termed pastoral fantasias. Schama describes landscape as "a work of the mind" (7), and while Rosen also connects landscape with memory and persuasively places them both in the musical achievement of the "Romantic generation," nature's meanings both capacious and contested were not unknown to the composer who yearned for urban pleasures from his country "wasteland" (CCLN 96; Briefe 228). But inflecting nature with "pastoral" and "landscape" inevitably introduces the artifices of genre, the reach of myth, the AESTHETICS of BEAUTIFUL, SUBLIME, and picturesque, and the controversies over description and tone-painting (PROGRAMMATIC ELEMENTS).

> From a Tour of this kind, in which the beauties of Nature are the object of our search, we experience a pleasure that few other amusements can furnish. The picturesque views, which at every step present themselves to an observant eye, while they pass unnoticed by the plodding or hasty passenger, afford the sentimental one a fund of entertainment, which at once delights and improves the mind.

So began the illustrated *Tour of the Isle of Wight* (Hassell, 1790). Nature tourism rewarded the properly receptive "man of feeling" with pleasure and moral improvement. Haydn brought this book back with him from London, after having been a guest of the island's governor, Thomas Orde, in July 1794. His diary noted only the "splendid view of the sea" from the governor's house (CCLN 288; Briefe 530). He might not have seen ruined Netley Abbey (near Southampton), whose "melancholy greatness," apostrophized in a 1769 elegy by George Keate, was quoted in the *Tour*, but on a subsequent excursion out of London Haydn had a comparable experience at the "remains" in the "beautiful wilderness" of ruined Waverley Abbey: his heart was "oppressed" that "all this once belonged to my religion" (CCLN 304; Briefe 551). Griesinger quoted this (from the missing Fourth London Notebook) in the context of Haydn's Catholicism, but this mis-frames the experience: that Haydn was gripped by such a feeling places him squarely in the tradition of the melancholy landscape. Churchyards and ruins evoking lost possibilities and gloomy imaginings were a staple of mid-century English poets popular in German translation: Thomas Gray's "Elegy in a Country Churchyard" (1750; *Musenalmanach*, 1771), Thomas Warton's "Pleasures of Melancholy" (1747; trans. Zachariä 1765), and Edward Young's *Night Thoughts* (1742; trans. in Haydn's library) mined a vein that re-emerged with Romanticism.

Haydn's sensitivity to his English environments included admiring references to gardens (Hampton Court, Cambridge), an expensively installed grotto with waterworks and an English garden (Oatlands), and Bath's white stone buildings ("one of the most beautiful cities in Europe") (CCLN 294, 272, 295; Briefe 539, 508). Plausibly, he had no less acute an appreciation of the elaborate gardens of the landscape-obsessed Esterházy princes, who spent astounding sums on their hunting grounds and parks to raise game birds (Körner 73–91). Haydn told Griesinger that his main forms of relaxation during the "long stays in Hungary" were hunting and fishing, recalling his proud moment of bringing down three hazel-hens with one shot (29–30). The extended hunting scene in "Autumn" of *The Seasons* opens with an aria detailing the way a countryman (striding in eighth-notes), his obsessive dog (running and circling in sixteenth-notes), and his gun (with a "flash" and loud "bang") successfully bring down a bird (its sudden ascent when flushed out by the dog, high trilling call, the singer's gleeful and repetitive modeling of its fall). We are enjoined to "see" the broad fields and the dog in the grass, the third of five numbers in which the audience is asked to visualize seasonal aspects of nature (or, at the end, the stunning moment of heaven's gate opening for the "great Morning"). The raucous stag hunt that follows introduces actual hunters (and their hounds) to the chorus of peasants, a "sphere of aristocratic pastimes, which are otherwise lacking in the oratorio." As with the dog stalking the bird, the hunting chorus enacts a narrative, exploding with the energy of well-known hunting-horn calls (also notated in Diderot's *Encyclopédie*) in the order corresponding to that of the hunt from the "Quest" to the kill (see Heartz).

Arguments over the propriety of pictorialisms, too-literal imitations of nature, erupted immediately, continuing the thread of critique in response to *The Creation* but actually reviving a much older strand of thought about the IMITATION of nature and tone-painting in general. Nature-related topics in operatic and instrumental music – the pastoral in swaying sicilianas in slow movements or rustic drones in the trios of minuets, the hunting-horn figures and triadic melodies primarily in Allegros – never excited the same comment, perhaps because the intentionally stylized distance of a musical "TOPIC" prompted the pleasures of shared experience and recognition rather than seeming explicitly to correspond to an aspect of nature. Only human nature and affective states were fit subjects for imitation, and critics had to hold the line against popular enjoyment of what was theorized and valued as "picturesque" in England. Thus, stormy-sounding music (string tremolos in minor mode, say) in an untitled symphony might rank higher than similar passages for the "foaming billows" in *The Creation*, the violent storm in *The Seasons'* "Summer," or the thunderstorm in Beethoven's *Pastoral* Symphony (itself heavily indebted to those foaming billows). Does the storm topic of the overture to Haydn's Metastasian opera *L'isola disabitata* (1779) "represent" or "depict" the storm that shipwrecked the protagonists on the uninhabited island of the title, the painful emotions of the abandoned Constanza, or does it simply prepare the audience for the turbulence that lies ahead (as theories of the overture prescribed)?

Raymond Monelle's rich investigations into the cultural history of the "outdoor" musical topics related to the huntsman, soldier, and shepherd reveal that pastoral, military, and hunting topics "map whole tracts of human reality," and their resonances move far beyond a listing of signifiers. In considering Haydn's brilliant musical evocations of celestial bodies, weather, birds, animals, and landscapes bleak or fecund, we similarly become aware of the human in the landscape, the persona, character, or sensibility engaging with nature. In the Adagio recitative of Symphony No. 7 ("Le midi") the solo violin enacts the despair and panic caused by noontide's overwhelming sun; in Hannah's aria in "Summer," coursing blood and vibrating nerves rise chromatically to awaken the soul; when the storm inverts the chromatic line, the human sensibility is terrifyingly challenged. Connecting Haydn to "nature," in its multiple meanings "perhaps the most complex word in the language" (Williams), may not make it essential to know that he enjoyed hunting, was highly sensitive to changes in weather, kept fruit trees, owned books on growing and using "kitchen plants," and jotted down impressions of marvelous vistas and melancholy ruins. But his compositional sensibility was strikingly attuned to the natural world. (See also THE AMERICAS.)

ELAINE SISMAN

FURTHER READING
Briefe; CCLN; Groves (2012); Hajós (1989); Hassell (1790); Heartz (1976); Hirschfeld (2001); Körner (2008); Monelle (2006); Porter (2000); Rosen (1995); Schama (1995); Sisman (2013); Stalnaker (2010); Williams (1985).

Networks – see People and

Opera – see Theater and Theatricality

Orchestras – see Leading Large Ensembles

Orchestration To speak of Haydn's "orchestration" is an anachronism: the term was not in use until the nineteenth century. Haydn's music, however, contains the hallmarks of modern orchestration *avant la lettre*. Indeed, his orchestral music seen across the span of his career paints a picture in miniature of the development of orchestral writing in the second half of the eighteenth century.

One necessary precondition for the birth of modern orchestration was the solidification of the orchestra as an institution and musical body. As Spitzer and Zaslaw have shown, this process took place over the course of the eighteenth century. During this time, more wind instruments became regular members of the orchestra. This change is reflected in Haydn's ensembles. Many (though by no means all) of Haydn's earlier symphonies, for example, employed only oboes in the upper wind parts; it was not until the mid-1770s that the flute became a regular member of Haydn's orchestra. As Zaslaw has argued, it is important to understand the ways in which Haydn's pre-1779 orchestral compositions were not composed in total isolation, but rather reflected (and influenced) broader orchestral trends of this period.

Three strands in Haydn's orchestral writing are worth teasing out here: Haydn's attention to individual instruments, his creation of VARIATION through instrumentation, and the ways in which his music calls attention to the status of the orchestra as an ensemble. Taken together, these might be said to constitute the basic elements of modern orchestration. The prevalence of *concertante* writing can be found throughout his compositional career, from the numerous solos in his Symphonies Nos. 6–8, the English horn and horn dialogues in Symphony No. 22 in E♭ major, the cello solo in the trio of Symphony No. 95 in C minor, and the keyboard solo in the finale of Symphony No. 98, to name just a few. Haydn did not shy away from unusual and striking instrumental combinations and his writing embraced the particularities and peculiarities of his instruments. These unusual sounds sometimes evoked objects outside of the orchestra. The arresting beginning of the primary theme of the first movement of his Symphony No. 100 in G major, "Military," with just a flute and two oboes, resembles the squeaky musical clocks popular in the late eighteenth century.

The second strand – Haydn's creation of variation through changes to his instrumentation – is one facet of his larger preoccupation with a range of techniques of variation that can be seen throughout his career and across

241

genres. In the first movement of his Symphony No. 85 in B♭ major, for example, the primary theme first appears *piano* in the strings alone; this anemic theme becomes more robust in subsequent appearances. Haydn sometimes uses a particular instrumentation of a theme to indicate a triumphant arrival at a recapitulation or else to undermine the strength of a theme in a false recapitulation. For example, in the first movement of his Symphony No. 102 in B♭ major, the theme reappears at the end of a long development in C major, but a more immediate give-away than the wrong key is the *piano* presentation of the theme with flute and string accompaniment. This relationship between the thematic material and instruments suggests a way of distinguishing orchestration and instrumentation: both require the thoughtful deployment of instruments, but orchestration involves the large-scale use of reinstrumentation.

The third strand – the calling attention to the status of the orchestra as an ensemble – is related closely to the second idea. It refers to the prevalence of gestures that play out the coming together of the orchestra. For example, in first movements of his later symphonies, Haydn often begins primary themes with a reduced number of instruments and then dramatically introduces the whole orchestra, culminating in a loud and grand *tutti* exclamation. In finales, Haydn employs this same gesture of what we can call "orchestral growth"; here, in conjunction with the prevalence of dance-like themes, this kind of gradual coming together imbues the music with a sense of collective social celebration. Slow movements often pit sweet, lyrical themes against loud, aggressive intrusions, creating large-scale form through sonic contrast. The "Representation of Chaos" in *The Creation* can be heard – as it was by Haydn's contemporaries – as a random assortment of un-ordered instruments; the moment of creation of light is also the first bringing together of the instruments as a coherent orchestra.

While old-fashioned narratives describe Haydn learning how to orchestrate only later in life (and only by following Mozart's model), Haydn was in fact both sensitive to and experimental with his instrumental forces from his early years. Indeed, for many of Haydn's contemporaries, Haydn was both model and innovator. His approach to the orchestra at once balanced sensitivity towards individual instruments while also bringing them together in the service of a greater whole. Ernst Gerber, for example, invoked this idea of instrumental equality in his *Historisch-biographisches Lexikon der Tonkünstler* (1790–92), praising Haydn's careful attention to instrument parts that might otherwise be considered unimportant interior lines. Such admiration continued into the early nineteenth century. Writers like Giuseppe Carpani and E. T. A. Hoffmann described the evolution of orchestral music in Haydn's hands as the emergence of a more democratic ensemble in which individual instruments had their own, distinct voices.

From the 1790s onward, we find a growing preoccupation with orchestral sonority: critics complained about the misuse and abuse of instruments – in particular wind instruments – and the increasing obsession with effect, which was often done in imitation of Haydn's orchestral style. Carl Zelter, for example, cautioned composers against blindly imitating Haydn (referring to things such as using trumpets and drums in slow movements). Such criticisms ultimately point to the widespread popularity of this approach to the orchestra. The power of Haydn's legacy is attested to by its later invisibility: during the nineteenth century, rich, colorful orchestration became normative.

EMILY I. DOLAN

FURTHER READING
Dolan (2013); Gerber (1790–92); Gerlach (1981); Spitzer and Zaslaw (2004); Zaslaw (2012); Zelter (1798).

Organology – see Instruments and

Originality – see Genius

P

Pannonia – see Burgenland

Paris – see European Contexts

People and Networks The Esterházy court musicians formed just one part of an interlocking network of patrons, musicians, and professionals with whom Haydn engaged across his lengthy and multifaceted career. His employers and co-workers were an important subset of a larger circle of STUDENTS, COMPOSERS, DEDICATEES, PUBLISHERS, PERFORMERS, PROFESSIONALS, FRIENDS, and social acquaintances within Haydn's orbit – an overlapping network of concentric circles around the common core figure: Haydn himself. Many different kinds of listeners, in multiple PLACES and venues (PERFORMANCE SPACES), also formed part of his extended social and communication networks. This essay, divided into two parts, provides an overview of the many networks Haydn cultivated and negotiated with, both inside and outside the Esterházy COURT milieu. (See also EISENSTADT AND ESZTERHÁZA.)

In configuring this study of people and networks, we adapt Richard Taruskin's methodology, presented in the Introduction to the *Oxford History of Western Music* (2005). Moving beyond a consideration of the everyday, Taruskin advocates an anthropological approach to music history, one where music is perceived not only as a social phenomenon but one where the collective activities of individuals forge networks to mobilize resources and positionality. In the words of Michael Gallope, throughout his magnum opus Taruskin "challenges the straightforward narration of historical facts, debunking appeals to aesthetic transcendence or trans-historical authenticity, and critiquing unqualified celebrations of 'poietic' greatness" (199) by focusing on human agents." "Real people," to quote Taruskin, are the doers and makers of history, and the more we focus on an "actor–network" methodology (Piekut), the more closely we approach a "true history" of music and gain a more realistic understanding of "how and why things happened as they did" (Taruskin, 2005b, I, xxii). By reconfiguring the standard narratives in new intersectional ways, and placing Haydn and his musical output in dialogue with others within his sphere, we point to possible new connections and potential lines of inquiry.

Haydn did not work alone, nor did he create in a vacuum. The many individuals and communities with whom he worked during his nearly three decades of close proximity to the music-making machinery and creative talent within the Esterházy court, and an even longer period beyond the confines of the court – all of these people form part of the "social elites" (a problematic term for sure) associated with literate music enumerated by Taruskin: "ecclesiastical, political, military, hereditary, meritocratic, economic, educational, academic, fashionable, even criminal" (xxii). To this list we would also add, in Haydn's case, less-literate types – including members of his own family – for whom music-making was sometimes a more oral affair (think of the young Haydn singing alongside his father, a harpist, or learning to write gestural, actor-centric music under the tutelage of Kurz-Bernardon), and to those living and working in his immediate surroundings from whom he drew so much inspiration. (See Biography; Burgenland; Theater and Theatricality.) Bruno Latour might disagree with Taruskin's assertion that "agents can only be people" when arguing that natural processes or technical objects (a keyboard, for instance?) might also be agents in our social world (however, in the case of the keyboard, the instrument still requires human intervention to create change). But for the purposes of this essay, we focus on the range of people Haydn encountered within and beyond the court over the course of his long and productive life – his many "art worlds" as it were (with acknowledgment to art historian and cultural sociologist, Howard Becker, via Taruskin, xxviii). An actor-network approach opens up a richer context for possible discourses surrounding Haydn's music than we are traditionally accustomed to recounting. As Becker theorizes, "all artistic work, like all human activity, involves the joint activity of a number, often a large number, of people, through whose cooperation the art work we eventually see and hear comes to mind and continues to be" (cited in Taruskin 2005b, xxix). By inserting greater human agency and collective activity into Haydn historiography, we stand to enrich the field by acknowledging the importance of everyday acts of encountering, engaging, inspiring, and doing.

Within the Court The range of peoples Haydn interacted with inside the Esterházy court is vast. And within this environment the lens of social class and the unequal distribution of wealth are especially palpable. How did these factors affect individual autonomy? Did working under a patron, even an Enlightened one, confine the spirit seeking greater autonomy and squelch or suffocate individual and collective creativity? Were individuals operating in court environments less able to express agency than those working in other, more autonomous settings? Were talented individuals, whether working in the arts, in literature or philosophy, able to manipulate situations of unequal power to their advantage by outwitting or cajoling their superiors, or winning them over through their talents and intellect? Haydn's experience of living together in isolation with an engaged network of peers and collaborators appears to have fostered his creativity and originality – although it's possible that, by acknowledging this, he was just being diplomatic towards his patron and colleagues. All of these possibilities and more deserve our attention when considering the role of artistic creators (of all kinds) within the court ecosystem.

Haydn's initial tasks at court related to secular composition. Hired to write entertainment music for chamber and theatrical events, Haydn worked closely with numerous copyists employed at court – initially Anton Adolph, followed by three successive members of the Elssler family (Joseph father and son, and brother Johann) – in preparing manuscript parts for instrumentalists and VOCALISTS in advance of REHEARSALS and performances (Jones 2009, 52–53). Among the earliest singers Haydn collaborated with were Leopold Dichtler and his first wife, Barbara, for whom he wrote his first Italian operas, Acide (1763) and La canterina (1766). Barbara Dichtler's initial start as a chorister in the sombre church choir at Eisenstadt in the late 1750s contrasted markedly with her later portrayal of two comic trouser roles in opera buffa productions at court, first in Eisenstadt and then in Eszterháza. For instance, in the role of Don Ettore in La canterina, she performed alongside her cross-dressed husband, who played the role of the "false mother" Apollonia – with Leopold, a tenor, presumably singing in falsetto and adopting effeminate gestures when portraying this elderly female character. Then, as Volpino in Lo speziale (1768), Barbara-in-drag interacted directly with her husband singing the part of Mengone, the young apprentice apothecary. Later in the opera, the scheming Volpino (Barbara) further disguises him-(her)self – this time as an emissary of the Turkish Sultan – in an attempt to lure the older apothecary, Sempronio, to Constantinople singing the farcical aria "Salamelica" (see EXOTICISM; JEWISH CULTURE). The transition to Sunday morning choral worship services following these over-the-top operatic and theatrical performances suggest that penance was sought and forgiveness readily obtainable at this fun-loving Catholic court (see RELIGION AND SPIRITUAL BELIEFS).

How the strict estates director, Peter Ludwig von Rahier, viewed this kind of ribald behaviour is unclear. But as a former military man who administered the court and landed estates with a stiff hand, he was likely concerned that these on-stage shenanigans might spill over into everyday life, with the potential to threaten his ability to maintain order and stability in other aspects of court life – even though he was well aware that courtly splendour was necessary to propagate princely status. It appears his fears were founded, since Haydn was required to step in periodically to defend his musicians and colleagues from Rahier's wrath (see Landon II). Known for his quick temper, Rahier probably found it difficult to manage a court where all manner of comedic performance and "staginess" prevailed, including musical comedies of the kind described above, musical inserts in theatrical performances, and high-spirited productions presented by travelling theatrical troupes, all of which were a regular part of Prince Nicolaus's entertainment fare. Discipline meted out in regular measure, as was the military man's wont, helped Rahier maintain control over the many actors, musicians, singers, set designers and all manner of theater personnel – resident and itinerant – engaged in theatrical performance at court. Regular outside performers invited to perform at Eszterháza during the summer months in the mid-1770s included the well-known travelling theatrical troupe of Carl Wahr, for whom Haydn wrote incidental music to insert during performances of plays (see Sisman 1990). Haydn's six-movement symphony, "Il distratto" (Hob.I:60) provides apt musical commentary to the irrational actions of the absent-minded man depicted in this stage work, and Haydn even prescribes a role to the upper string players who, sixteen measures into the finale, stop and listen to their open strings and then tune the G string – presumably having "absentmindedly" begun to play before tuning.

Prior to the engagement of Wahr in 1772, several other troupes performed at court, including those of Riersch Hellmann and Koberwein in 1769, and Passer in 1770–71, which specialized in Hanswurtian-style comedies performed by actors skilled in traditional roles and improvisational delivery (H-L 831). Franz Diwald's troupe, contracted in 1778 and for several seasons thereafter, may even have contributed dancers and supernumeraries to productions of opera at court, including Haydn's *Armida* (1784). In contrast to the travelling players, all the operatic singers resident at Eszterháza – not just Luigia Polzelli – must have been fairly close to Haydn in order for him to adapt imported arias to their voices or write entirely new ones for them. And each new operatic encounter would provide yet further information for the composer to build on. Moreover, the networks by which opera reached Eszterháza were vast – extending from Milan (where Wenzeslaus Pichl, chapel master to Archduke Ferdinand, was the agent) and Venice, to Dresden and, of course, VIENNA. As a collective creative enterprise, opera is an ideal exemplar of Becker's "art worlds."

Many of these travelling players would have interacted with the THEATER painter and stage designer Girolamo Bon in the early years, together with his wife and daughter, both of whom were singers. By this time Bon had published six sonatas for violin and basso continuo (1752), and may even have written some texts for Esterházy cantatas (H-L). And Pietro Travaglia, who arrived at Eszterháza in 1777 to head up the design teams for costumes and scenery at both theaters – the marionette theater and the opera house – was front and center in all theatrical productions at court thereafter, preparing for performances by in-house singers as well as those by travelling singing-actors. He also oversaw theatrical lighting, which included gas or alcohol lanterns (rather than candles) in the auditorium and on the scenery flats, with mirror deflectors to intensify the light source. These performances were enjoyed by the prince and many others employed at court, including "actors, architects, gardeners, guards, officers, servants, and so on – as it was their entertainment too" (Jones 2009, 83).

AUDIENCES at the Eszterháza court were mixed, and frequently included more than just members of the Esterházy family, as Emily Green observes. Indeed, in 1781 the Hungarian poet Márton Dallos claimed that local lower nobility, soldiers stationed nearby, servants, and even peasants living in the rural countryside attended musical, operatic and theatrical performances (Gates-Coon 179) – perhaps pointing to the prince's enlightened values. Many works composed there were for court consumption, including music for larger semi-private listening at family and dynastic celebrations, often in the company of visiting dignitaries and guests. Other more personal music-making tributes included the sonatas Haydn wrote for the sixteen-year-old Princess Marie Hermenegild Esterházy, wife of the philandering Prince Nicolaus II (r. 1794–1833). Beghin (2005) seeks to understand why Haydn composed the Sonatas Nos. 40–42 in G major, B♭ major, and D major (Hob. XVI:40–42), in the manner he did, and the many ways in which they respond to the recipient's keyboard skills, GENDER, and deportment as a young princess newly resident at court.

Haydn's interactions with the royal horse guards, hussars, soldiers, grenadiers, and other military personnel at court is less well documented, but still vital. As former members of the military decorated for their service, all of the Esterházy princes Haydn served would have required ceremonial music and marches for a variety of different occasions, including fanfares and Feldparthie or Harmonie (field or outdoor wind band) music for welcoming dignitaries, initiating the hunt, displaying military might in tattoos and pageants, or celebrating elaborate outdoor banquets and other festivities. (See Figure 9 showing Prince Anton's 1791 installation in the entry Eszterháza and Eisenstadt.) Indeed, Prince Nicolaus was Captain of the Hungarian Guard from 1760 to 1787, demanding that he make frequent trips to Vienna to fulfil military duties (see Gates-Coon), with appropriate music marking his send-offs and homecomings. Members of the Esterházy Feldmusik, consisting of six players (two oboes, two horns, and bassoons – or sometimes clarinets), performed wind divertimenti by Haydn and others for ceremonial purposes. Soldiers also frequently served as extras on stage at Eszterháza, presumably dressed in uniform, and on one occasion performed with their instruments – Haydn having written a military march for them directly into the dramatic action: a March in two–four in B♭ major (for two clarinets, two horns, and two bassoons) in Act 1, sc. 4 of Armida marks the arrival of the Christian knights at the enchantress's castle to rescue their captive leader, Rinaldo.

With Eszterháza increasingly the home of pageantry and display, Eisenstadt held onto traditions associated with religion and sacred music. Under head Kapellmeister Gregor Werner, who was in Esterházy employ from 1728 until his death in 1766, church music and the court chapel choir flourished. But the split between generations and between changing musical styles – the old Baroque church style versus the new Italian chamber and theater styles – only entrenched the rift between Haydn and his superior, resulting in a nasty written complaint penned by an elderly and unwell Werner in Eisenstadt and sent to Prince Nicolaus in Eszterháza on October 8, 1765. (Rahier may even have written the complaint, with Werner – who was putting his affairs in order in the last months of his life – providing the ammunition.) An *ad hominem* attack on Haydn's immaturity and inattention to musical affairs in Eisenstadt, this letter attests to the insular microcosm of the Esterházy sphere, and to the interconnectedness of its disparate musical components during the early years of Haydn's employment at court. Church musicians absent for long periods without permission (presumably because they were doing double duty on the stage), instruments in poor repair, undisciplined musicians, and a music library in disarray – Werner carefully lays out Haydn's dereliction of duties. With increasing time spent "away" in Vienna, Eszterháza, Pressburg, Kittsee, and elsewhere, and with Nicolaus's attention focused less on the church and more on secular entertainments, including his new interest in the baryton (see INSTRUMENTS AND ORGANOLOGY), Haydn had only to bide his time until the old guard was gone. By diligently applying himself to composing for the prince's newfound instrument he would again find favor. In the meantime, organist and tenor Joseph Dietzl undertook the organizational and cataloguing tasks outlined by Werner. Under Dietzl and his successors, the prince's devout and retiring wife, Princess Maria Elisabeth, continued her routine of regular worship in the court chapel, where she oversaw many renovations. Sometimes she attended mass incognito, viewing the proceedings from a window installed off to the side above the altar so the attending priest could register her attendance.

The reprimand and directive from Regent Rahier was sent in November of 1765, rounding out a period of turbulent relations between Haydn and his superiors. Early in September Haydn had overstepped the manager to appeal directly to Prince Nicolaus on behalf of two musicians: the flautist Frantz Siegl and the tenor Carl Friberth. Both had recently crossed paths with the estates manager, resulting in detention for Siegl and threats against the talented singer Friberth, prompting Haydn to write a long petition that concluded: "These honorable men find this treatment very unfair and hope that . . . you will put a stop to such exercises of power where anyone can be his own judge without differentiating between guilty and not guilty." Music-making within the court may not always have been harmonious, but one thing is clear: Haydn was a man of character, and someone who could be counted on to defend the rights of others who wielded less power, and recognize and respond to injustices in their midst. Already Haydn was becoming a man of the ENLIGHTENMENT.

While the critical explanations and casual connections outlined above may be based on incomplete historical evidence, they do invite productive speculations – even if those speculations (to echo Gallope) appear over-reaching or even ideological in some instances (228). Indeed, actors and agents may, at times, be responding to larger political and cultural ideas circulating within a society – and the late eighteenth-century society and world of IDEAS in which Haydn lived manifestly affected his world view, helping to shape his musical output and its RECEPTION. Individual agents or "real people" working within and responding to the times in which they lived, and attentive to the circumstances within which they conducted their daily lives together, all helped determine the kinds of music Haydn created and its success or failure with players and listeners. Responsible to one another and to their individual and collective thoughts and times – both locally and beyond their circumscribed sphere – these people, and the social networks they created, as outlined above and below, played a large role in the creation and live (aural) dissemination of Haydn's music and the multiple ways in which it was received "in the moment."

Fixed notions of patronage do little to further our understanding of Haydn's personal interactions and dealings at court. While our established narratives would suggest that Haydn was able to exercise considerable freedom of a certain kind in "the land of opportunity" epitomized by the "thriving civic culture" of LONDON, this view could use further problematizing. Through negotiation with several different impresarios, appearances at social functions (a form of celebrity self-promotion increased through six separate portrait sittings), hard work, and worldly reputation, Haydn was able to earn considerably more money than he could earn under the Esterházys, and exercise greater purchasing power (see Jones 2013; see also ICONOGRAPHY; MATERIAL CULTURE). Numerous studies of patronage in the eighteenth century focus on artistic and cultural patronage, but few studies focus on the patronage of philosophers and creative thinkers, as political theorist Edward Andrew reminds us. In *Patrons of Enlightenment*, Andrew argues that the intellectual marketplace was insufficient to foster the ideology of Enlightenment, and that the eighteenth-century republic of letters depended upon both royal and aristocratic patronage. For him, the "Enlightenment was essentially plebian talent serving royal and aristocratic patrons while professing intellectual independence" (8). Like the arts, intellectual production was a collective project, with patronage underlying many of its foundations. So, while Adam Smith's "marketplace of ideas" was dependent upon an expanding middle-class readership and broader musical publication and circulation networks, many enterprises, including all major (male) writers in the eighteenth century were dependent upon royal or aristocratic patronage – and this is even true for Beethoven in the early nineteenth century. While everyone engaged in the public sphere celebrated the independence of thought as a characteristic feature of their time, especially in the market-driven economy of London, much intellectual thought was still being produced under the protection of patrons. Artists, actors, and creators of public opinion may have reshaped their images or cultural products in response to audience opinion or public approval, but much decision-making was still exercised from the top of the social class hierarchy. Much philosophizing in this period turned on questions about the superiority of republics to monarchies, with many liberal Enlightenment thinkers coming down on the side of abolishing the *ancien régime* and the power of the aristocracy. And the ultimate irony? – many patrons knowingly supported individuals and causes that would diminish the fortunes of their grandchildren.

In the British context, the transition from patronage through to the republic of letters and into the commercial marketplace of ideas was more gradual than abrupt. As Andrew writes, Edmund Burke understood patronage as "the tribute which opulence owes to genius" (7). Even Immanuel Kant acknowledged that it took time for men to learn to think for themselves without the guidance of priests or spiritual advisors. (And women are missing from the equation entirely; see IDEALISM.) Thus, for many late eighteenth-century artists and intellectuals, the republic of letters was a place of "imaginary independence." Only when the idea of a commercial marketplace took hold more broadly after the power of aristocratic patronage had dissipated, well into the early decades of the nineteenth century, did intellectual autonomy begin to take root in the creative sphere (aspects of patronage that continue even today). Haydn operated in a patronage environment during his Esterházy years, but even in COMMERCIAL and COSMOPOLITAN LONDON, where a parliamentary democracy was in place, the British crown and many aristocrats continued to exercise considerable control, especially in artistic circles. For instance, Haydn was employed by the impresario John Gallini, who had married into the British aristocracy, and, by virtue of his political connections and status as well as his dancing and theatrical skillset, oversaw the running of both the Hanover Square Rooms and the King's Theatre Haymarket. Although the second contract Haydn signed with Prince Nicolaus in 1779 was more liberal and accommodating than the one he was grateful to sign back in 1761, and although he became a wealthy man working in the market economy of the late eighteenth century, we would do well to understand Haydn as operating within a rapidly changing social environment, but one still controlled by the aristocracy in some form or other – even beyond the walls of the court.

Beyond the Court Although Haydn's early biographers name only the most famous of his STUDENTS, Ignaz Pleyel and Sigismund Neukomm, it's clear that throughout his life – from youth to old age – Haydn privately tutored numerous pupils in COMPOSITION. He gave his first lessons shortly after leaving the music school at St. Stephen's Cathedral (see CHURCH), while a draft letter from 1804 records his last teaching activity. His earliest pupils, Theresia Helena Keller and Marianna Martines, rather than study composition with Haydn, pursued singing and keyboard lessons respectively, while his first composition students, including Abund Mykisch and Robert Kimmerling, probably also sought out his tutoring services in the 1750s. Only with his rising fame as a composer, however, did the number of students also increase; there's a noticeable uptake after 1780, and again after his relocation to Vienna in the 1790s. The bond with some of his students was close, exceeding a purely teaching relationship: Ignaz Pleyel, for instance, lived at Haydn's house from 1772 to 1777 during his tuition, with his expenses being paid by count Ladislaus Erdődy; Martines lived in the same building as both Haydn and Metastasio (who probably recommended the latter as a teacher, as Federico Celestini argues in TEACHING AND STUDENTS); and Pietro Polzelli, son of Haydn's mistress Luigia, received lessons in composition (as did his brother Anton), and was also accepted into Haydn's household. The reverse was the case with Franciszek Lessel, a former student, who tended to the AGED and increasingly debilitated Haydn at the end of his life.

In addition to formal composition students, many of Haydn's contemporaries also deserve to be counted among his extended network of students, since many paid their respects to the world-famous composer in Vienna while also seeking his advice and guidance. Haydn himself appears to have enjoyed such interaction, as the young Carl Maria von Weber reported after meeting him in 1804: "He is always cheerful and lively, likes to talk of his experiences, and particularly enjoys having up-and-coming artists about him. He is the very model of a great man" (Walter 1975, 63). This relationship between teacher and student, or between colleagues, frequently became manifest in reciprocally DEDICATED musical works. Many who did not actually study with Haydn also dedicated works to him, referencing his importance as a "father" figure in composition as well as his generosity in imparting guidance and understanding. The most famous example of this is Mozart's Italian-language dedication of his six "Haydn" Quartets (K. 387, 421, 428, 458, 464 and 465) in 1784. Joseph Eybler also prefaced his String Quartets Op. 1 (1794) with an Italian letter of dedication to Haydn, which obviously references Mozart's text. In the Haydn dedication that Johann Brandl prefixed to his Quartets Op. 17, Mozart is even explicitly named as a model. And Haydn himself deliberately assumed the "father" persona when Luigi Cherubini visited him in Vienna in 1805/6, at which time Haydn gave him the autograph of Symphony No. 103 in E♭ as a gift, appending the words "Padre del celebre Cherubini" beneath his name on the first page. In passing along this valuable souvenir to the younger composer, Haydn acts the part of the patriarch ceding his power, giving way to the hungry and energetic younger generation (see also BIOGRAPHY). As for Haydn's own dedications, they can be split into two categories, as Katelyn Clark discusses in her entry on DEDICATEES. Haydn's string quartets, which are dedicated exclusively to men, reveal his use of dedications as a commodifying social device in comparison to the more personal dedications of his keyboard compositions.

Dedications also worked as a kind of exchange currency within a composer's network, a form of symbolic capital exceeding a simple demonstration of homage, as Green (2015) has shown. This is especially so in the case of Beethoven. Although the relationship between Haydn and his most famous pupil is often considered to have been strained, the fact that Haydn created an opportunity for the young Beethoven to perform one of his own piano concertos (Op. 15 or Op. 19) for the first time in an Academy hosted by Haydn in the small Redoutensaal on December 18, 1795, indicates that the relationship between teacher and student was probably closer than traditionally assumed (Webster). The dedication of Beethoven's Op. 2 to his teacher might also be considered not only as an expression of gratitude, but also as further evidence that their relationship was probably better than generally supposed. That *Accademien* also functioned as a place where sophisticated conversation about music was central, as Edward Klorman discusses in his entry on SOCIABILITY, suggests that Haydn and his music were central to evolving social networks during public performances of his chamber music in a salon or another social event – while also suggesting that the salon and other performing venues created a space where Haydn's music could also be in dialogue with works by other composers.

Mozart and Beethoven score the greatest cultural capital in relation to Haydn's evolving network. More than simply fellow COMPOSERS AND MUSIC PROFESSIONALS, they also frequently refer to each other's works in a musical network of allusions and quotations. The possible quotation of *Così* in Haydn's Symphony No. 97 in C major that Martin Nedbal mentions in RELATIONSHIPS AND FRIENDSHIPS points to this phenomenon. All three composers performed works by one another as well. Mozart played string quartets with Haydn (together with fellow composers Carl Ditters von Dittersdorf and Johann Baptist Vanhal), and Haydn ordered a copy of the score of Mozart's *Le nozze di Figaro* in summer 1789, possibly with the intent of performing the opera at Eszterháza later that year or the following year. And Beethoven took part in performances by the *Tonkünstler-Societät* in Vienna where he performed Haydn's pieces. The *Tonkünstler-Societät*, a benevolent SOCIETY founded by Florian Gassmann in 1771 that provided funds for the bereaved survivors of deceased professional musicians, was central to the performance of Haydn's oratorios. Although Haydn sought to become a member in 1778, he did not want to accept the conditions set by the society, so his admission was annulled the following year. But even this did not sever his connection to the society. For their performances of his oratorio *Il ritorno di Tobia* in 1775, Haydn even brought five musicians from the Esterházy orchestra, thereby linking these two independent institutions. In a later performance in 1784 some of Haydn's students also were involved. Finally, in 1797, the society admitted Haydn as an honorary member free of charge, appointing him "perpetuirlichen Assessor senior" (perpetual senior assessor). Once again Haydn appears as the central father figure when he is described as "father and reformer of the noble art of music" (quoted in Pandi and Schmidt, 278).

Haydn's networking potentiality also features prominently in his relationship with the Gesellschaft der Associierten Cavaliere. An aristocratic musical entity organized by Baron Gottfried van Swieten, their connection to Haydn began in 1796 with the premiere of his oratorio version of *The Seven Last Words* based on a revised text by Swieten. Other members included Count Franz Joseph Maximilian Lobkowitz and the Counts Anton Georg Apponyi and (later) Joseph Erdődy, to whom Haydn dedicated sets of string quartets: the Quartets Op. 71/74 composed in 1793 were dedicated to Apponyi; Lobkowitz commissioned the Quartets Op. 77 in 1799; and Haydn probably composed Op. 76 for Erdődy in the context of his work with *The Creation*. As such, Haydn's networks included those to whom he tailored his music – including performers and patrons. As Nedbal observes, continuing study of "Haydn's relationships with women and men of his time will continue to afford new insights into the composer's biography, his social and cultural milieu, and, perhaps most importantly, new interpretations of his music."

Other networks emerged when Haydn left Vienna for his two stays in London. On these trips, even before having arrived at his destination, he encountered many new individuals and met numerous colleagues. In Bonn, he was presented to the court chapel there (it was here that he met Beethoven, a member of the chapel), and they in turn performed a mass of his composition. Moreover, in Bonn (during his journey back in 1792) he met the publisher Nikolaus Simrock, who was to play an important role in publishing scores of the "London" Symphonies. During his stay in London, Haydn's networks expanded even further, as his London NOTEBOOKS attest. As Mark Ferraguto observes in COMPOSERS AND MUSIC PROFESSIONALS, Haydn's enumeration of some ninety professional and amateur musicians (including some duplications) fell under the categories of "Singers, male and female," "Composers," "Pianists," "Violinists," "Violoncellists," "Oboists," and "Doctors." For many of those new acquaintances, Haydn fulfilled many commissions, such as the flute trios (Hob.IV:2–4) for the Earl of Abingdon. In the concerts at the Hanover Square Rooms, he "presided" over the performance of his "London" Symphonies at the keyboard (see LEADING LARGE ENSEMBLES), and performed with numerous other musicians including Salomon, Madame Krumpholz, and Johann Ladislav Dussek. Haydn also entered into high society, including the royal family; in a letter to Marianne von Genzinger (December 20, 1791), he describes performing pieces of his composition together with the Prince of Wales and his sister-in-law.

The focal point of Haydn's London network was Johann Peter Salomon – the violinist and impresario who had brought Haydn to London in the first place. In addition to the pieces Haydn composed for Salomon's concert events, he also wrote for him as a soloist – the solo violin parts in Symphonies No. 97 and 98 as well as the *Sinfonia concertante*. Similarly, Salomon performed the role of Primarius at the premiere of the String Quartets Op. 71/74, the first quartets Haydn wrote for public performance. During Haydn's first stay in London from 1791 to 1792 he even shared a flat with Salomon in Great Pulteney Street, located in a fashionable area of London. As a native German speaker, Salomon also served as Haydn's translator in England.

Haydn's enormous fame, which made his visit to England possible, also lengthened his stay. This happened thanks to another special network – a flourishing music PUBLISHING industry that made the distribution of Haydn's works possible throughout Europe and beyond. Haydn's international fame grew based on the distribution of his works in print by prominent publishing houses, whereas in Germany handwritten copies were still dominant. Although Haydn's first contract of employment prohibited the distribution of his works in any form, many works nevertheless circulated in print as well as handwritten copies. Even the first printed edition authorized by Haydn – the keyboard sonatas Hob.XVI:21–26 issued by the Viennese bookseller Kurzböck in 1774 – was issued during a period when his contract prohibited such distribution. The dedication of this edition to Haydn's employer Prince Nicolaus Esterházy indicates that this clause in the composer's employment contract was no longer being upheld – at least by a Count who appears to be have been rather willing to associate himself with his subordinate's fame. (In 1779, the new contract dispensed with this publication ban.) As Deirdre Loughridge points out in her entry on AMATEURS, 1778 "marked a decisive transition point, when Haydn turned toward the public as a main audience for his chamber music," expanding exponentially the number of contacts in his publication network.

The simultaneous existence of printed editions and handwritten copies also suggests multiple audiences. Whereas the Keyboard Sonatas Hob.XVI: 27–32 were distributed in handwritten copies, Haydn permitted the following series, Hob.XVI:20, 35–39 (1780), to be published in print. This printed edition by the Viennese publisher Artaria initiated one of the closest relationships between Haydn and a publisher. Indeed, the majority of Haydn's preserved letters – the visible record of his networks, as it were, assessed by Laurel E. Zeiss in the entry CORRESPONDENCE AND NOTEBOOKS – were sent to Artaria as addressee, and moreover, most of the Haydn-authorised first editions were published by Artaria. Both ways of distribution – print and handwritten copies – did not just coexist; they also helped Haydn to maximise the profits. For instance, just before Artaria published the String Quartets Op. 33 in 1782, Haydn offered them for sale to music lovers in handwritten copies – enabling the clever composer/businessman to capitalize on his sales network. But this strategy of parallel publication could also lead to conflicts. For example, Haydn engaged in an argument with Viennese music-store owner Traeg over his score to the opera *L'isola disabitata*. After having given the publishing house Breitkopf & Härtel permission to revise the opera for a printed edition, Haydn, who apparently did not have a score at his disposal, had to fall back on Traeg's stock, for which the publisher demanded payment. Haydn initially protested, but eventually offered the publisher a keyboard sonata to print. Griesinger describes the course of events in a letter to Gottfried Christoph Härtel:

> The matter is as follows: Haydn let somebody bring him the manuscript of Isola disabitata from Träg, which he revised and sent to you [Härtel]. After

some time Träg demanded that Haydn return the manuscript, or a compensation payment of 12 ducats. Haydn, enraged about this demand, asked that Träg visit him in order to give him a piece of his mind. To avoid further fuss, however, he [Haydn] eventually handed over to him the sonata in question, which he had composed in London (Griesinger 200).

Working together with publishers, Haydn also tried to maximize his profits by selling the same piece to several publishers without their knowledge. Working in this network of market possibilities, Haydn had to be careful to keep this information secret. That the String Quartets Op. 76 were published by both Artaria in Vienna and Longman, Clementi & Co. in London in two successive series was a resulting precautionary measure. Because the publishers were in contact with each other, Haydn's strategy was risky. In 1788 and 1791 these activities led to a legal dispute between the London publishing houses Forster and Longman & Broderip. Which publisher held the rights to Haydn's works, which the composer had sold not only to Forster but also to Artaria in Vienna? In this case, problems arose because Longman & Broderip had taken on the task of selling Artaria's editions in commission, whereas Forster possessed a declaration of ownership written by Haydn in 1786. (Haydn testified twice as a witness at court, with Salomon acting as his translator). In this instance, Haydn's strategy to sell his works to several people cannot be explained only by his interest in profit, as Axel Beer explains, since it also reveals his intention "to prevent unauthorised or maybe corrupted reprints" (813).

The publishing house Breitkopf & Härtel in Leipzig played a special role in Haydn's network of publishers. For their project to publish a complete edition of Haydn's piano works they secured the composer's support, and in 1800 the first volume of the *Oeuvres complettes de Joseph Haydn* came out with a foreword by Haydn himself. (This foreword, addressing the audience via one-way communication, as it were, is similar to his autobiographical sketch for Ignaz de Luca's encyclopedia "Das gelehrte Österreich," where, for the first time, Haydn uses a printed publication as a means for communicating with the public.) Moreover, Breitkopf had published the *Allgemeine musikalische Zeitung* since 1789, which gave several reports about Haydn in reviews, thereby contributing to and promoting his fame (see PRESS). It is remarkable that Haydn's European publishers not only made him known throughout Europe, but also played an important role in the distribution of his works in North AMERICA. The publication history of Haydn's works – mostly compositions of chamber music for the amateur market – only started there 1789, and during the eighteenth-century, North American publishers neither edited symphonies, nor string quartets, and it is not known if the professional performances there were played with handwritten copies or printed editions. Nevertheless, the role of European editions must not be underestimated. Similarly, Ignaz Pleyel played an important role in connecting different networks through his series of *Bibliothèque musicale*, as Celestini observes in TEACHING AND STUDENTS. By providing study scores for both the public and for students, Haydn's ambitious former student served not only as an agent, but also enabled those who were unable to study with Haydn personally to have access to his music for the purposes of self-study.

Among the many visitors who came to Haydn during his last years in Vienna were individuals with additional networks. A key figure here is Griesinger, who worked in cooperation with Breitkopf & Härtel. A diplomat in Vienna, from 1799 onwards he acted as a kind of agent and mediator between the publisher and the composer. The correspondence between Haydn and Gottfried Christoph Härtel documents several visits; the publisher also encouraged Griesinger to use his conversations with Haydn as the basis of a biography of the composer. As a result, the *Biographische Notizen über Joseph Haydn*, published after the composer's death, is the earliest Haydn biography. As an individual networking in different circles, Griesinger was also more than a publisher's agent and a biographer. Indeed, on the occasion of Haydn's seventy-third birthday, where Mozart's son performed in public for the first time at a concert in Haydn's honor, Griesinger described to Härtel that he composed a Birthday Cantata for he which he wrote most of the text.

Griesinger was just one of many diplomats in Haydn's extended network, who fulfilled a diverse range of roles. In addition to his first and second Esterházy patrons, both of whom had worked in diplomatic service, LIBRETTIST Gottfried van Swieten too had been a diplomat (Berlin 1770–77) before meeting Haydn in Vienna. Among their many skills, including knowledge of foreign languages and cultures, diplomats assisted composers by offering an expansive network of international contacts and negotiation skills honed abroad; furthermore, since most were recruited from well-educated noble families, they maintained a strong commitment to music. To have one's works performed for an audience of international elites helped to promote careers, and assisted a composer in gaining greater recognition through an international web of disseminators. In Haydn's case, diplomats helped negotiate with foreign publishers on his behalf (i.e., General Jermingham worked with Forster in London), while in other instances they facilitated direct contact between the composer and royal dedicatees (i.e., Konstantin Jacobi, the Prussian ambassador to Vienna, helped facilitate the dedication of the String Quartets Op. 50 to Friedrich Wilhelm II, King of Prussia, in 1787). Russian diplomats were particularly adept at forging connections; for example, Dmitri M. Galitzin oversaw performances of several works by Haydn, and was the dedicatee of the 1782 Torricella print of Symphony No. 73 in D major, "La chasse." Moreover, noble men also assisted composers by providing letters of reference, fostering new international connections. On his journey to London in late 1790, for instance, Haydn carried three letters of introduction: one he requested from State Chancellor Wenzel Anton Kaunitz, for the Austrian envoy in London, Count Johann Philipp Stadion; and two other letters – one from Ferdinand IV of Naples (recent recipient of several works by Haydn for *lira organizzata*), and one for the Spanish envoy in London, Marquis del Campo (capitalizing on the composer's recent connections with SPAIN) (see Fuhrmann 120–25).

Another diplomat and frequent visitor to Haydn was Fredrik Samuel Silverstolpe from Sweden, with whom the composer developed a trusting friendship. Silverstolpe wrote regularly to his family in Sweden, and his letters offer many details about his visits with Haydn, as the following examples attests:

> A few days ago I went to Haydn ... On this occasion he played for me on the piano, violin quartets, which were ordered by Duke Erdödi for 100 ducats and that were only allowed to be printed after a specific number of years. They are done in a most masterly manner and full of new ideas. While he played, he let me sit next to him and watch him how he had divided the single parts in the score. He also sang some arias, which he wanted to publish as subscription when reaching the number of 24 ... He also told me, how he proceeds when he wants to compose something.

Silverstolpe's letters offer important detailed biographical information of this nature. He also was the driving force behind Haydn's election into the Swedish Music Academy in 1798, as well as the Swedish premiere of *The Creation* at the Riddarhuset in Stockholm in 1801, for which he translated the libretto. Silverstolpe also exemplifies overlapping connections in Haydn's network: during his time as a diplomat in St. Petersburg, Silverstolpe got to know Haydn's former student, Sigismund Neukomm, and befriended him. Neukomm is actually another example of a visitor who also acted as a messenger, delivering honorific awards and proving his international fame. For example, Neukomm delivered a medal to Haydn from the Philharmonic Society of St. Petersburg, which had performed *The Creation* with great aplomb. Luigi Cherubini transmitted greetings and another honorary medal to Haydn from the Paris Conservatoire (and it was on this occasion that Haydn presented the autograph of Symphony No. 103 to Cherubini). Again, Haydn's main role amidst all these networks was his patriarchal outreach. In a letter to his brother, Silverstolpe calls Haydn "the Father of music" (quoted in Mörner 232), and in Neukomm's catalogue of works, the inscription "for my father Haydn" is found in the entry beside his Scottish Songs (Angermüller 59; see also FOLK SONG SETTINGS). In both instances, and in similar statements from the same period, the term "father" is used as a sign of genuine of respect towards a towering patriarchal musical figure.

We wish to thank Wolfgang Fuhrmann for his timely help and advice in preparing this essay.
CARYL CLARK AND ULRICH WILKER

FURTHER READING
Andrew (2006); Angermüller (1977); Becker (2008 [1982]); Beer (2010); Beghin (2005, 2015a); Biba (1978, 1987); *Briefe*; Clark (2005a); Dack (2010a and 2010b); Finscher (2008); Fuhrmann (2010a); Gallope (2014); Gates-Coon (1994); Gerlach and Raab (2010); Green (2015); Griesinger; H-L; Jones (2009, 2013); Landon II; Larsen et al. (1981); Latour (2005); Lowens (1979); McVeigh (1989); Mörner (1952); NG Haydn; Pandi and Schmidt (1971); Pete (1996); Piekut (2014); Reinisch (2010); Ronge (2009); Scholz (2010); Siegert, Thomas, and Wilker (2009); Sisman (1990, 2005); Taruskin (2005b, 2014); Walter (1981, 1985); Webster (1984).

Performance

> "Ne vous expliquez point si vous voulez vous entendre."
> "Avoid explanation if what you want is a mutual understanding."
>
> Diderot, *Paradox of the Actor* (1773, 6)

A Beginning That Isn't Let us begin, as Haydn sometimes liked to do, with a conundrum – a very well-known conundrum too: the opening two measures of the String Quartet Op. 33, No. 5 in G major, which in the original Artaria edition was in fact No. 1 (see Example 12). A good deal of ink has been dedicated to this opening-that-sounds-like-an-ending, this obviously deliberate structural misplacement: what it might have meant (to Haydn or to AUDIENCES of his day) and mean (to audiences or to Haydn scholars today) (Wheelock 14–20). Why revisit it here?

We would answer, because there has been a perspective missing, or at best incompletely incorporated, in all these discussions: what Haydn's directions on the page meant and can mean, and to whom, *in the moment of performance*. We here dedicate ourselves to this perspective, which will tend to emerge as a complex of questions. Almost none of them are questions unique to Haydn's music; yet there can be no doubt that, as the rhetorical man he was, Haydn raises them with peculiar urgency and dexterity (see Beghin and Goldberg). His music is a wonderful laboratory for rethinking and deepening the study of performance in general.

Example 12 Quartet in G major, Op. 33, No. 5, first movement, opening measures, transcribed from the JHW score.

Some starter questions, then:

1. Who were the quartet players of Haydn's time and under what circumstances would they have encountered this opening?
2. How might those circumstances have conditioned their experience of it? What meanings, not necessarily implicated in the score, might have been created?
3. How can we improve our latter-day understanding of those circumstances? And how can that become a fruitful and interesting part of contemporary performance?
4. How can this mixture of historical evidence and living practice enter discourse about what this "work" is considered to be?

And some starter answers:

1. They may be four middle-class men, skilled AMATEURS, playing from separate parts, *prima vista*, for their own enjoyment, like the ones Haydn addressed in his "subscription letters" in connection with his Op. 33 Quartets. Neither the synoptic view of the score nor any aural synopsis through any previous hearings would have been available. Or they may have been four professional colleagues, intimately familiar with Haydn's previous work, perhaps members of his ESZTERHÁZA band. A few hours before some formal performance, Haydn might have handed out the handwritten parts of his new quartet, which the musicians might have played through once or twice.
2. The musicians would most probably have been seated in a circle, around individual assembled stands or around a quartet table – symbol of human interactivity and conviviality (see SOCIABILITY). Figure 19 shows a hybrid example of a quadruple stand that is foldable and that may be positioned on any table, easily transportable to any living room or music room.
3a. In a classical music culture that still revolves around abstraction and that still pretends to sublimate musical performance to sound alone, the scholar

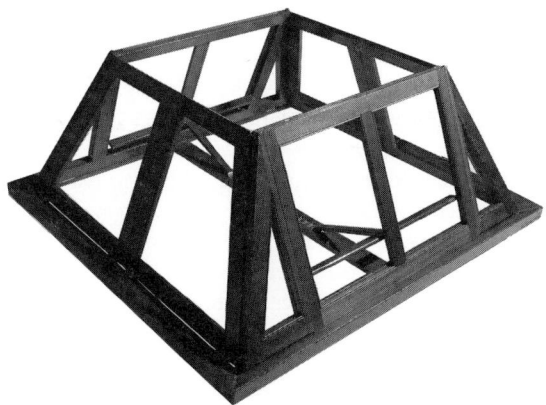

Figure 19 Foldable quartet stand. English, early nineteenth century. Collection of Pierre Bouckaert (Ghent, Belgium). Photo by Jonas Tavernier. Reproduced with permission of Orpheus Institute, Ghent, Belgium.

of performance must return again and again to the concrete and corporeal. We propose *historical impersonation* as a corrective to abstraction and as a stimulus to different ways of thinking and understanding historical music-making. We mean by it a fundamentally THEATRICAL manoeuvre in which the scholar-performer seeks to go beyond mere acquaintance with the social and cultural circumstances of their historical counterparts. While necessary, this acquaintance is always and inevitably superficial; it will not yield much insight without the further step of entering intuitively into the bodies and personas of those historical counterparts as they execute the music at hand, recreating their circumstances in our own bodies and minds in real time: in effect, *becoming them* to the extent possible.

3b. Things, objects, architecture, and accoutrements become very important in this exercise. The key role of using INSTRUMENTS appropriate to a given historical setting in generating new musical insight has long been recognized; but we want to suggest that similar levels of insight may come, at times, from furniture (like the quartet table), from room set-ups that do not assume the existence of a proscenium, even from costuming (we will return to the possible role of the corset in women's execution at the pianoforte). Such explorations have obvious practical limits, but within these we want to reassert their potential as part of the enterprise of scholarly performance. In addition, they can be a great deal of fun.

4. The question of how historical evidence and living practice may enter discourse about the "work" may be best answered with a Socratic manoeuvre. Just as Demosthenes was steadfast in his conviction that oratorical success hinges on delivery, delivery, and delivery, Haydn insisted on his "rights" as a master, to be enforced "by his presence and true performance [*wahrer Vortrag*] – playing and singing his new German songs "in the critical houses" of VIENNA (letter to Artaria of July 20, 1781; Bartha 101). Flanked by these two authorities in performative arts, we answer question No. 4 by rephrasing it: "If not music as embodied performance, then what is it that we study?"

This question-answering-a-question highlights a self-reflexive intention in this essay: an examination of the relation of the Performance section of this encyclopedia to all the other sections. As scholars of music who are also performers of music, we feel both obligation and desire to make a compelling connection/articulation between the study of performance and other aspects of musicology.

We assume that, for the communities likely to read and use this book, this connection/articulation has moved or is moving away from that vexed state of opposition whereby performance must be asserted as somehow ontologically prior to scholarship, or conversely, scholarship asserted as a necessary condition to "legitimate" performance – although it must be admitted that exactly such polarizations still characterize most of academia and professional performance, as manifested in administrative structures, curricula, concert presentation, editorial decisions, and the social habits of musicians, audiences, readers, scholars, and students. We are not interested in entering into this particular fray, much less proposing any kind of resolution to it. Such efforts, we feel, are ultimately sterile. We join the authors of other performance-related entries in this volume in preferring to concentrate on what we – from our positions as professionals who have managed to maintain careers that involve both performance and scholarship – consider to be the most fertile areas in the study of Haydn performance.

The historical study of performance has long favored a somewhat utilitarian approach: how scholarship may aid the living performers of Haydn's works who wish to get as close as they can to the conditions of performance in Haydn's day. This recreative enterprise can approach its object far more closely than anyone would have dreamed a generation ago. The flourishing contemporary industry of artisanal reproduction of historical instruments enables more musicians than ever before to use instruments very similar to those available to musicians during Haydn's career; Robert Giglio's entry on INSTRUMENTS AND ORGANOLOGY throws down the gauntlet to builders to note and reproduce the variety of those instruments, but also to players to demand them. Nicholas McGegan (LEADING LARGE ENSEMBLES) reminds us of the numbers of orchestral musicians documented in various theater and COURT payrolls, and of their dispositions in certain spaces shown in drawings or engravings, in an open invitation to reproduce these practices. Most astonishingly, the acoustics of Haydn's PERFORMANCE (and rehearsal) SPACES as detailed by János Malina and Edward McCue are now available to the living performer without travelling to the rooms themselves, thanks to the wizardry of digital sampling and room recreation (see Woszczyk). And "thick" research into period pedagogical and social practices, such as that modeled by Erin Helyard (VOCAL COACHING AND REHEARSAL), is detailed enough to enable us, should we wish, to experiment with learning and rehearsing Haydn's music in a manner that he might have recognized and even approved.

The phrase "should we wish" is key here. Some of the recreative strategies available to performers are heavily used – imitating period set-ups for orchestral concerts has been a common strategy for generations, and reproductions of historical instruments are now expected in many professional circles. Some of these strategies, however, are scarcely used at all, even though they would be much less stressful on the performer's pocketbook than a new instrument or a trip to Haydn's stomping grounds. For instance, the obvious importance of oral/aural learning among singers, mentioned by Helyard, presents us with a question: while no one in their right mind would recommend that today's singers of early music cultivate illiteracy, it does seem that scholars of historical performance could take oral learning and transmission more seriously than they have yet done, while pedagogues, repetiteurs, and even opera directors might take a page from the ongoing, orally derived experiments with partimenti being conducted by Gjerdingen, Sanguinetti, and Cramm (see COUNTERPOINT; COMPOSITIONAL PROCESS). Productions of seventeenth- and eighteenth-century THEATRICAL music that imitate period practices of movement, gesture, and blocking are still unusual – modernist and surrealist stagings proliferate even as the musicians in the pit are proudly advertised as "playing on historical instruments." And in all areas of contemporary early music performance, attempts to approximate period audience behavior are as rare as hen's teeth.

Some aspects of historical performance studies do not imply living performers in any direct way, yet serve to usefully elucidate the differences between ourselves and our historical counterparts; Head's work on the Gendering of North German keyboard treatises and repertory is a well-known example. Other aspects are only beginning to swim into the collective view. Giglio's essay on Instruments and Organology begs a section in this Encyclopedia that cannot yet be written, because the musicological field that it invokes is so new as to barely have a name: the intersection of medical, political, and environmental histories with organology, as audible or inferable through the evidence of compositions. For example, how are we to understand the choices available to a flautist wanting to play Haydn's Trios, Hob.XV:15–17? His likely amateur status already differentiates him from our contemporary, highly professionalized musical culture (an issue we take up later in this essay); furthermore, he likely lives in a London heavily polluted by coal smoke, and in an age where tuberculosis was rampant. The question of compromised breath control and lung capacity may be as important as that of the number of keys on his flute. Or again: the bows, long and short, used by violinists during Haydn's lifetime were made of tropical hardwoods harvested in Central and South America at horrific human and environmental cost; the ivory keys on most period pianos invoke a similar history based in Africa. These embedded, invisible stories imply forms of performance as well, and the sub-discipline of historical performance practice has yet to seriously ask itself how they matter and to what extent.

For now, we see the most fruitfulness in work that in some way acknowledges the tension between the ever-perishing present moment of performance and the documental, positivist tendencies of writing history. Haydn's music, like any music, is only available to us *as performance* in the present moment. And right there with us, thronging into that moment, are all the other people with whom our performance will create, alter, or sustain relationships: our hearers, our fellow performers, our concert agent (if we have one), our teacher (if we are studying), our students (if we teach), our instrument builder (if we maintain an ongoing relationship with one), the rancher in Brazil who supplied the wood for our bow, our neighbors who have learned to tune out the sounds of our practice, the chiropractor who corrects the damage done by years of sitting hunched over: they are, willy-nilly and in all their messy variety, our co-performers in this complex Network. We propose that their now-ness is also, and always, a proper part of the study of performance.

Speaking very broadly, we see fertile potential in approaching Haydn's music through in-depth, "thick" examinations of how the many acts of making this music create, alter, and sustain human relations of various kinds, both historical and in the present moment. This is the humanistic project; it is furthermore quite explicitly the goal of that archetypical humanistic endeavor, the encyclopedia.

The Orpheus Experiment, June 2016 As performers who are also historians of performance, our concern with this necessary doubleness – then and now, Haydn's time and our own – led us to design a particular experiment as a response to the invitation to write this essay. We proposed to address the durable metaphor of "chamber music as conversation" self-reflexively and on its own terms, that is, through real-time conversations among living performers about the supposedly conversational chamber music we were making. In effect, we designed a series of latter-day salons (see Le Guin). Like good *salonnières*, we invited special guests, with a careful eye toward compatibility; topics were fixed in advance, and so was the repertory: Haydn's Keyboard Trios Hob.XV:11–13, published by Artaria in 1788, and the String Quartets Op. 33, also published by Artaria in 1781. In addition, funding from the Orpheus Institute in Ghent, Belgium, enabled us to take a step into a level of SELF-REFLEXIVITY unknown to our *salonnière* forebears: nearly all of four days of structured programs of conversations and read-throughs, rehearsals, and a final concert, was sound- or video-recorded (see RECORDING; DISCOGRAPHY). This elaborate experiment bore many fruits – not all of which we expected – and informs much of the analytic content of this essay. (Selected video clips of the event may be found at https://orpheusinstituut.be/en/haydn-and-the-art-of-conversation.)

Our "hypotheses" for this experiment mostly took the form of questions. The scientific language we have invoked here – experiment, hypothesis – belies our para-scientific hope that in one way or another we would raise more questions than we answered: that the deliberate putting into dialogue of living performers' experience with different kinds of historical sources would refine and extend the kinds of questions we were asking, and in the process, enrich the experiences of all involved.

This is the (abridged) form in which we shared some of our guiding questions in advance with our salon guests:

> Can we experience Haydn's chamber music in ways that challenge today's conventional concert protocols? To what extent should historically informed performance also embrace historical social practice? In counterpoint to the broadness of this field of inquiry, we offer two concrete décors for experimentation: one is suggested by an antique quadruple music stand [Figure 19]; the other is a late eighteenth-century drawing of a female keyboardist flanked by two string-playing men [Figure 20]. What communicative qualities of Haydn's chamber musicking will the choreographies that unfold around these two décors reveal?

Returning to Op. 33, No. 5 Proposals made, terms established, and a multi-day experiment initiated, let us now return to the opening of Op. 33, No. 5. How might our exercises in historical impersonation serve understanding, and enrich experience, of this famous little paradox?

There is remarkable evidence that four seasoned professionals actually performed one of the Op. 33 quartets; it may well have been No. 5. The performance took place before a distinguished audience of guests (including the Emperor Joseph II) that had been assembled by Maria Feodorovna, alias Countess von Norden, in her Viennese apartments on Christmas Day 1781. (A nice additional touch: during her stay at Vienna, this future Russian Empress took piano lessons from Haydn.) Assembled for the performance were the violinists Luigi Tomasini (concertmaster at Eszterháza) and Franz Aspelmayr (erstwhile secretary at Count Morzin's); the violist Thaddäus Huber (active at the Nationaltheater and in the Schottenkirche in Vienna); and the cellist Joseph Weigl (first cellist at the Esterházy court) (Landon II 456). All four were composers of string quartets in their own right and all four knew Haydn well. They represented Haydn not just by proxy, since Haydn was present at the occasion, receiving a "magnificent diamond-covered enamel golden box" in recognition of his labors, as reported in the press (*Wiener Zeitung* 1782, 7; see also Material Culture).

The professionalism here would have supplemented what was probably, by modern string-quartet standards, a minimal amount of rehearsal. We will assume that they were able to catch and effectively render many of the subtleties that modern-day performers of this work explore and enjoy through more extended rehearsal processes. They would have been alert to witty possibility, ready to throw each other curve balls with Haydn's slightest encouragement, ready to explore and exploit the oddities visible in their parts, and skilled in subtly signaling the surprises for their knowledgeable listeners – perhaps placing some kind of silent parentheses around that understated opening-that-is-not.

Agreeing to Disagree Speaking in terms of historical impersonation, the musical insights and actions we may attribute to this one-time professional configuration are likely to feel familiar to the latter-day professional musician, schooled to seek and to produce subtlety and sophistication, to chart a path through ambiguity, and – crucially – to maintain interpretive and technical control at all times. But in the Orpheus experiment, we were particularly interested in exploring another possible scenario for this music: four well-to-do gentleman amateurs, musically experienced but by no means professional, reading the quartet down *a prima vista*. This scenario would have been far more typical for all quartets in the late eighteenth century. However, it proved very much less familiar to us, and was considerably more difficult to sustain, musically, intellectually, and interpersonally, than a professionalized attitude. In effect, our own musical training became a barrier to the understanding we sought.

We pursued historical impersonation of these amateurs in various ways. By previous agreement, none of us looked at our parts in advance of the first session. In addition, two members of the quartet – the violinists – did not identify as professionals on that instrument, although they are highly skilled and experienced musicians in other areas. Instead of reading off a modern score, we played from the original Artaria parts (see Example 13). (The mix of amateurs and professionals in this first session was a temporary arrangement until two professional violinists were to take over on the next day.)

Reading Op. 33, No. 5 Around a Period Table Holding our instruments on our laps, we conversed for a few minutes, but the shift from small talk to making

Example 13 "Quartetto I," first movement, opening measures, Artaria parts.

music around this imposing piece of furniture was less smooth than expected. Clearly, we had to get used to it. The music stand, well, "stood" – annoyingly blocking our respective lines of sight, and consequently making us perceive the set-up as much more formal than anticipated.

Tom wrote of this first foray:

> Great was my surprise when exchanging the keyboard for the violin (an instrument that like Haydn I studied in my childhood and early adulthood before choosing a career as a pianist), I sat around the quartet table, ready to play together for the first time the few measures that I had so often contemplated and, like so many Haydn scholars, had developed precise ideas about. When I play the cautious opening of the D major Piano Sonata Hob.XVI:42, a work similarly exemplary of Haydn's inimitable cleverness and wit, "understated" is exactly the effect I go for. [But this:] How clunky! Nothing of the deliberate finesse of a rhetorical understatement, but hesitant confusion: who's leading; why aren't we together; shouldn't we be playing *pianissimo*?

Haydn – like Tom – studied both the violin and the keyboard. Unlike Tom, he kept up playing both throughout his career, so he knew first-hand what he was submitting each of the players to in those opening measures. He also knew that these players would most likely be a mixture of *Kenner und Liebhaber*. In fact, he targeted his Op. 33 quartets explicitly to the "many gentlemen amateurs and great connoisseurs," reaching out to them in places as far as Zürich or Winterthur (letter to J. C. Lavater of December 3, 1781; Bartha 106). Haydn's professional colleagues at Eszterháza – like the violinist Tomasini, who may have read through the proofs with Haydn – may have immediately recognized a Haydnesque twist; but it is fair to assume that the four gentlemen in Winterthur may not have even realized that the two first measures can be heard as a misplaced tag-on, a rhetorical game. At least, upon opening their new set of Haydn parts, there would be no knowing up front. Playing off single parts, there's simply no way to tell what the others are or are not playing. And Haydn not only knew this: he must have planned for it.

Let's look at these parts, both one by one and together (see Example 13). The placement of the double bar *in medias res* (toward the end of m. 2) makes for some bizarre graphics. What's "in" and what's "out"? We're used to something like an upbeat being "out," but the upbeat is all too explicitly – and confusingly – included in the "real" beginning (the silent rests in the viola and cello parts look all the more important), while the opening/closing gesture stands strangely on its own. Someone reads the tempo indication aloud: *Vivace assai*. For a first movement? And what does *pf* even mean? The violist, the more musically literate of the four, knows that it means *poco forte* – but he shares this piece of knowledge only after we've stopped for our next pause, too late for first impressions. Then there's the strangely positioned turn for the first violinist in m. 3. Aiming for more notational precision than ever before in this first sanctioned publication of string quartets, Haydn also manages to plant confusion – is it to be played before or on the beat? (These "Op. 33" quartets, published in 1782, were Haydn's third production with Artaria, after his newly negotiated contract with Prince Nicolas II Esterházy had in 1779 cleared the way for out-of-court publishing [Webster and Feder 22]. Along with his keyboard sonatas, Hob.XVI:35–39, 20, of 1780, and German lieder, Hob.XXVIa:1–12, of 1781, these engraved quartet parts reveal an enhanced prescriptive awareness of Haydn vis-à-vis the printed page, to be read by the generic amateur.) The violist, again, knows: a turn on the beat is the only correct answer. A good source has it that Haydn swears by the teachings of C. P. E. Bach (see Somfai 1995, 38ff.). The turn is to be as lively and crisp as it will be in mm. 25ff., where Haydn reverts to his more familiar shorthand notation for what must be a fast turn, or (more correctly) a single fast trill with a suffix. But the very first time, "too explicitly" notated and coming hard upon the imbalanced feel of the opening, these turns come out fudged. Meanwhile, the second violinist had the unexpected task of starting the piece by playing double stops: in *pianissimo*? The violist, from his side, is the unwitting agent of the violation of an eighteenth-century custom: as his first note of the piece he plays a dissonant c', the seventh of the dominant. A structural dissonance, it should have been lengthened and emphasized, but this he realizes only in hindsight.

Seven micro-confusions in three measures! Only the cellist, finally, stood a reasonable chance of recognizing and shaping correctly at his first attempt the cadential pattern of V-I, though he too is befuddled by the presence of what appears to be a perfect closure at the beginning of a piece. The opening effect, inevitably, is one of awkwardness – a confluence of tiny but telling *faux-pas* and misunderstandings. We, in our gentleman-amateur *personae*, have been handed a deft facsimile of an awkward social situation by the composer, making it likely that we will search for clarity all the more energetically in what comes.

The "proper" G major tonic harmony on the downbeat of m. 3 lasts a reassuring two measures, and seems to stabilize things gesturally with its drum bass accompaniment; perhaps we can just agree to forget that awkward beginning? But the new theme proves awkward too, since the only way for the violinists to coordinate a down-bow on the downbeat in m. 5 is by retaking an up-bow at the end of the previous measure (which of course didn't happen the first time: more hindsight!). When Haydn raises the volume to *fortissimo* in m. 10, our mounting micro-frustrations threaten to find outlet in some gentlemanly aggression. The reason for this dynamic shift is not very clear, and to make matters worse, there's no coordination: the second violinist and violist are told to start shouting on the downbeat of m. 10, while the cellist and first violinist follow one and three eighth-notes later, respectively.

If we assume that this scripted play with awkwardness was what Haydn had in mind, we can further assume that he knew very well what its sequels might be. Repeat signs and the sectional repeats they trigger are an impossibility in conversation, and can be a problem for sophisticated listeners like André Modeste Grétry; but for the anxious *prima vista* reader, they are a boon, a second chance for understanding, an opportunity to gradually revise and replace initially confusing elements. (Grétry [356] started mocking the practice: "What would we think of a man who, cutting his discourse in half, were to repeat each half?" But Somfai [2007, 224] recognizes potential in a real-time *seconda vista*, giving "musicians a second chance" and bringing "*memoria* (the fourth stage of the rhetorical process) into the act of performance itself.") Haydn goes so far as to suggest in the parts themselves that reconciliation and clarification are possible: the "cadential" opening gesture, for example, returns just before the recapitulation, thus taking on a belated kind of motivic identity, and making its return an amusing memory-exercise (rather like recounting one's own painful *faux-pas* after the fact, for humoristic effect). As we work our way into the second half of the movement, we note that the puzzling *poco forte* disappears in the recapitulation (mm. 184ff., see Example 14). So does the apparently gratuitous *fortissimo* shouting, which is reduced to a more-in-character *forte*, and that point is now marked in entirely coordinated fashion (m. 191).

Example 14 "Quartetto I," first movement, mm. 182–93, transcribed from Artaria parts.

At a certain point, perhaps even as early as the second read-through, we are given the opportunity to recognize that there's a system, and possibly a definite Topos, in not playing "together." In effect, Haydn has handed us not only a series of small traps and barriers to understanding, but also a kind of road map for the processes of accommodation and coordination that are the stuff of Sociability and rehearsal alike.

The clarity of that opening cadential figure does not make it a less surprising one – on the contrary. For its "nonchalance" to work as a figure of speech in performance, and to be recognized as such by whomever is listening, the four gentlemen-players need a second, third, or fourth chance. The meaning of this moment will need to be agreed upon, collectively cherished, crafted, and only then (hopefully!) realized. Formalizing this realization for third-party listeners is yet another step, and a tricky one. Certainly for latter-day professional musicians, there is a danger of over-rehearsing, of replacing its delicious awkwardness with suavity, its peril with control, and in the process erasing an exquisitely original idea altogether. How do we keep alive the memory and the experience of those first, priceless moments?

Solo vs. Accompanied Keyboard Musicking In another room of the house where the four gentlemen stumble their way happily through Op. 33 sit the wife of the cellist and her young daughters, busy this night with needlepoint and reading aloud. The fortepiano, purchased for the daughters' benefit, sits closed and mute on quartet night, but in a few days' time it and the house will be opened for a musical soirée. These have been a regular feature of household life for some years; the girls have real talent as well as a dedicated music master, and their performances of sonatas and songs have graced the family's parties, giving real – not feigned – pleasure to their social circle. However, in a few days the stakes will be a little different. The father has recently acquired a brand-new Artaria print of Haydn's Trios, those we now know as Hob.XV: 11–13. A young gentleman of her father's acquaintance, new to the city, with decent prospects, had been invited to play second violin in the quartet session; he acquitted himself well both musically and socially, and has duly been invited back to read trios. The father will once again serve as cellist. No one mentions that he will also serve as chaperone, nor is it made explicit that the older daughter is approaching marriageable age.

Hob.XV:11–13 is the set of trios that had also made Haydn bite the bullet and finally buy a fortepiano: "In order to compose your 3 *Clavier* sonatas [trios] particularly well, I was forced to buy a new Forte-piano," he wrote to Artaria on October 26, 1788 (Bartha 195). The business-like tone of the letter nonetheless holds intriguing implications. Less than a decade into his relationship with Artaria, Haydn felt confident enough to share his Financial burden with his publisher, asking him to pay the instrument maker Wenzel Schanz as an advance or loan. These are *your* sonatas, Haydn suggests, and *only* a piano – that newly normative commodity in the Viennese salon – will allow me to write them *particularly well*. In other words, it's all about the details, and these details matter for the clientele that *both you and I* have in mind: the keyboard-playing *Liebhaberin* in Vienna.

Example 15 Sonata in B♭ major, Hob.XVI:41, first movement, mm. 1–8, original edition by H. Bossler (Speyer, 1784).

What kind of details? Since Haydn's thoughts are with the piano, let's zoom in on those that a good master would have imparted to his talented pupil through their daily lessons. One particularly fine example for such teacher–pupil interaction (in fact, entirely analyzable as a music lesson itself) is the Sonata in B♭ major, Hob.XVI:41, the second of a set of three that Haydn had published not long before (in 1784, dedicated to the young Princess Marie Esterházy née Liechtenstein) (see Beghin 2015a). The sonata (see Example 15) begins with a compact statement: a presentation phrase (mm. 1–4) that instead of sitting on the half-cadence in m. 4, elides with the continuation phrase (mm. 4–8). This eight-measure opening period ends elegantly and clearly on an authentic cadence. Both hands are engaged; that is to say, the left is just as melodically active as the right, and the right is just as harmonically active as the left. A daringly expressive G♭ in m. 2 calls to a halt the right hand's downward *tièrces coulées* – a rare notated instance in Haydn of what C. P. E. Bach in an anti-Quantz frenzy had called "those dreadful *Nachschläge*" (or "unaccented appoggiaturas"): Haydn's, we believe, are still *Vorschläge* (i.e., accented appoggiaturas) but these accents happen to take place ever so slightly "before the beat." (Bach [59, 64, 70], showing himself more rigid than Haydn, does not allow for this kind of inbetween-the-beat accented appoggiaturas.) The interiorizing G♭, suggesting an altered pre-dominant chord, finds its exteriorizing *alter ego* in the right hand's enthusiastic run towards G♮ (downbeat of m. 3), which on its own (as the ninth of the chord) sustains the dominant for an exquisite moment, before yielding to another *inégal* cascade down. The left hand's F♯ in m. 3 gently but firmly proceeds to a vi-chord, a chord progression that is mirrored and morphed in the right hand yet again, where that same high G from before is revisited in m. 5 and resolved to F♮. If fine semantic distinctions are to be drawn between the left hand's G♭ in m. 2 and then twice G♮ in the right (mm. 3 and 7), then the same can be said of the left hand's F♯ in m. 4, enharmonic nemesis of G♭, and the right hand's F♮ in m. 7.

In this opening statement, it is hard to call out a single special moment: there are several, each outdoing the other. Eyes, hands, and upper body enter in dialogue with the musical material read on the page, whether through the frowning and releasing of one's eyebrows, the moving upward and sideways of one's arms, or the swaying of one's torso and neck. Two self-centering poses occur exactly at the beginning (the two hands playing an assertive B♭ arpeggio) and at the end (the two hands collaborating again on a three-voiced V^7–I cadence): after this cadence, both hands have time to retreat upward together, allowing the keyboardist to recompose herself, before a next paragraph starts. (A Viennese five-octave fortepiano, it should be remembered, has a "middle f" – and not a "middle c" – making B♭ major also a well-balanced key in terms of keyboard choreography.)

This kind of playing sets the bar high in subtlety and daring – but to claim sole agency on the part of the keyboardist negates her constant and intimate relationship with her teacher. Especially for those opening and closing gestures, he may have picked up his violin. (This would be entirely in line with contemporary pedagogical practice: "If the student has progressed to the point where he can play without interruption, then the teacher should accompany him on the violin – for every keyboard teacher should be able to play this instrument adequately – or perhaps the flute" [Türk 19]). He would have played along with the keyboardist's right hand, bodily conveying the following instructions: "Here's your downbeat: let's start; now ease down, relaxed; now open up again to that high G; prolong it, and down again; listen to the decay of the dissonances, and don't be shy to mark them: *sforzato*; then resolve them, but the second time (m. 5) don't wait too long (do you feel the open-ended excitement of the resolving first-inversion tonic?), but let yourself be launched into that vivid passagework before the cadence." These unspoken directions would have allowed him to impart a good deal of fairly sophisticated theory in real time (see EDUCATION), without resorting to words and without interrupting the flow of the music, while coaching her out of her comfort zone, making her right hand sing with the fine rubato of a *prima donna*.

But team effort aside, the endgame of a solo sonata remains a performance *without* supportive partner. Recent historians of late eighteenth-century music have downplayed differences between "solo" and "accompanied" keyboard music – and Haydn, in his letter to Artaria, indeed refers to his Trios Hob.XV: 11–13 simply as "keyboard sonatas." Yet, try telling our marriageable-age pianist-daughter that there's little difference between performing on her own and with others. Her house is the place where the piano lives, as the least transportable instrument of the three; but she understands quite well the other motive behind the invitation of the gentleman violinist. It is in effect a kind of musical "blind date," enacted before her parents and their circle. She is used to the attention of an audience; but in the trios, that attention is explicitly shifted toward her performance of interaction. "Nothing is more adapted to give the last polish to the education of a young man than the conversation with virtuous and accomplished women," Baron von Knigge writes from the perspective of male etiquette (152). But from the moment when the cellist and violinist tune their instruments to her piano, it is the young woman who is suddenly forced to leave behind the protected environment of a solo sonata (where everything can be rehearsed and planned, with the caring help of her music teacher) in order to shine in the "real" world where accomplishment, nervousness, and

Example 16 Trio in E♭ major, Hob.XV:11, first movement, mm. 1–23, Artaria print.

the pressure of meeting that someone special, all make for unpredictable scenarios and emotions.

Might we imagine that Haydn anticipates this delicate situation? If through the score of his solo sonata and through the person of his avatar, the music master, he coached his virtual *protégée* out of her comfort zone, here, in the first accompanied sonata of the set (see Example 16), he keeps things simple and relatively risk-free. Whereas the rhythms in the solo sonata wove an intricate narrative from measure to measure, slurred articulations flirting with beats and barlines, the pace for the sixteen opening measures of Hob.XV:11 is by comparison notably straightforward, safely conforming to half or quarter note divisions. Stick to what we learned from C. P. E. Bach, her music teacher might have reminded her: play all ornaments *on* the beat. This includes the complex-looking upbeat to m. 7, which may well be Haydn's notation for what Bach calls a "snapped turn" or *geschnellter Doppelschlag* – or at least some relaxed version of it. Do not be fooled into thinking of the first B♭ as a mini-upbeat: it is the first note of a single ornament that spreads over the complete fourth beat. The first time around (i.e., before playing the repeat), in those delicate first moments of conversing with a new acquaintance, it may in fact be better to contain the whole ornament within the fourth beat (i.e., to "shift" the B♭ one eighth-note later), avoiding any awkwardness in not being quite together with the violinist, who keeps the simple, unornamented quarter note. (Somfai [1995, 63–74] gives an insightful overview of Haydn's snapped turns.) If we look for *je ne sais quoi* moments like the ones we cherished in the solo Sonata

Figure 20 Detail from title page of Haydn, Keyboard Trio Hob.XV:10, Artaria (Vienna) 1798, indicating ocular communication between the players. Reproduced by permission of Jean Gray Hargrove Music Library, University of California, Berkeley.

No. 41, we may rightly be disappointed: there's a three-tone slide, yes, in m. 9 (*Schleiffer von dreyn Nötgen*), followed by a turn in a dotted-note context (*Doppelschlag*) in m. 10, and a nice invariably short appoggiatura (*unveränderlich kurzer Vorschlag*) immediately after, but beyond demonstrating to our male partners that we know our C. P. E. Bach, these ornaments do not necessarily draw attention to our part as particularly BEAUTIFUL, intimate, or poetic. The display of reservedness in Haydn's score translates to physical composure: with the possible exception of m. 9 (where the left hand's thumb is made to reach f', forcing her elbow to brush her side), her upper body and bosom remain remarkably still, allowing her to look straight ahead at the music stand and not to feel too physically self-conscious quite yet.

But to mistake this kind of simplicity for disengagement or disinterest would be to miss the point of this highly codified social scene, as captured by the title page engraving of a different Haydn trio score (see Figure 20). By default, because of her long instrument, it is the keyboardist who delineates the physical space, which extends all the way from the tail of her instrument to the train of her skirt. She has perfect posture. Suspended by her corset-fixed shoulders, her elbows literally hang above the keyboard ("several inches higher," exactly as Türk [25] prescribes), keeping her delicate hands as relaxed as possible. She sits perpendicularly to the keyboard, in spite of the angle of her chair, turned counter-clockwise to allow her skirt to fall properly. (Here, one can only imagine the discomfort this causes: she may look properly seated, but from an ergonomic point of view this must be anything but.)

Right where the piano's vibrations are produced – literally "where the action is" – three music stands converge around the only partially opened piano lid to form an intimate triangle where vibrations of a different kind may emerge. (A piano lid would in principle remain closed; it could, at a more formal occasion or in the theater for a concerto, be taken off altogether, but using a lid prop to open up the piano sideways would have been highly exceptional [see Huber].) Clarity of sound is bound to be stunning – both sonically (bass parts uniting on the left side of the keyboard and treble parts on the right) and physically (the young woman's arms extending, as it were, into two full-bodied alter egos). Hers is the perfect listening spot from which to practice the musical interactions that are to be part of her performance tonight.

But it is not only her interactive skills that are under scrutiny here: her parents are ENLIGHTENED people, and her taste and sentiment matter to them in the choice of a potential suitor. Accordingly, it is the string players' responsibility to adjust their tone to hers, especially with that lid closed. (Taking off the lid may not have been necessary in the domestic setting of our historical counterparts, but for the public performance during our Orpheus workshop we found a solution in refurbished book stands to be fastened to the sides of a lid-less piano: see Figure 21.) "Women possess a peculiar facility in discerning those men who sympathize with them, feel interested in their conversation, and can accommodate themselves to their tone" (Knigge 152). Holding her neck perfectly straight on her upper body, she initiates a triangle of eye contact, but clearly, it is the violinist's attention she seeks, ever so modestly and if only from the side of her right eye, allowing him to engage in "a kind of ocular language ... which is understood and felt by a tender and sensible heart, without requiring the assistance of words" (Knigge 153). All the while, the cellist, her father, is in perfect position to keep the two in full view. In the historical engraving, he has an elegant (if

Figure 21 Enacting a domestic keyboard trio setting. Photo extracted from a video by marK Boone. Clockwise, from left: Rachel Stroud, Margaret Faultless, Ellie Nimeroski (violin), Satinder Gill, Mary Hunter, Tom Beghin (fortepiano), and Elisabeth Le Guin (violoncello). Reproduced with permission of Orpheus Institute, Ghent, Belgium.

peculiarly attached) leg, but his rather hunched posture allows us to imagine him as the senior member of the group – as Elisabeth was in our set-up (though it is Tom who was the most hunched of the three).

Impersonating the Drawing Room Our recreations of the engraving had the peculiarity of perfectly reversed genders: we were a male pianist and female string players. We took this as a special opportunity to reflect on how well gender delineates the great distances that historical impersonation must at times traverse, and of the provisional and even playful nature of the performing insights thus generated. None of us will forget Tom's trying on a whalebone corset – laughter or no, such experiences make real some of the crucial details in the keyboard-playing lives of the *Liebhaberin* for whom Haydn wrote this music, in an embodied way not otherwise possible.

Just as our hypothetical eldest daughter would have done, and unlike the string players, Tom did not come to Hob.XV:11 *a prima vista*. He was "permitted" to learn it beforehand. Let us read his account of this experience as if it were by our fictional daughter:

> After several sessions of anticipation (and nagging dread that I won't be capable of showing to as good advantage as I could in a solo piece), it's finally time to play with the others. I will admit that this accompanied sonata had seemed lacking in interest compared to my beloved solo sonata; but in the event, that simplicity was amply compensated. So much to pay attention to! and right from the very first moments: the initial upbeat and the potential anxiety of starting together. Haydn handed that one to me: he gave me the liberty of starting alone, and the string players were attentive, catching me on the downbeat of the first measure. When I practiced alone, mm. 5–8 had felt like a retracing of steps – twice in fact – and on the edge of dreary; but now I hear and see that the repetition allows me first to connect with the cellist (how much richer do those bass notes in mm. 5–6 sound with him, and how much more special that first accidental, B♮); and then with the violinist. He repeats my phrase in mm. 7–8, staying below me politely and gallantly. By this he seems to express his appreciation for being invited to come and play.
>
> The sounds of the bowed instruments feel a little overwhelming at first. I can't hear the decay of my piano's strings as well as I could during my practice alone. But it seems Haydn anticipated this, for he gives me a chance, in mm. 9–12, to play just by myself. I can reconnect with what's familiar to me. Again gently, not too aggressively, the strings join, now as a duo, in m. 13 (changing *maggiore* to *minore*) and together we head toward a cadence. It does not feel like an ending at all – we are just finding our stride together, and Haydn gives us some playful interactivity as we continue. The violinist takes the initiative in m. 16, but I'm ready for him: in m. 19, when I again respond to him, Haydn gives me a fine (one might almost say, "professional") variant of my first response. I dare say the violinist thinks well of me for that – it was deft enough, even gently witty...

Three "Auditions" In more than one respect, the trio scenario we have been developing here suggests a kind of mutual "audition" – of the gentleman-violinist as prospective suitor and of the young woman-pianist as a candidate for his attentions. While it is but one scenario, we chose it because it was common enough in the day for us to call it typical for this kind of music. From it, we can develop further hypotheses and questions about the social relations coded into Haydn's scores, as well as some of our possibilities for enacting and experiencing them. There is, for example, the exploratory nature of the relationships in our scenario: the two most active participants in the music-making are checking each other out, testing tender possibilities and sureness of response, perhaps even the very capacity for responsibility, while the third is observing and containing the energies of the situation. What are the ways in which the interactive forces appropriate to a given scenario may be traced in the score? How can we as performers develop these roles, allowing their basis in history and in human nature to inform and inspire our execution? And lastly, how does the resulting performance in turn create new interactive possibilities with an audience?

We found the "audition" aspect of Haydn's trios to be interesting and important enough that we dedicated one part of the Orpheus Experiment to developing it further. We invited each of the three different professional violinists involved in the experiment to "audition" with us – "us" being the authors of this essay: the pianist and cellist remained constant, as they would have done in our fictional household. We used the exposition of the first movement of Hob.XV:11. We videotaped these play-throughs, and later analyzed the performance of each "candidate" in some depth. What follows is a condensation of the very considerable amount of information thus generated. The incentive to summarize our notes as virtues and vices comes in part from André Morellet's 1812 essay "De la conversation," in which he elaborates on eleven "faults [*vices*] of conversation."

Candidate A

CELLIST: One's attention goes to this violinist right away, and tends to stay there. The extremely demonstrative gesturing often seems to signal what a phrase means before we've fully heard it. I would go so far as to call it exaggerated. What purpose does it serve? To whom is it communicating? Not very well to me, I have to say. The piano and cello become amiable (and I think slightly bemused) accompanists to this "show" about the piece.

Virtues: Clarity and definiteness. It's never in doubt what this individual is thinking.

Vices: It's never clear that this individual is really hearing the others involved in making the music.

PIANIST: After the cameraman's "OK," violinist A indicates with a nod to me that A is ready. I take the cue, but still catch A by surprise – was my upbeat too short? Our respective downbeats end up not quite together. Nevertheless A articulates clearly and without fear. As if making up for the first, at the second big chord (m. 3), we're very much together. A's upper body movement marks a subdivision of the opening phrase as 2 + 2 and makes sure to indicate its end (m. 4) with big and clear bow strokes. The facial expression of all three of us has been consistently

earnest so far, and in spite of a slight attempt by me in m. 3 to make eye contact with A, our gaze remains mostly on the score.
Virtues: Respect, earnestness, professionalism.
Vices: Attention to Haydn (and his crafting of a musical conversation) more than to me.

Candidate B

CELLIST: By sharp contrast to Candidate A, the visual element is almost wilfully suppressed here: the violinist presents as modest to the point of retiringness (their manner of sucking back the chest and hunching the shoulders is especially expressive of this). Very interesting to hear how, as a result, the piano's and especially the cello's sounds come forward. I notice this especially in mid-range (tenor to low alto) passages, and more extended notes, which "bloom" in this version to a much greater degree than in the previous. Does the absence of visual "directing" lead us to hear these things more? Or does it mean that the piano and cello felt freer in the moment to actually play out? Suspect it's some of both. This whole relationship feels both more spacious and more free. We can take the time we want for niceties.
Virtues: This individual models attentive listening very nicely.
Vices: It is unclear whether they could really step forward and lead assertively if that were called for.

PIANIST: Ready to play, Elisabeth and I cast our eyes in the direction of violinist B, who, seemingly unaware, makes a last-minute adjustment of the microphone cable. At the exact moment of B's bringing the bow to the string, I start my upbeat; B picks up on this opening gesture, and lands the downbeat perfectly with Elisabeth, turning to her and acknowledging her with a smile. Then B's attention returns to Tom, and after the second big chord (a subdominant in m. 3) their eyes interlock for a split second; they smooth into the feminine cadence together. B keeps out of the way from Tom's sound-space, allowing his snapped figures to reach a natural halt. All this time, Elisabeth has had a benevolent smile on her face; twice, on the long appoggiaturas and their resolutions (mm. 2 and 4), her smile shifted to a slightly more interiorized version.
Virtues: Goodwill, yielding, making sure I function well.
Vices: I feel like I carry the conversation, and would like to be surprised, inspired, or even contradicted once in a while.

Candidate C

CELLIST: This violinist seems uncomfortable throughout, worried about getting their part right. It draws attention, but in a way that makes one forget about the progress of the sounds being produced ("the piece"), and instead, one wonders a bit anxiously about the possible relationships of the people on camera. Why is this candidate there? Why are they doing this if it is so uncomfortable? At the same time, this violinist occasionally, seemingly almost without expecting it, comes right out of the shell of preoccupation and produces something communicative and brilliant – and then there is a flash of mutual recognition with Tom, signaled by a glance or a smile or a raised eyebrow – something that looks more like what I imagine chamber music "ought" to look like. We see the fundamental surprisingness of the real-time musical encounter, as opposed to the fulfilment (whether dutiful, mediating, ingratiating, or dominating) of a role. An interesting candidate . . .

Virtues:Shows quite a variety of interactive modes: not predictable or dull.

Vices: A little erratic, and seems to want to please more than to be really interested in communicating.

PIANIST: There's chitchat. During tuning (which takes a long time), C and I establish a connection, with Elisabeth looking on. When Elisabeth checks her own tuning vis-à-vis C's, I finally pay attention also to Elisabeth. Awaiting the beginning, C carefully watches me, also acknowledging Elisabeth ever so briefly. As I get ready to play my upbeat, I lean my head toward C, who picks up on my upbeat perfectly, even eagerly. The first downbeat ends up perfectly together – almost too perfectly – between the three of us. By m. 3, C takes control, the outspoken sway in the upper body (from left to right) indicating leadership. This draws me in, and together we end prematurely on the half-cadence (I barely have a chance to play my cascading figures) – but then we perfectly pace the ending. C smiles at me – either apologetically ("sorry for pulling") or reassuringly ("I'll carry you through"). Elisabeth's overall expression is mild, while one moment of closing her eyes (at the beginning of m. 2) conveys concentration and earnestness.

Virtues: Energy, vitality, initiative.

Vices: Trying too hard (Morellet's "eagerness to show esprit"), resulting in inattentiveness to what I have to say.

Was there a clear winner? In an essay where we argue that our interest lies not so much with "performing Haydn" but with "people performing Haydn," this must remain an open-ended question. There is no right or wrong – there is only human interaction. And in any case, marriage was not in the offing.

The Trios Nos. 11–13 as an Opus The kind of work we have been modeling tends naturally toward a focus on local detail, yet it does not preclude a broader one, as is suggested by the musical trajectory of the opus as a whole. If the first Trio in E♭ major is all about making first acquaintances, then the second, No. 12 in E minor, forces the participants to shed any remaining inhibitions – together, they plunge into a *Sturm und Drang* first movement on a shared downbeat: who will lead? In the second movement, with the cellist's blessing, keyboardist and violinist embark on a most tender love duet. And all three give in to abundant laughter in the third-movement rondo. But the interactive

Example 17 Trio in C minor, Hob.XV:13, first movement, mm. 1–8, transcribed from Artaria parts.

highpoint in our journey is undoubtedly the exquisite theme of the third Trio No. 13 in C minor (see Example 17), where cautious niceties of the first trio's opening period (Example 16) suddenly feel far away and superfluous. No repetition (we say in eight measures what previously needed sixteen); no second-guessing (we've gotten used to our respective ways of playing ornaments). When playing her first upbeat (the same leap of a sixth as before, solo), the keyboardist need not even look up: she's confident that her male partners will catch her. She may draw her focus inward, pretending to play that intimate solo sonata after all, not worrying about being covered by the bowed sounds. And she graciously yields to her new friend who, later on (in m. 21), gets to be the only star in the *maggiore* alternative of the *minore* theme. The position of this double-Variation movement, at this juncture of the opus, is no coincidence. As he wrote to Artaria on March 29, 1789, Haydn composed "the third sonata new with variations, according to your taste" (Bartha 202). Artaria, the local publisher which had its finger on the pulse of music-making Vienna, clearly knew what would work, and Haydn obliged.

Suggestions for Further Study It is important at this juncture to acknowledge that our intensive examination of sociability as constructed through performance, and of Haydn as an agent of sociability past and present, did not consistently result in the intensified and enriched sociability of shared analytical insights. Over the course of four days, in fact, the sociability among the Orpheus Experiment's participants was at times severely stressed. We did play the final concert together, but much of the video and audio recordings of the days before the concert cannot be used. Relations were badly strained along certain axes, and any kind of collective follow-up has not been possible.

What happened? What conclusions can be drawn from such an unexpectedly unhappy outcome? On one level, a sociologist or anthropologist could have seen it coming miles off. This was a first foray for Tom and Elisabeth into formal investigative work with living people, rather than with the personal "channeling" of their long-dead counterparts through our own bodies and musical sensibilities that each of us has explored over the course of years. Demanding as historical impersonation can be for the individual pursuing it – and we hope that the preceding accounts give some textured sense of that demandingness – our respective experiences with it simply did not prepare us for the immense messiness of inviting others, with their very different musical, professional, and historical preoccupations, into the core structuring of a project.

Our difficult experience as organizer-participants underlined the importance of respecting intentionality in the study of performance. The question is, whose? As historians, we stay scrupulously away from imputing intentionality to historical subjects – as promoters do not: what performer on historical instruments has not been marketed from time to time as playing "the way Haydn intended it to sound"? However, intentionality cannot be so easily set aside in working with living subjects. It is foundational to performers' sense of artistic and personal control, and must be acknowledged as such. An important question for future study of historical performance is the degree to which the living performer's intentions, whether conscious or not, must be acknowledged epistemologically in regard to the work of art.

One way that human intention can be effectively studied, and interpersonal collisions minimized, is through ethnography (see Hunter). It would seem advisable for scholars of musical performance to take ethnography seriously: to get training in it, to be familiar with the ethical and interpersonal situations it raises, and to learn to practice it as a regular part of a scholar-performer's analytical toolkit. A more pragmatic suggestion is to simply start filming oneself during informal practice and rehearsal: such a habit can help accustom musical performers to the visible, theatrical elements of their art and may eventually transform into a method of embodied research, as one invents scenarios that divert attention from Haydn's works to the people playing them.

We close by respectfully mirroring Haydn's strategy: we deliberately end this essay with gestures more like openings than like endings. The study of historical performance has tended in recent years toward becoming an ancillary industry to the commoditization of professionalized performances and recordings, rather than a field of real historical inquiry – that is, a field in which product is far less important than process, and solutions, no matter how elegant, are secondary in interest and importance to good and sometimes even uncomfortable questions. It is a lot to ask of musicians who sustain their livings and their reputations through maintaining certain standards of execution, to call the very historicity of these standards into radical question; yet we submit that if we do not do so, with ourselves and with those we work with, we will have abdicated our core responsibilities as scholars and as artists.

TOM BEGHIN AND ELISABETH LE GUIN

FURTHER READING

Bach (1994, [1753/62]); Bartha (1965); Beghin (2009/11); Beghin (2015a); Beghin and Goldberg; Brown (1999); Cramm (2014); Diderot (1773, 1883); Gjerdingen (2007); Grétry (1797); Head (1999); Hellwig (1987); Huber (1987); Hunter (2015); Klorman (2016); Knigge (1788); Landon II; Le Guin (2007); Morellet (1812, 1995); Rink et al. (2017); Sanguinetti (2012); Somfai (1995, 2006, 2007); Türk (1789); Webster and Feder (2002); Wheelock (1991); *Wiener Zeitung* (1782); Woszczyk (2009/11).

Performance Spaces During his career as performer, composer, and conductor, Haydn worked in dozens of rooms and performance spaces, most of which were not specifically designed as public concert venues. This concise survey reveals the wide variety of environments that Haydn worked in during his lifetime and, in a few cases, suggests how Haydn may have responded to the acoustical conditions he encountered. (Some of the statements in this entry are based on actual site visits or on still unpublished documents of the Esterházy ARCHIVES [Esterházy Privatstiftung Archiv, Burg Forchtenstein]. Additional information appears in the chart found at the end of this entry.)

Building upon his early training as a vocalist, violinist, and keyboard player near and in VIENNA, the young composer sought patronage among the many aristocrats of the Habsburg Monarchy who cultivated music-making at both their country and city residences. In the mid-1750s, Baron Carl Joseph von Fürnberg invited Haydn to compose and perform string quartets at Schloss Weinzierl, which is situated today in Wieselburg in Lower Austria. Also associated with Haydn's early instrumental output is the extant mansion of the Counts Morzin located in Lukawitz, Bohemia (now Dolní Lukavice, near Plzeň, in today's Czech Republic). There, in a low-ceilinged parlor nearly square in plan, Haydn performed symphonies of his own composition in the late 1750s and 1760. The "Times of Day" Symphonies (nos. 6–8), composed in 1762, were very probably written for and first performed in the elegant hall of the Esterházy palace that still stands, although extensively remodeled, on the Wallnerstrasse in central Vienna. All of these spaces most likely would have been furnished primarily for the comfort of Haydn's patrons and their guests, with, at best, accommodations for the performers consisting of a slightly raised podium.

Haydn also became acquainted with theatrical performance environments early in his career. During the 1750s, *Der krumme Teufel* and its revival, *Der neue krumme Teufel*, introduced him to the Kärntnertortheater in Vienna. After its destruction by fire in 1761, an even larger replacement theater, capable of seating well over two thousand, featured five levels of boxes completely lining the side and rear walls of a relatively shallow audience chamber. Such an arrangement would have afforded a clear sound that promoted the intelligibility of spoken and sung texts, but such an acoustic would have been so "dry" that Haydn was compelled to employ extraordinarily large vocal and instrumental forces when he returned to the Kärntnertortheater in 1775 for the first performance of *Il ritorno di Tobia*. Perhaps this experience influenced Haydn's decision to allow a performance of *Il ritorno* with an expanded orchestration by his STUDENT Sigismund Neukomm at the even less-responsive Burgtheater in 1808.

Haydn's first proper opera, *Acide*, was premiered in January 1763 as a part of the wedding festivities of Prince Nicolaus Esterházy's eldest son, Anton, in the great hall of the palace that still dominates the skyline of EISENSTADT, Austria (then Western Hungary). Temporary modifications to the ceremonial hall were substantial in that they included protecting the white marble tiles with timber floorboards; building an elevated stage at one end of the room, complete with a proscenium arch, stage sets and stairways (thereby blocking from sight the usual view of a huge, water-spouting statue of Adam or Eve); erecting a decorative pyramid; and setting up benches for the spectators. In the summer of that same year, Haydn's *comedia La marchesa nespola* and an *opera buffa* by Fischietti were also performed there, and it is highly likely that the great hall was called upon again to serve as a THEATER for Haydn's *La canterina* in 1766. An examination of the monumental dimensions, room finishes, and furnishings of today's "Haydn-Saal" in the palace in Eisenstadt, however, which had been altered in the early nineteenth century during an overall updating of the palace by the French architect Charles Moreau, suggests that the acoustic of the great hall in Haydn's time was likely much too "live" and unwieldy to foster opera performances by singers and small instrumental ensembles playing to relatively small audiences. Archival documents confirm that music was provided for the balls and banquets that took place the great hall, but the absence of any evidence of other music-making there, beyond the initial attempts at opera performance, suggests that instrumental concerts for distinguished audiences at Eisenstadt, should they have occurred, might have taken place in one of the smaller, first-floor rooms known today as the Mirror Hall and the Empire Room.

Prince Nicolaus also resided for extended periods of time in the 1760s at his residence in Kittsee, now in Austria on the border with Slovakia. Between July and September in 1764, Haydn and his orchestra joined him in Kittsee while the Hungarian diet was meeting in Pressburg (now Bratislava). Maria Theresia, Queen of Hungary, visited Kittsee, only a pleasant excursion's distance from Pressburg, at least twice in 1764 and again in the summer of 1770, but the musical repertoire that she enjoyed there has not been recorded. The former Esterházy palace in Kittsee, more recently associated with the Batthyány family, still features an elegant ceremonial room with a pleasing acoustic.

The autumn of 1768 marks the beginning of the ESZTERHÁZA era with Prince Nicolaus's completion of his first opera house and the premiere of Haydn's *Lo speziale*. We know little about the physical characteristics of this first opera house at Eszterháza, but the performances were free and open to everyone. This was the opera house Maria Theresia saw when she visited Eszterháza in 1773. During its eleven-year lifetime it was the site of as many as three hundred performances of at least twenty-eight operas, including all of Haydn's operas through *La vera costanza*, along with frequent *Accademien*, concerts with mixed programs of instrumental and vocal music (see Malina 2016a).

When fire destroyed the first opera house at Eszterháza in late 1779, the marionette theater, originally built in 1773 on the opposite side of the formal gardens, was pressed into service as a temporary replacement. (The majority of marionette performances, consisting mostly of German singspiel-type pieces, had already taken place in this small theater by 1779.) With an interior praised by its visitors for its grotto-like décor (shells, mirrors, precious stones, and fountains activated by the entering public), the sets and machinery of the marionette theater were quickly enlarged so that they might accommodate opera performances featuring human actors. Until November 1780, the modified marionette theater supported over a hundred opera performances, beginning with the November 21, 1779 performance of Felici's *L'amore soldato* and, already on December 6, 1779, Haydn's *L'isola disabitata*. In spite of exhaustive archaeological efforts, however, a recent renovation of the surviving building shell was able to preserve little to nothing of the original marionette theater interior.

With its function and design being something of an amalgamation of the public Burgtheater in Vienna and the imperial private theater at Schönbrunn, a larger theater, seating approximately four hundred spectators, rebuilt on the same site as the first opera house at Eszterháza, was inaugurated with the premiere of Haydn's *La fedeltà premiata* on February 25, 1781 (see Figure 22). As at the Burgtheater, the repertoire presented at the second opera house at

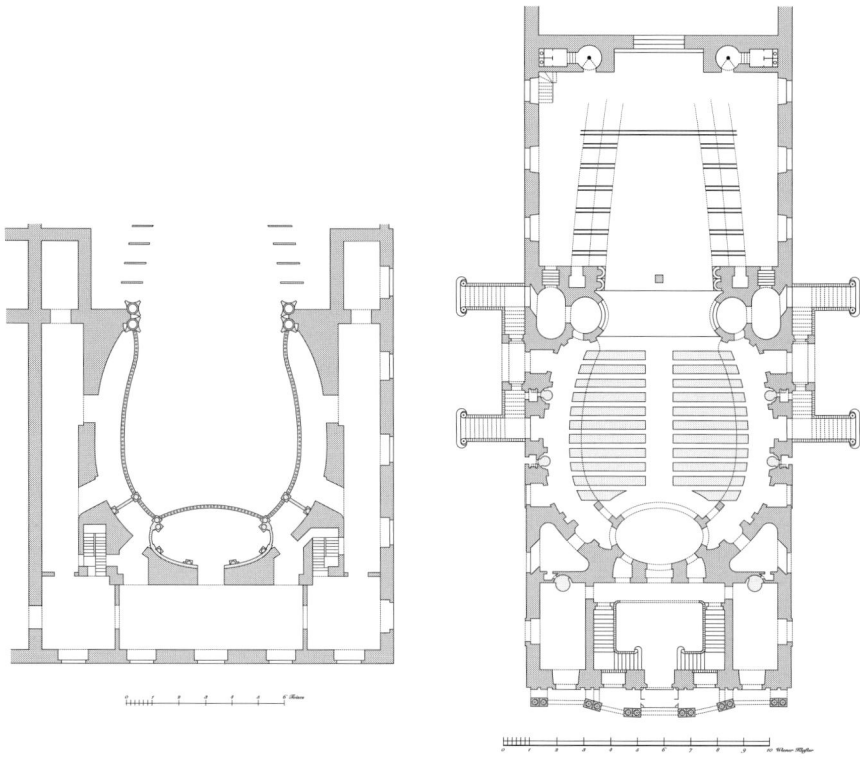

Figure 22 Comparison of the size and shape of the Schlosstheater at Schönbrunn (l) and the second opera house at Eszterháza (r). After a gallery level and partial stage plan by Carl Schütz, around 1778, Wien Museum, HMW 19.160/1, Vienna (copyright Wien Museum, used with permission); and a ground floor and stage plan by Joseph Ringer, 1789, Magyar Országos Levéltár (Hungarian National Archives), Fond T2, no. 1222, Budapest. Used with permission.

Eszterháza was open to the public, and PROFESSIONAL musicians, seated at the same level as the parterre AUDIENCE, accompanied professional actors playing within a square-shaped proscenium portal opening into stage decorations that could create illusions of deep perspective. This second opera house also resembled the Schönbrunn model in that admission was free of charge, the audience chamber was similar in size and also oval in shape, and a large box reserved for the sovereign was strategically placed at the center of a single elevated seating gallery that terminated in boxes at either side of the proscenium. A contemporary poet, Márton Dallos, observed Hungarian, German, Italian, and French nationalities in attendance. STUDENTS, noblemen, peasants, clerics, monks, soldiers, and "Saracens" were seated on benches in the parterre, while visiting dignitaries found their places in the gallery and proscenium boxes of the theater.

A computer model of the second opera house at Eszterháza shows that, while it was less grand in size and capacity than the Kärntnertortheater and

Burgtheater, it was warmer in tone and more supportive for both voices and instruments. This was primarily due to the fact that the upper volume of the second opera house was entirely free of encumbering, sound-absorbing seating galleries (see McCue). During the decade in which this second opera house was in use, a total of 69 or 70 operas were played in about 930 performances. Four of Haydn's operas and many of the most successful operas of the contemporary European scene were produced here, along with occasional *ballets d'action*, including Gluck's pivotal *Don Juan*. After 1781, the regular alternation of plays and operas in the second opera house left little or no room in the calendar for concert dates, but symphonies, and possibly concertos, were incorporated into the overall structure of opera evenings in the form of introductions and insertions, a practice also known in Vienna and at the Erdődy opera in Pressburg. All of this came to an end with Haydn's release from regular duties after Nicolaus's death in 1790.

Haydn's subsequent trips to ENGLAND in the 1790s gave him ample opportunity to fully experience and adjust to the performance conditions of his concert venues. The nine symphonies commissioned by Salomon, along with the Opp. 64, 71, and 74 string quartets, were performed in the Hanover Square Rooms, an acoustical environment designed to seat only 800, but sometimes occupied by up to 1,500. As a result, it was less sympathetic to instruments than the second opera house in Eszterháza. The last three "London" Symphonies were composed for Viotti's Opera Concerts that took place in the much larger and more resonant concert hall ("New Room"), built in 1793–94 as an extension to The King's Theatre building – a room that comfortably seated around 1,300 listeners. Neither of these two concert halls survives today.

Haydn's London orchestras were considerably larger than the one he had led at Eszterháza, where the number of players rarely exceeded twenty-four (see LEADING LARGE ENSEMBLES). For the Hanover Square Rooms, Haydn expanded his orchestra by augmenting the woodwind section and increasing the number of strings, for a total of thirty-five to forty players, thereby improving overall orchestral balance and increasing the loudness of the tutti ensemble. In the case of the King's Theatre concert room, the acoustical characteristics of the space, in association with orchestral forces as large as fifty-five players, allowed Haydn to explore further dynamic contrasts and timbral variety (see ORCHESTRATION).

After returning to Vienna from England, Haydn was finally at liberty to manage most of his musical affairs. Already in December 1795 he rented the Kleiner Redoutensaal (small ballroom) in the Hofburg for a concert showcasing three of his last six "London" Symphonies, along with the premiere of Beethoven's Piano Concerto in C major, Op. 15, allowing us to surmise that he found the acoustical response of this room, which was even more resonant than the King's Theatre concert room, to be at least adequate for performances of his latest symphonies. Haydn, however, appears to have been less eager to appear at the comparatively enormous Grosser Redoutensaal (large ballroom), which was judged by some critics to be excessively resonant. Today, the interior of the Kleiner Redoutensaal reflects renovations made shortly after Haydn's death, while the Grosser Redoutensaal has been fully rebuilt in a modern style following its complete devastation by fire in 1992.

In 1796 Haydn privately premiered the oratorio version of *The Seven Last Words* in the Schwarzenberg Palace that once stood on Vienna's Neuer Markt, which also was the site of the first private performances of *The Creation* and *The Seasons*. In each case, public performances of the oratorios followed in the Burgtheater or Grosser Redoutensaal, and, shortly before his death, Haydn attended a performance of *The Creation* in the Neue Aula of the Old University.

Haydn was eventually interred in the Bergkirche at Eisenstadt, where four of his final six masses had been first celebrated. Extremely resonant and bright in tone, the acoustic of the CHURCH, combined with the interplay of daylight with the exuberant decorations of Pietro Travaglia, Prince Nicolaus's stage designer, creates an exhilarating atmosphere of joy and resplendence.

Overview of Performance Spaces The following chart summarizes basic information about the primary music performance spaces in Haydn's career, arranged chronologically according to the first documented experience of each venue during his lifetime, and offering observations concerning their architectural condition at the beginning of the twenty-first century, estimated or actual seating capacity and geometrical size. Of primary importance are the venues where Haydn personally conducted his own compositions or the works of others. Included too are spaces Haydn knew personally and for which he provided scores but did not lead performances.

Excluded from this summary are spaces for which Haydn composed on commission, but never visited, such as the Santa Cueva oratory in Cádiz (*The Seven Last Words*), the abbey at Zwettl (*Il ritorno di Tobia*), and the Tuileries Palace in Paris (Symphonies nos. 82–87). Places in Vienna where Haydn's compositions were performed without his involvement, such as the concert series arranged by Ignaz Schuppanzigh at the Augarten and Schikaneder's productions of Haydn operas at the Freyhaus-Theater auf der Wieden, are not included. Similarly, the venue of the Erdődy opera in Pressburg, where four of Haydn's operas were performed in German translation, does not appear in this summary, since the actual venue cannot be identified. Two speculative concert spaces in the Eisenstadt palace, known today as the Mirror Hall and Empire Room, are also not included since no direct contemporary references to these rooms as music spaces survive. It is possible, however, that concerts (or *Accademien*) took place in these two well-appointed rooms, as well as those documented to have occurred in the Officers' Room during Haydn's earliest years with the Esterházys. Also excluded are additional spaces where Prince Esterházy's musicians provided musical entertainment for banquets, balls and similar occasions under Haydn's direction (e.g., the large hall, summer dining room and picture gallery of the Eszterháza palace; the Chinese ballroom, destroyed by fire in 1779 along with the first opera house; and the Grassalkovich palace at Pressburg).

Sites of domestic music-making, such as Haydn's home in Eisenstadt, Prince Hildburghausen's salon at Mannersdorf, Frau Genzinger's and Stephen Storace's homes in Vienna, and Anne Hunter's parlor in London, are excluded, as are details of less important churches first experienced by Haydn as a youth (e.g., the parish church of St. Philip and St. James in Hainburg, Count Haugwitz's Chapel in Vienna, and Mariazell).

Location/Identity	Modern Address	Status	Seating Capacity	V(m³) = L×W×H	Musical Importance
Vienna, St. Stephen's Cathedral (Stephansdom)	Stephansdom A-1010 Wien Stephansplatz Austria	Repaired after damage in 1809; rebuilt after 1945 bombing.	3,000	91,000 = 107×34×25	1739/40–c. 1749: Haydn sings as a choirboy.
Vienna, Kärntnertortheater (1)	Formerly stood at the site of Hotel Sacher A-1010 Wien Philharmonikerstrasse 4 Austria	Destroyed by fire in 1761.	Unknown	V = 19×15×H (audience chamber only, original ceiling height is unknown)	1750s: *Der krumme Teufel* and *Der neue krumme Teufel*
Vienna, Hofburg, Chapel	A-1010 Wien Hofburg Schweizerhof Austria	Baroque interior regothicized in 1802.	200 (nave only) 500 (with balconies)	2,900 = 24×8×14	1754–56: Haydn sings November 8, 1800: Heiligmesse (Haydn conducted?)
Weinzierl, Baron Fürnberg's Estate (unknown space)	Francisco Josephinum A-3250 Wieselburg Schloss Weinzierl 1 Austria	Repeatedly renovated, large hall reworked as a multipurpose space.	Unknown	Unknown	Mid-1750s: string quartets (Opp. 0, 1 and 2)
Vienna, Church of the Brothers Hospitallers (Barmherzige Brüder)	Klosterkirche "Hl. Johannes der Täufer" der Barmherzigen Brüder	Restored after 1830 flood.	180	4,300 = 37×9×13	1755–58: Haydn plays violin; March 25, 1768: *Stabat mater* (with Hasse present)

Location/Identity	Modern Address	Status	Seating Capacity	V(m³) = L×W×H	Musical Importance
Lukawitz, Count Morzin's Palace (unknown space, but possibly the parlor on the first floor)	A-1020 Wien Taborstrasse 16 Austria Zámek Dolní Lukavice CZ-334 44 Dolní Lukavice 1 Czech Republic	After World War II, used as a medical depot; since 1990, various attempts at renovation and cultural reuse.	Unknown	450 = 10×9×5 (first floor parlor)	Late 1750s (also 1760?): approximately 15 symphonies
Vienna, Esterházy Palace, Large Hall	The tenant occupying the relevant portion of the first floor is: Capital Bank A-1010 Wien Wallnerstrasse 4/1 Austria	Renovated in 1791; expanded between 1805 and 1820; repeatedly renovated since 1959.	Unknown	V = 14×11×H (original ceiling height is unknown)	1761: "Times of Day" Symphonies nos. 6–8
Eisenstadt, Esterházy Palace, Great Hall	Schloss Esterházy A-7000 Eisenstadt Esterházyplatz 1 Austria	Significant alterations between 1790 and 1810.	400–600	6,800 = 38×15×12	1762(?)–66: *Acide* (1763), *La canterina* (1766); no mention of Accademien
	Neues Schloss		150	1,200 = 13×13×7	

Location	Address	Alterations	Volume (m³)	Events
Kittsee, Esterházy Palace, Large Hall	A-2421 Kittsee Dr. Ladislaus-Batthyány-Platz 1 Austria	Renovated at the end of the nineteenth century; renovated 1969–74.	Unknown	July–September 1764: numerous performances of unidentified operas and instrumental music; 1770: Maria Theresia's short visit (musical program is unknown)
Eisenstadt, Esterházy Palace, Officers' Room	Schloss Esterházy A-7000 Eisenstadt Esterházyplatz 1 Austria	Renovated in the early nineteenth century.	$V = 10 \times 6 \times H$ (original ceiling height is unknown)	Late 1765 to 1768 and possibly through 1775: bi-weekly Accademien during the winter period
Eisenstadt, Esterházy Palace, Chapel	Schloss Esterházy A-7000 Eisenstadt Esterházyplatz 1 Austria	Few alterations since the eighteenth century.	$1{,}200 = 20 \times 6 \times 10$	1766–90: Haydn supervises liturgical music; 1773 through 1778 (or later): Haydn serves as organist during the winter periods
Pressburg, Primate's Summer Palace (Primasgarten), Large Hall	Úrad vlády Slovenskej republiky SK-813 70 Bratislava Námestie slobody 1 Slovakia	After 1859, insertion of a ceiling at the second floor; 1940–41 removal of Baroque interior and rebuilding of the ceiling at its original height	Unknown	February 16, 1767: La canterina

Location/Identity	Modern Address	Status	Seating Capacity	V(m³) = L×W×H	Musical Importance
Eszterháza, Esterházy Palace, The Prince's Private Chambers	Esterházy-kastély H-9431 Fertőd Joseph Haydn utca 2 Hungary	Interior ornamentation removed shortly after World War II; partially restored in the 1950s.	Unknown	200 = 7×7×4 (each of three similar rooms)	1768?–90?: baryton performances (some with Haydn's participation) as well as other forms of chamber music
Eszterháza, Opera House (1)	Formerly stood in garden of the Esterházy-kastély H-9431 Fertőd Joseph Haydn utca 2 Hungary	Destroyed by fire in 1779.	Unknown	Unknown	1768–79: c. 300 (or more) performances of 28 operas, including 8 by Haydn; a substantial, but unknown, number of Accademien
Vienna, Sumerau Residence (unknown space)	Formerly stood at A-1060 Wien Windmühlgasse 28 Austria	Demolished in 1969.	Unknown	Unknown	March 1770: two performances (one staged, the other unstaged) of Lo speziale
Vienna, Church of the Piarists (Piaristenkirche)	Piaristenkirche "Maria Treu" A-1080 Wien Jodok-Fink-Platz Austria	Renovated in 1997.	240	45,000 = 54×32×26 (overestimation of volume based on the maximum width at the crossing and the greatest height of the dome)	1771: Stabat mater; 1796: Paukenmesse (or Heiligmesse?); both directed by Haydn

Eszterháza, Marionette Theatre	In garden of the Esterházy-kastély H-9431 Fertöd Joseph Haydn utca 2 Hungary	Renovated in 1779 for use by human actors; marionette function reinstated in 1782; rebuilt as a multipurpose hall in 2013.	Unknown	1,400 = 26×9×6 (audience chamber only, assuming length extends from lip of stage to the west exterior wall)	1773–83: at least 6 marionette operas by Haydn; 1779–80: more than 100 performances of 8 operas, including 3 performances of Haydn's *L'isola disabitata* 1775: *Il ritorno di Tobia*
Vienna, Kärntnertortheater (2)	Formerly stood at the site of Hotel Sacher A-1010 Wien Philharmonikerstrasse 4	Opened in 1763; renovated in 1814; razed in 1870.	2,400	4,100 = 22×13×14 (audience chamber only)	
Eisenstadt, Church of the Brothers Hospitallers (Barmherzige Brüder)	Konventkirche der Barmherzigen Brüder A-7000 Eisenstadt Esterházystrasse 26 Austria	Renovated in 1945.	70	1,300 = 16×7×12	c. 1775–78: "Kleine Orgelsolomesse"
Eszterháza, Opera House (2)	Formerly stood in garden of the Esterházy-kastély H-9431 Fertöd Joseph Haydn utca 2 Hungary	Disappeared from maps after 1860.	400	3,400 = 20×15×11 (audience chamber only)	1781–90: nearly 70 opera productions, including 4 composed by Haydn, in c. 930 performances
Vienna, Burgtheater			1,500–1,800	3,700 = 26×11×13	

Location/Identity	Modern Address	Status	Seating Capacity	V(m³) = L×W×H	Musical Importance
	Formerly stood near today's Spanische Hofreitschule A-1010 Wien Michaelerplatz 1 Austria	Expanded in 1794; razed in 1889.	(audience chamber only)		1784, 1793, and every year between 1798 and 1803: Haydn conducts Il ritorno di Tobia, The Seven Last Words, The Creation, The Seasons or his symphonies; February 12, 1797: Gott erhalte 1808: Neukomm conducts his revised version of Il ritorno di Tobia
London, Hanover Square Rooms	Formerly stood at the site of Blain|Southern London 4 Hanover Square London W1S 1BP United Kingdom (gallery wing fronting Hanover Street)	Renovated in 1861 and 1875; demolished in 1900.	800–1,500	1,900 ≈ 24×10×8	1791/92: Symphonies Nos. 93–98 1794: Symphonies Nos. 99–101 and string quartets Opp. 64, 71 and 74
Oxford, Sheldonian Theatre	Sheldonian Theatre Broad Street Oxford OX1 3AZ United Kingdom	Repaired and redecorated in the 1790s; renovated in 2008.	800–1,000	7,000 ≈ 26×23×13 (taking amphitheater shape into account)	July 7, 1791: Symphony No. 92, "Oxford"

Vienna, Hofburg, Kleiner Redoutensaal	Kleiner Redoutensaal A-1010 Wien Heldenplatz Austria	Altered in 1816; restored after 1992 fire.	400–700	3,300 = 23×11×13	1793: Haydn arranges and possibly conducts a concert; December 18, 1795: Haydn conducts three London symphonies and the premiere of Beethoven's piano concerto in C major; 1796: Haydn conducts his symphonies
Vienna, Lobkowitz Palace, Large Hall	Österreichisches Theatermuseum A-1010 Wien Lobkowitzplatz 2 Austria	Interior modified in 1845; renovated in 1946 and 1991.	100	800 = 15×7×8	1793: unknown work; 1799: *Der Sturm* (Haydn probably conducts)
London, Carlton House (unknown space, possibly the "Music Room")	Formerly stood between Pall Mall and St James's Park, approximately in line with the long façades of today's Carlton House Terrace	Demolished in 1828.	Unknown	Unknown	1794 and 1795: Haydn sings and plays the piano

Location/Identity	Modern Address	Status	Seating Capacity	$V(m^3) = L \times W \times H$	Musical Importance
London, King's Theatre (Haymarket), Concert Room	London SW1Y 5AJ United Kingdom. Formerly stood at site of today's Her Majesty's Theatre London, St James's SW1Y 4QL Haymarket United Kingdom	Destroyed by fire in 1867.	1,300–2,000	$4,500 = 29 \times 14 \times 11$	1795: Symphonies Nos. 102–4
Eisenstadt, Bergkirche	Bergkirche A–7062 Eisenstadt Joseph-Haydn-Platz 1 Austria	Renovated in 1880; Haydn mausoleum placed at the base of the North Tower in 1932.	154	$9,000 = 25 \times 19 \times 19$	1796–1802: performances of 5 of the 6 late masses
Vienna, Schwarzenberg Palace (Neumarkt) (unknown space, probably a salon on the first floor)	Formerly stood at A–1010 Wien Neuer Markt 8 Austria	Razed in 1894.	Unknown	Unknown	April 29, 1798: premiere of *The Creation* conducted by Haydn, and additional performances in 1799 and 1800 might also be conducted by Haydn.

Eisenstadt, St. Martin Church	Dom St. Martin A–7000 Eisenstadt Domplatz 1a Austria	Interior regothicized 1890–1904, extensive alterations in 2003.	Unknown	18,700 = 41×19×21 + 17×8×17 (apse)	1798: "Nelson Mass". Performances of The Seasons in April and May 1801 might also be conducted by Haydn.
Buda, Castle, Throne Room	Magyar Nemzeti Galéria H-1014 Budapest Szent György tér 2 Hungary	Seriously damaged in 1945, new interior constructed 1960–70 within the original structure.	Unknown	3,000 = 30×10×10	March 8, 1800: Haydn conducts The Creation.
Vienna, Hofburg, Grosser Redoutensaal	Grosser Redoutensaal A-1010 Wien Heldenplatz Austria	Altered in 1808 and 1816; rebuilt as a multipurpose hall after 1992 fire.	1,500–2,000	10,600 = 39×17×16	1801–3: Haydn annually conducts his oratorios and symphonies; December 26, 1803: last known appearance of Haydn as a conductor

Location/Identity	Modern Address	Status	Seating Capacity	V(m³) = L×W×H	Musical Importance
Vienna, Old University, Neue Aula, Great Hall	Österreichische Akademie der Wissenschaften A-1010 Wien Doktor-Ignaz-Seipel-Platz 2 Austria	Interior rebuilt in 1963 after fire.	300	5,100 = 23×17×13	March 27, 1808: Haydn makes his last public appearance during a performance of *The Creation*.

Glossary of Places

Bécs:	see Vienna
Bratislava:	see Pressburg
Buda:	(now part of Budapest; *Ger* Ofen), capital of the Kingdom of Hungary/Hungary
Dolní Lukavice:	see Lukawitz
Eisenstadt:	(*Hun* Kismarton), Sopron (Ödenburg) County, western part of Kingdom of Hungary/Burgenland, Austria
Eszterház:	see Eszterháza
Eszterháza:	(also Eszterház; now part of Fertőd), Sopron (Ödenburg) County, western part of Kingdom of Hungary/Hungary
Fertőd:	see Eszterháza
Kismarton:	see Eisenstadt
Kittsee:	(*Hun* Köpcsény, *Slo* Kopčany), Moson (Wieselburg) County, western part of Kingdom of Hungary/Burgenland, Austria
Kopčany:	see Kittsee
Köpcsény:	see Kittsee
London:	capital of England/United Kingdom
Lukawitz:	(*Cze* Dolní Lukavice), Bohemia, Austrian Empire/Czech Republic
Ofen:	see Buda
Oxford:	England/United Kingdom
Pozsony:	see Pressburg
Pressburg:	(*Hun* Pozsony, *Slo* Bratislava), Pozsony (Pressburg) County, western part of Kingdom of Hungary /capital of Slovakia
Vídeň:	see Vienna
Viedeň:	see Vienna
Vienna:	(*Cze* Vídeň, *Ger* Wien, *Hun* Bécs, *Slo* Viedeň), capital of Austria
Weinzierl:	(now part of Wieselburg), Lower Austria, Austrian Empire/Austria
Wien:	see Vienna

Cze	Czech
Ger	German
Hun	Hungarian
Slo	Slovak

JÁNOS MALINA AND EDWARD MCCUE

FURTHER READING

Beghin (2011, 2015); Clark (2009a); Dallos (1781); Dávid (2013); Dávid and Fatsar (2004); Dávid, Jung, Malina, and McCue (2015); Deleglise (1947); Edge (1992b); Feder (1970); Forsyth (1985); Koppány and Thúry (2013); Krähling, Koppány, Fekete, Halmos, and Józsa (2013); Landon I–V; Malina (2016a, 2016b); McCue (2004); McGrann (1998);

McVeigh (1993); Meyer (1978, 1995); Morrow (1989); NG *Haydn*; Pollheimer (2017); Pratl (2009b); Rotenstein (1793); Sisman (1990); Spitzer and Zaslaw (2004); Szentesi, Mentényi, and Simon (2013); Tank (1980, 1981); Weinzierl (2002).

Philosophy – see Idealism

Place To the music lover interested in Haydn, places may seem self-evident as objects of inquiry. Places are simply *there*. And, as the word implies, they generally stay put. They are the ancient buildings – some of which survive after all this time – which have played host to Haydn and his music. They are the landscapes and seascapes upon which Haydn gazed, and so can we. They are the statues and memorials – such as the monument erected to Haydn in his birthplace of Rohrau in 1793 – at which enthusiasts regularly pay their respects. But, even though one can still visit many of the places where Haydn lived and worked (for instance, the palace of EISENSTADT, or the Stephansdom in VIENNA) and marvel at their permanence, any place is, of course, made out of conglomerations of IDEAS and materials that are more changeable and more mobile than the appearance of self-evidence might let on. And music counts among this conglomeration of ideas and materials. For as anyone can attest who has heard a mass by Haydn performed as part of a CHURCH service, or one of his concertos in what is now known as the Haydn-Saal in the Esterházy palace in Eisenstadt – music works to produce places as much as the other way around.

Haydn's Places That places are more protean and multivalent than one might think is no clearer than in the church, the court, and the MARKET – three domains that, more than any other, shaped Haydn's music and career. To be sure, all of them were represented in physical locations that surrounded and encroached upon Haydn and his music. Consider Haydn's main place of residence in the 1750s, the attic room of the Michaelerhaus in the center of Vienna. He would have awakened most mornings to the bells from the Gothic tower of the ancient Michaelerkirche next door, where he probably assisted as a performer now and again. Descending into the street, Haydn would have seen the imposing gate of the Hofburg palace in one direction and, in the other, he could have walked to the hustle-bustle of the Graben, a centuries-old marketplace, whose open-air stalls were, by the end of the 1750s, giving way to high-class shop fronts. The church, the court, and the market thus lay at Haydn's door.

But each of these places was, of course, constituted by a great deal more than mere architectural fabric. Indeed, to Haydn, the church was an all-embracing idea and a widely distributed web of relationships. It supported the school that had conveyed him as a child from Rohrau to Hainburg, the fortress town close to Pressburg (today's Bratislava) where Haydn had first participated in the full choral mass in the Philippus-und-Jakobus-Kirche. It had also given him his rigorous EDUCATION as a chorister, living with the other boys in the Capellhaus that once abutted the Stephansdom. And it had hosted his many performances with the Hofkapelle and similar institutions. The court during this period was likewise scattered between locations, held together by a patchwork of ancient protocols and hierarchies. As a boy, Haydn would have performed in all the main seats of imperial rule, not only the Hofburg but also the palaces on the outskirts of Vienna, such as Schönbrunn and Laxenburg. And by the 1750s, Haydn regularly plied between various court centers dotted across the

Habsburg realm in search of patronage: the palace of the Austrian administrator Baron Carl Joseph Weber Fürnberg in the village of Weinzierl in the Danube valley, where Haydn produced his earliest trios and quartets; and the palace of the Morzin family in the Bohemian village of Lukawitz where Haydn was appointed Kapellmeister sometime before 1757, and produced his earliest symphonies. In the 1750s, the market had a much less prominent role in Haydn's professional life. This was to change radically, however, especially with the rapid expansion of music PUBLISHING in European capitals over the ensuing decades. In fact, one could fairly say that, during Haydn's long career, "the market" crucially changed its meaning: once a particular place designated for the purpose of truck and barter (on the Graben or Kohlmarkt, say), it was now an abstract principle potentially spanning the globe – both everywhere and nowhere.

To acknowledge the complexity and hybridity of place is to avoid articulating the relation of Haydn and his music to particular places in simplistic or univalent ways. As Philip V. Bohlman and Rudolf Pietsch observe in their entry on BURGENLAND, the borderlands in which Haydn was raised, and spent nearly all of his career, hosted a varied and tangled COSMOPOLITAN mix, change and motion rather than fixity. Haydn's experience of this mix would have been, from an early age, mediated by the INSTITUTIONS and strata in which he moved. In Vienna, Haydn encountered a type of cosmopolitanism produced not only by the porous nature of borderlands but also by the well-trodden paths leading between the EUROPEAN court-based hubs of Austria, Italy, and France. Thus, as a choirboy under the guidance of Georg von Reutter (one of the most prominent students of the Venetian composer Antonio Caldara), and during a short period of apprenticeship with the Neapolitan master Nicola Porpora in the 1750s, Haydn was to receive distinctively Italianate modes of musical instruction, both in singing and at the keyboard. And by the early 1760s, when Haydn began working for the Esterházy family, a series of pictorial pieces – the "Times of Day" symphonies ("Le matin," "Le midi," and "Le soir," Nos. 6–8; see TIME) – indicates that Haydn was now paying close attention to French musical AESTHETICS, fashionable at a time when the Habsburg dynasty was creating ties with the Bourbons. Though located mainly at the Esterházy's urban palace on Wallnerstrasse, Haydn experienced French music via the extensive collections of Prince Paul Anton, and, of course, Gluck, who was busy composing a series of French operas for the court THEATER, only a short walk away. Haydn's early years in the court circles of Vienna thus gave him access to Italy and France; these transnational contacts constituted his sense of place as much as the city or palace that surrounded him.

Haydn's career thus complicates what may seem a natural assumption about music and place: that an intimate connection between them requires a single story of co-presence – that a piece of music was performed in a particular room or by a particular institution or in front of a particular AUDIENCE. Granted, toward the beginning of his career, Haydn sought to manage this co-presence, as any responsible Kapellmeister of the period would have done. In 1768, he was obliged to send an *Applausus* (a sort of celebratory cantata) to the abbey of Zwettl in Lower Austria. Because Haydn was not going to be present at the performance, and had no knowledge of the players and singers, he sent extensive instructions for its REHEARSAL and execution, and complained, "I know neither the persons nor the place, and in truth the fact that these were concealed from me made my work very difficult" (CCLN 9–11). Yet this challenging division of music and place ultimately became normal for Haydn, much of whose music, by the 1780s, was constantly on the move. This had much to do with the increasingly de-territorialized realm of the market, with its cluster of technologies and formats that we would nowadays call media: journals and magazines (see PRESS), the ticketed public concert, and music publications, all of which enabled the distribution, CIRCULATION, and increasingly standardized reproduction of music over large distances. Soon, the multiple destinations of many of Haydn's works were no longer even known, let alone present, to their author. Particular locations now related to many of these works less as fixed points of origin or as places of termination, but as myriad stopping-off points in the wide-ranging journeys of print.

As early as 1775, the Vienna *Realzeitung* lauded Haydn as a "great artist whose works are loved throughout Europe" – a formulation as much about the media imagination as Haydn's burgeoning reputation: the proliferation of print nurtured fantasies of a world connected by music. And Haydn's music in turn cultivated marketable fantasies of distant climes: the Turkish EXOTICISM of *L'incontro improvviso*, the FOLK naivety of the Scottish songs, the self-othering "gypsy" rondo from the Keyboard Trio, Hob.XV:25. As Thomas Tolley explores in his entry on TRAVEL AND EXPLORATION, these imaginative geographies articulate an aesthetic rather than material relationship with place, though it was a relationship made thinkable in part by the reality of busy trade routes and colonial expansion.

Haydn's Court Haydn was appointed Vice Kapellmeister to the Esterházy court in 1761, and the Esterházy family was to furnish Haydn with many of the places that shaped, and were shaped by, his music throughout his long career. Though Haydn began his service in the Wallnerstrasse palace, this grand Viennese residence would surely have felt like but one node (and not a particularly important one) in a court system constituted by chains of ancestral territories, administrative seats and country retreats, and an ever-changing architectural fabric.

Until the later 1760s, Haydn divided his work mostly between Wallnerstrasse and the palace of Eisenstadt, not thirty miles from Vienna. The seventeenth-century baroque palace in Eisenstadt was a major administrative center, and attracted vast numbers of people into its orbit, with informal and formal, temporary and long-term relationships; even opera began in Eisenstadt as a seasonal entertainment provided by an itinerant Italian troupe – a troupe that was eventually hired by Prince Nicolaus on a more permanent basis. From 1761, the musicians in service at Eisenstadt were divided between church and chamber (the former was directed by Haydn's senior colleague Gregor Werner until his death in 1766). This division of roles matched the architectural layout of the palace: one side of the grand courtyard was occupied by the chapel, while a capacious banquet hall made up the extended back wall – one of the possible venues for *Tafelmusik*, concerts, and theater, decorated with lavish murals depicting episodes from Ovid and classical myth, which could comfortably hold several hundred people (see also COMMEMORATIONS AND FESTIVALS; PERFORMANCE SPACES). Haydn's daily life was split between his work inside the palace and his place of residence, together with the other court musicians in the Old (court) Apothecary, located just outside the main entrance to the palace. (The Old Apothecary was originally thought to be located in the Oberberg district near the Bergkirche, but Pratl relocates it within the town walls, opposite the pre-1670 JEWISH enclave.) And Haydn's musical output at this time reflected both the court's status as a multinational hub and its cloistered localism: Haydn turned his hand to the globetrotting Italian operatic genres that would occupy him for the next two decades, alongside many smaller-scale enterprises evidently shaped by the niche preferences of his new prince, such as the first of many trios featuring Nicolaus's obscure stringed INSTRUMENT of choice, the baryton.

Around the time when Haydn was promoted to the role of senior Kapellmeister, the attention of the Esterházy court began to turn from the imperial capital toward their rural seats in Hungary, in particular Nicolaus's former palace in Süttör, a further day's journey southeast of Eisenstadt, at the southern end of the Neusiedlersee. The new importance of Süttör had been signaled in a court directive issued only weeks before Werner's death: from now on it was to share the name of its noble occupants, "Eszterház." ESZTERHÁZA, as it was usually known – Haydn tended to call the palace "Estoras" in his letters – was already a large building in the early 1760s, its forty-one rooms and three floors situated in many acres of gardens and parkland. As Balázs Mikusi carefully shows in his entry, any architectural account of these court residences must acknowledge that they were, and remain, palimpsests, in which the new constantly overlaid and incorporated the old. While Haydn worked for the Esterházy family, his working environment was in a continual state of change. Over the next twenty years, a series of building projects transformed Eszterháza into the equal of the imperial palace of Schönbrunn, a sumptuous expression of the wealth and influence of the Esterházy family.

Though Haydn was in charge of church music after 1766, in Eszterháza his attentions would have been directed toward the church only rarely. A circular chapel extended upward through all three storeys of the palace, but its dimensions were such that it could have hosted only the most modest religious services. Some musical action within the palace may have taken place in the upstairs Prunksaal, with its elaborate ceiling fresco of Apollo and splendid statuary depicting the four seasons, and in the neighboring space that became known as the music room; as János Malina and Edward McCue explore, however, beyond the designated spaces for music such as the theater, present-day historians have had trouble establishing which parts of the palace complex hosted musical performances most frequently. This is in part because music must have been a fairly peripatetic business within the palace, accompanying dinners, rituals, and celebrations, and only intermittently taking center stage. Malina and McCue demonstrate, in fact, that the very concept of musical "Performance Spaces" (an idea that would have been relatively new even in the commercial concert culture of late eighteenth-century LONDON) may be unhelpful as a way of categorizing the many state rooms, chapels, and banquet halls in Haydn's court environments, and that "acoustic spaces" might be a more apt designation.

In 1768, new structures were completed outside the palace building itself where the bulk of Haydn's labor was eventually expended: a neo-classical theater and a Chinese ballroom next door. In 1773, a small marionette theater was added on the southeast side. The theater in which operas were performed had a capacity of around four hundred: seating was provided on eleven rows of benches; there was standing room further back. Stairs from the gardens took high-ranking guests up to a pair of boxes on either side of the stage, nearer to the action. Except during special visits and ceremonies, the bulk of the audience would have been made up of the servants and officers of the court and their families. Indeed, on occasion, it is likely that attendance would have been sparse, and limited to little more than the prince and his retinue. As was typical of eighteenth-century theaters, the architecture granted the prince the most advantageous perspective: two grand staircases in the foyer led up to a large oval box at the back of the theater; several adjoining rooms were available for entertainment and refreshment throughout the performance. Haydn would have directed most performances from a keyboard placed at the end of a long single music desk, which all of the musicians shared. The orchestra was seated on the same level as the audience, in front of a cavernous stage.

The theater in Eszterháza (and the ballroom next door) was destroyed by fire in 1779, but it was rebuilt with astonishing rapidity by early 1781, when the packed program of opera was resumed. Especially after its earliest full-length season (running from spring until the onset of winter) in 1776, the opera house dominated Haydn's daily life in Eszterháza. It was the point of origin not only for nearly all of Haydn's operas, but a great deal of music besides: the substitute arias for operas by other composers, which Haydn regularly produced in order to suit the singers at his disposal (see Vocal Coaching and Rehearsal); incidental music to spoken dramas; and symphonies that provided musical entertainment on their own, or during the breaks in longer theatrical presentations. The opera house was a space of vibrant musical circulation: new and old operas were brought in and extensively adapted by Haydn himself, including works by Gluck, Paisiello, Piccinni, and others, and singers continually came and went from the troupe, usually from Italian cities. The repertoire of the theater in Eszterháza was probably decided as much by the director of the opera as by Haydn himself – a role that, in the year of the reopening of the building in 1781 (and the premiere of Haydn's *La fedeltà premiata*), was taken up by one Nunziato Porta. In the decade that Porta was in charge, the operas were drawn from a largely north Italian repertoire markedly distinct from that sponsored by the Viennese court – works by figures such as Cimarosa, Sarti, and Zingarelli. Eszterháza, buried deep in the Hungarian countryside, was thus also a center of north Italian music and musicians. (See Composers and Music Professionals.)

From the late 1760s, then, Haydn's work took him mostly between Eisenstadt and Eszterháza, typically with a visit of only a few weeks to the Wallnerstrasse palace over Advent and Christmas. In 1766, he bought a large house and several acres of land a few minutes' walk east of the Eisenstadt palace – a major purchase that reflected the new Eisenstadt–Eszterháza focus of the prince, and also increased Haydn's physical separation, as Kapellmeister, from the other court musicians living in the nearby musicians' residence. He sold the house in 1778, after more than a decade of problems with it, including two fires, in which many of Haydn's possessions (including copies of his music) were destroyed. In Eszterháza, Haydn lived in a four-room apartment (an ampler living situation than any other court musician) in a substantial two-storey complex of dwellings west of the theater – completed in 1768 (the same year as the theater), but altered and expanded many times over the years. Almost all the servants and officers of the court lived together in this giant dormitory, with a nearby inn, also built by the Esterházy family, providing a good deal of their social life and recreation.

Haydn's City To the extent that Haydn ever expressed his feelings about the contrast between places – or even a sense of spatial dislocation – it concerned the relationship between the court and the city. Late in life, Haydn described to his earliest biographers his growing feeling of isolation as the court spent more and more time in Eszterháza: "I was cut off from the world," he told Griesinger. Haydn surely played up his earlier loneliness at a time when his international reputation was a given, and when Romantic tropes of the isolated artist were increasingly in vogue. Still, at the start of the 1780s, when Haydn began to feel the pull of Vienna more strongly, he already explained to Artaria, who had recently expanded into music publishing, that "my misfortune is that I live in the country." By the end of the decade, Haydn openly complained to friends in Vienna that he was regularly forced to return to his "wasteland," with its lack of social stimulation and terrible food. The ever-present spatial logic of imperial center and margin was frequently confusing to foreign visitors, especially those from London – a city now perpetually reorganized by the more variegated hierarchies of the market. When Gaetano Bartolozzi dropped by in 1786 or 1787, as part of a many-pronged effort to persuade Haydn to come to London, he exaggeratedly reported to the *Gazetteer* that the great musician lived "in a miserable apartment in the barracks" in a condition "unworthy of his Genius." The metropolitan whirl, in which Haydn had earned quite a reputation, was now conceivable – by some, at least – as the very opposite of the magnificent court centers within which Haydn spent his working days.

Though Haydn was widely recognized and respected in Vienna, until the late 1790s he existed at one remove from the imperial capital and the Habsburg court. His many operas were by and large not taken up by the court theater, and his connections with other Vienna-based institutions tended to be loose and ad hoc. When Haydn did connect with them, however, he tended also to access a wider world, mostly separate from Esterházy Court Networks. Having produced a setting of the *Stabat mater* for the traditional Good Friday service at Eisenstadt in 1767, Haydn arranged, in subsequent years, for performances in the church of the Barmherzige Brüder in Leopoldstadt and Vienna's Piaristenkirche. From here, the piece made its way into the busier concert scenes of Paris and London, as well as the church services of Catholic southern Europe: traveling in the slip-stream of Pergolesi's well-known setting of the text, Haydn's *Stabat* turned out to be one of the most widely circulated works of his lifetime.

To Haydn, then, the city was where his music was set in motion in wholly new ways, making its way from place to place in the increasingly busy thoroughfares of the music export market. The main infrastructural condition of this motion was a generation of music publishers based in Vienna and other European cities: London music sellers such as William Forster, Viennese ones such as Artaria, and Parisians such as Sieber, and the web of transnational exchanges between them, like those legally enshrined between Bland and Hoffmeister, and Longman & Broderip and Artaria. To the extent that Haydn himself encountered urban venues for music-making in Vienna, they were most frequently to be the parlors of city dwellers of the middling sort. In the 1780s, Haydn was often a guest of Peter von Genzinger (surgeon to Prince Esterházy) and his music-loving wife Maria Anna, who became an intimate friend. The genres that Haydn cultivated for publication in this decade, such as the keyboard sonata, the solo song, and the string quartet, were designed for non-aristocratic houses like these, all across Europe. As such, the intimate domestic places for which so much published music in the 1780s and 1790s was destined put Haydn in touch with a network of consumers in a way that the traditional court hubs of Eszterháza and Eisenstadt did not. (See SOCIABILITY; AMATEURS.)

Via the diffuse and distance-traversing mechanisms of import and export, the shape of even distant places could be imprinted on Haydn's music. By the early 1780s, many places in Paris had become crucial to Haydn's musical output, even though he was never to visit the city himself. Haydn's symphonies had achieved an unassailable position in the Concert Spirituel, and were the most frequently recurring items on its twenty or more annual performances in the 1780s, presented by an orchestra of several dozen players in the ornate Salle des Cent Suisses, and, from 1784, frequently in the cavernous Salle des Machines, both in the Tuileries palace. It is probable that one of these spaces witnessed the first performances of Haydn's so-called "Paris" Symphonies in 1786 or 1787. Haydn's older music underwent comparable transformations in London. The concert series organized by Johann Christian Bach and Carl Friedrich Abel had introduced several of Haydn's symphonies to English audiences by the early 1780s; indeed, Symphony No. 53 in D major was so closely associated with its London hosts that it became known as the "Festino," after the Festino Rooms in Hanover Square, where the concerts were held. Once the Bach-Abel concerts were dissolved in 1782, the various series of the later 1780s continued to be dominated by works by Haydn, not only the symphonies but also string quartets, such as the Op. 55 and Op. 64 sets – one-time parlor music, which was now projected, by virtuosos such as Johann Peter Salomon, into the teeming public spaces of the urban beau monde. Around this time, persistent rumors of Haydn's imminent arrival on London's concert scene began to spread. Once he did show up in London, however, Haydn was only catching up with the unceasing journeys of his own music.

The first of Haydn's trips to London, accompanied by Salomon, was the longest he had undertaken ever since his journey to Lukawitz back in the 1750s.

Setting out in mid-December 1790, Haydn took ten days to travel from Vienna to Munich, from Munich to the Wallerstein palace in the Swabian countryside, from Wallerstein to Salomon's birthplace of Bonn, from Bonn to Calais, from Calais to Dover (Haydn's first sea voyage), and from Dover to London. When Haydn arrived in London, on January 2, 1791, he stayed, appropriately enough, at the Holborn warehouse of the music seller John Bland, who had made the composer's acquaintance in Eszterháza, where Bland had traveled in 1789, on an expedition to purchase music by famous Continental musicians to publish in London. Haydn's experience of London was to be mediated in large part by these places of lively commercial exchange – places that gave a palpable sense, not only of London but of an interconnected world beyond it, a virtual world made from the relentless activity of communications and commodities. As Thomas Busby put it, the many music sellers of London provided "an open table at which professors and amateurs, from every part of the world, had the opportunity of meeting, and of eliciting from each other information of mutual and considerable advantage" (127). Haydn was frequently at this table – whether in the glamorous shop spaces of Longman & Broderip or in the small working studio he was provided in John Broadwood's instrument workshop on Great Pulteney Street, on the same street as the apartments where he eventually found a more permanent home.

London in the 1790s had a population of around a million people, and was nearly ten times the dimensions of Vienna. Haydn would surely have been struck by the city's density. An early letter to Maria Anna von Genzinger described the "endlessly huge city" whose "various beauties and marvels quite astonished me." In this vibrant urban marketplace, Haydn was alarmed by the "noise that the common people make as they sell their wares in the street," which, he noted, was "intolerable." The racket made by street criers was something of a point of pride among Londoners, celebrated in the pages of *The Spectator*, in some of the best-known prints by William Hogarth, in paintings by Francis Wheatley shown in the Royal Academy between 1792 and 1795, and on the London stage. The socialite Charlotte Papendieck later recalled in her journals (published in the mid-nineteenth century as *Court and Private Life in the Time of Queen Charlotte*) that Haydn opened the 1791 season of concerts with a movement that "was to imitate the London cries." This was surely an erroneous memory, yet it attests to the ways in which Londoners were inclined to experience Haydn's music as an elevated echo of their distinctive urban landscape.

More important even than London's extreme density, however, was what one might call its psycho-geographical layout. The middle of Vienna was, as Charles Burney had observed, with a certain English liberal disapproval, made up of palaces cheek by jowl – an imposing imperial center with a hierarchy of concentric layers surrounding it. London, by contrast, presented a less centralized and much more variegated civic landscape. Its physical expansion continued haphazardly to the north and west as its immense wealth increased, and its existing concentrations of grand residences and well-appointed homes provided evidence of an ever-growing class of rich entrepreneurs and well-to-do professionals, living alongside and among the landed gentlemen of England. Partly because of its tangled physical and social structure, London, more than any other European capital, made sense of itself – represented itself to itself – through print. Haydn reported in a letter to Maria Anna von Genzinger that his introduction to London consisted of going the "round of all the newspapers for three successive days." As Wiebke Thormählen shows in her entry, Haydn's perception of London was constantly mediated by newspapers and magazines, of which there were many more, embracing a wider range of opinion, than in Vienna.

The musical institutions hosted by this most modern of cities did more than echo its notorious street-level commotion, however. In fact, the places of greatest importance to Haydn's music during his visits of the early 1790s did not necessarily foster noisiness or mass proximity at all, as much as exclusive forms of musical attention and focus, and sometimes the sort of repose frequently sought out by busy urbanites. The concert series organized by Salomon – for which Haydn composed, among other smaller items, twelve new symphonies, which he directed from the keyboard – took place in the so-called Festino or Assembly Rooms at Hanover Square. This room, which had been purpose-designed as a venue for music and dancing in the 1770s, was around eighty feet in length with high vaulted ceilings, its windows decorated with translucent paintings by Thomas Gainsborough. In this splendid space, Haydn's new symphonies reached out in newly explicit ways to a discriminating audience who had purchased expensive tickets, and had a great many competing musical entertainments to choose from – especially once the Professional Concert began a rival series in the same space in 1792. Several of Haydn's "London" Symphonies would rapidly acquire nicknames that parsed their most novel and memorable moments, such as the "Military" (No. 100) and the "Surprise" (No. 94). That these names stuck was not only a consequence of Haydn's urgent musical appeals to audience attention in Hanover Square, but also a wider metropolitan culture of conversation and published criticism that converged upon such places. The String Quartets, Opp. 71 and 74, which were composed in the knowledge that they would be performed by Salomon and his colleagues in the Festino Rooms, just as the Op. 64 quartets had been, also seem to respond in noticeable ways to the particular dimensions and ambience of their new environment, not least in the new preponderance of theatrical slow introductions.

Salomon's concerts ran out of money in 1794, so the last of Haydn's "London" Symphonies was presented in the context of a new series, the Opera Concerts led by the violinist Giovanni Viotti, which took place in the concert room at the King's Theatre in the Haymarket. Haydn had one of the most lucrative musical evenings of his career here (see ECONOMICS AND FINANCES). He had already been paid handsomely by the King's Theatre for a new opera, *L'anima del filosofo*, which – because of institutional intrigues or perhaps political sensitivities about its treatment of the Orpheus theme – never reached the stage. Partly because of this, the King's Theatre could be counted among the London institutions that helped to promote Haydn as a symphonist above all else.

Far from the city's hubbub – yet in many respects distinctively urban in the way that it packaged a form of escapism that Elaine Sisman (in her entry on NATURE) calls "pastoral fantasia" – London's pleasure gardens were among the city's major musical venues during this period. Haydn visited the largest,

Vauxhall Gardens, on the south bank of the river Thames, at least once (in 1792) when he noted down his impressions of the music and musicians there (see Correspondence and Notebooks). The band who performed at the park's glamorous Rotunda had a great deal of Haydn's music in their repertoire, if the handful of surviving set-lists from this period are any guide. Surrounded by all the other distractions – sports and games, dancing, drinking and eating, and wandering the leafy paths in search of solitude or amorous encounters – the Rotunda performances promoted a decidedly more unfocused form of musical reception than Hanover Square or the King's Theatre.

In Vauxhall, Haydn had the opportunity to pay his respects to the statue of Handel by Roubiliac. The Monumentalizing aesthetic of late eighteenth-century Handel performance, and the prominent place of this music in English public life altogether, was crucial to Haydn's subsequent musical direction. Handel was cultivated with particular conviction in a couple of London locations that Haydn visited while in London. The refurbished New Rooms by the Tottenham Court Road housed the Concerts of Antient Music (in many respects, a court-sponsored vehicle of Handel veneration) until 1795. And the same body supported the Handel Commemorations in Westminster Abbey, which had been held annually since 1784, focusing for the most part on the chorus-driven English oratorios. In the last week of May 1791, Haydn almost certainly witnessed the Handel festival himself, and thus would have experienced, in the Gothic nave of the most important Royal Peculiar church in England, hundreds of singers and instrumentalists delivering a potent blend of national ritual and musical revival.

Many other scenes of musical activity that Haydn encountered during his London sojourn were small in scale. These included the clubs and Musical Societies that hosted Haydn as an honored guest, such as the Anacreontic Society, who met every week to make merry and hear music in the Crown and Anchor tavern on the Strand. And the everyday rhythm of Haydn's musical life in London was, perhaps above all, established by amateur performance in genteel domestic settings – the sort of thing that he was only beginning to experience with any regularity in Vienna, but which became the foundation of so much nineteenth-century musical culture. For Haydn, this meant parties at the home of Rebecca Schroeter (the widow who became his lover, and to whom he dedicated the Keyboard Trios Hob.XV:24–26), evenings of music and conversation with the accomplished Burney family and their circle, and musical evenings with the poet Anne Hunter, the equally celebrated wife of the celebrated surgeon John Hunter; it was Anne who provided most of the texts for Haydn's twelve Original Canzonettas – beautifully crafted and easily consumable songs, which were aimed at precisely this fashionable urban set.

Haydn's World As Martin Eybl observes in his entry on Vienna, Haydn's return to the imperial capital in 1795 – first to apartments in the Neue Markt and subsequently to a house he had purchased in Gumpendorf between his London trips – began a period when his focus was at once more Viennese than it had ever been, and more cosmopolitan. While the Bergkirche and the court chapel in Eisenstadt may have been the primary destinations for most of Haydn's late masses, these monumental and frequently experimental works nonetheless gestured to a European landscape far beyond the court, especially given the new wartime conditions. This is no clearer than in the *Missa in tempore belli* (*Mass in Time of War*), with its ominous "Agnus Dei" and charged "Dona nobis pacem," premiered in the Piaristenkirche on St. Stephen's Day 1796 during a period of popular mobilizations against the French (see McGrann).

In a time of perceived national peril, Austrian administrators now sought to harness the cosmopolitanism of Haydn's music to create cohesion across its historically disparate domains. Thus, the premiere of Haydn's song of dynastic loyalty "Gott erhalte Franz den Kaiser" took place on the emperor's birthday in 1797 in the Burgtheater – but also, at the same time, in theaters and other performance spaces across Vienna and its suburbs, and in Hungary and northern Italy. This was a remarkable bureaucratic feat, which aimed to create a sense of geographically dispersed simultaneity through Haydn's music. And the medium of print meant that the song could insinuate itself into middle-class parlors in keyboard reductions and other arrangements, including the variation movement of the String Quartet Op. 76, No. 3.

This enterprise doubtless made the near global ambitions of Haydn's *Creation* thinkable. The earliest performances of this oratorio, in the Palais Schwarzenberg in 1798 and 1799, were in many respects quintessentially Viennese and inward-looking. Yet the long-awaited and wildly successful Burgtheater performance on March 19, 1799 was reported by the European press as a major event in the world history of music. Haydn's oratorio, with the dimly Handelian lineage of its libretto (adapted from the English source by Baron Gottfried van Swieten) and its monumental London-derived aesthetic, was already transnational in conception, and it was accordingly published by Haydn in 1800 with both English and German texts. But the performances that followed the Vienna premieres reveal a still more radical geographical reach: performances in London by the Covent Garden Oratorio, and then in the King's Theatre, in 1800; a premiere in the Théâtre des arts in Paris and in Buda castle in the same year; and only a year later, a performance in St. Petersburg. By the end of 1815, there had been at least two performances of *The Creation* in North America – one by Moravians in Bethlehem, Pennsylvania and another by the Boston Handel and Haydn Society in the year of its foundation. To be sure, this kind of musical cosmopolitanism had been a feature of a few earlier works, not least *The Seven Last Words*. Sarah Day-O'Connell and Bertil van Boer remind us in their entry on the AMERICAS that this work, written for Spain, was commissioned by a Mexican-born churchman who claimed to be drawing on Peruvian liturgical traditions: it is an example, they argue, of the new colonial networks' ideological, if not physical, proximity. Still, by the time of *The Creation*, Haydn's music was engaged in travel of unprecedented scope, which helped to create a sense of the world – a world mapped out by music.

"My language is understood all over the world," Haydn supposedly retorted to Mozart when his younger colleague questioned whether the old man knew enough languages to undertake the journey to London. This kind of universalizing rhetoric was an important part of the self-image of the enlightened cosmopolitan gentleman. But Haydn was doubtless responding to a growing perception of the huge geographical reach of his music. By 1820, Haydn's music could be heard from Rio de Janeiro to Calcutta – a musical witness to the radical spatial upheavals and dislocations that characterized nineteenth-century modernity.

NICHOLAS MATHEW

FURTHER READING

Agnew (2008); Born (2013); Brown (1995); Busby (1825); Chandler and Gilmartin (2005); Chesser and Jones (2013); Clark (2009a); Diergarten (2011); Elias (2006); Eybl (2008); Feder (1970); Gericke (1960); Heartz (1995, 2009); Herter Norton (1932); Hiles (2009); Horányi (1962); Kassler (2011); Malina (2016b); McGrann (1998); McVeigh (1993); Morrow (1989); Pratl (2013); Rice (2003); Sanguinetti (2012); Schama (1995); Shesgreen (2002); Sisman (2005); Taylor (2010); Tolley (1992, 2001); White (2012); Williams (1973); Winkler (2006); Woodfield (1994, 2002).

Poets What drew Haydn to Johann Nikolaus Götz and Christian Friedrich Weisse but not Goethe and Schiller? Given that no literary canon then existed, it perhaps is more useful to inquire if Haydn turned to the poets he did because he, his friends, and his patrons in VIENNA and LONDON admired them. This is not to suggest limited literary discernment, but merely to acknowledge that the eighteenth century esteemed *Geselligkeit* – SOCIABILITY – and that verse and song reflected broad cultural values. Sociability readily meshed with other ambitions, as Haydn demonstrated in his first lieder collection (1781) when he resolved to best Leopold Hofmann by setting three poems the latter had composed "miserably" the year before. *Geselligkeit* certainly helps explain the attention Haydn accorded the poetry of Anne Hunter, wife of the prominent London surgeon John Hunter (whose patients included George III) and that resulted in an entire volume of musical settings, the 1794 *Six Original Canzonettas*. A similarly entitled publication the following year contains an additional Hunter poem, John Hoole's "Sympathy" (after Metastasio), "She Never Told her Love" from Shakespeare's *Twelfth Night*, and three others by unidentified poets. (On Hunter's biography, see Grigson 2009 and 2013.)

Sociability and its ally sympathy – linked as they are to EMPFINDSAMKEIT or sensibility – provide a fuller explanation for why Haydn set the poets he did. Scottish philosopher Adam Smith, in his widely read *Theory of Moral Sentiments* (a copy of which Haydn owned), defined sympathy as "the greatest pleasure of society," "a certain harmony of minds, which like so many musical instruments coincide and keep time with one another" (428). Haydn plumbed sympathy's pleasures when he based the second movement of Symphony No. 73 in D major ("La chasse," 1782) on his "Gegenliebe" (Mutual Love), part II No. 4 of his *Lieder für das Clavier* (composed 1781; published 1784). Using the hunting overture to his opera *La fedeltà premiata* (Fidelity Rewarded, 1781) as the symphony's finale, the presence of Gottfried August Bürger's poem at the heart of these works likely highlights an intertextual interrelationship. True to its title, "Gegenliebe" yearns for a future where the beloved "might meet my greeting halfway," a subject informing Haydn's opera as well, where only at the last moment are three pairs of lovers able to join in mutual love.

While Haydn's poets address a wealth of subjects – courtship, death, despair, flirtation, love (faithful and fickle), pastoralism, the sea, supernaturalism – Bürger helps locate common ground when he reserves his highest praise for poetry that imparts "a living breath that blows over the hearts ... of all humankind" (448). Whether in poetry read aloud or set to music, that breath arises from an animate, breathing human; it is aimed at another, whose heart – as sensibility theorists insisted – is a vibrating mechanism set in motion by sound. That is, physical sensation leads to the center of feelings: the heart. In Haydn's songs, imbued as they are by sensibility's heightened sounds, that breath also reaches the ear. As Johann Gottfried Herder put it, "sound seems to impart living reality to what we see ... that the *human voice and language* is the principal source of human sympathy" (249). In "The Wanderer," Haydn engages with Hunter's text paradoxically, linking while differentiating the two strophes' parallel yet textually antithetical climatic moments, dressing the words "add sound" in the first with a predominately two-line texture and "there's nothing for hopes" in the second with a three-line texture. Musical intensification likewise is at work in Haydn's setting of another Hunter poem, widely regarded during her day as her most celebrated, "O Tuneful Voice." Here the text recounts two separated lovers, a leave-taking made poignant by the protagonist's memory of the beloved's words, which, "tho' heard no more, still vibrate on my heart." Whereas up to this point the keyboard has contributed lively light-textured triplets in a single-voice alternation between left and right hands, the triplets thicken at the word "vibrate" to five-note chords in both hands, followed by a swift resumption of the lighter texture after two intensely emotional "vibrating" measures.

Given the range of Haydn's poets it is not surprising that the secondary literature is slim (though see Parsons and Glauert). As (A. Peter) Brown (2002) incisively puts it, another reason is that Haydn's songs were for many years "damned for their texts, which were regarded as unworthy of a composer" possessing his abilities, a judgment Brown persuasively refutes (77). One example is "Lob der Faulheit" wherein Brown argues that Gotthold Lessing's satirical poem inspired the composer to retain "the utter simplicity" of the eighteenth-century lied while dispensing with many of its conventions. Haydn's literary acumen is not so quickly granted by (Marshall) Brown, who provocatively inquires if there is "continuity between his songs and his greater accomplishments?" (2007, 232). One answer comes into view "by taking seriously" the "many tactics of avoidance" of ENLIGHTENMENT poetry in which one often finds a "furtive quality intentionally covered by the playful or placid sentiments of ... Anacreontic and sentimental" verse that "fascinate through what they conceal" (238). What it lacks in quantity, scholarship on Haydn and poetry makes up for in quality, drawing as it does on a variety of interdisciplinary-thinking approaches. Day-O'Connell asks the seemingly simple question "what canzonettas (both the genre at large and Haydn's contributions in particular) meant for contemporary creators, performers and audiences" (79). Seeking answers, she explores a variety of issues including anatomy, the border between life and death, femininity (GENDER), the female body, and the dynamics of Anne and John Hunter's marriage. The question however is not simple and so allows for no easy pronouncements. Pondering whether Anne pursued the themes she did guided by "inherited conventions deployed reflexively" or purposefully "to expand her scope" to the masculine public sphere, Day-O'Connell sagely responds "somewhere in between" (109). Interdisciplinary thinking also guides November's examination of the aesthetics of MELANCHOLY in the canzonettas and their probing of "concerns about the nature of emotions and interpersonal communication" (42). Haydn's musical response, she writes, reveals "his understanding and assimilation of contemporary ideas of melancholy" and also his "original development" of those ideas (49). JAMES PARSONS

FURTHER READING
Brown (1980, 2002, 2007); Bürger (1776); Day-O'Connell (2009a); Glauert (2004); Grigson (2009, 2013); Herder (1784); November (2008); Parsons (2004a, 2004b); Smith (1761 [1759]).

Politics Haydn lived through the Atlantic revolutions that fundamentally transformed politics across EUROPE and the AMERICAS, ushering in a new era in which political participation extended beyond a narrow elite and universal rights were argued and fought for. For most of his career, however, Haydn was insulated from these events through his position as Kapellmeister to the Esterházy princes, a leading Hungarian noble family who owed their allegiance to the Habsburg monarchy. Under the terms of the contract he signed on May 1, 1761, his compositions were for the exclusive use of the COURT. While this clause was dropped when the contract was revised in 1779, allowing Haydn to sell his work to PUBLISHERS and accept outside commissions, he remained a liveried court composer, largely confined within the rural isolation of ESZTERHÁZA until his two extended visits to LONDON in the 1790s. During his later years in London and Vienna, he continued to be an Esterházy employee but in effect enjoyed a large degree of independence.

Reflecting this history, the received political image of Haydn is of a conservative figure, a product of court patronage and servant of the *ancien régime*. In his 1776 autobiographical sketch, Haydn wrote "my sole wish is to offend neither my neighbor, nor my gracious Prince, nor above all our merciful God" (Landon II 399), although there is evidence of increasing dissatisfaction with the conditions of his employment from the 1780s. The view of Haydn as a politically conservative figure has been further entrenched by the patriarchal position he occupies within the classical canon, and particularly in relation to Mozart and Beethoven. Recent scholarship, however, points towards a much more complex relationship between the contexts and reception of Haydn's music and contemporary politics, from the rational, universal, COSMOPOLITAN ideals of the ENLIGHTENMENT to the ideological and military conflict that dominated European politics from the 1790s. As Mathew argues, in this period political appropriation represents the flipside – or perhaps the precondition – of emerging ideas of aesthetic autonomy.

Haydn famously declared that "my language is understood throughout the whole world" and the perceived ability of his music to transcend national and linguistic differences was an important part of his appeal for Enlightenment thinkers. As such, he could be seen as a member of the republic of letters, even a citizen of the world. The political significance of the world citizen shifted dramatically over Haydn's career, as the cosmopolite became increasingly linked, or tainted, with revolutionary politics. In these years, and in the wake of events in America and France, revolution began to acquire its modern meaning: no longer a return to an earlier political state, it began to signify instead a definitive break with the past and beginning of democratic modernity (see WAR).

Within this new concept of revolution, Haydn's ordinary background, as the son of a wheelwright and deputy mayor of Rohrau, a small village on the Austro-Hungarian border, made him a plausible representative of the post-revolutionary career open to talents. Although his success was established through the patronage of the Esterházys and owed nothing to any political revolution, he was celebrated as an example of phenomenal success without the advantages of rank and privilege. While one familiar image of Haydn is of a composer lionized by European elites, he told his biographer, "I have been in the company of emperors, kings and many great gentlemen, and I received many a compliment from them: but I do not wish to live on terms of intimacy with such persons and prefer to be with people of my class" (Landon III 23). The frequent inclusion of folk (FOLK SONGS) idioms within the popular style of Haydn's later symphonies, and above all in *The Seasons*, is one expression of this cultural and class identity.

Haydn's contemporaries were acutely sensitive to the political valence of particular musical FORMS and categories of AESTHETICS. This is especially true of his time in London, when events across the Channel colored all aspects of cultural life. When the Symphony No. 100, the "Grand Overture with the Militaire Movement," was first performed in 1794, reviewers focused on its purported SUBLIMITY, which they immediately connected to the war between the French Republic and the First Coalition, including both Britain and Austria. To the writer in the *Morning Chronicle*, the bursts of percussion and trumpet fanfare of the slow movement evoked "the advancing to battle; and the march of the men, the sounding of the charge, the thundering of the onset, the clash of arms, the groans of the wounded," as "the hellish roar of war" reached "a climax of horrid sublimity" (April 9). By "calling up all the ideas of the terror of such a scene," "discordant sounds" became "sublime" (May 5). In Edmund Burke's *Philosophical Enquiry into the Origin of our Ideas of the Sublime and Beautiful* (1757), the sublime describes natural or aesthetic experiences that are vast, obscure and overpowering. By the 1790s, such features were also politically coded as Burke and other writers used the language of the sublime to warn of the dangers of revolution. Haydn's integration of moments of sublimity within conventional symphonic form was welcomed by these commentators as serving NATIONALISTIC ends: a further stage in the anglicization of Haydn, which, as Jones shows, took place in the context of Austria's military alliance with Britain. Opera was always less stable, and consistently understood as a political medium capable of performing cultural work. *L'anima del filosofo*, based on the Orpheus myth, could not be performed at the King's Theatre due to its portrayal of mob violence, despite its "fundamentally conservative" view of revolution (Clark 121).

To understand the full range of political meanings Haydn's music held for his contemporaries we need to read against the grain of established narratives, both of European history and of Haydn's career. Haydn's visits to London were enthusiastically welcomed not only by an aristocratic elite and a burgeoning COMMERCIAL class but also by London's dissenting intelligentsia. To the latter group, Haydn's music held a new set of political meanings: the playwright, atheist, and radical reformer Thomas Holcroft published a poem celebrating Haydn's symphonies as the musical representation of "fitness, system, sense, and truth," and the "endless harmony" of a rational universe (*Morning Chronicle*, September 12, 1794). Holcroft met Haydn, provided lyrics for the second set of English Canzonettas (1795) – including, as Grigson shows, the sensual "Transport of Pleasure," an adaptation of "Der verdienstvolle Sylvius" (Hob.XXVIa:36bis) – and played chamber arrangements of the "London" Symphonies alongside Johann Peter Salomon (the impresario who brought Haydn to Britain). For him, the order, clarity and wit of Haydn's music, and the idea it conveyed of music as a philosophical system, upheld Enlightenment ideals in counter-revolutionary times. Haydn's "extraordinary achievement" in the late symphonies is to "devise procedures for instrumental music that would allow it an intelligibility previously thought possible only if words were present" (Schroeder). Intelligibility and radical ideas come together at the beginning of *The Creation*, where the creation of light is also, as Tolley observes, "the light of a new order, propounding freedom and justice ... the light Paine used as a metaphor for truth in the *Rights of Man*" (284). By contrast, many of Haydn's most popular and lucrative compositions in his final years were overtly nationalist in character. These ranged from settings of Scottish, Welsh and Irish melodies and "national airs" written for the Edinburgh publisher George Thomson, to a series of martial songs and patriotic odes, including, most famously, "Gott erhalte Franz den Kaiser." This national song, or "Volksleid," was commissioned in emulation of the British "God save the King" in 1796–97, when Austria was threatened by French invasion; its melody is still sung today as the German national anthem. By the mid-1790s, Haydn's music could be claimed by both the politics of nationalism and the utopian project of the radical Enlightenment. JAMES GRANDE

FURTHER READING
Morning Chronicle, April 8, 1794, p. 3; May 5, 1794, p. 3; September 12, 1794; Botstein (1997); Burke (1757); Clark (2012b); Grigson (2013); Jones (2013); Landon II–III; Mathew (2007); Schroeder (1990); Tolley (2001).

Popular Culture – see Reception 1950s–Present

Portraits – see Iconography

Press The eighteenth century witnessed an explosion of periodical publications in EUROPE and in the AMERICAS – both newspapers and literary or scholarly journals devoted to various subjects, though journals devoted solely to music (mostly found in Germany) were rare and short-lived (see Figures 23 and 24). Not until the founding of the *Allgemeine musikalische Zeitung* in 1798 did northern Europe have a stable, long-lasting musical periodical. While only music periodicals routinely provided detailed discussions of music, non-music journals and newspapers covered it in the form of advertisements for printed music,

Figure 23 Almanach Musical (1775–83), vol. 7 (1782). Frontispiece. Paris: Au Bureau de L'Abonnement Littéraire, 1782. https://hdl.handle.net/2027/mdp.39015027690703

notices of upcoming concerts (often with programs) or operas, as well as reviews of those prints and performances. PUBLISHERS' notices and announcements of musical performances were most often found in newspapers (usually issued three or four times a week) like the *Wiener Zeitung*, *Hamburgische Correspondent*, *Gazzetta di Bologna*, *Morning Chronicle* (LONDON), or the *Mercure de France*. Some of these newspapers also offered performance and brief publication reviews. In addition, discussion of operas occasionally appeared in THEATER journals, and general scholarly publications (like the *Allgemeine deutsche Bibliothek*) sometimes included detailed reviews of published music alongside their book reviews. Haydn received little attention from the Austrian press (mostly because of its weak tradition of journalism) and enjoyed some coverage in Italy and North America. However, it was the press coverage in Germany, France, and Britain that established his Continental reputation (see RECEPTION).

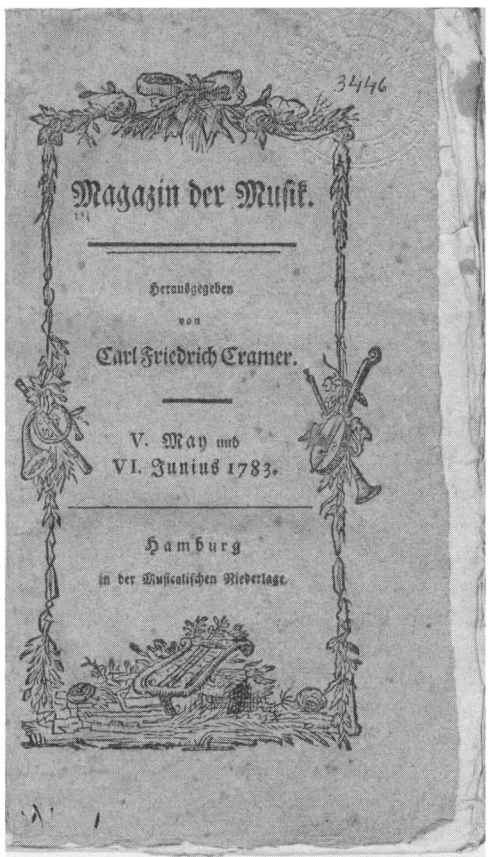

Figure 24 *Magazin der Musik*, vol. 1 (1783), Frontispiece. Hildesheim: Georg Olms Verlag, 1971. Image courtesy of The Irving S. Gilmore Music Library of Yale University.

In the German press, despite the occasional deprecating remark about his parallel fifths or distant modulations that disturbed the "unity of tonality," Haydn's music received almost universal approbation. The singularity of his style was noted as early as 1770 in a review in the *Wöchentliche Nachrichten* that questioned – correctly – whether all of the symphonies appearing under his name in a Parisian print were actually his, as they showed no sign of his "singular and original style." By the 1780s reviewers commonly referred to him as an "inexhaustible genius," the one who set the standards by which other composers were judged. For example, a 1783 review in the *Magazin der Musik* of keyboard sonatas by H. O. C. Zinck praised a rondo that was so full of drollery and wit that even Haydn would have been proud to have written it. One review in the *Musikalische Realzeitung* of keyboard trios from 1789 noted that Haydn's "original style," his BEAUTIFUL modulations and richness of ideas were so well known that "we don't need to say anything more to recommend these pieces." Again and again, Haydn's music was described as SUBLIME, rich in variety and originality (GENIUS), shot through with wit and HUMOR, replete with surprising modulations and skillfully worked-out MELODIES, and – especially – robust and masculine (see GENDER).

Though Haydn's vocal music never received the same attention in the press as his instrumental works, it was not ignored or undervalued. The general German prejudice against tone painting meant that he would be (and was) taken to task for illustrating things like "the quaking of frogs" in The Seasons, but that mostly academic debate did not deter audiences and critics from hailing his oratorios as masterpieces. His operas received less attention because they were not often performed outside ESZTERHÁZA. In 1805 the Berlinische musikalische Zeitung reviewed a Hamburg performance of Orlando paladino, and while the reviewer agreed with what he termed the "best critics," that Haydn's genius was less suited to vocal music, and while he found the opera's forms to be outmoded, he concluded that – as one would expect from Haydn – there was still a lot of excellent music in it. An 1805 review in the Neue allgemeine deutsche Bibliothek of a collection of Haydn's airs and chansons observed that they proved Haydn was also a master of vocal music.

In French periodicals, Haydn's name (usually spelled "Hayden" until late in the century) first appears in lists of recently published music in the late 1760s and in concert reviews (mostly of the Concert Spirituel) beginning in the 1770s. Most of the works on the programs were symphonies, though his Stabat mater was also performed and well received. One review in the Mercure de France from May of 1779 reported that the first two movements of a symphony were applauded (the second being in imitation of the ancient French style), but the third was received less well because of the incoherence of its ideas. In September of the same year a reviewer specified the reasons for Haydn's success: "his ideas are noble & passionate, always graceful, always varied, and the genius of the composer seems to be in fact inexhaustible; ... each [of his compositions] has its own distinct character." And while the Germans may have disdained any type of tone painting, the French liked music that conjured up images, a preference that Johnson has identified in the early nineteenth-century Parisian reception of Haydn.

Late eighteenth-century London had a lively daily press, and newspapers like the Morning Chronicle and the Morning Herald regularly ran announcements of new music publications and upcoming concerts and also published regular reviews of performances. Since the reviews from Haydn's two London trips are reproduced in Landon III, summarized here are the characteristics that so delighted his audiences: grandeur, variety and richness of ideas, sublimity, genius, and originality occurred most frequently, but there are also references to beauty and charm, wit, caprice and whimsy, surprise, expressiveness and profundity, imaginative HARMONY, imagination, taste, and his ability to take a simple idea and extend it "to a vast complication." Though most of the reviews address Haydn's instrumental works, the Morning Chronicle observed in 1791 that his newly published Scottish FOLK SONGS "will be a striking and lasting proof of how little the merit of Haydn was confined to inventing, or conquering instrumental difficulties."

There are few references in the Italian press to Haydn, in part because of Italy's preoccupation with opera. The Gazzetta Toscana reported in 1787 that

Haydn's *Stabat mater* was performed in Florence, and a private concert in Padua in the 1790s offered the "best symphonies" of Haydn and Pleyel. Haydn compositions occasionally turn up in the infrequent lists of music for sale, but his works do not appear to have had much of an impact on Italian musical life – at least not one that was reported in the press – until after his death. That was not the case in North America, where Haydn's name turns up not infrequently in the newspapers of the major northeastern cities. A concert reviewer in New York's *Daily Advertiser* in 1786 observed that the Haydn symphony on the program combined "harmony and melody ... with the happiest effect." Though programs and reviews rarely specified which work was performed, an 1802 concert announcement in the *New-York Evening Post* lets us know that the evening would conclude with "the celebrated Farewell Overture by Haydn, in which the performers take their leave of the audience." Haydn's music would no doubt have been appreciated and celebrated even without publicity, but the press played no small role in creating his celebrity status throughout Europe and the Americas.

MARY SUE MORROW

FURTHER READING
Johnson (1991); Landon III; McVeigh (1993); Morrow (1997, 2004).

Printing – see Publishers and Publishing

Professionals – see Composers and Musical

Programmatic Elements Attributed to Franz Liszt, the term "program music" refers to instrumental music in which the compositional or structural logic is dictated by extra-musical principles; these are usually explicated in a title, preface, or explanatory note. While often associated with later nineteenth-century genres such as the symphonic poem, the term also applies to earlier music. Haydn, who told his biographer Griesinger that he often portrayed "moral characters" (*moralische Charaktere*) in his symphonies (117), wrote several works that may be considered programmatic in the narrow sense, and many more whose effect is greatly enhanced by knowledge of their extra-musical references.

The three "Times of Day" Symphonies (nos. 6, 7, and 8, c. 1761), Haydn's first symphonic offerings as Vice-Kapellmeister at the Esterházy COURT, are "characteristic" works belonging to a long tradition of pastoral music that included Vivaldi's *The Four Seasons* (see NATURE; TIME). While their representation of the pastoral mode relies on TOPICAL and ORCHESTRATIONAL conventions, these works also include referential cues that suggest a programmatic design: No. 6 in D major, "Le matin," opens by depicting a sunrise; No. 7 in C major, "Le midi," includes an evocative instrumental recitative for solo violin that has been variously read as implying a domestic quarrel and a private confrontation with death; No. 8 in G major, "Le soir," opens with a movement based on a popular melody from Gluck's *Le diable à quatre* and concludes with a storm ("La Tempesta"), complete with raindrops, lightning strikes, and downpours. As Sisman has argued (2013), such cues go beyond the traditional associations of the pastoral, imparting a sense of extra-musical narrative to the trilogy, even if the details of that narrative remain elusive.

Borrowed tunes with their concomitant associations also figure prominently in other symphonies. Two symphonies conjure RELIGIOUS moods through their use of Austrian liturgical melodies known as the Passionston (No. 49 in F minor) and Lamentationston (No. 26 in D minor). Another quotes a Gregorian Easter "Alleluja" (No. 30 in C major). (See CHURCH.) Quotations of secular melodies such as the French tune "La Roxelane" (No. 63 in C major) and the "Night Watchman's Song" (No. 60 in C major and six other works) must have also been evocative for contemporary listeners. Not quite a borrowed tune, the posthorn signal that opens and closes Symphony No. 31 in D major imbues that work with extra-musical significance, programmatic and TOPICAL.

A more explicitly programmatic work, *The Seven Last Words of Our Savior on the Cross*, commissioned for Good Friday, 1783, consists of seven slow movements, each inspired by one of the last sayings of Christ, and a closing "Terremoto" (Earthquake) in C minor. While the slow movements could potentially stand on their own without the titles, the same cannot be said for the "Terremoto," a movement whose frantic juxtaposition of themes and unpredictable structure (a massively truncated sonata form) demand extra-musical explanation (see also EUROPEAN CONTEXTS – SPAIN; AMERICAS). Equally dependent on its programmatic title is the "Representation of Chaos" that opens *The Creation*; also in C minor, its harmonic instability and abrupt changes of mood strikingly depict an earth "without form and void." As Waldoff notes, Haydn's choice of C minor for both movements results from a contemporary association of this key with "astonishing and unrepeatable events" (169).

Haydn's THEATRICAL music, some of which was repurposed in his symphonies, also relies on extra-musical references for its effect. The most notable example is Symphony No. 60 in C major, the six movements of which originally served as the overture and entr'actes to the comedic play *Il distratto*. Throughout its movements, Haydn ingeniously depicts the play's absent-minded protagonist, Leander, using a variety of unconventional musical techniques that create the impression of absent-mindedness. The first movement conveys this impression through its extension of a subdominant harmony well past the point of its feeling like a subdominant. In the finale, the violin section, having "forgotten" to tune their instruments, must tune their scordatura F up to a G as they perform. Among Haydn's other "theater symphonies" are No. 63 in C major, which opens with the overture to *Il mondo della luna*; No. 73 in D major ("La chasse"), the finale of which first served as the hunting overture to *La fedeltà premiata*; and possibly No. 64 in A major (titled in some sources "Tempora mutantur" ["the times are changed"]), which Sisman (1990) conjectures might have served as incidental music to Shakespeare's *Hamlet*.

Haydn recognized that the suggestion of a program could also be a selling point (see COMMERCE). He did little to interfere with the circulation of unofficial nicknames for his symphonies during his lifetime; many of these, such as "Farewell" (No. 45 in F♯ minor), "La Reine" (No. 85 in B♭ major), "Surprise" (No. 94 in G major, known in German as "mit dem Paukenschlag"), and "Military" (No. 100 in G major) signal musically or contextually relevant aspects of the works to which they are attached. Haydn even approved the inauthentic title "Laudon" (a reference to the celebrated hero Field Marshal

Laudon) for the keyboard arrangement of Symphony No. 69 in C major, noting that it would "contribute more to the sale than [any] ten finales" (Landon II 474). More enigmatic is his offer to compose a "National Symphony" for a Parisian publisher just six weeks after the fall of the Bastille, an offer that never materialized. Haydn also used suggestive titles to highlight fashionable "Exotic" references in his music, as in the "Allegretto alla zingarese" (String Quartet in D major, Op. 20, No. 4), "Rondo all'ungarese" (Keyboard Concerto in D major, Hob.XVIII:11), and "Rondo in the Gipsies' style" (Keyboard Trio in G major, Hob.XV:25).

A riddle concerns Haydn's comment to both Griesinger and Dies that he composed an *Adagio* depicting a conversation between God and an unrepentant sinner. In his old age, the composer could not recall which symphony contained the programmatic movement; possibilities include Nos. 7 ("Le midi"), 22 ("Philosopher"), and 26 ("Lamentatione"). Another ambiguity concerns whether the "Times of Day" in fact concluded with a fourth symphony, "La nuit," since Haydn's tripartite division deviates from conventional visual and literary representations of the subject. (Dies, who attributes the idea for the "Times of Day" to Prince Anton, also speaks of four times of day, but of "quartets.") Zaslaw suggests that Symphony No. 40 in F major is a possibility, based on chronology, key, and topical associations.

Symphony No. 45, the "Farewell," is perhaps Haydn's best-known programmatic work. In the finale, the musicians depart one by one, snuffing out their candles, until only two violinists (Haydn and Tomasini, in the original performance) remain. This unusual ending was calculated to send a message to Prince Nicolaus that his orchestral entourage was eager to return home after an especially long season at Eszterháza. Webster has shown how, while the program is made explicit only in the finale, it is possible to read the entire five-movement symphony as representing the musicians' yearning for home – a reading supported by the symphony's exceptional key (F♯ minor), unorthodox design, and tempestuous character.

Haydn's incorporation of extra-musical content in his symphonies places him in step with such contemporaries as Dittersdorf (whose symphonies on Ovid's *Metamorphoses* he undoubtedly knew) and Paul Wranitzky. His dramatic fusion of extra-musical suggestion, Cyclic Integration, and end-oriented structure was, however, unrivalled in his day, and remained so until Beethoven's symphonies of the early 1800s. MARK FERRAGUTO

FURTHER READING
Bonds (2011); Chew (1974); Griesinger; Landon I–V; Schering (1949 [1939]); Scruton (2015); Sisman (1990, 2013); Waldoff (2012); Webster (1991); Wheelock (1992); Will (1997, 2002); Zaslaw (2012).

Publics – see Audiences and

Publishers and Publishing At the outset of Haydn's career, music was primarily distributed in the form of manuscript copies. When his compositions started gaining popularity in the 1750s, music printing played a marginal role in Austria. Even more advanced cities in Western Europe, including Amsterdam, London, and Paris, had only a handful of publishing houses.

By the early nineteenth century, however, most European cultural centers featured several music publishers who increasingly competed with each other both locally and internationally. Since Haydn's works were among the most merchantable commodities on this flourishing MARKET, he had to learn how to profit in this expanding marketplace.

Haydn has often been criticized for his lack of sincerity in his dealings with publishers, and not without reason. The young composer must have been shocked when he realized that, while he sought to make some money by selling manuscript copies of his early works, publishers in Paris and elsewhere made massive profits on the basis of these copies – arguably without his consent, let alone fair participation. Haydn's position was further complicated by his contract with Prince Paul Anton Esterházy, signed on May 1, 1761, which prohibited the "communication" of the composer's music outside of the court. Consequently, while Haydn's compositions were printed in Paris as early as 1764 (La Chevardière's edition of the Op. 2 Quartets), it took another decade until the first authorized edition of his works appeared (including the six keyboard sonatas Hob.XVI:21–26). Even then, Haydn's sonatas still retained a dedication to Nicolaus I Esterházy. While this edition may in part have indicated the prince's benevolent acceptance of the larger-scale distribution of Haydn's music, the old-fashioned printing technology used by the VIENNESE bookseller Joseph Kurzböck – who used typesetting rather than engraved plates – apparently did not inspire Haydn to have more of his music published.

In the late 1770s, the Viennese art dealer Carlo Artaria started issuing higher-quality engraved music prints of Haydn's music, and soon established a significant, long-term partnership with the composer until the latter's departure for England in 1790. Haydn's attachment to Artaria was no doubt prompted by their geographic proximity, which made the checking of proofs possible – a luxury he had to dispense with in the case of foreign publishers. Haydn nonetheless remained open to establishing contacts with other publishers across the continent. Due to increasing rates of piracy, he began to sell the same work simultaneously to different publishers in different countries, a tactic that allowed him to maximize his own profit while ensuring the relatively high quality of editions outside of Vienna. Furthermore, this practice facilitated his ability to fulfill the numerous requests arriving from publishers in a period when his compositional output lagged far behind international demand for his music – a circumstance compounded by his work related to the long opera (THEATER) seasons at Eszterháza. In one extreme case the composer even sold two keyboard trios (Hob.XV:3 and 4) by his pupil Ignaz Pleyel under his own name, leading to an embarrassing legal battle between two British publishers, Forster and Longman & Broderip (Artaria's London partner). This infamous case was representative of a much larger practice; indeed, although Haydn originally wrote the "Paris" Symphonies for a commission of Le Concert de la Loge Olympique, and accepted a sizeable sum for allowing Imbault to publish the works in Paris, he simultaneously sold the symphonies to Artaria in Vienna and Forster in London. Although such dubious dealings were underhanded, Jens Peter Larsen is arguably right in characterizing the relationship between composer and publisher at the time as "a game without fixed rules" (120). Who benefited from editions published abroad? "No one can blame me for attempting to secure some profit for myself after the pieces have been engraved," wrote Haydn to Artaria on November 27, 1787, "for I am not properly recompensed for my works, and have a greater right to get this profit than the other dealers" (CCLN 73). The composer was even more forthright in a letter written a few months later to Forster, who believed himself the sole proprietor of the quartet version of *The Seven Last Words*, only to find out that the work had also been sold to Artaria. This letter, dated February 28, 1788, states emphatically: "You certainly must realize that whoever wants to have the exclusive rights for six new pieces of mine must pay more than twenty guineas" (CCLN 76).

By the time Haydn traveled to London, his relationship with Forster had chilled considerably. But Haydn's two trips to the English capital also brought a change in his dealings with Artaria; from 1790 on, the first editions of Haydn's most important works were reserved for British publishers, including John Bland; Corri, Dussek and Co.; and Longman & Broderip. The twelve symphonies composed for London, however, were printed for Salomon, who evidently acquired not only the right of performance but also that of publication. Similarly, Haydn's arrangements of Scottish FOLK SONGS published with Napier and later Thomson are yet another facet of his publishing history.

By the late eighteenth century Haydn's main partner was the Leipzig firm Breitkopf & Härtel, whose agent Georg August Griesinger developed a friendly relationship with the composer – culminating in arguably the most trustworthy Haydn biography of the time. Given the composer's age and decreasing creative powers, Breitkopf's most important project proved to be the retrospective *Oeuvres complettes*, a twelve-volume collection of Haydn's works with keyboard, including a handful of unpublished works. The project was clearly modeled on Breitkopf's similar *Oeuvres de Mozart*, nine volumes of which Haydn possessed (most likely received as gifts from the publisher). Although this partnership with Breitkopf prompted Haydn to take account of his entire oeuvre, the publication of a true critical or complete EDITION was not the aim. The preface, signed in the name of the composer on December 20, 1799, clarified that the series sought to exclude inauthentic compositions as well as early works unworthy of reprinting. Breitkopf also launched a series each for Haydn's masses and symphonies (amounting to only seven and six works, respectively), and contemplated a "complete" edition of the string quartets. However, Pleyel, who launched a publishing house in Paris in 1795, preempted this plan. The latter's *Collection complette des Quatuors d'Haydn* became a standard edition, establishing the opus numbers for each set of quartets that are still in use today. Nevertheless, the slogan *avoués par l'Auteur*, with which Pleyel's thematic catalogue was advertised, may promise too much, as the authenticity of the Op. 3 set is today mostly doubted.

In London, Haydn even experimented with self-publishing, a practice that was commonplace there. Several of Haydn's works, including the English edition of the cantata *Ariana a Naxos*, and the first edition of the first set of English Canzonettas, appeared with the following remark on the title-page: "Printed for the Author & sold by him." These copies are also signed by

Figure 25 Title page of the London edition of Haydn's *Ariana a Naxos* with the clause "Printed for the Author & sold by him" and Haydn's signature as publisher. Copy from the former Esterházy Collection. Courtesy of the National Széchényi Library, Budapest.

Haydn, which, according to general practice, indicates him as the publisher (see Figure 25).

Presumably satisfied with the result of these attempts, Haydn chose to self-publish *The Creation* after his return to Vienna. Printed copies of the oratorio are stamped with his initials JH – apparently an equivalent of the publisher's signature in the earlier English prints. The vast CORRESPONDENCE related to the circulation of subscribers' lists and the dealings with stationers, however, proved too cumbersome for the AGING composer. Since the publication of *The Seasons* and the oratorio version of *Sieben Worte* had already been left to Breitkopf, Haydn also sold the plates and all remaining copies of *The Creation* to the Leipzig firm. Haydn's four-decade-long struggle with his publishers thus ended with a compromise, with the composer receiving his due while the value added by the publisher was also acknowledged. Indeed, the preparation of this kind of reconciliation appears to be yet another field in which Haydn's life work proves representative of an entire period.   BALÁZS MIKUSI

FURTHER READING
Biba (1987); *Briefe*; CCLN; Griesinger; Larsen (1939); entries on individual publishers in *Oxford Companion*.

R

Reception, Contemporary Among eighteenth-century composers, Haydn presents a distinctive case in terms of contemporary reception. For his three decades of service to the Esterházy court (1761–90), the composer recounted to Griesinger, his first biographer, that he viewed himself as "set apart from the world" to the extent that he "had to be original" (Gotwals 17) – or, as Bauman discusses, to "become original." Haydn's relative seclusion led his contact with wider EUROPEAN musical life to be intermittent rather than sustained, thereby limiting the possibilities for him proactively to shape his own reception, especially during the early part of his career. Conversely, several of his most esteemed contemporaries (not least Gluck and Mozart) traveled widely, disseminating and promoting their music, obtaining commissions, and familiarizing themselves with the local customs of specific musical centers to increase their own MARKETABILITY (see also COMPOSERS AND MUSIC PROFESSIONALS). Haydn's scores nonetheless enjoyed extensive CIRCULATION, appearing in PUBLISHERS' CATALOGUES across Europe with increasing frequency in the latter decades of the century, and demand for his music was such that he not uncommonly offered the same work to performing institutions or publishing houses in more than one different country.

Haydn's two visits to ENGLAND at Salomon's invitation in the 1790s heralded a new chapter in both his life and his reception history. While the composer was then approaching sixty, comparatively late to be undertaking the first significant traveling of his entire career, his time in England placed him more squarely within public musical markets less limiting than his previous feudal service, earning him laudatory press reviews and the respect of the Royal Family as well as bringing him greater visibility in his home country. Griesinger reported that the composer had often remarked that "he had become famous in Germany only by way of England," for instance, coming to the attention of Emperor Joseph II (Gotwals 36). Also during the period of Haydn's English sojourns, a monument was set up in his honor as part of the renovations of Count Karl Leonhard Harrach's gardens in Rohrau, the place of the composer's birth (Gotwals 161–64). The pyramidal monument subsequently received discussion in an article of March 12, 1800 in the newly founded *Allgemeine musikalische Zeitung* alongside similar memorials erected to Mozart, C. P. E. Bach, and Handel (see Figure 26).

The closing years of the eighteenth century yielded a variety of indications from the musical community of the recognition of Haydn's leading status among living composers, particularly following the death of Mozart. Haydn's frequently repeated endorsement of Mozart as "the greatest composer known

Figure 26 An engraving of the monument to Haydn at Rohrau, published in the *Allgemeine musikalische Zeitung*, March 12, 1800. The inscription reads: "TO THE MEMORY OF JOSEPH HAYDN THE DEATHLESS [I.E. IMMORTAL] MASTER OF MUSIC, TO WHOM EAR AND HEART CONTENDING DO HOMAGE, DEDICATED, BY KARL LEONHARD COUNT VON HARRACH. IN THE YEAR 1793 [recte: 1794]" (Gotwals 162; cf. Landon III 200). Courtesy of the University of Toronto Music Library.

to me either in person or by name," stated to his father Leopold in 1785 following a private performance of the last three of the "Haydn" quartets, provides insight into the reverence in which he and his opinion were held. He was also sought out by Beethoven as a composition tutor during the period between Haydn's two English sojourns. They cultivated a working relationship in 1792–94 that history has not tended to view kindly, uncharitably so in light of Webster's detailed re-evaluation of the available documentary evidence.

As Jones and Green explore, the number of published works dedicated to Haydn was remarkable for its day. Mozart's "Haydn" quartets Op. 10 and

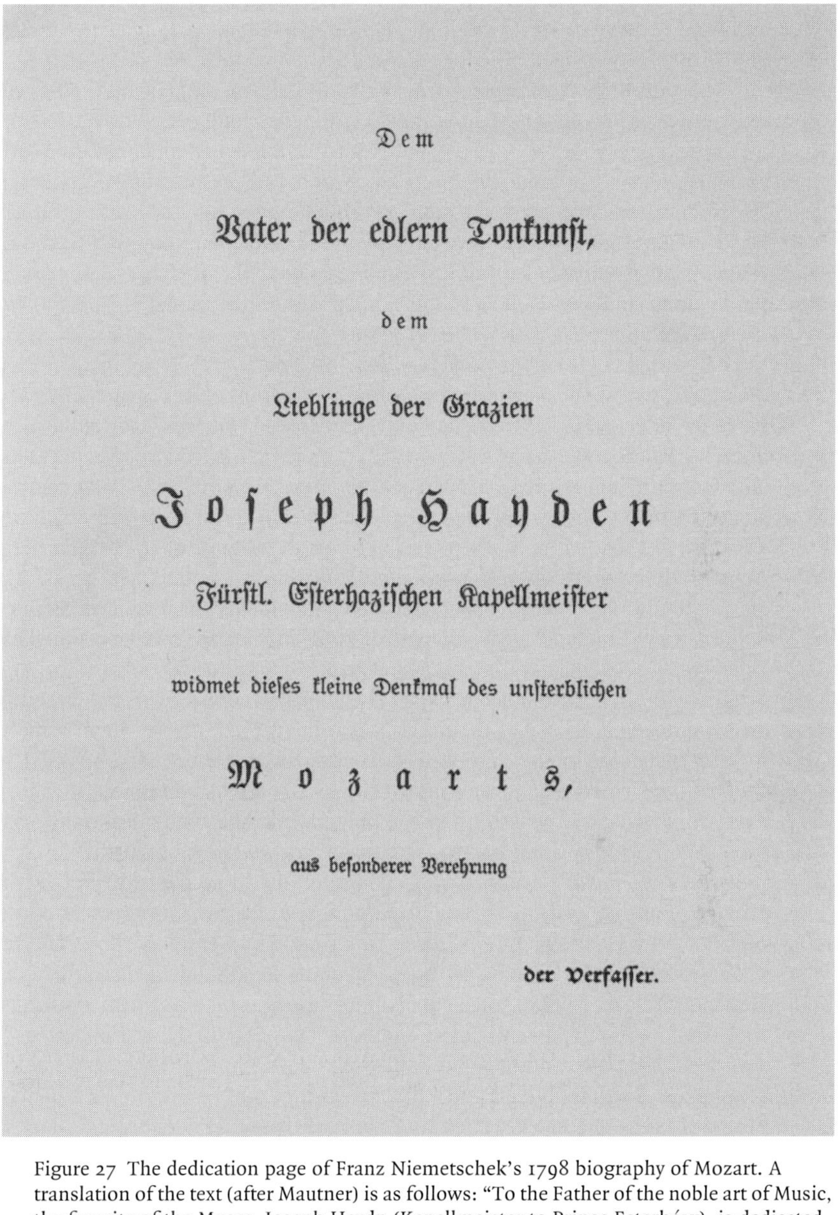

> Dem
>
> Vater der edlern Tonkunst,
>
> dem
>
> Lieblinge der Grazien
>
> Joseph Hayden
>
> Fürstl. Esterhazischen Kapellmeister
>
> widmet dieses kleine Denkmal des unsterblichen
>
> Mozarts,
>
> aus besonderer Verehrung
>
> der Verfasser.

Figure 27 The dedication page of Franz Niemetschek's 1798 biography of Mozart. A translation of the text (after Mautner) is as follows: "To the Father of the noble art of Music, the favorite of the Muses, Joseph Haydn (Kapellmeister to Prince Esterházy), is dedicated this little memorial to immortal Mozart, with deepest homage, [by] the author." Courtesy of the University of Toronto Music Library.

Beethoven's Op. 2 sonatas represent the pinnacle of some twenty-five sets of string quartets and keyboard sonatas by different composers bearing such gestures of homage (reciprocally, Haydn's scores encompass DEDICATIONS to a range of associates. Franz Niemetschek's seminal biography of Mozart was similarly dedicated, in its original version published in Prague in 1798 (see Figure 27).

A substantial body of music came to be misattributed to Haydn (just as some of his own was misattributed to others), often the result of a deliberate attempt on the part of a publisher or copyist to enhance the worth of a piece by a lesser-known composer by crediting it to a more renowned name. Such practices gave rise to hundreds of works of doubtful authenticity, in light of the magnitude of Haydn's reputation throughout Europe in his later years coupled to the continual need for newly composed music to feed the thriving AMATEUR and professional markets. Some of these misattributions persisted into the twentieth century (see EDITIONS).

The performance of The Creation in the Old University's Neue Aula in Vienna on March 27, 1808, as the culmination of a series of subscription concerts given by the SOCIETY of Amateur Concerts, marked Haydn's last public appearance. As Landon (V 364, n.1) identifies, it received much coverage in Austrian and German newspapers. Haydn's biographer Carpani, who had penned a sonnet in praise of the composer presented to him at the event and was himself a participant in the proceedings, related the attendance of over 1,500 people. Among them were members of the aristocracy, notably Princess Marie Hermenegild Esterházy, and celebrated musicians of the day including Salieri, who directed the performance, sung in Carpani's Italian translation; Wiley discusses the significance of various accounts having indicated the presence of Beethoven. Reports of the event describe how the assembled crowd cheered and rose to their feet as Haydn entered, carried in an armchair, to take his place in the audience as the guest of honor, accompanied by a fanfare performed on trumpet and timpani. The AGED composer, then just days from his seventy-sixth birthday, may have found the emotional occasion too overwhelming, as he had to leave at the end of the first part.

In view of Haydn's comparatively long life (set in even greater relief for its striking contrast with the premature demise of Mozart, his greatest contemporary), he was mistakenly believed to have died as early as 1805. The news soon spread across Europe, being particularly keenly felt in Paris, where, as Geiringer relates, works were specially composed to be performed alongside Mozart's Requiem at a planned memorial concert in Haydn's honor. The several biographical notices published in 1809–10 in the wake of the composer's actual death include texts by Mayr, Framery, and Le Breton. Reminiscence biographies by Griesinger, Dies, and Carpani also quickly appeared, marking a significant moment in the emergence of modern musical biography as well as playing their part in setting the agenda for Haydn's posthumous reception. All three authors knew their subject and benefitted from conversations with him during his final decade. However, as Gotwals (1959) observes, the composer's testimony could not always be taken at face value, given his apparently faltering memory and the disparities that became evident between different retellings of the same story.

Griesinger's is the most concise and reliable of the three biographies. Brought into contact with Haydn as an intermediary for Breitkopf & Härtel, Griesinger had originally published his account serially in the Allgemeine *musikalische Zeitung* between July 12 and September 6, 1809, before revising it as a single volume that appeared the following year. Dies, a landscape painter by profession, also published his biography in 1810, structured according to the thirty visits he had made to Haydn between April 15, 1805 and August 8, 1808 which collectively chronicle the composer's life story. Dedicated to its sponsor, Prince Nicolaus Esterházy II, Dies's text is nearly twice as long as Griesinger's, sacrificing brevity in favour of a more engaging prose style.

Carpani's biography, written as a set of seventeen letters dated April 15, 1808 to March 30, 1811, did not appear until 1812, enabling the author to consult both Griesinger's and Dies's narratives and thereby place himself in a position to surpass them, which he achieved in terms of level of detail, entertainment value, and commentary on Haydn's music, but not in factual accuracy. Stendhal, writing under the pseudonym Bombet, substantially plagiarized Carpani's text two years later in a volume that combined Haydn's life story with those of Mozart and Metastasio, which likewise drew heavily on previously published sources. Notwithstanding the wide circulation of Carpani's original in Italy and the later appearance of a complete French translation (1837), it was through Stendhal's mediation that Carpani's account of Haydn's life came to be disseminated, via translation, in England (1817) and AMERICA (1820).

While Griesinger's and Dies's biographies were translated by Vernon Gotwals (1963) some 150 years after their original publication, Carpani's less historically significant, but nonetheless interesting text has yet to receive a modern English translation. Between them, and despite their various inaccuracies and biases, they laid firm foundations for subsequent life-writing on the composer as well as establishing the enduring biographical tropes of "Papa" Haydn as a father figure for Viennese Classical music and its associated school of composition (particularly of the symphony, string quartet, and keyboard sonata), whose relative isolation throughout a substantial span of his career prompted artistic originality. (See also RECEPTION, POSTHUMOUS TO 1959; RECEPTION, 1950s–PRESENT.)

CHRISTOPHER WILEY

FURTHER READING
Bauman (2004); Carpani (1812); Dies; Gotwals (1959); Gotwals; Griesinger; Head (2000a); Jones (2005); Landon III–V; Mautner (1956); Niemetschek (1798); Stendhal (1814); Webster (1984); Wiley (2013).

Reception, Posthumous to 1959 Although Haydn died in 1809 as the most celebrated composer in EUROPE, there were numerous indications that his posthumous reputation would be challenged by a shift in AESTHETICS towards Romanticism. His works enjoyed a generally positive critical reception up to approximately the 1840s, but opinion turned markedly negative in the second half of the nineteenth century even as audiences continued to patronize concerts featuring them. The situation reversed in the early twentieth century, as the rejection of Romanticism fostered by neoclassicists and modernists fueled a resurgence of interest in Haydn's compositions. By 1959, the sesquicentennial of his death, Haydn's works enjoyed a newfound positive reception that has only increased in the years since.

A few factors contributed to the steep initial decline in Haydn's posthumous reputation. First, audiences and critics did not have the same attitude towards the musical canon as in the closing decades of the nineteenth century. New music was expected to supersede older music, and Haydn, keenly aware of this during his LONDON journeys, worked to seal his reputation in the same way Handel had: by writing oratorios. The Creation, especially, was a testament to his success in this regard, for it remained popular throughout the nineteenth century. Second, the very popularity of Haydn's music made it a target for those working to promote newer music. The critical reception of his symphonies shows this most concretely, as his works stood as a standard against which other composer could react. Haydn's decision to stop writing in the genre already in 1795 also meant that he would not participate in new stylistic developments. The ensuing fifteen years witnessed key stylistic changes, including the advent of Beethoven's "Heroic" style. E. T. A. Hoffmann's 1810 review of Beethoven's Fifth Symphony stands as the beginning point of this larger trend. While Hoffmann recognized the continuing importance of Haydn's symphonies, he urged audiences to turn their attention to Beethoven as Haydn's successor. Third, the ascendant generation of Romantic composers themselves attacked Haydn's music as part of a larger effort to situate their own music as rebelling against the outdated Classical style. Berlioz's writings were particularly critical (ironically he "detested" The Creation for its base programmatic depictions). Jealously may have played a factor in his critical stance, given the continuing popularity of Haydn's music and the troubles Berlioz had in gaining recognition for himself. Mendelssohn, whose works were very much in vogue, defended Haydn's compositions in a heated argument with Berlioz when the two met in Italy in 1831. Mendelssohn, unlike Berlioz, was also predisposed towards Haydn by nationality and training.

The uncertainty composers faced in dealing with Haydn's music is most evident in the writings of Robert Schumann. He can be credited with coining or popularizing a number of enduring and unflattering nicknames for Haydn: old, bewigged, papa, father, childlike, naive, and the "familiar friend" who has "ceased to arouse any interest." His negative comments on Haydn date primarily to 1835–41, a period of time during which he promoted Berlioz's music heavily. In 1841 Schumann underwent a private change of heart, brought about through extensive study of the string quartets and most clearly evidenced by the Second Symphony's direct quotation of Haydn's Symphony No. 104, "London." Nevertheless later writers such as A. B. Marx, Liszt, and Wagner latched on to his negative characterizations while his later more positive thoughts were largely forgotten. Haydn's reputation remained positive enough for George Sand to include a Romanticized version of him as a major character in her novel Consuelo (1842–43); however there is no evidence that Chopin shared Sand's views.

From the 1840s until the end of the century Haydn's music was largely dismissed, although some lesser-known critics continued to speak of its importance. Hans von Bülow's letters provide a number of remarkable insights into the late-century mindset. He heard the Sturm und Drang features of Haydn's works as "calming" and indicative of the composer's "eternal, divine serenity."

Bülow performed and conducted works by Haydn in concert on a regular basis, and he published his own edition of the Fantasia in C major, Hob.XVII:4 in the 1870s. But his performances in what he termed the "Haydn style" set the composer apart from music history and musical expression in such a way as to allow them to be dismissed as lighter fare (or worse as some kind of gimmick to attract audiences skeptical of the Wagner works he performed on the same concert). Brahms and Joachim stood as important supporters of Haydn's music (and scholarship on it) late in the century, but they were ultimately unsuccessful in changing critical opinion. Their lack of success may be partly attributed to Brahms keeping his own views private while supporting C. F. Pohl and others. Pohl's sudden death in 1887 ensured that Haydn would not receive biographical treatment in monumental fashion and also irreparably damaged the Gesellschaft der Musikfreunde's effort to organize a complete-works edition.

Haydn's reputation would begin to shift towards a more positive direction in the early years of the twentieth century. Unlike many other composer revivals, Haydn's was not the work of a single person or group of people; rather, a variety of individuals latched onto his music for disparate reasons. The French seem to have taken the lead, perhaps because Haydn's music was seen as anti-German, given that adherants of German Romanticism (the Wagnerians in particular) rejected it vehemently. The Haydn centennial of 1909 provided Jules Écorcheville with an excuse to convince leading French composers to write homages to Haydn in that year, including Debussy, Dukas, Ravel, and d'Indy. D'Indy's textbooks and teachings indicate a far more positive view towards Haydn's music than those typical elsewhere in pre-war Europe. Saint-Saëns and Landowska also encouraged a re-evaluation through their writings and performances, respectively. A meeting of the International Musikgesellschaft in Vienna in that same year, dedicated as the "Haydn Zentenarfeier," spurred on significant research into the composer as well. The conference included a number of Haydn-related activities, including a side-trip to EISENSTADT by the French attendees, and performances of *Lo speziale* and *L'isola disabitata*, though little formal scholarship on the composer was presented.

In spite of the Zentenarfeier, Germany and Austria were somewhat slower to readopt Haydn's music. The economic hardships created by World War I reparations led Schenker to point to the repertoire as a marker of a bygone but glorious era that needed to be recaptured. His personal connection with Anthony van Hoboken (see CATALOGUES), both a student and financial supporter, fostered a spirit of cooperation in using Haydn's music as a rallying point for a nation perceived to be on the brink of artistic collapse after centuries of musical dominance. In compositional circles Haydn's music also saw a resurgence. Schoenberg's efforts to situate himself within the Germanic tradition coupled with his interest in fostering a sense of intelligibility apart from tonality in a way that encouraged him to study Haydn's works in detail as he formulated his ideas on developing variation and coherence in the absence of tonality. This in turn led him to use examples from Haydn at a disproportionate rate in his textbooks on music theory, FORM, and composition (see MUSICAL MATERIALS).

In AMERICA Haydn's music made important inroads more through a string of coincidences than conscious design. The 1925–26 New York concert season featured eight works by Haydn in a four-month span. Six foreign conductors, including Toscanini on his first visit to the United States, and an appearance by Landowska playing the Harpsichord Concerto in D major (Hob.XVIII:11), coupled with unusually passionate program notes for the New York Philharmonic penned by Lawrence Gilman were noted in *Musical America* as the beginnings of a "back to Haydn movement" working to bring a "musical mummy" back to life.

Donald Tovey has traditionally been cited as the standard-bearer of the twentieth-century revival of interest in Haydn's music, and his *Essays in Musical Analysis* (published 1935–39) had a lasting impact on Haydn's critical reception. Tovey reacted to a larger interest in FOLK SONG and folk music among British composers that had already repopularized Haydn's music to a degree. William Henry Hadow translated and expanded upon the writings of Franjo Kuhač, who argued that most of Haydn's greatest works were based on Croatian folk songs; Vaughan Williams and Holst both furthered the argument to justify their own uses of folk song (see Proksch). Tovey's import can be seen as divorcing Haydn's importance from folk references in a way that encouraged others to hear Haydn's music as broader in scope and relevance than Hadow and his followers had argued.

The period after World War II saw the consolidation of these disparate positions in a way that would restore Haydn's music to a position within the canon requiring serious study and consideration in a way not seen since his death. The quantity and quality of scholarship, let alone RECORDINGS and prominence in the concert hall, increased markedly in the years leading up to the 1959 sesquicentennial of the composer's death. In 1959 Landowska offered a succinct overview of the events she had witnessed and taken part of, noting that while the old nineteenth-century views still were present and much work remained, others knew that "the works of Haydn are great not because they are stepping stones to Beethoven, but because they contain their own resources of inspiration and originality that mark them as masterpieces" (Proksch 165). (See also DISCOGRAPHY; RECEPTION, CONTEMPORARY; RECEPTION 1950S–PRESENT.)

BRYAN PROKSCH

FURTHER READING
Botstein (1998); Garratt (2005); Hoffmann (1999 [1810]); Proksch (2015); Tovey (1935–39).

Reception: 1950s–present The publication of Anthony van Hoboken's *Joseph Haydn: Thematisch-bibliographisches Werkverzeichnis* (1957–78), H. C. Robbins Landon's *The Symphonies of Joseph Haydn* (1955) and five-volume *Haydn: Chronicle and Works* (1976–80), G. Henle Verlag's *Joseph Haydn Werke* (1958-), and various collections of Haydn's CORRESPONDENCE and London NOTEBOOKS revitalized Haydn research in the post-war period and marked the beginning of the modern era of Haydn scholarship. By 1975 musicological engagement with Haydn was substantial enough to support an international conference devoted solely to Haydn in Washington, DC; another Haydn conference and festival soon followed in Vienna in 1982, the 250th anniversary of Haydn's birth. The flurry of publications and smaller conferences in the late twentieth and early twenty-first centuries, coinciding nicely with the reinvigorated and passionate Haydn promoted by the historically informed performance movement, brought interest in Haydn by both scholars and classical music enthusiasts closer to the levels enjoyed by Mozart and Beethoven.

If the construction of the tools of modern musicological research bears witness to a new era in Haydn scholarship in the mid-twentieth century, Haydn reception in the late twentieth century was shaped by rigorous interrogations of 1) the evolutionist ideology in the nineteenth- and early twentieth-century Haydn narrative, 2) linear histories of musical style, and 3) analysis dependent on deviation from a presumed stylistic norm. To be sure, Tovey's criticism had already undercut the "Papa Haydn" caricature, but reductive notions of Haydn as either a transitional composer or the requisite stylistic precursor to Mozart and Beethoven continued to reverberate. Rosen's landmark 1971 book *The Classical Style*, for instance, may have been the first to offer Haydn's string quartets and symphonies close readings within a sophisticated critical framework. A National Book Award winner, described as "brilliant," "epoch-making," and a "masterpiece" by highly respected critics and music scholars of the time, Rosen's hermeneutic engagement with Haydn's music had an impact that cannot be overstated. Indeed, the new seriousness with which AMERICAN musicology greeted Haydn in the years following its publication may have been largely inspired by Rosen's incorporation of extraordinary critical insights within eminently readable analyses.

But, as many of Rosen's critics over the years have articulated, his celebrated book sustains the reductive premises noted above that no longer find traction today. For example, in his discussion of relationships between a string quartet's opening motivic material and its later treatment in the movement, he writes: "Haydn had not yet arrived at Beethoven's conception of a musical idea unfolding gradually, let alone at Mozart's larger vision of tonal mass which in some ways surpassed even Beethoven's" (120). Directly answering critics of his insistence on Classical stylistic norms, Rosen doubles-down in the new preface to the 1997 expanded edition of *The Classical Style*. Mozart's excellence, he writes, "consists not only, or even primarily, in violating the expectations set up by the standard formulas of his time but also in the way he made the stereotypes appear graceful and determined by the piece at hand" (xvii). Sutcliffe's review cuts right to the heart of the "Rosen" problem for many late twentieth-century Haydn scholars: "For all the superb commentary ... [Rosen's] assessment of Haydn is also very often of its time, when at moments of stress Haydn must play the part of a precursor, 'prefiguring' what will be more fully realized by the two later composers" (604).

This problematic 150-year old evolutionist Haydn narrative receives its most rigorous interrogation in Webster's Kinkeldey award-winning 1991 book *Haydn's "Farewell" Symphony and the Idea of Classical Style*. As did Rosen's classic, this publication from arguably the world's leading Haydn scholar profoundly influenced Haydn reception. The "historiographical conclusion" to Webster's spectacularly detailed analysis of Haydn's "Farewell" Symphony challenged the traditional teleological stories of the development of Haydn's individual style as well as the idea of Classical style itself. By tracing the construction of *crisis* and *achievement* of style as central events in the Haydn narrative as told variously by Adolf Sandberger (1900), Théodore de Wyzewa (1909), Alfred Einstein (1924), Friedrich Blume (1931), Ludwig Finscher (1974), and ultimately Charles Rosen (1971/72) and exposing the reductive agenda, Webster (1991) takes down nothing short of the modern aesthetic construct of Classical style. At the same time, and with the weight of over three hundred pages of painstaking analysis in support, he effectively claims for Haydn Beethoven's most celebrated and revolutionary stylistic accomplishment: the integration of a multi-movement instrumental cycle. To be sure, Webster's sustained and multivalent attack hardly dethroned Beethoven from his top spot in the pantheon of Western composers (see, for example, Burnham's Wallace Berry Award-winning book *Beethoven Hero* which followed Webster's book by only four years), but the course of Haydn reception was substantially rerouted.

The reappraisal of Haydn's "early" music from the 1760s and 1770s, one of the many remarkable consequences of Webster's book, results also from at least two other influential articles published around the same time. In "Haydn's Theater Symphonies" (1990), Sisman challenges traditional understandings of Haydn's so-called *Sturm und Drang* style by hypothesizing that the dramatic rhetoric heard in Haydn's symphonies from these two decades originates in music composed for the stage. In "Haydn, Laurence Sterne, and the Origins of Musical Irony" (1991), Bonds explores ironic distance and the compositional techniques with which Haydn calls attention to the artificiality of his art. While the usual comedic suspects (e.g. the drumstroke in the slow movement of the "Surprise" Symphony, the finale of the "Joke" string quartet) are mentioned, Bonds's central example is Symphony No. 46 from 1772, an "earlier" work not generally regarded as humorous. But the many reinterpretations of Haydn's pre-1780 symphonies brought out especially by period-instrument ensembles during the last two decades of the twentieth century had perhaps the widest impact on the favorable shift in the reception of Haydn's "early" music, as these new recordings and performances were vigorously debated among scholars and music enthusiasts alike.

Much Haydn scholarship from the first two decades of the twenty-first century reflects the broader musicological turn toward new critical engagements with music and its cultural contexts. Five representative and recent publications can give some sense of the breadth of inquiry and diversity of repertory: Beghin and Goldberg's interdisciplinary, intertextual, and multi-mediated Solie Award-winning edited volume reconfirms the tremendous payoff of rhetorical Criticism (2007); Day-O'Connell explores femininity, the body, and death in Haydn's English Canzonettas in a fascinating exploration of music and anatomy (2009a); Dolan connects the materiality of sound in Haydn's orchestrations to the changing listening cultures of the late eighteenth and early nineteenth centuries (2013); Sisman situates the celebrated *Tageszeiten* Symphonies within the intense astronomical study of the time and rehears the trilogy though a poetics of solar illumination (2013); and Loughridge considers *The Creation* as an optical entertainment within the broader audiovisual culture of early Romanticism (2016).

A predictable surge in publications and academic symposia within the insular realm of musicological scholarship greeted Haydn Year 2009, the

200th anniversary of the composer's death, but there was also a flurry of Haydn activity aimed at a broader music-loving public. Commemorative events quite literally circled the globe: the World Creation Project, for instance, launched a performance of Haydn's most celebrated oratorio on the day of the composer's death in over a dozen cities across the time zones, from Toronto to Seoul. Among the more creative anniversary happenings was TRIOthlon, an International Haydn Festival concert of eighteen newly commissioned piano trios, all of which invoke some aspect of Haydn's life or music. Also exceptionally imaginative were exhibitions at the two palace residences of the Esterházy family in Hungary and Austria. At Eszterháza in Fertőd, visual artist Andreas Roseneder presented Haydn reloaded, an exhibition of new Haydn drawings, watercolors, acrylics, and polymer works created after the artist's extensive study of all of the historical representations of Haydn, from the contemporary portraits to the death mask (see link below). At Schloss Esterházy in Eisenstadt, Herbert Lachmayer curated the visionary Haydn Explosiv: eine europäische Karriere am Fürstenhof der Esterhazy, a multimedia extravaganza designed for "staging knowledge": video and sound instillations created living frescos and projected a levitating, life-size Hagen Quartet, while borderless, flat-screen monitors embedded in "hermeneutic" wallpaper explained the exhibition's content (see link below). To reflect on the significance of this anniversary year as a moment of transition in Haydn reception, Lowe chronicles many other celebratory exhibitions, performances, and scholarly events of Haydn Year 2009.

Before this latest anniversary and beyond the castles of central Europe, the Haydn Society of Great Britain has since its foundation in 1979 promoted greater public knowledge of Haydn's music and eighteenth-century musical life in general by sponsoring concerts, hosting exhibitions, and publishing a yearly journal for its members. Among the Society's most visible recent accomplishments is the commissioning of the Haydn plaque at 18 Great Pulteney Street, the site of the building in which Haydn lived during his first visit to London in 1791 (see link below). The plaque was unveiled in the City of Westminster on March 24, 2015 before a small but enthusiastic crowd. The Haydn Society of North America, established in 2008, likewise aspires to advance knowledge of Haydn among scholars, performers, and the broader classical-music-loving public through conferences, performances, and, since 2011, an online Journal. At present, however, the liveliest regular meeting place for Haydn enthusiasts is perhaps the Haydn listserv and discussion board, founded in 1999 and currently residing at Yahoo! Groups. Its community of over five hundred musicians, scholars, and music lovers welcomes any Haydn-related topic for conversation, from concert announcements, record reviews, and queries for information, to all-out gushing about all things Haydn.

Haydn reloaded
http://bglv1.orf.at/stories/380909
Haydn Explosiv
https://www.youtube.com/watch?v=cx__wm9AJWM
Haydn plaque
http://haydnsocietyofgb.co.uk/haydn-plaque/

MELANIE LOWE

FURTHER READING
Beghin and Goldberg; Bonds (1991a); Burnham (1995); Day-O'Connell (2009a); Dolan (2013); Hoboken; JHW; Landon I–V; Landon (1955); Loughridge (2016); Lowe (2010); Rosen (1971/72); Sisman (1990, 2013); Sutcliffe (1998b); Tovey (1935–39); Webster (1991).

Recording Recordings can be thought of as analogous to scores:

composer (Haydn) : musical work : score : performer
::   ::
performer : musical performance : recording : listener

Just as a composer creates a musical work and transfers it to a performer by way of a score, so also a performer creates a musical PERFORMANCE and transfers it to a listener by way of a recording. In both cases, we may (and often do) colloquially state that "the music" is conveyed from a creator to a receiver by way of a thing – something that can appear (and is often implicitly considered) to be both discrete and integral. But scores, we also know, are in fact quite incomplete representations of "the work." Recordings, meanwhile, are composites of multiple layers of creation.

This is the case even, or perhaps especially, when recording companies claim to have achieved the utmost "fidelity" to performance. Sterne and Weinstein provide an illuminating rundown and explication of how various forms of editing, sound compression, and "mixing" are applied to almost all recordings. Countless decisions significantly shape the recorded output – decisions that are not unlike those made by performers and analysts. Which voices or instruments, for instance, should be emphasized and at what times? In this case, the engineer becomes the fifth voice or even the moderator of a conversation in a string quartet. What should be the levels of resonance and rates of decay? The engineer creates the "space" in which a mass is performed, from dry or intimate to bright or resonant, which in turn affects the interpretive – indeed potentially even the spiritual – impact.

Even early recordings, despite predating modern editing and sound engineering, bear traces of values and choices beyond the performer's own. Acoustic recordings have limited dynamic range because performers were forced to accommodate the fickle temperament of the recording horn: too loud and the needle jumped, too soft and the sound was barely picked up. ORCHESTRATION was sometimes adjusted to suit the needs of the studio, and cuts were made to squeeze music into limited space. Furthermore, there is the creative reimagining by engineers as they transfer the product of earlier technologies into today's digital format. Although we call early recordings 78s, the rpm (rotations per minute) was not standardized until the 1930s; present-day transfer engineers must thus make decisions about pitch and key, and these, in turn, affect tempo. Engineers exert further decision-making power when dealing with recordings that are worn or damaged, prints that aren't centered exactly on the middle, and originals that were made in four-minute sections – how should they be woven back together? How much surface noise should one filter out to improve the sound quality without distorting the timbre or removing critical highs and lows?

In performance, "the music" is refracted through the lens of the performer and then the lens of the listener. In recording, the lenses multiply. Lowe makes this point in her "Symphonic Study" chapter – the principal critical study of Haydn recordings to date. To listen to a recording of a Haydn symphony is to experience a collaboration: "the musical performance is both practically and conceptually displaced by technological performance" (261). And yet, it is fair to say that the most influential writers on Haydn's music rarely mention, let alone acknowledge the unique features of, the recordings on which they base their analytical claims. Landon (in an interview with Brian Robins) recalled being introduced to certain Haydn symphonies by way of Sir Thomas Beecham's recordings with the London Philharmonic Orchestra; Tovey likely listened to these as well. How might the very distinct sounds, the filters – both interpretive and technological – of Beecham's Haydn on record have shaped Landon's and Tovey's understandings? To whom did Webster or Somfai listen when writing on Haydn's string quartets? To whom did Schenker listen when he produced his multiple influential analyses of Haydn keyboard sonatas? We know that even famously "idealist" Schenker listened to recordings (in a diary entry dated January 14, 1934, for example, he specifically mentions [and criticizes] a Toscanini recording of a Mozart work).

The factors of displacement and collaboration make this complicated work, but to study recordings with attention to the *act* of recording is to take up special opportunities to understand the people who have played and listened to Haydn's music since the early twentieth century. To date, only a few such studies have been undertaken. Again, Lowe serves as touch-stone; by considering recordings of Haydn symphonies she is able to document changes in performance practice. On a more specific level, Bazzana compares recordings by Glenn Gould of the keyboard Sonata in E♭, Hob.XVI:49, in order to highlight a changed aesthetic interpretation. Day-O'Connell considers Dietrich Fischer-Dieskau's recordings of the English Songs, Hob.XXVIa, and borrows from the theory of translation studies to argue that the recordings in effect "domesticate" passages that were conceived by Haydn's contemporaries as turbulent, unclear, and unresolved. These projects each shed light on "hidden" choices made in recording and go on to explain the implications and significance of those choices.

Although the Haydn-recording scholarship to date is comparatively limited and preliminary, extensive models and tools for such work are at the ready. Cook and others connected to the Centre for History and Analysis of Recorded Music (CHARM) Initiative (2004–9) have developed a range of techniques – from the study of spectrograms and the use of Sonic Visualizer to the analysis of large data sets comparing phrasing, dynamics, tempo, ornamentation and other musical features – that help us isolate and visualize performed moments (see charm.rhul.ac.uk and Cook 2009). As with more traditional modes of inquiry, the value of these studies is entirely dependent on the kinds of questions asked. But this kind of empirical musicology, supported by increased access to vast quantities of recordings (see DISCOGRAPHY) presents scholars with the opportunity to pose new questions and challenge current assumptions about performance, listening, and cognition that could very well push back at many claims made by historians and theorists. Meanwhile,

Zagorski-Thomas and Blier-Carruthers propose a "musicology of record production" which encourages performers to use the tools of recording technology as another means for presenting an acoustic argument about a given composition.

With regard to our understanding of Haydn and his music, it is neither desirable nor possible to avoid the pervasive influence of recording technology, so it becomes an obligation – and an opportunity – to consider its attendant assets and limitations. Just as technology has the ability to accentuate aspects of performance or to diminish them, it can also bring listeners closer or alienate them. Recording mediates between creators and audiences while also enabling, articulating, and subordinating different layers of creativity.

DANIEL BAROLSKY

FURTHER READING

Bazzana (1997); Blier-Carruthers (forthcoming); Borio (2015); Born (2013); Clark (2005a); Clarke (2013); Clarke and Cook (2004); Cook (2009, 2013); Day-O'Connell (2014b); Frith and Zagorski-Thomas (2012); Leech-Wilkinson (2009); Lowe (2005); McAdams, Depalle, and Clarke (2004); Robins (2009); Schenker (1934); Sterne (2012); Weinstein (2013); Zagorski-Thomas (2014).

Rehearsal – see Vocal Coaching and

Relationships, Friendships   Haydn's private life, unlike those of Mozart and Beethoven, has not been a subject of popular imagination, perhaps because of the long-standing perception of him as a venerated patriarch. At the same time, discussions of Haydn's mistresses and female friends take up a significant portion of the composer's biographies. Just like any artist, moreover, Haydn was strongly affected by romantic and platonic relationships that influenced his music and produced a lot of primary biographical material.

As noted already by early biographers, Haydn was not indifferent to, and thought of himself as desirable by, women. Haydn's first known love was Theresia Helena Keller (1733–1819), the sixth daughter of a Viennese wig maker. In 1755 Theresia entered a Franciscan convent, and Haydn might have composed the Organ Concerto in C (Hob.XVIII:1) and the *Salve Regina* in E (Hob.XXIIIb:1) to commemorate her investiture. In 1760, Haydn, similar to Mozart, married the initially not-so-desirable older sister, Maria Anna Theresia Keller (1730–1800). As Lorenz has shown in 2014, all of Haydn's biographers starting with Pohl confused Maria Anna Theresia with her younger sister Maria Anna Aloysia Apollonia, who was born in 1729 but died in 1730. The marriage remained childless, and most biographers depict Maria Anna as uninspiring. At the same time, there is little information about her beyond Haydn's own statements.

Haydn's one documented mistress clearly influenced his musical output. The Italian soprano Luigia Polzelli, née Moreschi (1750–1831), came to Eszterháza in 1779 with her husband, the violinist Antonio Polzelli. The younger of Luigia's two sons, Antonio (1783–1855), might have been fathered by Haydn; he became a violinist in VIENNA and EISENSTADT. Many biographers used the letters Haydn wrote to Polzelli from LONDON to portray her as a greedy and dissolute seductress. As Siegert has explained, however, these portrayals often reflect nineteenth-century views on morality and nationalistic biases. More widespread, even in recent scholarship, is the idea that Polzelli was not a talented singer, an attitude that mostly relies on circumstantial evidence.

Recent studies have in fact admitted that Polzelli was a source of inspiration for Haydn. The composer wrote only one operatic role for Polzelli (Silvia in L'isola disabitata), but reworked numerous minor roles specifically for her in revisions of Italian operas, composing new insertion arias and transposing and reorchestrating pre-existing ones to fit Polzelli's vocal technique. According to Siegert, although Haydn's music for Polzelli is not extraordinarily virtuosic and betrays a limited vocal range, it also points to a highly versatile singer.

Haydn met his next possible lover, Rebecca Schroeter, née Scott (1751–1826), during his first visit to London in 1791. Schroeter was the widow of the composer Johann Samuel Schroeter (1750–1788). Between March 1791 and June 1792, Schroeter and Haydn exchanged letters, some of which suggest that their relationship was not platonic. In 1795, Haydn dedicated a set of three keyboard trios (Hob.XV:24–26) to Schroeter. The trios reflect Schroeter's skills, acquired during her studies with her husband, an outstanding keyboardist, and with Haydn himself.

Haydn's biographers used various references in the composer's letters and his will to point out that the composer must have had other lovers. But aristocratic and middle-class women made an impact on the composer also as friends and patrons. From 1789 onward, Haydn was on friendly terms with Maria Anna von Genzinger (1750–1793), the wife of Prince Esterházy's physician. Genzinger received confidential letters from the composer, some of which detail his first trip to London. She was also an accomplished keyboard player, and Haydn composed his technically demanding Sonata in E♭ (Hob.XVI:49) for her. One of Haydn's most important aristocratic patrons after Genzinger's untimely death was Princess Marie Hermenegild Esterházy (1768–1845), the wife of Haydn's philandering last employer. Haydn wrote his six famous late masses (including his last major work, the Harmoniemesse) for the princess's name-day between 1796 and 1802. Towards the end of his life, the princess often visited the increasingly infirm composer in his Gumpendorfer house. In his late years, Haydn also received patronage from Empress Marie Therese (1772–1807), a trained singer who had Haydn's music performed in private concerts at the Viennese court. For the empress, Haydn wrote his second Te Deum (Hob.XXIIIc:2). He also presented her with a manuscript of his Mass in B♭ (Hob.XXII:12), which received the nickname Theresienmesse although it was first written for Princess Esterházy. Rice observes that the empress sought to impose her individual touch on the Gloria in the Schöpfungsmesse, originally dedicated to another woman, and asked Haydn to remove from it a reference to Adam and Eve's suggestive duet from The Creation. According to Mikusi, the Schöpfungsmesse might also reflect Haydn's amorous relations; the quote from the The Creation's racy duet coincides with the phrase "Qui tollis peccata mundi," perhaps to express the composer's remorse for past sexual immodesty.

The composer had many male friends, especially in Eszterháza and Eisenstadt, for whom he composed works that highlighted their skills. The Italian violinist Luigi Tomasini (1741–1808) was the long-time concertmaster of the Esterházy orchestra and the director of chamber music. For Tomasini Haydn wrote the Violin Concerto in C (Hob.VIIa:1), marking it as "fatto per il luigi" [made for Luigi] in his handwritten catalogue of works. Many other chamber pieces and virtuosic passages in Haydn's Eszterháza symphonies, such as the ones in the slow movement of Symphony No. 31 ("Horn Signal"), might have been written for Tomasini. For another friend in the Esterházy orchestra, the cellist Joseph Weigl (1740–1820), Haydn might have written his first cello concerto (Hob.VIIb:1), together with virtuosic passages in the symphonies of the 1760s. Haydn was godfather to Weigl's son Joseph (1766–1846), who was to become a famous composer of Viennese operas.

Friendships with fellow COMPOSERS AND MUSIC PROFESSIONALS were also significant for Haydn's output. Brief but influential was the encounter with Giuseppe Sarti (1729–1802), whose *Giulio Sabino* (performed at Eszterháza in 1783) influenced Haydn's *Armida* (1784). Haydn and Sarti supposedly met and admired each other's work during Sarti's 1784 visit to Eszterháza. More lasting were Haydn's relations with his own brother, Michael (1737–1806). The brothers met only sporadically after Michael became a court musician in Salzburg, but rekindled an affectionate relationship in 1798 when Michael travelled to Vienna. Joseph esteemed Michael as a composer of church music, and Michael arranged several of Joseph's compositions; for example, he turned the extremely popular "Gott erhalte Franz den Kaiser" into a set of keyboard VARIATIONS and a vocal quartet. Throughout his career, Haydn remained in contact with Carl Ditters von Dittersdorf (1739–1799), whom he met in the 1750s in Vienna. In Eszterháza, Haydn performed numerous symphonies and operas by Dittersdorf, and Dittersdorf's instrumental oratorio *Giobbe* influenced Haydn's *Seven Last Words*. The two composers also apparently occasionally met during temporary stays in Vienna, as illustrated in the famous story by the tenor Michael Kelly about a 1784 quartet party at the house of the composer Stephan Storace, where Haydn and Dittersdorf played the first and second violins. During the same party, Wolfgang Amadeus Mozart (1756–1791) supposedly played the viola. Mozart and Haydn struck up one of the most famous friendships ever to exist in the history of Western music. In the early 1780s, Mozart demonstrated his high esteem of Haydn's chamber music by dedicating six string quartets to him. As Leopold Mozart recalled in a letter dated February 14–16, 1785, Haydn was so struck with the quartets that he pronounced Mozart as "the greatest composer I know" (1785, 2). Haydn also admired Mozart's operas, as suggested by his plans to produce *Figaro* in Eszterháza and the possible quote from *Così fan tutte* in Symphony No. 97, written shortly after Haydn learned of Mozart's death.

Haydn's friendships with men of letters were particularly important for the reception of his works. The English critic Charles Burney (1726–1814) idolized Haydn in his *General History of Music*, assisted Haydn during the London trips, and incited enthusiasm for Haydn's music in the English public. Haydn also became personally acquainted with his first two biographers, Georg August Griesinger (1769–1845) and Albert Christoph Dies (1755–1822). The Elssler family was significant for the dissemination of Haydn's compositions. Joseph Elssler Sr. (d. 1782), the music copyist at Eszterháza from 1764 until his death, created manuscripts of Haydn's works that were distributed throughout Central Europe. His son Johann Elssler (1769–1843) became Haydn's copyist in the late 1780s and accompanied the composer on his second London trip.

Elssler, and his wife, lived with Haydn during his last years and left behind a description of the composer's daily routine. The personal diary of Joseph Carl Rosenbaum (1770–1829), a secretary in the service of the Esterházy COURT at first and later active in Vienna, represents another source on Haydn's final period. Haydn interceded on his friend's behalf with the Prince Esterházy during Rosenbaum's scandalous courtship of the singer Therese Gassmann. The couple eventually married in 1800 and visited Haydn regularly. After the composer's death, Rosenbaum became the initiator of the plot to steal Haydn's skull for Franz Joseph Gall's phrenological research.

The study of Haydn's relationships with women and men of his time will continue to afford new insights into the composer's biography, his social and cultural milieu, and, perhaps most importantly, new interpretations of his music, which was often tailored to specific performers and patrons.

MARTIN NEDBAL

FURTHER READING
Beghin (2006); Genesi (1993); Landon II; Lorenz (2014); Mikusi (2009); Radant (1968); Restle (2007); Rice (1984, 2003); Scull (1997); Siegert (2006, 2009, 2012).

Religion and Spiritual Beliefs Haydn's religious beliefs remain a complex issue not reducible to tropes of the composer's earnest and naive Catholic faith. In the first place, this faith encompasses both institutional and personal dimensions, and investigation of Haydn's liturgical music necessarily places central emphasis upon the general climate of piety within the Holy Roman Empire where the composer worked most of his life. At the apex of this world stood the Habsburg imperial family for whom the doctrine of *Pietas Austriaca* represented an essential facet of dynastic identity; as Coreth has revealed in an important documentary study, the intensive cultivation by the Habsburgs of Eucharistic and Marian worship revolved around the belief that worldly power received divine legitimation from the consecrated Body of Jesus Christ and from the Virgin Mary. Thus, religious and POLITICAL concerns in Haydn's Austria intertwined to a great degree. Even so, the extent of pious devotion among specific members of the Viennese ruling classes varied notably, with a significant impact upon the production of sacred music. It is not accidental that Haydn was least active as a composer of liturgical works during Emperor Joseph II's rationalist and pragmatic reforms, which included the radical simplification of religious practice in 1780s – a period coinciding with Nicolaus I Esterházy's overarching patronage of opera (see THEATER). By the following decade, however, with the reversal of Joseph's program under his successors Leopold II and Franz II as well as the different employment conditions at the Esterházy COURT provided by Nicolaus II, Haydn produced some of his most powerful Catholic liturgical music: the six late masses (Hob.XXII:9–14), including several for Princess Marie Hermenegild Esterházy, the young wife of Prince Nicolaus II (see McGrann), and the *Te Deum* in C major (Hob.XXIIIc:2), for Empress Marie Therese, the dynamic female patron at the apex of the social pyramid in Vienna at the turn of the nineteenth century (see Rice; WAR).

Counterbalancing these broad sociocultural considerations is the manifest sincerity of Haydn's personal religious convictions. In a letter from July 1801 regarding *The Creation* (1798), Haydn notes the music's potent role in fostering piety: "to accompany this great work [God's creation of the world] with appropriate music could certainly have no other result than to heighten these sacred emotions in the listener's heart, and to make him highly receptive to the goodness and omnipotence of the Creator" (quoted in Webster, 64). The idiosyncrasy of Haydn's sacred output diverges notably from a de-individualized, "corporate" model of sacred musical practice dominant in Austria since the time of Johann Joseph Fux (see White) and still represented by his younger brother Michael. Functional requirements do not fully account for the diversity in Haydn's sacred music; rather, they prompt a careful examination of the complex nature of the composer's religious outlook. At once a firm adherent of the Catholic CHURCH and sympathetic to a number of unorthodox tendencies, Haydn cannot be taken as exemplary of the antagonistic divide between collective and individual pursuit of faith that would come to mark the Romantic world view. By the turn of the nineteenth century, however, some sense of individual belief as a transcendence of institutional worship becomes apparent in the related influences of a SUBLIME AESTHETIC and the rationalistic Deist theology, which exerted their impact most directly in the late oratorios and masses.

Haydn's sacred music fully spans the half-century of his creative activity and indeed bookends it: his earliest composition is the *Missa brevis* (Hob. XXII:1) of 1749, evidently written during his service as a choirboy at St. Stephen's Cathedral in Vienna, while his final completed work is the *Harmoniemesse* (Hob.XXII:14) of 1802. Furthermore, the category of *musica da chiesa*, one of the three commonly recognized styles of music during the eighteenth century, extended beyond his vocal oeuvre to encompass symphonies that were sometimes used in church services, including not only those featuring overt religious elements such as Symphony No. 30 in C major, whose opening movement employs the Gregorian Easter Alleluia as the principal basis for its melodic material, but also those which today might seem to belong firmly within a secular domain, among them Nos. 37, 39, and 41 (see Riedel).

Haydn's efforts in writing music for liturgical or para-liturgical use roughly falls into two distinct phases. The first, comprising a group of stylistically heterogeneous works diffusely covering the period from 1749 to 1782, reveals Haydn's absorption of the broad range of conventional idioms forming the category of *musica da chiesa* in Austria during the mid- to late eighteenth century; while the second, represented by the oratorios and masses of 1796 to 1802, demonstrates an intensive and more overtly individualistic engagement with striving to express faith through music.

The first phase consists of seven authenticated Mass Ordinary cycles (one, the *Missa "sunt bona mixta malis,"* surviving in a fragmentary state), the *Stabat mater* (Hob.XXbis) of 1767, and the *Salve Regina* (Hob.XXIIIb:2 of 1771). In this group of compositions, Haydn conveys an accomplished familiarity with the prevailing styles and techniques of Catholic religious music within his milieu. The most general division of liturgical music in eighteenth-century Austria distinguished *solenne*, *mediocre*, and *a cappella* types, based on considerations of function and occasion as well as instrumentation: concerted accompaniment with clarini trumpets and timpani (*solenne*), without these instruments (*mediocre*), or colla parte accompaniment (*a cappella*).

Haydn's sacred works of 1749–82 encompass all three of these categories. The remarkably ambitious *Missa Cellensis in honorem BVM* (Hob.XXII:5), probably completed in 1766, exemplifies the *solenne* type, but also went far beyond the practical requirements of its intended liturgical use (which has not yet been fully clarified), particularly in its exceptional length as well as the elaborate choral fugues that conclude four of its six movements. Though such contrapuntal perorations represent a typical feature of masses in this period, adherence to convention does not account for the riches, especially of the Credo fugue, whose complex technique and sustained energy over a span of more than one hundred measures, admired by two centuries of commentators, must reflect a particularly deep commitment on Haydn's part to music's capacity for embodying religious belief. Wholly contrasting in scale is the *Missa brevis Sancti Joannis de Deo* (Hob.XXII:7), a work from the mid-1770s illustrating the practice of allocating different segments of the Gloria and Credo texts to the individual voice parts and simultaneously presenting them, in order to proceed at high speed through these movements, evidently out of pragmatic considerations (see also Jewish Culture).

Joseph II's measures against concerted sacred music, promulgated in 1783 and intended to curtail what he regarded as an unnecessary and wasteful luxury, probably account for the disappearance of such music from Haydn's output for a fourteen-year period. The single exception here is *The Seven Last Words*, a generically unique composition comprised of seven slow orchestral movements and written not for an Austrian church but for the Oratorio de la Santa Cueva in Cádiz, Spain, in 1786–87 (see European Contexts). But when Haydn became Kapellmeister for the Esterházy Chapel under Prince Nicolaus II, *musica da chiesa* regained a central place. Haydn's late liturgical works include six masses (of which, as mentioned above, at least three can be linked to the name-day celebrations of Princess Marie Hermenegild) as well as the para-liturgical oratorios, *The Creation* and *The Seasons*. These large-scale works, concentrated within the six years from 1796 and 1802, attest to Haydn's idiosyncratic exploration of resources lying beyond the orthodox traditions of Catholic religious music – including a new aesthetic of the sublime, and a Deistic outlook with strong rationalist leanings while still recognizing a Creator (see also Freemasonry).

In a study of the relation of the sublime to Haydn's late sacred vocal music, Webster emphasizes three categories of sublimity that emerged around the turn of the century, associated respectively with the awesome force of nature, mathematical infinitude, and incommensurability. The last of these particularly applies to the late masses and oratorios, in which Haydn develops a stylistic language of radical quality, vividly disjunctive and integrative at the same time, as a sonic analogue for the incommensurable mysteries of the Christian faith. Overlapping to a certain extent with the sublime aesthetic is the Deistic belief in a Natural world governed by rational Scientific principles and the foundational work of the Creator. This heterodox outlook, which flowered in England in the first half of the eighteenth century and enjoyed an active interest among intellectual circles in Austria during the late phases of the ENLIGHTENMENT, subverted official Christian theology in its de-emphasis of sin and preference for a celebration of the beauties of an existence ordered by an all-powerful yet benevolent deity. Deism displaced the religious dimension of mystery, moving it away from an awe-laden reverence for authority, and towards a passionate appreciation of the transcendent qualities of perceptible phenomena. As such, it shared with the sublime a non-conformist "re-siting" of the divine. Within Haydn's oeuvre, its tenets are most clearly realized in *The Creation* and *The Seasons*. Their overt and unembarrassed pastoral imagery – pictorialisms often criticized (not always justifiably) – link comfortably with grand choral apotheoses of unsurpassed splendor. That these oratorios encompass such a wide range of expression stands as clear evidence of the quintessentially vigorous and innovative nature of their composer's spirituality.

Finally, Haydn's views on Protestantism, which he encountered most directly while in England, are little known. A staunch adherence to the Catholic faith would seem apparent from a statement such as the following, from the London NOTEBOOKS:

> On 26th Aug. 1794, I went to Waverly Abbey, forty miles from London, to visit Baron Sir Charles Rich, quite a good 'cello player. Here there are the remains of a monastery which has already been standing for 600 years. I must confess that whenever I looked at this BEAUTIFUL wilderness, my heart was oppressed at the thought that all this once belonged to my religion (CCLN 304).

Haydn seems likely also to have worshipped regularly as a Catholic at least during 1791, when he lodged in Johann Peter Salomon's residence at 18 Great Pulteney Street, which was located a short distance from the chapel of the Lady of the Assumption and St. Gregory (see Jones (2009); Olleson). Yet he willingly contributed six English-language settings (Hob. XXIII: *Nachtrag*) to the first volume of the Reverend William Dechair Tattersall's *Improved Psalmody*, also published in 1794. Apparently, in his religious beliefs he did not cling to a denominational rigidity; indeed, his sacred music also encompasses a humane openness to the spiritual experiences of others, including Protestants and liberal JEWS.

JEN-YEN CHEN

FURTHER READING
CCLN; Coreth (2004); Erhardt (2013); HWorld; Jones (2000b, 2009); McGrann (1998); Olleson (2000); Rice (2003); Riedel (1992); Webster (1997); White (2013).

Revivals – see Commemorations and Festivals

Revolution – see War

Rhetoric – see Performance

Rhythm and Meter Haydn wrote his corpus of works during an era that saw a reconceptualization of TIME and, more specifically, of meter. At the beginning of Haydn's lifetime meter was generally theorized under the conceptual rubric of the beat. Tightly bound up with note values and characteristic rhythms, the beat indicated both a way of ordering musical temporality and also the rate at which that ordering took place – that is, the concept included within it both meter and what we today call tempo. The meter signatures and characteristic rhythms of Haydn's compositions demonstrate a sensitivity to this conceptual framework; these elements of composition are regularly adduced in the analysis of TOPICAL and affective references in his music. But toward the end of Haydn's career the relationships that had once joined meter signatures, characteristic rhythms, and tempi were reoriented, as meter signatures became more flexible and able to incorporate a wider range of affects and topics. This new malleability afforded Haydn important compositional innovations in the domain of rhythm and meter.

Haydn used the full range of eighteenth-century meter signatures in his compositions. In the analysis of his music it is useful to bear in mind three basic period distinctions: meters can be simple (*einfach*) meaning that they use duple subdivisions; they can be tripled (*triplirt* or *vermischt*) meaning that they use tripled subdivisions; they can also be compounded (*zusammengesetzt*), meaning that each written measure actually contains two smaller measures within it (note the difference from our twenty-first century term "compound," generally used for meters with tripled subdivisions). Both simple and tripled meters can be compounded. Haydn's compositions in simple meters of two, three, or four beats are many – they include minuet movements in three–four, and brilliant-style, first-movement allegros in four–four (C), two–four, or sometimes cut-C (¢). Haydn also availed himself of the ¢ meter signature's *stile antico* use in conjunction with long note values, as in the Missa "sunt bona mixta malis." Tripled meters such as six–eight and nine–eight are also common, especially used with the characteristic siciliano rhythms in an interior movement of an instrumental work, as in the six–eight slow movement of the String Quartet Op. 20, No. 5 (Example 18). But Haydn also used six–eight as a simple compounded meter (meaning that each measure actually contains two smaller measures of three–eight). The English Canzonetta "Pleasing Pain," (Hob.XXVIa:29) with its cadences exclusively falling in the middle of each notated measure, is a prime instance (Example 19).

In addition to the straightforward employment of a huge range of meter signatures, Haydn also experimented with the alteration of the meter mid-composition. Because many meter signatures could indicate more than one metric structure, he was often able to achieve this without changing the notated meter signature. The Adagio from the String Quartet Op. 50, No. 6,

Example 18 String Quartet Op. 20, No. 5, third movement, mm. 1–4.

Example 19 "Pleasing Pain," mm. 8–18.

"Frog," begins in simple, compounded six–eight, similar to "Pleasing Pain" in its use of mid-measure cadences. But after the opening phrase comes to an authentic cadence, the first violin leads the ensemble in a quickening of the rhythmic pace and a corresponding broadening of the metric structure: Haydn has changed the meter to a tripled six–eight with two beats per measure. Mirka has used this example among many others to demonstrate how this sort of play with meter is a hallmark of Haydn's style.

The exploitation of the multiple properties of meter signatures on the part of Haydn and his contemporaries was one component of a slow reconceptualization of meter. The eighteenth-century witnessed the birth of a new way of thinking about temporality – one that allowed composers and theorists to see meter as a mutable way of dividing the ongoing flow of time. This rendered meter signatures less defining in their semiotic capacity, and it afforded experimentation with structures of meter not contained by barlines. An example of the former is Haydn's use of the cut-C signature for music that layered *stile antico* durations and procedures on top of music written with the shorter durations and the characteristic gestures of the galant, as in the finale to Symphony No. 40 (Example 20).

This finale's admixture of styles took advantage of the mutability of cut-C, thereby undercutting the particularity of its designations. The first movement of the String Quartet Op. 76, No. 5 contains an instance of Haydn playing with durations longer than the notated measure. In the allegro portion of this movement there is a regular alternation between the stronger, even-numbered measures and weaker odd-numbered measures: a duple hypermeter. This pattern is subsequently upset with the arrival of the structural dominant in m. 101 and the subsequent resolution to the tonic in m. 107. Between these measures, a hypermetrical transition takes place. Haydn effectively changes the meter of the music without altering the meter signature or the barlines.

Precisely because Haydn's career spans a transformation in ideas concerning time, his music has held an important place in the scholarly study of rhythm and meter. On the one hand, some scholars identify in Haydn's music the quintessence of classical phrase structure (as in the work of Rosen and Sisman) and of the characteristic use of meter signatures (as in Ratner). On the other, scholars have been drawn to precisely those aspects of his work that frustrate these norms and expectations (see Rothstein; Temperley).

Example 20 Symphony No. 40, fourth movement, mm. 46–54.

Scholars have also begun to use Haydn's music to better understand the historical transition in rhythm and meter to which it bears witness (see Mirka; Grant). Taken together, these endeavors contribute to the ongoing importance of Haydn's work to music theory and analysis.

ROGER MATHEW GRANT

FURTHER READING

Allanbrook (1983); Caplin (2002); Cone (1968); Grant (2014); Grave (1985); Houle (1987); Kirnberger (1771–79); Koch (1782); Lester (1986); Marpurg (1750); Mattheson (1739); Maurer Zenck (2001); Mirka (2009, 2014b); Ratner (1980); Rosen (1971/72); Rothstein (1989, 2008); Schwindt-Gross (1989); Sisman (1982); Temperley (2003, 2008); Waldura (2000).

S

Science An anachronism in the eighteenth century, the term science was the realm of philosophers of the natural world, hence "natural philosophy," and could include highly speculative arguments like the "extraterrestrial life debate" of mid-century in which Kant participated. Observation, classification, measurement, and experiment drove theories and new knowledge; both found their way from burgeoning national academies to local bookshelves. Whether from genuine curiosity or from the recognition that broad knowledge was necessary to his career, as Mattheson advised in an important reference work (*Der vollkommene Kapellmeister* 1739), Haydn collected sources of information about many fields that today we would recognize as scientific. His library shows us a man interested in astronomy, geography, botany, meteorology, medicine, and encyclopedic reference (see MATERIAL CULTURE). Among his acquaintances or correspondents were pioneers in physiognomy (J. C. Lavater), anatomy (John Hunter), mineralogy (Ignaz von Born), thoracic percussion (Leopold Auenbrugger), and public health (Johann Peter Frank), and when learning or reporting new information he showed a fascination with details lending themselves to numerical reportage – sizes, amounts, costs, durations – though these would hardly add "mathematics" to the list of his possible interests.

During the 1780s, when Herschel discovered the planet Uranus, Haydn attended in the salon of court councilor Franz Sales von Greiner, whose wife Charlotte was passionately interested in astronomy and broadened the social sphere of literature and fine arts. Hörwarthner speculates that the dramatic increase in the size of Haydn's library beginning in the 1780s may be one outcome, and his foray into FREEMASONRY in 1785, with some of the same participants, may have had a similar effect. In LONDON in the 1790s, Haydn's circle included Charles Burney, whose fascination with comets and the Mongolfier hot-air balloon would likely have been congenial. Although Haydn's reactions to the two most spectacular comet events of the eighteenth century are unknowable – the first of 1744 with its three tails and the second of 1759 being the return of Halley's comet, which proved the truth of the predictable Newtonian universe – his career with an Esterházy COURT bent on acquiring instruments of celestial knowledge and his 1792 visit to Herschel's forty-foot telescope at Slough suggest that he too was fascinated by a science called "SUBLIME."

Haydn's first two Esterházy patrons, Prince Paul Anton and Prince Nicolaus, were educated in the early 1730s at the University of Leyden, a center of experimental and medical knowledge, and his mentor and librettist, imperial librarian Baron Gottfried van Swieten hailed from Leyden, the son of Maria

Theresia's court physician Gerhard van Swieten (1700–72), who had studied there with the celebrated Dutch professor Herman Boerhaave, a pioneer in the teaching of clinical medicine (see Berkel et al.; Hans). A favorite at the imperial court despite his disastrous failure to recommend the smallpox vaccine, the elder Swieten was given a mandate to eradicate superstition, traveling to Moravia to persuade the inhabitants that vampires did not exist. Haydn owned an English-language biography and account of Boerhaave's writings, by John Burton (1743). Boerhaave's other famous student was Albrecht von Haller, the naturalist, anatomical theorist of irritability and sensibility (see EMPFINDSAMKEIT), and influential poet of *The Alps* (1729), which Haydn owned in an edition of 1789; did Haydn know of his enduring scientific relevance even to the surgeon-anatomist John Hunter? (See Porter; Day-O'Connell.) Porter; Day-O'Connell) Haller's poetry appeared in English during Haydn's London visits in the 1790s, when didactic poetry renewed its long vogue. Indeed, Erasmus Darwin was then enjoying a huge if scandalous success with his didactic poem, "The Loves of the Plants" (1789), which sought to render the Linnæian system of botany, classifying plants by their sexual characteristics, into accessible and even playfully erotic terms. In his preface to the *The Botanic Garden* (1791), containing both "Loves" and the more science-and-technology-minded poem "The Economy of Vegetation," Darwin explicitly describes his intention: "to inlist [sic] the Imagination under the banner of Science; and to lead her votaries from the looser analogies, which dress out the imagery of poetry, to the stricter ones, which form the ratiocination of Philosophy." While we cannot place a copy in Haydn's hands, Darwin's work and the outpouring of botanical poetry it inspired, much of it by women, seems important to the climate of discovery around the natural world (see George; see also GENDER; PHILOSOPHY; IMAGINATION).

The extent to which tangential relationships and books attest to Haydn's knowledge of the scientific culture of his time is of course obscure. But at particular times his works seem to absorb and reflect topical scientific concerns in sophisticated and even moving ways. The global excitement over the Transit of Venus in June 1761 (occurring twice every *c.* 120 years, i.e. 1631 and 1639, 1761 and 1769, 1874 and 1882, 2004 and 2012) in which the movement of the planet across the sun's disk enables precise calculations of the distance between Earth and Sun when observations from different parts of the globe are compared, was widely reported. As Sisman (2013) shows, it focused attention on the diurnal positions of the sun that Haydn seemed to map in his Symphonies Nos. 6 through 8, written that month to impress his new patron who owned a celestial globe, a sundial clock that created an explosion at noon, and an unknown number of telescopes. To introduce morning ("Le matin," No. 6), the sun rises in a swelling, registrally increasing gesture turning toward the dominant. In the second movement, the clouds of morning reveal and dispel the moon from the sky. At noon ("Le midi," No. 7), the lordly sun becomes martial and imposing but in the second movement grows too strong: an instrumental recitative bespeaks bewilderment, panic, and debilitation, until the refreshing green shade can be found (*Adagio*). Finally, at evening ("Le soir," No. 8) the sun sinks below the horizon at the very end of the *Andante* (see TIME).

Remarkably, Haydn turned to the same musical gestures and even key relationships when setting the creation of the sun, moon, and stars in The Creation (1798, No. 12, "In splendor bright") and the details of the sun's day throughout "Summer" in The Seasons, making explicit the diurnal arc of the early trilogy. Tovey memorably asserted that Haydn's celestial formations in The Creation must have owed some of their vividness to "the nebular hypothesis of Kant and Laplace" (quoted in Meisel 315). While Haydn was in London, Herschel presented to the Royal Society his theory of nebular "condensation" into stars. Haydn's enduringly fascinating "Representation of Chaos," the task Swieten set him as Introduction to the oratorio, was instantly controversial; as Meisel puts it, "that Haydn avoids 'tone painting,' a mimetic literalism, in evoking the unimaginable has not prevented generations of critics from translating the experience of the music into images." He concludes, "in so far as it is chaos temporalized, it reconnects chaos and process, that is, chaos and creation, while delivering the imaginative experience of boundless drift and suspension" (314–15). (See MIMESIS; PROGRAMMATIC ELEMENTS.)

With the thin line separating alchemy from chemistry and astrology from astronomy, and the emergence of problems like Mesmerism, the risks of being taken in caused people to hedge their bets, a situation that could be mined for HUMOR. The English writer Nathaniel Wraxall wrote from VIENNA on December 20, 1777 that "natural philosophy has scarcely made greater progress in Vienna, than sound reason and real religion." He noted, amid the prevalence of superstition and credulity, the astounding detail that "the philosopher's stone is at this very time sought after here" by "at least three thousand persons" (272–73). Haydn's setting of Goldoni's durable comedy Il mondo della luna (1777), in which a daughter's suitor pretends to be an astronomer to trick the paterfamilias Buonafede into believing his false telescopes reveal a congenial lunar world, perhaps lampoons gullibility rather than astronomy. But as Polzonetti points out, the emblematic observatory and telescope, especially in the beautiful opening hymn to the moon sung by the faux-astronomer's acolytes, would have brought to mind serious science, heroic Galileo as well as newly venerated Benjamin Franklin, then an international symbol of "politically charged science" due to his work on electricity. During the scene in which Buonafede himself looks at staged "lunar" scenes during instrumental "intermezzos," the treatment of violins con sordino, in Loughridge's persuasive formulation, play the same trick on the listener by making "objects that are actually close seem far away," replacing Goldoni's "critique of credulity with the pleasures and promises of mediated listening" (197). Trying to have it both ways might also explain the persistence of humoral character types – melancholic, sanguinic, choleric, and phlegmatic – in the developing human sciences like empirical psychology and anthropology, even in Kant's Anthropology of 1798.

ELAINE SISMAN

FURTHER READING
Berkel et al. (1999); Darwin (1791); Day-O'Connell (2009a); George (2007); Hans (1957); Heilbron (2003); Hörwarthner (1997); Jones (2010); Loughridge (2013); Meisel (2016); Polzonetti (2011); Porter (2003); Sisman (2013, 2016); Wraxall (1799–1800).

Scotland – see Folk Song Settings

Self-Reflexivity Both within his music and in various non-musical ways, Haydn drew attention to his compositional prowess, to his desire to exert an unusual degree of control over performers, and to his consciousness of his image, both in and beyond his lifetime. This self-reflexivity – or in other words, his propensity not only to draw attention to his COMPOSITIONAL PROCESS, but to highlight the means of drawing attention, was certainly facilitated by the potentialities of late eighteenth-century style. However, it also stands in apparent or superficial contrast with the long-propagated (and, as Webster notes in his biographical entry for *Grove Online*, partly deserved) image of him as personally modest and unpretentious. All the individual elements of Haydn's self-reflexivity (or self-referentiality) have long been noted by scholars, and some (Agawu, Bonds, Dolan) have used the term. But to collect his compositional devices, his implied relation to performers and his public self-presentation under the single umbrella of self-reflexivity may suggest a particularly cohesive reading of his "life and works."

The Viennese Classical Style (of course partly created by Haydn himself), with its emphasis on variety of TOPICS and structural self-explanatoriness, was perfectly suited to bringing various aspects of the compositional act to the forefront of the listener's experience. That is, by virtue of the transparency and variety with which tonal processes, cadences and phraseology, melodic types, and textures could be deployed, the composer could directly engage the listener in the evolving processes of the music – raising, satisfying, and redirecting expectations all the while. (See MELODY, HARMONY, FORM.) Agawu, for example, notes that his category of "introversive semiosis" in Classical-period music (in other words, "pure" signs referring to the elements and devices of a work itself rather than to extra-musical phenomena) encourages the listener to listen to music "on its own terms," or as an endlessly iterative discussion about itself (109). However, although this late eighteenth-century style in general invites active reflection about musical processes, Haydn was the composer who most consistently, pervasively, and brilliantly deployed these processes to shed light on the choices he had made, and to make listeners aware that they are witnessing the processes of a creative activity.

Wit and HUMOR – surely the most widely noted aspects of Haydn's style (see Wheelock) – are the most obvious example of reflexivity. Bonds, among others, has related Haydn's wit to Laurence Sterne's, particularly in *Tristram Shandy*, a famously self-reflexive novel. Wit and humor are self-reflexive because, like many jokes, they draw attention to the manner of their own construction. But Haydn's capacity to draw conscious attention to his compositional devices does not always fall into the category of wit as we often understand it today. He may invoke an eighteenth-century sense of the term, as Mastic has argued about Haydn's recomposed recapitulations. But even an expanded sense of wit does not fully cover Haydn's compositional self-reflexivity. In a study of Haydn's Scottish FOLK SONG settings, Will demonstrates Haydn's "excessive" (though not inappropriate) compositional sophistication in relation to his original material. This kind of excess gently draws attention to Haydn's own creative contributions. And the recent interest in Haydn as rhetorician, deploying a variety of well-understood rhetorical strategies, not only to engage listeners, but to make them aware that they are being engaged, also falls into the category of self-reflexivity.

As Somfai and Webster have noted, Haydn's performance markings – especially dynamics and articulation – are particularly detailed, especially in genres, like the string quartet, that were widely disseminated for performance far away from Haydn's physical presence. This increased attention to the details of performance partly reflects the broader changing relationship between composer and performer at the end of the eighteenth and into the nineteenth century, whereby "following the intentions of the composer" became understood less as finding a legible Affekt and adding the necessary nuances to communicate that, and more as divining a numinous but also more particular "essence" for each work; an essence communicated in part by more, and more idiosyncratic, expression marks. But Haydn's PERFORMANCE indications, which include a number of string fingerings unique among non-pedagogical composers, also draw attention to his control of the performer's very body, not only creating some special effects, but also conspicuously denying performers choice in matters that were usually intimately their own. Thus, the famous sliding fingerings in the trio of the "Joke," string quartet Op. 33, No. 2 in E♭ may or may not refer externally to a drunken country fiddler, but they also draw attention to Haydn's capacity to control the performer's body.

Finally, Tolley has detailed Haydn's later-life preoccupation with his image in the context of a culture increasingly interested in connecting the visual emblems of composers with the sounds of their music (see RECEPTION; MATERIAL CULTURE). That Haydn was also concerned, especially in relation to *The Creation*, with marketing and controlling his posthumous reputation as a "great" composer, is also well-documented, as Mathew has shown. Griesinger's and Dies's first-hand biographical accounts reflect both Haydn's increasingly image-oriented cultural context and his own willingness to participate in it. This interest in his own image is not only telling in itself with respect to self-reflexivity, but it also provides a framework for thinking about the ways in which his compositions alert us to his extraordinary control of his tangible and intangible compositional resources.

MARY HUNTER

FURTHER READING
Agawu (1991); Beghin (2007); Bonds (1991a); Dolan (2013); *Grove Online*; Hunter (2012b); Mastic (2015); Mathew (2012); Somfai (1994); Tolley (2001); Webster (1979); Wheelock (1992); Will (2012).

Sensibility – see *Empfindsamkeit*

Sociability According to the oft-quoted founding myth, Haydn's supposed "invention" of the string quartet was motivated by a social occasion: Baron Fürnberg is said to have requested music for Haydn and two others to play together at his country estate in Weinzierl, and these "purely chance circumstances ... led him to try his luck at the composition of quartets" (Griesinger 15–16; Gotwals 13). More than any other genre, the string quartet has been regarded as a fundamentally social type of music since its PERFORMANCE seems to resemble a convivial exchange among familiars. That string chamber music often served as accompaniment for other, non-musical forms of sociability in aristocratic salons partly explains why it has been construed as an imitation of it. As Hunter (2012) puts it, the homogeneity of four parts engaging on an egalitarian (if not strictly equal) basis makes the quartet well suited to both "stimulate ... and in performance simulate" social intercourse.

To compare the string quartet (or related chamber genres) to artful conversation was to pay a high compliment, since the eighteenth century had elevated the social arts to new heights as a domain worthy of meticulous cultivation and serious philosophical examination (see Burke; Halsey and Slinn). If the wittiest, most refined discourse was to be found in Parisian salons – and if (as de Staël 1813 laments) German conversation did not achieve the same high mark – a fascination with the social had nevertheless firmly taken root in German-speaking lands. Haydn himself owned a copy of Adolph Knigge's (1788) influential treatise on social relations, which was widely republished in many editions and translations (Hörwarthner 462).

The influence of sociability on musical style (or at least on musical thought) is evinced by contemporaneous critical responses to Haydn's and Mozart's quartets emphasizing role-exchange and turn-taking among the four parts, principles that imitate a sociable dynamic among friends. Heinrich Christoph Koch contrasts the style of "sonatas" (meaning any chamber music, including trios and quartets) and "symphonies," noting that the former "portray the sentiments of individual people ... [and] must be exquisitely cultivated and seem to represent the subtlest nuances of the sentiments," whereas the latter depend less on subtlety than on "power and force" (Koch 315–16; Baker 203). Koch's remarks about "sonatas" hint at interpreting parts in a chamber piece as distinct musical characters or agents engaged in social intercourse (as in the "multiple agency" concept developed by Klorman).

This notion became more explicit (and colorful) in Carpani's famous description of Haydn's quartets resembling "a conversation among four amiable people": (1) the first violin, "a man of spirit and affability, middle aged, [and] a good speaker who sustained the major part of the discourse"; (2) the second violin, a "friend of the first" who strove to "make him shine" by "agreeing to what he had heard ... [rather than advancing] his own ideas"; (3) the cello [*Basso*], a "solid man, learned, and sententious" who "as a prophet ... predicted what the principal speaker [i.e., first violin]" would say, contributing "strength and direction [*norma*]" to the discussion; and (4) the viola, a "loquacious matron" whose "delightful chattering [*cicalate*] ... gave the others a chance to breathe" and "seasoned the conversation with her grace," and who "was more a friend of the cello" than of the others (Carpani 91–92n). Carpani thus imputes various human and social attributes to each instrument, including GENDER, age, personality, and a propensity toward forming allegiances informed by established dominant and subservient roles within their circle. Carpani's account – which was widely disseminated through a (liberally plagiarized) French adaptation (Stendhal 61–62; Coe 35–36) – reinforced a paradigm that remains influential to this day. The view of individual instruments representing distinct characters engaged in conversation has been espoused by figures as diverse as Anton Reicha and Johann Wolfgang von Goethe, one the one hand, and Charles Ives and Elliott Carter, on the other.

If the quartet-as-conversation concept has by now become a cliché, scholarship by Bracht and, in particular, Sutcliffe has challenged its validity on a variety of grounds, chiefly its over-simple equation of melody with speech and its dubious claims of an *equal* exchange among the four parts. Wheelock further notes the tendency, in focusing on intercourse among the players, to exclude *listeners* from a sense of participation. She writes of a "conflict between conversation and music . . . [since] the audience must abandon their own conversations to attend to that of the players" (1992, 73). I have suggested elsewhere (2016) that the very term "audience" may confuse matters, since it applies more properly to modern-day concert rituals than to Enlightenment-period domestic musical gatherings: events described as "concerts" or *Accademien* in eighteenth-century documents were fundamentally social affairs, running the gamut from formal gatherings (possibly approximating modern recitals) to noisy parties in which individuals playing (or sight-reading) were almost certainly drowned out by the company's conversation. In an imagined, fictional reconstruction of a Parisian salon, Le Guin depicts a kind of "parallel play" between musicians playing a Haydn trio and a coterie of *philosophes* musing and theorizing about musical performance. The "audience" members (if we must call them that) are thus highly engaged with the music-making, which animates their own social involvement (compare to the broadened concept of musical participation, or "musicking," advanced by Small). To the extent that the read-through of the trio constitutes a *musical* "performance," the conversation constitutes a *sociable* one.

It is only natural that "the social" has attracted particular attention in recent decades as musicology has broadened from a primary focus on musical works, scores, and structures to a purview that encompasses sites of music-making, the physicality of musical performance, and the involvement of listeners in musical gatherings. If these trends have tended at times to shift attention away from "the music itself" and toward the ambiences in which it was played, there remains an open question how these perspectives might best be integrated with analytical readings of COMPOSITIONAL PROCESS and MUSICAL MATERIALS.

Perhaps they are to remain separate and in productive tension; Parker, for instance, explains her turn to social metaphors of "conversation" in string quartets of the period 1750–97 as a rejection of traditional, formalist analytical methods. Another approach (exemplified by Le Guin and Beghin) has been to advocate a style of analysis deeply informed by each author's performance experience, infusing analysis with sensitivity to physical performance gestures. Beghin in particular draws in social considerations through his focus on Haydn's relationships with his DEDICATEES and their claviers. A third perspective emerges in a series of publications by Sutcliffe (2013) that abandon a focus on interplay among players, drawing attention instead to a kind of sociable ethos expressed in successive passages or musical gestures. He traces the "shapes of sociability" through exchanges wherein an initial, assertive gesture is followed by a gracious riposte. Tellingly, Sutcliffe finds this pattern not only in trios and quartets but equally in solo keyboard and symphonic contexts, demonstrating that

Figure 28 This engraving appeared on the title page of Artaria's edition of Haydn's Piano Trio in E♭, Hob.XV:10, published in 1798. Eighteenth-century depictions of figures playing chamber music often emphasize the intimate exchange among the players. Reproduced by permission of Jean Gray Hargrove Music Library, University of California, Berkeley.

sociability is a broader, more encompassing category for eighteenth-century music beyond the small-ensemble chamber repertoires for which it has most commonly been invoked. (See also AMATEURS; AUDIENCES; PERFORMANCE SPACES; RELATIONSHIPS AND FRIENDSHIPS; SELF-REFLEXIVITY).

EDWARD KLORMAN

FURTHER READING
Baker and Christensen (1996); Bashford (2003); Beghin (2015a); Bracht (1994); Burke (1993); Carpani (1812); Coe (1972); Gotwals; Griesinger; Halsey and Slinn (2008); Hanning (1989); Hörwarthner (1997); Hunter (1997a, 2012); Klorman (2016); Knigge (1788); Koch (1782, 1787, 1793); Le Guin (2007); Parker (2002); Schroeder (2000–1); Small (1998); de Staël (1813); Stendhal (1814); Sutcliffe (2003a, 2009, 2013); Wheelock (1992, 2003).

Societies – see Musical Societies

Spain – see European Contexts

Spiritual Beliefs – see Religion and

Sublime By the end of Haydn's career, the critical category of the sublime had achieved a central place in the network of terms that governed artistic production and reception. While it was frequently applied to artists and artistic works, it addressed, in particular, emphatic experiences characterized by sudden transport rather than persuasion, by power and passion rather than logic, and by resistance to classification and control. As a category of reception, it frequently worked in tandem with GENIUS, a category of production also linked with power, passion, spontaneity, and irregularity. But if the sublime had fame and fortune, it also had many guises. Depending on the artistic inclinations and the philosophical commitments of different times, it could describe the communicative act crystallized into a perfectly simple expression as well as it could the thrill of incomprehension at sensory perceptions that challenged the imagination. It could be an intensification of the BEAUTIFUL as well as its opposite. It could have clear theological implications, or it could be treated as physiological in essence.

Many of Haydn's works could be interpreted as sublime according to one of its various definitions, although there is no evidence that Haydn himself thought much about the category until his trips to England after 1791, where the category had been much in vogue for almost a century. Haydn reacted most palpably to the debate on the sublime in *The Creation* (1798), which features a setting of an exemplum of sublimity that was already canonical: "God said, let there be light, and there was light" (Genesis 1:3). Haydn himself held the passage in especial esteem, as did many of his contemporaries. There is still no music of greater sublimity" wrote Gustav Schilling in 1830 (Webster 1997, 65). The work can serve as an index of different conceptions of sublimity that echoed in Haydn's time, despite their origins at different points in the long history of the aesthetic category.

The category of sublimity (literally, "below the threshold," designating the place of the recipient with respect to something of great height) has a dual origin in the high or grand style taught in Roman treatises on rhetoric and in a fragmentary Greek treatise ascribed to Longinus, *Peri hypsous* (*On the Height of Eloquence*, 1st or possibly 3rd century CE). The first of these two traditions, the rhetorical grand or sublime style, taught how to transport audiences through figures of speech and thought. It was not difficult for musicians to develop procedures that invite comparison to such rhetorical amplification. Webster (1997) and Sisman describe how a musician could elaborate a stylistic lingua franca – such as the galant texture of imitative motivic exchanges within a homophonic and largely diatonic harmonic framework – by drawing upon stereotypical manipulations or accretions, such as TOPICS, complex HARMONIC progressions, disruptions of musical syntax, and generous ORCHESTRATIONS. Grandeur was the effect. In *The Creation*, the "Representation of Chaos" offers mysterious harmonies and intricate voice leading, while arrival of light showcases orchestral might and splendour.

Although Longinus wrote from within the rhetorical tradition and took up many of its propositions, he attended in particular to the ways in which the tricks of the rhetorical trade were not sufficient to achieve grandeur. It was not enough to elaborate style and to disrupt syntax, as useful as those procedures could be. It needed to be done well, and to do this the artist could draw upon innate powers of forming great conceptions and violent passion, often thereby falling away from stylistic perfection. The anti-regulatory spirit of Longinus allowed his writings to inspire many eighteenth-century enthusiasts of GENIUS. While this label as applied to Haydn fell into disuse beginning in the nineteenth century, critics have continued to find fascination in Haydn's play with and subversion of convention.

Longinus's anti-regulatory impulse also led him to point out that simplicity could produce height as well as amplification, so long as an utterance effectively communicated grandeur of conception or spirit. In his sole example from the Judaic tradition, he noted how the creation of light conveyed the idea of unbounded divine power. Elsewhere, he noted that amplification was not the same as elevation. In the translation of *Peri hypsous* into French (1674), the influential neo-classical poet and critic Nicolas Boileau combined example and principle and thereby ensured that many eighteenth-century writers would identify simplicity as an essential characteristic of the sublime. But simplicity was not just a matter of style. The reduction of means ensured that the moral nobility of an utterance or the truth of an idea shone through in a text or oration. These can be heard at work in *The Creation*, especially for a religiously minded auditor. Concentrated choral and orchestral forces report in hushed tones on the creation of light, and the event itself is represented in a singularly direct crescendo that contrasts diametrically with the intricate convolutions of chaos. Later in the work, the angelic commentators on the creation and the first humans confess awe and the expression of religious and moral truths with simple directness of vocal melody. As Webster (2005b) suggests, the neo-classical conception of sublimity was fully consonant with the pastoral mode, also represented in *The Seasons*.

Despite its central place in canonic texts on sublimity, high emotion often troubled critics up through the eighteenth century, suspicious as they were of physicality and immediacy. In his *Grounds of Criticism on Poetry* (1704), John Dennis, for example, suggests the "enthusiastic" passions characteristic of sublime sacred poetry (such as Milton and the Bible) transcended the "vulgar" passions because they sprang from reflection or meditation. In practice, critics sorted passions according to the contexts in which they were evoked or experienced, allowing as sublime only passions that served moral, religious, or patriotic attitudes. In his oratorios, George Frideric Handel so excelled at eliciting high emotions within the "safe" context of a moral and religious story that he would quickly become one of the century's primary exemplars of the sublime in music (see Johnson; Smith). Both homophonic and fugal choruses in Haydn's *Creation* show his debt to the tradition.

Most definitions of sublimity until the eighteenth century privileged the role of word or idea in the production of transport, as well as the close association of beauty and sublimity. Such approaches suited Haydn's music well, both vocal and instrumental, as it did the music of many of his contemporaries. With some notable exceptions, such as C. P. E. Bach, most musicians did not respond specifically to theorists of sublimity. Rather, the theorists crystallized issues in the production and reception of transport that occupied artists across media and were often communicated through genre traditions. Thus, the neo-classical play of nobility and simplicity was essential to FOLK SONG production and the early lied. As Bonds points out, amplification and syntactic disruption were essential to the ode, or, if one saw instrumental music as wordless vocal music, the symphony.

The approach to sublimity began to change mid-century, and the changes would strongly mark Haydn reception. In his *Philosophical Enquiry into the Origin of our Ideas of the Sublime and the Beautiful* (1757), Edmund Burke turned to the empirical process by which sensations are processed. Formal criteria such as magnitude, succession, uniformity, obscurity, magnificence, and difficulty, he argued, could produce physical discomfort that brought one's mortality into immediate experience. When attenuated through the knowledge of one's safety, however, these same qualities produced the delight characteristic of the sublime, so different from the positive pleasure associated with beauty. The bifurcation maps well onto Haydn's two oratorios, *The Creation* and *The Seasons* (Webster 2005b), and also supported the political use of musical monumentality for martial ends (see Mathew). Although Burke's catalogue of the formal causes of sublimity echoes in eighteenth-century celebrations of Haydn's chiaroscuro effects and disruptions of syntax, the philosopher's radical separation of sublimity from beauty would eventually have a pernicious influence on the composer's reputation. To those who enthused at the delightful horrors of Beethoven, Haydn would only seem beautiful.

In his *Critique of Judgment* (1790), Immanuel Kant followed Burke in opposing beauty and sublimity and in attending to the formal play of sensation. However, physiological response was less important to him than the cognitive and moral capacities that ensured that powerful experiences did not lead to a person's extinction as a free subject. These capacities underpinned the distinction between the mathematical sublime (arising from the response to a threat to a person's powers of understanding) and the dynamic sublime (arising from the response to a threat to a person's moral freedom). Webster (1997) and Sisman both suggest that even during Haydn's lifetime critics such as Christian Friedrich Michaelis productively misread Kant's idealist approach to hear Haydn's formal processes as sublime. The approach assisted in the gradual negligence of Haydn's vocal music and especially his religious music.

Haydn saw his masses as his greatest achievements, though they would quickly fall from the repertoire. This fall from fortune says much about the underpinnings of the sublime. Weiskel has written that "All versions of the sublime require a credible god-term, a meaningful jargon of ultimacy, if the discourse is not to collapse into 'mere' rhetoric" (36). For Haydn and many of his contemporaries, confidence in the divine nature of Creation stood as a guarantor that the transport provided by words and ideas was more than a tickling of the senses. Truth was what was conveyed. In the nineteenth-century, the shift to idealist versions of the sublimity would relocate sublimity from heavenly heights to the depths of subjectivity. Haydn's excellences did not fare well in the new regime. The category of sublimity has had new fortune with post-modern theorists such as Jean-François Lyotard, but it is not clear that Haydn's music suits their focus on shock as radical disruption to consciousness. Haydn's sublimity, so convincing to his contemporaries, may now be a matter of rhetoric, but his music continues to transport audiences without the metaphysics, providing both pleasure in the present and insight into the past.

KEITH CHAPIN

FURTHER READING
Bonds (1997); Dennis (1704); Doran (2015); Johnson (1986); Kant (1790); Mathew (2007); Monk (1960); Sisman (1993b); Smith (1995); Webster (1997, 2005b); Weiskel (1976).

T

Teaching and Students In Austria in the seventeenth and eighteenth centuries, initial musical studies (singing and instrumental training) were offered in primary schools, which were run by Catholic parishes (see EDUCATION; CHURCH). Further musical training was possible in other religious institutions such as monasteries and larger churches (cathedrals) as well as in the courts. The first public music schools in Austria were founded by SOCIETIES of citizens in the early nineteenth century (Graz 1816, Vienna 1817, Innsbruck 1818, Linz 1823, Klagenfurt 1828). Composition studies were neither systematic nor institutionalized in the eighteenth century. The first publically funded educational institution for music in EUROPE was the Paris Conservatoire, founded in 1795. Even here, it was possible to study COUNTERPOINT and figured bass, but not composition. Compositional training was still a personal matter between master and apprentice. Haydn's teaching activities extended over fifty years from the first keyboard lessons he gave in the early 1750s until only a few years before his death in 1809. Today we know of twenty-five COMPOSERS who verifiably or most likely studied with Haydn, and a further thirteen who may have done so.

In his autobiographical notes from 1776, Haydn reported that after completing his period as a chorister at St. Stephen's Cathedral in Vienna c. 1749, he managed to live on a small income from teaching voice and instrument lessons (mainly keyboard and violin) for eight years (*Briefe* 77). His first known (keyboard) student was Marianna Martines, to whom Haydn was likely recommended by the court poet Pietro Metastasio. At the time, Haydn, Metastasio and Martines all lived in the same building, the Michaelerhaus in VIENNA. Martines became a renowned pianist, singer, and composer in and beyond Vienna and in 1773 was the first female composer admitted to the Accademia Filarmonica in Bologna. Haydn also taught singing to Theresia Helena Keller, the sister of his future wife, Maria Anna Theresia. Among Haydn's first counterpoint students in Vienna were Abund Mykisch, from Bohemia, and Robert Kimmerling, who became the choral director of the Melk Collegiate Church in 1761. That same year, Haydn was appointed to the Esterházy COURT, where the duties listed in his contract included coaching singers (see VOCAL COACHING AND REHEARSAL). The young violinist George Polgreen Bridgetower whose father had been a page to Prince Esterházy from 1779 to 1785, presented himself as a pupil of Haydn on his tours through Germany (1786) and England (1789) (see Walter).

The many and frequent rehearsals Haydn directed as Kapellmeister to Prince Nicolaus Esterházy across nearly three decades of tenure at court suggest that, in the broadest sense, all of the musicians and singers he worked with at the court may be considered his students. He also taught composition to some members of the court orchestra, including Bohemian harp virtuoso Johann Baptist Krumpholz, the cellist Anton Kraft, whom Haydn greatly admired, and Haydn's successor as Kapellmeister at the court, Johann Nepomuk Fuchs. Another composition student was the Esterházy court librarian Father Primitivus Niemecz, with whom Haydn used Johann Joseph Fux's *Gradus ad Parnassum* – the same counterpoint instructional manual he had studied as a young adult, and in which he made numerous marginalia and corrections over several years. Haydn collated extracts from Fux's treatise into an album he called *Elementarbuch*, of which two copies survive – one from F. C. Magnus (1789) and another from Franz Lessel (1800), both Haydn's students – indicating that Haydn held Fux's guidelines in high regard into his later years. From the Esterházy years onwards, Haydn had many private composition students, including Ignaz Pleyel, who lived with Haydn in Eisenstadt between 1772 and 1777, his expenses underwritten by Duke Ladislaus Erdődy, Pleyel's first employer. Pleyel remained a close friend of Haydn's for the remainder of his life, even in London in 1792, when master and student were direct rivals in the London concert scene, performing in Johann Peter Salomon's concert series and in Wilhelm Cramer's "Professional Concert" series respectively. After establishing a music Edition in Paris in 1795, Pleyel Published many of Haydn's works, including the *Collection complette des Sonates de Piano d'Haydn* in six volumes in 1801–2 and the *Collection complette des Quatuors d'Haydn* 1801, extended respectively in 1802–3 and 1806. Finally, in the series *Bibliothèque musicale*, for which Pleyel invented the pocket score, he printed several of Haydn's "London" Symphonies and many string quartets. With the study of exemplary works continuing to form a major part of compositional studies, we can readily imagine what an important role the broad and relatively cheap distribution of pocket scores played in the Reception and assimilation of Haydn's works by an interested and competent Public as well as among composition students.

As Haydn's fame grew, more and more young composers claimed to be his students. Composition students in the 1780s included Anton Wranitzky, Fritz and Edmund von Weber (stepbrothers of Carl Maria von Weber), Johann Friedrich Kranz, Franz Seraph von Destouches, and the aforementioned Magnus, and among those in the 1790s were Ludwig van Beethoven, Peter Haensel, Pietro and Antonio Polzelli, Johann Spech, Paul Struck, Sigismund Neukomm and Lessel (see Walter). During his time in England, Haydn taught composers John Wall Callcott and Thomas Haigh, as well as Rebecca Schroeter, with whom he developed a close relationship. Haydn Dedicated his three Piano Trios Op. 73 (Hob.XV/24, 25 and 26), composed in London in 1795, to Schroeter.

Haydn's first meeting with Beethoven, his most famous student, was probably in Bonn in December 1790, when Haydn stayed there on his way to London. When he stopped in Bonn again on his return journey to Vienna in 1792, his high praise for Beethoven most probably played a role in the patronage of Archduke Maximilian Franz, enabling Beethoven to study with the master in Vienna starting in November 1792. A report by Johann Baptist Schenk (1753–1836), which mentions that Beethoven had lessons from him secretly as he was discontented with Haydn's tuition, influenced early literature on Haydn in particular (see Nottebohm); on the historical misrepresentation of Beethoven's relationship with Haydn see Reception, Contemporary.

When Haydn left for his second trip to London in January 1794, he referred Beethoven to his friend Johann Georg Albrechtsberger for further lessons. Even if the teacher–student relationship between Haydn and Beethoven may have been strained, Beethoven did admire Haydn's compositions, commenting respectfully on Haydn's music and purchasing many of his scores. Beethoven's own counterpoint guidelines, *Materialien zum Kontrapunkt*, written in 1809, demonstrate a close affinity with the ideas of his teacher Haydn on the topic.

Haydn continued to teach throughout his life. One of his last students was the keyboard virtuoso Friedrich Kalkbrenner, who had composition lessons with Haydn starting in 1803. During the last years of Haydn's life, Anton Reicha, Johann Nepomuk Hummel, Anton Diabelli, Conradin Kreutzer und Carl Maria von Weber all benefited from instructive discussions with Haydn (see Walter).

Several decades lay between the authorship of Fux's treatise and Haydn's use of this manual in his later years. During this period there were significant developments in compositional practice, which raises questions about the status and function of this treatise in Haydn's teaching. In Fux's conception, there are four different levels or steps (*gradus*) necessary in order to master the art of composition: (1) teaching the numerical relationship between intervals as a mathematical fundament; (2) strict counterpoint ("strenger Satz"), i.e., two, three and four-part counterpoint in the five species, as the fundament of correct composition; (3) fugal writing; and (4) free composition ("freier Satz"). Haydn used only the second and fourth levels – strict counterpoint and free composition – in his teaching, and understood studies in counterpoint as a necessary prerequisite for free composition. The idea that counterpoint forms the immovable basis and free composition the stylistically and historically variable superstructure of composition was already expressed in the mid-seventeenth-century by Marco Sacchi, Christoph Bernhard, Angelo Berardi, and others. It is striking that Haydn radicalizes these thoughts by retaining Fux's modal approach (in contrast to Albrechtsberger, who transferred counterpoint into the system of major and minor scales), thereby underlining the ahistorical character of counterpoint. Haydn's annotations and comments show, however, that he expanded the use of dissonances in counterpoint in comparison to Fux. Haydn's appreciation of Fux's treatise seems to have impressed Mozart, who began to teach Fuxian counterpoint to his own students in the 1780s, the decade in which Mozart and Haydn met frequently in Vienna. If we consider that Beethoven also adopted Haydn's modal attitude to counterpoint in his own teaching, then we are presented with an astonishing bond connecting the most prominent composers in Vienna at the time with the Baroque counterpoint tradition.

Although only vague insights into Haydn's free compositional teaching survive (see Mörner 27; Griesinger 113f.), we are able to recognize Haydn's pedagogical principles. These are based on the dichotomy between the rigorous study of counterpoint, which makes no concessions to practices of the period (style, genre, enforcement of major/minor TONALITIES), and the informal instruction in free composition, which mainly comprises the examination of exemplary works and critical discussion of compositional exercises. Compositional creativity, which Haydn viewed as innate (Griesinger 113f.), should be formed and honed through the fundaments of counterpoint in the first instance, and only then through a critical view of contemporary works. Further skills required to round off a consummate education in composition included knowledge of figured bass, singing, piano and/or instrumental playing – subjects that Haydn taught up until 1790. Haydn influenced his students not only through his direct intervention as a teacher, but also with his whole personality, his works, and the enormous authority that he enjoyed in the last decades of his life throughout Europe. FEDERICO CELESTINI

FURTHER READING
Briefe; Dies; Finscher (2008); Griesinger; H-L; Mann (1970a, 1970b); Mörner (1969); Nottebohm (1873); Walter (1982); Webster (1984).

Theater and Theatricality Haydn was a man of the theater. Throughout his career he composed and arranged music for a wide variety of genres, including incidental music for stage plays; German and Italian operas such as the lowbrow Singspiel *Der krumme Teufel* and the comedic intermezzo *La canterina*; heroic operas on well-known themes like Armida, Orlando, and Orpheus; numerous arias with orchestral accompaniment for insertion in stage productions of operas by other composers; dramatic scenes with orchestral or keyboard accompaniment (*Berenice, che fai?* and *Ariana a Naxos* respectively); and puppet opera performances.

Theatricality also played an important role in Haydn's musical development; indeed, the theater bears on Haydn studies in a broader sense, since critics and AUDIENCES have long understood his music to imitate human utterance, character, and action in ways suggestive of theatrical performance. Allanbrook captured this affinity between later eighteenth-century music and the theater under the venerable heading of "comic MIMESIS," a rubric loosely equivalent to the current critical notions of "meta-theatricality" and "performativity." Haydn's music – whether vocal or instrumental, written for the stage or not – is frequently connected to and imbued with contemporary theatrical AESTHETICS, in particular that of Italian comic opera.

Haydn's first impressions about the world of theater were formed during his youth in VIENNA. In the 1750s Haydn worked closely with the popular German-language theater troupe operating out of the Kärntnertortheater; as Melton points out, his dire financial straits probably motivated sustained collaboration. Here, Haydn worked alongside Joseph Felix von Kurz, the comic actor prized for his extemporized roles in Hanswurstian improvised comedy (see Figure 5), and for employing a wide range of performing gestures, facial expressions and vocal effects when playing the "Narr" or fool on stage – including "Judenmimus" –

when performing JEWISH caricature. Known by the stage name "Bernardon," Kurz-Bernardon was at the height of his career when, in 1752, he collaborated with Haydn on the composer's first work for the stage, *Der krumme Teufel* (The crooked or limping devil). Haydn provided musical inserts, now lost, but the surviving LIBRETTO for a revival, *Der neue krumme Teufel* (1759), indicates that the Singspiel included extensive incidental music, numerous arias, and choruses. Exaggerated movements, gesticulation, and theatrical histrionics were part and parcel of Hanswurstian performance, as evidenced in the "limping" of the title, or the swimming actions Kurz mimicked when instructing Haydn in how to coordinate musical gestures to physical movement (see COMPOSITIONAL PROCESS). Performed regularly in the Habsburg capital until 1783, and a staple of travelling theater troupes in the third quarter of the century, *Der (neue) krumme Teufel* was one of Haydn's best-known and most frequently performed stage works during his lifetime (see Clark 2009a; BURGENLAND).

Haydn's activity as an opera director and composer for the Esterházy COURT readily divides into three unequal phases or periods. First, from 1763–67 Haydn worked in various impromptu theater spaces at EISENSTADT, in Pressburg (Bratislava) and in the Kittsee palace (see PLACE). Second, from September 1768 to the end of 1775 Haydn directed performances in the first opera house at ESZTERHÁZA and in the marionette theater (opened 1773); these were either connected with festivities and social events at court, or formed part of a miscellaneous summer series. Third, 1776 initiated a series of fifteen full opera seasons at Eszterháza, during which the opera house, which was destroyed by fire in November 1779, was replaced with a larger 400-seat theater that opened early in 1781 with Haydn's *La fedeltà premiata*. Opera productions did not cease during the construction phase, but were moved to the smaller stage of the marionette theater, which was approximately the same size as the first opera house, as described by Pollheimer. (The first opera house, where twenty-two productions of Italian opera were staged from 1776–79, was similar in size to the marionette theater; this latter PERFORMANCE SPACE, still standing, has recently been renovated into a 170-seat concert hall.)

Although in Haydn's lifetime the Esterházy family owned and operated a proper and permanent theatrical enterprise only at Eszterháza, Prince Nicolaus initiated the first phase of opera productions at Eisenstadt shortly after his inauguration. In the summer of 1762, staged performances of some sort took place in a makeshift theater erected inside the glasshouse standing in the park, and may have included Haydn's lost short Italian *commedias* – probably a form of *commedia dell'arte* scenes with music.

Proper opera soon followed. With the festivities accompanying the wedding celebrations of Nicolaus's eldest son and heir, Prince Anton (m. Princess Maria Theresia Erdődy) in January 1763, the new prince offered a foretaste of multiple events to come; in addition to spoken theater, the cultural festivities also included two operas, one *buffa* the other *seria*. While the *opera buffa* is not known, the *opera seria* was Haydn's one-act allegorical *festa teatrale*, *Acide*, an Ovidian mythological pastoral adapted from a libretto by Metastasio (Haydn's former neighbor in Vienna), performed in the great hall of the palace in Eisenstadt on January 11, 1763. And that same summer Fischietti's *buffa Il mercato di Malmantile* was premiered at Eisenstadt, preceded by Haydn's fourth Italian *commedia*, *La marchesa Nespola* – laying the foundation for future theatricalizing of courtly musical entertainments. The meeting of the Hungarian legislative assembly in Pressburg (Pozsony, Bratislava) in 1764–65, for instance, provided Prince Nicolaus with an excellent opportunity to impress Hungarian and Austrian nobility with musico-theatrical entertainments. Concerts and opera performances began in July at his palace in Kittsee – a short excursion from Pressburg – and lasted until September. A further series of performances resumed in December and continued into January, this time in Pressburg and Eisenstadt. Besides the earlier repertoire, Esterházy performers may have performed two unknown operas whose existence is documented by an invoice referring to the printing of two opera librettos, dated early 1765 (Radant and Landon 63). The parodic *intermezzo per musica*, *La canterina*, which premiered at the palace in Eisenstadt in July 1766, was revived in Pressburg the following February during carnival season.

With the introduction of opera to Eszterháza in 1768, the occasional character of the theatrical performances did not change. The inauguration of the new building in September of that year took place during the festivities commemorating a visit by the royal governor of Hungary, and featured a performance of Haydn's *Lo speziale*, an adaptation of a mid-century libretto by Carlo Goldoni. Haydn's setting encodes the apothecary as a JEWISH stereotype, a racist caricature that had its place among the many stock characters common in eighteenth-century theatrical performance (see Clark 2009a, 2016; Pollheimer). Sacchini's (or possibly, Giacomo Rust's) *La contadina in corte* followed in 1769, and Haydn's *Le pescatrici* a year later – the composer's first full *dramma giocoso* by Goldoni and longest opera to date. For the next two summer seasons, the practice of arranging operas for visiting dignitaries to Eszterháza continued – including the visit of Prince Louis de Rohan, the French ambassador in Vienna, in July 1772 (see Landon II).

In September 1773, Eszterháza hosted its highest-ranking dignitary ever, Empress Maria Theresia, the Queen of Hungary. Her visit also marked the inauguration of the newly built marionette theater, with grottos encrusted with glittering precious stones and mother-of-pearl shells, automatic wall-fountains, and sophisticated stage machinery – all designed to enhance the luster and enchantment of this magical fairyland venue. Cultural events planned for the first night of her visit on September 1 included Haydn's peasant-styled comic opera *L'infedeltà delusa* – premiered a few weeks earlier to mark a family occasion while also ensuring the production was ready for the Empress's important visit. The next day saw the premiere event of her visit – the inauguration of the marionette theater with Haydn's *Philemon und Baucis* (with Vorspiel *Der Götterrath*), followed by a display of fireworks in the garden (see Landon II).

A short-lived Viennese theater periodical, *Historisch-kritische Theaterchronik von Wien*, offers a fascinating and detailed window into theatrical events at Eszterháza in the summer of 1774. This season featured a retrospective of previous stage works produced at Eszterháza, including the revival of many earlier operas beginning with *Acide* and ending with *L'infedeltà delusa*; only *Le pescatrici* and Fischietti's *buffo* are missing from these accounts. Opera revivals may have continued into the next summer, but for sure Haydn's "seraglio" opera, *L'incontro improvviso*, with its exotic Cairo setting, premiered on August 29, 1775, marking the visit of Archduke Ferdinand (youngest brother of the future Joseph II) and his consort. Unlike Mozart's *Die Entführung aus dem Serail*, which stages a European-Christian and Ottoman-Islamic encounter, this opera portrays the pasha/sultan and the young lover, Ali (who comes to rescue his abducted Rezia) as belonging to the same religion. According to Head, "antagonism to Islam does not figure in *L'incontro improvviso* but ambiguously, as part of a critique of an aspect of the 'home' religion: Catholic monasticism" (319). The Calandro's exoticized alms-begging performance "Castagno, Castagna," a song that, as Jerome argues, serves to undermine the character's credibility and integrity, invites audiences to probe the meta-performance of a European singing-actor portraying a devious imposter, and encourages reflection on religious wrongs perpetrated from within. Furthermore, the seraglio of *L'incontro improvviso*, "far from being a site of female enslavement and male tyranny" (as Head puts it) serves to "stage the civilizing, refining influence of 'woman'" (327). Musical productions such as this, part of celebratory festivities at court lasting for several days, aimed to overwhelm participants through an accumulation of spectacles, creating a "totalizing theatricality" in which "sovereign power elided distinctions between nature, theatre, fantasy and fact" (325).

The primacy of vocal and theatrical music in Haydn's oeuvre is articulated most persuasively in his biographical letter of July 1776, where he singled out his recent operas – *Le pescatrici*, *L'infedeltà delusa*, and *L'incontro improvviso* – for special approbation. At this time, a regular opera company was just getting underway at Eszterháza in response to the prince's waning interest in the baryton (see INSTRUMENTS) and his growing fascination with the wider world of the stage – a self-defining as well as competitive shift marked by the existence of not one, but two free-standing opera houses at Eszterháza. In the main theater where Italian opera and *Accademien* were performed (see Figure 29), and in the rococo marionette theater where mostly German-language stage productions took place utilizing puppets (probably 60–70 cm tall), Prince Nicolaus could physically "stage" his power and prestige and that of the talented musical establishment he sustained – indulging his passions for courtly spectacle while also affording Haydn the opportunity to hone the theatrical skills necessary to any eighteenth-century Kapellmeister. At least two productions in the marionette theater were sung in Italian: *Il cavaliere errante* and *L'assedio di Gibilterra*.

By far the greatest period of operatic activity at Eszterháza was the fifteen full seasons from 1776 to 1790. Each year, four to eight operas premiered alongside revivals from earlier seasons. The repertoire consisted exclusively of Italian operas by native and non-Italian composers – the one exception being Grétry's *Zemira ed Azor*, originally in French, but widely successful, as Loughridge points out, throughout Europe in this Italian version – and most had premiered recently, with the exception of emblematic works like Gluck's *Orfeo*, Piccinni's *La buona figliuola*, and Traetta's *Ifigenia in Tauride*, which were produced at Eszterháza after a delay of fourteen, sixteen, and twenty-three years respectively. This delay most likely reflected a self-conscious and retrospective

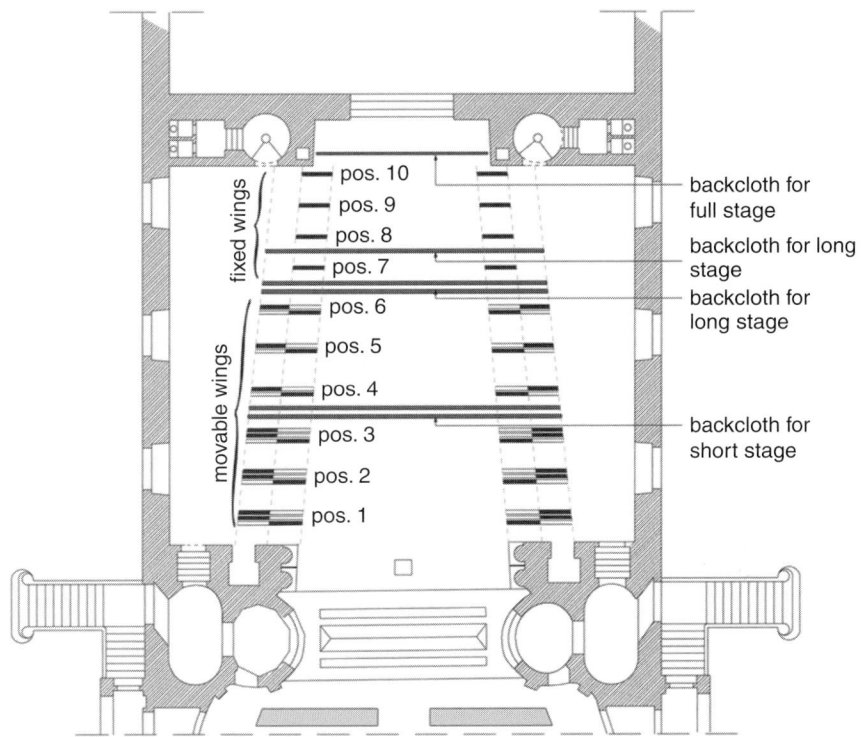

Figure 29 Plan of the stage and orchestra of the second opera house at Eszterháza, showing the position of the wings and backdrops for stage sets of different depth or length. Reproduced by permission of Oxford University Press.

interest in celebrating the important operatic achievements of the recent past (back to 1760) and the court's growing theatrical interests.

The oft-repeated objection that the Eszterháza repertoire was "provincial," mirroring the old-fashioned and amateurish preferences of Prince Nicolaus (promulgated by Horányi and Landon), is no longer tenable, due to the recent research of Malina and Pratl. Unlike truly provincial residential theaters, such as the one overseen by the Schwarzenbergs in the Krumau (Český Krumlov) castle, which relied strongly on local composers, the Esterházy repertory overlapped considerably with that presented in Vienna (especially after the Italian troupe took up residency there in 1783), and also at the King's Theatre in London and the court opera in St. Petersburg. This also undermines the other charge commonly leveled at Eszterháza – that it was just a rural imitation of the Burgtheater. On the contrary, both Prince Nicolaus and Haydn maintained a wide international network of correspondents, who provided scores of successful new operas. Specific characteristics exhibited by the Eszterháza operatic atelier include its self-consciously "retrospective," canon-forming approach; a conspicuous preference for operas by Dittersdorf during the late 1770s; and the near absence of *opera seria* between 1778 and 1782 – with Haydn's *L'isola disabitata* (1779) being a notable exception.

Sisman (2012) analyzes this "operetta" as a triple honorific: a testament to Calzabigi's and Gluck's reformist dramaturgy in their *festa teatrale*, *Orfeo*; a name-day and sixty-fifth birthday homage to Prince Nicolaus, sovereign of the "island" Eszterháza; and a tribute to the octogenarian poet Metastasio and his libretto's depth of characterization – a legacy continued into the new century with Haydn's many revisions to the score for a concert performance in Leipzig in April 1802 (see Wilker). Increasingly, the theater became a symbol of Esterházy identity – a symbol of its aristocratic and transnational NETWORKS, sovereignty, and royal alliances.

The institution of a regular theatrical season at Eszterháza began with the production of Gluck's *Orfeo ed Euridice* on March 21, 1776, which remained in the repertory until autumn of the following year. But operatic history and demonstrations of sovereign power were not the only matters addressed in the Esterházy theater; on the contrary, the old aristocratic order was sometimes undermined – or subtly critiqued – in *opera buffa*. Haydn's first opera for the new operatic regime, *Il mondo della luna*, a Goldoni libretto set for wedding festivities in the summer of 1777, revolves around the archetypal plot of young lovers tricking the old patriarchal figure in order to break away from his control. As Polzonetti notes, this could be understood as a revolutionary conceit "during the era of great revolutions, when philosophical or fictional attacks on the principle of patriarchy became potent critiques of the monarchic political system" (31; see also THE AMERICAS). In the utopian world of the moon, American ENLIGHTENMENT values abound, as do the promises of the new SCIENTIFIC revolution, witnessed by the grand telescope on stage and in the floating lightness associated with weightlessness and reduced gravitational pull characterized by the spare, muted strings-only orchestral writing at the opening of the Act 1 finale, where the old man believes he is flying to the moon. It was also the occasion when the accomplished Italian set designer, Pietro Travaglia, joined the opera company, helping to realize the technological innovations in the observatory scene of Act 1 – its telescopic shadow play of "sensory extension as well as sensory deception" offering a critique of science (Loughridge 30–31) – and the exotic lunar landscape of the second act (see also TRAVEL AND EXPLORATION). Apart from a couple of singers who had been employed earlier, only Italian singers were contracted as opera performers for extended periods of time. Although there were no celebrated "stars" among the members of the opera troupe, the limited number of eyewitness accounts that describe individual singers are overwhelmingly positive – with the exception of Haydn's mistress at the time, Luigia Polzelli, for whom the composer lovingly rewrote many arias (see RELATIONSHIPS, FRIENDSHIPS).

The opera season typically began around Ash Wednesday, when the prince returned from Vienna at the end of the Carnival season. Following the conclusion of the opera season in the city at the commencement of Lent, Prince Nicolaus initiated his own season at Eszterháza, enabling him to enjoy nearly continuous opera performances. In the beginning, two opera performances were given each week, on Sundays and Thursdays; then, starting in August 1780, a Tuesday performance was added. Before the change, the number of performances per year never exceeded 82; but after 1780, this figure rose to between 84 and 125 (apart from two incomplete seasons – in 1781 when the prince left for Paris on September 30, and in 1790 following his death on September 28). The total number of performances across the 15 seasons was approximately 1,270; the total number of operas performed was almost certainly 90, with Cimarosa's *Giannina e Bernardone* most likely the last opera premiered in August 1790, a month before Prince Nicolaus's death. Only two operas – Haydn's *L'incontro improvviso* and Sacchini's *La contadina ingentilita* – were revivals from the earlier repertoire of 11 operas. In total, then, Haydn oversaw the production of approximately 100 operas at court.

Among them were many remarkable operas. From the early years, these include: Gassmann's extremely popular *L'amore artigiano*, revived in 1790, following the request of the prince, seeking consolation after his wife's death; Anfossi's *Il geloso in cimento*, a musically ambitious *opera buffa* that achieved considerable success throughout European (and an exceptionally long run at Eszterháza, with 53 performances); and Alessandro Felici's *L'amore soldato*, which was premiered November 21, 1779, at the impromptu venue of the marionette theater just 3 days after the main opera house was destroyed by fire – a disastrous end to a rich season featuring, exceptionally, two operas by Haydn (*La vera costanza* and *L'isola disabitata*). Haydn's *dramma pastorale giocoso*, *La fedeltà premiata*, inaugurated the second opera house in February 1781, and later that year the all-round Italian opera expert, Nunziato Porta, became director of the opera. Much more than a place for celebrating royal alliances, dynastic weddings, and diplomatic visits, the Esterházy theater also commemorated personal loss and INSTITUTIONAL renewal.

Highlights from the new and enlarged opera house include two new operas by Haydn: *Orlando paladino* (1782), his most frequently performed opera outside Eszterháza; and *Armida* (1784), his last *seria* work for Eszterháza. Other notable performances include Traetta's *Il cavaliere errante*, which parodies Orfeo's famous aria "Che farò senza Euridice" by Gluck; Sarti's extremely popular *Giulio Sabino*, an early rescue or "liberation" opera that initiated a series of tragic productions in 1783; Francesco Bianchi's astonishingly modern conscientious drama, *Il disertore*, that skirts the generic border between *comédie larmoyante* and *dramma serio*; Bertoni's celebrated version of *Orfeo ed Euridice* on the same Calzabigi text as Gluck's earlier work; *opera buffa* gems like Martín y Soler's lyric comedy, *L'arbore di Diana*, based on a libretto by Da Ponte; and two more by Paisiello, *Il barbiere di Siviglia* and *L'amor contrastato* (also known as *La molinara*). Towards the end of 1789, preparations were initiated for a production of Mozart's *Le nozze di Figaro*, but for unknown reasons (perhaps because of casting difficulties) the plan was abandoned by the beginning of 1790.

Haydn's later operas were performed in many opera houses throughout Europe during his lifetime, mostly in German translation. *Orlando paladino* achieved the greatest success as *Ritter Roland*, with stagings in numerous cities including Prague, Pest, Königsberg (today Kaliningrad, Russia) and St. Petersburg. Beginning with *La vera costanza*, all of Haydn's later operas for Eszterháza were performed in Viennese theaters during his lifetime, in either staged or unstaged concert performances. Emanuel Schikaneder was responsible for three of the five productions – *La fedeltà premiata* in the Kärntnertortheater, and *Orlando paladino* and *Armida* in the Theater auf der Wieden (Freyhaus Theater).

Prince Nicolaus's eponymous Eszterháza was famous for the monumental festivities regularly taking place there (and its post-World War II reputation is also growing, see COMMEMORATIONS AND FESTIVALS). Still, the overwhelming majority of musical and theatrical performances presented there formed part of everyday life at court. Regular productions of operas in Italian by in-house singers alternated with performances of spoken theater by travelling troupes that resided at Eszterháza for the full season – most notably Karl Wahr's troupe (1773–77), for whom Haydn wrote incidental music (see Sisman 1990). All of the resident dramatic troupes were of a high professional level; their repertoire ranged beyond the fashionable comedies, and included works by German and foreign celebrities such as Goethe, Schiller, Lessing, Beaumarchais, Molière, Diderot, and Shakespeare. Of particular interest is Haydn's incidental music to Wahr's 1774 production of Der Zerstreute, a German revival of Le Distrait by Jean-François Regnard consisting of an overture, four interludes, and a finale repurposed as the six movements of Symphony No. 60. As Sisman observes, much of Haydn's instrumental music from the 1760s and 70s, once described as a Sturm und Drang phase, may more accurately be understood as derived from or intended for theatrical use.

So-called "pantomimes" constituted the lightest stage genre produced at Eszterháza. Although the titles were German, the characters were the typical ones from Italian commedia dell'arte (or the French equivalent, Théâtre de la foire), and included well-known Harlequinesque slapstick and charades. These performances were overseen by Albert Bienfait, the leading "machinist" or puppet manipulator at the marionette theater, who hired additional personnel to assist with productions.

Marionette productions consisted mainly – but not exclusively – of puppet operas. The first performances took place in 1772, using the portable marionette stage owned by the high-ranking imperial official and playwright, Karl von Pauerspach. The following year the prince had a permanent marionette theater constructed opposite the park from the main opera house, and invited Pauerspach to direct the performances. The permanent marionette theater was inaugurated on September 2, 1773, during Maria Theresia's visit to Eszterháza. More than twenty productions were carefully staged, including German parodies of Italian operas, an original Italian opera buffa by Traetta, and Romantic-heroic stories. Haydn himself composed music to half-a-dozen pieces, but only one, Philemon und Baucis, survives in a later arrangement. The marionette performances were directed by Pauerspach until his departure after the 1777 season, and continued with waning intensity until disappearing altogether after 1783 (see Pollheimer). During their heyday, puppets offered an alternative means of perceiving music through a unique form of gestural mimesis. Yet, precisely how did lifeless puppets cast in the form of miniature humans animated by strings and ventriloquizing voices mediate musical perception or allow for different sensory experiences in the theater? It's plausible that, like mechanical androids and musical automata (see Voskuhl), theatrical manipulation and musical embodiment of marionette bodies and souls similarly served Enlightenment pretentions to refine and ennoble the passions by illustrating the sentimental culture of civil society – with Philemon und Baucis being a prime example. (Awakening social conscience also permeates Haydn's *La vera costanza* staged later that decade; see Clark 2005a).

The princely court also hosted full-evening ballet productions with dramatic action, in the manner of Angiolini and Noverre. These required the involvement of professional ballet troupes, like the Schmalögger company, which performed its own version of Goethe's *Werther* in 1777, just three years after its publication (Landon II 403). The greatest achievement in dance was the production of Gluck's celebrated reform ballet, *Don Juan* (Vienna 1761) early in 1788 (just a couple of months after Gluck died, so possibly as a commemoration), with unknown dancers and choreographer (according to unpublished commissions and receipts in Esterházy Privatstiftung Archiv, Burg Forchtenstein). How these particular ballets – steeped with depictions of inner struggle, social alienation, and sentimentality (EMPFINDSAMKEIT) and ending in catastrophe – were received at Eszterháza remains unknown, although it's possible that Haydn echoed the terrifying final scene of Gluck's pantomime ballet in his Orpheus opera for London.

A counterpoint to the Esterházy use of theater as a symbol of absolutism is the commercial theater in LONDON. (See COMMERCE AND THE MARKET.) Here, radical POLITICS were smuggled into Haydn's last opera, *L'anima del filosofo* (The soul of the philosopher), which was composed for the King's Theatre Haymarket in 1791 but never performed. How an Orpheus opera by the world's leading composer failed to reach the stage is a tragedy with far-reaching implications. If it had been greeted with critical acclaim that season, imagine how Berlioz, Liszt, and Wagner – all of whom championed Gluck's *Orfeo* – might have responded to this powerful opera, or how Haydn's operatic legacy might have played out differently had performances of his London opera continued throughout the nineteenth century. Probably only the overture (appended to Johann Peter Salomon *Windsor Castle* in 1795) and an aria for Euridice (performed by Nancy Storace in May 1791) were heard in public performance in London. Breitkopf & Härtel published eleven solo and choral excerpts from *Orfeo* in a German-language piano–vocal adaptation in 1806, followed by orchestral version with Italian text in 1807. Not until 1951 was the opera premiered on stage – at the May Festival in Florence, with Maria Callas singing the role of Euridice under the baton of Erich Kleiber (see Figure 30), laying the foundation for diva-driven revivals by Joan Sutherland (Edinburgh 1966; Vienna 1967) and Cecilia Bartoli (Vienna and Zurich 1995; London 2001; see also Clark 2012a). Petty opera house rivalries and theater licensing issues do not fully explain why this quixotically titled opera failed to reach the stage in 1791 (see Heartz 2009; Price et al.).

· Commissioned by Sir John Gallini for the newly rebuilt theater, Haydn's Orpheus opera was calculated to help restore the theater license and prestige of the Haymarket Theatre after fire destroyed the building in June 1789, forcing the theater to yield its privilege to produce Italian opera to the Pantheon. The libretto, by the experienced house poet Carlo Francesco Badini, is cast in five acts, and features four main characters and multiple choruses (that could readily accommodate sumptuous ballets performed by Auguste Vestris and the resident ballet troupe). Badini's propensity for satirical and topical allusions in his libretti, as well as scurrilous criticism in the press, suggests that allegorical

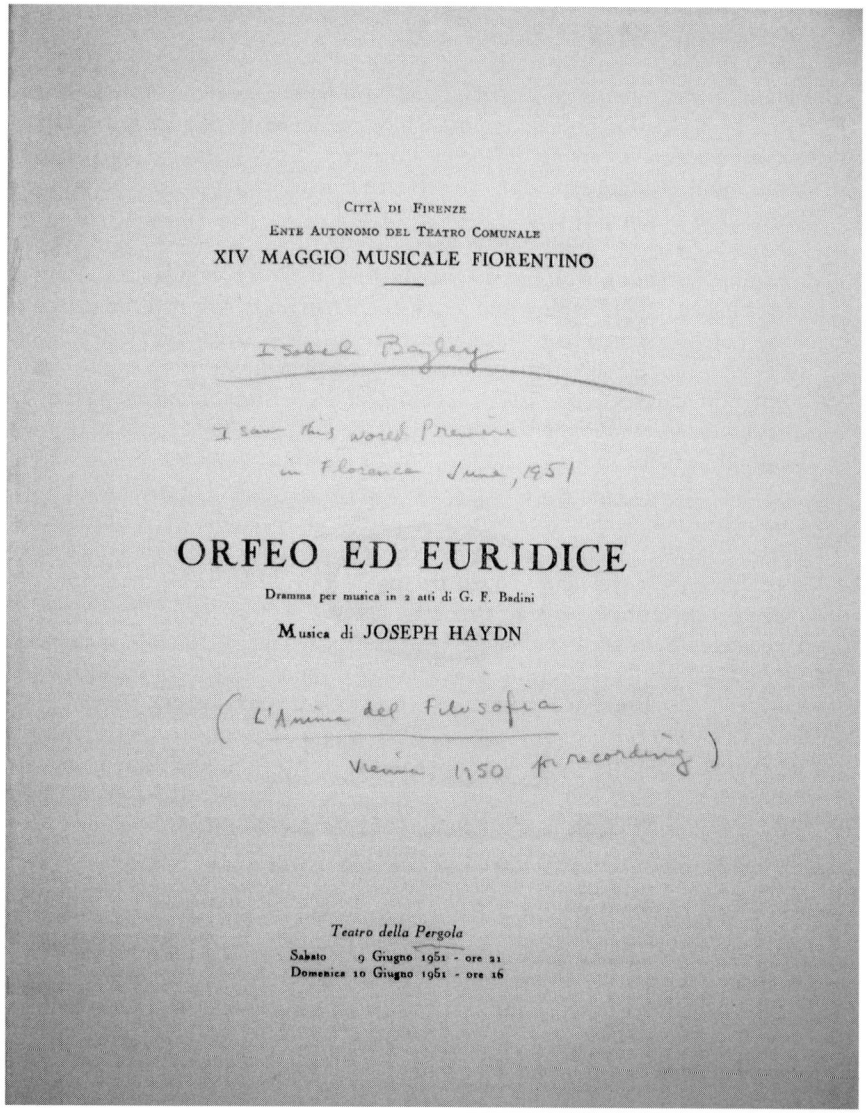

Figure 30 Title page and cast list from the printed program of the first production of Haydn's *Orfeo ed Euridice* (original title *L'anima del filosofo*,1791), premiered at Teatro della Pergola in Florence on June 9, 1951, as part of the XIV *Maggio Musicale Fiorentino*. Inscribed by Isabel Bayley, who attended this "world Premiere," the program shows that the original five-act opera was divided into two acts. Reproduced with permission of the Faculty of Music Library, University of Toronto, and *Maggio Musicale Fiorentino*, Florence.

readings are essential to understanding this unusual retelling of the Orpheus myth. Especially remarkable is the tragic ending, where the Thracian singer is poisoned by a vengeful mob of Maenadic women, after which all are destroyed

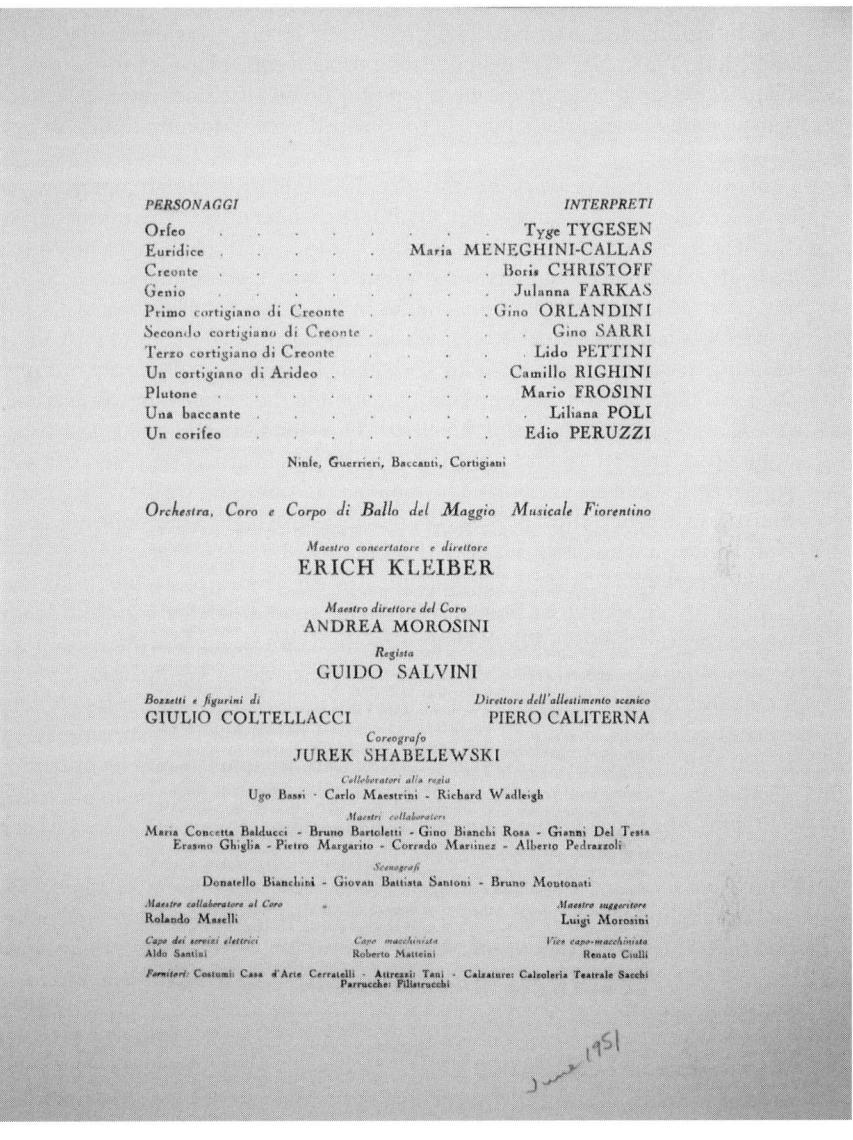

Figure 30 (cont.)

in a catastrophic storm. Indeed, the opera's terrifying narrative trajectory, which portrays the downfall of Orpheus (written for the tenor Giacomo Davide, rather than a castrato), closely resonates with contemporary politics during William Pitt's "reign of alarm" (see Johnston) – including campaigns of intimidation and censorship aimed at writers, artists, and other potential radicals during a period of political turmoil. Recent tumults included King

George III's temporary insanity in 1788–89, the outbreak of the French Revolution in 1789, and polarizing responses in the British press by Burke and Paine. When placed in dialogue with these events, reasons for the opera's demise appear related to the hero's pitiful downfall caused by a rebellious female mob echoing the kinds of civil disobedience unfolding in France (see Clark 2012b).

Haydn's formative work on this deeply troubling Orpheus opera in the intellectually stimulating and culturally liberating environment of COSMOPOLITAN London provided the catalyst for manifold changes in his late style. Haydn's enriched musical vocabulary was now firmly rooted in the SUBLIME, articulated by Edmund Burke in his treatise *A Philosophical Enquiry into the Sublime and Beautiful* (1757), of which Haydn owned a copy of the revised edition. Passions associated with the sublime, including obscurity, infinity, vastness and privation, are especially apparent in the Act 4 Underworld scenes (see Clark 2012b). After losing his beloved a second time, Orpheus lashes out at his cruel fate at the end of Act 4 in a breathless "allegro agitato" aria rife with jagged melodic leaps, chromatic instability, and pulsating rhythmic accompaniment – a loss of control perhaps overly suggestive of the king's recent mental disturbance and agitated state.

The opera ends in total annihilation. On the shores of Lesbos, a forlorn Orpheus accepts an elixir from the Bacchantes and dies a Socrates-like death, suggesting the demise of democracy (see Clark 2014). But the revelries of the rowdy Maenads are short-lived, their rustic *contredance* ("Andiamo, amici") suddenly interrupted by a violent storm that engulfs the Bacchantes ("O che orrore" chorus in D minor, with timpani and trombones), destroying everything – a natural catastrophe that aligns with other representations of natural disasters on Parisian stages during the early years of the French Revolution (see Hibberd) while also echoing the "hellish" ending of Mozart's *Don Giovanni* and the tormenting furies and fiery inferno concluding Gluck's *Don Juan*.

To quote Siegert, Haydn was "an opera expert" (2013, 466). In addition to performing many tasks associated with producing opera on stage – including composition, transcription, manuscript preparation and adaptation, instruction, REHEARSAL, and direction (see Clark 2005a) – Haydn's musical style was recognized in its day for its theatricality, its rhetorical strategies, gestural language, and referential content steeped in the conventions of operatic characterization and narrative. Of Haydn's music, the Spanish poet Tomás de Iriarte rhapsodized: "His music is pantomime without gestures, painting without pigments, poetry without syllables, rhetoric rhythmized. The instruments for which he writes declaim, recite, paint, [and] express sensible ideas" (Stevenson 3). Mimetic *buffo* elements abound in secular music of the second half of the eighteenth century, what Allanbrook describes as the "affective postures" and "diorama of the passions" portrayed in the "theater of surface" found in, for instance, the opening of Symphony No. 59 in A major, "Das Feuer" (25–28). During Haydn's time at Eszterháza, both opera and symphony were considered to be theatrical genres (see Sisman 1990; Malina 2016a). And this is further corroborated by recent research on the second opera house in particular (Malina 2016a), which demonstrates that this space functioned well for both concerts and operas. Indeed, "all four movements of Haydn's Symphony No. 73 "La chasse," rather than only the final *Presto*, might well have served as the orchestral prelude to his *La fedeltà premiata* on particularly festive occasions" (Dávid et al. 123). Acoustic modeling of the building shows how the unique use of dynamics in the symphony appears designed to function in tandem with the architectural and auditory properties of the audience area. With the semiotics and location of late eighteenth-century instrumental music so deeply intertwined with operatic aesthetics, it's likely that later eighteenth-century audiences listened more theatrically than structurally. Cross-genre fertilization also supports this view (see Siegert 2011a). So too does the notion that "the music itself" was, at this time, understood "as pure and original utterance, rather than a performance before spectators of something pre-composed" (November 27).

Around 1800, conceptions of symphony, chamber, and theater music differed substantially from those commonly held today. As November observes, our views have been shaped anachronistically by the music of Beethoven (7), obscuring our ability to celebrate Haydn as one who cultivated operatic aesthetics in his string quartets – and in many other repertoires too. PERFORMANCE parameters (including location and function) rather than compositional parameters (such as instrument complement or size of ensemble) defined music for the CHURCH, chamber, and theater. VOCAL works – including operatic arias and ensembles – could be performed staged or unstaged in either the theater or the chamber, while symphonies, which were extremely versatile in Haydn's day, could be performed in chamber, church, or theatrical contexts. Haydn's "Overtures," as his symphonies were called in London, were performed as part of a potpourri where audiences were offered a range of vocal and instrumental selections from contemporary operas, songs, choruses, concertos, string quartets, and keyboard works, etc. – mixed repertoires for secular entertainment. Underpinning all these musical offerings was a binding aesthetics of theatricality and spectacle.

Haydn's second season in London offers an apt example. As Burnham observes, "like a clown stepping on stage," Haydn's finale themes frequently "prepossess the listener towards the humorous" (61) – the finale of Symphony No. 98 in B♭ major from March 2, 1792 being a perfect example (69–71). Here the coda stages a miniature duel between the musical actors Salomon and Haydn – the violinist on his podium and Haydn at the "cembalo" morphing into sparring protagonists engaging in a comedic exchange of one-upmanship. In this *buffo* enactment, Haydn temporarily emerges from behind his continuo-playing mask to exert his position as composer-soloist (mm. 365–75, marked "piano"), temporarily usurping Salomon's leadership role with his brilliant upper-register salvoes which exploit the shimmering upper-register of the English keyboard (for staging, see LEADING LARGE ENSEMBLES, Figure 15; see also SELF-REFLEXIVITY).

According to Allanbrook, the multiplicity of motives, affects, and surface gestures in later eighteenth-century instrumental music enact a kind of "miniature drama in which characters" from recognizable social milieus "interact and emotions shift and collide as if played out on notional stage sets that evoke such concrete if metaphorical occasions as hunts, dances or battles" (xiii). She theorizes that the classical doctrine of *enargeia* or "lively essence" – the vivid character depiction and lively action of characters "at work" as found in the "mimetic units" of the musical surface of *opera buffa* – pervades galant instrumental music of the eighteenth century (15–16). It's as if the hierarchies and social stratification so palpable in *opera buffa* migrated to instrumental music as the raw materials for motivic manipulation – a veritable social microcosm ripe for interaction and interrogation via MELODIC variation, timbral differentiation (see ORCHESTRATION), HARMONIC motion, and other elements of character identity and SOCIABILITY. So, while theorists in the early nineteenth century valorized a newly "German" instrumental music – the ineffable, autonomous, "absolute" symphonic music associated with Beethoven, vaunted for its organicism, structural organization, interiority, and sublimity – this view was entirely antithetical to the aesthetics of Italianate eighteenth-century instrumental music, for which Haydn became famous.

And this is precisely why a greater appreciation of theater, comic mimesis, and the kaleidoscopic *buffo* style of Italian comic opera in general is essential to understanding Haydn's music. The short phraseology of Haydn's instrumental music is especially indebted to intermezzo and *opera buffa* accompaniment patterns. Both Haydn and Mozart are Italianate composers; Mozart's lyricism aligns to *opera seria*, whereas Haydn leans towards comedy. Rather than "pure music" to be interpreted through the lens of German opinion-formers of the nineteenth and twentieth centuries, Haydn's instrumental music presupposes a complex of operatic listening modes oriented toward rhetorical appeal and TOPICAL reference – the very things that enabled the composer's famous musical wit and HUMOR.   CARYL CLARK AND JÁNOS MALINA

FURTHER READING
Allanbrook (2014); Betzwieser (2007); Buch (2006); Burke (1757); Burnham (2005); Clark (2005a, 2009a, 2012a, 2012b, 2014, 2016); Dávid et al. (2015); Green (1997); Head (2014); Heartz (1995, 2009); Hibberd (2012); Horányi (1962); Hunter (1999); Hunter and Will (2012); Jerome (2015); Johnston (2013); Landon I–III; Loughridge (2016); Malina (2006, 2016a, 2016b); Melton (2007); November (2017); Pollheimer (2016); Polzonetti (2011); Price et al. (1995); Radant and Landon (1993); Siegert (2011a, 2013); Sisman (1990, 2012); Stevenson (1982); Voskuhl (2013); Wilker (2013).

Time Toward the end of "Summer" in Haydn's oratorio *The Seasons* (1801), Hannah, Lucas, and Simon call attention to the horns' eightfold tolling of the "Abendglocke," the evening bell or curfew. Immediately afterwards, in the rustic landscape of people going home to the welcome of a night's rest under the benign gaze of Venus the evening star, a sonic tapestry enhanced by birds and other creatures, the eight peals return twice, not in the horns but sung iambically by the chorus, again on a single pitch. Human time expressively transfers the sound of evenly spaced bells to the short–long pattern of the words and the bodily pulse. This emphatic insertion of the sounds of time into a temporal work of art whose theme is the cycle of life points both to the new importance of evening as a lyric location (as described by Miller) and to Haydn's rich understanding of the layering of temporal elements, as well as the forms of attention they command from an AUDIENCE never far from his mind.

The Seasons crowned a career in which time was often of the musical essence: for Haydn, time was a musico-poetic theme, a source of humor, and a characteristic topic. It also crowned a century in which time was a subject of literary preoccupation (epistolary novels, diaries, and the satiric reaction of *Tristram Shandy*), mechanical invention (the Harrison H4 clock that finally determined longitude), astronomical discovery (the Transit of Venus observations that used time to measure distance in determining the size of the solar system), and, after the French Revolution, self-conscious historical transformation and reaction (the new calendar and local fin-de-siècle epiphanies). Karol Berger locates the emergence of modernity itself in the change from a cyclic to a linear sense of time. A Viennese conference devoted to "Joseph Haydn and Time" in 2009 (Dittrich et al.) included considerations of time and GENDER in Haydn's LONDON (Day-O'Connell 2012; see also Day-O'Connell 2009b) and metaphysical time, rhythm, and tempo in *The Creation* (Grant), among other fascinating subjects whose implications are still being explored.

The clock-based rituals of courtly and city life differed from the sun-based rhythms of the country. In a short essay in the *Journal des Luxus und der Moden* on the "the uses and divisions of the day and the night" (1786) Friedrich Bertuch confidently asserted that "an entirely new order of things" had arrived: daytime activities were pushed later and later, and evening was less a time of rest than a time filled with pleasurable activities like theater-going and conversation (see Koslofsky). Society's increasing refinement was the cause. In Henry VIII's time, the "bon ton" in England ate lunch ("Mittag") at ten in the morning; "today no one in polite society lunches before five in the evening." Indeed, Haydn's experience was even more extreme: as he wrote to Marianne von Genzinger on January 8, 1791 soon after arriving in London, he had his "Mittag" with the Neapolitan ambassador "NB at 6 pm, as is the custom here" (CCLN 112, *Briefe* 251). In November 1791, he stayed two days with the Prince of Wales and Duke of York where they made music from 10 pm to 2 am, then supped and went to bed at 3 am. London society was clearly different both from the "daily order" of Viennese life humorously detailed according to class by Johann Pezzl in the late 1780s (*Skizzen von Wien*, trans. Landon) and from Haydn's well-ordered life as a house officer at Eszterháza, where for decades he had been required to visit the Prince both before and after midday to determine his daily musical assignments, as well as compose, rehearse, produce, and organize a complex schedule of operatic and other performances, not to mention special efforts for Prince Nicolaus's name-day on December 6.

Haydn was thus by both temperament and profession inclined to care a great deal about what we would now call time management. But time also turned out to be one of his great subjects. His first "opus" of symphonies for his new employer in 1761 was a cycle on the fashionable Times-of-the-Day theme, in which he drew impressively on cultural and mythic imagery of the sun as well as pastimes of court and countryside to forge a solar poetics. A consciously designed trilogy, the symphonies move from sunrise and morning hunt in "Le matin" (no. 6), to the symbols of power, panic, and search for pastoral refreshment caused by the noonday sun in "Le midi" (no. 7), to the theater-going, sunset and tempest of "Le soir" (no. 8) (see Sisman 2013). Haydn might also have wanted to demonstrate a more up-to-date musical evocation of time than the old but still active Kapellmeister Gregor Joseph Werner, whose *Curious Musical Instrument Calendar* for two violins and bass (1748) had been dedicated to the Prince. One of Haydn's last symphonies, No. 101 in D, written for the 1794 season in London, was quickly nicknamed the "Clock" because of the *Andante*'s "ticking" accompaniment, an even eighth-note ostinato in pizzicato strings and staccato bassoons. The movement's sense of temporal mechanism extends even to the dotted rhythms of its MELODY. An especially witty touch is the reorchestrated ticking in this rondo, pared down to high flute and low bassoon in the first return of the refrain (m. 63), alarmingly restarted in the wrong key (♭VI) in strings alone after a general pause (did the watch stop?), thickened into tutti in the second return (m. 112), doubled into a heartbeat in the viola's final measures.

The sense of time as a pattern to be disrupted comes to the fore in the metrical irregularities of Haydn's dance movements, and in his use of silences and skewed phrase rhythms. A celebrated case of the latter is the Largo slow movement of Symphony No. 64 (c. 1773), titled "Tempora mutantur" ("the times are changed"). The first phrase lacks a single beat on which to resolve, and is marked instead by a rest, Haydn's storied way of calling attention to the time "behind" the music. The second phrase falls further behind, with two beats of silence instead of the notes of resolution. As the timing becomes progressively more distorted, and dark evocations of earlier styles raise the dramatic temperature, the listener's consciousness of rhetorical or theatrical purpose is inevitably engaged. Is the time out of joint? Is the composer channeling Hamlet for a THEATER symphony or calling attention to the relationship between temporal processes and affective rhetoric? (See Sisman 1990; Mirka.)

At the peak of Haydn's international fame around 1800, a "MEMORIALIZING and historicizing" tendency on the part of PUBLISHERS enabled him to gain financially from an edition of his collected works (see Head; see also EDITIONS and MEMORIALS). Yet the journal of the same house, the *Allgemeine musikalische Zeitung*, serialized Triest's lengthy evaluative periodization of the eighteenth century that extolled Haydn's instrumental works but kept up the critique of his vocal works to which the composer was unusually sensitive (1801, trans. in HWorld). Haydn was right to worry: his radical late oratorios were generationally misunderstood ("didactic," sniffed Beethoven) by those who wanted the father to get off the stage. (See also SCIENCE.)

ELAINE SISMAN

FURTHER READING
Berger (2007); *Briefe*; *CCLN*; Day-O'Connell (2009b, 2012); Dittrich et al. (2012); Dohrn-van Rossum (1996); Grant (2012); Head (2000a); HWorld; Koselleck (2002); Koslofsky (2011); Landon (1991); Miller (2006); Mirka (2012); Sisman (1990, 2013); Tomalin (2016); Triest (1997 [1801]).

Tonality Tonality is a historiographical principle that has had a dramatic and abiding effect on the reception of Haydn's music. The term gives name to a theoretical system that describes the orientation of musical material toward a central tonic pitch class. Writers on music have also used this discursive construct to distinguish a particular type of repertoire – tonal music – from its others, both historically and anthropologically. Emerging in the early nineteenth century, the conceptual development of tonality does not overlap with the period during which Haydn composed; however, his music has played an important role in the consolidation of both the concept and the repertoire it has come to define. Thus, since the time of Haydn's death his music and the concept of tonality have participated in a complex of mutually reinforcing scholarly endorsements. However, the methods through which this occurs and the qualities that Haydn's works are said to exhibit have evolved since the nineteenth century, creating a distinct strand of Haydn RECEPTION.

Among the early theorists of the concept, François Joseph Fétis identified Haydn as one of the "grand masters who had a profound tonal sense [*sentiment tonal*]" (100). For Fétis, Haydn's music exemplifies transparent structural integrity and simplicity. The French theorist draws on specific passages from Haydn's works or refers to his oeuvre in general when he wants to discuss the considered and measured use of rare harmonies or the ornamentation of a simple MELODY. For Gottfried Weber too, Haydn's music is a paragon of restraint. Weber was well acquainted with Haydn's music and regularly included examples drawn from Haydn in his treatises. Haydn provided for Weber models of the correct handling of dissonant seventh chords, the inclusion and resolution of dissonant chromatic elaborations, and the just use of the deceptive cadence. Of the many works Weber refers to, a particular favorite is Haydn's *Creation*.

The Creation would go on to have an illustrious career in the history of tonality. Perhaps most famously the overture of the work was the subject of a detailed analysis by Heinrich Schenker, which was designed to show the internal structure and coherence of "Chaos." Schenker's theory of tonality – which became widely influential, especially in North AMERICA – saw all tonal works as the elaboration of basic contrapuntal patterns. These patterns could be said to exist independently of the compositions as autonomous, Platonic forms (in one instance Schenker compared the fundamental structure of a Haydn piano sonata to "Leibniz's concept ... [of] the pre-established harmony of the composition" ([1925] 1994, 109)). The overture of *The Creation* thus presented Schenker with the ideal challenge: to find the underlying order in the tonal evocation of disorder. As Schenker described the work, "it is only with its strict principles that art is able to convey the meaning of Chaos! Thus Haydn, in his portrayal of Chaos, remains faithful to his basic artistic principles; but he is, of course, committed to stretching the means of his art, to increase the tension to the point that they – mysteriously – suggest the very mysteries of Chaos" (1996 [1926], 97). In Schenker's view, Haydn's music held firm to the underlying principles of tonal structure and order while nevertheless deviating from them on the musical surface in order to produce chaos as an emergent effect. Here Haydn's work is again held up as an ideal example of technical mastery over MUSICAL MATERIALS and adherence to tonal principles.

The past fifty years have seen new configurations of the relationship between Haydn's music and the concept of tonality. One strand of Haydn reception derives from the Schenkerian view, for which Haydn's music continues to provide an ideal model. Aldwell and Schachter's undergraduate HARMONY textbook – a chief exponent of the Schenkerian understanding of tonality – employs some twenty-one examples drawn from Haydn's music. But an alternative strand sees in Haydn's works the incipient use of highly chromatic techniques that augur the dissolution of the tonal system. Early instances of this sort of scholarship include Cuyler's work on what she calls "bimodality" in Haydn's late string quartets. Bimodality "premises the inclusion, within one supramode, of all the pitch elements of the diatonic major and minor modes of the eighteenth century" (138). That is, the use of the melodic and harmonic resources of the parallel minor key for music in major or vice versa. Cuyler sees in Haydn's late string quartets the use of bimodality as a means of motivating the connection to distant key areas, which sometimes occupied an entire movement of a multi-movement work (as in Haydn's String Quartet in G major Op. 77, No. 1 with its E♭-major second movement). With these "bold juxtaposition[s]" Haydn was, for Cuyler, a "joyful innovator" (137). In a similar vien, Chapman calls attention to Haydn's use of enharmonic modulations to distant keys in the keyboard trios of the 1790s. More recently, Anson-Cartwright has found in Haydn's development sections a habit of moving through the submediant that is typically associated with Schubert.

The shift in the practice of using Haydn's music to exemplify the quintessential procedures of tonality to one in which his music is shown to prefigure later, more chromatic styles indicates a corresponding shift in the value systems of music scholarship more broadly. While once Haydn's music was used to buttress a developing theory of tonality, the two have now so thoroughly shaped each other that to report on their connection is the work of undergraduate music theory textbooks. Newer scholarship has therefore begun to emphasize the ways in which Haydn's music challenges our understandings of tonality both as a theoretical model and as a historiographical principle.

ROGER MATHEW GRANT

FURTHER READING
Aldwell and Schachter (2011 [1979]); Andrews (1981); Anson-Cartwright (2000); Burstein (2010, 2011); Chapman (1981); Cuyler (1970); Fétis (1844); Heyer (2015); LaRue (1992); Schenker (1994 [1925]), 1996 [1926]); Weber (1817–21).

Topics. Theoretical Background Certain musical materials, processes, or events in the Classical style are stable enough to be recognized as categories (i.e., *style types*), and many of these have familiar expressive entailments. They only become *topical* when they can be freely *imported* into a context differing from their prototypical source. Topics are generally foregrounded to some degree, but they may also be subsidiary to other compositional techniques. The two primary criteria for a topic are thus (1) its initial stability as a style type with expressive associations, and (2) its characteristic identity (whether in whole or in part) when it appears in a novel context.

Much confusion exists over the hierarchical organization of topical categories. We begin our account with *figurae*, following Rumph (2014), defined as the non-signifying features that help articulate topics, but that are not in themselves fully topical (e.g., two–four meter, major mode). But what may appear as component parts may also be potentially topical, as motivated by various associations (sighs and fanfare figures have iconic and indexical motivations; the major 6–3 chord may trigger a recitative-like moment), and these we term *figures*. Figures may signal a larger topic due to a part-for-whole (synecdochic) allusion (e.g., the dotted-quarter/sixteenth/eighth rhythm is associated with the *siciliano*). Textures may also function topically in this way (e.g., homophonic as suggestive of hymn, imitative as learned, MELODY-and-accompaniment as singing or aria, virtuosic passagework as brilliant), although they may also exist as *figurae* contributing to various different topics (e.g., melody-and-accompaniment texture may be used for various dance topics).

The first level of association where identification is also topical – that is, the level at which musical material can be imported and retain its expressive associations – is thus the sub-level of the figure (see Figure 31). The next level is filled with those familiar style types that exist as characteristic genres (marches, dances, French overture, romance, aria, recitative, hymn, fugue, fantasia, etc.). When these genres appear in new contexts – whether represented in whole or in part – their expressive associations may acquire further interpretations. For example, the French overture may signal high, ceremonial dignity, or more generally, "nobility," when imported into the context of a symphony, quartet, or sonata. In the case of dances, a minuet movement, for example, may be considered topical due to the imported effect of marked stylization. Furthermore, genres may be imported into another movement or context either in whole or in part – either as an integrative thematic-textural unit or more allusively as a characteristic RHYTHM or texture. At this same topical level, we include variously termed "styles." Each style or genre is

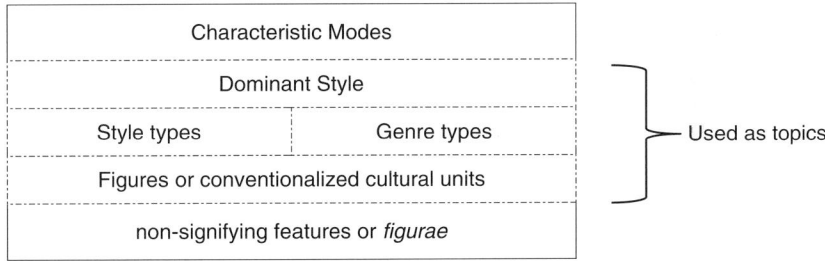

Figure 31 The hierarchical organization of topical categories, and the interaction of topics in String Quartet Op. 50, No. 5, i.

composed of a constellation of *figurae* and more topical figures. Sturm und Drang (or *tempesta*), EMPFINDSAMKEIT, pastoral, military, and hunt are all examples of broader styles that are found in Haydn's works.

Any style or genre may serve as a dominant topic for a given passage or movement, with imported topics serving as inflections of the central expressive purport of the dominant style or topic. The galant style, however, functions as the unmarked, dominant style for many Classical works. Various topical importations may in turn creatively *inflect* that dominant style, in a process Hatten explains as "troping" (1994; 2014). For example, the learned style may be imported into a galant context, where it contributes a topical association of "authoritativeness" or "high seriousness." The mixing of topics is either consonant (compatible), dissonant (creative, tropological), or enhanced (inflecting). Lowe (2002) notes that the dominant topic of the third movement of Symphony No. 23 in G major is a minuet, the simplicity of which is challenged by the importation of learned contrapuntal imitation, creating topical "dissonance." For instance, the slow movement of String Quartet in B♭ major, Op. 50, No. 1, is in the style of a *pastorale*, with features of sensibility imported in different ways in each of the variations to heighten the level of pathetic expression first suggested in mm. 9–11 of the theme. In some movements, the dominant topic is marked in terms of stylization, as removed from its original experienced activity and imported into a new context. Thus, while the galant style is often the dominant style in the Classical period, other styles can function as dominant. This is especially true for Haydn's slow movements, where the dominant style often draws from sentimental styles.

Yet another level for those styles that take on a more *comprehensive* role in *coordinating the larger expressive discourse* of a movement or cycle we term "mode" (Hatten 2004, 53). The sensibility mode, for example, has an expressive process that features expansion and elaboration. The pastoral mode presupposes simplicity, amelioration of dissonance, and serenity, as in the opening of Symphony No. 6 in D major, "Le matin," or the third movement of String Quartet in B minor, Op. 33, No. 1. The comic mode appears in Haydn's play with the expectations of tonal syntax and meter, what Rosen calls "a genuinely autonomous musical wit" (96). The comic mode can be powerful enough, as Sisman claims for the finale of Symphony No. 102 in B♭ major, to cause a listener to tropologically reinterpret "episodes of tempest, learned style, and eerie wind 'voices'" as "mock bluster rather than elevated or dark turns" (2014, 114–15). The hierarchy of mode and topic is clearly significant: modes can direct the interpretation of topics, potentially supporting ironic readings.

Furthermore, modes often – but not always – suggest topical content for movements. For instance, movements exhibiting the mode of sensibility often include features imported from sentimental opera (longed-breathed melodies, pulsing or undulating accompaniment, and "breathless" pauses and sighs), or the *empfindsamer* keyboard style of C. P. E. Bach, a particularly important influence for Haydn's sentimental style (see Boisjoli). Some modes draw on multiple styles and genres that are related, such as the comic mode, which typically employs *buffa* style types and dances; and the *galant* style, which, as Hunter describes, typically presupposes a juxtaposition of contrasting topics, as in the play of galant and learned styles in the third movement of Symphony No. 23 in G major.

Haydn's Conception of Topical Importation: History Lowe summarizes the theoretical treatises of the eighteenth century that explain concepts now included under topic theory, suggesting "topical references were the product of conscious compositional decisions" (2007, 27). How this reflects Haydn's personal use of topics is harder to know with certainty (see AESTHETICS). Haydn's biographer, Dies, said he once asked Haydn whether "he sought in his instrumental pieces to work out some verbal problem or other selected at will."

> "Seldom," answered Haydn. "In instrumental music, I generally allowed my purely musical fantasy free play. Only one exception occurs to me now, in which in the Adagio of a symphony, I chose as a theme a conversation between God and a heedless sinner." On a later occasion the talk turned again to this Adagio, and Haydn said he always expressed the Deity by love and goodness (Gotwals 155).

However, earlier in the biography, when discussing the programmatic work *The Seven Last Words of Christ*, Dies offers a more specific interpretation of Haydn's intentions:

> [Many,] for example, take the modulation from minor into major for a usual phenomenon of the century and at most believe that it was intended to indicate a transition from a sad into a happy state of mind. But that is much too indefinite. Haydn wanted in the oratorio to express such a state of mind as rises above earthly imperfection to heavenly bliss. The words *Hodie mihi*, and so on, are the theme [of the second Adagio]. What a great uplift is thereby given to the above-mentioned shift from minor to major that he makes use of toward the end of the Adagio! (Gotwals 102–103)

Through this statement Dies implies that Haydn and his contemporaries were concerned with whether music could express with the same specificity as language, and assumed that music could "indicate" changing emotional states.

The number of nicknames given to symphonies or quartets by others also suggests a contemporaneous interest in hearing more literal meanings in instrumental music. For example, the picturesque associations with animals (Lark, Bird, Frog, Hen, Bear, Rider), humor (the "Joke" Quartet, "Surprise" Symphony), "Times of Day" ("Le matin," "Le midi," "Le soir" Symphonies; "Sunrise" Quartet), effects (Echo, Palindrome), states ("Dream," "Miracle," and "Il distratto" Symphonies), or objects (the "Bell" Quartet; "Clock" Symphony). This kind of pictorialism, whether intentional or not, need not involve direct importation of topics. Instead, Haydn may be inventing new means of representing or expressing particular objects or emotions. Such inventions become fertile ground for future style types, which may then be exploited topically. For example, Sisman describes Haydn's development of the "sunrise" topic in the "Time of Day" Symphonies (nos. 6–8), and later in *The Creation* and *The Seasons* (2013) (see TIME). While not original to Haydn, his use of the topic for works with programmatic titles or texted oratorios strengthens the association of the musical features with the image of the sun. New means of representation may thus provide newly minted figures to enhance established topics. For example, a newly created bird-call figure in one work may be topically referenced in the pastoral mode of another work.

Haydn also participated in the creation of new figures and topics, especially through his use of text painting, such as the croaking of frogs or drunkenness in "Juhe, juhe! der Wein ist da!" from *The Seasons* (Gotwals 186–87). As Webster relates, according to the Swedish diplomat Fredrik Samuel Silverstolpe, Haydn described his depiction of waves by "notes [that] run up and down," and the depiction of chaos through unexpected resolutions in *The Creation* (32).

Haydn's Figures, Genres, Styles, Modes, and Topical Imports Haydn's compositions feature a combination of contrapuntal scaffolding (based on both Fuxian counterpoint and Italian partimenti); the syntactic implications of tonal harmony, periodic forms, and meter; and the enhancement of surface elaborations (diminutions, timbral and registral variation). Expressive content can be inferred from the shaping of any of these musical parameters, but prefabricated topical material offers the advantage of more immediate orientation toward and clarification of that content. Jones notes that the scherzo of String Quartet in E♭ major, Op. 33, No. 2, "Joke," begins in the style of a *Deutsche*, a dance associated with lower levels of society. Registral shifting in the first phrase, the disruption of hypermeter by filler material, and the imitation of a conventional cadential figure in the digression are further indicators of potential comic excess. In the trio, a topical importation of the *Schuhplattler* (a humorous folk dance) clinches an interpretation of the mode as comic (see HUMOR).

Topics in Haydn's music rarely appear as single, independent musical objects; there is often some ambiguity or fusing of topics. If some topics are present only as bare allusions, they may nonetheless contribute to the interpretation of expressive meaning emerging from topical fusions, when considered as tropes. The dimensions of interaction among topics – their degrees of compatibility, dominance, creativity, and productivity – are often dependent on their features (Hatten 2014). For example, the pastoral style is compatible with an aria style from *opera seria* (as in the slow movement of String Quartet in G major, Op. 33, No. 5) because of a number of common *figurae*, including the undulating accompaniment and lyric melody.

Topics can inflect either simultaneously or successively. An example of both is found in the finale of Symphony No. 104 in D major, "London," as discussed by Hunter (62–65). The movement opens with a simultaneous "light-footed peasant dance" and a "musette drone"; successive topics (governed by the comic mode) include learned-style COUNTERPOINT and the Turkish style. Another example is the Sonata in E♭ major, Hob.XVI:52 (see also Ratner's topical analysis, 412–21). The first two measures present a French-overture enhancement of a common-time march. Measure 3 echoes m. 2, transforming the melodic idea up the octave and alluding to the singing style. This is followed successively by a filled-in breathless sigh figure that tropes with the pastoral through harmonization in parallel thirds (see Example 21).

Example 21 Topics in the first 5 measures of Sonata in E♭ major, Hob.XVI:52.

Transition from one topic to another (topical "modulation") may occur in two ways. When there is compatibility of topical *figurae* between two topics, a shared *figura* may underlie what might be termed a "common-*figura*" topical modulation, following Rumph (2012, 97). Consider the opening theme from the String Quartet in D minor, Op. 42. While Rumph would likely consider the sigh figure as a signifying feature of sensibility, we would suggest it is similar to the pedal point in that it functions as an "abstract structure," articulating multiple styles. In this movement the sigh figure is initially associated with a more negative emotional state, perhaps topically alluding to tragic *opera seria*. But when the sigh figure develops into a portamento, and then becomes thematized and accompanied by an undulating texture, the music has "modulated" to the pastoral mode; both the major mode and the positive associations with the pastoral help to "neutralize" the previously dysphoric sigh. Thus, the sigh figure, as the pivot of the topical modulation, is reconceived in a way that progressively undermines the authoritative style of tragic opera and substitutes a more popular "middle style."

A similarly gradual topical modulation, which Sutcliffe calls "stylistic modulation," can occur when one or more non-signifying elements are held in common without any "marked points of discontinuity" (224). The opening of String Quartet in F♯ minor, Op. 50, No. 4 begins with a foreboding character that features a head motive of three staccato eighth-notes. This head motive remains constant while changing to the major mode and the first violin adds grace notes in m. 16, shifting the music to a galant topic. In m. 28, the intervallic distance of the head motive is expanded and accompanied by undulating sixteenth-notes, cueing the pastoral topic.

Genres and Compositional Techniques as Referential As often as Haydn included topics in his compositions, they are not necessarily the main signifying material. Instead, many of his pieces are in the unmarked galant style and are more concerned with techniques of motivic elaboration, along with contrapuntal and harmonic development. Although a 6–4–5–3 suspension over a tonic resolution (as in the first theme of the third movement of String Quartet in C major, Op. 33, No. 3, "Bird") might hint at the topic of sensibility, or a moment of imitation might hint at the learned style, many times the appearances of these features remain unconnected to any larger topical discourse. According to Griesinger, Haydn claimed that "once I had seized upon an idea, my whole endeavor was to develop and sustain it in keeping with the rules of art" (Griesinger, 61). Agawu, in his analysis of the String Quartet in D minor, Op. 76, No. 2, "Quinten," describes this focus on compositional technique as a self-referential (SELF-REFLEXIVITY) discourse (involving introversive, as opposed to extroversive, semiosis). In the so-called "Quinten" quartet, the interval of a fifth becomes thematized, emerging as "single musical element" that undergoes a "transformational process" (100). The process of transformation thereby becomes the premise of the movement, and as Agawu notes, "for Haydn, sonata form itself could be taken as a semiotic object, complete with a normative set of relations between signifier and signified" (106). The expressive content in Haydn may in some cases arise from the discourse of thematic and tonal design, without recourse to intertextual or topical enhancements. (See also COMPOSITIONAL PROCESS; FORM; HARMONY; IMITATION AND MIMESIS; PROGRAMMATIC ELEMENTS.) ELOISE BOISJOLI AND ROBERT S. HATTEN

FURTHER READING
Agawu (1991); Boisjoli (2018); Dies; Griesinger; Hatten (1994, 2004, 2014); Hunter (2014); Jones (2000a); Lowe (2002, 2007); Ratner (1980); Rosen (1971/72); Rumph (2012, 2014); Sisman (2013, 2014); Sutcliffe (2003); Webster (2005).

Transatlantic Studies – see Americas, The

Travel and Exploration Although Haydn's first extended journey, travelling from VIENNA to LONDON in late 1790, took place when he was aged fifty-eight, the idea of travel and conceptions of remote places had long before this held a special fascination for him.

Mapping and Music One item owned by Haydn that provides an insight into his early interest in such notions was a school atlas with maps designed by the leading German cartographer Johann Baptist Homann, Imperial Geographer to Charles VI between 1715 and his death in 1724. Although the evidence that Haydn owned this atlas (his copy, like all his books, is lost) comes from an inventory of the composer's possessions drawn up following his death, the fact that the item was intended for the young suggests he had owned it since childhood, retaining it because its contents appealed to him (see CATALOGUES). Homann's "small" atlas was reissued many times during the first half of the eighteenth century in various formats. The precise version Haydn owned is uncertain. In its most extended form the atlas featured twenty-six elaborate maps, including those showing the whole world (with representations of the celestial sphere and views of remote regions), each of the continents, all the major countries in EUROPE, and finally the Holy Land.

An indication that Haydn's imagination was fired by this atlas is the evidence that it led him to acquire a still more extensive publication by Homann, a large-format atlas of the world featuring many more maps, all with greater detail, first published in 1716. The expense entailed for the adult Haydn in purchasing this atlas, one of the most celebrated cartographical publications of the eighteenth century, suggests the degree of the composer's interest in its contents. This is corroborated by a separate collection of "various maps" he owned, now unidentifiable.

In Vienna, music sellers offered maps for sale. For example, the firm of Artaria, one of Haydn's main PUBLISHERS after 1779, sold maps before taking up music and continued to do so long after its music business folded. There was therefore a COMMERCIAL connection between the retailing of music and of maps, which an ambitious composer, like Haydn, might consider worthwhile understanding. Of equal importance from Haydn's perspective, the atlases he owned enabled him to chart the extent of his reputation as commissions flowed to him from distant part of Europe, like Cádiz (see EUROPEAN CONTEXTS, SPAIN) and as he received admirers from abroad, like the Venezuelan revolutionary Francisco de Miranda, who visited Eszterháza with the specific intention of meeting Haydn in 1785 (see AMERICAS).

Pilgrimage The concept of pilgrimage, journeys of spiritual significance with sacred shrines as their destinations, would have been familiar to Haydn, a devout Catholic (see RELIGION AND SPIRITUAL BELIEFS). The composer told his first biographers that after he was obliged to leave the choir school at St. Stephen's Cathedral in Vienna before reaching the age of twenty, he decided to make a pilgrimage to the huge Benedictine basilica at Mariazell, Austria's most famous shrine, where a medieval statue of the Virgin Mary was reputed to have miraculous powers. Like other pilgrims from Vienna, Haydn probably made the sixty-mile journey on foot. As Haydn related it, however, the purpose of the trip was more than just spiritual. He took with him "several motets" of his own composition, probably his earliest vocal works (some of which possibly survive), in the hope of their performance leading to some recognition for him. Although his plan did not succeed, he appears to have ingratiated himself sufficiently with the resident singers at Mariazell to be rewarded for his trouble. The connection remained important for him since he later made two substantial mass settings in connection with Mariazell, both entitled *Missa Cellensis*, the first begun in 1766, possibly conceived in fulfilment of a personal vow to the Virgin Mary, and the second composed in 1782 for a retired military general.

While Haydn was probably too busy to engage with extended pilgrimage later in his career, one form of related spiritual journey arguably remained important to him. Adjacent to the lodgings where Haydn resided at EISENSTADT when he first entered Esterházy employment is the Bergkirche, featuring another Marian shrine, largely developed in the eighteenth century as a focus for local devotion. At the center was a statue of the Virgin, which was claimed to work miracles, housed in an elaborate structure suggestive of Calvary. This, the *Kalvarienberg*, contains a series of winding passages and grottoes featuring twenty-four scenes denoting the Stations of the Cross, each with life-sized statues of the Biblical character painted in eye-catching colors. The devout might thus retrace Jesus's final journey on earth, ascending and descending the mount, and meditating on the significance of the events portrayed at each Station.

The experience is likely to have played a role in the creation of some of Haydn's compositions, especially those with para-liturgical associations such as the *Stabat mater* (1767) and *The Seven Last Words* (first composed in 1786). Since some of Haydn's late settings of the mass were first performed in the Bergkirche, these too may have been conceived with something of the spirituality of such sacred journeys in mind. The musical form of the last two masses – the *Schöpfungsmesse* (1801) and the *Harmoniemesse* (1802), both in B♭ major – in particular conveys a sense of a spiritual journey, transcending earthly considerations and implying progress towards a divine goal. *The Seasons*, Haydn's final oratorio, composed during the same period, presents a comparable journey, yet more explicit in meaning. The seasons are revealed as a metaphor for Man's progress through life. In *Winter*, the physical hardships of old AGE transport the listener to a vision of Heaven and the promise of everlasting peace.

Imagining Remote Places After Prince Nicolaus I chose to spend most of his time at Eszterháza, opera became a more intensive focus for Haydn's activities as Kapellmeister. Operas selected for performance there include a number set in regions far beyond Europe, often with EXOTIC associations, which evidently appealed to the Prince. Examples include Zingarelli's *Montezuma* and Sarti's *Idalide*, both with action taking place in Latin America, performed in 1785 and 1786 respectively. Documentation relating to decorations for *Montezuma* shows that one set portrayed "a view over the city of Mexico." In a cost-cutting measure, other sets for this opera reused those originally created for Haydn's operas *Orlando paladino* (1782) and *Armida* (1784), suggesting that attempts to provide non-Western settings for these operas were taken seriously. Haydn's *L'incontro improvviso* (1775), set in Cairo with characters exclusively from the Middle East, is an example of a "seraglio" opera, a favorite European stage convention of the eighteenth century. This setting enabled librettists to satirize notions of slavery, especially subjugation of women, by ultimately revealing the ruling sultan as a paradigm of ENLIGHTENMENT values, not the tyrant he is set up as. When the TOPOS was treated THEATRICALLY in other contexts, the target of the satire was often revealed as a topical example of servitude or oppression, something also likely in the case of Haydn's opera.

An indication that Haydn's imagination was captured by the settings of these operas is his choice of historical and travel literature, known from an inventory of books that comprised his personal library (see MATERIAL CULTURE). He owned, for example, William Robertson's *History of America*, one of very few objective accounts of Spanish-speaking America that had then been written, in an edition in English published in Vienna in 1787.

Among books concerning travels owned by Haydn was one of obvious relevance to music, Reichardt's *Briefe eines aufmerksamen Reisenden die Musik betreffend*, published in two volumes in 1774 and 1776. In a subsequent travelogue, Reichardt recounted visiting the elderly Haydn in Vienna and, contrary to expectations, was delighted to discover the old composer knew all about him, evidence that Haydn had actually read Reichardt's earlier volumes. A different kind of travel writing was represented in Haydn's library by eight volumes of Joachim Heinrich Campe's *Erste Sammlung merkwürdiger Reisebeschreibungen für die Jugend*, a collection of extraordinary and varied journeys, mostly based on true accounts, rewritten in a form suitable for young people. As well as travels within Europe, the volumes Haydn owned covered voyages to polar regions, the Indies, the Americas, as well as global explorations such as Captain Cook's first voyage to South Pacific. From Haydn's perspective Campe's version enabled him to explore the nature and scope of global travel in a quickly digestible form.

Haydn also owned literature helpful for imagining otherworldly or fabulous settings, a characteristic of many operas performed at Eszterháza, including his own. For example, he acquired Tomaso Garzoni's *Il serraglio de gli stupori del mondo*, a bibliographical rarity published in Venice in 1613. Its fantastical contents could have provided inspiration for an opera like his own *Il mondo della luna*, which evokes imaginary travel to an enchanted lunar world (see THEATER AND THEATRICALITY).

Journeys to England On the first outward journey from Vienna to London, Haydn took advantage of travel through Bavaria to accept a longstanding invitation to visit Wallerstein Castle, the main residence of his most ardent supporters in the German aristocracy. On the same journey Haydn, travelling in the company of the violinist and impresario Salomon, stayed in Bonn where Salomon was born. During this visit and again on the return journey Haydn was received by the Elector and by court musicians, occasions when he is likely to have had contact with Beethoven, who subsequently studied with the older composer in Vienna (see COMPOSERS). Since French territory had to be avoided during his second return journey because of the Revolutionary WARS, Haydn travelled via Hamburg, where according to his biographer Dies he hoped to meet C. P. E. Bach. Haydn would certainly have known, however, that Bach had actually died six years earlier. The real reason for including Hamburg on his itinerary was probably to see Bach's collection of portraits of composers preserved by Bach's widow and a fundamental source for musical portraiture of the period, as Richards confirms. Haydn perhaps knew about it from a published catalogue of Bach's collection, which was available in London before he left in 1795.

Being resident in London, then one of the most COSMOPOLITAN cities in the world, enabled Haydn to form connections with people who had considerable experience of global travel. His interest in this is evident from numerous entries made in his NOTEBOOKS. For instance, Haydn was certainly curious about British attempts to expand trade in China. He noted a series of facts about the Chinese capital and monarchy, which he probably heard directly from Lord Macartney, who had headed this diplomatic initiative. Haydn also came into contact with Sir Joseph Banks, the distinguished explorer and botanist, who had participated in Captain Cook's first great voyage, visiting South America, Tahiti, New Zealand, and Australia (see SCIENCE). Banks's family attended Haydn's concerts.

After finally returning to Austria, Haydn's interest in new travelogues did not diminish. He acquired, for example, a translation into German of Jean-Jacques Barthélemy's popular *Voyages de jeune Anacharsis en Grèce dans le milieu du quatrième siècle* (first published in 1788). This imaginative, though scholarly reconstruction of ancient Greek civilization is seen through the eyes of a young visitor from Scythia, who recounts his experiences of the Greek world from the perspective of old age, having returned home. Haydn was perhaps drawn to this wide-ranging work (there were seven volumes of it in his library, each illustrated with a plate) because it incorporated an extended account of music (first published in 1777). In revolutionary France, this volume was celebrated for its advocacy of the moral dimension of music in society, promoting all that was virtuous, though castigating music of the kind intended merely for the purposes of pleasure. Arguably this AESTHETICS of music was relevant to Haydn in developing the final phase of his career. Adopting many of its principles enabled him to retain the favor he had previously held in France during the final decade of the *ancien régime* despite the considerable change in aesthetic outlook in revolutionary times and into the Napoleonic era.

Haydn on Tour During the time Haydn spent in England he undertook much travel. Specific destinations included Oxford, Cambridge, Bath, Bristol, Winchester, and Windsor Castle. His notebooks systematically record details of places visited and impressions of what he saw. He was exceptionally able and willing to comment on works of art and architecture, often distinguishing styles or identifying artists by name. The experience of one particular trip he made, travelling alone and incognito, is of special interest in that it shows him indulging in a British craze of the time – a "picturesque tour," an early form of popular tourism. Haydn's destination was the Isle of Wight, a region that at the time was gaining appreciation for the natural beauty of its countryside, coastline, and architectural monuments. Although those concerned with the aesthetics of the picturesque at the time were unlikely to make the Isle of Wight a first choice for such a tour, from Haydn's point of view this was the most convenient way to experience the concept. His seriousness of purpose is suggested by his purchase of a recent guidebook, Hassell's *Tour of the Isle of Wight* (published in two volumes in 1790), an example of a new kind of travel literature drawing attention to historical and geographical curiosities that the traveler might consider worth exploring. A particular point recommending this publication is a series of striking aquatint illustrations (a new technique for illustration, then unavailable in Austria) depicting many of the landscape views tourists were encouraged to seek out to experience for themselves. Haydn probably followed the text only in so far as it gave him a sense of what such a tour was about, an experience that may have helped him in developing new musical effects, the kind of musical pictorialism later explored in *The Creation* and in *The Seasons* (see PROGRAMMATIC ELEMENTS). In his notebook Haydn records a visit to Mr. Orde, the island's governor, whose house "commands the most magnificent view over the ocean." Orde was a skilled amateur caricaturist and print-maker, possible factors in Haydn's interest in him.

A sense that English notions of travel and the range of experiences associated with them remained meaningful to Haydn after finally returning to Vienna in 1795 is his acquisition of Laurence Sterne's *Sentimental Journey through France and Italy by Mr Yorick*, in an English edition published in Vienna in 1795. Bonds explores how Haydn's musical language was often compared with Sterne's writings to illustrate his use of wit and irony.

Journeys in Music Music composed specifically to convey notions of travel was explored by Haydn relatively early in his career. The opening chorus and possibly the preceding overture of his first marionette opera, *Philemon und Baucis* (1773), represents in dramatic terms the journey of Jupiter from the summit of Olympus to the world of mortals, as underlined by the opera's subtitle: *Jupiters Reise auf die Erde*. Haydn's first oratorio composed two years later, *Il ritorno di Tobia*, explores notions of departure and arrival through musical means (reinforced by stage directions) notwithstanding the static nature of the oratorio form. Though more conventional and less powerful conceptually, the use of instrumental marches in his operas *Il mondo della luna* and *Armida* suggests Haydn's continuing interest in pursuing a sense of journeying through musical means, as does the overture to *La vera constanza* (1778/9), which depicts vessels at sea tossed by the ravages of a storm.

According to an account provided by his biographer Carpani, Haydn developed these compositional procedures still further by devising what he calls a *romanzo* ("romance") or *programma* ("program") for use in sustaining what the biographer calls "the musical colors" of an instrumental composition. Carpani illustrates this with an account of one program, elucidated for him by the composer himself. Haydn, Carpani claims, imagined an impoverished friend seeking fortune in America. The composition, a symphony, opens with the friend's departure, his family watching the ship sail away and waving farewell with tear-filled eyes. Waves drive the vessel forward on its journey until it reaches not America, but unknown lands. Following contact with inhabitants, native music, dancing, and primitive language are heard. Interaction between Europeans and natives leads to commercial exchange. Once laden with valuable merchandise, the ship sets sail once more for the return journey to Europe, aided by a favorable breeze. An episode follows during which the sea gradually grows rougher and skies darken. The ensuing storm brings complete disorder, terrifying the crew. Slowly the waves subside, and propitious winds ensure a safe homecoming. Finally, Carpani states that the composition concludes with joyful reunions and celebrations.

While Carpani's account might easily be dismissed as fanciful, a sense that he accurately recorded what Haydn actually told him comes from one of the most exceptional books contained in the composer's library. Haydn owned a complete collected edition of accounts of journeys of discovery made around the globe, including all the celebrated voyages of Captain Cook, published in London in 1784. What makes the volume he owned outstanding was that it features 125 illustrations and 32 maps copied from the original publications of the voyages in question, in many cases the earliest Western representations of remote regions of the globe. These include depictions of all the key details mentioned in Carpani's account of the Haydn symphony, an indication that the composer was genuinely inspired by viewing pictures in the volume he owned, with compositional consequences.

Although identifying the precise symphony Carpani mentions is problematic, its significance in terms of imagined journeys playing roles in Haydn's compositional procedures is clear. In both of his late oratorios Haydn followed up on this by composing music that unambiguously conveys people undertaking journeys in varied circumstances. *The Seasons*, for example, features episodes portraying a man hunting with his gun and dog, riders in pursuit of a stag, and a traveler on foot lost in drifting snow.

It seems likely that Haydn's late instrumental music, compositions conceived after he had himself experienced long-distance travel, also drew on the idea that music might be conceived like a journey, with its sense of departure, purpose, destination, and arrival. When listeners in the nineteenth century detected an impression of a rider in the final movement of Haydn's Quartet Op. 74, No. 3, they were probably more perceptive than is generally recognized.

THOMAS TOLLEY

FURTHER READING
Bonds (1991a); CCLN; Hassell (1790); Hörwarthner (1997); Landon V; Richards (2011, 2012, 2013, 2014); Sisman (2013).

Variation as Principle The variation – and its manifestations as a family of Classical forms, a process for development of musical ideas, a multivalent rhetorical tool, and a performance practice – was central to Haydn's creative persona. Variation came naturally to this composer whose professional day started with IMPROVISATION at the keyboard and whose training in classical rhetoric had taught him the value of leavening repetition with artful ornamentation, elaboration, and intensification. (See also COMPOSITIONAL PROCESS.)

As Viennese music theorist Johann Friedrich Daube observed in 1773, "everything that has been and will be composed is subject to the art of variation" (148). By then Haydn's transformation of mid-eighteenth-century variation technique from a decorative to an interpretive resource – from surface to structure – was well underway. Haydn's exploration of this principle intensified in the late 1770s, concurrently with his new Esterházy contract granting him license to MARKET his music commercially to a growing international audience (see PUBLISHERS AND PUBLISHING). Unlike Mozart and Beethoven, however, for whom the stand-alone variation set provided a popular vehicle for audience outreach, Haydn preferred to embed variation movements into larger instrumental works. Beginning with the symphonies numbered in the 70s, followed over the next several years by the String Quartets Op. 33, the "Auenbrugger" and "Bossler" keyboard Sonatas (Hob.XVI:35–39, 20, and 40–42), and the first published set of keyboard Trios (Hob.XV:6–8), Haydn's music regularly features one or more movements in variation forms. According to Sisman's taxonomy these include the strophic "theme and variation" set, alternating (or double) variation of two contrasting themes, the ABA_1 ternary variation favored in central movements, varied reprises (repetition replaced by written-out ornamentation of a larger formal unit), and the rondo-variation and its hybrids. By 1790 Haydn's lifelong engagement with variation as FORMAL and AESTHETIC principle had so imbued his creative practice that one can say his late instrumental music is essentially about the art of variation in its broadest sense.

Haydn's most vigorous contributions to the variation lie among his strophic, alternating, and ternary variations in lyrical style, in which slower tempo and relaxed pace allowed for wealth of musical detail. Here the prevailing association of variation forms with the marketplace is turned to higher purposes of expression and exploration. Exemplary is the first movement of the Sonata in D major (Hob.XVI:42), the last of three short keyboard sonatas published by Bossler in August 1784. Its opening set of three variations on an *Andante con espressione* theme embodies for all its brevity the depth and diversity of Haydn's

Example 22 Sonata in D major, Hob.XVI:42, mm. 1–4.

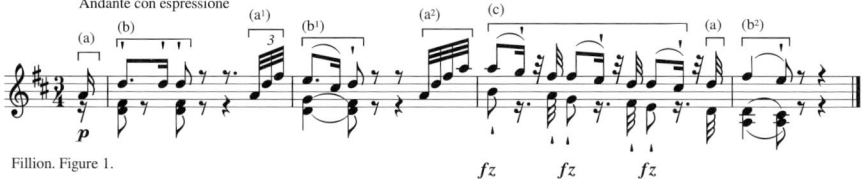

Fillion. Figure 1.

emerging variation principle. The theme itself (see Example 22) is an essay in ongoing elaboration of three tiny gestures, the upbeat impulse (a), the downbeat tap (b) and its outgrowth, the chain of "sighs" punctuated by *forzati* (c), all of which gather rhythmic momentum and rhetorical nuance with each transformation. This process unfolds with sustained purpose through the brilliant first variation and the learned *minore* variation two, reflecting the qualities of spontaneous virtuosity and compositional forethought, the *Spielmanieren* and *Setzmanieren* extolled by Marpurg (36). Haydn's return to the original theme initiates the culminating third variation with varied reprises, in which the ornamentation reaches a highpoint. Little occasion remains for further embellishment by the performer beyond the odd *fermata* or cadential flourish.

In his later movements in sonata and rondo forms Haydn often resorted to developing variation to offset their concentration on relatively few musical ideas. Several examples speak for his broad practice. The sonata-rondo finale of the Symphony No. 101 (1793–94) caps its steadfast hold on the refrain theme with a triple variation as recapitulation/coda: a quiet four-voice fugato for strings, a forceful multi-layered outburst for full ensemble, and a pastoral close over tonic drone (mm. 189–261). The Sonata in C major (Hob.XVI:50, 1794–95) opens with one of Haydn's most single-minded sonata-form movements, with permutations of a single theme used for each structural area; the most mysterious exploits an "open pedal" effect in a distant A♭ (m. 73). In Haydn's farewell to the variation, the exquisite rondo-variation slow movement of the String Quartet Op. 77, No. 2 (1799), the sheer loveliness of its theme and the resourcefulness of its elaboration mask its limitation to a single subject.

One of the most forward-looking aspects of Haydn's variations after 1790 is their use of instrumental color and ORCHESTRATION as variation techniques, anticipating in this regard the Romantic variation from Beethoven to Brahms. For example, when he revised the *Adagio cantabile* of the Trio in F♯ minor (Hob. XV:26) for use in the Symphony No. 102 (1794), Haydn added a varied reprise of the gracious exposition intensified by stirring undercurrents of trumpets and timpani. The *Largo assai* of the String Quartet Op. 74, No. 3 (1793), a ternary variation conceived for the concert halls of LONDON, enhances the extravagant violin ornamentation of the reprise with "orchestral" tremolos for full ensemble (mm. 49–50). Finally, the *Andante* of the Symphony No. 103 (1795), hailed by Sisman as "the richest variation movement in Haydn's symphonies" (1993a, 170), exploits contrasting orchestral groupings in its alternating variations of two Croatian tunes.

Haydn's variations for fortepiano, the majority in his solo sonatas and keyboard trios, constitute a special class. The range of color, accentuation, and dynamics facilitated by the Viennese fortepiano of the 1780s appears to have provided Haydn with fresh resources for elaboration. Again, the "Bossler" Sonatas of 1784 are the pathway to his new manner. His eventual acquisition of a Schanz fortepiano initiated a spate of variation movements that probe the expressive and dramatic resources of this INSTRUMENT. Variation movements are given first position in the alternating variations of the Trio in C minor (Hob.XV:13, 1789) and the hybrid rondo-variation of the Sonata in C major, Hob.XVI:48 (1789). While fantasy and imagination are given free rein in the exquisite ternary variation slow movement of the Sonata in E♭ (Hob.XVI:49, 1789–90), the meticulous planning of its unfolding ornamentation suggests a subtle logic that assists the pianist who can unearth it.

Many of Haydn's finest keyboard variations are DEDICATED to women. These include discriminating patronesses such as the Princess Marie Hermenegild Esterházy (Sonata in D major, Hob.XVI:42, and Piano Trio in D minor, Hob. XV:23) and cherished friends such as Marianne von Genzinger (Sonata in E♭ major, Hob.XVI:49) and Rebecca Schroeter (Trio in G major, Hob.XV:25). Therese Jansen-Bartolozzi, a superb London pianist who had studied with Muzio Clementi, merited the dedications of the Trio in E major (Hob.XV:28, 1795?), with its retrospective slow movement variations on a ground bass, and the London Sonatas Hob.XVI:50 in C major and 52 in E♭ major (1794), both of which feature powerful varied reprises. Finally, the Variations in F minor, Hob. XVII:6 (1793) were dedicated to pianist Barbara Ployer, a former student and Viennese colleague of Mozart. In the process of probing the two themes of its alternating variations, a solemn arietta with dotted upbeat and its lyrical F major complement with swirling arabesques, the movement broke free, circling back to the original F minor theme (m. 146). It also acquired a massive rhapsodic coda of overwhelming intensity (mm. 168–205) before subsiding into a closing meditation on the dotted figure. Suggestive of a musical "return trip" culminating in new insight into its root experience, this work heralds the variations of Beethoven and demonstrates Haydn on the cusp of what Robert Schumann would in 1836 term the "new variation" that strives for "thoughts, for inner connection, for poetic wholeness, the whole bathed in fresh fantasy" (I:224).

MICHELLE FILLION

FURTHER READING
Beghin (1997); Daube (1773); Harrison (1997); HWorld; Marpurg (1755b); Schumann (1854); Sisman (1993a, 2002).

Vienna "Wien bleibt Wien" (Vienna will always stay Vienna). The fact that everything remains the way it has always been in the Danube metropolis and that new things can only overcome entrenched traditions with difficulty, if at all, is a topos from the rhetorical arsenal of modernity. The expression "Wien bleibt Wien" first gained popularity after 1850 and was used by conservatives and progressives alike – those who wanted to maintain the status quo and those who advocated for change.

> A cultured COURT and educated circles of dilettantes [AMATEURS] can never in itself create such a primordial and richly prolific musical life, as is the case in Vienna. The musical root must be located in the FOLK itself, its temperament, its disposition and its basic nature, from which the more educated musical endeavours sound forth organically like harmonic overtones, and in which autonomously created art still finds resonance

wrote Eduard Hanslick in 1869 (64). In contrast to this alleged stability in the nineteenth century, the Austrian capital underwent extensive changes in the preceding century – a time of upheaval, reformation, and the threat of WAR. New impulses came from the outside, with immigration and cultural transfer (see COSMOPOLITANISM) creating the preconditions for the city's ascent as the "undeniable capital of the musical world," as Louis Spohr experienced Vienna in 1812 (155).

Born in a village less than fifty kilometres from Vienna, Haydn spent long periods of his life in the Austrian capital and was closely tied to Viennese society throughout his life. During this period the city underwent considerable social and economic change. The War of the Austrian Succession (1740–48), the Seven Years War (1756–63) and the Austro-Turkish War (1787–91) compromised the court budget and to some extent impacted cultural activities. During the Napoleonic Wars the French army even invaded the city in 1805 and 1809, but did not affect its continuous growth in the long run. Alongside LONDON, Paris, Istanbul, Naples, and Amsterdam, Vienna was one of the largest cities in EUROPE, and by far the largest city in the German-speaking countries (see Figure 32). As a result of economic developments, the number of inhabitants grew remarkably during Haydn's lifetime, from 175,000 in 1750 (including the suburbs) to 230,000 in 1800. Following the principles of mercantilism, Empress Maria Theresia promoted the foundation and expansion of manufacturers and COMMERCE, primarily producing luxury goods such as top-quality drapery, porcelain, gloves, music instruments, watches, wallpaper, and so forth. Gumpendorf, for instance, where Haydn purchased a house in 1793, developed into a center of silk manufacturing. Vienna's burgeoning industries enticed many entrepreneurs and skilled workers to move to the city from abroad, while its close proximity to the Danube also made it a prime location for traders. From the 1750s onwards, the middle class consisting of gentry, manufacturers, academics, and high officials, increasingly took part in cultural life.

Governmental reform policy stemming from ENLIGHTENMENT principles promoted economic growth and social transformation. These reform efforts simultaneously aimed to achieve emancipation and discipline, expanding legal protections and creating opportunities for underprivileged segments of society while also promoting the rising influence and control of the state in various areas – as in the case of manors and monasteries, which had, under feudalism, been considered legally autonomous. State reform and the centralization of public administration under the guise of the Enlightenment, although closely associated with Emperor Joseph II in the 1780s, were started by his mother Maria Theresia (ruled 1740–80) and continued by his brother Leopold II and

Figure 32 Map of Vienna from John Stockdale's *A Geographical, Historical, and Political Description of the Empire of Germany, Holland, the Netherlands, Switzerland, Prussia, Italy, Sicily, Corsica, and Sardinia* (London, 1800). The city of Vienna was surrounded by a strong fortification outside of which independent villages existed that were incorporated as suburbs about 1850. Most of his years in Vienna, Haydn lived in the city, but late in life he decided to move to Obere Windmühle, a village situated at the lower right corner of the map (close to No. 34 "Mariahilf Gate"). Although published in 1800, the map presents the layout from when Haydn moved to Vienna as a boy. The site where Haydn's house was erected in the 1780s is still shown as an agrarian area, not yet developed. Since then Vienna has expanded considerably. Reproduced with the permission of Wiener Stadt- und Landesarchiv (WStLA, Pläne und Karten: Sammelbestand, P5: 6175).

his nephew Franz II through the 1790s and into the new century. These reforms, in turn, influenced CHURCH policy, which regulated the establishment of many new parishes, and led to the Tolerance Patents of 1781–82, which guaranteed protestant Christians and JEWS the right to practice their beliefs freely. At the same time, many monasteries were dissolved and significant restrictions were placed on church music. Inspired by ideas of Enlightenment, the government promoted SCIENCE and EDUCATION, fought superstition, propagated literacy among the common folk, introduced German as the everyday language in the church and the THEATER, and stimulated German language literature. Freedom of the PRESS was also guaranteed in 1781. Simultaneously, however, censorship authority was strengthened, and attempts were made to repress dialects.

In Austria, the Enlightenment manifested itself as a top-down revolution. In addition to being driven by state institutions, parts of the church were also active ("Catholic Enlightenment"), as was FREEMASONRY, which rose up in the middle of the eighteenth century in the Austria monarchy in support of the core principles of freedom, equality, fraternity and tolerance. In the lodge "Zur wahren Eintracht," founded in 1781, Haydn had contact with the leading figures of the Austrian Enlightenment who, like the composer, moved to Vienna from other places and earned their reputations in various disciplines, including the author and scholar of public administration Joseph von Sonnenfels (1732/33–1817), and the scientist and mining expert Ignaz von Born (1742–1791). Whereas the freemasons embodied the ideas of the Enlightenment in the 1780s, suspicion grew after 1789 that they were sympathetic to the ideas of the French Revolution. Viennese lodges were closed in 1793, and a Jacobin Conspiracy was uncovered a year later, in which freemasons were said to have been involved.

Haydn was connected with several musical fields in Vienna including church music and concert life, PUBLISHING and copying, private education, and, in the early part of his career, with opera. All these areas were affected by the reform policy of the court in some way. Despite the instability of institutional support, Vienna continuously played host to various kinds of music theatre. Generally speaking, *opera seria* was losing its privileged position, while *opera buffa* was gaining in importance – a process mirroring the declining influence of the court on the Burgtheater repertoire. Starting in 1752, the Viennese theaters were administered by directors who had to manage the program, the staff, and the budget more or less independently from the court. After a period with French comedies dominating the repertoire of the Court Theater, Italian troupes started performing *opera buffa* in the 1760s. Although *opera seria* was staged regularly, it almost disappeared later that decade under the commercial approach of the new management.

At the Kärntnertortheater, the second major stage in town, traditional German farces and Singspiel were performed. Johann Joseph Felix Kurz (called Bernadon), an actor famous for his farces, and his troupe were regularly engaged at this theater, and it was for this troupe that Haydn wrote his first Singspiel, *Der krumme Teufel* (1752). In their efforts to raise German theater to a higher literary level, however, Enlightenment activists attempted to repress this kind of lowbrow popular theater. In 1770, Sonnenfels succeeded in implementing a permanent prohibition of extempore performance on stage, ultimately forcing Bernadon, famous for his improvised performances in the role of Hans Wurst, to leave Vienna. To compensate for this loss, from 1776 to 1783 Joseph II opened the Court Theater to a German troupe for the exclusive production of Singspiel. The Emperor's theatrical regulations also led to new theaters opening in the suburbs dedicated primarily to German comedies and Singspiele, thus reviving the tradition of Viennese popular theater. Although Haydn's subsequent Italian operas were restricted to the Esterházy court and not performed publicly in Vienna, his opera buffa, Lo speziale (1768), received a private staging at Baron Sumerau's Vienna residence in 1770 (see Landon II; Clark). Unlike Wagenseil, Gluck, Gassmann and Salieri, who dominated the repertoire among the local composers, Haydn never achieved a position at the Habsburg court; compared to other genres, his operas were less internationally favoured and distributed – setting the course for their future critical Reception.

Before Joseph II reformed religious services in the 1780s, drastically reducing the role and scope of music in masses and processions, many Viennese churches offered music of the highest quality to all classes. The Hofmusikkapelle represented the most important institution of church music under Empress Maria Theresia. Kapellmeister Georg von Reutter Jr. (1708–72), who became Kapellmeister at St. Stephen's Cathedral in 1738, dominated Vienna's church music for decades (see Composers and Music Professionals). After being elected to serve as Second Hofkapellmeister in 1747 (alongside the First Hofkapellmeister Luca Antonio Predieri, who was responsible for opera), he singlehandedly managed the church music at the Imperial Court. By combining these positions, Reutter gained considerable influence, benefiting Haydn. Indeed, Reutter picked out the seven-year-old boy at Hainburg and accepted him into St. Stephan's choir. Haydn used his time as a choirboy to learn several instruments and begin composing. He probably wrote a Missa brevis (Hob.XXII:1) for the choir before leaving. Aside from the court and the cathedral, several other places of worship performed high quality music during services, including the Schottenkirche (Scottish Church), the Jesuitenkirche (Jesuit Church), and St. Peter's Church, and many other churches – in both the city and the suburbs – regularly played orchestrated masses, among them the church of the Order of the Barmherzige Brüder (Brothers Hospitallers) in Taborstrasse, where Haydn played first violin from 1755 to 1758.

Musicians without a position in an ecclesiastical institution normally composed church music only on commission. This might explain why, apart from a couple of organ concertos, there is little extant church music by Haydn from the 1750s. Haydn's second mass for Vienna, the Missa in tempore belli (Mass in Time of War), was composed in 1796 when a recently ordained priest and friend celebrated his first mass. Haydn's Te Deum in C (1799/1800?) is dedicated to the wife of Emperor Franz II, Marie Therese, who (Rice surmises) probably commissioned the piece. While religious music by Leopold Hofmann and Tobias Gsur, for example, was written for the specific church where they had their positions as regentes chori (Hofmann at St. Peter and St. Stephen's Cathedral, Gsur at the Schottenkirche) Haydn's Mass in Time of War and late Te Deum were not composed for a specific place. From the beginning, they were widely available; collectors scrambled for copies, and soon after the first performance the works appeared in print (see PUBLISHING).

The earliest public concerts in Vienna took place during Lent. The first recorded concert was in 1745, and for the next twenty years Lenten concerts were given at the Court Theater three times a week. Programs normally included oratorios, solo concertos, and symphonies. Additionally, starting in November 1761, regular concerts, called *Accademien*, were held in the Court Theater every Friday throughout the year – presumably to increase profits, since Friday was a free day in the theater.

Starting in 1772, the concerts of the Tonkünstler-Societät took place four times a year: two with the same (or similar) programs before Easter, and two others before Christmas. The earnings were used to fill a pension fund for musicians and their families. In several respects these concerts followed the model of the earlier Lenten concerts. They were played in the theater on free days in Lenten and Advent periods. The programs also featured oratorios, framed or interrupted by symphonies and solo concertos.

The similar setting of both concert series makes comparison easy; it also reveals the extent to which taste changed within just ten years. With few exceptions, all the composers predominant in the Lenten concerts around 1760 (Wagenseil, Gluck, Holzbauer, Porpora, Jommelli, Galuppi, Sammartini) were rarely if ever played in the academies of the Tonkünstler-Societät. Only Hasse, Bonno and Dittersdorf continued to be performed, at least in the early years. Oratorios by new composers were introduced in the circle, such as works by Gassmann, Salieri, Starzer, Handel, Albrechtsberger and Marianna Martinez. In the same context, Haydn conducted the first performance of his oratorio *Il ritorno di Tobia* in 1775, involving more than 180 musicians. From 1780 symphonies and choral works by Haydn were included in the program, regularly every year or two. In 1784 *Tobia* was repeated, conducted by the composer. From 1798 the politics of programs changed remarkably. Starting with *Die sieben letzten Worte*, again with Haydn conducting, for a couple of years the programs included only oratorios by Haydn.

In addition to these concerts performed in the theater by professional musicians, beginning in the 1780s dilettante concerts were also performed in restaurants (e.g., Mehlgrube, Augarten) or at the university for a mixed bourgeois and aristocratic audience. Haydn's last public appearance occurred in conjunction with a performance of *The Creation* in March 1808 when aristocratic music lovers organized a concert in the university auditorium. At this and other concerts, the orchestra often consisted of bourgeois or aristocratic dilettantes, while professional musicians often performed the solos (see LEADING LARGE ENSEMBLES). Local and visiting virtuosos held their own concerts, principally in the theater with orchestra accompaniment.

In the early years of public concerts, Austria's old aristocratic families played only a minor role (if the few available sources truly reflect the aristocratic activities). Two concert series in the Lenten period of 1747 and 1759 reported in the diaries of Prince Johann-Joseph von Khevenhüller-Metsch mark the transition from academies for a distinct circle to concerts for a broader public, including the middle class. These concerts were organized (and partly funded) by a group of music-loving aristocrats. Furthermore, in March 1759, Giuseppe Bonno's oratorio *Isaaco, figura del Redentore* was performed in a staged version at the palace of Prince Joseph Friedrich von Sachsen-Hildburghausen (1702–87). The prince presented the piece first to the high nobility, but later repeated it for a larger audience.

Thirty years later oratorio performances were organized in a similar way. Starting in 1786, a group of noblemen calling themselves "Gesellschaft der Associierten Cavaliere" held annual academies at the Court Library, the Schwarzenberg Palace, and the Esterházy Palace in Vienna. The members of the exclusive SOCIETY belonged to the most prestigious families in the Empire. Again, the program consisted primarily of oratorios including a number of works by Handel and Haydn; *The Creation* was performed here for the first time in May 1798. Baron Gottfried van Swieten (1733–1803), who initiated the founding of the society and organized this concert, was not a member of high nobility but of the middle class, suggesting that significant social transformation was underway. A diplomat and a scholar, Swieten succeeded his father Gerard as director of the court library. Musically educated, and a composer as well as a tenor vocalist, he dedicated his weekly Sunday concerts held in his home to the music of G. F. Handel and J. S. Bach and inspired Mozart to arrange their music. He was not only influential in the early reception of Handel's oratorios in Vienna, but also supported Haydn in selecting and adapting his oratorio texts – not coincidentally following Handel's lead in choosing English originals in both cases (see CIRCULATION).

Members of the nobility arranged regular weekly concerts in their palaces, and members of the middle class also held them in their houses. The Prince of Sachsen-Hildburghausen, for instance, hosted a weekly musical academy for "high nobility" in the 1750s and 60s (see Dittersdorf 54 and 87). Even Haydn performed here as Nicola Porpora's accompanist (see Griesinger 14). Count Karl von Zinzendorf reports in his diary of regular concerts with various princes and counts. According to him, there was little social interchange among audience members from different classes: mainly high-ranking nobility attended (see Morrow). Zinzendorf himself rarely attended concerts of the middle class. Joseph Haydn, on the contrary, attended weekly concerts hosted by Franz Bernhard Ritter von Keeß (1720–95), a jurist and high court official, as well as those of Swieten and the salon of Marianne von Genzinger (1754–93) (see Eybl 1998).

The market for musical INSTRUMENTS boomed in Vienna in the second half of the eighteenth century. The number of keyboard-instrument makers increased from six in 1730 to twelve in 1760, a development linked to social transformation and later on the rise of the fortepiano. The aristocratic educational ideal was progressively adapted by middle-class families; it included dancing and performing music, increasing the demand for private music lessons. An article in Johann Adam Hiller's *Wöchentliche Nachrichten* from 1766 mentions several keyboard teachers, who were most likely the most prominent among the many other teachers working in Vienna. The article also lists a number of women from both the nobility and the middle class skilled at the keyboard or in singing (see Heartz 727). This is Haydn's field of activity in the 1750s and an important source of income: "Unfamiliar with the amenities

Figure 33 Kohlmarkt with Grosses Michaelerhaus immediately beside St. Michael's church, engraving by Karl Schütz 1786. Haydn lived here from 1750 to 1755. In this house he accompanied the singer and singing teacher Nicola Porpora, met the famous court poet and librettist Pietro Metastasio who resided here, and advised the latter's protégé Marianna Martinez in keyboard playing. Reproduced with the permission of Österreichische Nationalbibliothek, Bildarchiv.

of life, all his time was divided between TEACHING, the study of his art, and performing music. He played at serenades and in the orchestras for money and diligently exercised composing" (see Griesinger 12–13, own translation). In the 1750s Haydn worked for several, mostly private patrons in Vienna as a freelance composer, keyboard accompanist, violinist, organist, and keyboard teacher. From 1750 to 1755 he lived in a house, still extant today, the Grosses Michaelerhaus at Kohlmarkt (No. 11) (see Figure 33). There he accompanied the singer and singing teacher Nicola Porpora, met the famous court poet and librettist Pietro Metastasio who resided in the same building, and advised the latter's protégé Marianna Martinez in keyboard playing. Similar to the divertimentos by Georg Christoph Wagenseil and Joseph Anton Steffan (Stěpan), Haydn used many of his early keyboard sonatas and chamber music with keyboard instruments for teaching purposes.

Vienna relied on the distribution of musical manuscripts much longer than in Paris, London or Amsterdam. Therese Ziss (c. 1702–1777), Boniface Charles Champée, Simon Haschke and others worked partly for the court and partly for other customers (see Eybl 2008). Music that formerly was reserved exclusively for the court was now available in Vienna and throughout the empire. Very rarely was music printed in Vienna, and most of this was keyboard music. However, when the music engraver Antoine Huberty moved from Paris to

Vienna in 1777, music printing increased, gradually replacing the older practice of manuscript distribution (see CIRCULATION). Haydn figured prominently in the music market. The first two advertisements published by Haschke in the *Wienerisches Diarium* at the end of the 1760s included piano works and chamber music by Haydn. Joseph Kurzböck printed his piano sonatas in 1774, and following the music printing boom in 1780, Haydn's presence in the musical marketplace continued to be strong. As Haydn's most important Viennese publisher, Artaria offered in his shop not only his own products, but also numerous prints of Haydn's music from abroad (see Fuhrmann).

In keeping with his international reputation, Haydn was viewed by the Viennese public first of all as a composer of instrumental music and oratorios. By 1800 he was a powerful presence in both Viennese concert life and the local music market. Unlike Mozart, he did not manage to develop close connections with the Habsburg court. Throughout his career he preferred to move in middle-class circles in Vienna rather than with the high nobility, in clear distinction to Beethoven. Haydn's appearance in middle class salons may also have contributed to the great popularity he enjoyed in Vienna at the end of his life.

MARTIN EYBL (TRANSLATED BY SCOTT WITMER)

FURTHER READING
Brown (1995); Clark (2009a); Czeike (1992–2004); Dittersdorf (1801); Edge (1992b); Eybl (1998, 2008); Fritz-Hilscher (2011); Fuhrmann (2010); Gericke (1960); Griesinger; Hanslick (1869); Heartz (1995); Hochstein (1993); Melton (2007); Mitchell (2007); Morrow (1989); Pohl (1871); Rice (2003); Spohr (1968); Zechmeister (1971).

Vocal Coaching and Rehearsal In his role as the conductor of numerous operas composed by himself and others, Haydn coached individual singers and directed many rehearsals of operatic productions. Clause eight of his 1761 Vice-Kapellmeister contract specifically states that he should "coach the singers" (Jones 136). In 1784 Haydn listed seventy-three operas produced at Eszterháza: eleven are by him, and the rest are by COMPOSERS as varied and diverse as Mysliveček, Dittersdorf, Gluck, Gretry, Anfossi, Gazzaniga, Salieri, Piccinni, Gassmann, Paisiello, Gugliemi, Astarita, Cimarosa, Righini, Sacchini, Sarti, and Naumann. Haydn wrote many insertion arias for performances in these operas. These new arias, along with the complete operas themselves, must have been effectively rehearsed and coached to ensure the praise that commentators heaped on the productions under Haydn's direction.

In the 1750s Haydn gained valuable first-hand experience as a coach in assisting one of Europe's greatest vocal pedagogues, Nicolo Porpora. Dies reports that "[w]hile Porpora taught the girl singing, Haydn, who had to accompany on the keyboard, found it a useful opportunity to gain a perfect knowledge of, and practice in, the Italian method of singing and accompanying," which Carpani adds was "an exercise much more thorny [*scabroso*] than is commonly supposed" (Diergarten 56–57). Haydn appears to have served as Porpora's valet and dogsbody, shining his shoes and putting up with Porpora's impatience, but he "was glad to suffer all this because he learned so much from the man" (Dies 32). This "perfect knowledge" of Italian diction, prosody, and word-setting was put to use in the busy schedule of opera performances that adorned the courtly calendar at Eszterháza. Years later, as a seventy-year old, Haydn recommended in a Correspondence of 1804 the same educational regime he had undertaken with Porpora (Briefe 448).

We know little of Haydn's direct vocal-pedagogical engagement with the singers he encountered throughout his career. Certainly he did not appreciate relinquishing artistic control of his compositions to others, as the famous letter to the monks at Zwettl Abbey (1768) attests. This document offers unique insight into the kinds of performance guidelines that he may have imparted to vocalists in productions under his direction. He comments that the genre of the piece (in this case, a celebratory *Applausus*) should inform the overall *Affekt*, and that the tempi should be on the whole faster than usual "since the whole text applauds." He cautions that the singer should enter after the orchestra in accompanied recitatives, even if the "score shows the contrary," as it would be "ridiculous if you would fiddle away the word from the singer's mouth, and understand only the words 'quae metamo . . . '. But I leave this to the harpsichord player, and all the others must follow him." This suggests that, in vocal music, Haydn expected the keyboardist to direct proceedings accordingly, and desired that the text be clearly understood. Haydn is concerned not only with prosody, inserting a short digression on the ambiguities of the pronunciation of "metamorphosis" in Latin and Italian, but he is also apprehensive about clear diction. Comprehension is valued above all: "I suggest that the two boys in particular have a clear pronunciation, singing slowly in recitative so that one can understand every syllable" (CCLN 9–10). This sentiment is echoed in two 1790 letters to Genzinger: "My good friend Fräulein Peperl will (I hope) be reminded of her teacher by singing the Cantata [*Ariana a Naxos*] frequently; she should remember to have a distinct articulation and a correct vocal production . . . [Peperl should] articulate the words clearly, especially the passage 'chi tanto amai'" (CCLN 97, 99; see also Day-O'Connell). In the *Applausus* letter he explains his preferred execution of the prosodic appoggiatura in recitative (in "metamorphosis," the penultimate appoggiatura on the accented syllable receives a full quarter note for emphasis and not two eighth notes, which weakens the prosodic accent). Here he relies "on the skill of the tenor, who will explain such things to the boys." Importantly, Haydn implies that both instrumentalist (the harpsichordist directing the orchestra) and vocalist (the older tenor with musical skill) will act as coaches and directors for both rehearsal and performance.

On the whole, Haydn seems to have preferred to Teach and coach through demonstration and imitation. As we find in his letter to the monks, Haydn is frustrated when he cannot coach in person. In 1790 he writes to Genzinger: "Oh! How I do wish that I could play this Sonata to you a few times"; earlier he says that "it contains many things which I shall analyze for Your Grace when the time comes" (CCLN 105). Certainly his keyboard duet "Il maestro e lo scolare" (Hob.XVIIa:1) teaches articulation, ornaments, and varying patterns through imitation: the maestro plays first in the bass and then the student copies in the treble (see Beghin). And in London in 1794, Haydn demonstrated timpani technique by example to George Thomas Smart (see Landon III).

Some eighteenth-century singers were not able to read music at all. These were the so-called *orecchianti* (literally "ear-ers") who were adept at picking up music astonishingly quickly. Brigida Giorgi Banti, for example, was musically illiterate, but after "hearing an air once played over, and that but indifferently, she sang it most divinely" (Rosselli 93). Salieri played a 132-measure hallelujah for her three times in 1785 and afterwards she sang it back note-perfect and with the appropriate expression. In 1768, Leopold Mozart wrote that some of the cast of his son's *La finta semplice* could only learn from the young boy, as they learned everything by ear (see Feldman 2007). Some of the singers Haydn coached at Eszterháza were probably skilled *orecchianti* too. This kind of imitative pedagogy is most often evident in the portrayal of singing lessons or rehearsals in eighteenth-century comic opera. Salieri's 1781 *Der Rauchfangkehrer*, for example, has the fake maestro (a hustling chimney sweep with a musical bent) correct the diction of his students and suggest cadenzas and trills, which are dutifully repeated by the two singers. A similar scene appears in Gassmann's 1769 *L'opera seria*, where the maestro instructs the orchestra in matters of correct articulation, the length and execution of appoggiaturas, and dynamics (see Bellini).

Haydn himself set a singing lesson in his 1766 intermezzo, *La canterina* (Hob. XXVIII:2). Here we encounter the familiar trope of the singing-lesson-as-seduction, a scenario Haydn knew from personal experience. He recounted to Griesinger his erotically charged embarrassment at observing the bosom of Countess Morzin at a music lesson, and as Beghin points out, he most likely first encountered his mistress Luigia Polzelli in coaching sessions for operatic performances at Eszterháza. Unusually, in *La canterina* there is no imitative pedagogy; rather, the singing student Gasparina sings fragments of recitative simultaneously with her teacher Don Pelagio, a scene witnessed by her pretended mother Apollonia (a trouser role) who offers satirical commentary.

Like any eighteenth-century composer who achieved international fame, Haydn considered his operatic output as central to his EDUCATION, training, and his own prestige as an artist. When asked to provide an autobiographical note in 1776, Haydn mentioned his operatic output first, then his sacred works, and, finally, his compositions for the chamber (see Schroeder). Haydn also mentioned that his works had met with the approbation of Hasse, the then pre-eminent composer of *opera serie*. Unlike Hasse, however, Haydn's operatic work did not bring him into sustained contact with the great castrati singers of the day, a still-vital presence in operatic culture of the 1770s. The only castrato employed at Eszterháza during Haydn's tenure was Pietro Gherardi, from 1776–78. Geiringer describes how at first Haydn had Gherardi in mind for the central character of Ecclitico in *Il mondo della luna* (1777), but ultimately cast him instead in the small role of Ernesto. An alto castrato, Gherardi had previously worked with Haydn in the title role of Gluck's *Orfeo* (1776). Jones suggests that the absence of castrati at Eszterháza and – more importantly – the large-scale *seria* works that were their speciality, appears to have been the result of a stylistic preference at court for *dramma giocoso*.

Despite limited contact with castrati during his career on the continent, Haydn had fond relationships with older, retired castrati during his trips to England. Haydn's own near brush with castration as a teenager (it was forbidden by Haydn's father, according to Griesinger), if true, might have led the composer to consider these musicians more sympathetically than some. In Bath in 1794, Haydn was a guest of Venanzio Rauzzini (1746–1810), who had also studied with Porpora. Haydn also befriended Gaspare Pacchierotti (1740–1821) in London in 1791; Pacchierotti was a castrato universally liked by the notoriously fickle English during his sojourn there.

On February 18, 1791, Haydn performed *Ariana a Naxos* with Pacchierotti to rapturous applause (see Feldman 2015a). Absent from contemporary accounts is the dissonance of GENDERS between the protagonist, Ariana and castrato performer; Pacchierotti had played female characters in his youth, as was normal for young castrati (e.g., Livietta in Galuppi's 1759 *Le nozze di Dorina*). Indeed, Richard Edgcumbe, who was present at the performance where Haydn accompanied at the keyboard, described Pacchierotti in his *Musical Reminsicences* as a "forcible and impressive" actor: "even those who did not understand the language could not fail to comprehend, from his countenance, voice, and action, every sentiment he expressed" (14–15). Haydn destined the part of the Genio for an anonymous castrato in the failed London production of *Orfeo ed Euridice* in spring 1791. Haydn's writing for the Genio demonstrates the flashy virtuosity that was the classic hallmark of heroic castrati roles.

Haydn's relationship with the voice was a deeply felt one, as witnessed in his emphatic comments regarding expression. A well-documented anecdote reveals that his connection with the voice was not as "flat as a sheet of typing paper," to quote Feldman's critique (2015b), in which the timbre of the voice is considered merely as a "secondary parameter ... a befouling of the 2D purity of the score" (654). Haydn notes in his First London NOTEBOOK:

> 8 days before Pentecost I heard 4000 charity children in St. Paul's Church sing the song noted below [Example 23]. One performer indicated the tempo. No music ever moved me so deeply in my whole life, so full of devotion and innocence. N.B.: All the children are newly clad, and enter in procession. The organist first played the melody very nicely and simply, and then they all began to sing at once (Landon III 173–74; see also EMPFINDSAMKEIT).

Dies spoke with Haydn about the event and received an augmented account:

> He told me in addition, "I stood there, and wept like a child." He remarked that the voices sounded like angels' voices; that the descent in the first three measures to the low B worked in a uneasy (*bange*), heart-breaking (*herzergreifende*) way whilst the notes of the tender young voices died away, and the [low] B with the fermata sounded only like a floating breath; that in the continuation of the melody the ascending tones gradually gained in life and strength and that thus the melody took on light and shadow and made a powerful impression on the feelings (Dies 128).

Here is an expressive account of the different "grains" of the voice. Haydn is overwhelmed by the effect of 4000 young voices, and moved by the "heartbreaking" struggle that the voices undertake as a community when attempting to sing the low B, poignantly too low for their "tender voices." This struggle appears to bring up a wealth of associations for Haydn (perhaps reminding

Example 23 Haydn's notation of a children's chorus heard in St. Paul's Cathedral, London, recorded in his First London Notebook

him of his own childhood as a chorister), and he is moved to tears; he weeps "like a child." Encountering forms of vocal extremes (in tessitura), as well as extremes of age (youthfulness) and of the voice on the verge of being altered by puberty ("full of innocence"), he experiences his own humanity. His vivid account, with its three-dimensional assessment of minute and differing qualities of the voice, reinforces how attuned he was to all aspects of timbre (as also explored by Dolan).

The celebrated Bologna pedagogue Lorenzo Gibelli (1719–1812), a contemporary of Haydn's, opined that a perfect singer must "besides enjoying a fine, well-tuned voice, know all that concerns music and the essentials of her own language and of acting, and should also have furnished her mind with knowledge of the civil, political, and religious history of the peoples of the world, of the civilization and customs of different social classes, if possible of all times, not to mention enough philosophy to teach her the course of human passions" (Rosselli 102–3). Here, then, was the ideal, although clearly not every singer that Haydn or indeed any other eighteenth-century composer worked with had all the requisite skills Gibelli lists. The few comments we have from Haydn on his coaching and rehearsal methods for vocalists are overall quite pragmatic and concern themselves with diction, prosody, clarity, and appropriate expression. His relationship with castrati was limited to fond friendships rather than active professional contacts and, finally, his association with the highly expressive powers of the human voice was an extremely sensitive and responsive one.

ERIN HELYARD

FURTHER READING
Beghin (2015a); Bellini (2009); Bianconi (1998); Briefe; CCLN; Day-O'Connell (2014a); Diergarten (2011); Dies; Dolan (2013); Durante (1998); Edgcumbe (1834); Feldman (2007, 2015a, 2015b); Geiringer (1982); Jones (2009); Kelly (2004); Landon II, III; Rosselli (1992); Schroeder (2005).

War Haydn was born during the Seven Years War, traveled to VIENNA during the Austro–Turkish War of 1787–90, and traversed Western EUROPE during the Revolutionary Wars with France. He died during a dramatic sequence of battles between Napoleon and allied European powers that arguably initiated something like modern warfare – with popular levies and even conscription widespread, and a growing tactical orientation towards the bombardment and capture of enemy cities. Many of Haydn's patrons and employers were veterans of the bloodiest and strategically most important conflicts of the eighteenth century: all four Esterházy princes under whom Haydn served had pursued military careers, as was the tradition among the Austro-Hungarian nobility – from Paul Anton's victorious service in the War of the Austrian Succession and the Seven Years War to Nicholas II's honorable but troubled leadership of largely Hungarian regiments during the Napoleonic Wars. In 1800, Haydn even met Horatio Nelson, the skilled naval strategist of the Napoleonic wars who was passing through EISENSTADT along with a sizable retinue, and the admiring English hero presented Haydn with a gold watch, requesting in return a worn pen. By this time, Haydn had clearly become fascinated by contemporary battles and war heroes: during his LONDON visits of the 1790s, when he encountered the lively English culture of the print shop amid an increasingly bellicose public ambience, he acquired an engraving of Nelson's famous naval victory in the Battle of Aboukir Bay. (He also came to own a 1798 engraving of Nelson issued by his main Viennese PUBLISHER Artaria.) For all that, Haydn did not experience the grim realities of war at first hand until the last days of his life, when the elderly musician, along with his servants, sheltered in his house in Gumpendorf as Napoleon's troops bombarded the Viennese suburbs in advance of their second occupation in May 1809.

It should come as no surprise, then, that Haydn's music frequently echoed and spurred on the warlike preoccupations of his patrons and AUDIENCES. This was especially true in his last two decades, not only because the wars with France became an abiding geopolitical preoccupation during the 1790s, but also because representatives of the political establishment in Britain and Austria increasingly required musicians and other artists to shape and mediate wartime public sentiment in newly prominent ways (see NATIONALISM AND COSMOPOLITANISM). This tendency was most plainly illustrated by Count Joseph Franz Saurau's 1797 commission of Haydn's "Gott erhalte Franz den Kaiser," a song of state loyalty soon to be ubiquitous on stages and in parlors across the Habsburg realm.

To be sure, many of Haydn's compositions from this period contain warlike episodes or have a broadly martial character. Symphony No. 100 in G major, "Military," dating from 1793–94, might appear the most obvious case, though this composition is only one among a family of comparably warlike and at times explicitly TOPICAL compositions. These include at least three works associated with Nelson: the grand *Missa in angustiis* or "*Nelson Mass*" of 1798, which acquired its nickname only after Nelson's visit to Eisenstadt; the song for voice and keyboard, "Lines from the Battle of the Nile" (Hob.XXVIb:4), a two-part-song produced and performed during Nelson's stay, based on excepts from a rather turgid Pindaric Ode in praise of the Briton's recent victory in Egypt; and the magnificent *Te Deum* in C major (Hob.XXIIIc:2), which was also performed during Nelson's time at Eisenstadt, ostensibly as part of name-day celebrations for Princess Marie Therese, but undoubtedly with a broader topical resonance, given that the *Te Deum* traditionally served to give thanks for military victories.

One could add to this trio of Nelson-associated works a selection of patriotic and warlike music by Haydn originating both in England and the Habsburg realm. Examples from the second of Haydn's London trips include the unfinished cantata known as the *Invocation of Neptune* – a single aria and a boisterous Handelian chorus celebrating the might of the British navy, which Haydn began to set at the behest of Willoughby Bertie, Fourth Earl of Abingdon but quietly set aside when the earl was sentenced to prison in 1795. In a similar rhetorical vein, but representing a contrast of genre, was the "Sailor's Song" from the second book of Original Canzonettas (Hob.XXVIa:25–36, 1795), which glorified British marine power in a sort of sea shanty punctuated by striking martial gestures.

Back in the Viennese orbit the following year, Haydn started to produce music that participated in a rapidly expanding culture of state-sponsored popular resistance. In September 1796 an adaptation of Alexander Bicknell's patriotic play *Alfred, King of the Anglo-Saxons* was staged at Eisenstadt, and Haydn provided three incidental numbers – the last a rousing C-major *Kriegerischer Chor*. And, later that year, on the Feast of St. Stephen (the day after Christmas), and with Vienna under serious threat of invasion, Haydn's *Missa in tempore belli* (*Mass in Time of War*) was performed under his own direction in the Piaristenkirche in the Viennese suburb of Josefstadt. The Agnus Dei of this mass, which incorporates ominous timpani rolls and abrasive brass tattoos, has elicited a cluster of related interpretations over the years: Georg August Griesinger, in his 1810 biography of Haydn, concluded that it depicted "the enemy approaching in the distance," while another contemporary heard "the human heart thudding with anxiety" before the victorious fanfares of the "dona nobis pacem" – a plea with obvious relevance in the winter of 1796.

The RECEPTION of this mass in particular shows how Haydn's later music was called upon by aristocratic patrons and the state not only to mark or adorn unfolding wartime events, but actively to shape the public understanding of these events, to create collective feelings about them, and to move people to further action. The 1796 performance of the *Missa in tempore belli* was the centerpiece of a public celebration staged by Johann Franz von Hofmann, a treasurer in the War Department whose son had recently been elevated to the priesthood: "There hasn't ever been a sermon to pack 'em in like that," remarked Joseph Richter in his chronicle of Viennese daily life, the *Eipeldauer Briefe*. Indeed, such was the perceived power of Haydn's musical voice, that his compositions were continually reused in charged wartime contexts until the end of the Napoleonic era. This not only applies to explicitly political fare such as "Gott erhalte Franz den Kaiser," but also untexted works such as the "Military," which was performed with great regularity at wartime celebrations through the lavish events of the Congress of Vienna. Even Haydn's chorus of victorious warriors from *Alfred* resurfaced during the Congress period, reprinted in piano reduction in 1814 by the Leipzig *Allgemeine musikalische Zeitung*, which presented the chorus to its readers as an especially appropriate contribution to the burgeoning genre of topical wartime music. Thus did Haydn's unprecedented celebrity, won relatively late in his life, give him the opportunity to become an especially potent "wartime artist." (See also POLITICS.)

NICHOLAS MATHEW

FURTHER READING
Deutsch (1982); Jones (2013); Mathew (2007).

Women – see Relationships and Friendships; Gender

Worklists – see Catalogues

Bibliography

"A Musical Graduates Society" 1892. *Musical Times and Singing Class Circular*, 33 / 598: 713–14.

Abrams, Meyer Howard 1953. *The Mirror and the Lamp: Romantic Theory and the Critical Tradition*. New York: Oxford University Press.

Acker, Yolanda 2007. *Música y danza en el Diario de Madrid (1758–1808). Noticias, avisos y artículos*. Madrid: Centro de Documentación de Música y Danza.

Adams, Sarah 1994. "International Dissemination of Printed Music during the Second Half of the Eighteenth Century" in Lenneberg (ed.) 21–42.

Adler, Guido (ed.) 1909. *Haydn-Zentenarfeier. III Kongress der Internationalen Musikgesellschaft Wien: Bericht*. Vienna and Leipzig: Artaria.

Adorno, Theodor W. 1982 [1959]. "Verfremdetes Hauptwerk. Zur Missa Solemnis," *Gesammelte Schriften* 17: 145–61.

Agawu, V. Kofi 1991. *Playing with Signs*. Princeton University Press.

Agnew, Vanessa 2008. *Enlightenment Orpheus: The Power of Music in Other Worlds*. Oxford University Press.

AHRC Centre for the Research and History of Recorded Music [website]: charm.rhul.ac.uk (accessed July 13, 2018).

Al-Taee, Nasser 2010. *Representations of the Orient in Western Music: Violence and Sensuality*. Farnham and Burlington: Ashgate.

Aldwell, Edward and Carl Schachter 2011 [1979]. *Harmony and Voice Leading*, 4th edn. New York: Schirmer.

Allanbrook, Wye Jamison 1983. *Rhythmic Gesture in Mozart*. University of Chicago Press.

(ed.) 1998. *Strunk's Source Readings in Music History*, rev. edn. Vol. 5, *The Late Eighteenth Century*. New York: Norton.

2014. *The Secular Commedia: Comic Mimesis in Late Eighteenth-Century Music (Ernest Block Lectures)*, ed. Mary Ann Smart and Richard Taruskin. Oakland: University of California Press.

Allanbrook, Wye Jamison, Janet M. Levy, and William P. Mahrt (eds.) 1992. *Convention in Eighteenth- and Nineteenth-Century Music: Essays in Honor of Leonard G. Ratner*. Stuyvesant: Pendragon Press.

Almén, Byron 2008. *A Theory of Musical Narrative*. Bloomington: Indiana University Press.

Anderson, Emily (trans. and ed.) 1985. *The Letters of Mozart and his Family*, 3rd edn., rev. Stanley Sadie and Fiona Smart. London: Macmillan.

Andrew, Edward 2006. *Patrons of Enlightenment*. University of Toronto Press.

Andrews, Harold 1981. "The Submediant in Haydn's Development Sections" in Larsen, Serwer, and Webster (eds.) 465–71.

Angermüller, Rudolph 1977. *Sigismund Neukomm. Werkverzeichnis, Autobiographie, Beziehung zu seinen Zeitgenossen* (Musikwissenschaftliche Schriften 4). Munich: Katzbichler.

Anson-Cartwright, Mark 2000. "Chromatic Features of E♭-major Works of the Classical Period," *Music Theory Spectrum* 22/2: 177–204.

Appel, Bernhard R. and Armin Raab (eds.) 2015. *Widmungen bei Haydn und Beethoven. Personen – Strategien – Praktiken. Bericht über den internationalen musikwissenschaftlichen Kongress Bonn, 29. September bis 1. Oktober 2011.* Bonn: Verlag Beethoven-Haus.

Arlt, Wulf 1983. "Zur Handhabung der Inventio in der deutschen Musiklehre des 18. Jahrhunderts" in Buelow and Marx (eds.) 371–91.

Arnim, Ludwig A. von and Clemens Brentano 1806–8. *Des Knaben Wunderhorn. Alte deutsche Lieder.* Heidelberg: Mohr und Zimmer.

Aversano, Luca 2008. "The Transmission of Italian Musical Articles through Germany and Austria to Eastern Europe around 1800" in Rasch (ed.) 143–56.

Bach, Carl Philipp Emanuel 1994 [1753/62]. *Versuch über die wahre Art, das Clavier zu spielen.* Berlin and Kassel: Bärenreiter.

Badley, Allan 2012. "Two Composers and a Cellist: Haydn, Hofmann, and Joseph Weigl," *Haydn: The Online Journal of the Haydn Society of North America* 2/1: https://www.rit.edu/affiliate/haydn/two-composers-and-cellist-haydn-hofmann-and-joseph-weigl (accessed August 1, 2018).

Badura-Skoda, Eva 1972. "Teusche Comoedie-Arien und Joseph Haydn" in Schwarz (ed.) 59–72.

    1985. "Il significato dei manoscritti Scarlattiani recentemente scoperti a Vienna," *Chigiana* 40: 45–56.

    (ed.) 1986. *Joseph Haydn. Bericht über den Internationalen Joseph Haydn-Kongress, Wien, Hofburg, 5.–12. September 1982.* Munich: G. Henle Verlag.

Baker, Nancy Kovaleff and Thomas Christensen (eds.) 1996. *Aesthetics and the Art of Musical Composition in the German Enlightenment: Selected Writings of Johann Georg Sulzer and Heinrich Christian Koch.* Cambridge University Press.

Bakke, Gretchen and Marina Peterson (eds.) 2017. *Anthropology of the Arts: A Reader.* London and New York: Bloomsbury Academic Publishing.

Barker-Benfield, G. J. 1992. *The Culture of Sensibility: Sex and Society in Eighteenth-Century Britain.* University of Chicago Press.

Bartha (ed.) 1965: see Abbreviations (*Briefe*).

Bartha and Somfai 1960: see Abbreviations.

Bar-Yoshafat, Yonatan 2013. "Kenner und Liebhaber – Yet Another Look," *International Review of the Aesthetics and Sociology of Music* 44: 19–47.

Barz, Gregory F. and Timothy J. Cooley (eds.) 2008. *Shadows in the Field: New Perspectives for Fieldwork in Ethnomusicology*, 2nd edn. New York: Oxford University Press.

Bashford, Christina 2003. "The String Quartet and Society" in Stowell (ed.) 3–18.

Batteux, Charles 1746. *Les Beaux-arts réduits à un meme principe.* Paris: Chez Durand.

Bauman, Thomas 2004. "Becoming Original: Haydn and the Cult of Genius," MQ 87/2: 333–57.
Bazzana, Kevin 1997. *Glenn Gould: The Performer in the Work*. Oxford University Press.
Beach, David and Yosef Goldenberg 2015. *Bach to Brahms: Essays on Musical Design and Structure*. New York: University of Rochester Press.
Beal, Timothy (ed.) 2015. *The Oxford Encyclopedia of the Bible and Arts*. 2 vols. Oxford University Press.
Beales, Derek 2005. *Enlightenment and Reform in Eighteenth-Century Europe*. London and New York: I. B. Tauris.
Becker, Howard S. 2008 [1982]. *Art Worlds*. Twenty-fifth anniversary edn. Berkeley and London: University of California Press.
Beer, Axel (2000). *Musik zwischen Komponist, Verlag und Publikum. Die Rahmenbedingungen des Musikschaffens in Deutschland im ersten Drittel des 19. Jahrhunderts*. Tutzing: Hans Schneider.
  2010. "Verlage/Verleger/Verlagswesen," H-L 811–14.
Beer, Axel and Klaus Burmeister 1997. "'. . . in betreff des geizigen Caracters von Haydn'. Ein Brief Franz Anton Hoffmeisters als Quelle zur Musik- und Verlagsgeschichte der Zeit um 1800," *Die Musikforschung* 50: 36–47.
Beghin, Tom 1997. "Haydn as Orator: A Rhetorical Analysis of His Keyboard Sonata in D Major, Hob.XVI:42" in HWorld 201–54.
  2005. "A Composer, His Dedicatee, Her Instrument, and I: Thoughts on Performing Haydn's Keyboard Sonatas" in *Cambridge Companion* 203–25.
  2006. "'Votre très humble & très obeisant serviteur.' Männliche und weibliche Rhetorik in Haydns Sonate Hob.XVI:40" in *Perspektiven und Aufgaben der Haydn-Forschung. Bericht über den internationalen wissenschaftlichen Kongress Köln, 23.-25. Juni 2005*. H-St 9(1–4): 33–57.
  2007. "Delivery, Delivery, Delivery" in Beghin and Goldberg 131–71.
  2008. "Taking Oxford to Montreal and Other Adventures in Virtual Acoustics," *Haydn Society of North America Newsletter*, 1/1: 11–12.
  2009/2011. *The Virtual Haydn: Complete Works for Solo Keyboard*, box set of four Blu-ray discs, reissued as thirteen CDs/DVD, Naxos NBD 0001–04 and Naxos 8501203.
  2014. "Recognizing Musical Topics versus Executing Rhetorical Figures" in Mirka (ed.) 551–76.
  2015a. *The Virtual Haydn: Paradox of a Twenty-First Century Keyboardist*. University of Chicago Press.
  2015b. "The Lady Named on the Title Page: The Rhetoric of Dedication in Haydn's Keyboard Works" in Appel and Raab (eds.) 93–120.
Beghin and Goldberg 2007: see Abbreviations.
Bellini, Alice 2009. "Music and 'Music' in Eighteenth-Century Meta-Operatic Scores," ECM 6/2: 183–207.
Bent, Ian (ed.) 1996. *Music Theory in the Age of Romanticism*. Cambridge University Press.
Berg, Darrell 1990. "Carl Philipp Emanuel Bach und die 'empfindsame Weise'" in Marx (ed.) 93–105.
  2009. *The Correspondence of Christian Gottfried Krause: A Music Lover in the Age of Sensibility*. Farnham and Burlington: Ashgate.

Berger, Karol 2007. *Bach's Cycle, Mozart's Arrow: An Essay on the Origin of Musical Modernity*. Berkeley and Los Angeles: University of California Press.

Bergeron, Katherine and Philip V. Bohlman (eds.) 1992. *Disciplining Music: Musicology and Its Canons*. University of Chicago Press.

Berkel, Klaas van, Albert van Helden, and Lodewijk Oalm (eds.) 1999. *A History of Science in the Netherlands: Survey, Themes and Reference*. Leiden: Brill.

Bertoli, Bruno 2006. "La creazione di Joseph Haydn e la Bibbia," *Musica & Storia* 14/1: 5–31.

Betzwieser, Thomas 2007. "La vera costanza in Paris. Joseph Haydn's Laurette (1791) zwischen dramatischer und musikalisches Bearbeitung" in Raab, Siegert, and Konrad (eds.) 183–212.

Bianconi, Lorenzo and Giorgio Pestelli (eds.) 1998. *Opera Production and Its Resources*. University of Chicago Press.

Biba, Otto 1978. "Beispiele für die Besetzungsverhältnisse bei Aufführungen von Haydns Oratorien in Wien zwischen 1784 und 1808," H St 4: 94–104.

  1982. "Haydniana in den Sammlungen der Gesellschaft der Musikfrende in Wien," ÖMZ 37: 174–78.

  1987. "*Eben komme ich von Haydn...*". *Georg August Griesingers Korrespondenz mit Joseph Haydns Verleger Breitkopf & Härtel 1799–1819*. Zürich: Atlantis Musikbuch-Verlag.

  2013. "A Newly Discovered Libretto Edited by Haydn" in Chesser and Jones (eds.) 137–46.

Black, David Ian 2007. "Mozart and the Practice of Sacred Music, 1781–91." Ph.D. dissertation, Harvard University.

Blasius, Leslie David 1996. "The Mechanics of Sensation and the Construction of the Romantic Musical Experience" in Bent (ed.) 3–24.

Blažeković, Zdrakvo and Barbara Dobbs Mackenzie (eds.) 2009. *Music's Intellectual History*. New York: RILM.

Blier-Carruthers, Amy, forthcoming. "The Problem of Perfection in Classical Recording – The Performer's Perspective," MQ.

Bloechl, Olivia, Melanie Lowe, and Jeffrey Kallberg (eds.) 2015. *Rethinking Difference in Music Scholarship*. Cambridge University Press.

Bohlman, Philip V. 1992. "Die Vorstellung vom Judentum in der 'Schönen Jüdin'" in Dittmar and Stief (eds.) 79–81.

  2006. "Zweistromland. Die Vielfalt der jüdischen Klanglandschaften im europäischen Grenzgebiet" in Winkler (ed.) 37–58.

  2008. "Returning to the Ethnomusicological Past" in Barz and Cooley (eds.) 246–70.

  2011. *Focus: Music, Nationalism, and the Making of the New Europe*, 2nd edn. New York and London: Routledge.

  2017a. "Folk Song at the Beginnings of National History: Essay on *Alte Volkslieder* (1774)" in Herder and Bohlman 21–25.

  2017b. "The Folk Song Project at the Confluence of Music and Nationalism: Essay on *Volkslieder* (1778/79) and *Stimmen der Völker in Liedern* (1807)" in Herder and Bohlman 44–49.

Bohlman, Philip V. and Otto Holzapfel 2001. *The Folk Songs of Ashkenaz*. Middleton: A-R Editions (*Recent Researches in the Oral Traditions of Music*, 6).

Boisjoli, Eloise 2018. "Haydn's Aesthetics of Sensibility: Interpretations of Sentimental Figures, Topics, Mode, and Affect in the String Quartet Slow Movements." Ph.D. dissertation, University of Texas at Austin.

Bonds, Mark Evan 1988. "Haydn's False Recapitulations and the Perception of Sonata Form in the Eighteenth Century." Ph.D. dissertation, Harvard University.

1991a. "Haydn, Laurence Sterne, and the Origins of Musical Irony," JAMS 44/1: 57–91.

1991b. *Wordless Rhetoric: Musical Form and the Metaphor of the Oration*. Harvard University Press.

1993. "The Sincerest Form of Flattery? Mozart's 'Haydn' Quartets and the Question of Influence," Studi musicali 22: 365–409.

1997. "The Symphony as Pindaric Ode" in HWorld: 1–53.

1998. "Haydn's 'Cours complet de la composition' and the *Sturm und Drang*" in Haydn Studies: 152–76.

2011. "Symphonic Politics: Haydn's 'National Symphony' for France," ECM 8/1: 8–19.

2014. *Absolute Music: The History of an Idea*. Oxford University Press.

Bordas, Cristina, José María Domínguez, and José Antonio Gutiérrez 2011. "El Archivo de Música del Convento de las Claras de Sevilla" in Morales (ed.) 187–206.

Borio, Gianmario (ed.) 2015. *Musical Listening in the Age of Technological Reproduction*. Farnham and Burlington: Ashgate.

Born, Georgina (ed.) 2013. *Music, Sound, and Space: Transformations of Public and Private Experience*. Cambridge University Press.

Borthwick, E. Kerr 1990. "The Latin Quotations in Haydn's London Notebooks," M&L 71: 505–10.

Botstein, Leon 1997. "The Demise of Philosophical Listening: Haydn in the Nineteenth Century" in HWorld: 255–85.

1998. "The Consequences of Presumed Innocence: The Nineteenth-Century Reception of Joseph Haydn" in Haydn Studies: 1–34.

Bourdieu, Pierre 1984 [1979]. *Distinction: A Social Critique of the Judgement of Taste*. London: Routledge.

Bracht, Hans-Joachim 1994. "Überlegungen zum Quartett-'Gespräch'," Archiv für Musikwissenschaft 51/3: 169–89.

Brand, Carl Maria 1941. *Die Messen von Joseph Haydn*. Würzburg-Aumühle: Konrad Triltsch Verlag.

Brandenburg, Sieghard 1998. *Haydn, Mozart, and Beethoven: Studies in the Music of the Classical Period. Essays in Honour of Alan Tyson*. Oxford: Clarendon Press.

Braunschweig, Karl 2015. "Expanding the Sentence: Intersections of Theory, History, and Aesthetics," Music Theory and Analysis 2: 156–93.

Brévan, Bruno 1980. *Les changements de la vie musicale parisienne de 1774 à 1799*. Paris: Publications de la Sorbonne.

Broggini, Norberto 2010. "Haydn's Keyboard Music in Spanish and Latin American Sources," De Clavicordio 9: 151–64.

Brook, Barry S. 1975–76. "Piracy and Panacea in the Dissemination of Music in the Late Eighteenth Century," *Proceedings of the Royal Musical Association* 102: 13–36.

Brown, A. Peter 1975. "The Structure of the Exposition in Haydn's Keyboard Sonatas," *Music Review* 36: 102–29.

1986a. *Joseph Haydn's Keyboard Music: Sources and Style.* Bloomington: Indiana University Press.

1986b. *Performing Haydn's 'The Creation': Reconstructing the Earliest Renditions.* Bloomington: Indiana University Press.

1994. "Joseph Haydn and Leopold Hofmann's 'Street Songs'," JAMS 33: 356–83.

1996. "The Sublime, the Beautiful and the Ornamental: English Aesthetic Currents and Haydn's London Symphonies" in Jones and Biba (eds.) 44–71.

2002. "Notes on Joseph Haydn's Lieder and Canzonettas" in Scott (ed.) 77–103.

Brown, Bruce Alan 1995. *Gluck and the French Theatre in Vienna.* Oxford: Clarendon Press.

Brown, Bruce Alan and Daniel Heartz. 2001. "Empfindsamkeit," in *Grove Online;* www.oxfordmusiconline.com/search?q=Empfindsamkeit&searchBtn=Search&isQuickSearch=true (accessed August 11, 2018).

Brown, Clive 1999. *Classical and Romantic Performing Practice 1750–1900.* Oxford University Press.

Brown, Marshall 2007. "The Poetry of Haydn's Songs: Sexuality, Repetition, Whimsy" in Beghin and Goldberg 229–50.

Broyles, Michael 1992. *"Music of the Highest Class": Elitism and Populism in Antebellum Boston.* New Haven: Yale University Press.

Bryan, Paul 1973. "Haydn's Hornists," H-St 3: 52–58.

Buch, David J. 2006. "Supernatural Imagery in Haydn's Theater Music," H-St 9/1–4: 137–47.

2012. *Representations of Jews in the Musical Theater of the Habsburg Empire (1788–1807).* Jerusalem: Jewish Music Research Centre, The Hebrew University of Jerusalem.

Budday, Wolfgang 1983. *Grundlagen musikalischer Formen der Wiener Klassik an Hand der zeitgenössischen Theorie von Joseph Riepel und Heinrich Christoph Koch dargestellt an Menuetten und Sonatensätzen (1750–1790).* Kassel: Bärenreiter.

2002. *Harmonielehre Wiener Klassik.* Stuttgart: Berthold & Schwerdtner.

Buelow, George and Hans Joachim Marx (eds.) 1983. *New Mattheson Studies.* Cambridge University Press.

Burchell, Jenny 1996. *Polite or Commercial Concerts? Concert Management and Orchestral Repertoire in Edinburgh, Bath, Oxford, Manchester, and Newcastle, 1730–1799.* New York: Garland Publishing.

Bürger, Gottfried August 1776. "Herzensausguss über Volks-Poesie," *Deutsches Museum* 1: 443–50.

Burke, Edmund 1757. *A Philosophical Enquiry into the Origin of Our Ideas of the Sublime and the Beautiful.* London: R. and J. Dodsley.

Burke, Peter 1993. *The Art of Conversation.* Ithaca: Cornell University Press.

Burney, Charles 1773. *The Present State of Music in Germany, The Netherlands, and United Provinces.* London: Printed for T. Becket and Co., J. Robson, and G. Robinson.
  1785. *An Account of the Musical Performances in Westminster-Abbey, and the Pantheon, May 26th, 27th, 29th; and June the 3d, and 5th, 1784. In Commemoration of Handel.* London: printed for the benefit of the Musical Fund [e-resource].
Burnham, Scott G. 1995. *Beethoven Hero.* Princeton University Press.
  2005. "Haydn and Humor" in *Cambridge Companion* 59–76.
Burstein, Poundie 2010. "Mid-Section Cadences in Haydn's Sonata-Form Movements," *Studia Musicologica* 51/1–2: 91–107.
  2011. "Reassessing the Voice-Leading Role of Haydn's So-Called 'False Recapitulations,'" *Journal of Schenkerian Studies* 5: 1–37.
  2015. "Strolling Through a Haydn Divertimento with Two Heinrichs" in Beach and Goldenberg (eds.) 9–22.
Busby, Thomas 1825. *Concert Room and Orchestra Anecdotes of Music and Musicians Ancient and Modern*, vol. 1. London: Clementi and Co.
Cahan, Y. L. 1957. *Yidishe Folkslider mit Melodyes.* New York: YIVO – Yiddish Scientific Institute.
Caplin, William E. 1998. *Classical Form: A Theory of Formal Functions for the Instrumental Music of Haydn, Mozart, and Beethoven.* New York: Oxford University Press.
  2001. "The Classical Sonata Exposition: Cadential Goals and Form-Functional Plans," *Tijdschrift voor Muziektheorie* 6: 195–209.
  2002. "Theories of Musical Rhythm in the Eighteenth and Nineteenth Centuries" in Christensen (ed.) 657–94.
Caplin, William E. and Nathan John Martin 2015. "The 'Continuous Exposition' and the Concept of Subordinate Theme," *Music Analysis* 35: 4–43.
Carpani, Giuseppe 1812. *Le Haydine, ovvero Lettere sul la vita e le opere del celebre maestro Giuseppe Haydn.* Milan: C. Buccinelli.
Cassaro, James 2016. "Haydn in Latrobe: Providing Context to Manuscripts Held at St. Vincent College." Paper given at the Haydn Society of America Conference, Vancouver, 2016.
Castelvecchi, Stefano 1996. "From 'Nina' to 'Nina': Psychodrama, Absorption and Sentiment in the 1780s," *Cambridge Opera Journal* 8/2: 91–112.
  2013. *Sentimental Opera: Questions of Genre in the Age of Bourgeois Drama.* Cambridge University Press.
Chandler, James 1998. *England in 1819: The Politics of Literary Culture and the Case of Romantic Historicism.* University of Chicago Press.
Chandler, James and Kevin Gilmartin (eds.) 2005. *Romantic Metropolis: The Urban Scene of British Culture.* Cambridge University Press.
Chantler, Abigail 2003. "The 'Sturm und Drang' Style Revisited," *International Review of the Aesthetics and Sociology of Music* 34: 17–31.
Chapin, Keith 2008. "Scheibe's Mistake: Sublime Simplicity and the Criteria of Classicism," *ECM* 5: 165–77.
  2014. "Learned Style and Learned Styles" in Mirka (ed.) 301–29.

Chapin, Keith and Lawrence Kramer 2009. *Musical Meaning and Human Values.* New York: Fordham University Press.

Chapman, Roger E. 1981. "Modulation in Haydn's Late Piano Trios in the Light of Schoenberg's Theories" in Larsen, Serwer, and Webster (eds.) 471–75.

Chesser, Richard and David Wyn Jones (eds.) 2013. *The Land of Opportunity: Joseph Haydn and Britain.* London: The British Library.

Chew, Geoffrey 1974. "The Night-Watchman's Song Quoted by Haydn and its Implications," H-St 3/2: 106–24.

Christensen, Thomas 1992. "The Règle de l'octave in Thorough-bass Theory and Practice," *Acta Musicologica* 64/2: 91–117.

(ed.) 2002. *The Cambridge History of Western Music Theory.* Cambridge University Press.

Christiansen, Paul 2008. "The Turk in the Mirror: Orientalism and Haydn's String Quartet in D Minor, Op. 76, No. 2 ('Fifths')," *19th-Century Music* 31/3: 179–92.

Chua, Daniel 1998. "Haydn as Romantic" in *Haydn Studies* 121–51.

Clark, Caryl 2005a. "Haydn in the Theatre: The Operas" in *Cambridge Companion* 176–99.

2005b: see Abbreviations (*Cambridge Companion*).

2009a. *Haydn's Jews: Representation and Reception on the Operatic Stage.* Cambridge University Press.

2009b. "Haydn's Conversion Masses," JMR 28/2–3: 189–211.

2010. "Haydn's Judaizing of the Apothecary," *Studia Musicologica*, 51/1–2: 41–60.

2012a. "Encountering Others: Haydn's *L'anima del filosofo* as directed by Jürgen Flimm" in Gruber, Reicher, and Siegert (eds.) 411–26.

2012b. "Revolution, Rebirth, and the Sublime in Haydn's *L'anima del filosofo* and *The Creation*" in Hunter and Will 100–23.

2014a. "Encountering 'Others' in Haydn's *Lo speziale* (1768)" in Hüttler and Weidinger (eds.) 291–306.

2014b. "The Librettist's Dilemma in London: Badini's and Haydn's *Orfeo ed Euridice*" in Lichtenstein (ed.) 107–29.

2016. "Haydn's Judaizing of the Apothecary – Take 2" in Ingraham, So, and Moodley (eds.) 99–121.

2018. "Transcultural Contexts for Understanding *Die Schöpfung/The Creation.*" Paper given at the Annual Meeting of the American Musicological Society, San Antonio, TX, November.

Clark, Peter 2000. *British Clubs and Societies 1580–1800: The Origins of an Associational World.* Oxford: Clarendon Press.

Clarke, Eric F. 2013. "Music, Space and Subjectivity" in Born (ed.) 90–110.

Clarke, Eric F. and Nicholas Cook (eds.) 2004. *Empirical Musicology: Aims, Methods, Prospects.* Oxford University Press.

Clough, Francis F. and Geoffrey J. Cuming 1952. *The World's Encyclopaedia of Recorded Music.* London: Sidgwick & Jackson, in association with the Decca Record Co.

Coe, Richard N. 1972. *Lives of Haydn, Mozart, and Metastasio,* trans. of Stendahl 1814. London: Calder & Boyars.

Colburn, Glen 2008. *The English Malady: Enabling and Disabling Fictions*. Newcastle: Cambridge Scholars.
Cole, Malcolm S. 1998 "Mozart and Two Theatres in Josephinian Vienna" in Radice (ed.) 111–45.
Cole, Michael 1998. *The Pianoforte in the Classical Era*. Oxford: Clarendon Press.
Cone, Edward T. 1968. *Musical Form and Musical Performance*. New York: Norton.
Cook, Nicholas 2009. "Methods for Analyzing Recordings" in Cook, Clarke, Leech-Wilkinson, and Rink (eds.) 221–45.
   2013. *Beyond the Score: Music as Performance*. Oxford University Press.
Cook, Nicholas, Eric Clarke, Daniel Leech-Wilkinson, and John Rink (eds.) 2009. *The Cambridge Companion to Recorded Music*. Cambridge University Press.
Coreth, Anna 1959. *Pietas Austriaca. Ursprung und Entwicklung barocker Frommigkeit in Österreich*. Vienna: Verlag für Geschichte und Politik.
   2004. *Pietas Austriaca*, trans. William D. Bowman and Anna Maria Leitgeb. West Lafayette: Purdue University Press.
Cowart, Georgia J. 1984. "Sense and Sensibility in Eighteenth-Century Musical Thought," *Acta Musicologica* 56/2: 251–66.
Cramer, Carl Friedrich 1783. "Lieder für das Clavier..." *Cramer's Magazin der Musik*. vol. 1: 456–57.
Cramm, Tobias, with Alma Deutscher 2014. "Joint Improvisation." www.youtube.com/watch?v=nubC3dktQ24 (accessed January 8, 2018).
Crews, C. Daniel 1997. *John Antes*. Winston-Salem: Moravian Music Foundation.
Croll, Gerhard 1973–74. "Mitteilungen über die *Schöpfung* und die *Jahreszeiten* aus dem Schwarzenberg-Archiv," *Haydn Studies* 3 85–92.
Cuyler, Louise E. 1970. "Tonal Exploitation in the Later Quartets of Haydn" in Landon and Chapman (eds.): 136–50.
Czeike, Felix 1992–2004. *Historisches Lexikon Wien*, 6 vols. Vienna: Kremayr and Scheriau.
Dack, James 2005. "Sacred Music" in *Cambridge Companion* 138–49.
   2010a. "London," H-L: 476–80.
   2010b. "Salomon, Johann Peter," H-L: 657–60.
Dahlhaus, Carl 1967. *Untersuchungen über die Entstehung der harmonischen Tonalität*. Kassel: Bärenreiter.
   1978. "Satz und Periode," *Zeitschrift für Musiktheorie* 7: 16–26.
   1982. *Analysis and Value Judgment*, trans. Siegmund Levarie. New York: Pendragon Press.
   1989. *The Idea of Absolute Music*, trans. Roger Lustig. University of Chicago Press.
Dallos, Márton 1781. *Eszterházi várnak, és ához tartozandó nevezetessebb helyeinek rövid le-irása* [Short Description of the Castle of Eszterháza and of the Noteworthier Places Belonging to It]. Oedenberg (Sopron): Siess.
Damschroder, David 2012. *Harmony in Haydn and Mozart*. Cambridge University Press.

Darwin, Erasmus 1791. *The Botanic Garden: A Poem in Two Parts. Part I: The Economy of Vegetation. Part II: The Loves of the Plants. With Philosophical Notes.* London: J. Johnson.

Daube, Johann Friedrich 1756. *General-Bass in drey Accorden.* Leipzig: J. B. Andra.

— 1773. *Der musikaliche Dilettant: Eine Abhandlung der Composition.* Vienna: Trattner.

Dávid, Ferenc 2006. "Eszterháza: Palace, Park and Settlement" in Jung, Malina, McCue and Robberechts (eds.) 17–23.

— 2013. "Adatok az eszterházai bábszínházról [Data about the marionette theater at Eszterháza]" in Szentesi, Mentényi, and Simon (eds.) 107–16.

Dávid, Ferenc and Kristóf Fatsar 2004. "Esterházy 'Fényes' Miklós herceg itineráriuma és az általa rendezett ünnepségek hercegi rangra emelkedésétől haláláig (1762–1790) [Itinerary of Prince Nicolaus Esterházy 'the Magnificent' and the Festivities Staged by Him from his Acquisition of the Title of Prince until his Death (1762–1790)]." *Levéltári Közlemények* 75/1: 83–103.

Dávid, Ferenc, Carsten Jung, János Malina and Edward McCue 2015. "Haydn's Opera House at Eszterháza: New Archival Sources," *EM* 43/1: 111–27.

Davison, Alan 2009. "The Face of a Musical Genius: Thomas Hardy's Portrait of Joseph Haydn," *ECM* 6/2: 209–27.

— 2013. "Thomas Hardy's Portrait of Haydn" in Chesser and Jones (eds.) 59–76.

Day-O'Connell, Sarah 2009a. "The Composer, the Surgeon, His Wife, and Her Poems: Haydn and the Anatomy of the English Canzonetta," *ECM* 6/1: 77–112.

— 2009b. "Watches Without Pockets: Singing About Minutes in a London Drawing Room, circa 1800" in Eisen (ed.): 268–85.

— 2012. "'The Clock Still Points its Moral to the Heart': Singing About Time in Haydn's London" in Dittrich, Eybl, and Kapp (eds.) 153–78.

— 2014a. "The Singing Style" in Mirka (ed.) 238–58.

— 2014b. "Creative Fidelity: Insights on Musical Performance via Translation Theory." Paper given at the Performance Studies Network Third International Conference, University of Cambridge 2014.

Deldevez, Edouard Marie 1887. *La Société des Concerts, 1860 à 1885.* Paris: Firmin-Didot.

Deleglise, Oscar 1947. *Das Schönbrunner Schlosstheater.* Vienna: H. Bauer.

Dennis, John 1704. *The Grounds of Criticism in Poetry.* London: printed for Geo. Strahan, and Bernard Lintott.

Deutsch, Otto Erich 1982. *Admiral Nelson und Joseph Haydn. Ein britisch-österreichisches Gipfeltreffen*, ed. Gitta Deutsch and Rudolf Klein. Vienna: Österreichischer Bundesverlag.

Deutsch, Walter 1969. *Die Volksmusiksammlung der Gesellschaft der Musikfreunde in Wien (Sonnleithner-Sammlung).* Vienna: Schendl.

— 2000. "Zur Geschichte und Gegenwart der Volksmusik in Salzburg," *Jahrbuch des Österreichischen Volksliedwerkes* 49: 33–38.

Diderot, Denis 1773, 1883. *Paradoxe sur le comédien*, trans. Walter Herries Pollock as *The Paradox of Acting.* London: Chatto & Windus.

Diergarten, Felix 2008. "Anleitung zur Erfindung. Der Musiktheoretiker Johann Friedrich Daube," *Musiktheorie* 23: 299–318.
  2010. "Auch Homere schlafen bisweilen. Heinrich Christoph Kochs Polemik gegen Joseph Haydn," H St 10: 87–92.
  2011. "'The True Fundamentals of Composition': Haydn's Partimento Counterpoint," ECM 8/1: 53–75.
  2012. *"Jedem Ohr klingend". Formprinzipien in Haydns Sinfonieexpositionen.* Laaber: Laaber Verlag.
  2018. "'Zusetzen, wegschneiden, wagen.' Historische Aufführungspraxis, Historische Satzlehre und die Sinfonie Nr. 70" in Fuhrmann (ed.) *Eisenstädter Haydn Berichte.*
Diergarten, Felix and Markus Neuwirth. 2018. *Formenlehre 2018. Ein Lese- und Arbeitsbuch zur Instrumentalmusik des 18. und 19. Jahrhunderts.* Laaber: Laaber Verlag.
Dies 1810: see Abbreviations.
Dietrich, Thomas 2008. "'Dein Will ist Mir Gesetz' und 'Deine Liebe sey mein Lohn'. Hegemoniale Geschlechterordnung, Musiktheorie und Haydns Schöpfung" in Kreutziger-Herr and Losleben (eds.) 140–53.
Díez, Marcelino 2011. "Franz Joseph Haydn y Cádiz. El encargo de las Siete Palabras," MAR – *Música de Andalucía en la Red*, 1: 25–40.
Ditters von Dittersdorf, Carl 1967 [1801]. *Lebensbeschreibung. Seinem Sohne in die Feder diktiert*; Munich: Kösel.
Dittmar, J. and W. Stief (eds.) 1992. *Deutsche Volkslieder mit ihren Melodien. Balladen*, vol. 9. Freiburg im Breisgau: Verlag des Deutschen Volksliedarchivs.
Dittrich, Marie-Agnes, Martin Eybl, and Reinhard Kapp (eds.) 2012. *Zyklus und Prozess. Joseph Haydn und die Zeit.* Vienna: Böhlau Verlag.
Dohrn-van Rossum, Gerhard 1996. *History of the Hour: Clocks and Modern Temporal Orders.* Trans. Thomas Dunlap. University of Chicago Press.
Dolan, Emily I. 2013. *The Orchestral Revolution: Haydn and the Technologies of Timbre.* Cambridge University Press.
Donohue, Thomas (ed.) 2011. *The Maestro's Direction: Essays in Honor of Christopher Hogwood.* Lanham: Scarecrow Press.
Doran, Robert 2015. *The Theory of the Sublime from Longinus to Kant.* Cambridge University Press.
Dratwicki, Alexandre 2005. "La réception des symphonies de Haydn à Paris. De nouvelles perspectives de recherche," *Annales historiques de la Révolution française*, 340: 83–104.
Dreo, Harald and Sepp Gmasz (eds.) 1997. *Volksmusik im Burgenland. Burgenländische Volksballaden* (Corpus musicae popularis austriacae, 7). Vienna: Böhlau Verlag.
du Bos, Jean Baptiste 1748 [1719], *Réflexions critiques sur la poësie et sur la peinture*, trans. in Thomas Nugent, *Critical Reflections on Poetry, Painting and Music.* London: Printed for Joun Nourse.
Durante, Sergio 1998. "The Opera Singer" in Bianconi and Pestelli (eds.) 345–418.
Dwight, John Sullivan 1881. "Music in Boston" in Winsor 415–64.

Dwyer, John 1998. *The Age of the Passions: An Interpretation of Adam Smith and Scottish Enlightenment Culture.* East Linton: Tuckwell Press.

Ebenbauer, Melitta (2007). *Zur Geschichte der Dommusik.* www.dommusik-wien.at/Dommusik/media/ZurGeschichtederDommusik_Ebenbauer.pdf.

Edelstein, Dan 2010. *The Enlightenment: A Genealogy.* University of Chicago Press.

Edgcumbe, Richard 1834. *Musical Reminiscences, Containing an Account of the Italian Opera in England from 1773.* London: John Andrews.

Edge, Dexter 1992a. "Mozart's Viennese Orchestras," EM 20: 64–88.

1992b. "Review Article: Mary Sue Morrow, Concert Life in Haydn's Vienna," HYb 17: 108–66.

Edwards, Warwick 2004. "New Insights into the Chronology of Haydn's Folksong Arrangements: Reading Between the Lines of the George Thomson Correspondence," H-St 8: 325–40.

Eisen, Cliff (ed.) 1997. *Mozart Studies 2.* Oxford: Clarendon Press.

2009. *Coll' astuzia, col giudizio: Essays in Honor of Neal Zaslaw.* Ann Arbor: Steglein.

Eisen, Cliff and Simon P. Keefe 2006. *The Cambridge Mozart Encyclopedia.* Cambridge University Press.

Elias, Norbert 1969. *Die höfische Gesellschaft. Untersuchungen zur Soziologie des Königtums und der höfischen Aristokratie.* Neuwied: Luchterhand.

2006. *The Court Society.* Trans. Edmund Jephcott, ed. Stephen Mennell. Dublin: University College Dublin Press.

Engel, Johann Jakob 1780. *Über die musikalische Malerei.* Berlin.

Erhardt, Tassilo 2013. *Sakralmusik in Habsburgerreich 1570–1770.* Vienna: Verlag der Österreichischen Akademie der Wissenschaften.

Evans, R. J. W. 1979. *The Making of the Habsburg Monarchy.* Oxford: Clarendon Press.

Eybl, Martin 1998. "Franz Bernhard Ritter von Keeß – Sammler, Mäzen und Organisator. Materialien zu Wiens Musikleben im Geist der Aufklärung" in Hilscher (ed.) 239–50.

2008. "From Court to Public: The Uses of Keyboard Concertos in Austria 1750–1770," Ad Parnassum 6/2: 19–40.

Eyerly, Sarah 2008. Review of Nola Reed Knouse (ed.), *The Music of the Moravian Church in America. Journal of the Society for American Music* 2/4: 583–87.

2010. "Der Wille Gottes: Musical Improvisation in Eighteenth-Century Moravian Communities" in Lempa and Peuker (eds.) 201–27.

Fastl, Christian 2003. *Österreichischen Musiklexikon*, vol. 2: Hainburg an der Donau. Vienna: Verlag der Österreichischen Akademie der Wissenschaft.

Fauquet, Joël-Marie 1986. *Les Sociétés de musique de chambre à Paris de la restauration à 1870.* Paris: Aux Amateurs de Livres.

Feder, Georg 1970. "Haydn und Eisenstadt," *Österreichische Musikzeitschrift* 25: 213–21.

1979. "Joseph Haydns Skizzen und Entwürfe. Übersicht der Manuskripte, Werkregister, Literatur- und Ausgabenverzeichnis," *Fontes artis musicae* 26: 172–88.

1998. *Haydns Streichquartette. Ein musikalischer Werkführer.* Munich: C. H. Beck.

1999. *Joseph Haydn. Die Schöpfung*. Kassel and New York: Bärenreiter.
Feder, Georg, Heinrich Hüschen, and Ulrich Tank (eds.) 1985. *Joseph Haydn. Tradition und Rezeption. Bericht über die Jahrestagung der Gesellschaft für Musikforschung Köln 1982* (Kölner Beiträge zur Musikforschung 144). Regensburg: Bosse.
Feldman, Martha 2007. *Opera and Sovereignty: Transforming Myths in Eighteenth-Century Italy*. University of Chicago Press.
   2015a. *The Castrato: Reflections on Natures and Kinds*. Berkeley: University of California Press
   2015b. "The Interstitial Voice: An Opening' in 'Colloquy: Why Voice Now?'," *JAMS* 68:3: 653–58.
Ferraguto, Mark 2010. "Haydn as 'Minimalist': Rethinking Exoticism in the Trios of the 1760s and 1770s," *Studia Musicologica* 51/1–2: 61–77.
Fétis, François-Joseph 1844. *Traité complet de la théorie et de la pratique de l'harmonie*. Paris: Maurice Schlesinger.
Fillion, Michelle 2005. "Intimate Expression for a Widening Public: The Keyboard Sonatas and Trios" in *Cambridge Companion* 126–37.
   2012. "Form, Rhetoric, and the Reception of Haydn's Rondo Finales" in Hunter and Will 187–210.
Fink-Mennel, Evelyn and Ingo Rainer (eds.) 2009. *Haydns Volck's Lied. Gott erhalte: Inspectionen und Productionen anno 2009*, CD-Rom (klanglese 6). Vienna: Institut für Volksmusikforschung und Ethnomusikologie.
Finscher, Ludwig 2000. *Joseph Haydn und seine Zeit*. Laaber: Laaber Verlag.
   2008. "Joseph Haydn und seine Schüler," *Österreichische Musikzeitschrift* 63/1: 5–13, 63/2: 4–15.
Fischer, Wilhelm 1915. "Zur Entwicklungsgeschichte des Wiener klassischen Stils," *Studien zur Musikwissenschaft* 3: 24–84.
Fitzpatrick, Horace 1970. *The Horn and Horn-Playing*. Oxford University Press.
Fojtíkova, Jana 1997. "Musiksammlungen des Museums der Tschechischen Musik" in Loos (ed.) 393–97.
Forsyth, Michael 1985. *Buildings for Music*. Cambridge, MA: MIT Press.
Fortino, Sally 1997. "Women Composers Associated with Joseph Haydn: A Short Introduction to Some 'New' Keyboard Repertoire" in Galazzo, Brauchli, and Brauchli (eds.) 241–54.
Foucault, Michel 1994 [1969]. "What is an Author?" Trans. Josué V. Harari in *Aesthetics, Method, and Epistemology*, ed. James D. Faubion. New York: The New Press, 205–21.
Freeman, Robert N. (ed.) 2002. *Joseph Haydn and the Eighteenth Century: Collected Essays of Karl Geiringer*. Warren: Harmonie Park Press.
Frith, Simon and Simon Zagorski-Thomas (eds.) 2012. *The Art of Record Production: An Introductory Reader for a New Academic Field*. Farnham and Burlington, Ashgate.
Fritz-Hilscher, Elisabeth Th. and Helmut Kretschmer (eds.) 2011. *Wien Musikgeschichte. Von der Prähistorie bis zur Gegenwart*. (Geschichte der Stadt Wien, 7.) Vienna: Lit Verlag.
Frye, Northrop. 1956. "Towards Defining an Age of Sensibility," *English Literary History* 23/2: 144–52.

Fuchs, Ingrid 2009. "'... Spielt das Fortepiano mit vieler Empfindung und Präzision'. Damen im musikalischen Salon rund um Joseph Haydn" in Gabriel and Winkler (eds.) 144–53.
   2013a. "Die Londoner Notizbücher. Aspekte zu Persönlichkeit und Weltsicht Joseph Haydns" in Gruber, Reicher, and Siegert (eds.) 33–58.
   2013b. "The First Performers and Audiences of Haydn's Chamber Music" in Chesser and Jones (eds.) 147–62.
Fuhrmann, Wolfgang 2010a. "Haydn und sein Publikum. Die Veröffentlichung eines Komponisten ca. 1750–1815." Habilitation thesis, University of Berne.
   2010b. "Originality as Market-Value: Some Considerations on the Fantasia in C Hob.XVII:4 and Haydn as Musical Entrepreneur," *Studia Musicologica* 51: 303–16.
   2011. "Die Ordnung der Idylle: Haydns späte Oratorien" in Hohmaier (ed.) 169–95.
   2013. "Volck's Lied. Zum 'Gattungs'-Kontext von Haydns *Gott erhalte*," H-St 10/3–4: 467–91.
Gabriel, Theresia and Gerhard J. Winkler 2009. *Phänomen Haydn 1732–1809. Prachtliebend, Bürgerlich, Gottbefohle, Crossover.* Eisenstadt: Schloss Esterházy Management.
Galazzo, Alberto, Bernard Brauchli, and Susan Brauchli (eds.) 1997. *De Clavicordio III.* Magnano: Musica antica.
Galeazzi, Francesco 2012 [1796]. *Theoretical and Practical Elements of Music (Elementi teorico-pratici di musica),* parts III and IV, trans. with an introduction and annotations Deborah Burton and Gregory W. Harwood. Urbana: University of Illinois Press.
Gallagher, Sean and Thomas Forrest Kelly (eds.) 2008. *The Century of Bach and Mozart: Perspectives on Historiography, Composition, Theory, and Performance.* Cambridge, MA: Harvard University Press.
Gallope, Michael 2014. "Why was this Music Desirable? On a Critical Explanation of the Avant-Garde," JM 31/2. Special issue in honor of Richard Taruskin, with response by Richard Taruskin and a reply by Michael Gallope: 199–230.
Garratt, James 2005. "Haydn and Posterity: The Long Nineteenth Century" in *Cambridge Companion* 226–38.
Gartrell, Carol 2009. *A History of the Baryton and its Music: King of Instruments, Instrument of Kings.* Lanham: Scarecrow Press.
Gates-Coon, Rebecca 1994. *The Landed Estates of the Esterházy Princes: Hungary during the Reforms of Maria Theresia and Joseph II.* Baltimore: The Johns Hopkins University Press.
Gay, Peter 1966–69. *The Enlightenment: An Interpretation.* New York: Knopf.
Geiringer, Karl 1982. *Haydn: A Creative Life in Music,* 3rd edn. Berkeley: University of California Press.
   2002a. "Joseph Haydn: Protagonist of the Enlightenment" in Freeman (ed.) 55–64.
   2002b. "Gluck and Haydn" in Freeman (ed.) 171–74.

Geiringer, Karl and Irene Geiringer 1982. *Haydn: A Creative Life in Music*, 3rd edn. Berkeley: University of California Press.
Gelbart, Matthew 2007. *The Invention of "Folk Music" and "Art Music": Emerging Categories from Ossian to Wagner*. Cambridge University Press.
Genesi, Mario Giuseppe 1993. "Teatri d'opera ducali a Piacenza alla fine del Settecento: Ricognizione storiografica. La presenza della mezzo-soprano Luigia Polzelli protetta haydniana," *Archivio storico per le province parmesi* 45: 191–217.
George, Sam 2007. *Botany, Sexuality, and Women's Writing, 1760–1830: From Modest Shoot to Forward Plant*. Manchester University Press.
Gerber, Ernst Ludwig 1790. *Historisch-biographisches Lexicon der Tonkünstler*. Leipzig: Breitkopf.
Gericke, Hannelore 1960. *Der Wiener Musikalienhandel von 1700 bis 1778*. Graz: Böhlau.
Gerlach, Sonja 1981. "Over de originele bezetting van Haydns symfonieen," *Huismuziek* 5–6: 10–13.
  1998. "Haydn's 'Entwurf-Katalog': Two Questions" in Brandenburg (ed.) 65–84.
Gerlach, Sonja and Raab, Armin 2010. "Breitkopf & Härtel," H-L: 55–59.
Gibbs, Thomas Jordan 1972. "A Study of Form in the Late Masses of Joseph Haydn." Ph.D. dissertation, University of Texas at Austin.
Gieseke, Ludwig 1957. *Die Geschichtliche Entwicklung des Deutschen Urheberrechts*. Göttingen: Verlag Otto Schwartz.
Gjerdingen, Robert O. 2007. *Music in the Galant Style*. Oxford University Press.
Glauert, Amanda 2004. "The Lieder of Carl Philipp Emanuel Bach, Haydn, Mozart, and Beethoven" in Parsons (ed.) 63–84.
Godt, Irving 2010. *Marianna Martines: A Woman Composer in the Vienna of Mozart and Haydn*. New York: University of Rochester Press.
Goehr, Lydia 1992. *The Imaginary Museum of Musical Works: An Essay in the Philosophy of Music*. Oxford University Press.
Goehring, Edmund 2004. *Three Modes of Perception in Mozart: The Philosophical, Pastoral, and Comic in "Così fan tutti"*. Cambridge University Press.
Goldmark, Karl 1922. *Erinnerungen aus meinem Leben*. Vienna: Rikola Verlag.
Gon, Federico 2013. "Le influenze su Rossini della musica di Haydn." Ph.D. dissertation, Università degli Studi di Padova.
Gordon, Bonnie 2014. "What Mr. Jefferson Didn't Hear" in Bloechl, Lowe, and Kallberg (eds.) 108–32.
Gotwals, Vernon 1959. "The Earliest Biographies of Haydn," *MQ* 45/4: 439–59.
  1961. "Joseph Haydn's Last Will and Testament," *MQ* 47: 331–53.
  1963: see Abbreviations.
  1968. *Haydn: Two Contemporary Portraits*. Originally published as *Joseph Haydn: Eighteenth Century Gentleman and Genius*. See Abbreviations. Madison: University of Wisconsin Press.
  1982. "Haydn and the Organ," *American Organist* 16/7: 30–34.
Gramit, David 2002. *Cultivating Music: The Aspirations, Interests, and Limits of German Musical Culture, 1770–1848*. Berkeley: University of California Press.

Grant, Roger Mathew 2012. "Situating Time in Haydn's *Die Schöpfung*" in Dittrich, Eybl, and Kapp (eds.) 97–115.
   2014. *Beating Time and Measuring Music in the Early Modern Era.* Oxford University Press.

Grasberger, Franz 1968. *Die Hymnen Österreichs.* Tutzing: Hans Schneider.

Grave, Floyd K. 1985. "Metrical Displacement and the Compound Measure in Eighteenth-Century Theory and Practice," *Theoria* 1: 25–60.
   2008. "Recuperation, Transformation and the Transcendence of Major over Minor in the Finale of Haydn's String Quartet Op. 76, No. 1," *ECM* 5: 27–50.
   2016. "Narratives of Affliction and Recovery in Haydn" in Howe, Jensen-Moulton, Lerner, and Straus (eds.) 563–89.

Grave, Floyd K. and Margaret Grave 2006. *The String Quartets of Joseph Haydn.* Oxford University Press.

Green, Emily H. 2011. "A Patron Among Peers: Dedications to Haydn and the Economy of Celebrity," *ECM* 8/2: 215–37.
   2015. "On Giving and Taking: A Study of Dedications as Reception History" in Appel and Raab (eds.) 29–44.
   2017. "Music's First Consumers: Publishers in the Late Eighteenth Century" in Green and Mayes (eds.) 13–28.

Green, Emily H. and Catherine Mayes (eds.) 2017. *Consuming Music: Individuals, Institutions, Communities, 1700–1830.* New York: University of Rochester Press.

Green, Rebecca 1997. "Representing the Aristocracy: The Operatic Haydn and *Le pescatrici*" in *HWorld* 154–200.
   2005. "A Letter from the Wilderness: Revisiting Haydn's Esterhazy Environments" in *Cambridge Companion* 17–29.

Grétry, André Ernest Modeste 1797. *Mémoires, ou Essais sur la musique,* vol. 3. Paris: Imprimerie de la République.

Griesinger 1810: see Abbreviations.

Grigson, Caroline 2009. *The Life and Poems of Anne Hunter: Haydn's Tuneful Voice.* Liverpool University Press.
   2013. "A Matter of Words: Haydn, Holcroft and Anne Hunter" in Chesser and Jones (eds.) 77–91.

Grossegger, Elisabeth 1987. *Theater, Feste und Feiern zur Zeit Maria Theresias 1742–1776. Nach Tagebucheintragungen des Fürsten Johann Joseph Khevenhüller-Metsch, Obersthofmeister der Kaiserin.* Vienna: Österreichische Akademie der Wissenschaften.

Grove Music Online, Oxford Music Online, www.oxfordmusiconline.com.

Groves, Stephen 2012. "The Picturesque Oratorio: Haydn's Art in Nature's Clothing," *M&L* 93: 479–512.

Gruber, Gernot 2013. "Der späte Haydn, ein modernes Kanondenken und die Konstruktion des Klassischen," *Haydn-Studien* 10/3–4: 360–68.

Gruber, Gernot, Walter Reicher, and Christine Siegert (eds.) 2012. *Joseph Haydn im 21. Jahrhundert. Bericht über das Symposium der Österreichischen Akademie der Wissenschaften, der Internationalen Joseph Haydn Privatstiftung Eisenstadt und der Esterházy-Privatstiftung (Eisenstädter Haydn-Berichte 8).* Tutzing: Hans Schneider.

Grunwald, Max 1924/25. *Mattersdorf*, special edition of *Jahrbuch für jüdische Volkskunde*, 1924/25, no. 2.

Gürtler, Wolfgang and Rudolf Kropf (eds.) 2009. *Die Familie Esterházy im 17. und 18. Jahrhundert*. Eisenstadt: Landesmuseum Burgenland.

Habermas, Jürgen 1989 [1962]. *The Structural Transformation of the Public Sphere: an Inquiry into a Category of Bourgeois Society*. Trans. Thomas Burger and Frederick Lawrence. Cambridge: Polity.

HaCohen, Ruth 2011. *The Music Libel Against the Jews*. New Haven: Yale University Press.

Haimo, Ethan 1990. "Remote Keys and Multi-Movement Unity: Haydn in the 1790s," MQ 72: 242–68.

  1995. *Haydn's Symphonic Forms: Essays in Compositional Logic*. Oxford: Clarendon Press.

Hajós, Géza 1989. *Romantische Gärten der Aufklärung: Englische Landschaftskultur des 18. Jahrhunderts in und um Wien*. Vienna: Böhlau Verlag.

Halsey, Katie and Jane Slinn (eds.) 2008. *The Concept and Practice of Conversation in the Long Eighteenth Century, 1688–1848*. Newcastle: Cambridge Scholars.

Hanning, Barbara R. 1989. "Conversation and Musical Style in the Late Eighteenth-Century Salon," *Eighteenth-Century Studies* 22/4: 512–28.

Hans, Nicholas 1957. "Russian Students at Leyden in the 18th Century," *Slavonic and East European Review* 35: 551–62.

Hanslick, Eduard 1869. *Geschichte des Concertwesens in Wien*. Vienna: Braumüller.

Hárich, János 1962. "Das Repertoire des Opernkapellmeisters Joseph Haydn in Eszterháza (1780–1790)," HYb 1: 9–110.

Harrison, Bernard 1997. *Haydn's Keyboard Music: Studies in Performance Practice*. Oxford: Clarendon Press.

  1998. *Haydn: The "Paris" Symphonies*. Cambridge University Press.

  2002. "Genius" in *Oxford Companion* 116–17.

Haselböck, Martin 1982. "The Organ Concertos of Joseph Haydn," *American Organist* 16/12: 38–41.

Hassell, John 1790. *Tour of the Isle of Wight*. London: printed by John Jarvis for Thomas Hookham, 2 vols. Eighteenth-Century Collections Online; https://quod.lib.umich.edu/e/ecco/ (accessed July 13, 2018).

Hatten, Robert S. 1994. *Musical Meaning in Beethoven: Markedness, Correlation, and Interpretation*. Bloomington: Indiana University Press.

  2004. *Interpreting Musical Gestures: Mozart, Beethoven, Schubert*. Bloomington: Indiana University Press.

  2014. "The Troping of Topics in Mozart's Instrumental Works" in Mirka (ed.) 514–36.

Haydn, Joseph. *Entwurf Katalog*. Staatsbibliothek zu Berlin. Preussischer Kulturbesitz. Digital Collection. http://digital.staatsbibliothek-berlin.de/werkansicht?PPN=PPN857378139&PHYSID=PHYS_11&DMDID=DMDLOG_2 (accessed July 13, 2018).

Head, Matthew 1995. "Like Beauty Spots on the Face of a Man: Gender in Eighteenth-Century North-German Discourse on Genre," JM 13/2: 143–67.

1999. "'If the Pretty Little Hand Won't Stretch': Music for the Fair Sex in Eighteenth-Century Germany," JAMS 52/2: 203–54.

2000a. "Music With 'No Past?' Archaeologies of Joseph Haydn and *The Creation*," *19th-Century Music* 23/3: 191–217.

2000b. *Orientalism, Masquerade and Mozart's Turkish Music*. London, Royal Musical Association.

2005. "Haydn's Exoticisms: 'Difference' and the Enlightenment" in *Cambridge Companion* 77–92.

2012. "Interpreting 'Abduction' Opera: Haydn's *L'incontro improvviso*, Sovereignty and the Esterház Festival of 1775," *TheMA:Theater – Music – Arts – Open Access Research Journal* 1/1: 1–18.

2013. *Sovereign Feminine: Music and Gender in Eighteenth-Century Germany*. Berkeley: University of California Press.

2014a. "Fantasia and Sensibility" in Mirka (ed.) 250–78.

2014b. "Interpreting 'Abduction' Opera: Haydn's *L'incontro improvviso*, sovereignty and the Esterhàz Festival of 1775" in Hüttler and Weidinger (eds.) 315–30.

Heartz, Daniel 1976. "The Hunting Chorus in *Die Jahreszeiten* and the 'Airs de Chasse' in the *Encyclopédie*," *Eighteenth-Century Studies* 9: 523–39.

1982. "Nicolas Jadot and the Building of the Burgtheater," MQ 88/1: 1–31.

1993. "The Concert Spirituel in the Tuilleries Palace," EM 21: 241–48.

1995. *Haydn, Mozart, and the Viennese School, 1740–1780*. New York: Norton.

2003. *Music in European Capitals: The Galant Style 1720–1780*. New York: Norton.

2009. *Haydn, Mozart, and Early Beethoven, 1781–1802*. New York: Norton.

Heartz, Daniel, and Bruce Alan Brown 2001. "Empfindsamkeit." *Grove Music Online*. www.oxfordmusiconline.com.catalogue.ulrls.lon.ac.uk/subscriber/article/grove/music/08774 (accessed July 15, 2016).

Heilbron, J. L. 2003. "Natural Philosophy and Science" in Kors (ed.).

Heine, Claudia 2005. "*Il ritorno di Tobia*". *Die Geschichte von Joseph Haydns italienischem Oratorium. Mit Analyse und Quellenbeschreibung*. Lizentiatsarbeit, University of Zurich.

Heinichen, Johann David 1728. *Der General-Bass in der Composition*. Dresden: The Author.

Hellwig, Friedemann (ed.) 1987. *Studia Organologica. Festschrift für John Henry van der Meer zu seinem fünfundsechzigsten Geburtstag*. Tutzing: Hans Schneider.

Hepokoski, James and Warren Darcy 1997. "The Medial Caesura and Its Role in the Eighteenth-Century Sonata Exposition," *Music Theory Spectrum* 19: 115–54.

2006. *Elements of Sonata Theory: Norms, Types, and Deformations in the Late Eighteenth-Century Sonata*. New York: Oxford University Press.

Herder, Johann G. 1784. *Ideen zur Philosophie der Geschichte der Menschheit*, vol. 1. Leipzig: Johann Friedrich Hartknoch.

1778/79. *Volkslieder*, 6 folios in 2 vols. Leipzig: Weygandsche Buchhandlung.

2017. *Alte Volkslieder*, unpublished manuscript 1774, trans. in J. G. Herder and P. V. Bohlman, *Song Loves the Masses: Herder on Music and Nationalism*. Berkeley: University of California Press: 21–43.

Herter Norton, M. D. 1932. "Haydn in America (Before 1820)," MQ 18/2: 309–37.
Heyer, Brian 2001. "Tonality" in *Grove Music Online* https://doi.org/10.1093/gmo/9781561592630.article.28102 (accessed July 15, 2018).
Hibberd, Sarah 2012. "Cherubini and the Revolutionary Sublime," *Cambridge Opera Journal* 24/3: 293–318.
Hiebert, Thomas 1992. "Virtuosity, Experimentation, and Innovation in Horn Writing from Early 18th-Century Dresden," *Historic Brass Society Journal* 4: 112–59.
Hiles, Karen 2009. "Haydn's Heroic Decades: Music, Politics, and War, 1791–1809." Ph.D. dissertation, Columbia University.
Hilscher, Elisabeth T. (ed.) 1998. *Österreichische Musik – Musik in Österreich. Beiträge zur Musikgeschichte Mitteleuropas. Theophil Antonicek zum 60. Geburtstag*. Tutzing: Schneider.
Hirschfeld, C. C. L. 2001. *Theory of Garden Art*. Ed. and trans. Linda B. Parshall. Philadelphia: University of Pennsylvania Press.
Hirschman, Albert O. 2013 [1977]. *The Passions and the Interests: Political Arguments for Capitalism Before Its Triumph*. Princeton University Press.
Hirschmann, Wolfgang 1995. "Empfindsamkeit." MGG, Sachteil 2: 1765–71.
Hoboken, Anthony van 1957–78: see Abbreviations.
Hochradner, Thomas and Géza Michael Vörösmarty 2000. "Zur Musikpflege am Altar Mária Pócs (Maria Pötsch) in St. Stephan in Wien," *Studia Musicologica* 41: 133–75.
Hochstein, Wolfgang 1993. "Zum Entstehungsprozess der 'Paukenmesse' von Joseph Haydn," *Kirchenmusikalisches Jahrbuch* 77: 117–34.
Hoffmann, E. T. A. 1999 [1810]. "Review of Beethoven's Fifth Symphony," *Allgemeine musikalische Zeitung* 12, cols. 630–42, 652–59; trans. Robin Wallace in Senner (ed.) 95–112.
  1989. *E. T. A. Hoffmann's Musical Writings: Kreisleriana, The Poet and the Composer, Music Criticism*, ed. David Charlton. Cambridge University Press.
Hogwood, Christopher 1980. *Haydn's Visits to England*. London: The Folio Society.
  1996. "In Praise of Arrangements: the 'Symphony Quintetto'" in Biba and Jones (eds.) 82–104.
Holloway, Robin 1998. "Haydn: The Musicians' Musician," in *Haydn Studies*: 321–34.
Hohmaier, Simone (ed.) 2011. *Jahrbuch 2010 des Staatlichen Instituts für Musikforschung Preussischer Kulturbesitz*. Berlin: De Gruyter.
Holoman, D. Kern 2004. *The Société des Concerts du Conservatoire, 1828–1967*. Berkeley, Los Angeles and London: University of California Press.
Holtmeier, Ludwig 2007. "Heinichen, Rameau, and the Italian Thoroughbass Tradition: Concepts of Tonality and Chord in the Rule of the Octave," *Journal of Music Theory* 51/1: 5–49.
  2017. *Rameaus langer Schatten. Studien zur deutschen Musiktheorie des 18. Jahrhunderts*. Hildesheim: Olms.
Horányi, Mátyás 1962. *The Magnificence of Eszterháza*. Trans. András Deák. London: Barrie and Rockliff.

Hortschansky, Klaus (1993). "The Musician as Music-Dealer" in Salmen, Kaufman, and Reisner (eds.) 189–218.

Hörwarthner, Maria 1997. "Joseph Haydn's Library: Attempts at a Literary-Historical Reconstruction." Trans. Kathrine Talbot in HWorld 395–462.

Hörz, Peter F. N. 2005. *Jüdische Kultur im Burgenland. Historische Fragmente – volkskundliche Analysen*. Vienna: Institut für Europäische Ethnologie der Universität Wien.

Hosler, Bellamy 1981. *Changing Aesthetic Views of Instrumental Music in Eighteenth-Century Germany*. Ann Arbor: UMI Research Press.

Houle, George 1987. *Meter in Music: 1600–1800*. Bloomington: Indiana University Press.

Howe, Blake, Stephanie Jensen-Moulton, Neil Lerner, and Joseph Straus (eds.) 2016. *The Oxford Handbook of Music and Disability Studies*. Oxford University Press.

Hoyt, Peter 1999. "The 'False Recapitulation' and the Conventions of Sonata Form." Ph.D. dissertation, University of Pennsylvania.

Huber, Alfons 1987. "Deckelstützen und Schalldeckel an Hammerklavieren" in Hellwig (ed.) 229–50.

Hunter, Mary 1982. "Haydn's Aria Forms: A Study of the Arias in the Italian Operas Written for Esterháza, 1755–1783." Ph.D. dissertation, Cornell University.

  1985. "'Pamela': The Offspring of Richardson's Heroine in Eighteenth-Century Opera," *Mosaic* 18: 61–76.

  1997a. "Haydn's London Piano Trios and His Salomon String Quartets: Private vs. Public?" in HWorld 103–30.

  1997b. "Rousseau, the Countess, and the Female Domain" in Eisen (ed.) 1–26.

  1999. *The Culture of Opera Buffa in Mozart's Vienna: A Poetics of Entertainment*. Princeton University Press.

  2012a. "'The Most Interesting Genre of Music': Performance, Sociability and Meaning in the Classical String Quartet, 1800–1830," *Nineteenth-Century Music Review* 9/1: 53–74.

  2012b. "Haydn's String Quartet Fingerings: Communications to Performer and Audience" in Hunter and Will 281–301.

  2014. "Topics in *Opera Buffa*" in Mirka (ed.) 61–89.

  2015. "Werktreue and the Rhetoric of Agency." Paper given at the National Meeting of the American Musicological Society, Louisville, KY, November 2015.

Hunter and Will 2012: see Abbreviations.

Hurwitz, Joachim 1996. *Joseph Haydn und die Freimaurer*. Frankfurt am Main: Peter Lang.

Hüttler, Michael and Hans Ernst Weidinger (eds.) 2014. *Ottoman Empire and European Theatre. Vol. 2: The Time of Joseph Haydn: From Sultan Mahmud I to Mahmud II (r. 1730–1839)*. Vienna: Hollitzer Wissenschaftsverlag.

Ingraham, Mary, Joseph So, and Roy Moodley (eds.) 2016. *Opera in a Multicultural World: Coloniality, Culture, Performance*. New York: Routledge.

International Music Society 1909. *Haydn Zentenarfeier verbunden mit dem III. musikwissenschaftlichen Kongress der Internationalen Musik-Gesellschaft. Programmbuch zu den Festaufführungen (25.-29. Mai 1909)*. Vienna: Selbstverlag des Festkomitees.

Jacobshagen, Arnold, Armin Raab, Wolfram Steinbeck (eds.) 2013. "Retrospective und Innovation: Der Späte Joseph Haydn [Report of the International Musicological Congress, Cologne, June 4–6,2009]," *Haydn-Studien* 10/3–4.

Jaenecke, Joachim 1990. *Joseph und Michael Haydn. Autographe und Abschriften. Katalog*. Munich: G. Henle Verlag.

Jahn, Michael 2005. *Die Musikhandschriften des Domarchivs St. Stephan in Wien.* Vienna: Verlag Der Apfel.

Jerome, Erin W. 2015. "Haydn's *L'incontro improvviso*: Deceitful Dervishes, Greedy Servants, and the Meta-performance of *alla Turca* Style" in Libin (ed.) 114–30.

Johnson, Claudia 1986. "'Giant HANDEL' and the Musical Sublime," *Eighteenth-Century Studies* 19: 515–33.

Johnson, Douglas 1982. "1794–1795: Decisive Years in Beethoven's Early Development" in Tyson (ed.) 1–28.

Johnson, H. Earle 1981. *Hallelujah Amen! The Story of the Handel and Haydn Society of Boston*. Vermont: Da Capo.

Johnson, James H. 1991. "Beethoven and the Birth of Romantic Musical Experience in France," *19th-Century Music* 15: 23–35.

Johnston, Kenneth R. 2013. *Unusual Suspects: Pitt's 'Reign of Alarm' and the Lost Generation of the 1790s*. Oxford University Press.

Jones, David Wyn 2000a. "Minuets and Trios in Haydn's Quartets" in Young (ed.) 81–97.

2000b. *Music in Eighteenth-Century Britain*. Farnham and Burlington: Ashgate.

2002a. "Catalogues" in *Oxford Companion* 33–37.

2002b: see Abbreviations (*Oxford Companion*).

2004. "A Newly Identified Sketchleaf for Haydn's Quartet in D Minor, Op. 103," *Haydn Studien* 8/4: 413–17.

2005. "First Among Equals: Haydn and His Fellow Composers" in *Cambridge Companion* 45–57.

2006. "Haydn" in Eisen and Keefe (eds.) 211–15.

2009. *The Life of Haydn*. Cambridge University Press.

2010. "Becoming a Complete Kapellmeister: Haydn and Mattheson's *Der vollkommene Capellmeister*," *Studia musicologica* 51: 29–40.

2013. "Haydn, Austria and Britain: Music, Culture and Politics in the 1790s" in Chesser and Jones (eds.) 1–21.

2016. *Music in Vienna: 1700, 1800, 1900*. Woodbridge, Suffolk: The Boydell Press.

Jones, David Wyn and Otto Biba (eds.) 1996. *Studies in Music History Presented to H. C. Robbins Landon on His Seventieth Birthday*. London: Thames & Hudson.

Kant, Immanuel 1764. *Beobachtungen über das Gefühl des Schönen und Erhabenen* (*Observations on the Feeling of the Beautiful and Sublime*). Königsberg: Johann Jakob Kanter.

1790. *Kritik der Urteilskraft (Critique of Judgement)*. Berlin and Libau: Lagarde and Friedrich.

1991. "An Answer to the Question: What is Enlightenment?" in Hans Reiss (ed.), *Political Writings*, 2nd edn. Cambridge University Press, 54–59.

Kassal-Mikula, Renata and Reinhard Pohanka (eds.) 1997. *850 Jahre St. Stephan: Symbol und Mitte in Wien, 1147–1997. 226 Sonderausstellung, Historisches Museum der Stadt Wien, Dom- und Metropolitankapitel Wien, 24. April bis 31. August 1997*. Vienna: Museen der Stadt Wien.

Kassler, Michael (ed.) 2011. *The Music Trade in Georgian England*. Aldershot: Ashgate.

Kellner, David 1743. *Treulicher Unterricht im General-Bass*, 3rd edn. Hamburg: Herold.

Kelly, Linda 2004. *Susanna, the Captain and the Castrato: Scenes from the Burney Salon 1779–80*. London: Starhaven.

Kemp, Lindsay 2002. "Recordings" in *Oxford Companion* 322; 338–43.

Kerman, Joseph 1980. "How We Got into Analysis, and How to Get Out," *Critical Inquiry* 7: 311–31.

Kidd, Ronald R. 1987. "Jefferson's Music Library, His Catalogue of 1783, and a Revision of Lowens's Haydn in America," *Studies in Eighteenth-Century Culture* 17: 319–34.

Kielian-Gilbert, Marianne 2006. "Beyond Abnormality – Dis/ability Studies and Music's Metamorphic Subjectivities" in Lerner and Straus (eds.) 217–34.

Kirnberger, Johann Philipp 1771–9. *Die Kunst des reinen Satzes in der Musik*, 3 vols. Lübben: Christian Friedrich Voss.

Klampfer, Josef 1959. *Joseph Haydn und die Haydn-Gedenkstätten in Eisenstadt*. Vienna: Bergland Verlag.

Klancher, John 2013. *Transfiguring the Arts and Sciences: Knowledge and Cultural Institutions in the Romantic Age*. Cambridge University Press.

Klier, Karl M. 1932. "Das Volksliedthema eines Haydn-Capriccios: Eine kultur- und musikgeschichtliche Betrachtung," *Das deutsche Volkslied* 34/7–8: 88–93, 100–4.

Klorman, Edward 2016. *Mozart's Music of Friends: Social Interplay in the Chamber Works*. Cambridge University Press.

Knapp, Raymond 2018. *Making Light: Haydn, Musical Camp, and the Long Shadow of German Idealism*. Durham: Duke University Press.

Knigge, Adolph 1805 [1788]. *Über den Umgang mit Menschen*. Hannover: Schmidt. Trans. Peter Will, *Practical Philosophy of Social Life; or, The Art of Conversing with Men*. Lansingburgh: Penniman & Bliss.

Knouse, Nola Reed (ed.) 2008. *The Music of the Moravian Church in America*. New York: University of Rochester Press.

(ed.) 2011. "European Music in Colonial America: The Moravians as Transmitters of a Culture" in Murray (ed.) 221–25.

Koch, Heinrich Christoph 1782, 1787, 1793. *Versuch einer Anleitung zur Composition*. 3 vols. Rudolstadt and Leipzig: Böhme.

1795. "Über den Modegeschmack in der Tonkunst," *Journal der Tonkunst* 1: 63–121.

1802. *Musikalisches Lexikon*. Frankfurt am Main: Hermann dem Jüngern.

1983. *Introductory Essay on Composition*. Trans. Nancy Baker. New Haven: Yale University Press.

Kollmann, Augustus Frederic Christopher 1799. *An Essay on Practical Musical Composition*. London, n.p.

Komlós, Katalin 1987. "The Viennese Keyboard Trio in the 1780s: Sociological Background and Contemporary Reception," M&L 68: 222–34.

2005. "Miscellaneous Vocal Genres" in *Cambridge Companion* 164–75.

2012. "Haydn's English Canzonettas in their Local Context" in Hunter and Will 75–95.

Konrad, Ulrich 2008. "On Ancient Languages. The Historical Idiom of Wolfgang Amadé Mozart" in Gallagher and Kelly (eds.) 253–78.

2013. "'Ihm schweben öfters Ideen vor, wodurch seine Kunst noch viel weiter gebracht werden könnte'. Überlegungen zum Spätwerk Joseph Haydns," *Haydn-Studien* 10/3–4: 335–59.

2014. *Werkstattblicke. Haydn, Beethoven und Wagner beim Komponieren beobachtet*, Stuttgart: Franz Steiner Verlag.

Kopp, Margit and Susanne Felicitas Wolf 2014. *Esterházy Palace. History, State Rooms, Exhibitions, Palace Grounds*. Trans. Thomas Ball. Eisenstadt: Esterházy Betriebe GmbH/Colorama.

Koppány, András and László Thúry 2013. "A fertődi bábszínház régészeti módszerű kutatása [The Researching of the Fertőd Puppet Theater with Archeological Methods]" in Szentesi, Mentényi, and Simon (eds.) 117–28.

Körner, Stefan (ed.) 2008. *Fürstliches Halali. Jagd am Hofe Esterházy*. Munich: Prestel.

Kors, Alan Charles (ed.) 2002. *Encyclopedia of the Enlightenment*, vol. 3. Oxford University Press.

Koselleck, Reinhart 2002. *The Practice of Conceptual History: Timing History, Spacing Concepts*. Trans. Todd Samuel Presner et al. Stanford University Press.

Koslofsky, Craig 2011. *Evening's Empire: A History of the Night in Early Modern Europe*. Cambridge University Press.

Kramer, Lawrence 1992. "Music and Representation: The Instance of Haydn's *Creation*" in Scher (ed.) 139–62.

2009. "The Devoted Ear: Music as Contemplation" in Chapin and Kramer (eds.) 59–78.

Kramer, Richard 2008. *Unfinished Music*. Oxford University Press.

Kretschmer, Helmut 2009. *Haydns Beziehungen zu Wien: Vom Sängerknaben zum ersten Wiener Klassiker*. Vienna: Wiener Stadt- und Landesarchiv.

Kreutziger-Herr, Annette and Katrin Losleben 2008. *History Herstory: Alternative Musikgeschichten*. Cologne: Böhlau.

Kris, Ernst and Otto Kurz, 1979. *Legend, Myth and Magic in the Image of the Artist: A Historical Experiment*. New Haven: Yale University Press.

Krähling, János, András Koppány, J. Csaba Fekete, Balázs Halmos and Anna Józsa 2013. "The Marionette Opera and the Orangerie of Eszterháza (Fertöd, Hungary) Building Archeology Methods and

Theoretical Reconstruction," *Materiali e strutture: problemi di conservazione*, 2/4 (new series): 75–94, 123–28.

Kühl, Paolo M. forthcoming. "The Prince of Harmony, His Favorite Disciple and Other Geniuses: The Diffusion of a 'Classical' Repertory in Early 19th-Century Rio de Janeiro" in Reicher, Siegert and Fuhrmann (eds.) 99–112.

Lamkin, Kathleen 2007. *Esterházy Musicians 1790 to 1809 Considered from New Sources in the Castle Forchtenstein Archives* (Georg Feder and Walter Reicher (eds.) *Eisenstädter Haydn Berichte* 6). Tutzing: Hans Schneider.

Forthcoming. "Haydn's Heritage and Reception in the Moravian Communities of North America" in Reicher, Sieger, and Fuhrmann (eds.) 113–58.

Landmann, Ortrun 1986. "Die Dresdener Haydn-Quellen im Hinblick auf ihre Provenienzen," in Badura-Skoda (ed.), *Joseph Haydn. Bericht*: 519–25.

Landon, Else Radant (2002). "Dichtler Family" in *Oxford Companion* 63–64.

Landon, H. C. Robbins (1955). *The Symphonies of Joseph Haydn*. London: Universal Edition.

1976–80: see Abbreviations (Landon I–V).

1991. *Mozart and Vienna*. New York: Schirmer Books.

Landon, H. C. Robbins and Roger E. Chapman (eds.) 1970. *Studies in Eighteenth-Century Music: A Tribute to Karl Geiringer on His Seventieth Birthday*. Oxford University Press.

Landon, H. C. Robbins and David Wyn Jones 1988. *Haydn: His Life and Music*. London: Thames and Hudson.

Larsen, Jens Peter 1939. *Die Haydn-Überlieferung*. Copenhagen: Ejnar Munksgaard.

1962. "Sonateform-Probleme" in Anna Amalile Abert and Wilhelm Pfannkuch (eds.), *Festschrift Friederich Blume zum 70. Geburtstag*. Kassel: Bärenreiter.

(ed.) 1974. *Three Haydn Catalogues*, 2nd edn. New York: Pendragon.

1984. "Review of Lowens, *Haydn in America*," *American Music* 2/2: 82–86.

1988a. "The Haydn Tradition" in Larsen 1998c. Trans. Ulrich Krämer. Ann Arbor: UMI Research Press.

1998b [1962] "Sonata Form Problems" in Larsen 1998c.

1998c [1962] *Handel, Haydn, and the Viennese Classical Style*. Trans. Ulrich Krümer. Ann Arbor: UMI Research Press.

Larsen, Jens Peter, Howard Serwer, and James Webster (eds.) 1981. *Haydn Studies: Proceedings of the International Haydn Conference Washington, DC*. New York/London: Norton.

LaRue, Jan 1961. "Significant and Coincidental Resemblance between Classical Themes," *JAMS* 14: 224–34.

1982. "Multi-Stage Variance: Haydn's Legacy to Beethoven," *JM* 1: 265–74.

1992. "Bifocal Tonality in Haydn Symphonies" in Allanbrook, Levy, and Mahrt (eds.) 59–75.

Lászay, Judit G. 2009. "Lokalforschungen in Eszterháza/Fertöd am Anfang des Jahrtausends" in Gürtler and Kropf (eds.) 317–47.

Latour, Bruno 2005. *Reassembling the Social: An Introduction to Actor-Network-Theory.* Oxford University Press.

Leech-Wilkinson, Daniel 2009. *The Changing Sound of Music: Approaches to Studying Recorded Musical Performances.* London, CHARM www.charm.rhul.ac.uk/studies/chapters/intro.html (accessed July 13, 2018).

Le Guin, Elisabeth 2005. *Boccherini's Body.* Berkeley and Los Angeles: University of California Press.

  2007. "A Visit to the Salon de Parnasse" in Beghin and Goldberg 14–35.

Lehner, Ulrich 2016. *The Catholic Enlightenment: The Forgotten History of a Global Movement.* Oxford University Press.

Lehner, Ulrich and Michael Printy (eds.) 2010. *A Companion to the Catholic Enlightenment in Europe.* Leiden and Boston: Brill.

Le Huray, Peter and James Day 1981. *Music and Aesthetics in the Eighteenth and Early Nineteenth Centuries.* Cambridge University Press.

Lempa, Heikki and Paul Peuker (eds.). 2010. *Self, Community, World: Moravian Education in a Transatlantic World.* Bethlehem: Lehigh University Press.

Lenneberg, Hans (ed.) 1994. *The Dissemination of Music: Studies in the History of Music Publishing.* Lausanne: Gordon and Breach.

Leppert, Richard 1993. *The Sight of Sound: Music, Representation, and the History of the Body.* Berkeley: University of California Press.

Lerner, Neil and Joseph Straus 2006. *Sounding Off: Theorizing Disability in Music.* New York: Routledge.

Lester, Joel 1986. *The Rhythms of Tonal Music.* Carbondale: Southern Illinois University Press.

Lesure, François 1986. Preface in Fauquet 9–10.

Levy, Janet M. 1981. "Gesture, Form, and Syntax in Haydn's Music" in Larsen, Serwer, and Webster (eds.) 355–63.

  1987. "Covert and Casual Values in Recent Writings about Music," *JM* 5: 3–27.

  1992. "'Something Mechanical Encrusted on the Living': A Source of Musical Wit and Humor" in Allanbrook, Levy, and Mahrt (eds.) 225–56.

Libin, Kathryn L. (ed.) 2015. *Haydn and his Contemporaries.* Ann Arbor: Steglein.

Lichtenstein, Sabine (ed.) 2014. *"Music's Obedient Daughter": The Opera Libretto from Source to Score.* Amsterdam: Rodopi.

Lippman, Edward 1992. *A History of Western Musical Aesthetics.* Lincoln: University of Nebraska Press.

Lister, Warwick 2004. "The First Performance of Haydn's 'Paris' Symphonies," *ECM* 1/2: 289–300.

Locke, Arthur Ware and E. T. A. Hoffmann 1917. "'Beethoven's Instrumental Music': Translated from E. T. A. Hoffmann's *Kreisleriana* with an Introductory Note," *MQ* 3/1: 123–33.

Locke, Ralph P. 2009. *Musical Exoticism: Images and Reflections.* Cambridge University Press.

Lockwood, Lewis and Phyllis Benjamin (eds.) 1984. *Beethoven Essays: Studies in Honor of Elliot Forbes.* Cambridge, MA: Harvard University Press.

Loos, Helmut (ed.) 1997. *Musikgeschichte zwischen Ost- und Westeuropa. Symphonik–Musiksammlungen. Tagungsbericht Chemnitz 1995.* Sankt Augustin: Academia Verlag.

Lorenz, Michael 2014. "Joseph Haydn's Real Wife." michaellorenz.blogspot.com/2014/09/joseph-haydns-real-wife-11.html.
Loughridge, Deirdre 2010. "Haydn's *Creation* as an Optical Entertainment," JM 27: 9–54.
  2013. "Magnified Vision, Mediated Listening, and the 'Point of Audition' of Early Romanticism," ECM 10: 179–211.
  2016. *Haydn's Sunrise, Beethoven's Shadow: Audiovisual Cultures and the Emergence of Musical Romanticism*. University of Chicago Press.
Lowe, Melanie 2002. "Falling from Grace: Irony and Expressive Enrichment in Haydn's Symphonic Minuets," JM 19: 171–221.
  2005. "Recorded Performances: A Symphonic Study" in *Cambridge Companion* 249–63.
  2007. *Pleasure and Meaning in the Classical Symphony*. Bloomington: Indiana University Press.
  2010. "The Art of Transition: After Haydn Year 2009," JM 27: 1–8.
  2015. "Difference and Enlightenment in Haydn's Instrumental Music" in Bloechl, Lowe, and Kallberg (eds.) 133–69.
Lowens, Irving 1979. *Haydn in America*. Detroit: Information Coordinators.
Mace, Nancy A. 1996. "Haydn and the London Music Sellers: Forster and Longman & Broderip," M&L 77: 527–41.
MacIntyre, Alasdair 1984 [1981]. *After Virtue: A Study in Moral Theory*. 2nd edn. University of Notre Dame Press.
MacIntyre, Bruce C. 1986. *The Viennese Concerted Mass of the Early Classic Period*. Ann Arbor: UMI Research Press.
  1998. *Haydn: The Creation*. New York: Schirmer.
Magalhães-Castro, Beatriz 2009. "Robert Stevenson's Iberian World Connections: Haydn and Interconnected Music Histories in Latin American Studies" in Blažeković and Mackenzie (eds.) 353–63.
Malina, János, ed. 2006. *The Eszterháza Opera House: Past and Future*. Budapest: The Hungarian Haydn Society.
  2016a. "Az 1776 és 1790 közötti eszterházi operaévadok kronológiája [The Chronology of Opera Seasons at Eszterháza Between 1776 and 1790]." Ph.D. dissertation, Liszt Academy of Music.
  2016b. "On the Venues for and Decline of the *Accademies* at Eszterháza in Haydn's Time," ECM 13/2: 253–81.
  2017. "The Eszterháza Libretti: An Overall Survey," H-St 11/2: 223–65.
Mann, Alfred 1970a. "Haydn as Student and Critic of Fux" in Landon and Chapman 323–32.
  1970b. "Beethoven's Contrapuntal Studies with Haydn," MQ 56/4: 711–26.
  1973. "Haydn's Elementarbuch," The Music Forum 3: 206–237.
Mansel, Philip 2001. *Paris Between Empires 1814–1852*. London: John Murray.
Marpurg, Friedrich Wilhelm 1750. *Des critischen Musicus an der Spree*. Berlin: Haude and Spener.
  1755a. *Anleitung zum Clavierspielen*. Berlin: Haude and Spener.
  1755b. *Handbuch bey dem Generalbasse und der Composition*. Berlin: Johann Jacob Schützens Witwe.
Martin, Nathan John 2010. "*Formenlehre* Goes to the Opera: Examples from *Armida* and Elsewhere," Studia Musicologica 51: 387–404.

2014. "Larsen's Legacy: The Three-Part Exposition and the New *Formenlehre*," *HAYDN: Online Journal of the Haydn Society of North America* 4/2; www.rit.edu /affiliate/haydn/ (accessed July 11, 2018).

Marx, Hans Joachim (ed.) 1990. *Carl Philipp Emanuel Bach und die europäische Musikkultur des mittleren 18. Jahrhunderts. Bericht über das Internationale Symposium der Joachim Jungius-Gesellschaft der Wissenschaften Hamburg, 29. September–2. Oktober 1988.* Gottingen: Vandenhoeck & Ruprecht.

Mastic, Timothy 2015. "Normative Wit: Haydn's Recomposed Recapitulations," *Music Theory Online* 21: 1–16.

Mathew, Nicholas 2007. "Heroic Haydn, the Occasional Work, and 'Modern' Political Music," *ECM* 4/1: 7–25.

2012. "'Achieved is the Glorious Work': *The Creation* and the Choral Work Concept" in Hunter and Will 124–42.

Mattheson, Johann 1739. *Der vollkommene Capellmeister.* Hamburg: Christian Herold.

Maunder, Richard 1998a. "Viennese Wind-Instrument Makers, 1700–1800," *The Galpin Society Journal* 51: 170–91.

1998b. *Keyboard Instruments in Eighteenth-Century Vienna.* Oxford: Clarendon Press.

Maurer Zenck, Claudia 2001. *Vom Takt.* Vienna: Böhlau Verlag.

Mauss, Marcel 1966 [1923–24]. *The Gift: Forms and Functions of Exchange in Archaic Societies.* Trans. Ian Gunnison. London: Cohen & West.

McAdams, Stephen, Philippe Depalle, and Eric Clarke 2004. "Analyzing Musical Sound" in Clarke and Cook (eds.) 157–96.

McClelland, Clive 2014. "Ombra and Tempesta" in Mirka (ed.) 279–300.

McCorkle, Donald M. 1956. "John Antes, American Dilettante," *MQ* 42/4: 486–99.

McCue, Edward 2004. "Acoustics of the Second Opera House at Eszterháza," in Georg Feder and Walter Reicher (eds.) *Miscellanea. Referata Zweier Haydntagungen 2003* (Eisenstädter Haydn-Berichte 3) 101–35, Tutzing: Hans Schneider.

McCue, Kirsteen 1993. "George Thomson (1757–1851): His Collections of National Airs in their Scottish Cultural Context." D.Phil. dissertation, University of Oxford.

McGrann, Jeremiah W. 1998. "Of Saints, Name-days, and Turks: Some Background on Haydn's Masses written for Prince Nikolaus II Esterházy," *JMR* 17/3–4: 195–210.

McGuinness, Rosamond 2004. "Gigs, Roadies and Promoters: Marketing Eighteenth-century Concerts" in Wollenberg and McVeigh (eds.) 261–71.

McVeigh, Simon 1989. "The Professional Concert and Rival Subscription Series in London, 1783–1793," *Royal Musical Association Research Chronicle* 22: 1–135.

1993. *Concert Life in London from Mozart to Haydn.* Cambridge University Press.

Meisel, Martin 2016. *Chaos Imagined: Literature, Art, Science.* New York: Columbia University Press.

Melton, James Van Horn 1988. *Absolutism and the Eighteenth-Century Origins of Compulsory Schooling in Prussia and Austria.* Cambridge University Press.

2007. "School, Stage, Salon: Musical Cultures in Haydn's Vienna" in Beghin and Goldberg 80–108.
Mercer-Taylor, Peter 2015. "'Gems of Exquisite Beauty': Baker and Southard's 1850 *Haydn Collection* and American Hymnody's Path Toward a Classical Music Aesthetic." Paper given at the American Musicological Society National Meeting (Louisville, Kentucky) 2015.
Merten, Josef 1986. "Zu den Orgelinstrumenten Joseph Haydns" in Badura-Skoda (ed.) 72–75.
Meyer, Jürgen 1978. "Raumakustik und Orchesterklang in den Konzertsälen Joseph Haydns," *Acustica* 41/3, 145–62.
  1995. *Akustik und musikalische Aufführungspraxis*, 3rd edn. Frankfurt am Main: Erwin Bochinsky.
Michaelis, Christian Friedrich 1805. "Einige Bemerkungen über das Erhabene der Musik," *Berlinische musikalische Zeitung* 1/46: 179–81.
  1807. "Ueber das Humoristische oder Launige in der musikalischen Komposition," *Allgemeine musikalische Zeitung* 10/46 cols. 725–29.
Mikusi, Balázs 2009. "'The Dew-Dropping Morn . . . Miserere Nobis': Haydn's Worst Joke Reconsidered," *JMR* 28/2–3: 212–22.
  2010. "Between Tradition, Innovation, and Utopia: Haydn's Mehrstimmige Gesänge," *Studia Musicologica* 51: 179–91.
  2013. "Haydn's 'British Music Library'," in Chesser and Jones (eds.), *Land of Opportunity*: 112–36.
  2018. "Giuseppi Sartis 'Idalide' und Johann Gottlieb Naumanns 'Cora'. Die Eroberung Perus in Eszterház und Eisenstadt" in Reicher, Siegert, and Fuhrmann (eds.) 211–32.
Milhous, Judith, Gabriella Dideriksen, and Robert D. Hume (eds.) 2001. *Italian Opera in Late Eighteenth-Century London*. Vol. 2, *The Pantheon Opera and its Aftermath, 1789–1795*. Oxford: Clarendon Press.
Miller, Christopher R. 2006. *The Invention of Evening: Perception and Time in Romantic Poetry*. Cambridge University Press.
Miller, Norbert 2013. "Greisenavantgardismus. Thomas Mann und der Mythos des Spätwerks," *H-St* 10/3–4: 504–32.
Milligan, Thomas B. 1983. *The Concerto and London's Musical Culture in the Late Eighteenth Century*. Ann Arbor: UMI Research Press.
Mirka, Danuta (ed.) 2008. *Communication in Eighteenth-Century Music*. Cambridge University Press.
  2009. *Metric Manipulations in Haydn and Mozart: Chamber Music for Strings, 1787–1791*. Oxford University Press.
  2012. "Absent Cadences," *ECM* 9: 213–35.
  (ed.) 2014a. *The Oxford Handbook of Topic Theory*. Oxford University Press.
  2014b. "Topics and Meter" in Mirka (ed.) 357–80.
Mitchell, Brian R. 2007. *International Historical Statistics: Europe, 1750–2005*. Basingstoke and New York: Palgrave Macmillan.
Mőcsényi, Mihály 1999. *Eszterháza fehéren-feketén*. Budapest: Self-published by the author.
Monelle, Raymond 2000. *The Sense of Music: Semiotic Essays*. Princeton University Press.

2006. *The Musical Topic: Hunt, Military and Pastoral*. Bloomington: Indiana University Press.

Monk, Samuel 1960. *The Sublime: A Study of Critical Theories in XVIII-Century England*. Ann Arbor: University of Michigan Press.

Montero, M. del Rosario 2011. "La música de Franz Joseph Haydn en España. Recopilación, catalogación e interpretación de las fuentes musicales conservadas en Madrid hasta 1833." Ph.D. dissertation, Universidad de Granada.

Morales, Luisa 2011a. "Keyboards, Feast and Liturgy in Castilian Female Monasteries and convents during the Early Modern Era" in Morales (ed.) 1–27.

Morales, Luisa (ed.) 2011b. *Keyboard Music in the Female Monasteries and Converts of Spain, Portugal and the Americas*. Barcelona: LEAL.

Morellet, André 1812, 1995. *De la conversation. Suivi d'un essai de Jonathan Swift*. Paris: Rivages poche/Petite Bibliothèque.

Mörner, Carl-Gabriel Stellan 1952. *Johan Wikmanson und die Brüder Silverstolpe. Einige Stockholmer Persönlichkeiten im Musikleben des Gustavianischen Zeitalters*. Stockholm: Almqvist & Wiksell.

 1969. "Haydniana aus Schweden um 1800," H-St 2/1: 1–33.

Morrow, Mary Sue 1989. *Concert Life in Haydn's Vienna: Aspects of a Developing Musical and Social Institution*. Stuyvesant: Pendragon Press.

 1997. *German Music Criticism in the Late Eighteenth Century: Aesthetic Issues in Instrumental Music*. Cambridge University Press.

 2004. "Late Eighteenth-Century Instrumental Music from the Perspective of the Italian Press" in Radicchi and Burden (eds.) 713–35.

Mullan, John 1998. *Sentiment and Sociability: The Language of Feeling in the Eighteenth Century*. Oxford: Clarendon Press.

Müller, Hans 1932. "Joseph Haydns letztes Testament," *Die Musik* 24: 440–45.

Muller, Joseph 1932. "Haydn Portraits," MQ 18: 282–98.

Murray, Sterling, ed. 2011. *Haydn and his Contemporaries: Selected Papers from the Joint Conference of the Society for Eighteenth-century Music and the Haydn Society of North America, Claremont, CA, 29 February–2 March, 2008*. Ann Arbor: Steglein.

 2015. "Haydn and Prince Kraft Ernst of Oettingen-Wallerstein: A Study in Admiration, Deception, and Reconciliation" in Libin (ed.) 100–13.

Nedbal, Martin 2016. *Morality and Viennese Opera in the Age of Mozart and Beethoven*. Abingdon: Routledge.

Neuwirth, Markus 2013. "Recomposed Main Themes in the Recapitulations of Classical Sonata Forms: An Analytical, Typological, and Explanatory Approach." Ph.D. dissertation, Katholieke Universiteit Leuven.

Newman, Nancy 2010. *Good Music for a Free People: The Germania Musical Society in Nineteenth-Century America*. New York: University of Rochester Press.

Niedt, Friedrich Erhardt 1717. *Musicalische Handleitung. Dritter Theil*. Hamburg: Schillers Erben.

Niemetschek, Franz 1798. *Leben des K. K. Kapellmeisters Wolfgang Gottlieb Mozart, nach Originalquellen beschrieben*. Prague: In der Herrlischen Buchhandlung.

 1956. *Life of Mozart*. Trans. H. Mautner. London: Hyman.

Nottebohm, Gustav 1873. *Beethoven's Studien*. Leipzig: J. Rieter-Biedermann.

November, Nancy 2007. "Haydn's Melancholy Voice: Lost Dialectics in His Late Chamber Music and English Songs," ECM 4/1: 71–106.
   2008a. "English Malady, English Song: Melancholy Voice in Haydn's Canzonettas" in Colburn (ed.) 41–66.
   2008b. "Instrumental Arias or Sonic Tableaux: 'Voice' in Haydn's String Quartets Opp. 9 and 17," M&L 89/3: 346–72.
   2017. *Cultivating String Quartets in Beethoven's Vienna*. New York: Boydell.
Nowak, Leopold 1970. "Die Skizzen zum Finale der Es-Dur-Symphonie GA 99 von Joseph Haydn," H-St 2/3: 137–66.
Och, Gunnar 1995. *Imago judaica. Juden und Judenthim im Spiegel der deutschen Literatur 1750–1812*. Würzburg: Königshausen & Neumann.
Ogesser, Joseph 1779. *Beschreibung der Metropolitankirche zu St. Stephan in Wien, herausgegeben von einem Priester der erzbischöflichen Kur im Jahre 1779*. Vienna: van Ghelen.
Olleson, Edward 1965. "Georg August Griesinger's Correspondence with Breitkopf & Härtel," HYb 3: 5–53.
   1966. "The Origin and Libretto for Haydn's *Creation*," HYb 4: 148–66.
Olleson, Philip 2000. "The London Roman Catholic Embassy Chapels and their Music in the Eighteenth and Early Nineteenth Centuries" in Jones (ed.) 101–18.
Oppermann, Annette 2003. "Schreibraum und Denkraum. Joseph Haydns Skizzen zur *Schöpfung*," *Die Musikforschung* 56: 375–81.
Organ Database. Eisenstadt, Österreich (Burgenland) – Domkirche Sankt Martin 2017. www.orgbase.nl.
Page, Janet K. 2014. *Convent Music and Politics in Eighteenth-Century Vienna*. Cambridge University Press.
Panagl, Oswald 2013. "Sprachwissenschaftliche Beobachtungen zum Briefstil von Joseph Haydn" in Gruber, Reicher, and Siegert (eds.) 59–74.
Pandi, Marianne and Schmidt, Fritz 1971. "Music in Haydn's and Beethoven's Time as Reported in the Pressburger Zeitung," HYb 8: 267–93.
Parakilas, James (ed.) 1999. *Piano Roles: Three Hundred Years of Life with the Piano*. New Haven: Yale University Press.
Parker, Mara 2002. *The String Quartet, 1750–1797: Four Types of Conversation*. Burlington: Ashgate.
Parsons, James (ed.) 2004a. *The Cambridge Companion to the Lied*. Cambridge University Press.
   2004b. "The Eighteenth-Century Lied" in Parsons (ed.) 35–62.
Pederson, Sanna 1994. "A. B. Marx, Berlin Concert Life, and German National Identity," *19th-Century Music* 18: 87–107.
Pete, Claudia 1996. "Geschichte der Wiener Tonkünstler-Societät." Ph. D. dissertation, University of Vienna.
Piekut, Benjamin 2014. "Actor-Networks in Music History: Clarification and Critique," *Twentieth-Century Music* 11/2, 191–215.
Plaschka, Georg Richard (ed.) 1985. *Österreich im Europa der Aufklärung. Kontinuität und Zäsur in Europa zur Zeit Maria Theresias und Josephs II. Internationales Symposium in Wien 20. – 23. Oktober 1980*, vol. I. Vienna: Verlag der Österreichischen Akademie der Wissenschaften.

Plöckinger-Walenta, V. and G. J Winkler (eds.) 2011. *Alltag und Handwerk im burgenländisch-westunganischen Raum.* Eisenstadt: Wissenschaftliche Arbeiten aus dem Burgenland.

Pohl, Carl Ferdinand 1871. *Denkschrift aus Anlass des hundertjährigen Bestehens der Tonkünstler-Societät, im Jahre 1862 reorganisirt als "Haydn" Wittwen und Waisen-Versorgungs-Verein der Tonkünstler in Wien.* Vienna: Gerold.

    1875, 1882, 1927. *Joseph Haydn,* 3 vols. (ed. Hugo Botstiber). Wiesbaden: M. Sändig.

Pollheimer, Klaus M. 2016. *Das Marionettentheater zu Eszterház. Das Marionettentheater auf Schloss Eszterház zur Zeit Joseph Haydns und sein Begründer Karl Michael Von Pauerspach* (Walter Reicher [ed.] Eisenstädter Haydn-Berichte 9). Vienna: Hollitzer.

Polzonetti, Pierpaolo 2011. *Italian Opera in the Age of the American Revolution.* Cambridge University Press.

    2012. "Haydn and the Metamorphoses of Ovid" in Hunter and Will 211–39.

    2015. "Haydn, Joseph" in Beal (ed.) 401–5.

    2018. "Il mondo della luna. Von der Utopie zur Revolution" in Reicher, Siegert, and Fuhrmann (eds.) 265–84.

Porter, Roy 2000. *The Creation of the Modern World: The Untold Story of the British Enlightenment.* New York: Norton.

    (ed.) 2003. *The Cambridge History of Science.* Vol. 4: *The Eighteenth Century.* Cambridge University Press.

Porter, Roy and Mikuláš Teich 1981. *The Enlightenment in National Context.* Cambridge University Press.

Potter, Dorothy 2011. *Food for Apollo: Cultivated Music in Antebellum Philadelphia.* Bethlehem: Lehigh University Press.

Powell, Ardal 2002. *The Flute.* New Haven: Yale University Press.

Pratl, Josef 2009a. "Die Wohnorte Haydns und seiner Musiker in Eisenstadt" in Gabriel and Winkler (eds.) 34–37.

    2009b. *Acta Forchtensteiniana. Die Musikdokumente im Esterházy-Archiv auf Burg Forchtenstein* (Walter Reicher and Christine Siegert [eds.] Eisenstädter Haydn-Berichte 7). Tutzing: Hans Schneider.

    2009c. "Aus dem Morgendämmern der Eisenstädter Haydn-Zeit" *Burgenländischen Heimatblätter* 71/11: 3–31.

    2013. "Zur Topographie von Haydns Eisenstadt" in Gruber, Reicher, and Siegert (eds.) 513–44.

    2018. "Kostüme und Dekorationen für 'Amerikanische' Opern. Dokumente aus den Esterházy Archiven" in Reicher, Siegert, and Fuhrmann (eds.) 257–64.

Price, Curtis, Judith Milhous, and Robert D. Hume 1995. *Italian Opera in Late Eighteenth-Century London.* Vol. 1, *The King's Theatre, Haymarket 1778–1791.* Oxford University Press.

Prickler, Harold (ed.) 1988. *Österreichischer Städteatlas.* Vol. 3: *Eisenstadt.* Vienna: Wiener Stadt- und Landesarchiv.

Proksch, Bryan 2006. "Cyclic Integration in the Instrumental Music of Haydn and Mozart." Ph.D. dissertation, University of North Carolina at Chapel Hill.

2015. *Reviving Haydn: New Appreciations in the Twentieth Century*. New York: University of Rochester Press.

Raab, Armin 2003. "Haydns Briefe an den Verleger Boyer," H-St 8: 237–52.

2010. "Gesamtausgabe," and "Überlieferung" in H-L 795–98.

2013. "Ein Porträt des Künstlers als alter Mann. Joseph Haydn und seine Biographen [A Portrait of the Artist as an Old Man: Joseph Haydn and his Biographers]," in H-St 10/3–4: 369–80.

2017. "Joseph Haydn Werke Draws to Its Close," ECM 14/2: 322–23.

Raab, Armin, Christine Siegert, and Ulrich Konrad (eds.) 2007. *Bearbeitungspraxis in der Oper des späten 18. Jahrhunderts. Bericht über die Internationale wissenschaftliche Tagung Feb. 2005 in Würzburg*. Tutzing: Hans Schneider.

Raab, Siegert and Steinbeck (eds.) 2010: see Abbreviations (H-L).

Rabin, Ronald J. and Steven Zohn (1995). "Arne, Handel, Walsh, and Music as Intellectual Property: Two Eighteenth-Century Lawsuits." *Journal of the Royal Musical Association* 120/1: 112–45.

Racine, Karen 2002. *A Transatlantic Life in the Age of Revolution*. Wilmington: Scholarly Resources Inc.

Radant, Else (ed.) 1968. "Die Tagebücher von Joseph Carl Rosenbaum, 1770–1829," HYb 5: 1–159.

Radant, Else and H. C. Robbins Landon 1993. "Dokumente aus den Esterházy-Archiven in Eisenstadt und Forchtenstein, herausgegeben aus dem Nachlass von János Hárich," HYb 18: 1–114.

Radicchi, Patrizia and Michael Burden (eds.) 2004. *Florilegium Musicae. Studi in onore di Carolyn Gianturco*, 2 vols. Pisa: Edizioni ETS.

Radice, Mark A. 1998. *Opera in Context: Essays on Historical Staging from the Late Renaissance to the Time of Puccini*. Portland: Amadeus Press.

1999. "The Nature of the 'Style Galant': Evidence from the Repertoire," MQ 83/4: 607–47.

Randel, Don Michael 1992. "Canons in the Musicological Toolbox" in Bergeron and Bohlman 10–22.

Rasch, Rudolf (ed.) 2008. *The Circulation of Music in Europe, 1600–1900*. Berlin: Berliner Wissenschaftsverlag.

Ratner, Leonard G 1980. *Classic Music: Expression, Form, Style*. New York: Schirmer.

Ratz, Erwin 1951. *Einführung in die musikalische Formenlehre*. Vienna: Österreichischer Bundesverlag für Unterricht, Wissenschaft und Kunst.

Rehding, Alexander 2009. *Music and Monumentality: Commemoration and Wonderment in Nineteenth-Century Germany*. Oxford University Press.

Reiber, Joachim 1994. "Druck, Nachdruck, Urheberrecht" in Gunda Barth-Scalmani, Grigitte Mazohl-Wallnig, and Ernst Wangermann (eds.), *Genie und Alltag*, 259–80. Salzburg: Otto Müller Verlag.

Reicha, Anton 1832. *Traité de haute composition musicale*. Ed. and trans. Carl Czerny as parts 5–10 of *Vollständiges Lehrbuch der musikalischen Composition*. Vienna: Diabelli.

Reichardt, Johann Friedrich 1800/01. "Biographische Nachrichten. I. A. P. Schulz dargestellt von I. F. Reichard [sic] (Fortsetzung)," *Allgemeine musikalische Zeitung* 3: cols. 169–76.

1814. "Noch ein Bruchstück aus Johann Friedrich Reichardt's Autobiographie: Sein erster Aufenthalt in Hamburg," *Allgemeine musikalische Zeitung* 16: cols. 21–34.

Reicher, Walter (ed.) 2017. *Almanache der Internationalen Haydntage Eisenstadt 1989–2017*. Eisenstadt: Verein Burgenländische Haydnfestspiele.

Reicher, Walter, Christine Siegert, and Wolfgang Fuhrmann (eds.) 2018. *Joseph Haydn und die "Neue Welt"* (Eisenstädter Haydn-Berichte. 11). Vienna: Hollitzer.

Reinisch, Frank 2010. "Breitkopf & Härtel," H-L 124–27.

Restle, Nicole 2007. "'Viele Grüsse an alle schönen Weiber'. Haydn und die Frauen" in Ulm (ed.) 65–73.

Ribeiro, Alvaro 1991. *The Letters of Dr. Charles Burney*. Vol. 1, 1751–1784. Oxford University Press.

Rice, John 1984. "Sarti's *Giulio Sabino*, Haydn's *Armida*, and the Arrival Opera Seria in Eszterháza," HYb 15: 181–94.

  2003. *Empress Marie Therese and Music at the Viennese Court, 1792–1807*. Cambridge University Press.

  2012. "Did Haydn Attend the Handel Commemoration in Westminster Abbey?" EM 40: 73–80.

  2018. "Montezuma at Eszterháza: A Pasticcio on a New World Theme" in Reicher, Siegert, and Fuhrmann (eds.) 233–44.

Richards, Annette 2001. *The Free Fantasia and the Musical Picturesque*. Cambridge University Press.

  2007. "Haydn's London Trios and the Rhetoric of the Grotesque," in Beghin and Goldberg: 251–80.

  2011. "Picturing the Moment in Sound: C. P. E. Bach and the Musical Portrait" in Donohue (ed.) 57–90.

  2012. *The Portrait Collection of Carl Philipp Emanuel Bach*. Cambridge, MA: Packard Humanities Institute.

  2013. "C. P. E. Bach, Portraits and the Physiognomy of Music History," JAMS 66: 337–96.

  2014. "Listening for Likeness, or C. P. E. Bach and the Art of Speculation," EM 42/3: 347–62.

Ridgewell, Rupert 2013. "Publishing Practice in Haydn's Vienna: Artaria and the Keyboard Trios Op.40" in Chesser and Jones 163–94.

Riedel, Friedrich Wilhelm 1992. "Joseph Haydns Sinfonien als liturgische Musik" in Schlager 213–22.

Riepel, Joseph 1752. *De Rhythmopoeia oder von der Tactordnung*. Regensburg and Vienna: Bader.

Riethmüller, Albrecht 1987. "Joseph Haydn und das Deutschlandlied," *Archiv für Musikwissenschaft* 44/4: 241–67.

Riley, Matthew 2003. "Johann Nikolaus Forkel and the Listening Practices of 'Kenner' and 'Liebhaber'," M&L 84: 414–33.

Rink, John, Helena Gaunt, and Aaron Williamon (eds.) 2017. *Musicians in the Making: Pathways to Creative Performance*. Oxford University Press.

Riskin, Jessica 2002. *Science in the Age of Sensibility: The Sentimental Empiricists of the French Enlightenment*. University of Chicago Press.

Ritter, Frederic 1884. *Music in America*. New York: Charles Scribner's Sons and London: William Reeves.
Robbins Landon 1959: see Abbreviations (CCLN).
Robbins Landon 1976–80: see Abbreviations (Landon I–V).
Robertson, Patricia 2001. "Early American Singing Organizations and Lowell Mason," 42/4: 17–24.
Robertson, Ritchie and Edward Timms (eds.) 1991. *The Austrian Enlightenment and its Aftermath*. Edinburgh University Press.
Robin, William 2015. "Traveling with 'Ancient Music': Intellectual and Transatlantic Currents in American Psalmody Reform," JM 32/2: 246–78.
Robins, Brian 2006. *Catch and Glee Culture in Eighteenth-Century England*. New York: Boydell.
  2009. "An Interview with H. C. Robbins Landon," Early Music World, http://brianmartinrobins.powweb.com/id29.html (accessed July 13, 2018).
Ronge, Julia 2009. "Was Beethoven bei Haydn wirklich gelernt hat," H-St 10: 492–503.
Ronge, Julia and John Wilson 2013. "Beethoven's Studies with Joseph Haydn (With a Postscript on the Length of Beethoven's Bonn Employment)," The Beethoven Journal 28/1: 4–25.
Rosa, Mario 2002. "Roman Catholicism" in Kors 468–72.
Rosen, Charles 1971/72. *The Classical Style: Haydn, Mozart, Beethoven*. New York: Viking Press/Norton.
  1995. *The Romantic Generation*. Harvard University Press.
Rosenblatt, Jason 1994. *Torah and Law in Paradise Lost*. Princeton University Press.
Rotenstein, Gottfried von [Gottfried Stegmüller] 1793. *Lust-Reisen durch Bayern, Würtemberg, Pfalz, Sachsen, Brandenburg, Österreich, Mähren, Böhmen und Ungarn, in den Jahren 1784 bis 1791*, vol. 3. Leipzig: Schneider.
Rosselli, John 1992. *Singers of Italian Opera: The History of a Profession*. Cambridge University Press.
Rothstein, William 1989. *Phrase Rhythm in Tonal Music*. New York: Schirmer.
  2008. "National Metrical Types" in Mirka (ed.) 112–59.
Rowland, David 2013. "Haydn's Music and Clementi's Publishing Circle" in Chesser and Jones (eds.) 92–111.
Ruhling, Michael (forthcoming). "A New World Oratorio Society Springs Up: Haydn, The Creation, and Boston's Handel and Haydn Society" in Reicher, Siegert, and Fuhrmann (eds.) 159–78.
Rumph, Stephen 2012. *Mozart and Enlightenment Semiotics*. Berkeley: University of California Press.
  2014. "Topical Figurae: The Double Articulation of Topics" in Mirka (ed.) 493–513.
Russell, Tilden A. 1985. "Über das Komische in der Musik: The Schütze-Stein Controversy," JM 4: 70–90.
Rycroft, Marjorie 2004. "Haydn's Volksliedbearbeitungen – von Neukomm. Über die Authentizität einer Bearbeitungen," H-St 8: 341–56.
Sachs, Joel 1973. "Hummel and the Pirates: The Struggle for Musical Copyright," MQ 49/1: 31–60.

Salinger, Arthur 2009. "Aspekte zur historischen Frage der Standorte von Orgeln im Wiener Stephansdom," www.dommusik-wien.at/Dommusik/media//Orgelstandorte_im_Stephansdom.pdf (accessed July 13, 2018).

Salmen, Walter, Herbert Kaufman, and Barbara Reisner (eds.) 1993. *The Social Status of the Professional Musician from the Middle Ages to the Nineteenth Century.* New York: Pendragon.

Sandgruber, Roman 1985. "Einkommensentwicklung und Einkommensverteilung in der zweiten Hälfte des 18. Jahrhunderts – Einige Quellen und Anhaltspunkte" in Plaschka (ed.) 251–63.

Sanguinetti, Giorgio 2012. *The Art of Partimento: History, Theory, and Practice.* Oxford University Press.

Sauder, Gerhard 1974. *Empfindsamkeit.* Vol. 1: *Voraussetzungen und Elemente.* Stuttgart: Metzler.

  1980. *Empfindsamkeit.* Vol. 3: *Quellen und Dokumente.* Stuttgart: Metzler.

  1990. "Die empfindsamen Tendenzen in der Musikkulture nach 1750," in Marx (ed.) 41–63.

Schafer, Hollace Ann 1987. "'A Wisely Ordered Phantasie': Joseph Haydn's Creative Process from the Sketches and Drafts for Instrumental Music." Ph.D. dissertation, Brandeis University.

Schama, Simon 1995. *Landscape and Memory.* New York: Knopf.

Schaul, Johann Baptist 1809. *Briefe über den Geschmack in der Musik.* Karlsruhe: Macklot.

Scheideler, Ullrich 2012. Kontrapunkt, in H-L: 425–29.

Schenker, Heinrich 1994 [1925]. *The Masterwork in Music,* vol. 1. Ed. William Drabkin and trans. Ian Bent, William Drabkin, Richard Kramer, John Rothgeb, and Hedi Siegel. Cambridge University Press.

  1996 [1926]. *The Masterwork in Music,* vol. 2. Ed. William Drabkin and trans. Ian Bent, William Drabkin, John Rothgeb, and Hedi Siegel. Cambridge University Press.

  1934. "Diary entry by Schenker January 14, 1934," *Schenker Documents Online,* www.schenkerdocumentsonline.org/documents/diaries/OJ-04-07_1934-01/r0014.html.

Scher, Steven Paul (ed.) 1992. *Music and Text: Critical Inquiries.* Cambridge University Press.

Schering, Arnold 1949 [1939]. "Bemerkungen zu J. Haydns Programmsinfonien" in Arnold Schering and Friedrich Blume (eds.),*Vom musikalischen Kunstwerk.* Leipzig: Koehler & Amelang, 246–77.

Schindler, Anton 1988 [1860]. *Ludwig van Beethoven.* Leipzig: Reclam.

Schlager, Karlheinz (ed.) 1992. *Festschrift Hubert Unverricht zum 65. Geburtstag.* Tutzing: Hans Schneider.

Schleuning, Peter 1984. "Ordentlich chaotisch: Zur Freien Klavierfantasie," *Musica: Zweimonatsschrift* 38/1: 14–18.

Schmalfeldt, Janet 1992. "Cadential Processes: The Evaded Cadence and the 'One More Time' Technique," *JMR* 12: 1–51.

Schmid, Ernst Fritz 1959. "Haydns Oratorium 'Il ritorno di Tobia', seine Entstehung und seine Schicksale," *Archiv für Musikwissenschaft* 16: 292–313.

Schmuhl, Boje E. Hans, and Ute Omonsky (eds.) 2011. *Zur Aufführungspraxis von Musik der Klassik*. Michaelsteiner Konferenzberichte Augsburg: Wißner-Verlag.
Scholz, Gottfried 2010. "Tonkünstler-Societät," H-L 785–86.
Schroeder, David P. 1990. *Haydn and the Enlightenment: The Late Symphonies and their Audience*. Oxford: Clarendon Press.
   1999. *Mozart in Revolt: Strategies of Resistance, Mischief and Deception*. New Haven: Yale University Press.
   2000–1. "The Art of Conversation: From Haydn to Beethoven's Early String Quartets," *Studies in Music from University of Western Ontario* 19–20: 377–99.
   2002. "Folk Music" in *Oxford Companion* 99–101.
   2005. "Orchestral Music: Symphonies and Concertos" in *Cambridge Companion* 95–111.
Schubart, C. F. D. 1973 [1839]. *Gesammelte Schriften und Schicksale*. Hildesheim: Olms [Stuttgart: Scheible].
Schumann, Robert 1854. *Gesammelte Schriften über Musik und Musiker* vol. 1. Leipzig: Breitkopf & Härtel.
Schwarz, Vera (ed.) 1972. *Der Junge Haydn. Kongressbericht Graz 1970*. Graz: Akademischen Druck- und Verlagsansalt (*Beiträge zur Aufführungspraxis* vol. 1).
Schwindt-Gross, Nicole 1989. "Einfache, zusammengesetzte und doppelt notierte Takte: Ein Aspekt der Takttheorie im 18. Jahrhundert," *Musiktheorie* 4/3: 203–22.
Scott, Darwin (ed.) 2002. *For the Love of Music: Festschrift in Honor of Theodore Front on His 90th Birthday*. Lucca: Libreria Musicale Italiana.
Scott, Marion M. 1932. "Haydn: Relics and Reminiscences in England," M&L 13/2: 126–36.
Scruton, Roger 2015. "Programme Music," in *Grove Online* https://doi.org/10.1093/gmo/9781561592630.article.22394 (accessed July 1, 2018).
Scull, Tony 1997. "More Light on Haydn's 'English Widow'," M&L 78: 45–55.
Searle, Arthur 2013. "'A Scarce Specimen of that Unrivalled Master's Handwriting': Haydn Manuscripts in the British Library" in Chesser and Jones (eds.) 212–32.
Seedorf, Thomas 2002. "Saitengesänge: Instrumentale Kantabilität in Haydns Streichquartetten," *Musik-Konzepte* 116: 3–39.
Seeger, Horst 1959. "Zur musikhistorischen Bedeutung der Haydn-Biographie von Albert Christoph Dies (1810)," *Beiträge zur Musikwissenschaft* 1/3: 24–31.
Seletsky, Robert E. 2004. "New Light on the Old Bow – Parts 1 and 2," EM 32/2–3: 286–301, 415–26.
Senner, Wayne M. (ed.) 1999. *The Critical Reception of Beethoven's Compositions by His German Contemporaries*, vol. 2. Lincoln: University of Nebraska Press.
Sher, Richard 1985. *Church and University in the Scottish Enlightenment: The Moderate Literati of Edinburgh*. Princeton University Press.
   (ed.) 1995. *Conjectural History and Anthropology*. Bristol: Thoemmes Press.
Shesgreen, Sean 2002. *Images of the Outcast: The Urban Poor in the Cries of London*. New Brunswick: Rutgers University Press.
Siegert, Christine 2006. "Die Fassungen der Arie 'Dove mai s'è ritrovata' aus Pasquale Anfossis Oper *I viaggiatori felici*," in *Perspektiven und Aufgaben der*

Haydn-Forschung. Bericht über den internationalen wissenschaftlichen Kongress Köln, 23.-25. Juni 2005, 107–36. Munich: Henle Verlag.

2009. "Joseph Haydn und Luigia Polzelli: Perspektiven einer Beziehung" in Kreutziger-Herr and Losleben (eds.) 336–51.

2010. "Einkünfte / Finanzen," in H-L 187–90.

2011a. "Opernbearbeitungen Haydns in seiner Instrumentalmusik – Überlegung en zu Form, Musiksprache und Aufführungspraxis" in Schmuhl and Omonsky (eds.), 159–72.

2011b. "Von George Crumb zu William Bolcom. Zeitgenössische Amerikanische Komponisten in Dialogue mit Haydn." Paper given at Haydn-Symposium 2011: Joseph Haydn und die Neue Welt, Eisenstadt.

2012. "' … auf unser Personale (zu Esterház in Ungarn) gebunden'. Bemerkungen zu Joseph Haydns Opernbearbeitungen am Beispiel von Pasquale Anfossis *La finta giardiniera*" in Detlef Altenburg und Rainer Bayreuther (eds.), *Musik und kulturelle Identität. Bericht über den Internationalen Kongress der Gesellschaft für Musikforschung vom 16. bis 21. September 2004 in Weimar*, 150–55. Kassel: Bärenreiter.

2013. "Haydn als 'Theaterkritiker' und die Aufführungen seiner Opern heute," in Gernot Gruber, Walter Reicher and Christine Siegert (eds.), *Joseph Haydn im 21. Jahrhundert, Bericht über das Symposium der Österreichischen Akademie der Wissenschaften, der Internationalen Joseph Haydn Privatstiftung Eisenstadt und der Esterházy-Privatstiftung* (Eisenstädter Haydn-Berichte 8) 433–94. Tutzing: Hans Schneider.

Siskin, Clifford, and William Warner (eds.) 2010. *This Is Enlightenment*. University of Chicago Press.

Sisman, Elaine 1982. "Small and Expanded Forms: Koch's Model and Haydn's Music," MQ 68: 444–75.

1990. "Haydn's Theater Symphonies," JAMS 43/2: 292–352.

1993a. *Haydn and the Classical Variation*. Cambridge, MA: Harvard University Press.

1993b. *Mozart: The "Jupiter" Symphony, No. 41 in C Major, K. 551*. Cambridge University Press.

1997a. "Haydn, Shakespeare, and the Rules of Originality" in HWorld 3–56.

1997b: see Abbreviations (HWorld).

2002. "Variation" in *Oxford Companion* 422–25.

2005. "Haydn's Career and the Idea of the Multiple Audience," in *Cambridge Companion*: 3–16.

2007. "Rhetorical Truth in Haydn's Chamber Music: Genre, Tertiary Rhetoric, and the Opus 76 Quartets" in Beghin and Goldberg 281–326.

2008. "Six of One: The Opus Concept in the Eighteenth Century" in Gallagher and Kelly (eds.) 79–107.

2011. "Haydn's *Isola disabitata* and Other Desert Islands." Paper given at Haydn-Symposium 2011: Joseph Haydn und die Neue Welt, Eisenstadt.

2012. "Fantasy Island: Haydn's Metastasian 'Reform' Opera" in Hunter and Will 11–43.

2013. "Haydn's Solar Poetics: The Tageszeiten Symphonies and Enlightenment Knowledge," JAMS 66/1: 5–102.

2014. "Symphonies and the Public Display of Topics" in Mirka (ed.) 90–117.
2016. "Music and the Labyrinth of Melancholy: Traditions and Paradoxes in C. P. E. Bach and Beethoven" in Howe, Jensen-Moulton, Lerner, and Straus (eds.) 590–617.
Small, Christopher 1998. *Musicking*. Middletown: Wesleyan University Press.
Smidak, Emil F. 1996. *Joseph Boulogne, called Chevalier de Saint-Georges*. Trans. John M. Mitchell. Lucerne: Avenira Foundation.
Smith, Adam 1978. *Lectures on Jurisprudence*. Ed. R. L. Meek, D. D. Raphael, and P. G. Stein. Indianapolis: Liberty Fund.
1761. [1759] *The Theory of Moral Sentiments*. London: A. Milner.
Smith, Ruth 1995. *Handel's Oratorios and Eighteenth-Century Thought*. Cambridge University Press.
Smither, Howard 1987. *The Oratorio in the Classical Era. History of the Oratorio*, vol. 4. Oxford: Clarendon Press.
Somfai, László 1969. *Joseph Haydn: His Life in Contemporary Pictures*. London: Faber & Faber.
1982. "Haydn's Eszterháza: The Influence of Architecture in Music," *New Hungarian Quarterly* 23: 195–201.
1986. "'Learned Style' in Two Late String Quartet Movements of Haydn," *Studia Musicologica* 28: 325–49.
1989. "Haydn at the Esterházy Court" in Zaslaw (ed.) 268–92.
1994. "Authentic Text and Presumed Intention: Experiences of the Festetics Quartet," H-St 6/4: 288–97.
1995. *The Keyboard Sonatas of Joseph Haydn: Instruments and Performance Practice, Genres, and Styles*. University of Chicago Press.
2006. "Trends, Accomplishment, Deficiency in Haydn Performance Today," H-St 9/1–4: 58–67.
2007. "Clever Orator versus Bold Innovator" in Beghin and Goldberg 213–28.
Sorkin, David 2008. *The Religious Enlightenment: Protestants, Jews, and Catholics from London to Vienna*. Princeton University Press.
Sothebys 2007. *Printed and Manuscript Music Sale, 23 May 2007*, London; www.sothebys.com/en/auctions/ecatalogue/2007/printed-and-manuscript-music-l07402/lot.76.html (accessed July 19, 2017).
Spink, Ian 2005. "Haydn at St. Paul's: 1791 or 1792?" EM 33: 273–80.
Spitzer, John and Neal Zaslaw 2004. *The Birth of the Orchestra: History of an Institution, 1650–1815*. Oxford University Press.
Spohr, Louis 1968. *Lebenserinnerungen*. Ed. Volker Göthel. Tutzing: Hans Schneider.
de Staël, Anne-Louise Germaine 1813. *De l'Allemagne*, vol. 1. Paris: H. Nicolle: 95–121. 1861. *Germany*, Vol. 1. Trans. O. W. Wright, 77–93. New York: H. W. Derby.
Stalnaker, Joanna 2010. *The Unfinished Enlightenment: Description in the Age of the Encyclopedia*. Ithaca: Cornell University Press.
Steblin, Rita 2000. "Haydn's Orgeldienst in der damaligen Gräfl. Haugwitzischen Kapelle," *Wiener Geschichtsblätter* 55/2: 124–34.
Stendhal [Marie-Henri Beyle] 1814. *Lettres écrites de Vienne en Autriche, sur le célèbre compositeur Jh. Haydn*. Paris: P. Didot.

Sterne, Jonathan 2012. *MP3: The Meaning of a Format*. Durham: Duke University Press.

Stevenson, Robert 1982. "Haydn's Iberian World Connections," *Inter-American Music Review* 4/2: 3–30.

Stockdale, John 1800. *A Geographical, Historical, and Political Description of the Empire of Germany, Holland, the Netherlands, Switzerland, Prussia, Italy, Sicily, Corsica, and Sardinia*. London: n.p.

Stowell, Robin (ed.) 2003. *The Cambridge Companion to the String Quartet*. Cambridge University Press.

Strauss, Barbara 1976. "A Register of Music Performed in Concert, Nazareth, Pennsylvania from 1796 to 1845: An Annotated Edition of an American Moravian Document." M.Mus. dissertation, University of Arizona, Tucson.

Sulzer, Johann Georg 1771–74. *Allgemeine Theorie der schönen Künste*. Leipzig: M. C. Weidmanns Erben und Reich.

Sutcliffe, W. Dean 1992. *Haydn: String Quartets, Op. 50*. Cambridge University Press.

1998a: see Abbreviations (Haydn Studies).

1998b. "Review of Charles Rosen, *The Classical Style: Haydn, Mozart, Beethoven*. Expanded Edition," *M&L* 79/4: 601–4.

2003a. "Haydn, Mozart, and Their Contemporaries" in Stowell (ed.) 3–18.

2003b. *The Keyboard Sonatas of Domenico Scarlatti and Eighteenth Century Musical Style*. Cambridge University Press.

2009 "Before the Joke: Texture and Sociability in the Largo of Haydn's Op. 33, No. 2," *JMR* 28/2–3: 92–118.

2010. "Expressive Ambivalence in Haydn's Symphonic Slow Movements of the 1770s," *JM* 27: 84–134.

2013. "The Shapes of Sociability in the Instrumental Music of the Later Eighteenth Century," *JRMA* 138/1: 1–45.

2014. "Topics in Chamber Music" in Mirka (ed.) 118–40.

Svoboda, Hedy 2001. "Joseph Haydn als 'Extra Musicus' der Wiener Hofmusikkapelle. Neue Funde zu seiner Biographie," *Musikblätter der Wiener Philharmoniker* 56: 116–23.

Szabolcsi, Bence 1956. "Exoticisms in Mozart," *M&L* 37/4: 323–32.

Szentesi, Edit 2013. "Eszterháza 18. századi leírásai [18th-century Descriptions of Eszterháza]" in Szentesi, Mentényi, and Simon (eds.) 165–229.

Szentesi, Edit, Klára Mentényi, and Anna Simon (eds.) 2013. *Kő kövön: Stein auf Stein. Dávid Ferenc 73. születésnapjára – Festschrift für Ferenc Dávid*. Budapest: Vince Kiadó.

Tank, Ulrich 1980. "Die Dokumente der Esterhazy-Archive zur fürstlichen Hofkapelle 1761–1770," *H-St* 4/3–4 (entire issue).

1981. "Studien zum Esterházyschen Hofmusik von etwa 1620 bis 1790." Ph.D. dissertation, University of Cologne; published in *Kölner Beiträge zur Musikforschung* 101. Regensburg: Gustav Bosse.

Taruskin, Richard 2005a. "Introduction: The History of What?" in Taruskin (ed.), *The Oxford History of Western Music*, vol. 1: *Music from the Earliest Notations to the Sixteenth Century*. Oxford University Press: xxi–xxx.

2005b. *The Oxford History of Western Music*, vol. 2: *The Seventeenth and Eighteenth Centuries*. Oxford University Press.

2014. "Agents and Causes and Ends, Oh My," JM 31/2, 272–93.
Taylor, Ian 2010. *Music in London and the Myth of Decline: From Haydn to the Philharmonic.* Cambridge University Press.
Temperley, David 2003. "End-Accented Phrases: An Analytical Exploration," *Journal of Music Theory* 47/1: 125–54.
  2008. "Hypermetrical Transitions," *Music Theory Spectrum* 30/2: 305–25.
Temperley, Nicholas 1984–87. *The London Pianoforte School 1766–1860: Clementi, Dussek, Cogan, Cramer, Field, Pinto, Sterndale Bennett, and Other Masters of the Pianoforte.* New York: Garland.
  1991. *Haydn: The Creation.* Cambridge University Press.
Thomson, George 1822. "Dissertation Concerning the National Melodies of Scotland" in George Thomson (ed.), *The Select Melodies of Scotland, Interspersed with Those of Ireland and Wales*, vol. 1. Edinburgh: G. Thomson.
Thormählen, Wiebke 2010. "Playing with Art: Musical Arrangements as Educational Tools in Van Swieten's Vienna," JM 27: 342–76.
Todd, R. Larry 1980. "Joseph Haydn and the *Sturm und Drang*: A Revaluation," *Music Review* 41/3: 172–96.
Tolley, Thomas 1992. "Music in the Circle of Sir William Jones: A Contribution to the History of Haydn's Early Reputation," M&L 73: 525–50.
  2001. *Painting the Cannon's Roar: Music, the Visual Arts and the Rise of an Attentive Public in the Age of Haydn, c. 1750 to c. 1810.* Aldershot: Ashgate.
  2003. "Exemplary Patience: Haydn, Hoppner and Mrs Jordon," *Imago Musicae* 20: 109–41.
  2013. "Caricatures by Henry William Bunbury in the Collection of Joseph Haydn" in Chesser and Jones (eds.) 22–58.
  2018. "My Language Is Understood All Over the World" in Reicher, Siegert, and Fuhrmann (eds.) 61–98.
Tomalin, Marcus 2016. "Literature and Time in the Eighteenth Century and the Romantic Period." *Oxford Handbooks Online*; www.oxfordhandbooks.com /view/10.1093/oxfordhb/9780199935338.001.0001/oxfordhb-9780199935 338-e-131 (accessed August 11, 2018).
Tovey, Donald Francis, 1935–39. *Essays in Musical Analysis*, 6 vols. Oxford University Press.
Triest, Johann 1997 [1801]. "Remarks on the Development of the Art of Music in Germany in the Eighteenth Century," trans. Susan Gillespie, in HWorld 321–94.
Tschischka, Franz 1843. *Die Metropolitankirche zu St. Stephan in Wien.* Vienna: C. Gerold.
Türk, Daniel Gottlob 1789. *Klavierschule, oder Anweisung zum Klavierspielen für Lehrer und Lernende.* Leipzig and Halle: Schwickert.
Tyson, Alan (ed.) 1982. *Beethoven Studies 3.* Cambridge University Press.
Tyson, Alan and H. C. Robbins Landon. 1964. "Who Composed Haydn's Op. 3?" MT 105: 506–7.
Ulm, Renate (ed.) 2007. *Haydns Londoner Symphonien. Enstehung – Deutung – Wirkung.* Kassel: Bärenreiter.
van Boer, Bertil 2018. "Undermining Independence: The English Political and Cultural Views of American during Haydn's London Sojourns," in Reicher, Siegert, and Fuhrmann (eds.) 39–60.

van Tour, Peter 2015. *Counterpoint and Partimento: Methods of Teaching Composition in Late Eighteenth-Century Naples.* Uppsala University.

Vécsey, Jenő 1960. *Haydn Compositions in the Music Collection of the National Széchényi Library, Budapest, Published on the Occasion of the 150th Anniversary of Haydn's Death (1809–1959).* Budapest: Publishing House of the Hungarian Academy of Sciences.

Voskuhl, Adelheid 2013. *Androids in the Enlightenment: Mechanics, Artisans, and Cultures of the Self.* University of Chicago Press.

Wald-Fuhrmann, Melanie 2010. "Ein Mittel wider sich selbst". *Melancholie in der Instrumentalmusik um 1800.* Kassel: Bärenreiter.

Waldoff, Jessica 1998. "Sentiment and Sensibility in *La vera costanza*" in *Haydn Studies* 70–119.

  2012. "Does Haydn Have a C-Minor Mood?" in Hunter and Will 158–86.

Waldura, Markus 2000. "Marpurg, Koch, und die Neubegründung des Taktbegriffs," *Musikforschung* 53/3: 237–53.

Walter, Horst 1970. "Haydn's Klaviere" H-St 2, 256–88. (Typescript translation by Judith S. Britt, held by National Museum of American History [Smithsonian Libraries]).

  1981. "On Haydn's Pupils" in Larsen, Serwer, and Webster (eds.) 60–63.

  1982. "Haydns Schüler" in Gerda Mraz, Gottfried Mraz, and Gerald Schlag (eds.), *Joseph Haydn in seiner Zeit. Eisenstadt, 20. Mai-26. Okt. 1982. Ausstellung,* 311–15. Eisenstadt: Amt der Burgenländischen Landesregierung.

  1985. "Haydn gewidmete Streichquartette" in Feder, Hüschen and Tank (eds.) 17–53.

Waltham-Smith, Naomi 2017. *Music and Belonging Between Revolution and Restoration.* Oxford University Press.

Weber, Gottfried 1817–21. *Versuch einer geordneten Theorie der Tonsetzkunst,* 3 vols. Mainz: B. Schotts Söhne.

Weber, Max 1968. "Die 'Objektivität' sozialwissenschaftlicher und sozialpolitischer Erkenntnis" Johannes Winkelmann (ed.) 145–85.

Weber, William 2004. "Overview of the Subject," in William Weber (ed.), *The Musician as Entrepreneur, 1700–1914: Managers, Charlatans, and Idealists.* Bloomington: Indiana University Press: 3–24.

  2008. *The Great Transformation of Musical Taste: Concert Programming from Haydn to Brahms.* Cambridge University Press.

Weber-Bockholdt, Petra 2005. "Komposition oder Begleitung: Ein Vergleich der Bearbeitungen Schottischen Lieder von Haydn und Beethoven," H-St 8: 401–12.

Webster, James 1974. "Towards a History of Viennese Chamber Music in the Early Classical Period," *JAMS* 27: 212–47.

  1979. "The Significance of Haydn's String Quartet Autographs for Performance Practice" in Christoph Wolff (ed.), *The String Quartets of Haydn. Mozart and Beethoven: Studies of the Autograph Manuscripts.* Harvard University Press: 62–98.

  1981. "When did Haydn Begin to Write 'Beautiful Melodies'?" in Larsen, Serwer, and Webster (eds.) 385–88.

  1984. "The Falling-Out Between Haydn and Beethoven: The Evidence of the Sources" in Lockwood and Benjamin (eds.) 3–45.

1990. "On the Absence of Keyboard Continuo in Haydn's Symphonies," EM 18: 599–608.

1991. *Haydn's "Farewell" Symphony and the Idea of Classical Style: Through-Composition and Cyclic Integration in His Instrumental Music.* Cambridge University Press.

1997. "The Creation, Haydn's Late Vocal Music, and the Musical Sublime" in HWorld 57–102.

1998a. "Haydn's Sacred Vocal Music and the Aesthetics of Salvation" in Haydn Studies 35–69.

1998b. "Haydn's Symphonies between Sturm und Drang and 'Classical Style': Art and Entertainment" in Haydn Studies 218–45.

2005a. "Haydn's Aesthetics" in *Cambridge Companion* 30–44.

2005b. "The Sublime and the Pastoral in *The Creation* and *The Seasons*" in *Cambridge Companion* 150–63.

2007. "The Rhetoric of Improvisation in Haydn's Keyboard Music" in Beghin and Goldberg 172–212.

2009. "Haydn's Sensibility," *Studia Musicologica* 51/1–2:13–27.

2010. "Ausbuilding," in H-L: 71–72.

2013. "Gibt es einen Spätstil bei Haydn? Die mehrstimmigen Gesänge als Fallstudie," H-St 10/3–4: 432–52.

Webster, James and Georg Feder 2001. "Haydn, Joseph," in *Grove Online*, https://doi.org/10.1093/gmo/9781561592630.article.44593 (accessed November 16, 2017).

Webster and Feder 2002: see Abbreviations (NG Haydn).

Weibel, Samuel 2006. *Die deutschen Musikfeste des 19. Jahrhunderts im Spiegel der zeitgenössischen musikalischen Fachpresse, mit inhaltsanalytisch erschlossenem Artikelverzeichnis auf CD-ROM.* Berlin [u.a.]: Edition Merseburger Band 1268.

Weinstein, Gregory Ellis 2013. "Creativity in the Mix: Collaboration and Contingency in Britain's Classical Music Recordings." Ph.D. dissertation, University of Chicago.

Weinzierl, Stefan 2002. *Beethovens Konzerträume. Raumakustik und symphonische Aufführungspraxis an der Schwelle zum bürgerlichen Zeitalter.* Frankfurt am Main: Erwin Bochinsk.

Weiskel, Thomas 1976. *The Romantic Sublime: Studies in the Structure and Psychology of Transcendence.* Baltimore: The Johns Hopkins University Press.

Werfel, Franz 1982 [1955]. *Cella oder die Überwinder. Versuch eines Romans.* Frankfurt am Main: S. Fischer.

Wheelock, Gretchen 1990. "Marriage à la Mode: Haydn's Instrumental Works 'Englished' for Voice and Piano," JM 8/3, 357–97.

1991. "Engaging Strategies in Haydn's Opus 33 String Quartets," *Eighteenth-Century Studies* 25/1: 1–30.

1992. *Haydn's Ingenious Jesting with Art: Contexts of Musical Wit and Humor.* New York: Schirmer.

1999. "Haydn's Keyboard Sonatas: Genre Instruments, and Players" in Parakilas (ed.) 113–120.

2003. "The 'Rhetorical Pause' and Metaphors of Conversation in Haydn's Quartets" in Georg Feder and Walter Reicher (eds.), *Haydn und das*

Streichquartett (Eisenstädter Haydn-Berichte 2), 67–88. Tutzing: Hans Schneider.

White, Harry 2013. "Johann Joseph Fux and the Musical Discourse of Servitude" in Erhardt (ed.) 11–22.

White, Jerry 2012. *London in the Eighteenth Century: A Great and Monstrous Thing*. London: Bodley Head.

Wiley, Christopher 2013. "Mythological Motifs in the Biographical Accounts of Haydn's Later Life" in Chesser and Jones (eds.) 195–211.

Wilker, Ulrich 2013. "Haydns 'letzte Oper'. Die Bearbeitung von L'isola disabitata im Jahr 1802," H-St 10/3, 453–66.

Will, Richard 1997. "When God Met the Sinner, and Other Dramatic Confrontations in Eighteenth-Century Instrumental Music," in M&L 78/2: 175–209.

  2002. *The Characteristic Symphony in the Age of Haydn and Beethoven*. Cambridge University Press.

  2004. "Pergolesi's Stabat Mater and the Politics of Feminine Virtue," MQ 87/3: 570–614.

  2012. "Haydn Invents Scotland" in Hunter and Will 44–74.

Williams, Raymond 1973. *The Country and the City*. New York: Oxford University Press.

  1985 (rev. edn.). *Keywords: A Vocabulary of Culture and Society*. Oxford University Press.

Winkelmann, Johannes (ed.) 1968. *Gesammelte Aufsätze zur Wissenschaftslehre*, 3rd edn. Tübingen: Mohr.

Winkler, Gerhard J. 2005 "Notizen zum Thema: Haydn und die 'Volksmusik', 'Zigeunertrio', 'Gott erhalte' und 'Sauschneider-Capriccio'." *Österreichische Musikzeitschrift* 60: 34–43.

  (ed.) 2006. *Musik der Juden im Burgenland*. Eisenstadt: Wissenschaftliche Arbeiten aus dem Burgenland.

  2009a. "'Gott erhalte' – Rossini – Paris 1825. Hymne des europäischen Legitimismus," Musicorum 7: 37–46.

  2009b. "Zur Geschichte des Haydn-Hauses in Eisenstadt" in Gabriel and Winkler (eds.) 138–43.

  2011. "'Volksmusik' und 'Kunstmusik'. Aspekte einer problematischen Beziehung am Beispiel von Joseph Haydns 'Sauschneider'-Capriccio," in Plöckinger-Walenta and Winkler (eds.) 339–54.

Winsor, Justin (ed.) 1881. *The Memorial History of Boston*, vol. 4. Boston: James R. Osgood and Company.

Winter, Robert 1989. "The Bifocal Close and the Evolution of the Viennese Classical Style," JAMS 42: 275–337.

Wittgenstein, Ludwig 2009. *Philosophical Investigations*, 4th edn, ed. P. M S. Hacker and Joachim Schulte. Chichester: Blackwell Publishing.

Wollenberg, Susan 2001. *Music at Oxford in the Eighteenth and Nineteenth Centuries*. Oxford University Press.

Wollenbeg, S. and Simon McVeigh (eds.) 2004. *Concert Life in Eighteenth-Century Britain*. Aldershot: Ashgate.

Woodfield, Ian 1994. "Haydn's Symphonies in Calcutta," M&L 75/1: 141–43.

2000. "John Bland: London Retailer of the Music of Haydn and Mozart," M&L 81/2: 210–44.

Woodmansee, Martha 1994. *The Author, Art, and the Market: Rereading the History of Aesthetics*. New York: Columbia University Press.

Woszczyk, Wieslaw 2009/11. "Virtual Acoustics," liner note to Beghin (2009), 56–59 and (2011): 64–67.

Wraxall, Nathaniel William 1799–1800. *Memoirs of the Court of Berlin, Dresden, Vienna, and Warsaw, in the Years 1777–1779*, 2 vols. London: A. Strahan.

Young, David (ed.) 2000. *Haydn, the Innovator: A New Approach to the String Quartets*. Todmorden: Arc Music.

Young, Edward 1759. *Conjectures on Original Composition in a Letter to the Author of Sir Charles Grandison*. Dublin: Printed for P. Wilson.

Zacharasiewicz, Waldemar 2018. "Bilder der Neuen Welt im deutschsprachigen Raum im späten 18. Jahrhundert" in Reicher, Siegert, and Fuhrmann (eds.) 25–38.

Zagorski-Thomas, Simon 2014. *The Musicology of Record Production*. Cambridge University Press.

Zaslaw, Neal 1976–77. "Towards the Revival of the Classical Orchestra," *Proceedings of the Royal Musical Assocation* 103: 158–87.

(ed.) 1989a. *The Classical Era: From the 1740s to the End of the 18th Century*. New Jersey: Prentice Hall.

1989b. *Mozart's Symphonies: Context, Performance Practice, Reception*. Oxford: Clarendon Press.

2014. "Haydn's Orchestras and His Orchestration to 1779, with an Excursus on the Times-of-Day Symphonies" in Hunter and Will 302–21.

Zechmeister, Gustav 1971. *Die Wiener Theater nächst der Burg und nächst dem Kärntnerthor von 1747 bis 1776*. Vienna: Böhlau.

Zelter, Carl 1798. "Bescheidene Anfragen an die modernsten Komponisten und Virtuosen," *Allgemeine musikalische Zeitung*, 1 col. 141–44, 152–55.

General Index

Note: Page numbers in **bold** refer to main entries and to authors of main entries. Page numbers in *italics* refer to figures, tables, and musical examples.

Abel, Carl Friedrich (1723–1787), **197–98**, 302
Abingdon, Willoughby Bertie, 4th Earl of (1740–1799), 197, 201, 232, 253, 405
Absolute music, 149, 154–55, 174
Abrams, M. H. (1912–2015), 213
Accademien, 89, 111, 112, 185, 231, 234, 252, 281, 286, 287, 288, 351, 356, 362, 396
"Acht Sauschneider müssen seyn," 36, 37, 180, 212
acoustics, 59, 89, 137, 186, 261, 283, 300, *see also* Performance Spaces
actor-network theory, 244–45
Adams, John (1735–1826), 10
Adams, Samuel (1722–1803), 10
Adams, Sarah, 61
Adolph, Anton (fl. 1760s), 245
Adorno, Theodor W. (1903–1969), 144
advertisements, 17, 61, 311, 399
Aesthetic Idealism, 149
Aesthetics, **1–3**, 19, 156–57
  ancien régime, 21, 23
  correspondence and, 71–72
  Enlightenment and, 103
  exoticism and, 117–18
  gender and, 136
  humor and, 146
  Idealism and, 150
  melody and, 209, 210
  mimesis and, 213
  nature and, 238
  place and, 297
  politics and, 310
  reception and, 325
  theatrical, 359
  topics and, 379
  travel and, 386
  variation and, 389
Africa, 262
Agawu, Kofi, 348, 382
agency, 245
Aging, **3–4**, 205, 251
  finances and, 92
  reception and, 324
  sensibility and, 99

Albrechtsberger, Johann Georg (1736–1809), 7, 25, 64, 138, 358, 396
Aldwell, Edward, 375
d'Alembert, Jean le Rond (1717–1783), xv
alla turca, 117, 118
Allanbrook, Wye Jamison (1943–2010), 154–55, 157, 214, 359, 370, 371
Allgemeine deutsche Bibliothek, 312
Allgemeine musikalische Zeitung, 14, 20, 81, 145, 160, 176–77, 208, 255, 311, 322, 325, 406
allusions, 252
Almanach Musical (1775–1783), 312
Alsergrund (Vienna), 51
Al-Taee, Nasser, 152
Altomonte, Andreas (1699–1780), 49
Alvarez de Toledo, Duke of Alba and Marques of Villafranca (1756–1796), 113
Amateurs, **4–7**
  audiences, 16
  circulation and, 53
  counterpoint and, 74
  disability and, 89
  folk song settings and, 122
  gender and, 135
  in Vienna, 392
  large ensembles and, 186
  listed in London notebooks, 65
  musical societies and, 229
  performance by, 259
  place and, 302
  publications and, 254
  publishing and, 172
  reception and, 324
American Musicological Society, 235
American Revolution, 192–94, 236, 310, *see also* War
Americas, The, **7–15**
  Enlightenment and, 364
  German immigrant community, 229
  Haydn's perceptions of, 9–10
  instruments and, 262
  musical societies in, 232–33
  operas dealing with, 192–94

451

GENERAL INDEX

Americas, The (cont.)
  people and networks, 255
  perceptions of Haydn, 10–15
  place and, 306
  press and, 315
  reception, 327–28
Amsterdam, 317, 392
Anacreontic, 308
Anacreontic Society, 231, 305
ancien régime, 21, 22–24, 78, 100, 224, 250, 309, 386
Andrew, Edward, 250
Anfossi, Pasquale (1727–1797), 365, 399
Angermüller, Rudolph, 257
Angiolini, Gaspare (1731–1803), 367
Anglicans, 23
Anlage (plan, layout, disposition), 67, 127–28
Anson-Cartwright, Mark, 376
Antes, John (1740–1811), 9
Antonio I, Prince of Monaco (1661–1731), 178
Apollo (Greek god), 33, 299
appoggiaturas, 400, 401
Apponyi, Count Anton Georg (1751–1817), 80, 86, 253
archives. *See* Collections and Archives
arias, 64, 130, 247, 335, 359, 360, 364, 365, 399, *see also* Vocal Coaching and Rehearsal
Ariosto, Ludovico (1474–1533), 194
aristocracy, 16, 52, 117, 197, 250, 396, *see also* Courts
aristocratic patronage, 27, 175, 236, 245, *see also* patronage
Aristotle (384–322 BCE), 151
Arnold, Samuel (1740–1802), 32, 54, 232
arrangements, 6, 13, 54, 62, 86, 111, 115, 172, 202, 311, *see also* Circulation
Artaria, 5, 6, 17, 56, 61–62, 86, 92, 94, 115, 148, 172–73, 176, 180, 254–55, 258, 260, 263, 264, 266, 268, 270, 271, 272, 278, 301, 302, 319, 352, 383, 399, 404
  circulation and, 52–54
  correspondence with, 71
Artaria, Carlo (1747–1808), 318–19
articulation, 178, 271, 349, 400, 401
Ashe, Andrew (c.1758–1838), 198
Ashkenazic Jews, 42
Aspelmayr, Franz (1728–1786), 264
Astarita, Gennaro (1749–1805), 399
astronomy, 104, 162, 345–47, 373
atlases, 382–83
Audiences and Publics, **15–18**
  adapting works for, 66, 70
  amateurs and, 5
  commerce and the market, 62
  disability and, 89
  Enlightenment and, 104

exoticism and, 118
folk song settings and, 121
London, 54, 199
melodies and, 213
multiple, 254
musical education and, 120
musical societies and, 229
people and networks, 244
performance spaces and, 282
place and, 297
recordings and, 90
students and, 357
theater and, 359
war and, 404
Auenbrugger, Caterina von (1755–1825), 6, 62, 92, 389
Auenbrugger, Joseph Leopold von (1722–1809), 345
Auenbrugger, Marianna von (1759–1782), 6, 62, 92, 135, 389
Auersberg (Auersperg), Prince Karl Josef (1720–1800), 80
Augarten, 396
Augsburg University library, 57
Ausarbeitung (elaboration), 67
Austria, 10, 41
  Lower Austria, 116, 280
  Upper Austria, 97
Austrian melodies, 212
Austrians, 40
Austrian–British relationships, 53, 200, 207, 310
Austro-German compositional style, 236
Austro-Hungarian Haydn Orchestra, 59, 89
authenticity, 45, 47, 52, 94, 147, 324
autobiographical sketch, 173, 255, 309
autographs, 46, 56–58, 68, 105, 205, 206, 251, 332

Bach, Carl Philip Emmanuel (1714–1788), 5, 21, 27, 61, 64, 87, 97, 103, 150, 159, 166, 204, 225, 230, 266, 269, 271–72, 321, 354, 378, 385
  Heilig, 32
  Versuch über die wahre Art das Clavier zu spielen, 120, 166
Bach, Johann Christian (1735–1782), 21, 197–98, 302
Bach, Johann Sebastian (1685–1750), 21, 94, 95, 397
  Art of Fugue, 4
Bach-Abel Concerts, 188, 197–98, 302
Badini, Carlo Francesco (c.1735 – c.1810), 194, 367–68
  L'anima del filosofo, 194, 304, 310, 367, 368
Badiou, Alain, 164
Badley, Allan, 64
Bagatelle pavilion, 109
Baillot, Pierre (1771–1842), 234
Baker, Benjamin Franklin (1811–1889), 13

452

Baker, Nancy, 103, 157, 350
Balkan, 117
ballads, 41, 44, 54
balles de la Cour impériale, 112
ballets, 112, 113, 367
Banks, Sir Joseph (1743–1820), 385
Banti, Brigida Giorgi (1757–1806), 16, 65, 401
Barker-Benfield, G. J., 98
Barmherzige Brüder (Brothers Hospitallers), 50–51, 169, 182, 183, 184, 301, 395
Barolsky, Daniel, **332–34**
Baroque, 21, 120, 131, 153, 157, 222
Barrett-Ayres, Reginald (1920–1981), 95
Bartha, Dénes (1908–1993), 73–74, 95, 191, 265
Barthélémon, François-Hippolyte (1741–1808), 121
Barthélemy, Jean-Jacques (1716–1795), 386
Bartoli, Cecilia, 367
Bartolozzi, Francesco (1727–1815), 148
Bartolozzi, Gaetano Stefano (1757–1821), 301
Bartolozzi, Therese. *See* Jansen-Bartolozzi, Therese (c.1770–1843)
baryton, 5, 78, 156, 179, 217, 232, 248, 299, 362
Basilica in Frauenkirchen, 59
Bath (England), 238, 386, 402
Batteux, Charles (1713–1780)
  Beaux-arts réduits à un meme principe, 213
Batthyány family, 281
Battle of Aboukir Bay, 404
Bauman, Thomas, 321
Bavaria, 41
Bayley, Isabel, 368
Bazzana, Kevin, 333
beat, 340, *see also* Rhythm and Meter, Time, Performance
Beaumarchais, Pierre-Augustin Caron de (1732–1799), 366
Beautiful, **19–21**
  aesthetics and, 1–2, 156–58
  amateurs and, 5
  gender and, 136
  humor and, 145
  ideas and, 152
  line of beauty, 20
  melody and, 210
  nature and, 161, 238
  press and, 313
  religion and, 340
  sublimity and, 353
Becker, Howard, 245, 247
Becker, John Joseph (1886–1961), 15
Beecham, Sir Thomas (1879–1961), 333
Beer, Axel, 61, 91, 255
Beethoven, Ludwig van (1770–1827), 27, 121, 171, 317, 371–72
  audiences, 18
  counterpoint and, 358

courts and, 78
cyclic integration, 82–83
editions, 94
Fifth Symphony, 82, 84, 140, 224, 326
finances, 92
folk song settings and, 122
gender studies and, 137
harmony and, 143
Haydn and, 4, 149, 206, 252, 253, 309, 324, 328, 374, 385
Haydn, works dedicated to, 252, 323
Haydn's tutelage of, 66, 322, 357–58
Idealism and, 150–51, 152
Materialien zum Kontrapunkt, 358
melancholy and, 87
Missa solemnis, 144
musical societies and, 230, 233–34, 252
Ninth Symphony, 164
on thoroughbass, 142
Pastoral Symphony, 239
patronage and, 250
Piano Concerto in C major, Op. 15, 283, 291
promoters of, 205
Rasumovsky Quartets, 225
reception, 145, 329–30
relationships and friendships, 334
social background, 21
sublimity and, 158, 355
third-period style, 4
variations and, 389, 391
Vienna and, 399
Wellington's Victory, 217
Beghin, Tom, 6, 17, 40, 73, 74, 85, 89–90, 137, 166, 179, 180, 247, **258–279**, 273, 330, 351, 400–1
Bellini, Alice, 401
Benavente, Countess María Josefa Alonso Pimentel Téllez-Girón (1751–1834), 114
Benedictine monastery of Montserrat, 113
Berardi, Angelo (c.1636–1694), 358
Berg, Darrell, 97
Berger, Karol, 161, 373
Bergkirche, Eisenstadt, 50–51, 110, 182, 183, 284, 299, 305, 383
Berkel, Klaas, 346
Berlin, 173, 195, 256
Berlinische musikalische Zeitung (newspaper), 314
Berlioz, Hector (1803–1869), 326, 367
Bernardon. *See* Kurz, Johann Joseph Felix von (Kurz-Bernardon) (fl. 1751–1784)
Bernhard, Christoph (1628–1692), 358
Bernstein, Leonard (1918–1990), 15
Berry, Wallace (1928–1991), 330
Bertali, Antonio (1605–1669)
  La Zenobia di Radamisto, 203
Bertati, Giovanni (1736–1815)
  Il convitato di pietra (Don Giovanni), 192
Bertoli, Bruno, 195
Bertoni, Ferdinando (1725–1813)

453

Bertoni, Ferdinando (1725–1813) (cont.)
  Orfeo ed Euridice, 365
Bertuch, Friedrich, 373
Berwald, Johan Fredrik (1787–1861), 190
Bessenyei, György (1747–1811)
  Az eszter-házi vígasságok, 109
Bethlehem, Pennsylvania, 306
Bianchi, Francesco (1752–1810)
  Il disertore, 365
Bianchi, Joseph Anton von (fl.1780s), 134
Biba, Otto, 92, 191, 192
Bible, 184, 195, 354
Bibliothèque musicale, 255
Bicknell, Alexander (?–1796)
  Alfred, King of the Anglo-Saxons, 217, 405–6
Bienfait, Albert (fl.1770s), 366
Bildung, 26, 53
Billington, Elizabeth (c.1765–1818), 65, 72
bimodality, 376
biographical sketch. *See* autobiographical sketch
Biography and Identity, **21–32**
  ancien régime, 22–24
  canonization, 31–32
  Christian names, 168
  disability and, 89
  English, 197
  Enlightenment and, 24–27
  iconography and, 148
  ideas and, 153
  institutions and, 167
  musical materials and, 223
  people and networks, 245, 252, 256
  reception and, 321, 324, 325
  sensibility and, 100, 158
  social contexts, 27–30
Birchall (publisher), 94
Bland, John (c.1750–c.1840), 33, 53, 94, 148, 175, 178, 201, 302, 303, 319
Blier-Carruthers, Amy, 334
Blume, Friedrich (1883–1975), 94, 330
Boccherini, Giovanni Gastone (1742–1798), 195
Boccherini, Luigi (1743–1805), 195, 225, 233
Boerhaave, Herman (1668–1738), 346
Bohak, Johann (1755–1805), 206
Bohemia, 57, 169–70
Bohlman, Philip V., **34–44**, 44, 297
Boileau, Nicolas (1636–1711), 354
Boisjoli, Eloise, 227, **376–382**
Bolcom, William, 15
Bolivia, 14
Bologna, 112
Bologna Porta, Metilde (fl.1768–1790), 64
Bologne, Joseph, Chevalier de Saint-Georges (1744–1799), 187
Bombet, 325, *See* Stendhal, pen-name for Marie-Henri Beyle (1783–1742)
Bon, Anna (c.1739–?), 135

Bon, Girolamo (fl.1735–1770), 247
Bonds, Mark Evan, 1, 25, 26, 125, 139, 145, 149, 237, 330, 348, 354, 387
Bonn, 253, 357, 385
Bonno, Giuseppe (1711–1788), 396
  Isaaco, figura del Redentore, 397
Book of Tobias (Tobit), 195
Boone, marK, 273
Born, Ignaz von (1742–1791), 345, 394
borrowed tunes, 316
Bossler, Heinrich Philipp (1744–1812), 269, 389–90, 391
Boston Academy of Music, 13
Boston Handel and Haydn Society Collection of Church Music (1822), 13
Boston Public Library, Music Department Special Collections, 13
Bote & Bock (publisher), 94
Botstein, Leon, 58, 145, 149
Bourdieu, Pierre (1930–2002), 27, 91
bourgeois society, 16, 22, 27, 78, 117
bows. *See* violin bows
Boyer (publisher), 28
Bracht, Hans-Joachim, 351
Brahms, Johannes (1833–1897), 44, 57, 327, 390
  "Haydn Variations," 94
Brand, Carl Maria, 133
Brandes, Charlotte "Minna" (1765–1788), 136, 138
Brandl, Johann (1760–1837), 251
brass instruments, 178
Bratislava, 41, 79, 281, 360
Braunschweig, Karl, 132
Brazil, 14
Breitkopf & Härtel (publisher), 3, 17, 31, 32, 46, 57, 86, 92, 93–94, 176, 206, 254–56, 319–20, 324, 367
Brévan, Bruno, 231
Bridgetower, George Polgreen (1778–1860), 356
Briefkultur, 73
Bristol (England), 386
British Library, 89
British "national song" melodies, 121
Broadwood, John, 303
Brook, Barry S. (1918–1997), 61
Broschi, Carlo (1705–1782), 138
Brotherhood of the Santa Cueva, 114
Brown, A. Peter (1944–2003), 125, 135, 189–91, 231, 308
Brown, Bruce Alan, 103
Brown, Marshall, 308
Broyles, Michael, 13, 233
Bruckner, Anton (1824–1896), 97, 118
Brunetti, Gaetano (1744–1798), 224
Bryan, Paul, 178
Buch, David J., 182
Buda (Hungary), 306
Budday, Wolfgang, 125, 131, 144
Buenos Aires, 14

buffo style. *See* opera, comic (*buffa*)
Bülow, Hans von (1830–1894), 326–27
Bunbury, Henry (1750–1811), 204
Burgenland, **34–44**
　commemorations and festivals, 59
　ethnic diversity, 116
　folk song settings and, 122
　Jewish culture and, 182
　Jewish music in, 42–44
　map of, 35
　multiculturalism, 40–42
　musical contact zones, 44
　people and networks, 245
　place and, 297
　theater and, 360
Bürger, Gottfried August (1747–1794), 307–8
Burgtheater, 120, 171, 185, 189, 190, 280, 281, 283, 284, 306, 363
Burke, Edmund (1729–1797), 1, 157, 164, 207–8, 210, 250, 350
　A Philosophical Enquiry into the Origin of Our Ideas of the Sublime and Beautiful, 19, 310, 354, 370
Burmeister, Klaus, 91
Burney, Charles (1726–1814), 49, 65, 175, 191, 199, 202, 303, 305, 336, 345
Burnham, Scott, 154, 371
　Beethoven Hero, 330
Burns, Robert (Rabbie) (1759–1796), 121
Burstein, Poundie, 125
Burton, John (1710–1771), 346
Busby, Thomas (1755–1838), 303
businessperson, Haydn as, 27–30, 71, 254
BWV (Bach Werke Verzeichnis) numbers, 45, 47

"cabinet," Haydn's, 204–5
cadential scheme/schemata, 126, 144
Cádiz (Spain), 114–15, 339, 383
caesuras, 76, 126, 167, 209
Cahan, J. L., 43
Cairo, 384
Caldara, Antonio (1670–1736), 50, 119, 297
calendrical reforms, 161
Callas, Maria (1923–1977), 367
Callcott, John Wall (1766–1821), 232, 357
Calzabigi, Raniero (1714–1795), 194, 364, 365
Cambini, Giuseppe (1746–1825), 112
Cambridge (England), 386
Campe, Joachim Heinrich (1746–1818)
　Erste Sammlung merkwürdiger Reisebeschreibungen für die Jugend, 9, 385
Campo, Marquis del (1725–1803), 256
canonization, 31–32, 138
capitalism. *See* Commerce and the Market
Caplin, William, 125, 126–27
Carlos III of Spain (1716–1788), 114
Carlos IV of Spain (1748–1819), 114

Caroline of Brunswick, Princess (1768–1821), 80
Carpani, Giuseppe (1752–1825), 24, 31, 65, 112, 142, 209, 218, 242, 324–25, 350, 387, 399
Carter, Elliott (1908–2012), 351
Carus-Verlag (publisher), 95
Casals, Pablo (1876–1973), 15
Cassaro, James, 11
cassatios, 179
castrati, 401–2
Catalogues, Worklists, Nachlass, **45–47**
　editions, 95
　inventory of Haydn's possessions, 46, 382
　marketplace and, 61
　monuments and memorializing, 217
　musical materials and, 223
　reception and, 327
catch (genre), 231
Catholic Church. *See* Church, Religion and Spiritual Beliefs
Catholic Enlightenment, 101, 105, 160, 394, *see also* Enlightenment, Religious Enlightenment
celebrity, 21, 66, 80, 139, 147, 249, 254, 255, 315, 406
Celestini, Federico, 25, **118–120**, 251, 255, **356–359**
Celtic "Ossian" epics, 122
censorship, 171, 394
Central European music, 117
Centre for History and Analysis of Recorded Music (CHARM) Initiative, 333
Centre for Interdisciplinary Research in Music Media and Technology (CIRMMT), 89
Český Krumlov, 363
Champée, Boniface Charles (fl.1757–1775), 52, 398
Chandler, James, 102
Chapin, Keith, **138–141**, 156, 158, 159, **352–355**
characteristic symphonies, 154
"characteristic" works, 315
charity, 92–93
　bequests in Haydn's will, 73
　biography and, 100
　concerts, 92–93, 171, 234
　performance by "charity children," 51, 99, 402
　song settings as, 121
Charles VI, Holy Roman Emperor (1685–1740), 119, 382
Charlotte of Mecklenburg-Strelitz, Queen of England (1744–1818), 80
Chen, Jen-yen, 23, **77–81**, 160, 161–62, 169, **337–340**
Cherubini, Luigi (1760–1842), 4, 204, 206, 234, 251, 257

455

GENERAL INDEX

Chesser, Richard, 196
Chevalier de Saint-Georges. *See* Bologne, Joseph, Chevalier de Saint-Georges (1744–1799)
Chiari, Pietro (1712–1785), 192
chiaroscuro, 355, *see also* light and shade
Chile, 14
China, 385
Chinese Pavilion, 109, 118, 300
Chopin, Frédéric (1810–1849), 326
Christensen, Thomas, 103, 157
chronology, xvii, 45, 47
Chua, Daniel, 146
Church, **47–51**, *see also* Religion and Spiritual Beliefs
  aging and, 3
  Burgenland and, 40
  collections and archives, 57
  commemorations and festivals in, 59
  conversion and, 184
  counterpoint and, 76
  education and, 95–97, 118
  Eisenstadt and, 110
  Europe and, 113
  form and, 125
  institution of, 168
  musical styles, 248–49
  nature and, 238
  place and, 296
  programmatic elements and, 316
  teaching and students, 356
  Vienna and, 394
Cimarosa, Domenico (1749–1801), 114, 300, 399
  Giannina e Bernardone, 365
Circulation, **51–55**
  amateurs and, 6
  audiences and, 17
  biography and, 28–30
  commerce and the market, 61
  in Europe, 111–12, 115
  in the Americas, 11
  London and, 201–2
  mediation and, 156
  monasteries and, 51
  monuments and memorializing, 217
  people and networks, 250
  place and, 298
  printed works, 172
  reception and, 321
  Vienna and, 397, 399
city, as place, 301–5
Clam-Gallas family, 57
Clark, Caryl, 43, 80, 117, 118, 120, **182–184**, 192, 194, 197, **244–257**, 310, **359–372**
Clark, Katelyn, **85–86**, 252
class. *See* social class
"Classical Haydn," 153
Classical style, 21, 131, 224, 227, 233, 326, 329–30, 376, 389, *see also* Viennese Classical Style

Clement, Franz (1780–1842), 65
Clementi & Broderip, 202
Clementi, Muzio (1752–1832), 17, 53, 65, 148, 198, 209, 224, 391
Coe, Richard N., 350
Cole, Malcolm S. (1936–2013), 187
Collection complette des Quatuors d'Haydn, 93, 319, 357, *see also Oeuvres complettes de Joseph Haydn*
Collection complette des Sonates de Piano d'Haydn, 93, 357
Collections and Archives, **55–58**
  catalogues, 46
  correspondence in, 73
  discography and, 89
  Esterházy, 46, 280
  Europe and, 111, 113–14
  festivals and, 59
  Moravian Music Foundation, 11, 57
  musical societies, 234
collective activity, 245
colonialism, 262, 306
Coltellini, Marco (1719–1777)
  Piramo e Tisbe, 191
Comédie Française, 112
comet events, 345
comic mode, 378, 380, *see also* opera, comic (*buffa*)
commedia dell'arte, 36, 192, 360, 366
Commemorations and Festivals, **58–61**, 366
  American, 7
  court and, 299
  Eszterháza and Eisenstadt, 111
  reception and, 328, 331
Commerce and the Market, **61–62**
  audiences and, 17
  biography and, 22
  catalogues and, 46
  circulation and, 52
  courts and, 80
  dedications and, 86
  European, 113
  finances and, 92
  genius and, 140
  in Europe, 115
  institutions and, 167, 172
  London and, 199
  maps and, 383
  patronage and, 250
  place and, 296
  politics and, 311
  programmatic elements and, 316
  publishers and, 318
  reception and, 321
  theories on, 102
  variations and, 389
  Vienna and, 392
Communist era, 109
companionship, 73, *see also* Relationships and Friendships
componieren, 67–70

456

composer's "voice," 159
Composers and Music Professionals, 4, 22, **63–66**, 252–54, 385
  amateurs and, 6
  biographies, 176
  correspondence and, 72
  courts and, 79, 170
  education, 97
  experiential learning, 119
  gender and, 135
  gifts given to, 205
  in London, 197
  in Vienna, 395
  libretti and, 191
  people and networks, 244
  place and, 300
  portraits of, 147
  reception, 321
  relationships and friendships, 336
Compositional Process, **67–70**, 71, 159, 261
  aesthetics and, 1
  counterpoint and, 75
  cyclic integration and, 82
  form and, 125
  gender and, 135
  genius and, 139
  improvisation, 166
  melody and, 209
  musical materials and, 223–24
  posterity and, 32
  self-reflexivity and, 348
  sociability and, 351
  theater and, 360
  travel and, 388
  variation and, 389
compositional training. See Teaching and Students
Concentus Musicus Wien, 59
Concert de la Loge Olympique, 134, 231
Concert des Amateurs, 231
concert organizations, 174, 175, 229
Concert Spirituel (Paris), 13, 111, 187, 231, 302, 314
Concerts of Antient Music, 305
Congress of Vienna, 406
connoisseurs, 5, 7, 16, 17, 229, 265
Conservatoire (Paris), 177, 257, 356
Conservatorio de Madrid, 114
contemporaries. See Reception, Contemporary
contract. See employment contract
contredanse topic, 118
convents, 48, 115
Cook, Captain James (1728–1779), 9, 385, 385, 387
Cook, Nicholas, 333
copyists, 52, 55, 245, 336
copyright laws, 52, 61, 140
Corelli, Arcangelo (1653–1713), 178
Coreth, Anna, 168, 337
Correspondence and Notebooks, 22, **70–74**

aesthetics and, 1
commerce and, 61
composers and music professionals in, 65
editions, 95
folk song settings and, 122
iconography and, 148
London, 31, 46, 174, 238, 253, 305, 340, 385, 402, 403
melancholy and, 207
people and networks, 254, 256
publishing and, 320
reception and, 328
relationships and friendships, 335
sensibility and, 100
travel and exploration, 386
Corri & Dussek (publisher), 54, 62, 319
Corri, (Miss) Sophia Giustina (1775–1847), 198
Corri, Domenico (1746–1825), 53, 61, 319
cosmopolitanism. See Nationalism and Cosmopolitanism
Counterpoint, 50, 69, **74–77**, 197, 261, 358, 380
  Beethoven's exercises, 66
  education in, 356
  form and, 127
  harmony and, 142
  lessons in, 119
  musical materials and, 228
  topics and, 380
Counter-Reformation, 118, 168
Couperin, François (1668–1733), 214
  "La Distraite" (The Distracted One), 214
  "Le Rossignol en amour" (The Nightingale in Love), 214
  "Les Moulins à Vent" (The Windmills), 214
Court and Private Life in the Time of Queen Charlotte, 303
Court of St. James (London), 80
Court Theatre, Vienna, 394–96
Courts, 21, 62, **77–81**, 169–71, 175, 309, *see also* Eszterháza
  aging and, 4
  audiences and, 15
  church and, 96, 249
  correspondence and, 72
  dedications and, 85
  exoticism and, 118
  finances and, 91
  in Vienna, 392
  monuments and memorializing, 217
  performance and, 261
  place and, 296, 298–301
  Wallnerstrasse palace, 106
Covent Garden, 197, 306
Cowart, Georgia J., 97
Cramer, Wilhelm (1746–1799), 65, 148, 197–98, 357
Cramer's Magazin der Musik, 6

457

Cramm, Tobias, 261
creativity, 79, 87, 139, 140, 158–59, 166, 167, 218, 230, 245, 334, 359, 380, *see also* Genius
Crèvecoeur, J. Hector St. John de (1735–1813)
 "Letters from an American Farmer," 9
Crews, C. Daniel, 9
Cristofori, Bartolomeo (1655–1731), 180
Croatian melodies, 36, 42, 117, 212, 328, 390
Croll, Gerhard, 81
cross-dressed characters, 182, 246, *see also* trouser roles
Crotch, William (1775–1847), 1–2, 232
Crown and Anchor Tavern, 231, 305
Crumb, George, 15
cultural capital, 252
cultural diversity. *See* diversity
cultural hero status, 80
Cunningham, John (1729–1773), 54
Cuyler, Louise E. (1908–1998), 376
Cyclic Integration, **81–84**
 ideas and, 154
 musical materials and, 218, 224–26
 programmatic elements and, 317
Czech Republic, 280
Czernin, Count Johann Rudolf (1757–1845), 80

Da Ponte, Lorenzo (1749–1838), 192, 365
Dack, James, 97
Dahlhaus, Carl (1928–1989), 131–32, 143
Daily Advertiser (New York), 315
Dallos, Márton, 247, 282
Dance, George (1741–1825), 148
Daniel, William (1769–1837), 148
Danube River, 392
Darcy, Warren, 88, 125–31
Darwin, Erasmus (1731–1802)
 "The Loves of the Plants," 346
Das gelehrte Oesterreich ("Learned Austria"), 173, 255
Daube, Johann Friedrich (1730–1797), 389
 Der Generalbass in drei Accorden, 142–43
 Der musikalische Dilettant, 75
Dávid, Ferenc, 371
Davide, Giacomo (1750–1830), 369
Davison, Alan, **147–149**, 200
Day, James, 145, 213
Day-O'Connell, Sarah, **7–15**, 20–21, **86–89**, 98, **135–37**, 201, 210, 306, 308–9, 330, 333, 346, 373, 400
death (concept), 3, 98, 136, 194, 216, 307, 308, 315, 330, 370
death, Haydn's, 46, 51, 56, 57, 284, 337
Debussy, Claude (1862–1918), 327
Dedicatees, 31, **85–86**, 173, 251–52, 357
 amateurs, 4
 courts and, 77
 gender and, 6, 137, 391
 Mozart to Haydn, 65, 336
 people and networks, 244, 252, 254, 256
 publishers and, 62
 sociability and, 351
 variations and, 390–91
 works dedicated to Haydn, 322
deformations (in sonata form), 88
Deism, 338–40
Delacroix, Joseph (fl.1790s), 8
Deldevez, Édouard-Marie-Ernest (1817–1897), 234
Dello Joio, Norman (1913–2008), 15
Dennis, John (1658–1734)
 The Grounds of Criticism on Poetry, 354
Der musikalische Dilettant, 75
Des Knaben Wunderhorn (Arnim and Brentano 1806/1808), 43
Destouches, Franz Seraph von (1772–1844), 357
Deutsch, Otto Erich (1883–1967), 94
Deutsch, Walter, 36, 40
Deutsche (dance), 380
Deutschkreuz, 41
Devienne, François (1759–1803), 177
Diabelli, Anton (1781–1858), 358
Diario de Madrid, 113
Dichtler, Barbara (? – 1776), 246
Dichtler, Leopold (? – 1799), 79, 246
Dictionnaire de musique (Rousseau), xv
Diderot, Denis (1713–1784), xv–xvi, 239, 366
 Paradox of the Actor, 258
"Die Jüdin" (The Jewish Woman), 43–44
Diergarten, Felix, **67–70**, **74–77**, 125, 130, 142, 223, 228, 399
Dies, Albert Christoph (1755–1822), 3–4, 24, 31–32, 51, 67, 91–92, 96, 99–100, 147, 189, 207, 209, 218, 317, 324–25, 336, 349, 379–80, 385, 399, 402
Dietrich, Thomas, 137
Dietzl, Joseph (1719–1777), 248
Díez, Marcelino, 114
difference. *See* Exoticism
Dilettant, 4–5, *see also* Amateurs
diplomats, 256–57
Disability, **86–89**, 99, 135
 Dis/ability Studies, 87–89
Discography, **89–90**, 263, 333, *see also* Recording
dispositio, 67
Dittersdorf, Carl Ditters von (1739–1799), 64, 65, 173, 184, 192, 252, 317, 336, 363, 396, 397, 399
 Das rote Käppchen, 184
Dittrich, Marie-Agnes, 373
diversity, 34, 40–42, 116, 163
Diwald, Franz (fl.1769–1790), 182, 247
Doblinger (publisher), 95
Dolan, Emily I., **152–165**, 225–26, **241–243**, 330, 348, 403
Dolinszky, Miklós, 95
Dolní Lukavice, 280
Dragonetti, Domenico (1763–1846), 198

Dratwicki, Alexandre, 112
Dreo, Harald, 44
Dresden, 247
Drury Lane, 197
Du Bos, Jean Baptiste (1660–1742)
  Réflexions critiques sur la poësie et sur la peinture, 213
Dukas, Paul (1865–1935), 327
Dussek, Johann Ladislav (1760–1812), 65, 253
Dwight, John Sullivan (1813–1893), 233
Dwyer, John, 102
dynamics, 117, 225, 333, 349, 371, 391, 401

Early Modern Period, 22
Easter Alleluia, 316, 338
Eastern European music, 117, see also Burgenland
Ebenbauer, Melita, 47
Ecclesiastical Census of 1768, 115
Ecclesiastical Confiscations of Mendizábal (1835–37), 113
Economics and Finances, 28, 62, **91–93**
  artistic reputation, 92
  charity, 92–93
  circulation and, 52
  home ownership and, 106
  in London, 304
  instruments and, 268
  last will and testament, 72–73
  material possessions and, 203
  monetary, 91–92
  people and networks, 249
  will and testament, Haydn's, 24, 93
economy, compositional, 218–24
Écorcheville, Jules (1872–1915), 327
Eden, 184
Edgcumbe, Richard (1764–1839), 402
Edge, Dexter, 186
Edicts of Toleration (1782), 182, 394
Edinburgh Musical Society, 101
Editions and Edition-Making, 3, **93–95**, 357, 374
  audiences and, 18
  catalogues and, 46
  circulation and, 52
  dedications and, 86
  discography and, 89
  Enlightenment and, 105
  monuments and memorializing, 217
  musical societies and, 235
  people and networks, 255
  reception and, 324
Education, 25–26, 63, 69, **95–97**, 168, 356, see also Teaching and Students, Experiential Learning
  church and, 47
  Enlightenment and, 105
  form and, 125
  harmony and, 142
  melody and, 210
  performance and, 270
  place and, 297
Edwards, Edward (1738–1806), 191
effect(s), 120, 139, 189, 222, 242, 265, 267, 315–16, 353, 355, 375, 379, 386
egalitarianism, 136
Einstein, Alfred (1880–1952), 330
Eipeldauer Briefe, 406
Eisenstadt, 41–43, 42, 62, **106–111**, 296, 305
  charity funds, 73
  commemorations in, 58–59
  correspondence and, 71
  ethnic diversity in, 116
  Haydn's burial place in, 51, 110
  Jewish community in, 182, 183
  Nelson's visit to, 404–5
  organist in, 91
  performance spaces, 249, 280–81
  place and, 298–301
  relationships with composers and music professionals, 63
  summer palace, 169
  theater and, 360–61
  theater at, 63
EK (Entwurf-Katalog), 45, 46, 47
elaboratio, 67
Elementarbuch, 75, 357
Elias, Norbert (1897–1990), 78
Elssler, Johann (1769–1843), 46, 56, 205, 246, 336
Elssler, Joseph (father) (? – 1782), 245, 336
Elssler, Joseph (son) (1767–1843), 245
embodied performance, 260
emotions, 213–15
empfindsamer keyboard style, 378
Empfindsamkeit, 72, **97–100**, 156, 158, 160, 378, 402
  Enlightenment and, 101, 103
  gender and, 136
  libretti and, 194
  love, 97
  melancholy and, 87
  poetry and, 307
  science and, 346
  theater and theatricality, 367
Empire Room, 281
employment contract, 5, 29, 52–53, 63, 85, 91, 106, 111, 174, 250, 254, 266, 309, 318, 356, 389, 399
encyclopedias, xv–xvi, 255, 262
Encyclopédie (d'Alembert and Diderot), xv–xvi, 239
Engel, Johann Jakob (1741–1802), 161, 214
  Über die musikalische Malerey, 214
England. See London and England
"English humour," 207
English-style songs. See Canzonettas
Enlightenment, 21–22, 24, **100–106**, 156, 160–61, 165, 172, 194–95
  courts and, 79
  exoticism and, 118

Enlightenment (cont.)
  folk music and, 34–40
  Freemasonry and, 134
  gender and, 136
  iconography, 148
  Jewish culture and, 184
  London and, 199
  musical materials and, 221, 229
  nationalism and, 236
  nature and, 237
  people and networks, 245, 249
  performance and, 273
  poetry and, 308
  politics and, 309–11
  religion and, 184
  theater and theatricality, 364
  Vienna and, 392
entertainment music, 185, 245
environments. See Place
Érard, Sébastien (1752–1831), 206
Erdődy, Count Johann Nepomuk (1749–1794), 17, 257, 283
Erdődy, Count Joseph (1754–1824), 80, 86, 253
Erdődy, Count Ladislaus (1746–1786), 251, 357
Erdődy, Maria Theresia (1779–1837), 360
Erfindung (invention), 67
Essentialisten (musical ensemble at St. Stephen's Cathedral), 48
Estate Inventories (Nachlass), 46, 382
Esterházy Court, 309, 321, 356 see Courts, People and Networks
  archives, 46, 280
  Burgenland and, 41
  Cammer Musique court ensemble, 63
  Hauskapellen, 78
  in Vienna, 397
  musicians, 244
  patronage, 27–30
  people and networks, 244–51
Esterházy, Prince Anton (1738–1794), 16, 77, 80, 91, 108, 109, 170, 248, 280, 317, 360
Esterházy, Prince Nicolaus I (1714–1790), 5–6, 28–30, 45, 52, 70, 78, 79, 80, 86, 91, 106–11, 169, 173, 174, 187, 194, 203, 206, 217, 248–50, 254, 281, 298–99, 317, 318, 337, 345, 356, 360, 361, 362–65, 373, 384
Esterházy, Prince Nicolaus II (1765–1833), 51, 56, 65, 72, 80, 92, 109, 110, 170, 175, 176, 179, 266, 325, 337, 339, 404
Esterházy, Prince Paul Anton (1711–1762), 79, 106, 109, 170, 174, 297, 318, 345, 404
Esterházy, Princess Maria Elisabeth (m. Nicolaus I) (1718–1790), 107, 170, 248
Esterházy, Princess Marie Hermenegild (m. Nicolaus II) (1768–1845), 6, 80, 85, 110, 137, 175, 247, 269, 324, 335, 337, 339, 391
Eszterháza, 28, 62, **106–111**, 169, 248
  audiences at, 15–16
  correspondence and, 71
  court chapel, 249
  ethnic diversity in, 116
  festivals at, 331
  Freemasonry and, 133
  "Hungarian Versailles," 109
  iconography and, 147
  instruments in, 180
  isolation of, 139
  Jewish culture and, 182
  Miranda's visit to, 9
  monuments and memorializing, 217
  operas, 79
  operas at, 191–92, 247, 337, 360, 364
  performance spaces, 191, 281–83
  performances at, 185
  performances recorded at, 90
  place and, 298–301
  relationships with composers and music professionals, 63
  theater and theatricality, 360–67, 362
  theaters at, 63
ethnicity, 40–41, 88, 135, 182, 236
European Contexts: France, Italy, Spain, 14, **111–116**
  circulation and, 52–53
  composers and music professionals, 63
  courts and, 79
  place and, 297
  politics and, 311
  programmatic elements and, 316
  publishing in, 173
  religion and, 339
European Magazine and London Review, The, 148, 174, 197
Evans, R. J. W., 96
exercices publics des élèves, 234
Exeter Hall, 232
Exoticism, 42, **116–118**, 152, 163, 184
  Americas and, 10
  dedications and, 85
  folk song settings and, 122
  Idealism and, 152
  melody and, 212
  musical materials and, 228
  nationalism and, 236, 237
  people and networks, 246
  place and, 298
  programmatic elements and, 317
  theater and, 362
  travel and exploration, 384
Experiential Learning, **118–120**
exploration. See Travel and Exploration
Eybl, Martin, 52, 305, **391–399**
Eybler, Joseph Leopold (1765–1846), 251
Eyerly, Sarah, 11

false recapitulation, 242
fame, 55, See celebrity
fantasieren, 67–70, 159, 165–66

Fantasiestücke in Callots Manier (1814), 140
Farinelli/Carlo Broschi (1705–1782), 138
Faultless, Margaret, 273
Fauquet, Joël-Marie, 230, 233–34
Feast of St. Stephen, 405
Feasts of the Nativity of Mary, 80
Feder, Georg (1927–2006), 32, 94, 189, 190, 222, 266
Federico, Gennaro Antonio (?–1744)
   La serva padrona, 192
feelings, 213–15
Feldman, Martha, 401
Feldmusik, Feldparthie, 248, see also Harmoniemusik (wind band music)
Felici, Alessandro (1742–1772)
   L'amore soldato, 281, 365
femininity, 136–37, 138, 308, 330, see also Gender
Feodorovna, Maria, Countess of Württemberg (Countess von Norden) (1759–1828), 264
Ferdinand III (House of Habsburg), Grand Duke of Tuscany (1769–1824), 81
Ferdinand IV of Naples (1751–1825), 53, 112, 256
Ferdinand, Archduke d'Este (1754–1806), 247
Fernando VII of Spain, 114
Ferraguto, Mark, **63–69**, 117, 253, 315–317
Fertőd, 109
Festino Rooms (Hanover Square Rooms), 302, 304
festivals. See Commemorations and Festivals
Fétis, François Joseph (1784–1871), 375
feudal, feudalism, 321, 392
Fichte, Johann Gottlieb (1762–1814), 149
Field, John (1782–1837), 65
figurae, 377, 380
Fillion, Michelle, 131, 166, 220, **389–391**
film, 18, see also Reception, 1950s-present
finances. See Economics and Finances
Fink-Mennel, Evelyn, 36
Finland, 60
Finscher, Ludwig, 139, 218, 223, 330
Finsterbusch, Ignaz (? – 1753), 119
Fischer, Adam, 59, 89
Fischer, Wilhelm (1886–1962), 131–32
Fischer-Dieskau, Dietrich (1925–2012), 333
Fischietti, Domenico (c.1725–c.1810), 280
   Il mercato di Malmantile, 361
Fitzpatrick, Horace, 178
Florence, 315
fluent song (*fliessender Gesang*), 1
flutes, 177–78, 241, 253, 262
Folk Song Settings, 26, **121–125**, 314, see also Enlightenment
   Burgenland and Enlightenment, 34–40
   cyclic integration and, 84
   Enlightenment and, 101
   melody and, 211–12
   monuments and memorializing, 217
   musical materials and, 228
   nationalism and, 236–37
   people and networks, 257
   politics and, 310
   reception and, 328
   sublimity and, 354
Forkel, Johann Nikolaus (1749–1818), 178
Form, **125–132**
   counterpoint and, 75
   dedications and, 85
   disability and, 88
   folk music and, 42
   Idealism and, 151
   melody and, 209
   politics and, 310
   reception and, 327
   self-reflexivity and, 348
   sensibility and, 98
   topics and, 380
   variation and, 389
Formenlehre, 125, 132
Forster, William (1739–1808), 53, 71, 94, 255, 256, 302, 318–19
fortepiano, 46, 65, 86, 99, 180, 188, 190, 206, 268, 270, 391, 397, see also keyboards
Fortino, Sally, 135
Fortspinnungstypus, 131
Foucault, Michel (1926–1984), 153
Framery, Nicolas Étienne (1745–1810), 324
France, 29, 53
   commerce and the market, 61
Franck, Johann Mathias (1711–1760), 47, 96, 118, 138
Franconia, 41
Frank, Johann Peter (1745–1821), 345
Franklin, Benjamin (1706–1790), 9, 347
Franz II, Holy Roman Emperor (1768–1835), 163, 236, 337, 394, 395
Franz, Carl (1738–1802), 179
Frederick, Prince, Duke of York (House of Hanover) (1763–1827), 80
"free" style, 75
Freemasonry, 65, 111, **132–134**, see also Relationships and Friendships
   Enlightenment and, 105
   in Vienna, 394
   musical societies and, 229, 231
   religion and, 339
   science and, 345
   "Zur wahren Eintracht," 111, 132–34, 394
   "Zur Wahrheit," 133
Freemasons Hall, London, 234
Freistadt, 183
French Restoration, 237
French Revolution, 22, 161, 175, 194, 199, 236–37, 310, 370, 385, 394, 404, see also War
French overture, 380
Freunde der Tonkunst, 176
Frey, Johann Franz (fl.1730s), 50
Friberth, Carl (1736–1816), 249

461

Frieberth (Friebert), Joseph (1724–1799), 115
Friederike, Charlotte Ulrike, Princess of Prussia (1767–1820), 80
Friedrich Wilhelm II, King of Prussia (1744–1797), 79, 86, 173, 256
friendships. *See* Relationships and Friendships
Fries, Count Moritz Christian Johann (1777–1826), 80
Friesenhagen, Andreas, **55–58**
Fritz-Hilscher, Elisabeth, 59
Frölich, Mathias (before 1800– after 1841), 206
Frye, Northrop (1912–1991), 97
Fuchs, Ingrid, 72, 73, 85, 135
Fuchs, Johann Nepomuk (1766–1839), 357
Fuhrmann, Wolfgang, **21–32**, **91–93**, 257, 399
Fürnberg, Baron Carl Joseph Weber (c.1720–1767), 7, 280, 297, 349
Fux, Johann Joseph (1660–1741), 50, 63, 75, 119, 338, 380
  Emperor Mass, 119
  Gradus ad Parnassum, 74–76, 119, 120, 357–58
  Singfundamente, 119

Gainsborough, Thomas (1727–1788), 304
galant style, 75, 76, 144, 153, 222, 227, 343, 353, 372, 378, 381
Galeazzi, Francesco (1758–1819), 81, 157
  Theoretical-Practical Elements of Music, 157
Galileo Galilei, (1564–1642), 347
Galitzin (Golitsyn), Dmitri Mikhailovich (1721–1793), 256
Gall, Franz Joseph (1758–1828), 337
Gallini, John (Giovanni) (1728–1805), 175, 197, 201, 250, 367
Gallope, Michael, 244, 249
Galuppi, Baldassare (1706–1785), 120, 396
  Il mondo alla roversa, 206
  Le nozze di Dorina, 402
Gardel, Pierre-Gabriel (1758–1840)
  Jugement de Pâris, 112
gardens, 9, 87, 106, 107–9, 111, 161, 238, 299, 321
Gardiner, William (1770–1853), 20, 205
Garratt, James, 58, 149
Gartrell, Carol, 179
Garzoni, Tomaso (1549–1589)
  Il serraglio de gli stupori del mondo, 385
Gassmann, Florian (1729–1774), 64, 192, 252, 395, 396, 399
  L'amore artigiano, 365
  L'opera seria, 401
Gassmann, Therese (1774–1837), 337
Gates-Coon, Rebecca, 247–48
Gazetteer, 301
Gazzaniga, Giuseppe (1743–1818), 192, 399
Gazzetta di Bologna, 312
Gazzetta Toscana, 314
Gegenbauer, Adam (?–1753), 119

Geiringer, Karl (1899–1989), 94, 101, 324, 401
Gelbart, Matthew, **121–125**, 228
Gellert, Christian Fürchtegott (1715–1769), 73
  "Inkle and Yarico," 9
Gender, 88, 115, **135–137**
  amateurs and, 4–6
  courts and, 247
  cross-dressed characters, 182, 246
  dedications and, 85, 252, 391
  genius and, 138
  in the Americas, 11, 12
  musical societies and, 230
  operas and, 195
  patronage and, 250
  performance and, 260, 262, 270–74
  poetry and, 308
  press and, 314
  science and, 346
  theater and, 362
  time and, 373
Genesis, Book of, 195
Genius, 24–25, 53, **138–141**, 158–59, see also creativity
  aesthetics and, 1
  courts and, 79
  gender and, 136
  iconography and, 149
  Idealism and, 150
  improvisation and, 167
  melancholy and, 87, 208
  monuments and memorializing, 217
  press and, 314
  sublimity and, 353
  unruliness, 140
gentry, 52, 392
Genzinger, Marianne von (1754–1793), 26, 28, 72, 73, 85, 100, 110, 199, 253, 302, 303–4, 335, 373, 391, 397, 400
Genzinger, Peter von (1737–1797), 302
George III, King (1738–1820), 307, 370
George, Prince of Wales (later King George IV) (1762–1830), 80, 81, 148, 175, 253, 373
George, Sam, 346
Gerber, Ernst Ludwig (1702–1775), 77, 178
  Historisch-biographisches Lexikon der Tonkünstler, 242
Gerlach, Sonja, 45
German Enlightenment, 104
German Idealism. *See* Idealism
German language, 73–74, 394
German national anthem, 17, 24, 34, 311
German patriotism, 32
Germania Society, 233
Germans, 40, 116, 150
  English aristocracy and, 198
Germany, 53
Geselligkeit, 307, *See* Sociability
Gesellschaft der Associierten Cavaliere, 79, 80–81, 176, 230–31, 253, 397

462

Gesellschaft der Musikfreunde, 36, 46, 50,
    55–57, 60, 94, 176, 234, 327
  Archive of, 50
  Haydn festivals and, 59
Gesellschaft von Musikfreunden, 176
gestures (bodily, physical, performative,
    musical), 100, 117, 154, 210, 225, 228,
    242, 245, 261, 343, 346, 351, 359, 371,
    390, 405
Gherardi, Pietro (fl.1776–1792), 401
Gibelli, Lorenzo (1719–1812), 403
Gieseke, Ludwig, 61
gifts received by Haydn, 205
  stockings, 205
  watch, 404
Giglio, Robert, **177–180**, 261–62
Gill, Satinder, 273
Gillespie, Susan, 20, 146
Gilman, Lawrence (1878–1939), 15, 328
Giornovichi, Giovanni (1747–1804), 65
Gjerdingen, Robert, 132, 210, 261
Glauert, Amanda, 308
glee, 231
Glee Club, 232
Gleim, Johann Wilhelm Ludwig (1719–
    1803), 99
Gluck, Christoph Willibald (1714–1787), 29,
    120, 297, 300, 321, 395, 396, 399
  Don Juan, 283, 367, 370
  Le diable à quatre, 64, 212, 315
  Orfeo ed Euridice, 64, 194, 362, 364, 365,
    367, 401
Gmasz, Sepp, 44
Gnadenkapelle, 48
Godt, Irving, 64, 135
Goehr, Lydia, 154
Goethe, Johann Wolfgang von (1749–1832),
    149, 151, 307, 351, 366
  Werther, 367
Goldberg, Sander M., 89, 258, 330
Goldmark, Karl (1830–1915), 41
Goldoni, Carlo (1707–1793), 192–94, 361
  Il mondo della luna, 194, 347, 364
  La buona figliuola, 192
Gon, Federico, 112
Good Friday, 316
Gordon, Bonnie, 14
Göttweig Abbey, 50–51, 57
Gotwals, Vernon (1925–2002), 1, 20, 22,
    23–24, 25, 26, 29, 31, 32, 48, 67, 70, 82,
    91–93, 99, 189, 218, 321, 322, 324,
    325, 349
Götz, Johann Nikolaus (1721–1781), 307
Gould, Glenn (1932–1982), 333
Goya, Francisco de (1746–1828), 113
Graben marketplace, 296
Gramit, David, 150
Granada (Spain), 113
Grande, James, 162, **309–311**
Grant, Roger Mathew, 218, 226, **340–344**,
    373, **374–376**

Grassalkovics, Prince Anton (1734–1794), 79
Graupner, Gottlieb (1767–1836), 11, 233
Grave, Floyd, 86–87, 221
Gray, John (1724–1811)
  Allgemeine Weltgeschichte, 9
Gray, Thomas (1716–1771)
  "Elegy in a Country Churchyard," 238
Graz, 356
Great Pulteney Street, 253, 303, 331, 340
Greece, ancient, 386
Green, Emily H., **15–18**, **61–62**, 85, 171, 192,
    247, 252, 322
Greenwood, Andrew, **100–106**, 160–61
Gregorian chant, 84
Greiner, Charlotte (1740–1816), 345
Greiner, Franz Sales von (1730–1798), 26,
    134, 345
Grenser, August (1720–1807), 177
Grétry, André (1741–1813), 267, 399
  Zemira ed Azor, 362
Griesinger, Georg August (1769–1845), 1,
    3–4, 7, 20, 22, 23–24, 26, 29, 31, 48, 51,
    67–70, 79, 80, 82, 91–93, 99–100,
    118–20, 139, 166, 176, 179, 209–10, 218,
    238, 254–56, 301, 315, 317, 319, 321,
    324–25, 336, 349, 359, 382, 397, 398,
    401, 402, 405
Grigson, Caroline, 54, 201, 307, 311
Grosswardein, 170
Gruber, Gernot, 3
Grundbass, 143
Grundmann, Johannes Basilius (1726–
    1798), 147
Grunwald, Max (1871–1953), 43
Gsur, Tobias (1726–1794), 395
Guénin, Marie-Alexandre (1744–1835), 224
Guglielmi, Pietro Alessandro (1728–
    1804), 399
  La quakera spiritosa, 192
Gumpendorf, 4, 32, 51, 92, 109, 204, 305,
    335, 392, 404
Gunn, John (1765–1834), 177
Guthrie, William (1708–1770), *Allgemeine
    Weltgeschichte*, 9
Guttenbrunn, Ludwig (1750–1819), 67,
    147–48
Gypsy melodies, 117, 212, 298
Gyrowetz, Adalbert (1763–1850), 4, 65,
    148, 204

Habermas, Jürgen, *The Structural
    Transformation of the Public Sphere*, 23
habitus, 27
Habsburg Empire
  audiences, 17
  diversity in, 116–18
  monuments and memorializing, 216
  nationalism and, 236
Habsburg monarchy, 10, 21, 28, 36, 41, 168,
    169–70, 309, 337, 399
  education and, 96–97

Habsburg monarchy (cont.)
  Jewish culture and, 182
HaCohen, Ruth, 182
Hadow, William Henry (1859–1937), 328
Haensel (Hänsel), Peter (1770–1831), 357
Haigh, Thomas (1769–1808), 357
Haimo, Ethan, 83, 125
Hainburg, 25, 47, 95, 119, 168, 296, 395
Haller, Albrecht von (1708–1777), 346
Halley's comet, 345
hallgató style, 117
Halsey, Katie, 350
Hamburg, 385
Hamburgische Correspondent (newspaper), 312
Hamilton, Alexander (1755–1804), 10
Hampl, Anton Joseph (1710–1771), 178
Handel and Haydn Society, 11–13, 12, 232–33, 306
Handel Commemoration Concerts, 31, 51, 175, 187, 191, 205, 305
Handel, George Frideric (1685–1759), 22, 31–32, 162, 184, 197, 207, 230, 305, 321, 326, 354, 396, 397
  Hallelujah chorus, 233
  Messiah, 11
handwriting, in letters, 74
Hanover Square Rooms, 16, 18, 187–89, 250, 253, 283, 302, 304, 305
Hanoverians, 10
Hans, Nicholas, 346
Hanslick, Eduard (1825–1904), 392
Hans-Wurst (Hanswurst) (folk theater character), 36–40, 39, 247, 359, 360, 395
Hardy, Thomas (1757–1805), 33, 148
harem, 118, *see also* seraglio
Hárich, János (1904–1990), 191
Harmonie, 248
Harmoniemusik (wind band music), 54, 237, *see also* Feldmusik, Feldparthie
Harmony, 4, 49, **142–144**
  cyclic integration and, 83
  form and, 125
  genius and, 139
  melody and, 209–10
  musical materials and, 222
  press and, 314
  self-reflexivity and, 348
  sublimity and, 353
  theater and theatricality, 372
  topics and, 380
Harnoncourt, Nikolaus (1929–2016), 59, 90
harpsichord. *See* keyboards
Harrach, Count Karl Leonhard (1765–1831), 80, 321, 322
Harrison H4 clock, 161
Harrison, Bernard, 64, 111, 139, 161, 187, 212, 224, 231, 373
Härtel, Gottfried Christoph (1763–1827), 254, 256
Harvard Musical Association, 233

Haschka, Lorenz Leopold (1749–1827), 36, 236
Haschke, Simon (1726/27–1776), 52, 398–99
Hasse, Johann Adolf (1699–1783), 23, 32, 64, 120, 396, 401
Hassell, John (c.1767–1825), *Tour of the Isle of Wight*, 238, 386
Hatten, Robert S., 227, **376–382**
Haugwitz, Count Friedrich Wilhelm (1702–1765), 50
Hauskapellen, 78–79
Hawkins, Sir John (1719–1789)
  General History of the Science and Practice of Music, 200
Haydn Bibliothek-Verzeichnis, 56
Haydn centennial (1909), 327
"Haydn Days" (*Haydn-Tage*), 59
Haydn Explosiv, 331
Haydn Festival Society, Burgenland, 59
Haydn Nachlass-Verzeichnis, 56
Haydn reloaded, 331
Haydn Saal, 59, 111, 280, 296
Haydn Society, 89, 94, 235
Haydn Society of Great Britain, 235, 331
Haydn Society of North America, 235, 331
Haydn Year 2009, 330–31
"Haydn Zentenarfeier," 327
Haydn, Anne Marie (m. Mathias) (1707–1754), 118
Haydn, Maria Anna Theresia (née Keller) (1730–1800), 334, 356
Haydn, Mathias (1699–1763), 21, 25, 118
Haydn, Michael (1737–1806), 11, 59, 120, 170, 204, 336, 338
Haydn-Haus museum, 106
Haydn-Verzeichnis (HV), 46
Hayes, Philip, 229
Haymarket Theatre, 367
Head, Matthew, **97–100**, 117–18, 122, 135–37, 138, **152–165**, 184, 228, 262, 362, 374
health, 3, 72, 87, 99
Heanzen, 40
Heartz, Daniel, 63, 103, 113, 132, 187, 239, 367, 397
Hegel, Georg Wilhelm Friedrich (1770–1831), 149
Heine, Claudia, 32
Heinichen, Johann David (1683–1729)
  General-Bass in der Composition, 74, 142–143
Hellmann, Riersch, 247
Helmholtz system, xvii
Helyard, Erin, 261, **399–403**
Henle, Günter (1899–1979), 94
Henry VIII, King (1491–1547), 373
Hepokoski, James, 88, 125–31
Herbst Theater, San Francisco, 189
Herbst, Johannes (1735–1812), 11

Herder, Johann Gottfried (1744–1803), 103, 122, 149, 161, 308
   Alte Volkslieder, 36, 43
   Kalligone, 150
heroism, 80, 200, 208
Herschel, Sir William (1738–1822), 162, 345, 347
Herter Norton, Mary Dows (1892–1985), 7–8, 233
Hibberd, Sarah, 370
Hiles, Karen, 236–37
Hiller, Johann Adam (1728–1804), 397
Hirsch, Zacharias (c.1737–1812), 177
Hirschman, Albert, 155
Historisch-kritische Theaterchronik von Wien (theater periodical), 361
Hoboken, Anthony van (1887–1983), 45, 47, 94–95, 327
   Joseph Haydn: Thematisch-bibliographisches Werkverzeichnis, 328
Hochradner, Thomas, 48
Hofburg, 48, 169, 283, 296
Hofburgkapelle, 48, 51, 169, 296, 395
Hoffmann von Fallersleben, August Heinrich (1798–1874), 24
   "Deutschlandlied," 34–36
Hoffmann, E. T. A. (1776–1822), 82, 140, 150–51, 224, 242, 326
Hoffmeister, Franz Anton (1754–1812), 52, 93, 173, 302
Hoffstetter, Roman (1742–1815)
   Opus 3 string quartets, 46, 61, 93–94, 319
Hofmann, Johann Franz von (fl.1790s), 405
Hofmann, Leopold (1738–1793), 64, 307, 395
Hogarth, William (1697–1764), 19, 20, 303
Hogwood, Christopher (1941–2014), 54, 89
Holcroft, Thomas (1745–1809), 54, 311
Hölderlin, Friedrich (1770–1843), 149
Holland, 53
Holloway, Robin, 223
Holoman, D. Kern, 230, 234
Holst, Gustav (1874–1934), 328
Holtmeier, Ludwig, **142–144**, 222
Holy Roman Empire, 21, 170, 337
Holywell Music Room, 230, 232
Holzapfel, Otto, 44
Holzbauer, Ignaz (1711–1783), 396
Holzmeister, Joseph von (1751–1817), 132, 134
Homann, Johann Baptist (1664–1724), 382
Home, Henry (Lord Kames) (1696–1782), 207
honorary doctorate, 18, 232
Hoole, John (1727–1803)
   "Sympathy," 307
Hoppner, John (1758–1810), xvii, 148
Horányi, Mátyás (1928–1995), 182
Hörwarthner, Maria, 26, 73, 103, 205, 345, 350
Hörz, Peter F., 43

Hosler, Bellamy, 157, 213–14
Hoyt, Peter, 125
Huber, Thaddäus (1742–1798), 264
Huberty, Antoine (1722–1791), 52, 398
Hume, David (1711–1776), 103, 131
Hummel, Johann Nepomuk (1778–1837), 4, 358
Humor, 2, 27, 36, 100, **144–146**, 207
   genius and, 140
   Idealism and, 152
   melody and, 212
   musical materials and, 221
   opera and, 194
   performance and, 264
   press and, 314
   science and, 347
   self-reflexivity and, 348
   theater and theatricality, 372
   topics and, 380
Humphrey, Hannah (1745–1818), 148
Hundsturmer Friedhof, 51
Hungarian Guard, Captain of, 248
Hungarian melodies, 212, 237
Hungarian National Library, 46
Hungarian–Gypsy musicians, 117
Hungarians, 40, 116–18
Hungary, 41, 73, 169–70, 184, 299, 306
Hunter, Anne (1742–1821), 54, 201, 305, 307, 308
Hunter, John (1728–1793), 305, 307, 308, 345–46
Hunter, Mary, 7, 186, 227, 273, 279, **348–349**, 350, 378, 380
hunting, 30, 161, 215, 238–39, 248, 307, 316, 372, 373, 378, 388
Hussites, 10
Hutcheson, Francis (1694–1746), 103
Hyde (publisher), 53
hymn arrangements, 13

Iconography, **147–149**
   compositional process, 67
   gender and, 135
   material culture, 204
   people and networks, 249
   self-promotion and, 32
Idealism, 100, **149–152**, 195, 199, 250
Ideas, **152–165**, 249, 296
identity. *See* Biography and Identity
imagination. *see also* Improvisation
   science and, 346
Imbault, Jean-Jérôme (1753–1832), 33, 318
imitation. *See* Mimesis
imperial courts. *See* Courts
impresarios, 168, 196, 249
Improvisation, 1, 11, 36, 75, 159, **165–167**, *see also* Self-Reflexivity
   compositional process and, 67–70
   exoticism and, 117
   genius and, 139
   melancholy and, 87

Improvisation (cont.)
  theater and, 247
  incidental music, 246
d'Indy, Vincent (1851–1931), 327
  Cours de Composition Musicale, 82
influence, Haydn's, 164, 197, 200, 205, 242
influences, 14, 21, 34, 64, 96, 117, 149, 162, 172, 180, 338, 350, 378
innovation, 22, 242, 376
Innsbruck, 356
inspiration. *See* Improvisation
Institutions, **167–177**
  Enlightenment and, 101, 105
  place and, 297
  theater and theatricality, 365
instrumental music, 31, 156
  counterpoint and, 76
  programmatic elements, 315–17
Instruments and Organology, 11, 110, 115, 156, 163, **177–180**, 248, 262
  baryton, 5
  Enlightenment developments in, 104
  Haydn's personal collection, 206–7
  in large ensembles, 185–87
  orchestration and, 241–42
  performance and, 260–62
  theater and, 362
  variation and, 391
  Vienna and, 397
intellectual marketplace, 250
intentionality (in performance), 279
international contacts. *See* diplomats
International Haydn Festival, 331
International Joseph Haydn Foundation Eisenstadt, 59
International Musikgesellschaft, 327
International Piano Archives (University of Maryland), 89
Internationalen Haydntagen Eisenstadt festival, 59
internationalization of music, 167
inventio, 67
Iriarte, Tomás de (1750–1791), 370
  La música, 113
Irish melodies, 311
irony, 146, 330, 387
Islam, 362
Isle of Wight, 386
isolation, 28, 110, 139, 245, 301, 309, 325
Istanbul, 392
Italy, 29, 306
Ives, Charles (1874–1954), 351

Jacobi, Konstantin Ph. W. (c.1745–1817), 256
Jacoby, Nicolas (1733–1784), 107
Jaén (Spain), 113
Jahn, Otto (1813–1769), 56
Janissary style, 152
Jansen-Bartolozzi, Therese (c.1770–1843), 6, 17, 85, 391
Jefferson, Thomas (1746–1826), 9, 10, 13–14

Jena, 149
Jerome, Erin W., 362
Jesuitenkirche (Jesuit Church), 395
Jewish Culture, 40–44, 42, 117, **182–184**, 192, 339, 340, *see also* Burgenland
  Haskalah (Enlightenment), 184
  people and networks, 246
  religious freedom, 394
  Sephardic Jews, 42
  stereotypes, 361
Joachim, Joseph (1831–1907), 41, 327
Johnson, Claudia, 354
Johnson, Douglas, 66
Johnson, H. Earle (1903–1988), 13
Johnson, James H., 314
Jommelli, Niccolò (1714–1774), 396
Jones, David Wyn, xv, 3–4, 24, 29, 45, 53, 63, 77, 78, 97, 157, **167–177**, 179, 196, 199, 246, 247, 249, 310, 322, 340, 380, 399, 401
"Joseph Haydn & Die Neue Welt" (2011 conference), 8
Joseph Haydn and Time (2009 conference), 373
Joseph Haydn Kritische Gesamtausgabe, 94
Joseph Haydn Werke (JHW), 95
Joseph Haydn-Institut (Cologne), 94
Joseph II, Emperor (1741–1790), 28, 110, 133, 168, 171, 182, 264, 321, 337, 339, 362, 392, 395
Joseph, Saint, 168
Journal de musique, 187
Journal des Luxus und der Moden, 373
Journal für Freymaurer, 132
journals. *See* Press
Jung, Philippe (fl.1789–1808), 232
Junker, Carl Ludwig (1748–1797), 145

Kalkbrenner, Frédéric/Friedrich (1785–1849), 358
Kalvarienberg, 183, 383
Kant, Immanuel (1724–1804), 19, 131, 149, 157, 162, 164, 207–8, 250, 345, 347
  Anthropologie in pragmatischer Hinsicht, 208, 347
  Critique of Judgment, 1–2, 19, 139, 355
  Observations on the Feeling of the Beautiful and Sublime, 19, 208
  "What is Enlightenment?," 105
Kapellmeister, 27–30, 47, 50, 63, 78–79, 80, 96, 110, 119, 138, 170, 174, 297, 299, 309, 339, 356, 362, 384, 395
Kärntnertortheater, 63, 120, 171, 194, 280, 282, 359, 365, 394
Kaunitz, Wenzel Anton (1711–1794), 256
Keate, George (1729–1797), 238
Kees [Keeß], Franz Bernhard Ritter von (1720–1795), 46, 57, 397
Keller, Georg Ignaz (1699–1771), 119
Keller, Hans (1919–1985), 83

Keller, Maria Anna Theresia, see Haydn,
    Maria Anna Theresia (née Keller),
    (1730–1800)
Keller, Theresia Helena (1733–1819), 251,
    334, 356
Kellner, David (c.1670–1748), 143–44
    Treulicher Unterricht im General-Bass, 144
Kelly, Michael (1762–1826), 65, 336
Kemp, Lindsay, 89
Kenner, 4–5, 7, 76, 213, 265
Kerman, Joseph (1924–2014), 131
Kerner, Anton (fl.1773–1780), 178
keyboards, 115–16, 179–80, 185, 265
Khevenhüller-Metsch, Prince Johann-Joseph
    von (1706–1776), 396
Kidd, Ronald R., 13
Kielian-Gilbert, Marianne, 89
Kimmerling, Robert (1737–1799), 251, 356
King's Theatre (Haymarket, London),
    174–75, 189, 197, 198, 199, 201, 250,
    283, 304–5, 306, 310, 363
Kinsky, Prince Ferdinand (1758–1814), 80, 230
Kismarton. *See* Eisenstadt
Kittsee, 41, 59, 248, 281
    Kittsee palace, 360–61
Klagenfurt, 356
Klancher, John, 105
Klang und Raum Festival, 60
Kleiber, Erich (1890–1956), 367
Klier, Karl Magnus (1892–1966), 37, 40
Klorman, Edward, 252, **349–352**
Kloster Irsee, 61
Klosterneuburg Abbey, 48
Knapp, Raymond, **149–152**
Knigge, Baron Adolf Franz Friedrich (1752–
    1796), 270, 273, 350
Knouse, Nola Reed, 11
Kober, Ignaz (1756–1813), 180, 181
Koberwein, Georg (1820–1876), 247
Koch, Heinrich Christoph (1749–1816), 76,
    81, 82, 125–32, 126, 157, 209–10, 350
    Musikalisches Lexikon, 166–67, 214
    Versuch einer Anleitung zur Composition, 67, 209
Kohlmarkt (Vienna), 297, 398
Kollmann, Augustus Frederic Christopher
    (1756–1829), 81–82
Kolowrat family, 57
Komlós, Katalin, 54
Könemann (publisher), 95
Königliche Bibliothek, 56, *see also*
    Staatsbibliothek zu Berlin
Königsberg, 365
Konrad, Ulrich, 3, 67, 76
Körner, Christian Gottfried (1756–1831),
    150, 238
Korngold, Erich Wolfgang (1897–1957), 25
Koslofsky, Craig, 373
Koslowski, Kaleb (translator), **58–61**
Kozeluch, Anton Thomas (1752–1805), 52
Kozeluch, Leopold (1747–1818), 121, 122,
    173, 209, 225

Kracher, Johann Matthais (1752–ca.1830), 11
Kraft, Anton (1749–1820), 357
Kramer, Lawrence, 151, 164, 225
Kranz, Johann Friedrich (1752–1810), 357
Kraus, Joseph Martin (1756–1792), 31
Kreisleriana essays (Hoffmann), 140
Kremsmünster Abbey, 51, 57
Kretschmer, Helmut, 59
Kreutzer, Conradin (1780–1849), 358
Kreutzer, Franziska Liebe Edle von
    (fl.1780s), 173
Kreutzer, Rodolphe (1766–1831), 234
Kris, Ernst, 24
Krumpholz, Johann Baptist (1742–1790), 357
Krumpholz, Madame Anne-Maria (c.1760–
    c.1820), 253
Kuhač, Franjo (1834–1911), 328
Kühl, Paolo M., 14, 15
Kuhmo Kammermusik Festival, Finland, 60
Kuks Abbey, 57
Kunstfreunden, 5, 7
Kurz, Johann Joseph Felix von (Kurz-
    Bernardon) (fl. 1751–1784), 63, 70, 75,
    182, 245, 359–60, 394–95
Kurz, Otto, 24
Kurzböck (publisher), 17, 254, 318, 399
Kurzböck, Magdalena von (1767–1845), 86
Kussenics, Adalbert (1699–1767), 106

La Borde, Jean Benjamin de (1734–1794),
    Choix de chansons mises en musique, 204
La Chevardière (publisher), 318
La gentille et jeune Lisette (French folk
    song), 212
La Rue, Jan (1918–2004), 83, 223, 225
Lachmayer, Herbert, 331
Lady of the Assumption and St. Gregory, 340
Lake Fertő (Neusiedlersee), 107
Lambach Abbey, 51
Lamkin, Kathleen, 11
Landon, Christa (1921–1977), 95
Landon, H. C. Robbins (1926–2009), 24, 45,
    59, 73–74, 77, 79, 92, 94–95, 97, 120,
    121, 140, 147, 179, 189, 195, 205, 217,
    226, 230–31, 235, 246, 264, 314, 317,
    322, 324, 333, 361, 363, 367, 373, 395,
    400, 402
    Haydn Chronicle and Works, 328
    The Symphonies of Joseph Haydn, 328
Landowska, Wanda (1879–1959), 15,
    327–28
Laplace, Pierre-Simon (1749–1827), 162, 347
large ensembles. *See* Leading Large
    Ensembles
Larsen, Jens Peter (1902–1988), 13, 17, 45,
    125, 318
    Die Haydn-Überlieferung, 94
Las Claras convent, Seville, 116
Lászay, Judit G., 107
late career, 32, 78, 139, 162, 177, 185, 207,
    216, 217, 228, 393, 406, *see also* Aging

late style, 3, 162, 222, 370
Latin America, 14–15, 384, see also Americas, The
Latour, Bruno, 245
LaTrobe, Christian Ignatius (1758–1836), 9, 11
Laudon, Ernst Gideon von (1717–1790), 113, 216, 317
Laune. See Humor
Lavater, Johann Kaspar (1741–1801), 265, 345
Laxenburg, 296
Le Breton, Joachim (1760–1819), 324
Le Concert de la Loge Olympique, 111, 187, 318
Le Duc (publisher), 94, 172
Le Guin, Elisabeth, 136, **258–279**, 273, 351
Le Huray, Peter (1930–1992), 145, 213
Leading Large Ensembles, 63, **185–191**, 198, 253, 371, see also Orchestration
  in Europe, 114
  in Vienna, 396
  performance and, 261
  performance spaces and, 283
learned musicians, 138–39, 159
learned style, 25, 29, 74, 76, 142, 228, 377–79, 380, 390
Ledbetter, David, 95
Lehmann, Christian Friedrich (1772–1827), 93
Leibniz, Gottfried Wilhelm (1646–1716), 375
Leichnamschneider, Johann Michael (1676–1746), 178
Leipzig, 173, 176, 195, 255, 406
Lenten concerts, 76, 112, 113–14, 194, 230, 396
Leo, Leonardo (1694–1744), 120
León (Spain), 113
Leopold II, Holy Roman Emperor (1747–1792), 337, 392
Leopoldstadt (Vienna), 50, 182, 301
Leppert, Richard, 135–36
Lés woods (hunting area), 107
Lessel, Franciszek (c.1780–1838), 251, 357
Lessing, Gotthold Ephraim (1729–1781), 308, 366
Lesure, François (1923–2001), 233
Levy, Janet M. (1938–2004), 219
Leydecker, Johann (c.1690–1759), 180
Leyden, 345
libraries. see also Collections and Archives
  Allgemeine deutsche Bibliothek, 312
  Augsburg University library, 57
  Bibliothèque musicale, 255
  Boston Public Library, Music Department Special Collections, 13
  British Library, 89
  Hungarian National Library, 46
  Königliche Bibliothek, 56
  Library of Congress, Washington, 57, 114
  Morgan Library and Museum, New York, 57
  National Széchényi Library (Budapest), 55–56, 206
  Neue allgemeine deutsche Bibliothek, 314
  New York Public Library for the Performing Arts, Music Division (Lincoln Center), 57
  Sächsische Landesbibliothek – Stadts- und Universitätsbibliothek, 57
  Staatsbibliothek zu Berlin, 55–56
  Universidad Complutense Library, Madrid, 116
library (books), 1, 26, 238, 387, see also Material Culture, Travel and Exploration
library (books), Haydn's, 204, 345, 384–86
library (music), Haydn's, 205–6
Library of Congress, Washington, 57, 114
Librettos and Librettists, 46, 63, 112, **191–196**
  people and networks, 256
  printed libretti, 203
  sensibility and, 158
Lichnowsky, Prince Karl Alois (1761–1814), 80, 230
Lichtental (Vienna), 97
Lidl, Andreas (1740–1789), 179, 232
Liebhaber, 4–5, 7, 265, 268
Liebhaber Concerte, 176, 231
Liechtenstein, Prince Aloys I (1761–1814), 80
Liedtypen, 131
life-writing, 70, 73, 325
light and shade, 71, see also chiaroscuro
lighting, theatrical, 247
Linley, Thomas (1733–1795), 195
Linz (Austria), 356
Lippman, Edward (1920–2010), 213
lira organizzata, 53, 112, 156, 256
Lister, Warwick, 187
listservs and online discussion boards, 331
Liszt, Franz (1811–1886), 315, 326, 367
literacy, 394
literature, 70, 358, See Reception, 1950s–present
lithography, 206
Lobkowitz, Prince Franz Joseph Maximilian (1772–1816), 57, 80, 169, 175, 230, 253
Locatelli, Piero (1695–1764), 178
Locke, Arthur Ware (1883–1969), 151
Locke, Ralph P., 117
London and England, 31, 33, 112, 172, **196–202**, 385–86, 392
  America and, 9
  audiences in, 15–16
  circulation and, 52–55
  commerce and the market, 61
  composers and music professionals, 65–66
  courts and, 80
  dedications and, 85
  fame and, 139
  finances and, 92
  Freemasonry and, 133
  iconography and, 147–48
  musical societies and, 231–33
  nature and, 238–39

notebooks, 72, 174
patronage and, 250
people and networks, 249, 253–55
performance spaces, 283
performances, 187–89
place and, 302–5
politics and, 310–11
press, 173–74
publishers, 317
reception and, 321
royalty, 80
sensibility and, 100
sublimity and, 353
teaching and students, 357
theater and theatricality, 371
war and, 405
London Philharmonic Orchestra, 333
Longinus (fl.-1st century CE), 2, 164
    Peri hypsous, 353–54
Longman & Broderip (publisher), 17, 53, 172, 176, 180, 206, 255, 302, 303, 318–19
Longman, Clementi & Co. (publisher), 255
Loughridge, Deirdre, **4–7**, 162, 164, 254, 330, 347, 362, 364
Lowe, Melanie, 89, 118, 137, 152, 185, **328–331**, 333, 378, 379
Lowens, Irving (1916–1983), 7–8, 13
Luca, Ignaz de (1746–1799), 255
Luisa (Princess of Naples and Sicily), Grand Duchess of Tuscany (1773–1802), 81
Lukawitz, Bohemia (Croatia), 280, 297, 302
Lutherans, Augsburg Confession, 41
Lyotard, Jean-François (1924–1998), 355

Macartney, Lord George (1737–1806), 385
Mace, Nancy, 53
MacIntyre, Bruce, 195
Macpherson, James (1736–1796), 122
Madison, James (1751–1836), 10
Madrid, 113–14
Magalhães-Castro, Beatriz, 14
Magazin der Musik, 313
Maggio Musicale Fiorentino, 368
Magnus, F. C. (fl.1789), 357
Mährischen Nationalmuseum, Schloss Jevisovice, Brno Czech Republic, 178
Malina, János, 111, 185, 191, 261, **279–284**, 299, **359–372**
Malleck, Johann Gottfried (1733–1798), 51
Mandyczewski, Eusebius (1857–1929), 47, 57, 94
Mann, Alfred (1917–2006), 75
mannigfaltigkeit (many-sidedness), 81
Mansel, Philip, 234
Mansfeld, Johann Ernst (1738–1796), 147–48
manuscript copies of scores, 5, 52, **55–58**, 61, 254, 255, 317–18, 398
maps and mapping, 382–83, *see also* Travel and Exploration

Mara, Gertrud Elisabeth (1749–1833), 65, 232
march, 8, 36, 123, 248, 310, 380, 387
Maria Carolina of Austria (1752–1814), 112
Maria Leopoldina, Princess of Austria (1797–1826), 14
Maria Pötsch icon, 48
Maria Theresia, Empress (Queen of Hungary) (1717–1780), 16, 23, 49, 109, 133, 168, 169, 281, 361, 392, 395
Marian shrines, 383
Mariazell, 50, 383
Marie Therese, Empress (1772–1807), 335, 337, 395, 405
Marie-Antoinette (1755–1793), 204
marionette theater, 63, 109, 247, 281, 300, 360, 366–67
market and marketplace. *See* Commerce and the Market
marketplace of ideas, 250
Marmontel, Jean-François (1723–1799), 10
Marpurg, Friedrich Wilhelm (1718–1795), 390
    Handbuch bey dem Generalbass und der Composition, 143
Marsh, John (1752–1828), 200
Martín y Soler, Vicente (1756–1806), *L'arbore di Diana*, 365
Martin, Nathan John, **125–132**, 218
Martinelli, Anton Erhard (1684–1747), 107
Martines (Martinez), Marianna (1744–1812), 64, 135, 251, 356, 396, 398
Marx, Adolf Bernhard (1795–1866), 326
    Lehre von der musikalischen Komposition, 130
masculinity, 137, 138, 314, *see also* Gender
Mason, Lowell (1792–1872), 13
Masons. *See* Freemasonry
Mastic, Timothy, 144, 348
Material Culture, 1, 26, 120, 162, **203–207**, 264, 384
    correspondence and, 73–74
    Enlightenment and, 105
    estate inventories, 46
    Freemasonry and, 134
    gifts, 404
    Jewish culture and, 184
    people and networks, 249
    portrait collection, 147
    science and, 345
Mathew, Nicholas, 162–63, 200, 216, **296–307**, 309, 349, 355, **404–406**
Mattheson, Johann (1681–1764), 63
    Der vollkommene Capellmeister, 120, 157, 345
Maunder, Richard, 180
Mauss, Marcel, 91
Maximilian Franz, Archduke and Elector of Cologne (1756–1801), 66, 358
Mayes, Catherine, **116–118**, 162–63, **236–237**
Mayr, Johann Simon (1763–1845), 324
McCaldin, Denis, 235
McCue, Edward, 261, **279–284**, 299
McGegan, Nicholas, **185–191**, 261

469

McGill University, Multimodal Shared
   Reality Laboratory, 89
McGrann, Jeremiah W., 80, 306, 337
McGuinness, Rosamond, 230
McVeigh, Simon, 16, 188, 229–30
Mechem, Kirke, 15
mediation, 156
medicine, 26, 136, 345, 346
Mehlgrube (Vienna), 396
Méhul, Étienne Nicolas (1763–1817), 234
Meisel, Martin, 347
Melancholy, 2, 160, **207–208**
   disability and, 87–88
   genius and, 138–39
   humor and, 145
   poetry and, 309
   self-conquest, 207–8
Melk Abbey, 51, 57
Melk Collegiate Church, 356
Melody, 157, **209–213**
   circulation and, 55
   compositional process and, 67
   folk music and, 121
   form and, 125
   musical materials and, 226
   press and, 314
   self-reflexivity and, 348
   sensibility and, 99
   theater and theatricality, 372
Melton, James Van Horn, **95–97**, 168, 359
memorials and memorializing. *See*
   Monuments and Memorializing
Mendelssohn, Felix (1809–1847), 25, 326
Mendelssohn, Moses (1729–1786), 105, 184
Mercer-Taylor, Peter, 13
Mercure de France (gazette and literary
   magazine), 174, 312, 314
Mesmerism, 347
Metastasio, Pietro (1698–1782), 64, 120, 135,
   194, 251, 307, 325, 356, 360, 364,
   398, 398
   L'isola disabitata, 194, 239
metathematicism, 221
meter. *See* Rhythm and Meter
mezzo carattere, 192
Michaelerhaus, 64, 120, 296, 356, 398, 398
Michaelerkirche, 51, 296
Michaelis, Christian Friedrich (1770–1834),
   1, 19–21, 145, 157, 160, 355
middle class, 78, 121, 197, 392, 396, 397, 399
Mikusi, Balázs, 10, **106–111**, **132–134**, 135,
   137, 201, 299, **317–320**, 335
Milan, 247
military (Topic), 8, 36, 152, 162, 216, 239,
   248, 378, 405
military personnel, 248
Miller, Christopher R., 372
Miller, Norbert, 3
Milton, John (1608–1674), 19, 354
   Paradise Lost, 184, 195–96

Mimesis, 32, 154–56, **213–215**, *see also*
   Topics, Programmatic Elements
nature and, 239
science and, 347
theater and, 359
theater and theatricality, 366, 370
minuet, 75, 100, 239, 341
Miranda, General Francisco de (1750–1816),
   9–10, 383
Mirka, Danuta, 154, 226, 342, 344, 374
Mirror Hall, 281
misattributed works, 324, *see also*
   authenticity, spurious works
missa brevis style, 184
mobility, 36, 44
model. *See* influence, Haydn's
"Modern Haydn," 153
modernism and modernity, 15, 36, 307, 310,
   325, 373
Molière (Jean-Baptiste Poquelin) (1722–
   1773), 366
monarchy, 237, *see also* Habsburg monarchy,
   Courts
monasteries, 51, 57, 115
Monelle, Raymond (1937–2010), 239
monetary economy, 91–92, *see also*
   Economics and Finances
Monn, Georg Matthias (1717–1750), 64,
   120, 138
monothematicism, 209, 218, 221
Montbeillard, François Guéneau de (1759–
   1847), 234
Monticello (Jefferson residence), 13
Monuments and Memorializing, 3, 32, 163,
   216–217, 374, *see also* Sublime
   place and, 305
   reception and, 321, 322
moral characters, 82, 315
Morales, Luisa, **111–116**
Moravians, 10–11, 57, 306
Moreau le Jeune, Jean-Michel (1741–
   1814), 204
Moreau, Charles (1758–1840), 109, 111, 281
Morellet, André (1727–1819), 275, 277
Morelli, Teresina (fl.1758–1770), 63
Morgan Library and Museum, New York,
   57
Moricheli, Anna (c.1745–1800), 148
Mörner, Carl-Gabriel, 257, 359
Morning Chronicle (newspaper), 310, 311,
   312, 314
Morning Herald (newspaper), 197, 314
Morrow, Mary Sue, 135, 173, 230,
   311–315, 397
Morzin Hauskapellen, 78
Morzin, Count Carl Joseph Franz (1717–83), 79
Morzin, Count Franz Ferdinand Maximilian
   (1693–1763), 63, 79, 91, 168, 264,
   280, 297
Morzin, Countess, 401
Mosaic law, 184

Most Holy Name of Mary feast, 80
motives, 117
Mozart, Constanze (1762–1842), 4, 189
Mozart, Franz Xaver (1791–1844), 256
Mozart, Leopold (1719–1787), 170, 336, 401
Mozart, Maria Anna (Nannerl) (1751–1829), 65
Mozart, Wolfgang Amadeus (1756–1791), 4, 27–28, 135, 140, 170, 171, 173, 319, 391
  amateurs and, 7
  audiences, 18
  biography, 153
  Così fan tutte, 252
  counterpoint and, 358
  cyclic integration, 82–83
  death of, 324
  Die Entführung aus dem Serail, 150, 362
  Die Zauberflöte, 134
  Don Giovanni, 192, 370
  entrepreneurship, 29
  Freemasonry and, 133
  gender studies and, 137
  harmony and, 143
  Haydn and, 99, 149, 186–87, 236, 252, 306, 309, 321–24, 336
  Haydn's relationship with, 65
  Idealism and, 150–51
  images of, 204
  La finta semplice, 401
  Le nozze di Figaro, 192, 194, 252, 365
  melody and, 209
  musical societies and, 230, 233–34
  orchestration, 242
  reception, 145, 321, 329
  recordings, 333
  relationships and friendships, 334
  sociability and, 350
  social background, 21, 25
  Sturm und Drang, 103
  variations and, 389
  Vienna and, 397, 399
  works dedicated to Haydn, 173, 251, 322
Müller, Hans, 24
multiculturalism, 40–42, 237
multi-stage variance, 225
Murray, Sterling, 235
musette drone, 380
music criticism, 22, 29, 99, 131, 208, 215, 304, 329–30
music stand, pedal-operated, 9
musica da chiesa, 338–39
Musical America, 328
musical autonomy, 99
musical idealism, 151
Musical Materials, 27, **218–229**
  disability and, 87
  Enlightenment and, 105
  reception and, 327

reduction, 222
sociability and, 351
musical notation, xvii
Musical Societies, 11, 168, 171, **229–235**, 305, *see also* Leading Large Ensembles, Americas, The
  American Musicological Society, 235
  Anacreontic Society, 231, 305
  Edinburgh Musical Society, 101
  Freunde der Tonkunst, 176
  Germania Society, 233
  Handel and Haydn Society, 11–13, 12, 232–33, 306
  Haydn Festival Society, Burgenland, 59
  Haydn Society, 89, 94, 235
  Haydn Society of Great Britain, 235, 331
  Haydn Society of North America, 235, 331
  New Musical Fund, 229
  New York Oratorio Society, 233
  Oxford Musical Society, 230, 232
  Philharmonic Society (Boston), 11, 233
  Philharmonic Society (London), 197, 202
  Philharmonic Society (St. Petersburg), 257
  Royal Society of Musicians, 229
  Sacred Harmonic Society, 232
  Société des Concerts of the Paris Conservatoire, 234
  Société Lamoureux, 234
  Society for Eighteenth-Century Music, 235
  Society of Amateur Concerts, 324
  Tonkünstler-Societät, 71, 171, 176, 185–87, 230–31, 252, 396
musical sources, 47
Musical Times and Singing Class Circular, 232
Musikalische Realzeitung (newspaper), 313
Musikalisches Institut, 176
Musiktage Mondsee, 60
Musikverein, Bergen, 231
Musikverein, Vienna, 59
Musikwissenschaftliches Institut, Graz, 50
Mykisch, Abund (Abuud) (fl.1750s), 251, 356
Mysliveček, Josef (1737–1781), 97, 118, 399

Nachlass, 46, *see also* Catalogues, Worklists, Nachlass
Napier, William (c.1740–1812), 54, 121, 123, 124, 124–25, 175, 319
Naples, 112, 392
Napoleon Bonaparte (1767–1821), 234
Napoleonic era, 21, 53, 99, 172, 175, 199, 216, 386, 392, 406
Národni muzeum, Prague, 55
national ideology, 159
national melodies. *See* Folk Song Settings
National Museum, Prague, 57
National Széchényi Library (Budapest), 55–56, 206
National Theater, 182

471

Nationalism and Cosmopolitanism, 24, 53, 63, **236–237**, 250, 370, 385, *see also* Burgenland, Folk Song Settings
  Burgenland and, 34, 36
  categorical ambiguity of, 163
  Enlightenment and, 101
  exoticism and, 117
  folk song settings and, 121, 122
  Idealism and, 150
  Jewish culture and, 184
  London and, 199
  place and, 297, 305–7
  politics and, 309, 310
  Vienna and, 392
  war and, 404
Native Americans, 11
natural philosophy, 162, 345–47
Nature, 160–61, **237–240**, *see also* Americas, The
  cyclic integration and, 84
  London and, 304
  mimesis and, 213
  programmatic elements and, 315
  religion and, 339
  sensibility and, 99
Naumann, Johann Gottlieb (1741–1801), 399
  Cora, 10
Nazi government, 171
Nedbal, Martin, 157, 252–53, **334–337**
negotiation skills, 256
Nelahozeves castle, 57
Nelson, Admiral Lord Horatio (1758–1805), 175, 404–5
Neoclassicism, 325
Netley Abbey, 238
networks. *See* People and Networks
Neue allgemeine deutsche Bibliothek, 314
Neue Bach Ausgabe, 95
Neue Mozart Ausgabe, 95
Neue Schubert Ausgabe, 95
Neuer Markt (Vienna), 81, 284
Neukomm, Sigismund (1778–1858), 14–15, 17, 25, 54, 122, 170, 206, 251, 257, 280, 357
Neuwirth, Markus, 125, 127, 130, **209–213**, 226, 227
New Musical Fund, 229
"New Musicology," 131, *see also* Gender, Form
New Rooms, Tottenham Court Road, 305
New World, 8, *see also* Americas, The
New York, 328
New York Normal Music Institute, 13
New York Oratorio Society, 233
New York Philharmonic, 15, 328
New York Public Library for the Performing Arts, Music Division (Lincoln Center), 57
Newman, Nancy, 230, 233
newspapers. *See* Press

Newton, Isaac (1643–1727), 139–40, 159, 345
Newton, James (1748–c.1804), 148
New-York Evening Post, 315
Niedt, Friedrich Erhardt (1674–1717), 75
Niemecz, Father Primitivus (1750–1806), 357
Niemetschek, Franz (1766–1849), 323, 324
niggun, 117, 184
"Night Watchman's Song," 316
Nimeroski, Ellie, 273
Nitschmann, Immanuel (1736–1790), 11
nobility, 57, 77–78, 80, 118, *see also* aristocracy
North America. *See* Americas, The
nostalgia, 199, 207, 224
notebooks. *See* Correspondence and Notebooks
Nottebohm, Gustav (1817–1882), 142, 358
Notturni for King Ferdinand IV of Naples, 53
novelty, 139–40
November, Nancy, **1–2**, 87, 144–46, 156–58, 160, **207–208**, 309, 371
Noverre, Jean-Georges (1727–1810), 367
Nowak, Leopold (1904–1991), 67

O'Reilly, Robert Bray (fl.1789–1793), 197
Oatlands (Duke of York's estate), 80, 238
obbligato, 103, 121
Obere Windmühle, *393*
oboes, 177, 241
Och, Gunnar, 182
Oedenburg. *See* Sopron (Oedenberg)
Oettingen von Wallerstein, Prince Karl Ernst of (1748–1802), 18, 57
Oeuvres complettes de Joseph Haydn, 93, 255, 319
Oeuvres d'Haydn en partitions / Quatuors and Symphonies, 94
Oeuvres de Mozart, 319
Ogesser, Joseph, 48
Ogny, Comte Claude-François-Marie (1757–1790), 18, 134, 187, 231
Old Apothecary (Eisenstadt), 299
Old Testament, 184, 194
Olleson, Edward (1927– 2013), 195, 340
online discussion groups, 331
opera. *See* Vocal Coaching and Rehearsal; *opera seria*; opera, comic (*buffa*); Theater and Theatricality
Opera Concerts (London, 1795), 198, 201, 304
opera seria, 98, 192, 360, 380, 394, 401
opera, comic (*buffa*), 98, 191, 192, 214, 246, 280, 359, 360, 365, 366, 370, 372, 378, 394
Oppermann, Annette, 69
opus concept, 30, 277, 373
opus numbers, 47, 62
Oracle, 140
orality, music and, 245

Oratorio de la Santa Cuev (Spain), 339
orchestras. *See* Leading Large Ensembles
Orchestration, 55, 112, 156, 164, 186, 185, **241–243**, 372, *see also* Leading Large Ensembles
  genius and, 140
  musical materials and, 225–26
  performance spaces and, 283
  programmatic elements and, 315
  recordings and, 332
  sublimity and, 353
  variation and, 390
Orde, Thomas (1740–1807), 238, 386
Ordonez, Johann Karl von (1734–1786), 64
orecchianti ("ear-ers"), 401
organicism, 83, 372
organology. *See* Instruments and Organology
originality, 1, 139–40, 149, 165, 245, 321, 325, *see also* Genius
ornamental (*niedlich*) (aesthetic category), 1–2
Orpheus Experiment, June 2016 (Orpheus Institute, Ghent, Belgium), 262–79
Orpheus myth, 197, 304, 310, 368
Osek Abbey, 57
Ossian. *See* Celtic "Ossian" epics
Other. *See* Exoticism
Ott, A. M. (fl.1790s), 148
Ottoman Empire, 40–41, 184, 362
output, Haydn's, 45, 47
Ovid (43 BCE–17/18 CE), 154–55, 194, 298, 360
  Metamorphoses, 196, 221, 317
Oxford (England), 386
Oxford Musical Society, 230, 232
Oxford University, 18, 175, 229, 232
  Musical Society, 230, 232

Pacchierotti, Gaspare (1740–1821), 402
Padua, 315
Page, Janet K., **47–51**, 168
Paine, Thomas (1737–1809), 10, 311, 370
Paisiello, Giovanni (1740–1816), 192, 300, 399
  Il barbiere di Siviglia (Paisiello and Petrosellini), 192, 365
  L'amor contrastato (La molinara), 365
Palestrina, Giovanni Pierluigi da (1525–1594), 50
Palomba, Antonio (1705–1769), 192
Palotta, Matteo (c.1688–1758), 50
Pandi, Marianne, 253
Pannonia. *See* Burgenland
pantomimes, 70, 112, 228, 366, 367, 370
"Papa Haydn," 144–45, 153, 325, 329, *see also* patriarch, Haydn as (father-figure)
Papendieck, Charlotte (1765–1840), 303
Paradis, Maria Theresia von (1759–1824), 135
paradoxical contrasts, 208
Paris, 172, 302, 392
  circulation and, 52
  concerts in, 187
  Freemasonry in, 134
  Jefferson in, 13
  musical societies, 230–31
  musical societies in, 233
  press, 173–74
  publishers, 317
Paris Institut National des Sciences et des Arts, 231
Paris Opéra, 112
Parker, Mara, 351
Parsons, James, **307–309**
partimento, 69, 142–43, 261, 380
part-songs, 15
Passer, 247
passions, 98, 99, 155, 157, 158, 213, 214, 354, 366
Passionston, 316
pastoral, 2, 227, 315, 340, 354, 378, 380
patriarch, Haydn as (father-figure), 251, 253, 257, 309, 325, 334
patriarchal ideology, 159
patronage, 27, 61, 62, 66, 78, 80, 81, 85, 156, 169, 172, 175, 230, 233, 245, 249–51, 280, 297, 309, 310, 337, *see also* Courts, aristocratic patronage
patrons, 4, 16–17, 21, 62, 92, 110, 111, 118, 201, 229, 230, 244, 250, 256, 307, 335, 337, 345, 391, 398, 404, 405
Pauerspach, Karl Michael von (1737–1802), 366
Paul Petrovich, Grand Duke of Russia (later Tsar Paul I) (1754–1801), 79, 111
peasants, 16
Pederson, Sanna, 149
Pensionsgesellschaft bildender Künstler, 234
People and Networks, **244–257**, *see also* Theater and Theatricality, Burgenland, Biography and Identity
  disability and, 87
  Enlightenment and, 101
  gender and, 135
  performance and, 262
  theater and theatricality, 363
Peregrinikapelle, 51
Peregrinus, Saint (1265–1345), 24
Performance, 26, 72, 174, **258–279**
  disability and, 89
  discography and, 90
  Enlightenment and, 105
  gender and, 137
  improvisation and, 166
  monuments and memorializing, 217
  people and networks, 244
  place and, 297
  self-reflexivity and, 349
  sociability and, 349
  theater and theatricality, 371
Performance Spaces, 50, **279–284**
  acoustics, 261
  amateurs and, 7

Performance Spaces (cont.)
    court and, 299
    Eszterháza and Eisenstadt, 109–11, 185, 299
    in Europe, 114
    large ensembles and, 188–91
    people and networks, 244
    theater and, 360
performativity, 137, 359
Pergolesi, Giovanni Battista (1710–1736), 120, 301
period ensemble, instrument(s), orchestra, performance, 59, 261, 264
Perioden, Periods, 125, 126, 153, 209, 212, 269, 278, 338–39, 341, 380
periodicals. *See* Press
periodicity, periodization, 3, 110, 131, 162, 171, 177, 341, 360, 362, 374
persona, 70
Peter, Johann Friedrich (1746–1813), 11
Peters, C. F. (publisher), 93, 95
Petrosellini, Giuseppe (1727–1797), 192
Pezzl, Johann (1756–1823), 373
Pfarrschule, 95
phantasieren, 1, 67–70, 165–66
Philharmonic Society (Boston), 11, 233
Philharmonic Society (London), 197, 202
Philharmonic Society (St. Petersburg), 257
Philippus-und-Jakobus-Kirche (Hainburg), 296
philosophy. *See* Idealism
    science and, 346
phrase, 81, 100, 122, 125–26, 209–10, 221, 224, 226, 269, 342, 343, 374, 380
phrenology, 337
physiognomy, 147, 345
pianos, 181, 262, 268, *see also* keyboards
Piaristenkirche, 51, 301, 306, 405
Piccinni, Niccolò (1728–1800), 300
    La buona figliuola, 362
Pichl, Wenzeslaus (Wenzel) (1741–1805), 247
pictorialism, 215, 239, 340, 379, 386
picturesque, 1, 195, 238, 379
Piekut, Benjamin, 244
Pietas Austriaca, 24, 168, 174, 337
Pietsch, Rudolf, **34–44**, 297
piety, 24, 96, 168, 337, 338, *see also* Religion and Spiritual Beliefs, *Pietas Austriaca*
pilgrimage, 383–84
Pilgrims Lodge, 133
piracy, 61, 122
Pitt, William the Younger (1759–1806), 369
Place, **296–307**
    audiences and, 15
    Enlightenment and, 101
    monuments and, 216
    people and networks, 244
    theater and, 360
pleasure gardens (London), 174, 201, 231, 304

Pleyel, Ignaz Joseph (1757–1831), 3, 46, 47, 65–66, 93, 97, 114, 118, 121, 148, 172–73, 198, 234, 251, 255, 315, 318, 319, 357
Ployer, Barbara von (1767–c.1810), 391
Poelchau, Georg (1773–1836), 56
Poets, 54, 121, **307–309**
    Idealism and, 149
    in London, 201
    sensibility and, 158
    sublimity and, 354
Pohl, Carl Ferdinand (1819–1887), 25, 57, 212, 327
Politics, 53, 152, 162, **309–311**
    ancien régime, 21, 22–23
    Burgenland and, 36
    England and, 197
    in the Americas, 12
    nationalism and, 237
    religion and, 337
Pollheimer, Klaus M., 360–61, 366
Polzelli, Antonio (1783–1855), 251, 334, 357
Polzelli, Luigia (1750–1830), 64, 201, 207, 247, 251, 334–35, 364, 401
Polzelli, Pietro (1777–1796), 251, 357
Polzonetti, Pierpaolo, 10, 154–55, **191–196**, 220, 347, 364
popular culture. *See* Reception, 1950s–present
popularity, 55, 111, 112, 167, 174, 212, 231, 243, 317, 326, 399, *see also* celebrity
Porpora, Nicola (1686–1768), 25, 63, 64, 69–70, 120, 142, 210, 297, 396, 397–98, 398, 399–400, 402
Porta, Nunziato (fl.1770–1795), 63, 192, 300, 365
    Orlando paladino, 194
Porter, Roy, 237, 346
portraits, 32, 147–48, 204, *see also* Iconography
Potter, Richard (1726–1806), 178
Pougin, Arthur (1834–1921), 233
Prague, 57, 170
Pratl, Josef, 10, 299, 363
Predieri, Luca Antonio (1688–1767), 395
prejudices, 138
prelapsarian, 184
Prellmechanik, 180
Press, 66, 173, 298, **311–315**
    freedom of, 394
    gender and, 135
    Idealism and, 151
    in London, 198
    London, 201
    people and networks, 255
Pressburg [Preßburg], 41, 79, 92, 170, 248, 281, 360–61
prestige, 78
Price, Curtis, 367
Prickler, Harold, 183
print collection, **204**

474

printing. *See* Publishers and Publishing
privileges, publishing and, 61
productivity, Haydn's, 45–46
Professional Concerts, 16, 65, 175, 197–98, 304, 357
professionals. *See* Composers and Music Professionals
profits, 254, 318
Programmatic Elements, 32, 64, 70, **315–317**
   cyclic integration and, 82
   musical materials and, 228
   nature and, 238
   reception and, 326
   science and, 347
   topics and, 379
   travel and exploration, 386
progress (Enlightenment concept), 24, 153, 384
Proksch, Bryan, 15, 18, **81–84**, 149, 218, 224, 225, 233, **325–28**
Protestantism, 23, 41, 105, 118, 149, 195, 340
Prunksaal, 299
psychology, 98, 347
public appearance, Haydn's last, 324
public sphere, 23, 27, 250
   women in, 136
publics. *See* Audiences and Publics
Publishers and Publishing, 21, 22, 66, 168, 171–73, **317–320**
   amateurs and, 5
   Americas and, 8
   audiences and, 15
   autograph scores and, 56
   catalogues and, 45, 46
   circulation and, 52–55
   commerce and markets, 61–62
   correspondence and, 71
   dedicatees and, 62, 85
   editions and, 93
   Enlightenment and, 105
   European, 115
   finances and, 92
   folk song settings, 121
   Freemasonry and, 134
   iconography and, 147
   in Vienna, 394, 396
   London and, 201–2
   maps and, 383
   material culture and, 205
   monasteries and, 51
   monuments and memorializing, 216–17
   people and networks, 244, 250, 254–56
   politics and, 309
   press and, 312
   reception and, 321
   self-publishing, 61
   symphonies, 187
   variations and, 389
puppet operas, 366–67
Puttini, Francesco (c.1755–c.1776)
   La vera costanza, 192

Quakers, 10
Quantz, Johann Joachim (1697–1773), 177, 269
quartet parties, 6
quartet stand, 259
quartet-as-conversation, 351
Quartetto Toscano, 112
"quatuor féminin," 230
quotations, 15, 84, 205, 252, 316

Raab, Armin, xv, 3, 28, **93–95**
race, racism, 135, 138, 361
Racine, Karen, 10
Rahier, Peter Ludwig von (? – 1791), 170, 246, 248, 249
Rainer, Ingo, 36
Rameau, Jean-Philippe (1683–1764), 87
Randel, Don, 135
Ratner, Leonard (1916–2011), 154–55, 343, 380
Ratz, Erwin (1898–1973), 127
Rauzzini, Venanzio (1746–1810), 191, 402
Ravel, Maurice (1875–1937), 327
Real Teatro del Fondo, 112
realism, 98, 157
Realzeitung (newspaper), 298
reason, 101, 102, 105, 136, 160–61, 194, 234, 347
recapitulation, 267, 348, 390
   false, 242
Reception, 22, 52, 153, 163, 172, 207
   aging and, 3
   American, 7, 11, 15
   catalogues and, 45
   commemorations, 58
   commercial success and, 62
   editions and, 94
   European, 113, 202
   exoticism and, 117
   folk music and, 121
   genius and, 138
   humor and, 145
   iconography and, 149
   Idealism and, 149
   ideas and, 249
   medals of achievement, 205
   monuments and memorializing, 217
   musical materials and, 218
   musical societies and, 229
   press and, 312
   recordings and, 90
   self-reflexivity and, 349
   sensibility and, 100
   students and, 357
   sublimity and, 352
   tonality and, 375
   war and, 405
Reception, 1950s–present, 131, **328–331**
Reception, Contemporary, 31, **321–325**, 358
Reception, Posthumous to 1959, 3, **325–328**
Reckh, Anton (1770–1863), 119

Recording, 90, 263, **332–334**, *see also* Discography
  editions and, 94
  musical societies and, 235
  reception and, 328
Redoutensaal, 231, 234, 252, 283
  Grosser Redoutensaal, 283–84
  Kleiner Redoutensaal, 283
Reformation, 195
Regensburg (Germany), 57
Regnard, Jean-François (1655–1709)
  Le Distrait, 30, 366
Rehding, Alexander, 216
rehearsal. *See* Vocal Coaching and Rehearsal
Reiber, Joachim, 61
Reicha, Anton (1770–1836), 25–26, 74, 76, 351, 358
Reichardt, Johann Friedrich (1752–1814), 24, 166, 384
Reicher, Walter, **58–61**
Reinagle, Alexander (1756–1809), 13
Reinhardt, Johann Georg (1676–1742), 48
Reinhold, Karl Leonhard (1757–1823), 149
Relationships and Friendships, 26, 31, 158, 201, 252, **334–337**, 364
  amateurs and, 6
  dedicatees and, 85
  gender and, 135
  people and networks, 244, 257
  sensibility and, 100
  with composers and music professionals, 63
  with Jews, 184
  with students, 357
Religion and Spiritual Beliefs, 62, 105, 160, 161–62, **337–340**, *see also* Church
  ancien régime, 21, 23–24
  charity and, 93
  conversion and, 184
  in Burgenland, 40–41
  monuments and, 216
  people and networks, 246
  pilgrimage and, 383
  programmatic elements and, 316
  sensibility and, 158
  topics and, 379
Religious Enlightenment, 105, *see also* Catholic Enlightenment, Enlightenment
Republic of arts and letters, 159
Réti, Rudolph (1885–1957), 83
Reutter, Georg, Jr. (1708–1772), 47–48, 50, 63, 78, 96–97, 119, 138, 297, 395
Reutter, Georg, Sr. (1656–1738), 119
revivals. *See* Commemorations and Festivals
revolutions. *See* War, French Revolution, American Revolution
rhetoric, 70, *see also* Performance
Rhythm and Meter, **340–344**
  cyclic integration and, 83
  folk song settings, 123

Latin, 15
musical materials and, 226
sensibility and, 99
topics and, 380
Ribeiro, Alvaro, 2
Rice, John A., 10, 187, 335, 337, 395
Rich, Sir Charles, 340
Richards, Annette, 156, 159, **165–167**, **213–215**, 385
Richardson, Samuel (1689–1761)
  Pamela, 98, 103, 192
Richter, Jean Paul (1763–1825), 146, 149
Richter, Joseph (1749–1813), 406
Riddarhuset (Stockholm), 257
Ridgewell, Rupert, 53
Riedel, Friedrich Wilhelm, 338
Riepel, Joseph (1709–1782), 125, 130, 132
Rieter-Biedermann, Jakob Melchior (1811–1876), 94
Riethmüller, Albrecht, 216
Righini, Vincenzo (1756–1812), 192, 399
Riley, Matthew, 5
Ringer, Joseph (c.1726–1802), 282
Rio de Janeiro, 14
Riskin, Jessica, 161
Ritter, Frederic (1834–1891), 233
Robertson, William (1721–1793)
  History of America, 9, 384
Robins, Brian, 232, 333
Rockobaur, Mathias (c.1708–1775), 177
Rohan, Prince Louis de (1734–1803), 109, 361
Rohrau, Austria (Haydn's birthplace), 3, 22, 59, 73, 118, 168, 217, 296, 310, 321
Roma (ethnic group), 40, 43
"Romantic Haydn," 153
Romanticism, 15, 31, 146, 149, 153, 159, 195, 325
  nature and, 238
  reception and, 326, 327
  religion and, 338
Römer, Ferdinand, 48
rondo/rondeau, 130, 135, 159
Ronge, Julia, 66
Rosa, Mario, 105
Rosen, Charles (1927–2012), 79, 131, 159, 227, 237, 343, 378
  The Classical Style, 329–30
Rosenbaum, Joseph Carl (1770–1829), 231, 337
Rosenblatt, Jason, 184
Roseneder, Andreas, xvii, 331
Rosenfeld, Paul (1890–1946), 15
Rossau (Austria), 51
Rosselli, John (1927–2001), 401, 403
Rossini, Gioachino Antonio (1792–1868)
  Il viaggio a Reims ossia Il giglio d'ora, 237
  Mosè in Egitto, 165
rotation (development procedure), 127
Rothstein, William, 343

Roubiliac, Louis-François (1702–1762), 305
Rousseau, Jean-Jacques (1712–1778), 9, 157, 161, 212
Rowland-Jones, Simon, 95, 202
Royal Academy Exhibition (1792), 148, 303
Royal Monastery of las Descalzas, Madrid, 113
Royal Palace (Spain), 114
Royal Society of Musicians, 229
royalty, 118, *see also* aristocracy, Courts, monarchy
Rudolph, Archduke of Austria (1788–1831), 57
Ruhling, Michael, 11, **89–90**
rule of the octave, 69, 143–44, 222
rules, 382
rules of art, 1, 25, 82, 159, 166–67, 218
Rumph, Stephen, 376, 381
Rust, Giacomo (1741–1786), *La contadina in corte*, 361
rustic style, themes, 117, 122, 228, 236, 239, 370, 372

Sacchi, Marco (1600–1662), 358
Sacchini, Antonio (1730–1786), 399
  La contadina in corte, 361
  La contadina ingentilita, 365
Sachsen-Hildburghausen, Prince Joseph Friedrich von (1702–1787), 397
Sächsische Landesbibliothek – Stadts- und Universitätsbibliothek, 57
Sacred Harmonic Society, 232
sadness, 208, *see also* Melancholy
St. Agnes zur Himmelpforte (female convent in Vienna), 48
St. Ägyd church (Gumpendorf), 51
St. Florian Abbey (Austrian monastery), 51
Saint Francis of Paola (1416–1507), 168
St. Ivonis (St. Ivo of Chartres), 48
St. James's Chronicle (court newspaper, London), 80
St. John of God (1495–1550), 50, 184
St. Joseph convent (Vienna), 48
St. Martin's church, 50–51
St. Nikolai convent (Vienna), 48, 50
St. Paul's Cathedral, 51, 99, 402, *403*
St. Peter's Church, 395
St. Petersburg (Russia), 257, 306, 363, 365
St. Stephen's Cathedral, 25, 27, 47–50, 49, 63, 91, 119–20, 169, 296, 338, 356, 395
  courts and, 78
St. Stephen's Choir School, 69, 75, 95–97, 138
Saint Vincent Archabbey (Pennsylvania), 11
Saint-Saëns, Camille (1835–1921), 25, 327
Salieri, Antonio (1750–1825), 4, 65, 112, 324, 395, 396, 399, 401
  Der Rauchfangkehrer, 401
Salle des Cent-Suisses, 187, 302
Salle des Machines, 302

Salomon, Johann Peter (1745–1815), 16, 18, 53–54, 61, 65–66, 112, 133, 140, 148, 174–75, 184, 188, 188–89, 198, 200–2, 232, 253–54, 283, 302–4, 311, 321, 340, 357, 371, 385
  Windsor Castle, 80, 367
salons, 135–36, 252, 350, 351, 399
Salzburg, 27, 170, 336
Sammartini, Giovanni Battista (1700–1775), 396
San Pedro de las Dueñas (León), 116
Sand, George (1804–1886), 326
Sandberger, Adolf (1864–1943), 330
Sandgruber, Roman, 91
Sanguinetti, Giorgio, 261
Santa Ana de Ávila, 116
Santa Cueva chapel, 114
Sarti, Giuseppe (1729–1802), 31, 134, 300, 399
  Giulio Sabino, 336, 365
  Idalide, 10, 384
Satz. *See* phrase
Sauder, Gerhard, 97
Saurau, Count Joseph Franz (1760–1732), 236, 404
Saxony, 40
Scarlatti, Domenico (1685–1757), 115, 120
Schachter, Carl, 375
Schafer, Hollace Ann (1955–1995), 67
Schama, Simon, 237
Schanz, Wenzel (c.1750–c.1789/90), 180, 206, 268, 391
Schaul, Johann Baptist (1759–1822), 219–20
Scheideler, Ullrich, 76
Schelling, Friedrich Wilhelm Joseph (1775–1854), 149
Schenk, Johann Baptist (1753–1836), 358
Schenker, Heinrich (1868–1935), 127, 327, 333, 375
Schiavonetti, Luigi (1765–1810), 147
Schifrin, Boris Claudio "Lalo," 15
Schikaneder, Emanuel (1751–1812), 365
Schiller, Friedrich (1759–1805), 122, 149–50, 307, 366
Schilling, Gustav (1805–1880), 353
Schindler, Anton (1795–1864), 142
Schlegel, August Wilhelm von (1767–1845), 149
Schlegel, Friedrich von (1772–1829), 149–50
Schlesinger, Adolf Martin (1769–1829), 148
Schleuning, Peter, 158
Schloss Esterházy, 331
Schloss Kittsee, 59
Schloss Rohrau, 59
Schloss Weinzierl, 280
Schmalfeldt, Janet, 127
Schmalögger, Joseph (fl.1770s), 367
Schmid, Ernst Fritz (1904–1960), 32, 94, 253
Schmidt, Ferdinand (c.1693–1756), 48
Schoenberg, Arnold (1874–1951), 327

477

Schönbrunn Palace (Vienna), 48, 281–82, 282, 296, 299
schools. *See* Vocal Coaching and Rehearsal, Teaching and Students, Education, Experiential Learning
Schopenhauer, Arthur (1788–1860), 149
Schottenkirche (Scottish Church), 395
Schroeder, David, 73, 102, 103, 151, 311, 401
Schroeter [Schröter], Corona (1751–1802), 138
Schroeter, Johann Samuel (1750–1788), 335
Schroeter, Rebecca (1751–1826), 31, 72, 73, 85, 201, 305, 335, 357, 391
Schubart, Christian Friedrich Daniel (1739–1791), 166
Schubert, Franz (1797–1828), 94, 95, 97, 118, 376
Schuchart, John Just (1695–1753), 177
Schuhplattler (folk dance), 380
Schuke, Karl (1906–1987), Orgelbauwerkstatt, 51
Schulz, Johann Abraham Peter (1747–1800), 31
 Lieder im Volkston, 236
Schumann, Robert (1810–1856), 94, 326, 391
 Second Symphony, 326
Schütz, Carl (1745–1800), 282, 398
Schwarzenberg, Prince Joseph Johann von (1769–1833), 80–81, 169, 230, 284, 306, 363, 397
Schwarzenburg Palace, 189
Science, 160, 162, 194, 195, 206, **345–347**, 364, 385
 Enlightenment and, 101, 104–5
 religion and, 339
"Scotch snap," 123
Scott, Marion (1877–1953), 23
Scottish Enlightenment, 101–3, 160
Scottish song settings, 121–23, 257, 314
"Séances populaires de musique de chambre," 234
Seedorf, Thomas, 210
Seeger, Horst, 25, 30
Seletsky, Robert E., 178
self-publishing, 61, 92, 319
Self-Reflexivity, 146, **348–349**, 371
 exoticism and, 118
 Idealism and, 152
 melancholy and, 207, 208
 musical materials and, 227
 performance and, 260, 263
 topics and, 382
self-study, 118, 119, 256
sensibility, 72, 97–100, 158, 378
 melancholy and, 87
 poetry and, 307
 science and, 346
 topics and, 382
sentimental styles, 192, 378, 378
sentimentality, 98, 100, 102, 103
seraglio, 137, 362, *see also* harem

Servite church, Rossau (Austria), 51
setzen. *See* Compositional Process
Seven Years War (1756–63), 392, 404
Sewell, John (publisher) (c.1734–1802), 148
Shaftesbury, Anthony Ashley Cooper, 3rd Earl of (1671–1713)
 Characteristics of Men, Manners, Opinions, Times, 102
Shakespeare, William (1564–1616), 139, 145, 151, 159, 160, 175, 197, 204, 366
 Hamlet, 316
 "She Never Told Her Love," 208, 307
 Twelfth Night, 307
Sheldonian Theatre, 232
Shenstone, William (1714–1763), 54
Sher, Richard, 102
Shield, William (1748–1829), 121
Sieben Gemeinde (seven Jewish communities), 41, 182
Sieber, Jean-Georges (1738–1822), 94, 237, 302
Siegert, Christine, xv, 15, 92, 334, 335, 370, 371
Siegl, Frantz (fl.1760s), 249
Silverstolpe, Fredrik Samuel (1769–1851), 144, 215, 257, 380
Simrock, Nikolaus (1751–1832), 94, 253
singing style, 380
Singspiel, 394
Sinzendorf, Prince, 80
Siskin, Clifford, 105, 156
Sisman, Elaine, 1, 5, 10, 16, 30, 73, 87–88, 103, 130, 139, 145, 154–55, 160–62, 194, 197, 208, 219, **237–240**, 246, 304, 315, 316, 330, 343, **345–347**, 353, 355, 364, 366, 370, **372–374**, 378, 379, 389, 390
slavery, 14, 384
Slinn, Jane, 350
Slovaks, 40, 43, 116, 117
Small, Christopher (1927–2011), 351
Smart, George Thomas (1776–1867), 400
Smith, Adam (1723–1790), 102, 103, 160, 214, 250
 Lectures on Jurisprudence, 102
 The Wealth of Nations, 102
 Theory of Moral Sentiments, 102, 307
Smith, Charlotte Turner (1749–1806), 54
Smith, Ruth, 354
Sociability, 26, 252, **349–352**, 352
 amateurs and, 5–6
 Enlightenment and, 101, 102
 humor and, 146
 Idealism and, 152
 performance and, 259, 270–79
 place and, 302
 poetry and, 307
 theater and theatricality, 372
social capital, 79, 80
social class, 16, 55, 117, 122, 138, 236, 245, 250, 403
social development, 101
societies. *See* Musical Societies

Socrates (c.470–399 BCE), 194, 370
Soler, Antonio (1729–1783), 115
Somfai, László, 127, 147, 191, 266, 267, 271, 333, 349
Somis, Giovanni Battista (1686–1763), 178
Sonata Theory (Hepokoski and Darcy), 131
sonata-form, sonata form structures, 127, 131, 151, 223, 316, 382
Sonneck, Oscar (1873–1928), 15
Sonnenfels, Joseph von (1732–1817), 394
Sonnleithner-Sammlung (1819) (collection of Austrian folk songs), 36
Sopron (Oedenberg), 35, 41, 109
Sor, Ferdinando (1778–1839), 113
Sorge, Georg Andreas (1703–1778), 143
Sorkin, David, 105, 184
Southard, Lucien H. (1827–1881), 13
Spain, 14, 256, 306, 383
Spain, New, 10
Spech, Johann (c.1767–1836), 357
Spectator, The, 303
spiritual beliefs. *See* Religion and Spiritual Beliefs
Spitzer, John, 187, 241
Spohr, Louis (1784–1859), 392
spurious works, 47, 61
Staatsbibliothek zu Berlin, 55–56
stadial theory, 102, 160
Stadion, Johann Philipp (1763–1824), 256
Stadler, Abbé Maximilian (1748–1833), 206
Stadlmann, Johann Joseph (1720–1781), 179
Staël, Anne-Louise Germaine de, 350
Stamitz, Johann Wenzel Anton (1717–1757), 97, 118
Starzer, Joseph (1726–1787), 64, 396
Stations of the Cross, 383
Statute of Anne (1709), 61
Steblin, Rita, 50
Steffan (Stěpan), Joseph Anton (1726–1797), 398
Steinbeck, Wolfram, xv
Stendhal, pen-name for Marie-Henri Beyle (1783–1742), 144, 325, 350
Sterne, Jonathan, 332
Sterne, Laurence (1713–1768), 100, 139, 146, 159, 160, 348
  Sentimental Journey through France and Italy by Mr Yorick, 387
  Tristram Shandy, 348, 373
Stevenson, Robert (1916–2012), 14, 370
Stockdale, John (1750–1814), 393
Stockholm, 257
Storace, Nancy (1765–1817), 65, 194, 367
Storace, Stephen (1762–1796), 65, 336
Stossmechanik, 180
Strauss, Barbara, 11
Stroud, Rachel, 273
Struck, Paul (1776–1820), 357
Sturm und Drang, 103–4, 151, 277, 326, 330, 366, 378
Sublime, 1–2, 152, 156, 158, 161, **352–355**

beautiful and, 19–20
counterpoint and, 76
Enlightenment and, 101
genius and, 138, 140
humor and, 145
Idealism and, 151
improvisation and, 166
melancholy and, 208
mimesis and, 214
musical materials and, 221
nature and, 238
opera and, 194–95
press and, 313
religion and, 338, 339
science and, 345
subscription concerts, 15–16, 54, 61, 196–98, 232, 324
success, commercial, 62
Sulzer, Johann Georg (1720–1779), 142, 157
  Allgemeine Theorie der schönen Künste, 214
Sumerau (Sommerau), Baron Gottfried von (1741/42–1787), 395
superstition, 346, 347, 394
Sutcliffe, W. Dean, 86, **218–229**, 329, 351–52, 381
Sutherland, Joan (1926–2010), 367
Süttör (Eszterháza), 106, 299
Svoboda, Hedy, 91
Swabia, 41
Sweden, 257
Swedish Music Academy, 257
Swieten, Gerhard van (1700–1772), 346, 397
Swieten, Gottfried van (1733–1803), 79, 80, 115, 133, 176, 184, 195, 204, 215, 230–31, 253, 256, 306, 345, 347, 397
symbolic capital, 252
sympathy, 98, 136, 145, 155, 160, 307–8
Szabolcsi, Bence (1899–1973), 117

talent, 138, *see also* Genius
Taruskin, Richard, 224, 227, 244–45
Tasso, Torquato (1544–1595), 112, 194
Tattersall, Rev. William de Chair (1751–1829)
  Improved Psalmody, 340
Tauregui, Fernandez (fl. 1780s), 14
Taylor, Ian, 197
Teaching and Students, 63, 71, 97, **356–359**, *see also* Vocal Coaching and Rehearsal, Education
counterpoint and, 119
demonstration and, 400
gender and, 135
people and networks, 244, 251, 255
Vienna and, 398
Teatro de la Cruz, 113
Teatro de los Caños del Peral, 113
Teatro del Príncipe, 113
Teatro Reale, 112
Teatro Regio, Turin, 112
technology, 101, 104

Teimer, Philipp (fl.1790s), 81
Telemann, Georg Philipp (1681–1767), 22, 61
Temperley, David, 343
Temperley, Nicholas, 216, 233
tempo, 36, 42, 266, 332, 333, 341, 373, 389, 402
text painting, 32, 164, 208, 215, 308, 380
textures, 54, 103, 117, 140, 153, 184, 222, 228, 308, 377
Theater and Theatricality, 28, **359–372**, 384
  Americas and, 10
  at Eszterháza, 110
  audiences and, 15
  comedies, 246–47
  counterpoint and, 75
  court and, 337
  courts and, 245–47
  form and, 125
  in Eisenstadt, 63
  in Europe, 112–14
  in London, 175, 197
  in Vienna, 182, 394–95
  Jewish culture and, 182
  libretti and, 192
  musical education and, 120
  people and networks, 245
  performance and, 260, 261
  press and, 312
  programmatic elements and, 316
  publishers and, 318
Theater auf der Wieden (Freyhaus Theater), 365
Theatre an der Wien, 90
Théâtre des arts in Paris, 306
Third Estate, 237
third-period style. *See* late style
Thomas-Mifune, Werner
  Haydns Südamerikanische Saitensprünge, 15
Thompson, Samuel (fl.1780–90)
  Twelve Elegant and Familiar Canzonetts, 6
Thomson, George (1757–1851), 121–23, 160, 311, 319
  "Dissertation Concerning the National Melodies of Scotland," 102
  Select Collection of Original Scottish Airs, 102, 123
Thomson, James (1700–1748)
  The Seasons, 195
Thomson, William (fl.1695–1753)
  Orpheus Caledonius, 102
Thormählen, Wiebke, 6, 31, **51–55**, 196–202, 304
thoroughbass, 69, 75, 142–44
Thurn und Taxis family, 57
Tieck, Johann Ludwig (1773–1853), 149–50
timbre, 179, 226, 332, 402, 403
Time, 136, 152, 155, 160–61, **372–374**, 380
  meter and, 340
  programmatic elements and, 315
  science and, 346

Tolley, Thomas, 9, 26, 28, 140, 201, **203–207**, 214, 215, 298, 311, 349, **382–388**
Tomasini, Aloisio Luigi (1741–1808), 63, 79, 109, 170, 179, 185, 264, 265, 317, 335–36
tonadillas (comic intermezzi), 113
Tonality, **374–376**
  folk song settings, 123
  harmony and, 143
  musical materials and, 218
  teaching and students, 359
Topics, 76, 97, 151, 154, **376–382**
  folk song settings, 122
  hunting, 30, 161, 215, 238–39, 248, 307, 316, 372, 373, 378, 388
  military, 8, 36, 152, 162, 216, 239, 248, 378, 405
  musical materials, 225, 227–28
  nature, 239
  programmatic elements and, 315–16
  rhythm and meter and, 341
  self-reflexivity and, 348
  sublimity and, 353
  troping, 378
törökös, 117, 184
Torricella, Christoph (c.1715–1798), 52, 173, 256
Toscanini, Arturo (1867–1957), 15, 328, 333
Tost, Johann (1759–1831), 173
Tour of the Isle of Wight (1790), 238
tours and tourism, 238, 356, 386, *see also* Travel and Exploration
Tourte, François (1747–1835), 179
Tovey, Donald Francis (1875–1940), 162, 329, 333, 347
  Essays in Musical Analysis, 328
Traeg, Johann (1747–1805), 254–55
Traetta, Tommaso (1727–1779), 366
  Ifigenia in Tauride, 362
  Il cavaliere errante, 365
tragédies lyriques, 112
Transatlantic Studies. *See* Americas, The
transcultural composition, 117
Transformationism (cosmogony), 195
translation studies, 333
transnational experiences, 184
Trautmannsdorf, Prince Franz Ferdinand (1749–1827), 80
Travaglia, Pietro (fl.1770–1790), 247, 284, 364
Travel and Exploration, 8, 182, 364, **382–388**
  composers and music professionals and, 63
  place and, 298
  traveling theatrical troupes, 52, 182, 246–47, 360, 366
Treaty of Paris (1814), 234
Treaty of Union (1707), 101
Tres horas (Three Hours) passion service, 114
Trias-harmonica tradition, 143
Triest, Johann Karl Friedrich (1764–1810), 20, 32, 145–46, 226, 374

TRIOthlon, 331
Tromlitz, Johann George (1725–1805), 177
trouser roles, 246, 401, *see also* cross-dressed characters
trumpet, keyed, 156
Tuilleries, 187, 302
Tůma, František Ignác Antonín (1704–1774), 50, 120
Türk, Daniel Gottlob (1750–1813), 272
Turks, 80, 152, 392, 404
turquerie, Turkish style, 118, 163, 184, 298, 380, *see also* alla turca
Twining, Rev. Thomas (1735–1804), 2

United States. *See* Americas, The, American Revolution
Unitel Classica/ORF, 90
universality, 159, 172, 199–200
universality (of Haydn's style), 14
Universidad Complutense Library, Madrid, 116
University of Leyden, 345
Unterberg ghetto (Eisenstadt), 183
Uranus, discovery of, 345
Uruguay, 14

Van Boer, Bertil, **7–15**, 306
Vanhal, Johann Baptist (1739–1813), 64, 65, 252
Variation as Principle, 61, **389–391**
  audiences and, 15
  counterpoint and, 75
  experiential learning and, 119
  form and, 130
  melody and, 212
  musical materials and, 220
  performance and, 278
  reception and, 327
variety, compositional, 30, 36, 81, 123, 145, 161, 219, 224–26, 313–14, 348
Vaughan Williams, Ralph (1872–1958), 328
Vaux Hall Gardens (New York), 8
Vauxhall Gardens (London), 31, 305
Venice, 112, 247
Venus, Transit of, 162, 346, 373
Verlag, G. Henle, *Joseph Haydn Werke*, 328
Vestris, Auguste (1760–1842), 367
Vice Kapellmeister, Haydn as, 50, 63, 78, 91, 106, 315, 399
Vienna, 25, 31, 168, 175, 248, **391–399**
  audiences in, 17
  charity funds, 73, 93
  composers and music professionals, 64–65
  courts and, 78, 80
  education in, 356
  Freemasonry in, 111, 133
  instruments in, 180
  map of, *393*
  music publication in, 173
  people and networks, 247, 251–53

performance spaces, 283–84
performances, 189
place and, 297, 301–2
theater and, 359
theater and theatricality, 363
theaters in, 182
Turkish siege of, 80, 152
war and, 405
Vienna University, 175
  Old Hall, 4, 112, 189, 191, 284
Viennese Classical Style, 153–54, 159, 325, 348, *see also* Classical style
Vinci, Leonardo (1690–1730), 120
violin bows, 178–79, 262
violins, 265
Viotti, Giovanni Battista (1755–1824), 65, 283, 304
Virgil (70–19 BCE), 194
Virgin Mary, 383
virtue(s), 98, 151, 157, 168, 200, 223, 224
virtuoso, 5, 22, 138–39, 159, 178, 302, 357, 358, 396
visiting card, Haydn's, 3–4
Vivaldi, Antonio (1678–1741)
  The Four Seasons, 315
Vocal Coaching and Rehearsal, 25, 63, 261, 356, **399–403**, *403*
  people and networks, 246
  place and, 300
Volkston style, 34, 36, 43, 122, 163, 236, 311
Vörösmarty, Géza Michael, 48
Voskuhl, Adelheid, 161, 366

Wackenroder, Wilhelm Heinrich (1773–1798), 149–50
Wagenseil, Georg Christoph (1715–1777), 50, 64, 120, 395, 396, 398
Wagner, Richard (1813–1883), 326, 327, 367
Wahr, Carl (1745–1811), 28, 30, 182, 246, 366
Waldoff, Jessica, 98, 103, 194, 316
Waldstein, Count Ferdinand Gabriel von (1762–1823), 57, 150–51
Wales, Prince of. *See* George, Prince of Wales (later King George IV) (1762–1830)
Wallerstein Castle, 385
Wallnerstrasse palace, 50, 106, 169, 280, 297, 298, 300
Walter, Horst, 251, 356–58
Waltham-Smith, Naomi, 164
War, 48, 152, 162, 199, 310, 337, **404–406**, *see also* French Revolution, Politics, American Revolution
  Austro–Turkish War (1787–91), 392, 404
  in Spanish America, 10
  inflation and, 91
  musical societies and, 234
  Napoleonic Wars, 404
  political revolutions, 155
  Vienna and, 392

481

War (cont.)
    War of the Austrian Succession (1740–8), 392, 404
    War of the first Coalition, 24
    World War I, 327
Warner, William, 105, 156
Warton, Thomas (1728–1790), "Pleasures of Melancholy," 238
Washington, George (1732–1799), 10
Waverley Abbey, 238
Weber, Carl Maria von (1786–1826), 4, 121, 151, 251, 357, 358
    Der erste Ton, 164
Weber, Fritz and Edmund von, 357
Weber, Gottfried (1779–1839), 375
Weber, Max (1864–1920), 132
Weber, William, 29
Webster, James, 2, 3, 66, 80, 81, 89, 98, 125, 130, 131, 151, 153–54, 159, 162, 166, 185, 210, 215, 222, 225, 230, 252, 266, 317, 322, 333, 338, 339, 348–49, 353–55, 380
    Haydn's "Farewell" Symphony and the Idea of Classical Style, 83–84, 329–30
Weidinger, Anton (1766–1852), 64, 156
Weigl, Joseph (1740–1820), 64, 179, 190, 264, 336
Weigl, Joseph (son) (1766–1846), 336
Weimar, 149
Weinstein, Gregory Ellis, 332
Weinzierl (Austria), 297
Weiskel, Thomas, 355
Weiss, Johann Baptist (1814–1850), 97
Weisse, Christian Friedrich (1726–1804), 307
Welsh songs, 121, 311
Weltschmerz. *See* Melancholy
Werfel, Franz (1890–1945), 41
Werner, Gregor Joseph (1693–1766), 25, 28, 50, 106, 111, 178, 248, 298
    Curious Musical Instrument Calendar, 374
Werner, Johann (fl.1750–1755), 178
Westminster Abbey, 51, 175, 187, 191, 305
Whateley, Mary (1738–1825), 54
Wheatley, Francis (1747–1801), 303
Wheelock, Gretchen, 6, 54, 135, 139, 144, 258, 348, 351
White, Harry, 338
Whyte, William (1771–1858), 121
Wieland, Christoph Martin (1733–1813), 2
Wiener Urtext (edition), 95
Wiener Zeitung (newspaper), 7, 9, 54, 173, 264, 312
Wieselburg, 280
Wigand, Balthazar (1771–1746), 189, 191
Wiley, Christopher, **321–325**
Wilker, Ulrich, **244–257**, 364
will and testament, Haydn's, 24, 72–73, 93
Will, Richard, 32, 103, 114, 122, 137, 154–55, 162–63, 186, 201, 214, 215, **216–217**, 348

Williams, Raymond (1921–1988), 239
Winchester (England), 386
wind instruments, 177–78, 241
Windsor Castle (England), 386
Winkler, Gerhard (1956–2012), 34, 40, 43, 237
Winter, Robert, 127
Wipplingerstrasse (Vienna), 50
wit, 145, 221, *see also* Humor
Witmer, Scott (translator), **391–399**
Wittgenstein, Ludwig (1889–1951), 101
Witzay, Countess Marianne (née Grassalkovich) (c.1760–c.1815), 17
Wöchentliche Nachrichten, 397
Wöchentliche Nachrichten (newspaper), 313
Wölfl, Joseph (1773–1812), 55
Wollenberg, Susan, 171, **229–235**
women. *See* Gender, Relationships and Friendships
Woodmansee, Martha, 140
word painting. *See* text painting
Wordsworth, William (1770–1850), 213
working class, 16
worklists. *See* Catalogues, Worklists, Nachlass
World Creation Project, 331
World's Encyclopædia of Recorded Music (WERM), 89
Woszczyk, Wieslaw, 261
Wranitzky, Anton (1761–1820), 17, 54, 65, 191, 357
Wranitzky, Paul (1756–1808), 65, 186, 190, 317
Wraxall, Nathaniel (1751–1831), 347
Wyzewa, Théodore de (1763–1917), 330

Yiddish folk songs, 43
Young, Edward (1683–1765), 167
    Night Thoughts, 238

Zacharasiewicz, Waldemar, 9
Zachariä, 238
Zagorski-Thomas, Simon, 334
Zaslaw, Neal, 186, 187, 188, 188, 189, 241, 317
Zatta, Antonio (fl. 1757–1797), 112
Zeiss, Laurel E., 31, **45–47**, **70–74**, 223, 254
Zelem. *See* Deutschkreuz
Zelter, Carl Friedrich (1758–1832), 215, 226, 242
Ziani, Marc'Antonio (1653–1715), 50
Zinck, Hardenack Otto (1746–1832), 313
Zingarelli, Niccolò Antonio (1752–1837), 300
    Montezuma, 10, 384
Zinner, Anton (1676–1751), 107
Zinzendorf, Karl von (1739–1813), 397
Ziss, Therese (c.1702–1777), 52, 398
Zwettl Abbey, 16, 51, 297, 400

Index of Compositions

Baryton works (Hob.X, XI, XII), 156, 179
   Baryton Trios, Hob.XI, 5, 16, 29, 62, 76, 78, 110
   Baryton Trio in A major, Hob.XI:5, 64
   Baryton Trios per violino, viola e violoncello, Hob.XI:57–62, 112
   Baryton Trio in D major, Hob.XI:95, 222

Concertos (Hob.VII, XVIII), 62
   Cello Concerto in C major, Hob.VIIb:1, 57, 64, 336
   Cello Concerto in D major, Hob.VIIb:2, 15
   Cello Concerto (spurious), 61
   Concerto for Organ and Violin (possibly Hob.XVIII:1 or Hob.XVIII:6), 50
   Concertos for Organized-Lyre, Hob.VIIh:1–5, 112
   Horn Concerto in D major, Hob.VIId:3, 57
   Keyboard Concerto in D major, Hob.XVIII:11, 15, 117, 317, 328
   Organ Concerto in C major, Hob.XVIII:1, 334
   Trumpet Concerto in E♭ major, Hob.VIIe:1, 64
   Violin Concerto in C major, Hob.VIIa:1, 179, 335

Divertimentos (Hob.II)
   Eight *Notturni* for 2 Organized-Lyres (for King Ferdinand IV of Naples), Hob.II:25–32, 112
   Hob.II:1, iv 11,iv, 119, 177
   Hob.II:41–46, "Feldparthien," 94
   Hob.II:47, "Toy Symphony," 94
   II:8, 177

Folk Song Settings and Vocal Arrangements (Hob.XXXI), 102, 160, 217, 298, 311, 319, 348
   "Maggie Lauder," 123
   Selection of Original Scots Songs in Three Parts, the Harmony by Haydn, 54
   "Strephon and Lydia," 123, 124
   Twelve Sentimental Catches and Glees, Hob.XXXIc:16, 201

Keyboard Sonatas (Hob.XVI), 6, 59, 209
   Sonata in D major, Hob.XVI:14, 132, 210, 211
   Sonatas, Hob.XVI:21–26 (Prince Esterházy sonatas), 6, 17, 254, 318
   Sonatas, Hob.XVI:27–32, 254
   Sonatas, Hob.XVI:20, 35–39, "Auenbrugger," 6, 61–62, 92, 254, 266, 389
   Sonata in C♯ minor, Hob.XVI:36, 62, 224
   Sonata in G major, Hob.XVI:39, 62, 224
   Sonatas, Hob.XVI:40–42, "Bossler," 6, 85, 247, 389–90, 391
   Sonata in E♭ major, Hob.XVI:41, 269, 269, 272
   Sonata in D major, Hob.XVI:42, 265, 389–90, 390, 391
   Sonata in E major, Hob.XVI:47, 127–30, 131, 180
   Sonata in C major, Hob.XVI:48, 391
   Sonata in E♭ major, Hob.XVI:49, 85, 100, 333, 335, 390–91
   Sonata in C major, Hob.XVI:50, 6, 27, 86, 390, 391
   Sonata in E♭ major, Hob.XVII:52, 6, 86, 144, 180, 380, 391

Keyboard Trios (Hob.XV), 59, 85, 234, 313, 331, 376
   Keyboard Trios, Hob.XV:3 and 4 (by Pleyel), 318
   Keyboard Trios, Hob.XV:6–8, 17, 112, 389
   Keyboard Trio in E♭ major, Hob.XV:10, 272, 352
   Keyboard Trios, Hob.XV:11–13, 180, 263, 268, 270, 278
   Keyboard Trio in E♭ major, Hob.XV:11, 7, 271, 274, 275
   Keyboard Trio in C minor, Hob.XV:13, 61, 278, 391
   Keyboard Trio in A♭ major, Hob.XV:14, 84, 136
   Keyboard Trios, Hob.XV:15–17, 177, 220, 262
   Keyboard Trio in B♭ major, Hob.XV:20, 7
   Keyboard Trio in D minor, Hob.XV:23, 391
   Keyboard Trios, Hob.XV:24–26, 85, 305, 335, 357
   Keyboard Trio in G major, Hob.XV:25, 42, 391

INDEX OF COMPOSITIONS

Keyboard Trios (Hob.XV) (cont.)
  Keyboard Trio in G major, Hob.XV:25, iii, "Rondo in the Gipsies' style," 85, 118, 298, 317
  Keyboard Trio in F♯ minor, Hob.XV:26, 6, 17, 86
  Keyboard Trios, Hob.XV:27–29, 6, 17, 86
  Keyboard Trio in C major, Hob.XV:27, 221
  Keyboard Trio in E major, Hob.XV:28, 391
  Keyboard Trio, Hob.XV:31, 6

Masses (Hob.XXII), 15, 16, 51, 76, 80, 96, 110, 114, 130, 292, 337–39, 355
  Harmoniemesse, Hob.XXII:14, 3, 206, 335, 338, 384
  Late Masses, Hob.XXII:9–14, 337
  Missa brevis in F major, Hob.XXII:1, 50, 119, 338, 395
  Missa brevis Sancti Joannis de Deo, "Kleine Orgelsolomesse," Hob.XXII:7, 50, 56, 184, 289, 339
  Missa Cellensis in honorem BVM, "Cäcilienmesse," Hob.XXII:5, 25, 50, 339, 383
  Missa Cellensis, "Mariazellermesse," Hob. XXII:8, 50, 56, 383
  Missa in angustiis, "Nelson Mass," Hob. XXII:11, 184, 221, 293, 405
  Missa in tempore belli (Mass in Time of War; Paukenmesse), Hob.XXII:9, 51, 288, 306, 395–96, 405–6
  Missa Sancti Bernardi von Offida, "Heiligmesse," Hob.XXII:10, 56, 285
  Missa "sunt bona mixta malis," Hob. XXII:2, 25, 76, 338, 341
  Schöpfungsmesse, Hob.XXII:13, 335, 384
  Theresienmesse, Hob.XXII:12, 184, 335
Miscellaneous Instrumental Works
  flute trios, Hob.IV:2–4, 253
  Hungarischer National Marsch, Hob.VIII:4, 237
  Prince of Wales March, Hob.VIII:3bis, 229
Miscellaneous Vocal Works – arias, cantatas, choruses and incidental music with orchestral accompaniment (Hob. XXIVa, XXIVb, XXX)
  Alfred, King of the Anglo-Saxons, Hob.XXX:5, 217, 405–6
  Applausus cantata, Hob.XXIVa:6, 15, 51, 72, 92, 400
  Berenice, che fai? Hob.XXIVa:10, 16, 65, 226, 359
  Da qual gioia improvvisa, Hob.XXIVa:3, 110
  Destatevi o miei fidi, Hob.XXIVa:2, 110
  "Gott erhalte Franz den Kaiser" (Kaiserhymne, "Volck's Lied"), Hob. XXVIa:43, 17, 34–36, 42, 163, 164, 216, 236–37, 306, 311, 404, 406
  Invocation of Neptune, Hob.XXIVa:9, 53, 405
  Qual dubbio ormai, Hob.XXIVa:4, 110
  Secular cantatas, Hob.XXIVa:1–5, 217

Sturm, Der (The Storm), Hob.XXIVa:8, 291
"Vada adagio signorina," Hob.XXIVb:12, 192
Miscellaneous Vocal Works – multi-voice partsongs, songs with keyboard accompaniment, and vocal canons (Hob.XXV, XXVIa, XXVIb, XXVII)
  Ariana a Naxos, Hob.XXVIb:2, 319, 320, 359, 400, 402
  "Betrachtung des Todes", Hob.XXVb:3, 3
  "Der Greis," 3, 99
  Canzonettas, Hob.XXVIa:25–36, 6, 20, 53–54, 98, 124, 201, 208, 210, 305, 307, 308–9, 311, 319, 330, 341, 405
  "Fidelity," Hob.XXVIa:30, 124
  "Pastoral Song, A," Hob.XXVIa:27, 20, 208, 210
  "Pleasing Pain," Hob.XXVIa:29, 341, 342
  "Sailor's Song," Hob.XXVIa:31, 405
  "She Never Told Her Love," Hob. XXVIa:34, 208, 307
  "Sympathy," Hob.XXVIa:34, 307
  "Transport of Pleasure/Content," Hob. XXVIa:36bis, 311
  "The Wanderer," Hob.XXVIa:36, 308
  German Lieder/songs, Hob.XXVIa:1–24, 6, 173, 266, 307
  "Gegenliebe," Hob.XXVIa:16, 307
  "Lob der Faulheit," Hob.XXVIa:22, 308
  "O Tuneful Voice," Hob.XXVIa:42, 6, 21, 308
  "The Battle of the Nile," Hob.XXVIb:4, 53, 216, 405
  "The Spirit's Song," Hob.XXVIa:41, 6
Miscellaneous Works for Keyboard (Hob. XVII)
  Adagio in F major (Divertimenti per cembalo o pianoforte facili e piacevoli), Hob.XVII:9, 112
  Capriccio, "Acht Sauschneider müssen seyn," Hob.XVII:1, 17, 36–40, 119, 180, 212
  Capriccio/Fantasia in C major, Hob. XVII:4, 160, 167, 327
  Five Variations in D major, Hob. XVII:7, 119
  "Il maestro e lo scolare" Hob.XVIIa:1, 180, 400
  Variations in A major, Hob.XVII:2, 119, 180
  Variations in F minor, Hob.XVII:6, 57, 208, 391

Operas, Singspiele and Marionette works for the Theater (Hob.XXVIII, XXIX), 29, 62, 79, 90, 399
  Acide, 16, 110, 194, 246, 280, 286, 360, 361
  Armida, 112, 194, 247, 248, 336, 359, 365, 384, 387

Der Götterrath, 361
Der (neue) krumme Teufel, 63, 117, 182, 194, 280, 285, 359–60, 394
Dido, 194
Il mondo della luna, 10, 90, 117, 162, 193, 194, 316, 347, 364, 385, 387, 401
L'anima del filosofo (Orfeo), 64, 174, 176, 194, 197, 304, 310, 359, 367–370, 368, 402
L'incontro improvviso, 23, 118, 137, 298, 362, 365, 384
L'infedeltà delusa, 228, 361–62
L'isola disabitata, 10, 16, 114, 194, 239, 254–55, 281, 289, 327, 335, 363, 365
La canterina, 246, 280, 286, 287, 359, 361, 401
La fedeltà premiata, 30, 281, 300, 307, 316, 360, 365, 371
La marchesa nespola, 280, 361
La vera costanza, 98, 103, 114, 160, 192, 281, 365, 367, 387
Le pescatrici, 192, 361–62
Lo speziale, 110, 117, 182–84, 192, 228, 246, 281, 327, 361, 395
Orlando paladino, 16, 17, 29, 114, 194, 314, 359, 365, 384
Philemon und Baucis, 109, 194, 361, 366–67, 387
Oratorios (Hob.XXI), 76, 80, 90, 144, 338
Il ritorno di Tobia, 32, 112, 114, 185–87, 194–95, 230, 252, 280, 289, 290, 387, 396
The Creation/Die Schöpfung, 2, 3, 4, 11, 12, 15, 17, 21, 23, 32, 54–55, 57, 61, 62, 65, 69, 71, 80–81, 83, 87, 92, 99, 112–13, 114, 134, 137, 152, 158, 162, 163–65, 171, 176, 184, 185, 189–91, 190, 195–96, 202, 214–15, 216–17, 230–31, 232–33, 234, 239, 242, 253, 257, 284, 290, 292, 293, 294, 306, 311, 316, 320, 324, 326, 330–31, 335, 338, 339–40, 347, 349, 353–55, 373, 375, 379, 386, 396–97
The Seasons/Die Jahreszeiten, 2, 3, 32, 51, 80–81, 99, 113, 114, 158, 164–65, 171, 176, 189, 195, 214–15, 222, 230–31, 233, 234, 238–39, 284, 290, 293, 310, 314, 320, 339–40, 347, 354, 355, 372, 379, 384, 386, 388

Sacred Works (Hob.XX, XXa, XXIII)
Ens aeternum, 50
Nachtrag, Hob.XXIII:a-f, 340
Non nobis domine, 76
Salve Regina in E major, Hob.XXIIIb:1, 96–97, 334
Salve Regina in G minor, Hob.XXIIIb:2, 56, 83, 112, 338
Stabat mater, Hob.XXbis, 23, 25, 32, 51, 64, 111, 112–13, 137, 174, 286, 288, 301–2, 314–15, 338, 384

Te Deum, Hob.XXIIIc:1, 48
Te Deum, Hob.XXIIIc:2, 335, 337, 395–96, 405
The Seven Last Words of Our Savior on the Cross (Die sieben letzten Worte) Hob.XX, 14, 51, 82, 99, 114–16, 115, 172, 226, 230, 253, 284, 290, 306, 316, 320, 336, 339, 379, 384, 396
String Quartets (Hob.III), 6–7, 27, 54, 59, 79, 85, 86, 90, 110, 156, 234, 258, 326, 349–51
Quartet, Op. 0 in E♭ major [NG Op. 1 No. 0; Hob.II:6], 258
Quartets, Op. 1, 16, 318
Quartet in B♭ major, Op. 1, No. 1, 210
Quartets, Op. 2, 16
Quartet, Op. 2, No. 6, i in B♭ major, 119
Quartets, Op. 3 (inauthentic, by Hoffstetter), 46, 61, 93–94, 319
Quartets, Op. 9, 5, 30
Quartets, Op. 17, 5, 30, 56
Quartets, Op. 20, 5, 25, 30, 56, 77
Quartet in C major, Op. 20, No. 2, 103, 104, 145, 160
Quartet in D major, Op. 20, No. 4, 117, 228, 317
Quartet in F minor, Op. 20, No. 5, 341
Quartet in A major, Op. 20, No. 6, 77, 123
Quartets, Op. 33, 7, 17, 65, 71, 79, 172, 254, 263–68, 389
Quartet in B minor, Op. 33, No. 1, 378
Quartet in E♭ major, Op. 33, No. 2, "Joke," 144, 330, 349, 380
Quartet in C major, Op. 33, No. 3, "Bird," 84, 382
Quartet in G major, Op. 33, No. 5, 26, 258, 258–59, 263–68, 380
Quartet in D minor, Op. 42 (Hob.III:43), 112, 381
Quartets, Op. 50, "Prussian," 71, 79, 86, 172, 173, 256
Quartet in B♭ major, Op. 50, No. 1, 378
Quartet in F♯ minor, Op. 50, No. 4, 381
Quartet in D major, Op. 50, No. 6, "Frog," 221, 341
Quartets, Op. 54/55, 172, 302
Quartet in C major, Op. 54, No. 2, 117, 146
Quartets, Op. 64, 7, 173, 290, 302, 304
Quartets, Op. 71/74, "Apponyi," 33, 62, 86, 253, 290, 304
Quartet in D major, Op. 74, No. 2, 220
Quartet in G minor, Op. 74, No. 3, 388, 390
Quartets, Op. 76, "Erdödy," 17, 86, 253, 255
Quartet in G major, Op. 76, No. 1, 87
Quartet in D minor, Op. 76, No. 2, "Fifths/Quinten," 88, 382
Quartet in C major, Op. 76, No. 3, "Emperor" (Hymne de Haydn), 17, 24, 234, 306
Quartet in D major, Op. 76, No. 5, 26, 220, 225, 343

String Quartets (Hob.III) (cont.)
  Quartet in E♭ major, Op. 76, No. 6, 208, 222
  Quartets, Op. 77, 253
  Quartet in G major, Op. 77, No. 1, 376
  Quartet in F major, Op. 77, No. 2, 390
  Quartet in D minor, Op. 103, 4, 58
String Trios (Hob.V)
  Hob.V:7, ii, 8, i, 11, ii, and 18, 119
Symphonies (Hob.I), 54, 59, 79, 90, 110, 113–14, 174, 187–89, 241, 286, 313, 371
  Symphony No. 3, 76
  Symphonies Nos. 6–8, "Times of Day" (*Tageszeiten*) Symphonies, 109, 162, 164, 165, 241, 280, 286, 297, 315, 317, 330, 379
  Symphony No. 6, "Le matin," 315, 346, 373, 378
  Symphony No. 7, "Le midi," 177, 239, 315, 317, 346, 373
  Symphony No. 8, "Le soir," 64, 212, 315, 346, 373
  Symphony No. 16, 226
  Symphony No. 21, 75
  Symphony No. 22, "Philosopher," 241, 317
  Symphony No. 23, 378, 379
  Symphony No. 26, "Lamentatione," 82, 84, 212, 316, 317
  Symphony No. 30, 212, 316, 338
  Symphony No. 31, "Horn Signal," 30, 83, 316, 336
  Symphony No. 32, 75
  Symphony No. 37, 338
  Symphony No. 39, 338
  Symphony No. 40, 317, 343
  Symphony No. 41, 338
  Symphony No. 42, 209
  Symphonies Nos. 45–47, 25
  Symphony No. 45, "Farewell," 30, 83, 84, 103, 131, 151, 154, 160, 170, 187, 234, 315, 316, 317, 329
  Symphony No. 46, 83, 330
  Symphony No. 47, 6, 75, 209
  Symphony No. 49, "La passione," 82, 83, 316
  Symphony No. 51, 221
  Symphony No. 53, "Festino/L'Impériale," 212, 232, 302
  Symphony No. 57, 26
  Symphony No. 59, 154, 214, 370
  Symphony No. 60, "Il distratto," 30, 246, 316, 366
  Symphony No. 62, 26
  Symphony No. 63, "La Roxelane," 232, 316
  Symphony No. 64 ("Tempora mutantur"), 210, 316, 374
  Symphony No. 65, 30
  Symphony No. 67, 226
  Symphony No. 68, 26
  Symphony No. 69, "Laudon," 113, 216, 317
  Symphony No. 70, 77
  Symphony No. 73, "La chasse," 30, 256, 307, 316, 371
  Symphony No. 75, 113
  Symphonies Nos. 76–78, 173
  Symphonies from No. 76 onward, 30
  Symphonies Nos. 82–87, "Paris" Symphonies, 71, 79, 111, 134, 172, 187, 231, 234, 302, 318
  Symphony No. 82, "L'Ours," 234
  Symphony No. 85, "La Reine," 151, 212, 212, 234, 242, 316
  "National Symphony" for France (unwritten), 237, 317
  Symphony No. 88, 137, 222, 225
  Symphonies Nos. 90–92, 79, 134
  Symphony No. 90, 18
  Symphony No. 91, 18, 58
  Symphony No. 92, "Oxford," 18, 189, 232, 234, 290
  Symphonies Nos. 93–104, "London" Symphonies, 16, 44, 176, 202, 211, 227, 232, 234, 253, 283, 290, 292, 304, 311, 357
  Symphony No. 93, 84, 152, 189
  Symphony No. 94, "Surprise," 18, 212, 234, 304, 316, 330
  Symphony No. 95, 84, 241
  Symphony No. 97, 252, 253, 336
  Symphony No. 98, 241, 253, 371
  Symphony No. 99, 67–69, 68
  Symphony No. 100, "Military," 152, 164, 189, 217, 232, 234, 241, 304, 310, 316, 405, 406
  Symphony No. 101, "Clock," 26, 374, 390
  Symphony No. 102, 56, 242, 378, 390
  Symphony No. 103, "Drumroll," 2, 84, 144, 211, 251, 257, 390
  Symphony No. 104, "London," 84, 211, 227, 326, 380
Sinfonia concertante, Hob.I:105, 56, 253